D1256701

DANTE GABRIEL ROSSETTI

PLATE I

CHATHAM PLACE, BLACKFRIARS BRIDGE

ENGRAVING BY J. C. STADLER, FROM A DRAWING BY JOSEPH FARINGTON, R.A. (*1747-182*

(*D. G. Rossetti's home is the first house on the left ;
the balcony is the top of the higher of the two bay windows*)

DANTE GABRIEL ROSSETTI

A Victorian Romantic

★

by

OSWALD DOUGHTY

NEW HAVEN
YALE UNIVERSITY PRESS
1949

FIRST PUBLISHED IN GREAT BRITAIN BY
FREDERICK MULLER LTD.
AND IN THE UNITED STATES OF AMERICA BY
YALE UNIVERSITY PRESS
IN 1949

PRINTED IN GREAT BRITAIN BY
UNWIN BROTHERS LTD.
LONDON AND WOKING

Some lives of men are as the sea is, continually vexed
and trampled with winds.

———

St. Agnes of Intercession   D. G. ROSSETTI

PREFACE

NO BIOGRAPHER OF ROSSETTI may flatter himself that the poet-painter would have approved his labours. "A devil," he wrote in 1878, appealing for help to his friend and legal adviser Watts-Dunton, "has written some rot to me about a biography for some series. I don't want him to be writing mine. If not answered he may scribble some malignity . . . a biographical Devil, . . . a scandal-mongering Devil."

That Rossetti did not wish to be the subject of any intimate biographical study, that he feared anything of the kind would lead to "scandal-mongering," is therefore beyond dispute. Nor was it solely that he feared a public revelation of his own tragic experience and unconventional way of life. The "private" life of artists as of other persons should, he believed, be really private; their works were all that the public had a right to know. This was his attitude in 1869 to Mrs. Beecher Stowe's accusations against Byron. "The vital interest of his poetry," Rossetti declared, "is all we have to do with."

Yet even in days before the advent of that self-contradictory hybrid the "fictional" biographer, Rossetti seems to have had melancholy premonitions of his ultimate fate. "Rossetti," wrote an anonymous reviewer, "used to be much delighted with the account a friend gave him of the peculiar biographical methods that obtain among the Kalmuk Tartars. . . It seems that when a Kalmuk high priest dies, the reverend gentleman next in rank sets about composing his biography in this wise: first he burns his hero's body to ashes, and then, moistening the ashes with water and his own saliva, he kneads them into a dough—'the sacred dough'—and then kneads the dough into a statuette, taking care that the statuette's face shall suggest as far as possible a kind of amalgamated expression representing both artist and subject. 'I wonder what officious kneader will try his hand on *my* "sacred dough," ' Rossetti used to say."

Despite Rossetti's wishes, however, from the moment of his death there was a scramble amongst his friends for priority as his biographer. Hall Caine won, to the disgust of the Rossetti family; William Sharp was a close second, and Oscar Wilde wittily remarked: "Whenever a great man dies, Hall Caine and

William Sharp go in with the undertakers." Dr. Johnson once declared that only those "who live with a man can write his life with any genuine exactness and discrimination"; but the personal friends of Rossetti who became his biographers cannot be cited as proofs of this. Caine exploited him as sensational "news," Sharp buried him under a mass of verbose adulation, and when in 1887 Joseph Knight's short study appeared, Rossetti's friends united in dismissing it as unsatisfactory. Five years later, one of its most severe critics, W. B. Scott, incurred much odium for his bitter comments on Rossetti when his own *Autobiographical Notes* were posthumously published.

Watts-Dunton, who might have produced the best biography of all, and is said to have been actually appointed "official" biographer by Rossetti himself, meditated such a work almost to the end of his life. As late as 1896 he denied in the *Spectator* an assertion that he had abandoned his intention to write it. He would, he said, write the biography and so correct the general impression that Rossetti was essentially an unhappy man. Indeed the fear lest he should die before he had done this, was, he said, "the only terror that death has for me now." Yet when he died eighteen years later, he had produced nothing on Rossetti save one or two discreet articles in various journals— unless we include the ridiculous novel *Aylwin*. In the meantime, William Rossetti stepped into the breach, and, in default of Watts-Dunton's volume, produced in 1895 his own dull, discreet and colourless *Memoir* of his brother, supplemented by a volume of carefully selected and censored letters written by Rossetti to various members of his family.

"After Rossetti's death," complained Ford Madox Hueffer in 1911, with characteristic exaggeration, "the biographers began. They poured forth, official and unofficial, sending out smuts or deluges of whitewash. . . . For thirty years or so they poured from the press, nearly all of them exceedingly dull, nearly all of them misleadingly accurate in things that did not matter. For thirty years or so Rossetti's figure was perpetually before the public, getting more and more pompous, more and more priestly, more and more like a German professor of the beautiful, growing duller and duller, and at last he was dead. Last year he was as dead as a doornail. And that was a thousand pities, a triumph of obscuring pompousness over a man who was very great, and a poet who was very rare."

Of the later biographers of Rossetti, however, Hueffer could have made no such complaint. Their weakness lay in sensationalism and superficiality, the opposite extreme from a laborious dullness, or they made no pretence of giving more than a general view of their subject. Yet without a franker, more accurate and detailed account of Rossetti's life, the true significance of much of his work could not be perceived, and consequently, even to the present day, much of the accepted criticism of Rossetti's verse is mistaken. As Edward Shanks wrote in 1928, during the temporary revival of interest occasioned by Rossetti's centenary: "The full story of Rossetti's life has not been told and probably never will be. The intimate details of his private life have not been recounted and his full character has not been drawn save with the most decorous understatement."

Besides the general Victorian ban upon intimate, truthful portraiture, which Mr. Harold Nicolson has so well described in his work on Biography, there were in the case of Rossetti, as the following pages show, overwhelming reasons why no full account of his life could appear during the lifetime of those with whom he was most closely associated. Of this Watts-Dunton was very conscious. "There is," he wrote, excusing himself in his ponderous way for his failure to produce the promised *Life*, "such a thing as knowing a man too well to be his biographer. Can any biography, by whomsoever written, be other than inchoate and illusory—nay, can it fail to be fraught with danger to the memory of the dead, with danger to the peace of the living, until years have fully calmed the air around the dead man's grave? So long as the man to be portrayed cannot be separated from his surroundings, so long as his portrait cannot be fully and honestly limned without peril to the peace of those among whom he moved—in a word, so long as there remains any throb of vitality in those delicate filaments of social life by which he was enlinked to those with whom he played his part—that brother, or that friend, or that outsider, who shall attempt the portraiture must feel that heavy responsibilities are his—must not forget that with him to trip is to sin against the head. And how shall he decide when the time has at last come for making the attempt. . . . What is the proper time for giving the world the truth, the whole truth, and nothing but the truth—what is the proper time?"

As some of the leading characters in Rossetti's life-time outlived Watts-Dunton, for him the time never came. For he knew, as Rossetti knew, that in this case the honest biographer must inevitably become "a scandal-mongering devil." Nor should we forget that Rossetti himself, in his desire to frustrate the biographers he feared, periodically destroyed his letters and private papers, as well as the references to himself and Lizzie Siddal that he did not like in his brother's *Preraphaelite Diary*, besides leaving strict orders, strictly carried out by the Rossetti family, for the destruction of various letters and documents after his death. And in this same spirit they carefully censored his own correspondence before its posthumous publication.

It seemed worth while, therefore, in the hope of obtaining a more accurate portrait of Rossetti, and, what is perhaps more important, a clearer understanding of those obscure poems which compose *The House of Life*, to attempt a new biography based on a detailed, impartial examination of all available published and unpublished material, a close adherence to authenticated fact, and the avoidance of mere sensationalism. Accuracy, sincerity and detachment were my aim, leading to an objective but understanding presentation of Rossetti through his life. My method was to arrange all my material (much collected over a long period), in chronological order, including Rossetti's literary and pictorial works which could thus be seen in their correct biographical contexts and perspective.

As I proceeded, a consistent and persistent design appeared, almost as in a jig-saw puzzle, and one that in some of its aspects I had not expected. Through a thousand details of the whole interlocking pattern, the facts overwhelmingly insisted upon two almost inescapable conclusions, one suggesting that uncertainty as to whether Mrs. Rossetti's death was accidental or suicidal aggravated Rossetti's hereditary tendency to anxiety, the other, a passion for Mrs. Morris, which through its frustrations and complexities, together with the burden of debt, ill-health and demoralization through chloral, intensified his morbid tendency until it assumed at least some of the aspects of paranoia. The literary importance of this, perhaps its chief importance, is that seen in this frame of reference, the sonnets of *The House of Life* and other poems, hitherto exceedingly obscure, acquire a definite, consistent biographical significance, and through that referential significance, an equally definite but generalized meaning; become, in fact, the "transfigured life" which Rossetti himself, in the sonnet of that name, defined as his poetic aim. In this connection, a comment by William Rossetti upon the last poem of *The House of Life*, *The One Hope*, is particularly illuminating in its definite assertion of a double significance in these sonnets, one their derivation from and reference to personal experience, the other, their generalized, ideal concepts. "The One Hope's one name," he writes, "is the name of the woman supremely beloved upon earth," and adds of another expression in the sonnet, " 'our kiss' is certainly— according to the scheme of the imagery and of the diction—the kiss of the speaker and of (his allegorical bride) Life. But here —as in so many other cases in poetry—it is fair to understand a something implied, as well as a something defined; and one perceives the poet to be thinking more of some actual experience in love than of his symbolic union with Life."* This is but one example out of many, but the reader of the following pages will see how mistaken has been the traditional interpretation of most of these sonnets in *The House of Life*, as also of *The Stream's Secret*; mistaken in their assumed biographical references, and consequently in their wider, general significance; for in fact, Rossetti's wife was the inspiration of very few of these sonnets or of the other poems usually associated with her name.

Nor was the external evidence as to the justness of my conclusions entirely lacking. Mr. T. J. Wise, when I discussed the question with him, agreed with my view as to the manner of Mrs. Rossetti's death, remarking that W. M. Rossetti had always appeared very doubtful and non-committal when expressing his opinion on the subject.

My conclusion as to Rossetti's passion for Mrs. Morris, I submitted to the one person living who was best able to speak with authority on the matter, asking if he could give me a

* *v. inf.* pp. 382-3 and 477.

A*

categorical denial of its truth. In two long, courteous and tactfully informative letters, he tacitly admitted its accuracy. As these letters were confidential and he did not wish his name, well known and highly respected in scholarly circles, to be mentioned, I consider myself to be still bound by his wishes despite his recent death.

For these as well as for purely literary reasons, I have preferred to present much of the actual material for Rossetti's life in detail, to show the actual pattern, not merely to present summary conclusions of my own. This has made the work longer than I should have desired, but it is only a fragment of the almost embarrassingly large quantity of material available and relevant. At any rate, the reader, being presented with the actual facts can judge of them for himself.

Previous biographers, concentrating their attention almost exclusively upon Rossetti's long association with Elizabeth Siddal, have made little more than a pretence of continuing his life in any detail after her death in 1862. Yet it was during these later years that he achieved eminence in both the arts he practised as painter-poet, found the most profound passion of his life and chief inspiration of much of his best verse as well as of his most ambitious though not his best efforts in painting. Hence the various periods of Rossetti's career are here treated on a new scale and in different proportions. The long, monotonous years of his decline, I have tried to abbreviate as far as possible without destroying the true perspective of Rossetti's life, the cumulative effect of detail and the artistic unity of the work. Nor is it without interest as a revelation of Rossetti's later life and its vicissitudes: its Indian Summer and rural wanderings with Janey usually in the background until near the end.

Finally, whether wisely or not, I could not resist, with the material to hand, the temptation to sustain "local colour," to remind the reader of the Victorian environment against which Rossetti in his life-time permanently rebelled, by concluding, in the manner of the novel of the time, with a churchyard scene, not invented, but correct in every detail.

Canty Bay House,
Muizenburg,
Cape Province,
South Africa.   July 27, 1946

AUTHOR'S NOTE

This book is not

1 *A History of Preraphaelitism or of the Preraphaelites*
2 *A critical study of the Preraphaelites' (or of Rossetti's) painting and poetry*
3 *A biography of the Rossetti family.*

It is, as its title states, a study of the development of the personality of an individual, *A Victorian Romantic*, D. G. Rossetti. The present is not the time nor is this the place for a critical evaluation of Rossetti's contribution to pictorial and poetic art.

Where the text of Rossetti's poems as here quoted differs from that in the edition of his works published in 1911, it is taken from earlier MS. versions, and consequently more closely reflects the original sources of inspiration drawn from his experience than do those versions which underwent later revision before publication.

ACKNOWLEDGMENTS

I gladly record my indebtedness to all—some no longer living—who kindly assisted in the preparation of this work, particularly to the following:—

For placing at my disposal letters by or relating to D. G. Rossetti

The late Lord Brotherton; R. E. Flower, Director of the Department of Manuscripts in the British Museum; Miss Belle da Costa Greene, Director of the Pierpont Morgan Library, New York; M. L. Howe of New Haven, Connecticut, U.S.A.; J. Purves, of the University of Edinburgh; G. Smetham (son of Rossetti's friend, James Smetham) of Somerset West, Cape Province, South Africa; J. A. Symington, formerly librarian of the Brotherton Collection; Dr. C. H. Wilkinson, Dean of Worcester College, Oxford; the late T. J. Wise of London.

For use of copyright material

The Directors of William Heinemann Limited, London, for permission to quote the hitherto only privately printed poem by Swinburne on pages 630–1.

For information of various kinds relating to Rossetti

The late Sir Edmund Gosse for personal reminiscences of D. G. R., etc; Miss E. G. Norton (daughter of Rossetti's friend Professor C. E. Norton) of Boston, Mass., U.S.A.; F. Page of the Oxford University Press for copies of various early texts of Rossetti's poems; Professor Max Förster; Professor Georges Lafourcade of Grenoble; and to the Council of the University of Cape Town for generous research grants towards the expenses involved in this work.

CONTENTS

Book III 'CHANGE AND FATE'—*continued*

Book IV THE LAST PHASE

ILLUSTRATIONS

15

PROLOGUE
1783-1824

A veritable scarecrow to Kings.

Letter to D. G. Rossetti GABRIELE ROSSETTI

IN APRIL 1824, there arrived in London an Italian political refugee, Gabriele Pasquale Giuseppe Rossetti, just forty-one years of age. Behind him lay a varied, even romantic past. His mother, Maria Francesca Pietrocola, a simple, uneducated peasant, had married in 1763, Nicola Rossetti, a blacksmith of Vasto, who, insulted by the French during their invasion of the Kingdom of Naples in 1798—some said beaten for neglecting to furnish provisions when ordered—and unable to retaliate, had drooped and died. Nicola had left four sons, including Gabriele, the youngest, and three daughters. Two of Gabriele's brothers showed intellectual ability, one becoming a Canon of Vasto, the other a lawyer, scholar and poet. His remaining brother, more versatile, combined the functions of barber and poetaster, adorning the head both without and within.

Born in 1783, Gabriele soon won so high a reputation, locally, for verse-writing and drawing, that the feudal lord of the town, the Marchese del Vasto, became his patron, saw to his schooling, and sent him in 1804 to the University of Naples. The following year the Emperor Napoleon made of the Northern part of the peninsula the Kingdom of Italy, saying as he placed the iron crown of Lombardy on his head: "God has given it to me, woe to him that touches it." When, shortly afterwards, Napoleon's brother, Joseph, appeared with a French army and seized the throne of Naples, the Marchese del Vasto's power was destroyed, and, incidentally, Gabriele's university career brought to a sudden close.

Nevertheless, Gabriele was not overwhelmed in the political maelstrom. The French he now saw as upholders of liberty, opponents of the tyranny of petty kings. Believing himself a poet, he joined those who welcomed the invaders with song, and though "scorning any cringing phrase"—as he afterwards declared in his verse autobiography—he none the less struck his lyre so vigorously as to gain the post of librettist to the San Carlo

19

Opera in Naples. In this capacity he wrote several works, greatly enjoyed the "unanimous applause" he believed he aroused, and dreamed of revealing his "genius" in the "arena of glory" which the theatre provided. But his joy was chequered by the first of those real or imaginary plots of jealous rivals, which, he believed, pursued him throughout life.

Then, within the Opera itself, troubles arose. The conflicting desires and sensitive nerves of managers, singers and composers soon exhausted Gabriele's limited patience. Complaining that the Opera too closely resembled a "madhouse," he obtained instead the post of Assistant Curator in the Naples Museum. There, surrounded by austere momuments of antiquity, he for a time found peace—and a salary of £32 2s. 6d. a year. To the end of his life he regretted his abandonment of the theatre, believing it had deprived Italy of a dramatist greater than Metastasio.

In 1808, Joseph Buonaparte, becoming King of Spain, left Naples, while Murat, assuming regal honours, mounted the vacant throne. Once again Fortune was kind to Gabriele. Well received at Murat's court, he was made Secretary of the Department of Public Instruction and the Fine Arts, and in this capacity even visited Rome.

But with the fall of Napoleon in 1815, Murat fell also. The exiled King, Ferdinand IV of Naples, returned in triumph as Ferdinand I of the Two Sicilies. "Exile," Gabriele reflected, "must have reformed the King. Besides, the Queen, his evil genius, was dead." So, ambitious as ever, though still jealously preserving his personal independence and dignity, Gabriele joined the chorus of welcome to the new king who was the old tyrant restored. Later, upon the King's recovery from a fever, Gabriele wrote such flattering verses that Ferdinand was moved to tears, and on re-reading them in after years even their author blushed.

Naïvely vain and self-important, Gabriele rejoiced in the belief that he had secured the favour of the King. Once again, he imagined, jealous rivals plotting against him were discomfited. An improvisatore, he dined with an applauding company of "Princes, Dukes and Marquesses," whom he amused with his recitations and songs, delivered in his rich and beautiful tenor voice, while the wine, "Massic or Falernian," went round.

But once again a blight fell upon his enjoyment. The King, he found, showed partiality to those who had accommodated themselves less readily than himself to the rule of Murat. Failing to secure the Chair of Eloquence in the University of Naples, he imputed his rejection to political prejudice, and regarded the King and his government with bitter hostility.

Meanwhile the spirit of revolt against the restored Bourbons was sweeping Europe like a flame. In 1820, Spain rose in successful rebellion, and Naples immediately followed suit in a bloodless revolution which compelled Ferdinand to grant a constitution permitting freedom of speech, and even membership of the rebel society of the Carbonari. Although Rossetti had hitherto played no part in politics, his delight in this era of liberty found expression in an ode of political ecstasy to the *Dawn of the Constitution Day*, beginning: "Lovely art thou with stars in hair," an ode which the Neopolitans at once took to their warm and tempestuous hearts. And at the same time, Gabriele joined the Carbonari.

Intoxicated with his popularity, Rossetti decided to become "the poet of the revolution," "the Tyrtaeus of Italy," as he named himself. But to the King he showed no open disrespect. Doubtless, as people believed, Rossetti had Ferdinand in mind when, under the threat of an Austrian invasion secretly supported by the King, he wrote:

> I vindici coltelli
> Sapran passarvi il cor;
> I Sandi ed i Luvelli
> Non son finiti ancor.[1]

It was a daring stanza, for Sandt had assassinated Kotzebue, and Louvel had murdered the Duc de Berry. Nor was it forgotten when the King's fortunes changed.

So Rossetti's political and poetic fame increased, until he reached, or so it seemed to him, the last pinnacle of fame. With simple pride he heard his name, linked with that of the musician

---

[1] The daggers of Vengeance
Thy heart's blood shall wet;
The Sandts and the Louvells
Have not finished yet.   [O. D.]

Rossini, sung by the people as they went about the streets of Naples.

> Rossini, Rossetti
> Divini, imperfetti . . . .

Those were the happiest days of Gabriele Rossetti's life.

But they were not to last. A year later, when Ferdinand, with an Austrian army at his back, abolished the constitution which had inspired Rossetti to lyric enthusiasm, the "poet of the revolution" found himself in no enviable position. Ferdinand proscribed the rebel leaders, including Gabriele. There were hangings and scourgings; eight hundred revolutionaries are said to have perished before the King's thirst for vengeance was satisfied. For a time, Gabriele's life was in danger. From March to June he lay concealed in Naples, eluding his pursuers.

His ultimate escape was remarkable. Part of the English fleet lay in the Bay of Naples, under the command of Sir Graham Moore, brother of the·ill-fated hero of Corunna. The admiral's wife, first attracted by Gabriele's songs and political enthusiasm, had formed with him a close personal friendship. "A great favourite of hers," the admiral described Rossetti to a friend, adding: "but I am not jealous, as I know that it is never of any use." Still obedient to his wife's wishes, Sir Graham Moore, disregarding international law, now exerted himself to save the unhappy refugee, and smuggled him, disguised as a British naval man, on to his ship, which carried him to Malta.

At Malta, Rossetti's romantic escape brought him notoriety. The leaders of society on the island, anxious to see "Italy's Tyrtaeus," invited him to sing his songs and improvisations, which inevitably received enthusiastic applause. Amongst his new associates, Rossetti specially noted:

> "One beneficent and reverend mien,"

that of John Hookham Frere, ex-diplomat, translator of Aristophanes, and, according to his friends, witty author of the greater part of *The Loves of the Triangles*, generally attributed to Canning. With Frere, now in studious retirement at Malta, whither he had gone for the sake of his wife's health, Rossetti quickly formed a friendship that was to last till Frere's death. Frere attempted to secure a pardon for Rossetti but in vain.

From the amnesty which Ferdinand ultimately granted the rebels, Gabriele and twelve others were excluded. This also Gabriele imputed to the plots of jealous rivals in poetry, rather than to his own threatening verses. But Frere knew better. "Nous sommes convaincus," he wrote to Gabriele, after informing him of the failure of his efforts to abtain a pardon for him, "que les paroles ne sont faites que pour être rhimées et chantées, pendant que la partie anti-poétique des hommes se persuade que les paroles doivent toujours signifier quelque chose, ainsi ils ne sentiront jamais la nécessité de mettre Louvello pour rhimer avec coltello."

With pleasant irony, Frere contrasted Gabriele's gentle nature with that of the assassins Sandt and Louvel named in his verses. "Pour l'example de Sandt," he wrote, after having dealt with Louvel, "c'est encore pire, car ce pauvre Kotzebue était un poète comme vous—c'était à ce qu'on m'a dit, un homme de génie, dont le coeur était excellent, et l'estomac encore meilleur, et qui à force de vivre avec des gens raisonnables, avait renoncé à des idées romanesques sur la liberté et le bonheur des hommes. Cette idée me fait trembler, car je craindrai tous les jours de voir arriver quelque nouveau Sandt expedié par les Carbonari pour plonger un couteau dans le ventre de cet excellent Rossetti qui ne voudrait jamais que les couteaux fussent employés que contre les pâtés de pigeon." Was the curious suggestion that the Carbonari, Rossetti's former friends, wished to murder him, merely part of Frere's jest, a slip of the pen, or did it touch upon some unknown incident in the exile's past?

Perhaps Rossetti's fellow conspirators had some grounds for suspecting his stability. Certainly "the poet of the revolution" who under Ferdinand, Joseph, Murat, and at first even under Ferdinand restored, had shown such extraordinary powers of accommodation, was little likely to become voluntarily a political martyr. Yet a political martyr he was, as five years later, from England, he complained to Frere, lamenting: "Of political news I cannot give you a syllable, because I know not and care not; and to tell the truth, I understand these matters not at all. Truly it is a strange thing that I, who don't at all understand what politics are, should for politics be persecuted

23

and exiled. Such is Fate! If the King of Naples knew me, he would indeed have something to laugh over. But this is not the first absurdity which people make him commit, and probably it will not be the last." And he mused with regret over the days when the King had wept over his loyal verses.

That he *had* meddled with politics could not, in fact, be truthfully denied, even by an ex-Carbonaro. But in a sense far truer than Gabriele intended, his complaint was justified. The apparent paradox is resolved by a casual warning to him from Frere, some years later, in 1833. "There are many things, my dear Rossetti," wrote Frere, "which induce me to fear the worst for you. Your openness to adulation such as that of Count Segovi—(which my sister when she saw it, said was an affront to your understanding) and which is just a repetition of the same sort of encouragement which induced you to put yourself forward at Naples. 'They are persuading him,' she said, 'to go forward and set fire to a mine!' "

Personal pique and a naïve vanity as much as political passion or idealism, seem to have been the chief cause of Gabriele's exile. The fame which came to him in Naples and Malta, which still haunts the Piazza Gabriele Rossetti in Vasto and the mural tablet in his honour in Santa Croce at Florence, is not unlike that which came to a similar man of action—The Playboy of the Western World. . . .

Cheered by the friendship of Frere and other influential residents in Malta, Rossetti settled down for a time to the teaching of Italian. But real or imaginary agents of King Ferdinand arrived in pursuit of the revolutionary poet. Frere's jest about pigeon pie might prove a tragic prophecy. So, early in 1824, after a stay of some two and a half years on the island, Rossetti, accepting the ever-obliging Admiral Moore's offer to take him, sailed away on H.M.S. *Rochfort*—the ship which had brought him to Malta—for the central stronghold of political plotters, London. On the way they called at Naples; and from the deck of the ship Rossetti, during the five days they waited in harbour, looked for the last time upon his native land. For London, although he did not suspect it on the morning of his arrival, was henceforth to be his home.

BOOK I

THE CARELESS YEARS
1828–1852

'Twas thus, thus is, and thus shall be:
The Beautiful—the Good—
Still mirror to the Human Soul
Its own intensitude!

Letter to W. M. Rossetti D. G. ROSSETTI

I

C H I L D H O O D
1828–1836

That indefinable sense of rest and
wonder which, when childhood is
once gone, poetry alone can recall.

Article in The Critic, December 1850 D. G. ROSSETTI

ARMED WITH LETTERS of introduction from Lady Moore and
Frere to influential persons, Gabriele soon established himself
in London as a teacher of Italian. But despite aristocratic
patrons he needed all the resources of his flamboyant optimism
when contemplating his position as a poor, undistinguished
foreigner in a strange vast city. More than ever he found support
and consolation in his intercourse with Frere, to whom in
many letters he poured out his doubts, difficulties and sorrows
—few readers of Italian, many instructors, "arduous truths for
me! But my hopes are not very soaring, and hence my disappointment will not be very painful. I also will enter the ball,
and we shall see who has the best legs. Good conduct, love of
work, few needs, many acquaintanceships, abundant assiduity,
talent not deficient, must surely produce *some* result." The
earliest omens, however, were distinctly unpropitious. Twice
Gabriele's pockets were picked, and from the first his new
acquaintances in London amusedly remarked in him "a certain
Parson-Adams-like simplicity."

Before Rossetti's departure from Italy, passion as well as
politics had already embittered his life. An illegitimate son—
who died shortly after birth—he long and deeply mourned.
The child's mother, having followed Gabriele to Malta, remained there in constantly declining health, and had probably
died before Gabriele's departure for London. As a result,
Gabriele had entered England in contrite mood, dedicating
himself to a new, exemplary life: "like that of Dante's *Vita
Nuova*," as he told himself.

Large in this "new life" loomed literary and scholarly

27

ambitions. At Malta, Gabriele had studied the Italian classics, claiming indeed to have memorized them all. In London, he quickly turned to a critical study of Dante, hoping to obtain from that unlikely source considerable financial benefits supplementary to his slender tutorial fees. Investigating Dante, Gabriele, like the Shakespearian critic described by Dr. Johnson, "did not easily miss what he desired to find," and it soon became evident to him that Dante's writings were really a secret allegory expressing the political and social opinions of Gabriele Rossetti, but so cleverly that no one save Gabriele Rossetti himself could discover their hidden meaning. To elucidate that secret was obviously Gabriele's mission in life. And having started this hare, he was sustained to the end by the excitement of the chase. An extreme anti-papalist in his enthusiasm for Italy's political liberation, although, nominally at least, a Catholic, he rejoiced to find Dante secretly confirming, as it seemed to him, in the *Divina Commedia*, his own opinions on freemasonry and the Pope. The first result of these studies was his publication, late in 1825, of Dante's *Inferno*, with a *Comento Analitico* by himself, revealing to the world his interpretation of the poem, which was indeed almost overwhelmed by the flood of his editorial comment. Although widely ridiculed, the *Comento* won Gabriele the friendship and support of another enthusiastic student of Dante, Charles Lyell, whose son in after years won fame as a geologist.*

On April 8, 1826, Gabriele Rossetti, with Catholic rites, married Frances Mary Lavinia Polidori. As his wife was an Anglican, the ceremony was repeated two days later in the traditional form of the Church of England. Gabriele was forty-three, his wife almost twenty-six. Mrs. Rossetti, the daughter of Gaetano Polidori (a teacher of Italian in London, and son of an Italian doctor), had been governess in English families of good standing. From her English mother, also once a governess, came the only English blood in the future Rossetti family.

Gaetano, solid, stolid, economical, now "in easy circumstances" and "highly respectable," had written some poems and moral tales, besides translating Milton, and Lucan's *Pharsalia*. Despite Gaetano's phlegmatic constitution, his

* *v. Notes.*

family of four sons and four daughters showed an obvious nervous strain. Maria Margaret was quick-tempered and subject to perpetual fits of hysterical laughter which reminded her irreverent nephews and nieces of a laughing hyena. Her brother Henry, an unsuccessful solicitor, was tense and eccentric; another brother was definitely weak-minded; a third, the vain, jealous, excitable physician of Byron's last journey, challenged Shelley to a duel, continuously exasperated Byron, and, shortly after dismissal from Byron's service, poisoned himself in London, as the best way of meeting his gambling debts. "Poor Polidori is gone," wrote Byron on hearing of his suicide; "when he was my physician, he was always talking of Prussic acid, oil of amber, blowing into veins, suffocating by charcoal, and compounding poisons!"

Two of the sisters, however, Eliza—who later helped Florence Nightingale in the Crimea—and Mrs. Rossetti herself, inherited the mental strength of their father Gaetano. The strength, the sanity, of Dante Gabriel's cultured, intellectual mother were eminent and life-long. Her character speaks in a comment she made on her family, when an old lady over seventy years of age. "I always had a passion," she said, "for intellect, and my wish was that my husband should be distinguished for intellect and my children too. I have had my wish; and I now wish that there were a little less intellect in the family, so as to allow for a little more common sense." She was, of course, quite right, as always, but, vague and shadowy though she is to us, we come to feel in time, unfairly it may be, that perhaps some touch of human weakness in the excellences of Dante Gabriel Rossetti's mother, might have been better for the son.

Although in his verse autobiography Gabriele Rossetti romantically described himself as the happy victim of love at first sight, sober truth and Italian shrewdness speak in his letter to a friend, written shortly before his marriage: "It was necessary for the sake of my studies, to take up a more regular way of life, and that has counted for something in my decision." Nevertheless, and despite the great difference in their respective ages, the marriage of Gabriele Rossetti and Frances Polidori seems to have been a happy one. Mutual affection, confidence, esteem, bound husband and wife, nor did the long trials of sickness and poverty awaiting them break the bond. Although to casual observers the volatile Gabriele doubtless seemed the dominant partner of the marriage, he came, in reality, increasingly to depend upon the superior strength of will of his quiet, unobtrusive, dignified wife. Whatever Mrs. Rossetti thought at times of her impulsive, excitable, child-like husband she characteristically kept to herself. Mrs. Rossetti's morally admirable gift of silence is unfortunate for the biographer, for it combines with the hazards of documentary survival to make her, for the modern reader, something of a mystery.

In London, in the small house, No. 38, he had taken, in dingy, dreary, decaying Charlotte Street (which later became 110 Hallam Street)[1] between Great Portland Street and Portland Place, the four children of the marriage were born: Maria Francesca in 1827, Gabriel Charles Dante (to give him his correct baptismal name), in 1828, and in the two following years, William Michael and Christina Georgina. For the children came with that rapidity which seems to have been one of the most signal rewards of Victorian virtue.

When on May 12th, 1828, Gabriele's eldest son was born, he determined to call him Dante in honour of his own recondite studies, and for the same reason chose Charles Lyell to be his eponymous godfather. So, with Lyell in attendance, "il picciolo Dantino," "il nostro Dantuccio"—for his father's affection overflowed in tender diminutives—was christened "Gabriel Charles Dante" at All Souls' Church, Langham Place. Gabriele also celebrated the occasion in extremely bad verse.

Over the early years of his son's childhood, Gabriele watched with an almost tremulous solicitude. "Our little Dante is lively as a sparrow and fresh as a flower; he kisses your hand"; "plump, fat, playful and affectionate"; "un caro impertinente," a cheeky little chap,—such were the proud father's descriptions of the baby as the months passed. When in the summer of 1829 Mrs. Rossetti, taking Dante Gabriel with her, went to stay at the Polidori's country cottage at Holmer Green, in Buckinghamshire, to rest before the expected birth of William,

---

[1] Nos. 110–116 Hallam Street were demolished in 1928 to make way for a block of flats, named "Rossetti House." The memorial tablet to Rossetti, which had been erected, was replaced—over the main entrance.

PLATE II

PROFESSOR GABRIELE
ROSSETTI
BY D. G. ROSSETTI
1853

MRS. GABRIELE ROSSETTI
BY D. G. ROSSETTI
1854

PLATE III

DANTE GABRIEL ROSSETTI
SELF PORTRAIT
1847

CHRISTINA ROSSETTI
BY D. G. ROSSETTI
1848

DANTE GABRIEL ROSSETTI
SELF PORTRAIT
1855

Gabriele, in nervous agitation, anxiously awaited news of Dante, rejoiced to hear of his "running away shouting with glee and staggering with his little hand to his ear," wondered at his fearing the lowing of the cows, laughed affectionately at his large ears and hoped that his legs, which were weak, would soon be strong.

Gabriele missed both wife and child terribly in absence. In the summer of 1832, Dante Gabriel, who was again in the country, with his mother and the other children, fell ill. Gabriele was at once overwhelmed with anxiety. "Every word you wrote," he told his wife, "pierced like a dagger into my heart." He tortured himself with endless self-questionings. "What was the cause?—the weather?—the country air?—or, most horrible thought of all, some figs *he* had sent them?" "I should be the most frantic and inconsolable man in the world if I were to lose a son, that dearest little Gabriel, the very core of my heart, and lose him thus, far from my sight. My eyes are already full of tears whilst writing these words and unless I dry them I cannot continue writing, as I do not see the paper. But take heart, my wife, it may turn out to be nothing serious."

Evidently Dante Gabriel Rossetti's father possessed, in addition to the tendency he had shown to belief in plots and persecution by jealous rivals, a strong disposition towards self-torture and anxiety. At times, he mistook his own imaginings for reality, as indeed he well knew, complaining to a friend of "this wretched fancy of mine which often forms the strangest illusions, and takes them for unquestionable realities." It was thus that now, under the stress of his nervous fear for his sick son, he mistook the red sealing wax on his wife's letter for black, the agreed signal of a fatal ending, and believed all was over. Finding better news within, however, he burst into tears of joy. The news came to him, he declared, "like dew to a dying flower," and he thanked God a thousand times for restoring his dear Gabriel whom he seemed to love, he said, so much more than his other children.

For a year now, Gabriele had been Professor of Italian at King's College, London. His academic environment disappointed him. "This shall be the last time. I don't want to spend money on being bored," he lamented after dreary professorial dinners. He was, he well knew, fallen on evil days since those proud and joyous nights when, as the "Massic and Falernian" went round, the aristocracies of Naples and of Malta repaid his improvisations with enthusiastic applause. To see himself now described on the title pages of his works as "Professore nel Collegio del Re," pleased him, but was only a pale afterglow to his former glory. Nor did his professorial chair, bringing him but one or two students and £10 a year, provide much solid cause for rejoicing.

Nevertheless, to the Rossettis, even this diminutive windfall was important, for times were often hard and Frere's occasional help, although accepted with much dignity and show of independence, very welcome. During the earliest years of family life, however, in a household managed with Latin economy, the professor was able to live without undue privation. The number of his students had increased. In the little box in which he hid his savings in the manner of the Latin peasantry from which he sprang, the pile of sovereigns had actually risen to a hundred and fifty one. He could now regard with less anxiety than before, a family rapidly growing up.

But soon to Gabriele came physical evils: gout, bronchitis, failing sight; and when shortly afterwards his father-in-law, Polidori, received a legacy and retired to his cottage at Holmer Green, Gabriele as reversionary legatee innocently but anxiously surveyed his own prospects. For his wife, upon her mother's death, two thousand pounds; upon that of her father, the reversionary thousand for himself. His petition to the King of Naples to be allowed to return to his beloved Italy had recently been rejected. But hope died hard. Some day, perhaps, dreamed the exile, he might return. If not in Italy, at least somewhere on the Continent he might find a corner to live in, and sufficient to buy bread.

Gabriele's chief source of consolation in exile was his intensive and protracted investigation of Dante. Roused by the opposition and ridicule his *Comento Analitico* had provoked, he determined to present to adversaries and scoffers, such indisputable proofs of the truth of his theory as would silence their derisive laughter and cover them with shame. Poor, married to a wife whose virtues were eminently domestic, the professor, no longer playing any part in the social world, devoted his hours of leisure to the pursuit of his extraordinary researches. From deep to deep, from mystery to mystery he gradually descended, until No. 38 Charlotte Street became the very Scotland Yard of letters.

With delight he saw the secret society he believed he had detected, the mysterious, masonic "sect" of Dante's occult propaganda, gradually spreading far beyond Dante until it covered the whole field of literature, from the dawn of the Christian era to his own day. Petrarch, Boccaccio, Swedenborg and Chaucer were, he found, members of this secret "sect" whose God was "man in freedom." In ecstasy, fear, and not without pride, he penetrated the "Great Secret," the "Mysterium Magnum." "I now comprehend," he wrote, "why the Mysterium Magnum was never manifested to the world. It is confided to very few persons, of well approved prudence, and at an age of thorough maturity; and to discover it by one's own scrutiny is a work of immense labour, and (I will venture to say) of no ordinary talent." Upon occasion, wrestling with some singularly occult problem, he would retire to the solitude of the tiny drawing-room upstairs reserved for such crises; but more frequently, for he was at heart sociable though often remote, he would sit over his books in the little "front parlour" with his family about him.

At long intervals Gabriele bestowed upon an indifferent or contemptuous world the results of his unwearying industry. Thus the *Comento Analitico* of 1825 was followed in 1832 by his *Disquisizione: Sullo Spirito Antipapale che produsse la riforma, e sulla segreta influenza ch'esercito nella letteratura d'Europa e specialmente d'Italia. Come risulta da molti suoi classici, massima da Dante, Petrarca, Boccaccio*; a title hardly calculated to achieve his frequently avowed aim of filling the family coffer.

The *Sullo Spirito Antipapale* however, converted Frere, hitherto so sceptical that Gabriele had suspected him for a time of being himself a member of the secret sect. Frere, infected, quickly discovered Erasmus, Tristram, and Iseult to be members of the secret society. Milton resisted Frere's efforts, but on his complaining to Gabriele, the professor, now a practised hand, brought Milton in, as well as St. Paul and St. John. Delighted,

Frere sent Gabriele a donation, which produced the grateful acknowledgment: "How many anxieties you have soothed in my mind by your unexpected gift. . . . How timely and appositely it has come to relieve me from a state such 'che poco è più morte.' "[1]

With the publication of *Sullo Spirito* and its anti-papal sentiment, Gabriele's growing horror of the blasphemies he was committing—for his moods varied from Catholic to rationalist—came to a head. Despite his literary enthusiasm, he reflected that he had been "brought up in a pious family," that religion was to him "a cherished sentiment," and confessed to Frere: "I repent of having plunged into water so deep and dangerous, my conscience has sustained a severe shock." In place of such interests, he determined he would substitute "matters of religion, which shall not cease to be my guide for the rest of my life." In this contrite mood he produced a psaltery, *God and Man—Iddio e l'Uomo. Salterio*, intended, as it were, to be the budding staff of this professorial Tannhäuser. Published with great expectations in 1833, it was promptly placed on the pontifical *Index Librorum Prohibitorum*, to poor Gabriele's intense indignation; for the writing of the psaltery had been an act of genuine penitence and piety.

Meanwhile, in a strange domestic atmosphere of politics, cosmopolitanism and literary mystery, Gabriel, the bright little boy with shining eyes, auburn hair and fresh complexion, played with his brothers and sisters, and began to look out on life as it revealed itself through the drab windows of 38 Charlotte Street. Although situated in the heart of London, Gabriele's home was Italian in tongue and spirit. His parents had few English friends, but many Italian ones. Their house was a centre to which, night after night, it seemed as if all the Italian refugees in London must have come. The variety of the professor's acquaintance was indeed extraordinary, ranging from counts, barons, cavalieri, to organ-grinders, macaroni-sellers and plaster-cast vendors. Amongst the most distinguished of these political exiles were a count turned coal-dealer, and a clay-modeller who was rumoured to have fought with brigands

---

[1] *cf.* Dante: *Inferno*, I. 7. *"Tanto è amara, che poco è più morte. . . ."*
"So bitter is it, that scarcely more is death. . . ."

and also to have murdered somebody. Some of these visitors were merely eccentric; others were clearly insane. Beneath Gabriele's hospitable roof the gentleman who believed himself Jesus Christ nightly met and chatted with the gentleman who boasted of having "a double stomach" and being "a ruminating animal." Another, who claimed to be a prophet, cut his throat in disgust when Austria beat Italy at Novara. Old Gabriele, reporting his suicide, declared that but for his family he would have done the same! Thus, into the little sitting-room where the Rossettis' family meals were taken, there crowded nightly as motley an assemblage as any house in London could show.

More distinguished acquaintances there were also: the great Mazzini, the scholar Panizzi, assistant librarian at the British Museum, Ugo Foscolo the writer, and Paganini the famous violinist. But these seldom if ever joined the throng in Rossetti's home.

The hospitality dispensed by Gabriele to these visitors was simple—bread and butter with coffee or tea. Smoking was not allowed. From the dull and dirty street, the strangely mingled crowd filed quietly into the room, greeted the silent "Signora Francesca" as hostess, and passed on to form an animated, gesticulating group round Gabriele. The chief joy of these gatherings was talk—talk of their beloved Italy, of their hopes for her freedom and for the overthrow of her hated tyrants. The visitors' voices rose with their enthusiasm as they rained invectives upon their political enemies, and their gesticulations were unrestrained.

Occasionally in their conversation literature would intrude upon politics, and often, at the request of the company, Gabriele would recite his poems—poems of Italy's impending liberation, delivered in the rich, sonorous voice that had once charmed the social worlds of Naples and Malta. But the applause that followed was accorded to the political and national sentiments expressed rather than to poetic quality. Mrs. Rossetti, a little apart from the voluble crowd, would occasionally interject a remark, while the children, busy with their play, looking at pictures, reading, colouring prints, would take in the scene not as a strange, exotic life, but as a normal incident of their daily life.

In later years, these nightly meetings in Charlotte Street were amongst the most vivid of Gabriel's early memories.

Another of his early recollections was an oft-repeated fire-light scene. Old Gabriele found the London climate but a poor substitute for that of Italy, and in winter he loved the fireside. He would often return at dusk, tired with his lessons, and lie flat on the hearthrug for an hour or two to sleep—and snore—before the fire, where the tabby cat, whose tastes were similar, kept him company. At other times, less fatigued, the professor would sing to them. The idealized memory of those evenings Gabriel described in after years. Amid the gathering darkness the little boy would sit on the hearthrug, gazing intently between his bent knees at the glowing fire, while his father, basking in its warmth, sang in his sweet tenor voice songs of home, or in more martial mood songs of revolution such as the *Marseillaise*. Then for little Dante "the music and the fire and my heart burned together," and taking paper and pencil he would try to fix the shapes that rose within him, and dream of becoming a great painter.

There were too, for Gabriel, other, slighter memories: the first things his eyes fell upon in the outside world: the Punch and Judy show that regularly played before the house opposite; the public house at the corner with its little crowd of permanent loungers and the cab-rank at its door; early walks in Regent's Park; visits to the Zoo. One such walk especially, Christina long remembered, when she and Gabriel visited the Zoo together. Troubled by the animals' captivity, Christina suggested the writing of woeful, sympathetic verses, but instead, Gabriel made such amusing biographies for the animals that Christina's unhappiness dissolved in laughter. Most vividly of all, she remembered their return: two small children, hand in hand, crossing a deserted park lit by a flaming sunset which, Gabriel declared, was setting on fire the trees and housetops in the distance.

Gabriel and Christina were uncommon children; imaginative, and Christina, so she declared later, ill-tempered too. Gabriel was whimsical and at times moody. Maria, their sister, though less imaginative and original, had the best memory, and would become, they thought, the scholar of the family.

William, their brother, was solid, reliable, self-controlled. His father, because of these qualities, believed William most resembled himself! Maria used to declare that she had the good sense, Christina the bad temper, William the good nature, and Gabriel the good heart, of their parents.

Between Christina and Gabriel there were resemblances in physical appearance, as well as in mind and natural disposition. Both had rich, musical voices, with softly cadenced speech, brown hair, and eyes of changing lights, "hazel and blue-grey." Besides the same imaginative, poetic bent, brother and sister had at this time other qualities in common. In each was the same intensity, the same sensitiveness, the same secret tendency towards idealism and mysticism. They shared too the same quick temper, the same slightly cynical humour and somewhat bitter speech. Both took pleasure in a somewhat "slangy" style of writing, which Christina in later life used only to Gabriel. Time, suffering, and stern self-discipline curbed many of the characteristics in which Christina resembled her brother, but despite occasional differences and even temporary estrangement, the two were, by nature, in closer mutual sympathy than others of the family. Of this fundamental harmony, however, there was so far little sign. Gabriel and Christina would quarrel, fight, shout at one another, and cry. "The storms," their father called them in contrast to the peaceable Maria and William who were "the calms."

Although Gabriel in later life particularly appreciated his poetic sister, the dominating elder sister, Maria, aroused his greatest admiration in these earliest years. "*She* was the Dante of our family," he once said, "Maria was a born leader; Christina a born apostle. In my boyhood I loved Maria better than anyone in the world." That Maria attracted Gabriel's admiration is not strange, for he too loved to dominate. Lyell's pious hope (expressed in a letter to Gabriele in 1835), that his godson "has ceased to be rebellious when turned out of the drawing-room," doubtless illuminates one otherwise unrevealed aspect of Gabriel's childhood.

Despite poverty and their drab, monotonous existence in Charlotte Street, the Rossettis were a happy family. Proud of his wife and children, Gabriele would sometimes grandiloquently exclaim: "Princes, ye have persecuted me in vain!" Italian rather than English, and so, in a "foreign" country, both children and parents made their home their world. Their interests and pleasures were artistic and intellectual. Games, save for the professor's occasional indulgence in chess, were seldom played. The two brothers and sisters were good companions together. To Dante Gabriel, drawing appealed even in his youngest days. "I saw a baby making a picture," said the surprised milkman to Rossetti's servant one morning. It was Gabriel, four years old, sketching his rocking horse. From that time onwards, drawing was a favourite amusement. He soon abandoned the attempt to sketch real objects, preferring to draw "out of his head," a natural bent which even his Preraphaelite associations and later development did not destroy! The few earliest letters of Gabriel which survive show a precocious interest in colour and form, for they describe a favourite amusement of the two brothers who spent their scanty pocket-money in buying cheap prints and old engravings of actors and actresses, which they delighted to colour.

Mrs. Rossetti's influence over the children was far greater than her husband's. "Gabriel," wrote the chief friend of Rossetti's last years, "even to the end of his life, accepted her dicta as oracles not to be challenged." She undertook the early education of all the children, and her daughters had no other teacher. Nor did she fail to bring them all up strictly in her own Protestant faith. Although Italian was the language spoken in the home, almost all Gabriel's reading at this time was in English. In 1836, his father proudly reported to Charles Lyell: "Gabriel Charles Dante is continually reading; this is his first passion, his second is for drawing. He knows many passages of Shakespeare by heart, and recites them energetically. He devours a book with more appetite, and perhaps more quickly, than I do." And a few months later he added the information: "Our Dantuccio is beginning to study Latin with attention and pleasure."

Gabriel was, in fact, already gripped by the romantic literature of the day. Scott's novels and poems, "Monk" Lewis's *Tales of Wonder*, Maturin and the rest, opened for him a world of delight, wild, mysterious, supernatural. Pictures too he loved—

an illustrated translation of *Faust*, Ariosto with eighteenth-century French engravings, and similar works. But a collection of scriptural engravings from the old masters bored him. His brother in later life found in these the cause of that indifference to the pictorial conventions of the old masters which led Gabriel ultimately to the Preraphaelite Brotherhood. Mrs. Rossetti taught them not only the usual fairy-tales of childhood, but also a good knowledge of the Bible. Gabriel's admiration for the Bible endured throughout his life. Their watchful parents gave them also the popular moral tales for children, but these were received without enthusiasm.

Outside their home their pleasures were few. Very rarely, friends would give the professor tickets for the opera, and then the children would have an unaccustomed treat. For they seldom heard music, save that of the organ-grinder in Charlotte Street, or of their mother, who would sing in her sweet but untrained voice or play on the pianoforte *The Battle of Prague*. Once, the delighted children saw a ballet in which fiends appeared, and henceforth they would play at "demons," a pastime which Gabriel, afterwards so fascinated by diabolism, doubtless much enjoyed. At long intervals also would come a memorable visit to the National Gallery.

Meanwhile, the children, gazing in awe upon their father as he sat surrounded by ponderous folios, mystical works, treatises on alchemy, freemasonry, Swedenborg, the Cabbala, and Brahminism, to which his Dante studies had led him, acquired (almost inevitably in a domestic atmosphere so intolerably overcharged with Dante and his secret propaganda), a dislike of the great Florentine, who indeed became for them the very symbol of dullness. Consequently, although they delighted in Shakespeare, Scott and other English writers, they had so far no desire to make acquaintance with the *Divina Commedia* or any other of Dante's works. That the influence of their father's intellectual pursuits was strong, however, is clearly revealed in the later life of the children, all of whom, on some occasion, made Dante the subject of their writing.

As for Gabriel, his tendency in childhood towards romantic mystery and the supernatural not only developed under the influence of his father's researches, but even found in them a focus. Although ignorant of all details, and indeed uninterested, he sensed the atmosphere of his father's works with the intuition of an intensely imaginative child. His father's "study" seemed to him in these early days "a haunted room." For him, "the very books had a conscious and external life of their own." Alone there, he grew afraid, feeling a strange presence beside him, while one copy of the *Vita Nuova* seemed to give out "a faint light," which "filled him with a happy terror." To the child, Dante was not only his father's friend; he was also a "sacred and benign, though mysteriously invisible visitor to, if not indeed inmate of, the Charlotte Street household." On the staircase, little Gabriel would run past an unpleasantly dark corner of the second landing, fearing to meet there the tall gaunt figure of Dante. Nor would he dare to enter that study of strange influences and dreams, in the twilight, if no one else was there, and the fire was not casting a glow into the gathering darkness. Like his father who had seen the red seal as black, little Gabriel was obviously prone to suggestion.

In later years, Rossetti came to know and love the poet who had so darkly haunted his childhood. A quarter of a century later, he wrote of his Italian translations, *The Early Italian Poets*, "In relinquishing this work . . . I feel, as it were, divided from my youth. The first associations I have are connected with my father's devoted studies, which, from his own point of view, have done so much towards the general investigation of Dante's writings. Thus, in those early days, all round me partook of the influence of the great Florentine; till from viewing it as a natural element, I also, growing older, was drawn within the circle." But unfortunately, within the circle of Dante as interpreted by Gabriele Rossetti, mysteries and secret conspiracies predominated, and the influences of these too, it may be, Gabriel unconsciously absorbed in his early days. Endowed as he was, by his father, with a nervous, impressionable temperament, and a similar, though long quiescent tendency towards a persecution complex and paranoiac belief in secret conspiracies of enemies, Gabriel, in after years, when the anxieties and disappointments of later life opened a way for the return of these early suggestions, largely fell a victim to their disastrous effects.

Such then, was the physical and mental environment of Rossetti in his earliest childhood. In this frugal home of strict principle yet cultured freedom, where indeed he generally had his way, Gabriel early asserted his intention to become a painter, and this was accepted without question by all. "Gabriel means to be a painter," they said, when friends discussed his future. Amid such encouragement the little boy made drawings from Shakespeare and, at the age of five or six, an inevitably naïve attempt at literature in which prose and blank verse mingled. It was entitled *The Slave*, and consisted of an unintelligible plot, of much mutual defiance and fighting, with many expletives, working up to a highly satisfactory climax in which, as in *Hamlet*, almost everyone is killed. Doubtless the indefatigable professor could have discovered in its incoherences, secret anti-papal propaganda.

II

SCHOOL
1836–1841

*A track of dust and dead leaves that merely led to
the fountain.*

Hand and Soul D. G. ROSSETTI

AFTER THE MIDSUMMER HOLIDAYS in 1836, Gabriel was withdrawn
from his mother's tuition and sent to school; first, to "Mr.
Paul's," a neighbouring preparatory day school attended by
some thirty sons of local tradesmen, where, after the Christmas
vacation, William joined him, and then, after a year, to King's
College School. For the ill-paid professors of King's College
were allowed to send to the school one son without payment,
and a second at reduced fees. Thus it was that after the midsummer vacation of 1837, when the as yet uncrowned Victoria
had barely succeeded to the throne, the Rossetti brothers, aged
respectively nine and eight years, entered King's College
School, a Church of England day school, staffed chiefly by
clergy, and with a few boarders.

Placed together in the lowest class upon entry, Gabriel and
William endured for the next four years an educational experience of average stupidity, from which they derived little
benefit. Even at school Gabriel was "temperamental." His
work lay at the mercy of moods, of sympathies and antipathies
which dominated him. Science and mathematics he detested,
and the multiplication table held for him only the romantic
charm of the vague, mysterious and uncertain. It was Arthur
Cayley, afterwards a noted mathematician at Cambridge, who
bore off all the class prizes. Yet Gabriel, largely helped of
course by the circumstances of his parentage and home life,
showed some linguistic ability. Despite his Italian origin and
environment, English was his native tongue. Long afterwards
he insisted that only in his dreams (and in youth only), was
Italian an instinctive, unconscious mode of expression. Nor did
he even attract the attention of his art-master, who was, for a

42

time, the painter John Sell Cotman. "In the highest degree commendable," was the enthusiastic verdict of the first quarter's report upon William; but Gabriel was merely described as "in every respect satisfactory." At this early period of their school life Gabriele boasted of his sons' "decided inclination for study," and contemplated their attainments with such satisfaction as he usually reserved for his own.

Gabriel's foreign origin was supposed to explain his dislike of sports and all athletic activities, as well as of the scuffling, fighting, and horseplay then accounted an important educational influence in English schools. Although his constitution was strong, an occasional snow fight or similar diversion marked the extreme limit of his physical activities. His later self-accusations of early timidity, however, were probably exaggerated, for in his last, sad days of physical and moral wreck, he magnified all his weaknesses, seeing even the scattered shadows of remembered childhood more darkly. Certainly, at no time of life was Rossetti's appearance that of a sportsman, and his ignorance of such pursuits remained abysmal to the end. There is no reason to doubt the story that in later life, when boating with a friend, he calmly suggested throwing one of the boat's stretchers overboard because it inconvenienced him!

The manners of both William and Gabriel, affected by the general tone of the school, sank somewhat below the high standard exacted in the Rossetti home. The moral influence of Mrs. Rossetti, however, was still strong. How completely it dominated Gabriel is shown in his reporting to his father, while still at Mr. Paul's, a mischievous youth who had drawn his attention to various intriguing incidents described in the Bible. Old Gabriele had in turn reported the boy to Mr. Paul, and the precocious Bible-student was given a seat apart. Nevertheless, Gabriel was easily influenced by the less estimable qualities of his companions, and during these school years, as his temper deteriorated, he became more imperious and self-centred. These defects were mitigated by an easy good nature and readiness to forget and forgive, rather than to forgive and forget. He became increasingly moody, while fits of idleness alternated with periods of almost feverish activity. His father, viewing him with increasing uneasiness, playfully called him "a born rapscallion."

Gabriel's temperament was too remote from those of his school-fellows to produce real friendships. The nearest approach to such were a few casual acquaintances he made, including a grandson of Sir Walter Scott and a son of Westall the landscape painter. Some little popularity he acquired by his sketches of school incidents and his colouring of prints, but he chafed against a consciousness of isolation, and although the school, in its rejection of flogging and similar fashionable educational brutalities, was better than most of that time, he spoke in later years with bitter disgust, of his life there as an unhappy experience, from which, without the support of his mother's affection, he would have fled.

School days brought him widening horizons. Outside school Gabriel probably learned more than within its walls. Too poor to travel by bus, the brothers daily tramped from their home in Charlotte Street to the school and back again. At first they chose leading thoroughfares: Regent Street and the Strand; but soon, attracted by the hum and stir and variety of life in the humbler districts, they went by way of Tottenham Court Road and St. Giles. It was thus that as a child Gabriel first felt the fascination and acquired the knowledge of London which time only intensified and extended, until at length he was compared in this respect to Dickens.

Writing *Jenny* in later years, Gabriel described one incident of this period, when some precocious schoolmate proudly imparted to him an element of street-knowledge carefully hidden from the boys in their decorous Victorian home. For when over the sleeping Jenny, Gabriel afterwards recalled:

> . . . the wise, unchildish elf,
> To schoolmate lesser than himself,
> Pointing you out, what thing you are,

he was describing an incident of his own past. During these school journeys he was by no means always on his best behaviour. At times, pretending to be lame or deformed, he would arouse the sympathy of some kindly observer and then run off, laughing at the effect achieved.

The brothers' entry into King's College School had occurred

in a short season of comparative prosperity for old Gabriele, during which the family removed to No 50 Charlotte Street, a slightly larger house, allowing separate rooms for his sons and daughters. But this short season quickly passed, and for several years various misfortunes beset the Rossettis—illness, theft, financial loss, poverty. Frere as usual sent aid, and Gabriele's Dantesque studies went on. The condemned psaltery instead of preventing a return to his unhallowed mysteries had merely exacerbated his anti-papalism, intensified his enthusiasm for his endless task. Obtaining secret documents, petitions from inquisitors, antique tomes of the fifteenth and sixteenth centuries revealing the secrets of the Freemasons and "sects of love," Gabriele advanced once more against his adversaries, confident of victory.

His only fear was the inevitable consequence when his discoveries should be placed before the world. His triumph must involve the fall not only of the Catholic Church but even of religion itself. Thus his anxiety "to impose silence on the wordy disbelievers" of his theories was checked by a disconcerting prevision of himself as a supreme disrupter of Church and State, despite his desire for the fall of the papacy which, he considered, was retarding the day of Italy's freedom. Gradually a megalomaniac's dream was enfolding Gabriele. Henceforth, save for an occasional, transitory, outbreak of scepticism from Frere, their correspondence proceeds in an ever thickening atmosphere of mystery. It breathes of hushed voices, whispered warnings, of tremendous secrets upon which hang all human destinies. Frere's apprehensions were, if possible, even greater than Rossetti's. But Frere's worldly wisdom was also greater, his fears for religion at least equalled by his fears for Gabriele himself. It seemed to him that once again, as in Naples, personal vanity was to be Rossetti's undoing. "Would it be in my power," he wrote, "to persuade any man that the author of a dangerous work might nevertheless be a safe instructor for his family?" And he offered Gabriele £50 for Christmas, which, on the ground that some of his benefactor's last bounty still remained, the professor politely declined. Frere's warning was an unpleasant descent into sordid reality, from Rossetti's grandiose dream of staggering the world.

Amidst the enchantment of his task Gabriele barely noted the flying years. The far-flung tentacles of his suppositional secret sect led him to a deep investigation of the Platonic Love of the Middle Ages, which in turn drew him to the love-poetry of Mediaeval Italy and of Provence. Charles Lyell, preparing a translation of Dante's lyrical poetry, begged from Rossetti an *Introduction* of some hundred pages, on Platonic Love. Gladly consenting, he seized the opportunity, publicly to "unmask the old fox Petrarca," and set to work. "When the mask falls," he promised Frere, "you will perceive the Platonic lover disappearing and the Patarin sectary coming out." Henceforth "discoveries" came fast and furious. Dante's Beatrice, he found, was no woman but only a symbol of wisdom; Gabriel, in later years, ridiculing his father's theories, said Gabriele thought Beatrice was "the twopenny post." Petrarch's Laura, the professor found, was really a masonic lodge. Secret propaganda of the "sect" were *The Pilgrim's Progress*, Tom Moore's *Epicurean* and Victor Hugo's *Notre Dame de Paris*. Joyfully, he became increasingly aware that the sect's secret activities still continued and were all about him. "How many masked sphinxes in the literary world!" he exclaimed. "I have come upon so many that it is a true marvel." It was indeed! To Victor Hugo he sent, unsolicited, his *Sullo Spirito*, with a friendly hint that he had discovered, "not by knowledge communicated to me, but by my sole cogitation," the occult significance of his novel, but would not give the secret away. Hugo, well knowing how to humour *une marotte*, returned *Sullo Spirito* with the truthful yet ironical reply that having read it, he was not surprised that Gabriele had discovered a secret in his own story!

The discovery of these occult significances was, however, far from profitable, and without Frere's occasional charity the Rossetti family could hardly have survived. But to Gabriele came no thought of turning. After two more years of investigation, the hundred pages on Platonic Love promised Lyell had become two large volumes, and the sect had been increased by the addition of many more members, including St. Basil, Origen, Tertullian, Synesius, and the writers of the Old and New Testaments! Frere, appalled, filled with "alarm and astonishment," and convinced that readers of Gabriele's work would "be led to this short inference, that all religions are alike, all equally the result of human policy and contrivance," increasingly protested against publication. In his fear for his own and Rossetti's reputation, as well as, apparently, for the future welfare of Gabriele's soul, he even offered to pay him the profits he anticipated on the sale of the work, if only he would refrain from publishing it. But Gabriele refused to be thus silenced. Pointing out to Frere that his writing was being done in the pecuniary interest of his family, and ignoring Frere's delicately hinted rejoinder that of all people his family were the least likely to profit by it, he declared it had received the approval of eminently religious persons, and settled down yet more resolutely to his task.

In 1840, when Michelangelo, Pico della Mirandola, and Poliziano had joined the sect, and the work itself embraced five formidable volumes, *Il Mistero dell'Amor Platonico del Medio Evo derivato dai Misteri Antichi, etc., etc.*, was privately printed with the financial aid of Frere and Lyell. At this critical moment, however, both Gabriele's supporters lost courage and increasingly clamoured for the suppression of the work. Frere even demanded its destruction. Before the combined attack, Gabriele at last gave way. "I have not the courage (according to a phrase of Petrarca's)" Gabriele replied, "to burn with my own hands a beloved offspring that costs me so much pain; and if *you* would lend yourself to this necessary office (excuse my boldness), I would despatch to you the remaining edition. Whether Neptune or Vulcan be the devourer of my vigils, I shall not see it, but I will endure it. However this may be I will never put on sale here or elsewhere, a writing of such quality." "Most injudicious and might be ruinous," Lyell meanwhile reported on the work to Frere, "for (as I long since told him), an enemy could make it a bolt to shut the door of every ladies-school against him as a teacher, and thus deprive him of bread." Lyell was greatly perplexed, for Gabriele, he explained, "is half distracted, and implores me to write to you, and entreat you to revoke the order which condemns his book to the flames."

Worn out by the long years of overwork and arduous endeavour into which he had poured all the energy and intensity of his nature, an energy and intensity for which, since his departure from Italy, his Dante studies provided almost the sole outlet, the ageing scholar was deeply distressed to think of the destruction of the work which held so much of his life, his hopes, his pride, his self-assertion, his proof to the world of his unrecognized and ridiculed ability. The pleasure of publicity, the joy of refuting, of overwhelming his opponents, were to be snatched from him in the very hour of victory. He became obsessed, could not sleep, began to fear his own shadow he said, and complained: "I have become like one of those people of exaggerated piety who think that in their most insignificant action they have committed a mortal sin." That was the state to which the son of whom he was so proud, Dante Gabriel, would also be reduced one day.

In these circumstances, Frere, to spare Gabriele the additional pain of parting with his unlucky offspring, and relying on his promise not to sell the work, left most of the copies in his hands. Upon Gabriele's death, Mrs. Rossetti, eminently strong-minded, orthodox and pious, found them amongst her husband's effects and committed the great work which had absorbed the best years of his life, and was to have changed the destiny of Europe, to the flames. "Vulcan" not "Neptune" was to be the "devourer," after all!

Meanwhile, to divert his mind from his disappointment, old Gabriele composed "a little poem on the cholera morbus," then particularly active, and interested himself in his children, who were happily oblivious of these tremendous happenings. In recent years the children had spent their summer holidays in the country, in their grandparents' cottage at Holmer Green to which Gaetano Polidori and his wife had retired. There, Gabriel, even less active physically than in London, loitered about the house and garden, or caught frogs in the pond, although his love of animals would not allow him to harm them, while Christina, delighting in the little garden, already sadly observed the ruthless strife of nature, and made reflections thereon which in later days found expression in her devotional writings. These occasional delights however had ceased after three years, for the Polidoris, wearying of country seclusion, had returned to London in 1839, and with their

return the children's country excursions had come to an
end.

At home in the evenings, Dante Gabriel, the schoolboy,
continued the pursuits of his earlier childhood. Amidst the
strange assemblage which still nightly crowded the little parlour, he continued to draw and read with unabated zest.
Byron displaced Scott in the order of his affections, but Shakespeare still retained his unchallenged supremacy. Gabriel's
taste in literature was, from the beginning, widely varied
rather than nicely discriminative or sure. He delighted in
Dickens, in tales of chivalry, of brigands, of terror, and in the
Newgate Calendar. He continued to collect and colour prints, generally choosing mediaeval subjects in accordance with the literary
fashion of the time, and he made similar illustrations to his reading, including a series of bad pen-and-ink designs for the *Iliad*.

During these school years Gabriel gave little attention to the
writing of verse or prose. The *Arabian Nights* inspired an attempt
at *Aladdin*, a prose story, of which, however, only the first few
lines were written. In 1840, when each of the children decided
to compose a romantic tale, Gabriel contributed *Roderick and
Rosalba: A Story of the Round Table*, obviously inspired by Scott.
"It was a dark and stormy night," was the highly original
opening, and there in the darkness we may leave it. Now too,
influenced by Scott's *Marmion*, and by a tale of Allan Cunning-
ham's, one of the *Legends of Terror*, he began his first printed
poem: *Sir Hugh the Heron*. To induce his indolent grandson to
complete it, grandfather Polidori promised to print it, when
finished, on his private press, and it duly appeared, in 1843,
labelled—and rightly—"for private circulation only." "There
is no knowing what fool may some day foist the absurd trash
into print," Gabriel, perhaps with an eye upon his brother,
wrote of it in later years: "It is curious and surprising to
myself, as evincing absolutely no promise at all."

Gabriel, who had increasingly shown an interest in painting,
now, at thirteen, would do "nothing but invent groups and
designs." Impelled by declining health as well as by poverty
to reduce his expenses, and anxious to start his son as soon as
possible upon a career which he hoped would quickly be successful and lucrative, old Gabriele allowed him to follow his

artistic ambitions, and abandon his formal education at an exceptionally early age. Thus it was that in the summer of 1841, Gabriel left school for good and without regret. "Not wanting to thwart his inclination," wrote Gabriele, "I have started him on pursuing the profession he covets. If he succeeds, he will aid my old age. A hundred times do I thank God that my four children are all studious and all good. If I can leave them a good education, leading them to an honourable path in life, I shall die contented in the fogs of England, without regretting the sun of Italy." "As I became older," wrote Gabriel, a few years afterwards, putting his own experience into the speech of a character in *St. Agnes of Intercession*, "my boyish impulse towards art grew into a vital passion; till at last my father took me from school and permitted me my own bent of study."

At school Gabriel had learned little. Nevertheless, save for some lessons in German, at home, and his art lessons, he was to have no other formal instruction. He knew some Latin and had just commenced the rudiments of Greek, but knew so little of that, that after a few years he had forgotten even the alphabet, and probably could not even read Greek characters. He had, however, a fair knowledge of French, and was reading French novels and Hugo's poems with keen appreciation. Despite his knowledge of Italian, he knew of Italy's literature little more than the works of Ariosto. To these limited acquisitions he added a smattering of history and geography. On the other hand, he knew nothing of science, algebra, or geometry. Introspection, fancy, imagination, intuition, sympathy, rather than knowledge, were to form the basis of Rossetti's intellectual life, nor did he ever show any interest in the acquisition of mere encyclopedic information. But the insufficiency of his education was not without effect upon his character and taste. These defects were, however, less formidable than they may appear, for history shows that the artist's achievement is not the gift of schoolmasters, but the creation of his own genius.

III

ART STUDENT
1841–1848

I may say, briefly, that I was wayward enough in the pursuit, if not in the purpose; that I cared even too little for what could be taught me by others.

St. Agnes of Intercession D. G. ROSSETTI

"GABRIEL MEANS to be a painter," they had long said at home. Now the time for action was come. Those ineffable dreams of the little boy sitting by the parlour fire must be translated into form and colour. So, for seven years, from 1841 to 1848, Rossetti ostensibly applied himself to the practical, formal study of painting.

For the first four years he attended "Sass's," a Bloomsbury drawing-school kept by a Mr. Cary, whose father, the well-known translator of Dante, was a friend of Gabriele Rossetti. Much favoured by Academicians, Sass's, three years before, had trained Millais, the nine-year-old prodigy, now a distinguished student in the Academy Schools. Holman Hunt, however, a plodding student yet also to be famous, had recently refused to enter Sass's because of its "mechanical precision."

Loving art but detesting technical training, and finding no charm in the antique, Gabriel was soon bored and disgusted by the dull, rigorous discipline of Sass's, and openly contemptuous of his teachers. Although his vivacity was tireless, he was but a desultory student, and made little or no effort to improve his conspicuous weakness in technique. Careless, indifferent to reality, in sketching the human lower leg he gave it, despite his study of anatomy, but one bone! During these intermediate years between boyhood and manhood, he was a not entirely agreeable person. To Mr. Cary he showed a studied insolence, singing loudly when silence was requested, using charcoal when forbidden, giving "idleness" as his excuse for absence even while pasting into fellow-students' hats, under the master's eye, the sonnets he had absented himself to write. Temperamental, critical, sarcastic, mimicking those he disliked, somewhat "spoilt" in fact, Rossetti left upon his class-mates an impression of waywardness, irregularity, brusqueness and unapproachability, varied at times by moods of even boisterous gaiety, during which he revealed a generous, warmly affectionate nature usually concealed. He was not above playing an occasional practical joke, and so loved to caricature the hated antique held up for the students' admiration, that Redgrave the Academician, seeing his drawing-board so ornamented, was moved to protest.

At Sass's as at school, Gabriel made few acquaintances and no friends, and already showed that nervous fear of public criticism which was to become so conspicuous in his later life. Nevertheless, unhampered by authority, he showed interest and determination. He joined a sketching club, worked for it with enthusiasm, and, so he said, "derived great improvement from it." Inheriting from his father an extraordinarily rich and beautiful voice, he also had "personal magnetism," and soon began to use it for his own ends.

It was thus, in the autumn of 1843 and again in the winter of 1844, that in two visits he made to Boulogne for the sake of his health, he captured the affections of his father's friends, the kindly Italian artist Signor Maenza and his English wife, with whom he stayed there. The picturesqueness of life in the old town, its quays and market-place thronged with quaintly-garbed fishermen and peasants, its ancient buildings, its old Gothic church and the Catholic services with pictures and images, music and singing, while the old fisherwomen knelt praying beneath the flickering lights in the dim aisles, all delighted him. The Maenzas, charmed by his "elevated spirit," nursed him through an attack of smallpox fortunately too mild to leave any permanent trace. "His imagination promises much," wrote Signor Maenza to Gabriele Rossetti, on the eve of Gabriel's second, and final, departure, "and I am persuaded that he will reach the goal all right." But Gabriel ignored the old man's shrewd hint to his father, that he should take up fencing or gymnastics, "to check the sedentary habits to which he is greatly inclined."

In December 1845, two years later than he had originally intended, Gabriel entered the Antique School of the Royal Academy, and the two years which followed were largely a repetition of those he had passed at Sass's. Rumours of his poetic and artistic ability, of his independence and eccentricity, had preceded him, and his entry into the Academy Schools created something of an "impression." "Dear me, Sir, you *have* a fine name," Mr. Jones the venerable keeper of the Academy Schools stammered on hearing Gabriel's rich, sonorous declaration of identity: "Gabriel Charles Dante Rossetti." Poor, proud, shabby in his old, ill-fitting, unfashionable, swallow-tail coat, Gabriel faced his new associates with a defiant, arrogant air of assumed indifference to their opinion. To one of them, indeed, he seems to have appeared almost as the fashionable "Byronic hero" of the day, with deep-set, sunken eyes in which smouldered a "lurid light," "roseless and hollow" cheeks revealing a "waste of life and midnight oil." Such was the effect of literary suggestion and Rossetti's foreign appearance upon at least one observer: of darkening, thick, curly, uncut, neglected hair, deep eye-sockets, dark eyebrows, pale cheeks, and spare, unathletic figure.

To Gabriel, the Academy Schools proved as disappointing as Sass's; even more so, indeed, as he had expected more from them. Once again he proved the truth of his admission in later life that what was "imposed on him as an obligation," what he ought to do, he could not do. As uninterested in the technique of painting, as bored by art-discipline as before, he again rejected advice and control, showed neither enthusiasm nor assiduity, and, despite his later references to frugal and hasty breakfasts snatched at street-stalls on his way to classes that apparently began almost at dawn, it is not strange that of his studies at Sass's and the Academy Schools little trace remains. "A vanishing quantity," said one who knew him, of his work at both places, nor need we question the accuracy of that description.

As at Sass's, but now with increasing confidence, his dominating character asserted itself. By his sketches, poems and personal presence, Rossetti quickly gained a following among the more impressionable students, and, moving about the

Academy Schools and British Museum with a crowd of admirers at his heels, soon became a conspicuous figure. To this bodyguard he would present his sketches, showing armoured knights rescuing fair ladies, picturesque mediaeval lovers, and similar themes culled from the works of his favourite romantic poets.

While still at Sass's, Gabriel had drawn his brother and sisters to join him in primitive attempts to create manuscript family journals. In this way, under the influence of Byron and of Retzsch's *Outlines to Goethe's Faust*, he had already begun to write and illustrate a prose romance of diabolism, *Sorrentino*, in which the Devil as principal character, thwarted the course of true love. But when Gabriel read it aloud his sisters, denouncing it as "horrible" and "indecent," left the room, and soon wearying of it, he destroyed the unfinished manuscript, to William's lasting regret. Next, in a sudden passion for poetic fame, he had written a tragic ballad, *William and Marie*, had sent it with an illustrative design to the editor of a magazine, and had neither seen nor heard of either again.

In later years, Gabriel chose to consider his doggerel stanzas on Napoleon at Waterloo, entitled *The End of It*, written in 1845, as "my first poem." From this, a year later, he had advanced to the free yet cadenced music of *A Prayer*, with its characteristic idealization of woman and love:

> Lady has not my thought
> Dared much?—for I would be
> The ending of darkness, and the dawn
> Of a new day to thee,
> And thine oasis, and thy place of rest,
> And thy time of peace, lady.

By this time, his early fear of Dante had yielded to a growing interest, and he had begun to make verse translations from the poet, as well as from Dante's Italian contemporaries, the men whose works old Gabriele had studied for his *Amor Platonico*.

Another year passed, and Rossetti at nineteen showed himself not only a promising verse-translator from Italian, but also by various tentative versions of *My Sister's Sleep*, *The Blessed Damozel*, *Jenny* and *The Portrait*, an original poet of some promise. Nor did his attempts at these poems by any means exhaust his first season of poetic creation. He soon began *A Last Confession*, the opening part of *Dante at Verona*, and much of *The Bride's Prelude*—some twelve years before his continuation of that never-finished poem.

In addition to these major poems, Gabriel at this time wrote many slighter pieces, including the first version of *Ave*, as well as the first of his sonnets on pictures, *For an Annunciation: Early German*, the painting inspiring it being one seen in an auction room. Poetically, Rossetti's early adolescence was to be conspicuously productive, until, in his twenty-fifth year, the rapidly dying flame of his inspiration flickered down into smouldering embers, not to be requickened for many years.

Thus, amidst diverse interests, and marked by but moderate achievement in painting, Gabriel's period of artistic tutelage slowly passed. Reading and writing seemed to absorb more of his attention than the profession he had chosen as a career. Shakespeare still, as ever, delighted him; but Scott and Byron now yielded place to Browning, whose passion, mediaevalism, and psychological analysis included all that most appealed to Rossetti in both literature and life. While the British public, bewildered by Browning's incomprehensibilities, feared, like Douglas Jerrold, for its reason, or grumbled like Tennyson, Gabriel travelled happily through *Paracelsus*, *Pippa Passes*, *The Blot on the Scutcheon*, *Bells and Pomegranates* and even *Sordello*.

For such minor contemporaries as Charles Wells, author of *Stories after Nature* and *Joseph and his Brethren*, or the poet, Ebenezer Jones, Rossetti conceived the deepest admiration, enthusiastically advertising them as unappreciated geniuses to the end of his life. Borrowing ten shillings from William, he bought from a British Museum attendant, a now famous manuscript of William Blake, with the never by him fulfilled intention of editing and publishing it some day. His devout, watchful mother was not always at ease about her son's reading. "Evidently written by a religious person," he added, to soothe her, after declaring Samuel Warren's *Ten Thousand a Year* "one of the most splendid works (not to say *the* most splendid), which I ever read." When, shortly afterwards, Mrs. Rossetti was alarmed by a complaint of Aunt Margaret, that Gabriel was reading indecent books, he indignantly denied the accusation, due, he discovered, to his having expressed a vague intention of buying Shelley's works. His desire for them was, he explained, "solely on account of the splendid versification, and not from any love of his atheistical sentiments." He wished, he indignantly declared, "that Aunt Margaret would refrain from circulating such falsehoods." It is to be hoped that his mother was comforted, for in the following year he bought a Shelley and, as his brother remarked, "surged through its pages like a flame."

For Gabriel, despite the boredom of the schools, these were indeed enthusiastic years. The poet-painter William Bell Scott, who had already caught Gabriel's fancy with his dreary *Rosabell* and *A Dream of Love*, intensified his admiration by another even drearier poem published in 1847, *The Year of the World*, in "five books"—so its author described it—"treating the different forms of religion underlying the periods of time occupied by the civilization of the world." Gabriel read it, and decided that, above all, he must make the personal acquaintance of the ineffable Scott. So, to Scott, in November 1847, he despatched a long, rambling, incoherent letter of enthusiasm for the poet's works known to him, begging at the same time to be told where the remainder might be obtained. To this impassioned epistle, the pleased but "canny" Scott replied with native caution. Gabriel's immediate response was to send Scott his own manuscript poems, entitled *Songs of the Art Catholic*.

Shortly afterwards Scott, visiting London, called on the Rossettis. Gabriel was not at home, but in the small "front parlour" Scott found the old professor, a black cap on his head, "with a great peak or shade for his eyes . . . sitting by the fire in a great chair, the table drawn close to his chair, with a thick manuscript book open before him, and the largest snuff-box I ever saw beside it conveniently open." Christina, "a slight girl with a serious, regular profile, dark against the pallid, wintry light without," stood near the window, writing at a "high narrow reading-desk."

Scott was at this time teacher in a Government art-school in Newcastle. Born in Scotland of Scottish parents, he had early absorbed the less happy qualities of his domestic environment.

The untimely demise of several elder brothers and sisters in infancy had plunged his parents into a permanent melancholy which proved contagious. Almost with his first words Scott had lisped to his mother of the ethics of suicide, while his entry upon school-life was darkened by a firm conviction of having committed "the unforgivable sin" against the third person of the Trinity. In addition, his sense of guilt was peculiarly complicated by the fact that he had not the least idea what "the unforgivable sin" might be. For Scott, later experience of life had been as little hilarious as its beginnings, and an eight years' struggle to live by poetry and painting in London had ended, three years before, in retreat to Newcastle. Nor was the teaching of art to ambitious Novocastrians an adequate solace to one who combined strong literary and artistic aspirations with no mean opinion of himself.

The Rossettis, pleased with their visitor, found him tall, rather bony but well developed; they noticed his dark hair (left thick and flowing in the manner of "artistic" people of the day), his "very pale clear blue" eyes, deliberately penetrating, his bushy, lifted eyebrows slanting in Mephistophelian fashion upwards from the nose. To their southern ears, his slow, guttural, pure-vowelled, Northern speech was strange and amusing. Despite his "pondering and somewhat melancholy" air, they found in Scott a certain naïveté, suggesting a nature more genial than his appearance had led them to expect. William Rossetti thought him "handsome and highly impressive," and the whole family agreed that he was "not only attractive but even fascinating."

Gabriel's enthusiasm for Scott, though genuine, had not perhaps been entirely disinterested. More and more he wearied of the academic routine which kept him drawing from casts when he hungered to paint from life. He craved self-expression, and this the schools had denied him. Instead, as he shortly afterwards complained in his early tale, *St. Agnes of Intercession*, they offered only "a toil rigidly exact and dealing often with trifles." He was, too, eager for success and its rewards. These were more alluring than a long, slow and deliberate apprenticeship to art. Poetry perhaps, he began to think, might offer a shorter and easier way to his goal. Thus, more insistently, his thoughts turned to poetry. To impress a poet like Scott might open the road to literary success and fame.

Poverty intensified Rossetti's impatience for "success" as a painter and poet. For several years now, Gabriele's failing health and consequent loss of pupils had gradually brought the fortunes of the Rossettis to a low ebb. Mrs. Rossetti had been forced to resume her French and Italian lessons; Maria was a somewhat unhappy governess in the family of Lady Charles Thynne; William, a clerk in the Excise Office. Christina, unfortunately, was too weak in health to do more than help in the house. Frere, unfailingly generous, had continued his assistance from time to time until his death in 1846. On hearing the news of his friend's death, old Gabriele had fallen on his knees, crying, as the tears trickled from his dim eyes: "Anima bella, benedetta sei tu, dovunque sei" (Noble soul, blessed be thou wherever thou art). It was a fitting end to an honourable friendship.

A year later, too blind and infirm to continue even a pretence of teaching, Gabriele resigned his chair at King's College, and (as he informed the Principal in his note of withdrawal), himself to God's will. "I have ever considered it a high honour," he concluded, "to be connected with so noble an institution, and shall with pride entitle myself to the day of my death, 'late Professor of King's College'." "I have personal feelings, arising out of relations to the Crown Prince of Hanover, which make me sympathize most sincerely with you in the calamity with which it has pleased God to afflict you," was the Principal's extraordinary reply, beginning with a brief and purely formal expression of "great regret." "Like my beloved pupil, however," he continued and concluded, "your secret for consolation is the only source of comfort and there you will, I doubt not, find it abundantly." After reading this note we may perhaps cease to wonder why poor Gabriele had so often returned from Professorial dinners at the College in a state of profound depression, vowing that he would never attend one again.

As for Gabriel at this time, even deepening poverty failed to stimulate him to greater exertions in the Academy Schools. While his mother, Maria and William plied their dreary tasks to support the home, he would sit translating mediaeval Italian verse in the British Museum, or writing poems in Charlotte Street. He was moved neither to active assistance nor to a more vigorous pursuit of art. Maria's woes, however, drove him to a momentary protest. "I hope you told Lady Charles," he wrote to his mother, who was then on holiday with Christina, "that poor Maggy is not to be bullied and badgered out of her life by a lot of beastly brats; and that Lady C. fully understands the same, and has already provided the said Maggy with a bamboo." Nevertheless, "Maggy" soon returned to Charlotte Street to help her mother with the daily Italian lessons in the homes of her private pupils.

Perhaps it was the drabness of real life which, despite his poverty, sent Gabriel so often at this time to the warmth and light of the theatre, for imaginative and emotional relief. His taste in the theatre was as catholic as in literature. All he asked was that a play should be interesting, and interest he found in bad plays as well as in good. Shakespeare or Webster, an amusing comedy or farce, a bad melodrama, would bring him infinite amusement. He had too his favourite actresses, and would go to the Adelphi to see Miss Woolgar or to Sadler's Wells to see Miss Glyn. But in musical matters he was no Italian. "I abhor concerts," he said, and when given tickets to hear Jenny Lind, he passed them on to friends. Oratorios, then so popular, he detested. Once, on returning from a performance of the *Messiah* at the Crystal Palace, it had seemed to him, he declared, that "everybody got up and shouted at him as loudly as possible." "Music," said Holman Hunt, his fellow-student and friend, "Rossetti regarded as positively offensive; for him it was nothing but a noisy nuisance." Nevertheless, at this time opera could on occasion please. He went to Covent Garden to see *Lucrezia*, found the singer Grisi "most tremendous," and "Alboni's song, with the funeral chaunt between the stanzas, very fine." The end of the first act specially delighted him, for, as he told William, "in this Grisi screamed continuously for about ten minutes, and was immense. We must go and see it together." For Gabriel, the dramatic rather than the musical qualities of opera were obviously its greatest charm.

As the spring of 1848 and Rossetti's twentieth year drew near, ineffectuality, failure in art and poetry seemed to dog his steps. Already his divided nature, unable to achieve a unified, integrated state, began to reveal itself. Lethargy and indecision were to frustrate the first half of his career. Once again he showed his inherent inability to do what was imposed upon him. Disgusted with difficulties of technique, increasingly bored by routine, vainly longing to express the emotions and dreams rising within him, he suddenly refused to endure longer the discipline of the schools. "As to which statue at the Museum I drew most or learned least from—or which professor at the Academy 'set' the model in the worst taste—these are things which no one need care to know," he wrote a few months later in *St. Agnes of Intercession*, adding, probably long afterwards with the illumination of retrospect: "I may say, briefly, that I was wayward enough in the pursuit, if not in the purpose; that I cared even too little for what could be taught me by others; and that my original designs greatly outnumbered my school drawings."

In later years he was bitterly to regret his inadequate training and technique. But now, in his impatience with academic instruction, he had no desire to proceed to the schools of Life and Painting. Above all he desired freedom—freedom to express the hauntings of ideal love and beauty which now flashed upon him. In poetry he was free from supervision and interference. The years of monotonous copying from the antique seemed to him wasted. This was not the way to "success." The independent spirit of the father rose in the son. In painting as in poetry he would be his own master. So, in a mood of dissatisfaction and revolt, from the Academy Schools he drifted away.

IV

THE PRERAPHAELITE BROTHERHOOD
1848-1849

Loin d'être "Chef de l'École" par priorité ou par mérite, je puis à
peine me reconnaître comme y appartenant, si le style du peu que j'ai
fait en peinture venait à être comparé avec les ouvrages des autres
peintres nommés Préraphaëlites. . . . C'est la camaraderie, plutôt
que la collaboration réelle du style, qui a uni mon nom aux leurs dans
les jours d'enthousiasme d'il y a vingt ans.

Letter to M. E. Chesneau D. G. ROSSETTI

FOR GABRIEL, the "year of revolution," 1848, was of singular
importance. In it, he made new and stimulating friends,
finally chose painting in preference to poetry as a career,
organized an aesthetic revolt.

Increasingly conscious of the technical difficulties to be
overcome in painting, he now made an impetuous attempt to
master the art. Since first seeing works by a little-known artist,
Ford Madox Brown, at the exhibition of competitive designs
for wall-paintings for the new Houses of Parliament, in 1844,
Gabriel had looked on Brown as the ideal artist. Now, having
received the financial support of generous Aunt Charlotte
Polidori—a governess in the Earl of Wicklow's family—
Gabriel wrote to the unknown Brown, begging him to accept
him as a pupil. So extravagantly laudatory was the letter,
however, that Brown, an unsuccessful painter and embittered
widower of twenty-six, suspecting a hoax, set off for Charlotte
Street with a stout stick, intending to inflict summary chastisement on the offender. What else could one think of a stranger
who declared he "listened with avidity" whenever Brown's
name was mentioned; "rushed first of all" to see Brown's
"glorious works" at exhibitions, and there remained, "standing
on the same spot for fabulous lengths of time"? On Brown's
arrival, however, Gabriel's sincerity was so manifest, his
charm so potent, that Brown not only accepted him on the
spot, as a pupil, but even refused any fee. For both men it

was the beginning of a life-long friendship. "By far the best man that I know—the really good man," Rossetti was one day accurately to describe this new acquaintance.

In the day-time Rossetti now worked in Brown's studio in Clipstone Street, Marylebone, and at nights, following Brown's advice, he attended a life class which he thought admirable and much enjoyed. For a time, he found Brown's tuition beyond all praise. "His kindness and the trouble he takes about me are really astonishing," he told his aunt: "I cannot imagine what I have done to deserve them." Soon, Brown was "a most delightful friend," their relations so "confidential" that Brown was privileged to see and admire his poems. For Gabriel's poetic ambitions, never entirely relinquished, were reviving. Before approaching Brown, Gabriel had sent his verses to the *doyen* of contemporary English letters, Leigh Hunt, begging his advice as to the choice of poetry or of painting as a career. Hunt, in a kindly reply, had greeted Rossetti as "an unquestionable poet, thoughtful, imaginative, and with rare powers of expression," but after his own bitter experience of literary poverty, had naturally advised painting, exhorting Gabriel: "If you paint as well as you write, you may be a rich man. . . . But I need hardly tell you that poetry, even the very best—nay, the best, in this respect, is apt to be the worst—is not a thing for a man to live upon while he is in the flesh, however immortal it may render his spirit." Nothing could have more certainly damped Rossetti's poetic ardour.

The enthusiasm with which he had entered Brown's studio also quickly waned. Brown, thoroughly trained by Baron Wappers of Antwerp in all the details of painting, from etching to oils, soon proved, to Gabriel's disgust, as exacting and laborious a master as any at Sass's or the Academy Schools. Reluctantly copying under Brown's supervision, pickle-jars, medicine bottles, and Brown's own picture, *The Seraphs' Watch*, which showed "cherub angels" guarding the crown of thorns, Rossetti soon lost heart and fell away. "Brown," he told Scott some years later, "is the dearest and kindest of old fellows. He would take no pay; had been educated at Brussels, and had a system of education which he would gladly apply to me. He set me to fag at some still life—drawing and painting both; but I could not stand that kind of thing; and after a time or two gave it up." Thus it was that Gabriel, his small patience quickly exhausted, abandoned Brown for a new mentor in pictorial art. But his faith in Brown's knowledge and talent never wavered. That, as well as his awareness of his own technical inadequacy, is clearly shown in his life-long habit of referring to Brown for advice in all difficulties of composition and technique.

"Old Brown" was six years older than Gabriel. Holman Hunt, his new teacher, was Rossetti's senior by but one year. Quiet, retiring, hard-working, obstinate and ambitious, as laborious an artist as Brown himself, Hunt had won his way, despite poverty and parental opposition, from a City office to the Academy Schools. For long, the two art-students were unacquainted. Peacefully working in some remote corner, Hunt would see Gabriel pass from time to time, accompanied by a noisy throng of admirers. The King of such a court Hunt made no effort to know. Not until he one day chanced upon Gabriel alone and sketching a single female figure from a cast of the exquisite Ghiberti doors of the Florence Baptistry, which Hunt too admired, did he speak to Gabriel for a moment before passing on. Nor was it till Rossetti saw Hunt's *Eve of St. Agnes* at the Royal Academy Exhibition of 1848 that they became friends. Rossetti, like Hunt an admirer of Keats, loudly declared the painting the best of all the exhibits. But he would hardly have approved Hunt's characteristically sober respect for the subject as an illustration of "the sacredness of honest, responsible love and the weakness of intemperance." A few days after seeing the picture at the exhibition, Gabriel called at Hunt's studio, and soon the acquaintance between them ripened into close friendship.

To Hunt, Gabriel confessed himself "very disheartened" about his painting, poured out indeed his tale of woe—his weariness of Brown's method, his impatience at being restricted to the copying of "pickle jars" and similar objects. Ignoring the facts of chronological sequence, he described his letter to Leigh Hunt as the consequence of the actually subsequent letter to Brown, and described himself as one driven by despair from the futilities of Brown's tuition, to poetry, and back again by Leigh Hunt, to painting. Such at least was Holman Hunt's story, which, if correct, was certainly a fantastic version of the truth. Gabriel, Hunt learned, had withdrawn from Brown's instruction, and was working without aim or direction in the studio of a sculptor friend. There, indeed, he had "broken down" again, baffled by difficulties of technique, unable to paint the themes he desired, yet unwilling to return to the humble subjects Brown had set him.

Upon this, Hunt suggested a compromise to lighten Gabriel's burden. Both belonged to a sketching club, *The Cyclographic*, which circulated amongst its members, for mutual criticism, the members' own designs. Recalling a design of Gabriel's recently circulated, and admired by Millais, Hunt suggested that Gabriel should attempt a painting from it. In this way, even while painting the abhorred still life of the accessories, Rossetti would be stimulated by the interest of an original composition expressive of an idea—for such was his bent. Rossetti liked the suggestion and wished to begin work at once, in Hunt's own studio and under his personal supervision. Hunt, who had already taken a pupil, refused to share his studio with Gabriel, but promised to see much of him, and to help him with criticism and advice. Gabriel then showed Hunt his poems, including *The Blessed Damozel*, *My Sister's Sleep*, and an early version of *Jenny*, asking him to read them and give him a frank opinion of their worth. For even now, poetry could not be given up.

Whatever the opposition, Rossetti seldom failed to achieve his desires, and when Hunt, on selling his *Eve of St. Agnes* for seventy pounds, took a studio of his own, Gabriel, overbearing Hunt's objections, soon established himself there as day-partner, paying, of course, a part of the rent. But the natural indolence which was so largely to contribute to the frustration that marked Rossetti's career, was already revealing itself. Impressed by a small head of Christina that Gabriel had painted, his godfather, Lyell, now commissioned a portrait of old Gabriele, and unwisely paid him ten pounds in advance. On receiving the money, Rossetti, baffled and angered by difficulties of technique, at once ceased painting, despite his father's protests, and, with Hunt, made holiday jaunts to

Rochester Castle, Greenwich and Blackheath, giving the cleaning of Hunt's studio in preparation for his own entry, as his excuse.

Together on the Thames steamer they read Monckton Milnes's recent *Life and Letters of Keats*, while Rossetti, at the various places visited, sketched and poetized to his heart's content. At times, discarding his usual moodiness, he would play the clown, as when, for instance, on the almost deserted pier at Greenwich, he advanced threateningly upon a single intimidated and retreating urchin, declaiming revolutionary lines from Shelley's *Rosalind and Helen* against "tyrants" and "priests of the bloody faith." During the ten days that Lyell's ten pounds lasted, Gabriel made holiday, while his father, with increasing anger, watched his disquieting son. "I say nothing to him for fear of some insulting reply. You know him well enough," he reported to Gabriel's absent mother; "The money has simply led him astray, not reconciled him to his work." It was often to be thus with Rossetti and his art.

In a few days, however, Gabriel's money was exhausted, while he, installed in Hunt's bleak studio, No. 7 Cleveland Street, at the corner of Fitzroy Square, and with the assiduous Hunt's example ever before his eyes, experienced a marked revival of enthusiasm. "Hunt and I," he told William on August 20th, "are now settled down quite comfortably." With apologies for delay as well as for his father's exaggerated praise of it, he sent Lyell the portrait of Gabriele, whose only merit, he declared, was "its resemblance, which all pronounce to be striking," and he added, modestly, "I endeavour to persuade myself that its unsatisfactory character in other respects is owing in a great measure to its being my first attempt in oils of the size of life." "A funny piece of painting, but no doubt considerably though not perfectly like," he described it thirteen years later, on seeing it again. Meanwhile, conscious of its imperfections, he promised Lyell, as a gift, another portrait of Gabriele already begun.

It was under Hunt's somewhat fussy supervision that Gabriel now turned to his first important work in oils, *The Girlhood of Mary Virgin*. Technical skill, as Bell Scott on calling immediately remarked, was conspicuously absent. The picture Scott thought akin to Gabriel's *Songs of the Art Catholic*. This Italian, he wrongly concluded, must be a "Romanist." Noting Rossetti's clumsy, ignorant method, his unskilful use of chalk, his oils thin as water-colours, his use of water-colour brushes although painting in oils, his canvas primed with white, smooth as cardboard and with every tint transparent, the sceptical Scott, as observant of other's failings as of his own virtues, found the scene amusing, agreeable; yet, in some obscure way, impressive.

Together in the studio, Hunt and Rossetti discussed their various interests. Hunt, in revolt against contemporary taste, despised the English painters of the time as trite, affected, and conventional, offering only "pictured wax works" for figures and "inane prettiness for beauty." His own attitude to art, exacting truth, self-restraint and humility in painting, an attitude moral rather than aesthetic, found fortuitous encouragement in the chance discovery of Ruskin's first volume of *Modern Painters*. The future Preraphaelite must have hailed with delight Ruskin's denunciation of art in Rome, where "among all students, the authority of their predecessors in art is supreme and without appeal, and the mindless copyist studies Raffaelle, but not what Raffaelle studied."

To Millais, two years his junior but already the idol of the schools, Hunt had confided his rebellious opinions as they worked together in the evenings in Millais' studio in Gower Street. Millais, understanding little of this revolutionary enthusiasm, and at heart indifferent, chose the easiest course. Acquiescing in Hunt's denunciation of Raphael as careless of truth, false in anatomy, prone to pompous posturing of figures, Millais was gratefully welcomed by Hunt as a fellow rebel. "Then," retorted unconverted students ironically to Hunt the proselytizer, "you are Preraphaelites;" and this name, despite the intended disparagement, Hunt at least readily accepted.

In Gabriel, Hunt now saw a potential ally, while Rossetti, angry at Brown's recent attempt at art-discipline, and even more at his own technical weakness and the difficulties his picture presented, on hearing of his friend's revolutionary mood, allowed his own discontents to flame up in sympathy, and welcomed revolt. Although he shocked Hunt by denouncing in theory and ignoring in practice the rules of perspective which Hunt vainly strove to instil, he accepted his friend's love of "Preraphaelite detail," and to some extent his belief in "going to Nature" for his models. Adherence to "Nature" in painting his *Girlhood of Mary Virgin*, necessitated, however anachronistically, a raid upon Professor Rossetti's *libri somma-mente mistici* for mediaeval tomes on which to place the vase holding the lily, the passing of a week in a conservatory painting a vine, and the posing of Christina and his mother as The Virgin and St. Anne.

In this, Hunt joyfully recognized Gabriel's conversion to the Preraphaelite cause. Yet that Rossetti, temperamentally indifferent to all abstract principles, genuinely accepted Hunt's confusion of general moral precepts and detailed literal transcription with art, that like Hunt he yearned "to make art a handmaid in the cause of justice and truth," is incredible both in the light of his own nature and of his own later comments and career. Rather, the independent spirit of the father, the poet of political revolution in Naples, was finding new expression in the son, moving him to join the aesthetic revolt in Gower Street. For Gabriel at least, the chief incentive was the excitement of an attack upon the Academicians, the supporters of the system he had so hated at Sass's and the Academy Schools, and the assertion of his own individuality, of the rising generation against the generation that was already established.

Nevertheless, Rossetti's impetuosity in finding new converts, quickly turned Hunt's rejoicing to anxiety. First, Gabriel brought into the fold his brother William, who, fired by the aesthetic enthusiasm and ambitions about him, now crowned arduous days in the Inland Revenue Office with laborious nights at a drawing-school, making conscientious but rigid studies in the nude. Next, Gabriel claimed an impecunious student-sculptor, Thomas Woolner, whose ambition and self-confidence were more obvious than his talent. James Collinson, an uninspired and uninspiring art-student, whose perpetual somnolence rivalled that of the fat boy in *Pickwick*, was also seized upon by Gabriel who approved his recent painting of a workhouse boy in his dismal uniform. "A born stunner,"

Gabriel declared Collinson, and despite Hunt's hesitation, brought him into the rebel band.

Alarmed by such facile extension of the conspiratorial ranks, with enthusiasm rather than achievement the test for entry, Hunt now decided that if Rossetti could introduce three such members, he, Hunt, an *original* member of the circle, might surely introduce one more, and brought his "painting pupil" Stephens, the rhetorical cripple, into the company. To the objection that Stephens had painted nothing, Hunt retorted with the severe and irrefutable logic of the Mad Hatter, that as he had done nothing, nothing could be brought against him! At the same time, fearing Gabriel's further activities, Hunt firmly declared that the extreme limit of admissions had now been reached. Such, in fact, was the almost Gilbertian creation of the "Preraphaelite Brotherhood," as it soon chose to be called.

When Millais—who, humiliated by the Academy's rejection of his *Cymon and Iphigenia*, had retired for the summer to Oxford —returned to town, he disappointed the expectant Hunt. Although he accepted Rossetti, he ridiculed the rest of what he flippantly termed "Hunt's flock." "I can't understand so far, what you are after," he said. "Are you getting up a regiment to take the Academy by storm?" To Hunt's somewhat lame explanations he turned but a sceptical ear. He was disquieted and displeased. He had no wish to invite public ridicule, especially after his recent mishap at the Academy Exhibition, and a society for the reform of painting, consisting largely of persons who could not paint, was, he knew, less likely to reform art than to excite derision. He had no wish to associate himself with an amateur society for the possible inspiration of beginners in painting, which was what Hunt seemed to have formed. So Millais decided that this ragged regiment should not be accepted until he had inspected them.

When, a few evenings later, the probationers duly appeared in Millais' studio for this crucial test, there was, amongst the various books in the room, a borrowed volume of engravings of those remarkable fourteenth-century frescoes that look out upon the Campo Santo at Pisa[1]—a work which Ruskin later

---

[1] Much damaged, I understand, in the recent war.

68

described as "Lasinio's execrable engravings," after having declared three years before that the frescoes themselves had opened to him "a veritable Palestine." The book aroused Hunt's enthusiasm, and, so at least he believed, that of the whole circle. The frescoes, they decided, should be their model. They would seek to emulate, said Hunt, "the innocent spirit which had directed the invention of the painter," and attempt to create "a kindred simplicity." The largely unknown imitators of Giotto, who had painted these frescoes, were mistaken by the band for careful observers of "Nature" and so, for exponents of Hunt's basic principle. In this erroneous belief all accepted them, at Hunt's instigation, as exemplars of their own revolutionary aims and ideals in art.

Although at the close of the meeting Millais was still sceptical as to the value of their new allies, there was no obvious excuse for withdrawal, and this decisive September evening they regarded in later years as the original birthnight of the Preraphaelite Brotherhood, although as yet it had no name. Their sole unity of view and certainty of aim was revolt against contemporary English art as represented in the Academy. Their principles were vague and confused, their name so far undetermined, their theories without unity or clarity. In the many discussions which followed, conflicting aims and theories battled together. Hunt, however, despite all drawbacks, rejoiced to think that art was now being placed, by himself and his friends, on the moral foundation of "Truth to Nature." Honest, careful toil would now obtain, he thought, the praise it morally deserved. For Woolner and Stephens there was the satisfaction of association with Millais and Hunt, painters who were already attracting attention; for William Rossetti there was a pleasant sense of being caught up by vast aesthetic forces gathering to shape a new universe of art; and for Gabriel, there was, above everything else, the fun, the exquisite "lark" of it all! For at heart, like Millais Gabriel was sceptical. He was not impressed by the book of frescoes. He even went to Brown to laugh at Hunt's enthusiasm for them. But Brown told him to go and look at them again, as they were "the finest things in the world"—which sobered Gabriel.

Thus, the Preraphaelite Movement, in its inception, how-

ever disappointing to the modern historian of art seeking
unity of ideas and a definite aesthetic theory, appealed to its
founders at the time, chiefly because it lacked all unity save
the common principle of revolt against contemporary fashion
in painting. But Millais, a shrewd judge of the world, was
a little uneasy, a little regretful that the movement had
ever begun—or rather, that he had been caught up in its
progress.

With principles so vague, practice—so far as there *was* any
practice—so varied, a name for the circle was specially necessary to give it an appearance of unity. Even after the meeting
at Millais', there was much confusion. Rossetti and Brown, for
instance, mistakenly identified it with the "Early Christian"
style of the contemporary German Preraphaelites led by Overbeck and Cornelius, whose aim was the propagation of "Catholic Art." Brown, years before, had visited the two "Early
Christian" leaders in Rome, though even then the movement,
as much religious as artistic, was in decay. The monastic
atmosphere of the palazzo which Overbeck and Cornelius
shared with the remnant of their band, had impressed Brown.
Overbeck, clad in a black velvet gown of monastic type,
corded at the waist, had received him with marked humility,
and shown him his paintings, in which, to eliminate the
sensuous, human flesh was made to resemble that of a wooden
doll or lay figure. Cornelius too, less unworldly, a short, red-
haired, active, somewhat impatient man, had shown him his
painting of *Death on the Pale Horse*, pointing out its features
with a stick—like a showman. The primitive rigidity and
plaster-like colouring of their works had held Brown with a
strange, impossible charm.

In the Italian and German painters of the Quattro Cento
these German Preraphaelites had found exemplars of their
own devotional aestheticism. Raphael's predecessors they
admired for being religious and ascetic artists devoted to the
decoration of churches and monasteries. Brown's own art,
under the influence of these Germans, had changed in sympathy, tending towards their "Early Christian" style, and it
was largely under Brown's influence that Gabriel had made
his design for *The Girlhood of Mary Virgin*, which, consequently,

was more closely related to the school of Overbeck and Cornelius than to that of the English Preraphaelites.

Rossetti, however, for some time believed that the two
Preraphaelite movements were identical. He continued like
Brown to call Hunt's Preraphaelitism "Early Christian,"
until Hunt, shocked, explained to him how different were the
aims of the English Preraphaelites. The Germans in flesh
painting and other elements had rejected "Nature"; the
Germans must not be imitated.

During these discussions, the name "Preraphaelite Brotherhood" ultimately given to the movement, established itself.
Gabriel proposed the romantic title of "Brotherhood," with
its suggestions of secrecy and revolt. It was in the monastic
tradition also, combined for him the world of the mediaeval
Dante and that of his own father the ex-Carbonaro. Nor was
revolt in this year 1848 a mere anachronism. It was, indeed,
"the year of revolutions" on the Continent, and even London,
England's nerve-centre, was restless and disturbed fearing a
Chartist uprising. In April there had been a great Chartist
demonstration, while the city trembled, and the Duke of
Wellington secretly fortified the capital, hiding his soldiers in
cellars, and behind sand-bags on house-tops.

Amongst the Preraphaelites, several at least sympathized
with political as well as aesthetic revolt, supporting not only
Chartism in England, but also the overthrow of Louis Philippe
and the establishment of a new republic in France. Even old
Gabriele, in his poverty-stricken home, looked up for a moment
from his study of Dante, felt for a moment a new hope for
liberty, the cause in which he deemed his own life sacrificed.
William Rossetti was ardently but "Platonically" revolutionary, and even Gabriel, though usually indifferent to actual
politics, was moved by poverty, the mood of the time and
what he had inherited of his father's liberalism, to join in
revolutionary talk with the rest. "Like most young men,"
wrote Hunt, long afterwards, "I was stirred by the spirit of
freedom of the passing revolutionary time." Yet how far
Gabriel was from sympathy with revolutionary ideals, the
verses he now wrote, *The English Revolution of 1848*, clearly
reveal. So far as he considered the Chartist demonstration—

71

and that was very little, for his interests were almost solely aesthetic—it appeared to him but a fussy and futile demonstration of low class "cads."

Although Hunt's moral enthusiasm had created the Preraphaelite Brotherhood, it was Rossetti who now took practical control, stimulating, organizing with unaccustomed energy. It was doubtless he who added to this "lark" the last touch of conspiratorial mystery by inducing the Brethren to paint henceforth on their pictures, the initials "P.R.B."—for Preraphaelite Brotherhood—as a sign of their solidarity. To the uninitiate world outside the Brotherhood, including the Academy itself, these mysterious characters must bring all the nameless terror of a "writing on the wall." Nor should the Academy learn what were the secret powers arrayed against it. But that the Brotherhood was little more than a schoolboys' conspiracy, Brown from the first, shrewdly saw. To him, this adoption of the secret initials seemed specially childish. Older, more experienced than the others, critical yet largely sympathetic, Brown, although evading official membership of the Brotherhood, nevertheless remained in intimate association with the Preraphaelites.

To Brown as to the rest, the Brotherhood's greatest charm lay in its social convenience, which indeed was the Brethren's strongest bond. Without family ties, social distractions or definite responsibilities, the Preraphaelites, bound by common interests, and by a common poverty which excluded them from so much that London offered, found in the Brotherhood a defence against mental and physical isolation in the great city. So congenial indeed was the atmosphere of mutual encouragement and high hopes which it created, that the original formal monthly meetings in members' studios, were quickly supplemented by almost nightly informal reunions of the Brethren and their friends.

Soon, Rossetti intellectually, Millais artistically, and Hunt morally, had established a kind of unofficial leadership over the rest. Too poor—except Collinson—to hire models, the Preraphaelites posed for each other, and thus Gabriel sat to Brown for the fool in *Lear*, and to Millais for one of the figures in his *Lorenzo and Isabella* from Keats's poem. For by this time, the admiration of Keats which Hunt and Rossetti felt, had spread to others of the circle. Hunt had introduced Keats's works to Millais, and Brown too joined the Keats cult. Millais and Hunt, in fact, had already begun a series of illustrations to Keats's *Isabella*, and Rossetti had promised to join them in the task, a promise which, like many others later, he failed to keep. The poet who almost thirty years before had died believing his name but "writ in water," was now coming into his own, and largely through the Preraphaelites. Nor was Keats's influence on them entirely confined to poetry. In painting too, they found in him a kindred spirit, for Gabriel, reading Milnes's *Life and Letters of Keats*, had joyfully noted the passage in the poet's letter to his brother and sister-in-law in which he expressed his admiration for the frescoes in a church in Milan—"the name of which I forget"—on seeing copies of them at Haydon's. "In it," Keats continued, "are comprised Specimens of the first and second age of Art in Italy. I do not think I ever had a greater treat out of Shakespeare. Full of romance and the most tender feeling—magnificence of draperies beyond everything I ever saw, not excepting Raphael's. But Grotesque to a curious pitch—yet still making up a fine whole—even finer to me than more accomplished works—as there was left so much room for Imagination." "He seems," Gabriel told William, speaking of Keats, on reading this, "to have been a glorious fellow, and says in one place (to my great delight) that having just looked over a folio of the first and second schools of Italian painting, he has come to the conclusion that the early men surpassed even Raphael himself." That was not quite what Keats had said, but it was sufficient to make him, for the Brotherhood, a "Preraphaelite" before his time. Nor was the rich pictorial detail in so much of Keats's verse without a marked influence upon Preraphaelite painting. Indeed, some eight or ten years later, when a new circle had gathered about Rossetti, led by Burne-Jones and Morris, it became a saying of these new "Preraphaelites" that as Keats had carried English verse to the limits of its finest possibilities, there was nothing left for poets but to turn painters and do for painting what Keats had done for poetry.

The meetings of the Brethren were by no means always

serious. With gaiety and song they often gave vent to the high spirits of youth, or set off on animated excursions by moonlight to the more attractive villages near London. Hunt long remembered one such expedition, when the sleepy Collinson was brought out of bed to join the others and tramp (through streets which to their fancy still seemed to echo to Keats's footsteps), to Hampstead and the open country beyond. In the little village which marked the limit of their journey they awakened the relapsed Collinson (and the inhabitants) with a mighty shout, and then returned, supporting their somnolent comrade on the way. Such were the chief ties between the Preraphaelites: simple good fellowship rather than any clearly comprehended, much less defined, aesthetic theory. And this also explains the rapid demise of the Brotherhood as "success," greater means, and marriage brought to the Brethren and their associates, new interests, and a wider social life.

For Hunt and Rossetti, working and talking together in their studio, a temporary revolt in religion followed their revolt in art and politics. Gabriel, like his father, was ever divided between a naturally rationalistic mentality and the emotional and sensuous appeal of religious mysticism, especially as embodied in the creed and ritual of the Catholic Church. His racial tendency towards Catholicism was strengthened and developed by his mediaeval reading, especially of Dante; the impact of a mediaeval mind upon his own, impressed his sensitive imagination with the full significance of the grotesque and terrible, as well as of the delicate and beautiful figures of mediaeval Christianity. His indifference to modern science, his early passion for diabolism, his tense imagination, his love of self-dramatization, made him an easy prey to the suggestions presented by the literature and art of the Middle Ages. Against this, his innate scepticism contended. This was an important part of his self-conflict, an added uncertainty in one who was ever divided by doubt.

Gaining temporary supremacy, this scepticism now led Rossetti and even the devout, unsophisticated Hunt, to reject the strict teaching of their parents and deny whatever in Christianity appeared to transcend natural law. They made an absurd class list of "immortals," which began with Christ and Shakespeare in a special division for those two alone, and, ignoring such "immortals" as Plato, Aristotle, Napoleon and Molière, ended with Haydon, Longfellow, and Mrs. Browning! To this remarkable assemblage they appended a somewhat illiterate profession of faith, asserting: "We, the undersigned, declare that the following list of immortals constitutes the whole of our creed, and that there exists no other immortality than what is centred in their names and in the names of their contemporaries in whom this list is reflected." In some incomprehensible manner, they for the moment associated this creed with their Preraphaelite dogmas, and posted it on the wall of their studio "for," as Gabriel said, "the affixing of all decent fellows' signatures." Rossetti gloated over the dismay their hair-raising heresy would arouse, and this indeed was probably its chief *raison d'être*. "It has already caused considerable horror amongst our acquaintance," he wrote, "I suppose we shall have to keep a hair brush."

For Hunt at least, this naughty fit of scepticism soon passed. Within a few weeks he was busy painting with religious fervour his picture *Christian Missionaries Pursued by Druids*. Gabriel's rationalism, however, continued to wage an increasingly victorious struggle with his desire for a comfortable faith. Yet in his last years he expressed astonishment that considering his poetry and painting—certainly the offspring of emotion rather than of reason—anyone should doubt his belief in immortality.

In the manner of youth, Hunt and Rossetti would turn serious discussion into jest, jest into serious discussion. Debating the ethics of suicide, Gabriel, with no premonition of an evil day to come, jocularly suggested the foundation of a suicide club. They discussed the debased state of applied art in Victorian England, the need of a revival of the sense of beauty in architecture, furniture, fabrics, and ornaments, as well as in painting. For Hunt, Rossetti and Brown, long before Morris, saw the need which Morris was to meet later. Rossetti also disliked the clothes of the period, and, long anticipating in this as in other things the aesthetes of the 'nineties, dreamed of a world set free from the ugliness of Victorian dress. Gabriel took Hunt home to dinner; and his insular guest's surprise at the macaroni and other unfamiliar dishes, was almost as great as that caused by the foreign revolutionaries jabbering away in French and Italian, while William and Gabriel shrugged their shoulders, saying it was always so.

Nor, during these talks in the studio, did the young idealists lose sight of more worldly aims. Even Hunt, that rigorous disciple of Art as handmaid to Truth and Justice, was led by Gabriel to contemplate with pleasure the delights of personal success. Together they dreamed of a golden future in which each would have a house with a suite of studios to accommodate themselves, their disciples, and the enthusiastic crowds of admirers clamouring for admission. And when Hunt turned sceptical, Gabriel would declare that there were "hundreds of young aristocrats and millionaires growing up who would be only too glad to get due direction how to make the country as glorious as Greece and Italy had been." For Gabriel, although he found neither interest nor inspiration in the world about him, was shrewdly observant of the opportunity it offered the artist. Ambitious, he at once and with sure insight appraised the spirit of his own industrial epoch, and in the result, led unromantic manufacturers and shipowners to support a painter of antique or idealized dreams!

It is surely not without significance that, as Gabriel now wrote to his brother: "I picked up the other day for sixpence a book I had long wished to see, called *An Exposition of the False Medium and Barriers precluding Men of Genius from the Public*." He did not mean to fail as his father had failed. He desired "success" in the profession he had chosen, a speedy success that could be enjoyed, and yet one attained without prostituting his art as Millais was to do later. That he had many of the qualities for securing such a success, above all that of quiet and dignified self-assertion, even domination, he was doubtless well aware. Impatient for success, he had left the dull art schools for Brown, the slow method of Brown for Hunt. Now, with Hunt ever at his elbow, Gabriel's mounting hopes of impending prosperity brought renewed confidence. Religious paintings were popular, so, spurred by hope, Rossetti worked away at *The Girlhood of Mary Virgin*. "It belongs," he said, "to the religious class which has always appeared to me the most adapted and the most worthy to interest the members of a

76

Christian community." How rightly Gabriel gauged contemporary taste was shown a few months later, for in the first
published criticism of his work, the *Athenaeum*, discussing the
Free Exhibition, at which Rossetti's painting appeared, after
dismissing the other exhibitors with some impatience, remarked:
"It is pleasant to turn from the mass of commonplace—the
records of mere fact or the extravagant conceits exhibited in
the illustrations of some of our most cherished writers, prose
and poetic—to a manifestation of true mental power; in which
Art is made the exponent of some high aim, and what is 'of
the earth earthy' and of the art material is lost sight of in
dignified and intellectual purpose."

Although Hunt found Gabriel a congenial companion, their
life in common was not without vicissitudes. Rossetti's Italian
temperament, his quickly changing moods, the "scenes" he
made when, faced by insuperable difficulties of technique he
fell into depression, despair or violent rage, all severely tried
even Hunt's comparatively phlegmatic nature. Besides, in a
thousand ways, Gabriel, careless, spontaneous, unthinking,
would unconsciously irritate his somewhat "touchy" friend. At
all hours of the day and night Gabriel with his comrades would
flock into the studio, interrupt Hunt's painting, and even get
him to prepare for them supper or tea. Also, to Hunt's
great annoyance, his pictures, carefully left with their faces
turned to the wall, were calmly turned round by Gabriel to
show to visitors and friends.

It was *The Girlhood of Mary Virgin* which Rossetti was
hurrying to complete for the exhibition of 1849 that brought
these differences to a head. Obstacles in his work quickly provoked Gabriel to a rage almost beyond the bounds of sanity—
at least so it seemed to his English friends. The Virgin's
drapery drove him into what Brown described as "an almost
maudlin condition of profanity," and Brown, amazed, watched
him "lying howling on his belly in my studio." His greatest
trouble, however, was the child-angel, who proved in fact his
final damnation. No suitable model could be found, for none,
when it came to posing, could be made to stand still. In a
cloud of studio dust Gabriel stormed and stamped at them,
or flung his paints and brushes on the floor; but this only

77

moved the angel to sob and scream. At last, Hunt, in desperation, took his friend out into Regent's Park, and there, as
in the wintry sunlight they paced the Broad Walk together,
warned him that such scenes meant separation. Gabriel thereupon calmed down, promised reform, got a new and better
angel and finished the picture in peace.

Nor did Hunt find Rossetti the respectful, obedient pupil
he had expected and desired. Instead, like some casual fellow-
student he contradicted Hunt's views on perspective or
admonished him for not appreciating the works of Brown. Yet
he amazed Hunt by the freedoms he took with Brown himself,
criticizing his work not only in Brown's absence, but to his
face. Hunt was, in fact, moved to protest, but Rossetti laughingly replied that "Bruno" admired his poems, respected his
opinion, and would not mind. With a touch of regret not
devoid of unconscious self-satisfaction, Hunt had anticipated
in Brown some resentment at Gabriel's abandoning his tuition
for that of Hunt himself. But on their first meeting, in the old
carpenter's workshop in Clipstone Street which was Brown's
studio, Hunt's expectations were pleasantly disappointed; for,
probably relieved by the abdication of so unpromising a pupil,
Brown cordially welcomed both Gabriel and his friend.

Busy with the Preraphaelite circle, and concentrating upon
the completion of his picture, Rossetti, by the beginning of
1849, had ceased all pretence of continuous attendance at the
Antique Class, nor did he ever enter the schools of Life and
Painting. Like the other Preraphaelites he had intended his
picture for the Royal Academy Exhibition; but as spring and
the hour of opening drew near, he suddenly changed his
intention. Conscious of its technical inadequacy, and fearing
rejection, he silently diverted *The Girlhood of Mary Virgin* to
the Free Exhibition at Hyde Park Corner, where (on the
principle of *Lucus a non lucendo*) all exhibitors paid for wall-
space, but from which no aspirant was rejected. In choosing
the Free Exhibition, Rossetti was following in the wake of
Brown, who had also exhibited there. But as this exhibition
opened some time before that of the Academy, Hunt, on
hearing of Rossetti's change of plan, immediately, and no
doubt quite wrongly, suspected treachery; that Gabriel was

trying to steal a march on his friends by being first in the field. The "treachery," if there was any, was more probably due to Rossetti's fear of rejection by the Academy, perhaps also to a fear of too close an association with his rebel Brethren, in case their work and the movement they represented should prove unpopular.

If such considerations influenced Rossetti, they were un-necessary. The Preraphaelites need have had no fears. When the Academy exhibition opened, Hunt's *Rienzi*—frantically finished at the last moment, and carried down to the exhibition by Hunt himself at midnight—was found safely hung with Millais' *Lorenzo and Isabella*. The two works, although attracting some adverse comment, were favourably received by the critics in general, while Rossetti's *Girlhood of Mary Virgin*, at the Free Exhibition, received mild blame and generous praise. *The Athenaeum* thought his "personification of the Virgin . . . an achievement worthy of an older hand," and pontifically declared: "its spiritual attributes and . . . great sensibility . . . inspire the expectation that Mr. Rossetti will continue to pursue the lofty career which he has here so successfully begun. . . ."

Upon the completion of his picture, however, Gabriel returned no more to Hunt's studio. A few weeks later, to Hunt's surprise, a porter arrived to remove Gabriel's property, explaining that on the preceding Lady Day Rossetti had withdrawn himself from the joint tenancy with Hunt. Poor, almost at the end of his limited resources, and thus saddled with the full rent of the studio as well as of the additional bedroom which Gabriel's advent had compelled him to take, Hunt resented Rossetti's action. Soon, indeed, to such desperate straits was he driven, Hunt had to evacuate his studio and, depositing most of his property at Brown's, make a strategical retreat to his home, to face a father who had long but vainly warned him that art, although an excellent avocation, was but a bad means of subsistence.

Already, thanks to Gabriel, Hunt the moralist had learned that altruism must be its own reward. Rossetti, too, had wearied of Hunt's well-intentioned but fussy supervision, had perhaps taken his exhortations less graciously than Hunt believed, and must have remarked Hunt's annoyance at his preferring the

Free Exhibition to the Academy. At any rate Rossetti had once again proved too independent, too capricious, to be a good pupil. Hunt was certainly disappointed in him. But Gabriel, untroubled by conscientious scruples, or by his friend's opinions, was now hard at work again. Beneath the stern gaze of a copy —cut out of an illustrated journal—of Brown's *Spirit of Abstract Justice*, a work he much admired, Gabriel, too poor to rent a private studio, now resumed his conquest of art in a bleak attic of his father's house.

V

THE FOREIGN TOUR—
THE GERM
1849–1850

When whoso merely hath a little thought
   Will plainly think the thought which is in him,
Not imaging another's bright or dim,
Not mangling with new words what others taught;
   When whoso speaks, from having either sought
   Or only found, will speak, not just to skim
   A shallow surface with words made and trim,
But in that very speech the matter brought;
Be not too keen to cry—"So this is all!—
   A thing I might myself have thought as well,
   But would not say it, for it was not worth!"
Ask: "Is this truth?" For is it still to tell
That, be the theme a point or the whole earth,
   Truth is a circle, perfect, great or small?

Sonnet in "The Germ" W. M. ROSSETTI

IT WAS GOOD Aunt Charlotte who acted as Gabriel's first art-agent, persuading the Marchioness of Bath to buy *The Girlhood of Mary Virgin* for eighty guineas. Even in this, his first business transaction, Rossetti showed the shrewdness and ability for which he afterwards was famous. Only in Lyell's letters to old Gabriele do we find any reference to the details of this sale, for only his half of the correspondence has come down to us, and hence there is considerable obscurity. It is, however, clear that the Marchioness at first sent only sixty guineas for the work, and that Gabriel thereupon, but most diplomatically, extracted eighty. Lyell, "exceedingly anxious" on learning that Gabriel had "exposed his modesty to be called in question by demurring to accept at once the munificent offer for his picture by the Marchioness of Bath," heard of the happy result with delighted surprise, and congratulated old Rossetti upon his son's success in obtaining his price without annoying his patroness. "Her conduct," wrote Lyell, unctuously, "was certainly very noble in sending him the full sum which he himself had determined to ask for his picture; and without a word

81

having passed to show that sixty guineas was below the estimate of G.C.D.R. (for Lyell employed Gabriel's full baptismal initials). This first success," Lyell concluded, "is most encouraging to the artist, and gives me great confidence in his future prosperous career."

Hunt, meanwhile, sold his *Rienzi* for a hundred and sixty guineas. With such means for the first time at their disposal, Gabriel and Hunt found the temptation to make a long-contemplated tour of continental art galleries irresistible, and in the last days of September set out for Paris. At first delighted with the French capital, Gabriel, from the top of Notre Dame, "shouted in the spirit," finding the old church itself "inconceivably stunning" and with "most glorious things to put in pictures." Everywhere his interest turned to the pictorial and poetic. Gobelin tapestry suggested to him a new design for his painting of *Kate the Queen*, from Browning's *Paracelsus*. The mediaeval exhibits in the Musée de Cluny inspired the continuation of his unfinished poem *Bride Chamber Talk*, afterwards renamed *The Bride's Prelude*.

To the enthusiastic but inexperienced and insular youths the Louvre and Luxembourg seemed chiefly filled with ancient incompetence—"slosh." Claude, Correggio, Rubens, even Michelangelo, and Delacroix whom Rossetti in later years much admired, aroused only their pity or contempt, though to other great names, including Fra Angelico, Leonardo, Giorgione, Titian and Ingres they paid various degrees of homage. But it was Hippolyte Flandrin's paintings in St. Germain des Prés of *Christ's Entry into Jerusalem*, *Departure*, and *Death*, which seemed to Gabriel "the most perfect works taken *in toto* that we have seen in our lives . . . wonderful! wonderful!! wonderful!!!"

Rachel, acting in one of Scribe's plays, left them "inexpressibly astounded," while the "cancan" at Valentino's moved Rossetti to write a sonnet of such moral indignation that when William printed it long afterwards, asterisks became its most conspicuous feature. One glimpse, too, of tragedy, Paris gave them, when, passing the Morgue, they saw the corpse of a man who had been stabbed and flung into the Seine.

But Gabriel's first pleasure in Paris quickly passed. He went about in a spirit of nationalistic pride and insular superiority, grumbling incessantly because France was not England. He frowned upon the poor Parisiennes, calling them in a sonnet, "bland smiling dogs with manes" at whom, "knowing of England one's eye demurs." "We have not seen six pretty faces since we have been in Paris," he wailed, "and those such as would not be in the least remarkable in London." "Fine churches" and "splendid inns," Paris, he reluctantly admitted, possessed; but of "first rate paintings" not more than a mere forty to fifty. Above all other crimes, in his eyes, Paris was ignorant of Browning.

Debarred from painting, Gabriel as ever, sought relief in poetry, venting his feelings in a "journal" written in weak verse, and also in "quelques méchants sonnets—real humbugs" as he described them. The best, most serious of these sonnets, he had written on the cliff-top at Boulogne, looking out over the sea. Later, after some changes, it became *The Sea-Limits*. In Paris, another sonnet had come "whole into his head" as he climbed the tower of Notre Dame, while the great bells pealed about him. The distractions of the moment had banished it immediately, but four days later it had returned, though "with some deterioration," and, copying it out, he preserved his original vision, of France emerging from the recent revolution, as he himself from the thunderous sound and darkness of the church tower, into the peace and brightness of open day.

The political unrest still prevalent was impressed upon Rossetti and Hunt by the sudden disappearance of a band of painters of revolutionary sympathies, who regularly patronized the *laiterie* in which the two artists took their morning roll and coffee. One of the revolutionaries, at first unrecognized as he had shaved off his beard and wore new clothes, momentarily reappeared to whisper to Gabriel and his friend that news of police enquiries about the political activities of the band had caused their secret departure. Such was the state of Paris during Rossetti's first visit, in 1849.

With growing English patriotism and a keenly conscious, half-humorous self-abandonment to prejudice, the Italian from England gloried in his English superiority as he walked the streets of the city. In one of the half-ironical sonnets he was

83

now writing he even hinted at personal encounters, and anathematized the police as:

> Fierce sentinels, (toy-size without the stands),
>   Who spit their oaths at you and grind their "r"s,
> If at a fountain you would wash your hands;

nor did he forget to make an ironical allusion to

> One Frenchman (this is fact) who thinks he spars.

"Can even good dinners," Gabriel demanded, in verse, "cover all these sins?" His personal grievances he exalted to national significance, expecting for every pain he suffered, England's gratitude. Hence, although the French, he believed, thought him

> A fool, and just a little cracked. Thy smile
>   May light on us, Britannia, healthy wench.

As for the million French in Paris,

> Cast up, they'll make an Englishman—perhaps.

And, finally, he made, doubtless in the same half-ironical vein, such a claim upon England's gratitude as no Englishman ever made—he has consistently lied to exalt and defend her:

> Should England ask, "Was narrow prejudice
>   Stretched to its utmost point unflinchingly,
>   Even unto lying, at all times, by ye?"
> We can say firmly: "Lord, thou knowest this,
>   Our soil may own us!"

Such was Gabriel's state of mind when, after a fortnight in Paris he and Hunt left for Brussels, which Rossetti found equally unsatisfactory. "A few fine Early German pictures, among them a wonderful Van Eyck" won his admiration, but Rubens he would not deign to look at, and Brussels itself he condemned for its "servile apeing of the French," and "beastly" victimization of English travellers, with not even a sonnet "to be got out of its utter muffishness." A visit to Waterloo inspired two sonnets and the candid comment in a letter to his brother: "Between you and me, William, Waterloo is simply a bore."

At Antwerp, the Van Eycks and Memling pleased as Gabriel had expected; but, to his annoyance, Rubens's paintings he found everywhere. One only did he wish to see, the famous

Descent from the Cross; but this, being at the restorers, was to his great annoyance temporarily inaccessible. In a denunciatory sonnet almost as violent as that on Valentino's, he expressed his disgust with the ubiquity of Rubens in Antwerp, which indeed drove him to Ghent.

In Ghent, Rossetti's frequent mood of somewhat crude and boisterous gaiety, especially prominent during this continental holiday, not only dominated him, but even infected the serious Hunt. In the famous Béguinage, the friends laughed to see the name of a patron saint over each door, and only with difficulty refrained from knocking and asking if the saint were at home. Whatever was unfamiliar seemed to their insularity absurd. At vespers they pretended to recognize in the music, comic English tunes then popular: the nuns' veils reminded them of towels, their collecting boxes suggested policemen's lanterns. With such subtleties of mirth the two cockneys beguiled their pilgrimage.

Bruges aroused Gabriel's enthusiasm: "a most stunning place, immeasurably the best we have come to," with "miraculous works" by Memling and Van Eyck, some "first-rate architecture, and very little or no Rubens"; this last being a strong recommendation in his eyes. Memling he now found not only a "stunner," but possibly even superior to Van Eyck, chiefly because of his devotional mysticism, which Gabriel praised in two sonnets. "I shall not attempt any description," he wrote to Collinson: "I assure you that the perfection of character and even drawing, the astounding finish, the glory of colour, and above all the pure religious sentiment and ecstatic poetry of their works, is not to be conceived or described. Even in seeing them, the mind is at first bewildered by such Godlike completeness; and only after some while has elapsed can at all analyse the causes of its awe and admiration; and then finds these feelings so much increased by analysis that the last impression left is mainly one of utter shame at its own inferiority."

At Antwerp he had begun a poem on the carillon, and this he now completed at Bruges. Before the last stanza was written, he sent it to Collinson with the comment: "The song is, of course, quite original; there is in particular a Yankee of the name of Longfellow with whose works it has no affinity."

Bruges marked the final limit of their wanderings. Soon they turned homewards, Gabriel celebrating the city in a parting sonnet as its towers receded into a distance of grey, sunless sky. Two souvenirs of a practical kind the friends brought back with them—"an extraordinary self-concocting coffee-pot for state occasions of the P.R.B." as Gabriel described it, and a "book containing a receipt for raising the Devil," which, judged by Gabriel's later life, seems to have been remarkably effective.

Their return was speedy. At Dover, Gabriel rejoiced to see once more an English policeman, and voiced his emotion in a final and execrable sonnet contrasting England's virtues with the abominations of the Continent.

For Gabriel, this short tour was to be the longest and most extensive continental wandering of his life. Hunt, with some manifest exaggeration, declared long afterwards that on this journey Gabriel was "a perfect travelling companion, ever in the best of temper," that their short tour "was overbrimming with delight in the beauties both of nature and art." They "came back," he said, "with richer minds but without change of purpose." Gabriel, however, in his last years, speaking of this, his first continental journey, apart from his two visits to Boulogne, told his friend William Sharp, that "he saw nothing when abroad," meaning that paintings had excluded all other interests. This was certainly true. He ignored in general the strange and picturesque incidents of foreign travel, was too prejudiced to appreciate unaccustomed modes of life. England and the English he liked better than any other country and nation. London he preferred to any other town. The tour in fact, provoked a surprising exhibition of cockney crudity in both Rossetti and Hunt. But if they had learned little, they had the satisfaction of retaining unimpaired their original faith in the absolute superiority of Preraphaelitism—even if they did not know clearly what it was.

By November 1st they were back in London, glad to tread once more the familiar ways. Their first need was a studio. For a moment the whole Brotherhood considered taking a house in Cheyne Walk as a kind of Preraphaelite monastery. On the door bell they would carve "P.R.B." which to the profane, they said, might suggest "Please Ring Bell." But reflection upon the rental of £70 a year cooled their ardour and the project was reluctantly abandoned. Finally, some days of dreary house-hunting culminated in Gabriel's taking a studio at No. 72 Newman Street, in the old quarter near Oxford Street and Fitzroy Square. Showing his usual skill in financial transactions, he succeeded in reducing the rent, which had once been £40, to £26 a year. He tried to persuade Hunt to share the place with him; but Hunt, mindful of Gabriel's sudden departure from Cleveland Street, was too wary to be caught again, and settled in Cheyne Walk, near the river.

Gabriel, who loved the river, often called at Hunt's. For hours he would sit with Hunt, drawing and writing, as if they still shared the studio. Sometimes the two would set off on night excursions, occasionally taking out a little rowing boat, and sailing on the river. Rossetti could neither row nor swim. Hunt long remembered their first voyage, when Gabriel, who never became either oarsman or sculler, clumsily attempted, to his companion's amusement, to turn boatman. Generally they sped silently along the dark water-way, absorbing, in a mood which curiously anticipated that of Whistler's well-known painting, the shadowy beauty and strangeness of the scene. In the long aftertime, Hunt recalled these excursions in Preraphaelite detail: "the star-checked gloom, the long deep-draggled lamps, making the water into a bottomless pit, the black piles of the timber bridges, the tides empty of all but floating barges, slowly guided with deep-falling, splashing sweeps, the challenged echoes, the ghostly houses on the bank, with windows glaring as the dawn stared into them as into the wide-opened eyes of a corpse; and last the jocund day uprose, cloud garlanded—these things were worth the seeing, the hearing, and the learning, for they had a voice for each."

The social meetings of the P.R.B.s, interrupted by the summer dispersal, were now resumed. Round Woolner's glowing stove they gathered in the cold, autumn evenings, to discuss amidst clouds of tobacco smoke, artistic, social, political and religious topics: debates in which Woolner, talkative and excitable, was conspicuously revolutionary, denouncing both the "governing classes" and democracy, and scorning wealth and power.

By this time, the small Preraphaelite band had increased. A number of sympathizers, although never admitted to formal membership of the Brotherhood, which Hunt jealously restricted to its original seven, were, especially as all possible assistance was needed for a projected magazine, now welcomed at the various meetings and discussions of the Brethren. In this way, sponsored by Hunt, came John Lucas Tupper, formerly his fellow student, but in sculpture, at the Academy schools, and now anatomical designer at Guy's Hospital. Millais introduced Arthur Hughes the painter, and Charles Allston Collins, the son of a painter and the brother of Wilkie Collins the novelist. Rossetti brought into the circle not only William Bell Scott, but also a sculptor Alexander Munro, a painter Walter Howard Deverell, and a bohemian novelist and journalist James Hannay. Woolner brought John Hancock and Bernard Smith, two sculptor friends, and Coventry Patmore the poet. Ford Madox Brown and his friend the painter William Cave Thomas, similarly joined the band of sympathizers. In addition to these, were George Tupper a printer, the brother of John Lucas Tupper, Thomas Seddon a painter, with his brother John Seddon an architect, sons of a cabinet maker in the Gray's Inn Road, and Lowes Dickinson, portrait painter, who with his brother Robert, ran a print-selling business in Bond Street and the drawing Academy in Maddox Street which the Rossettis had attended.

Gabriel, an admirer of Patmore's *Poems* since the publication of the volume in 1844, gladly welcomed the poet whose work was considered essentially "Preraphaelite," probably because of its elaboration of detail. To Patmore, who like Brown was some years older than the Preraphaelites, the Brethren looked up almost with veneration, envying his poetic achievement, his general maturity of thought as it seemed to them, and his acquaintance with distinguished persons. Patmore in return introduced the Brotherhood to wider literary circles, including even the great Tennyson himself. Thus for some four years Patmore was closely associated with the Preraphaelites, until as the Brotherhood disintegrated he drifted away.

Patmore's interest in the Preraphaelite Brotherhood was purely personal, and he afterwards disclaimed all conscious relationship to their aesthetic creed. "I was intimate with the Preraphaelites when we were little more than boys together," he wrote long afterwards; "they were all very simple, pure-minded, ignorant and confident." Hunt he preferred personally amongst the Brethren because of his integrity and high moral code. Millais, as the wealthiest and best known, was, he said, then regarded in general as leader, though his personality and conversation were not striking. Woolner he considered the "brilliant talker"; Rossetti, he thought "completely Italian," in manners, mind and appearance. "He had," said Patmore, "very little knowledge of or sympathy with English literature; and always gave me the impression of tensity rather than intensity." He recalled their poverty, remembering how Hunt once offered for sale at a meeting of the Brotherhood, forty sketches at £1 each, and how shortly afterwards Lord Houghton[1] commissioned Patmore himself to obtain for £100 a little Rossetti drawing of a boy and girl dancing before Borgia, for which a few months before, Gabriel had asked only £5.

So far, the movement had little of the high seriousness later imputed to it. Seriousness indeed was seldom the dominant note of their meetings, and often on leaving, the high spirited Preraphaelites and their allies would march down the street with Gabriel at their head, singing the *Marseillaise* or *Mourir pour la Patrie*.

Installed in Newman Street, Gabriel resumed his painting in earnest. He began his picture of the Annunciation, *Ecce Ancilla Domini*, completed preparations for a large painting of Browning's "Kate the Queen," worked at a picture of the Passover, and began a design for *Paolo and Francesca*. "Gabriel began making a sketch for the *Annunciation*," wrote William on November 25th—"The Virgin is to be in bed, but without any bedclothes on, an arrangement which may be justified in consideration of the hot climate"; as Gabriel had explained to him. The picture was to be "almost entirely white" as was a projected companion piece, *The Death of the Virgin*, never painted.

[1] Richard Monckton Milnes (1809–1885).

In painting, Gabriel still found many difficulties. The design
for the *Annunciation* would not come right; that for the *Death
of the Virgin* would not come at all. Fearing the picture would
not be ready for the spring exhibition, he thought of abandoning the two designs and returning to the *Francesca*. However,
he painted the Virgin's head, and, taking William as his model,
began the head of the angel in the *Annunciation*.

But by this time, Gabriel's literary interests were again
actively threatening his enthusiasm for pictorial art. From the
first, literary associations had played a large part in the for-
mation of the Preraphaelite Brotherhood. Often, in his enthral-
ling voice, Gabriel recited to the Brethren favourite passages
of verse, including some from his own poems, besides bringing
his own designs and verse translations for an illustrated edition
he was preparing of Dante's *Vita Nuova*. Fired by his enthusiasm
and example, Woolner, Millais and Brown for a time turned
poets and critics, generally with unhappy results. William
Rossetti, now "honorary secretary" to the Brotherhood, was
already keeping a *Preraphaelite Diary*, which, despite an occasional lapse, he sustained for four years.

Eager to distinguish himself in poetry as in painting, Gabriel
had quickly seen that to found a journal as an organ of the
Preraphaelites would provide not only a means of expressing,
exemplifying and advertising their aesthetic creed, when discoverable, but also a medium for the publication of his own
writings. During the months immediately preceding his foreign
tour, while the Brethren constantly discussed the journal at their
evening meetings, Gabriel had finally, by sheer power of domination, overcome their objections and secured their acquiescence
in the establishment of a monthly Preraphaelite magazine, of
which, by a subscription of a guinea each, the brethren would
become proprietors. Working strenuously to make the project
a practical success, Rossetti had found publishers, and, as the
means of the seven original Preraphaelites proved inadequate
to the needs of the occasion, had secured the financial aid of
sympathizers and of friends.

Having found publishers, the Preraphaelites next became
uncomfortably aware of the need of something to publish. For
the first number, Hunt made an etching, while Stephens,

knowing little or nothing of Italian art, wrote an essay on the subject. William Rossetti, yielding to his brother's demand that as he did not paint he should be editor, wrote for the cover one of the worst sonnets in the English language, intended to be explanatory of Preraphaelite aims, and here reprinted as epigraph to this chapter. But Gabriel himself was fully occupied in finishing his translation of the *Vita Nuova*.

The name of the journal was long and eagerly debated, and many bad suggestions were made. Finally, *Monthly Thoughts on Literature and Art* yielded to Gabriel's *Thoughts Towards Nature*, whatever that might mean. By September 24th, the prospectus was printed, and the first number, it was agreed, should appear in December. Gabriel, besides holding innumerable discussions with printers, publishers and Preraphaelite comrades, appealed to William Bell Scott for poetic aid, and also secured the help of Coventry Patmore who sent him an exquisite little lyric, *The Seasons*, afterwards published among Patmore's poems as *The Year*. Before the close of September Rossetti's energy had overcome all obstacles, and preparations for the first number of *Thoughts Towards Nature* were well begun.

The demands of the magazine, engrossing Gabriel's attention, had delayed his departure for Paris until summer was almost over and when at the last moment he tore himself away, it was largely because William had agreed to assume his brother's literary responsibilities during his absence. Almost to the day of departure, Gabriel's attention was centred upon the venture, and his last letter to his brother, before leaving, was a strict injunction to send the prospectus when ready "to every friend you can possibly think of, as well as to all literary men and artists of anything like our own views." William was also exhorted to "look sharp about advertising." Finally, William informed him, members, reasonably dissatisfied with the magazine's title, suggested *The P.R.B. Journal* instead. Gabriel, on the eve of departure, too busy packing to reply personally, had dictated to Christina an answer, sending details of the contents and arrangement of the first number, and advice on the points raised. Nothing could make Gabriel forget the magazine. Even during his tour the thought of it was ever on his mind. From Paris and Brussels he had sent William advice and exhortation about advertisements and similar details, while William busily hunted up subscribers in London, and a friend at Oxford aided his efforts in the University town.

Upon Gabriel's return, events moved swiftly towards the accomplishment of his plans. At the various meetings of the circle, the magazine was constantly discussed and new decisions were taken. Religion and politics were to be excluded. The intention to advertise was abandoned owing to the expense. As the financial difficulties revealed themselves, the enthusiasm of the circle waned. Gabriel persuaded them to produce at least *one* number of the journal, but the majority were inclined to refuse further support, even if this first number were successful. The title was again debated. Cave Thomas suggested *The Seed*, but finally, by a majority of six to four, *The Germ* was chosen from a list of sixty-five names drawn up by Thomas himself. Contributors' names they decided not to publish. They discussed the propriety of including an article explaining Preraphaelite principles in art, but decided that, as the number contained so many papers on art, this was unnecessary. For themselves it was certainly convenient. They always found *some* reason for not stating their aesthetic creed. George Tupper they chose as printer.

During the last two months of 1849, as the time for the appearance of the Preraphaelite journal approached, the atmosphere of the Brotherhood vibrated with energy and expectation. William anxiously begged members to provide him with material. Gabriel's difficulties in painting had prevented the intended completion of *Bride Chamber Talk* for No. 2. Woolner was dilatory about his promised poems: *My Beautiful Lady* and *My Lady in Death*. On December 19th, Tupper warned the worried editor that time was running out. In the evening Brown brought a sonnet on *The Love of Beauty*. William himself contributed a long review of Clough's *Bothie of Tober-na-Vuolich*. Christina's *Dreamland* was also appropriated, although Christina had at first refused to help, fearing that the journal would expound revolutionary politics and atheism. Gabriel having promised to complete a prose tale, *Hand and Soul*, succeeded in doing so by sitting up all night. William copied out the least decipherable parts of the manuscript and it was ready in time.

Even when proofs began to arrive from the printer's, William's troubles were not over. There were objections to Thomas's opening address, which was consequently rejected. Hunt's etching was to appear and some proofs of this were taken by Mr. Wyatt of Oxford, a printseller, for display in his shop. It was with obvious relief that on the last day of 1849, William wrote in his diary: "To-day before noon fifty copies of *The Germ* were in the hands of the publishers," and took home twelve copies for himself.

Throughout the earlier months of 1850 *The Germ*, or as they called it in fun, *The Gurm*—an American professor once proved in a lecture that this pronunciation was the correct one, and due to a strict adherence to Preraphaelite principles!—took precedence of all other interests. For despite their intention to abandon it after the first number, Gabriel, unwilling to lose this literary opportunity, persuaded them to continue their efforts. To promote advertisements and circulation, they sent *Germs* everywhere; to Lord John Russell, Sir Robert Peel and other distinguished persons; to the porter at Somerset House with a promise of ten shillings if he sold them to the students at the School of Design. They sent *Germs* to the best London booksellers and clubs. They visited their friends like newsboys with copies under their arms for sale. Such were the tactics employed by the brethren in their attack on the intellectual and aesthetic world of the day.

These attempts were not quite vain. The editor of the *Art Journal*, Samuel Carter Hall—whom Brown christened "Shirt-Collar Hall" because of his "starchy" appearance—promised to review *The Germ*, prophesying that its sponsors would be "the future great artists of the Age and Country." John Abraham Heraud, whose poem *The Descent into Hell* had brought him ephemeral fame—"Have you seen Heraud's *Descent into Hell*?" asked an early admirer. "No," replied Douglas Jerrold, "I only wish I had!"—invited William to tea and congratulations. At Heraud's William met the editor of the *Athenaeum*, and West-land Marston the dramatist, both of whom invited him to call on them. Before leaving, he also secured as subscribers to *The Germ* a painter and Miss Glyn the actress, much admired by Gabriel. Thus on the frail raft of *The Germ* was

William launched on the treacherous sea of London literary society.

Gabriel meanwhile worked hard providing new material for the next numbers of the magazine, and obtaining contributions from friends. He revised his *Blessed Damozel*, got more poems from Christina, from Collinson a poem *Child Jesus*—"a very first-rate affair," said Gabriel—with an illustrative etching; from Brown, despite the author's distrust of aesthetic theory, an article on *The Mechanism of an Historical Picture*, and two poems from Bell Scott's stock of dreary verse.

But the omens were unpropitious for the future of *The Germ*. Early reports of good sales proved delusive, and when on the last day of January the second number appeared, with *The Blessed Damozel*—signed by Gabriel, for anonymity was now largely abandoned—it was already known that of the first number only two hundred had been sold, and a deficit of £20 must be faced. The meeting of the Brotherhood in Gabriel's studio on January 20th, St. Agnes's Eve, was, in these circumstances not unnaturally, dull. Rossetti described it to Christina in a humorous sonnet: *St. Wagnes' Eve*; for to the "wag," the temptation to parody Keats's title was irresistible:

> By eight, the coffee was all drunk. At nine
> We gave the cat some milk. Our talk did shelve,
> Ere ten to gasps and stupor. Helpless grief
> Made, towards eleven, my inmost spirit pine . . .

Such was now the depression of the Brotherhood.

Nevertheless, spurred by Gabriel, the Preraphaelites gallantly fought, from the opening of February until the close of April, a losing battle to save *The Germ*. Of the second number only forty copies were sold; "the last knockdown blow," moaned William. This would have been the end, had not the printers offered to continue *The Germ* at their own risk, and brought out, very late of course, two more numbers renamed *Art and Poetry, being Thoughts towards Nature*, dated respectively for March and May. Despite advertising placards "paraded about daily before the Academy," by the Preraphaelites, in a vain attempt to save the journal, it failed to attract public support, and no further number was issued.

So, in the spring of 1850, the magazine which was to spread the Brotherhood's fame, if not definite Preraphaelite propaganda, died, leaving its supporters a debt of £33. William, despite his unenviable position as editor, mourned its fate, and John Tupper, the indefatigable "wit" of the Preraphaelite band, wrote a monody *On the Death of "The Germ" otherwise known as "Art and Poetry,"* calling upon the P.R.B.s to

> Bring leaves of yew to intertwine
> With "leaves" that evermore are dead,
> Those leaves as pallid-hued as you
> Who wrote them never to be read.

But the fate of *The Germ* is not surprising. Despite William's belief that the magazine was improving in quality when "it succumbed to its doom," it had in fact declined after the third number. It was indeed a rash literary venture, forced by Gabriel upon a Brotherhood of painters and would-be painters. Even Rossetti could not make good and bad painters—some even illiterate—into good writers, and for the magazine to succeed good writers were essential. Yet of all the contributors, the only ones with literary talent were Gabriel, Christina, and Coventry Patmore. Gabriel had contributed in *Hand and Soul* a single story, besides various poems which included some of the results of his continental tour. His sister had helped with verses which in general were superior in tone, finish, maturity, to her brother's; Patmore had given two poems—one exquisite—and a piece of critical prose. The rest of the contributors varied from a very plain mediocrity to absolute badness. Woolner generally wrote lines which not only failed to scan, but also verged on bathos. William, no master of verse or prose, wallowed in a perpetual flatness of thought and phrase which were often ludicrous. William Bell Scott's Helicon was a mudbank of pompous and dreary platitudes. These alone were a publisher's funeral. In addition, Gabriel had weighted his literary venture with Collinson's somnolent poetry, and Stephens' empty, pretentious prose. Nor were the prospects of *The Germ* improved by Tupper's weakly facetious verse and ignorant aesthetics, drearily written when not unconsciously absurd. His article *The Subject in Art*, for example, insisted that "the dead pheasant in a picture will always be as *food* [*sic*] while the same at the poulterer's will be but a dead pheasant."[!] John Orchard's *Dialogue on Art*, in the last number, was simply unreadable. Poor Orchard never saw it in print for immediately after writing it he died. Even William Rossetti, in later years, was troubled by the impossibility of deciding whether some of the contributions to *The Germ* were intended to be funny or serious!

Millais, astute in worldly interests, did not perhaps unduly regret that "pressure of work" which prevented his contributing to *The Germ*. Even the much vaunted etchings by Hunt, Collinson, Brown and Deverell had little merit. All were stiff, badly drawn, some also badly designed. They were in fact merely illustration, and clearly showed the Preraphaelites' fundamental defect—their frequent failure to distinguish between illustration and art.

Nor did *The Germ* contain any brilliant exposition of Preraphaelite theory. There was, however, a certain rough coherence in the various articles dealing with aesthetic matters. Stephens' two essays on *The Purpose and Tendency of Early Italian Art*, were, despite their title, little more than a repetition of Hunt's belief in the detailed copying of "Nature" and Rossetti's largely contradictory ideal of painting the "soul." In most of the aesthetic articles in *The Germ*, whoever the writer, the matter is clearly taken from Hunt or Rossetti.

The moral aspects of art were not forgotten. Ironically enough at the beginning of this movement which was to end in charges of "fleshliness" against Rossetti and in the "aestheticism" of the 'nineties, "the arts" wrote Stephens, "have always been most important moral guides." "Sensuality of mind" he strongly deprecated, "for sensuality is a meanness repugnant to youth, and disgusting in age; a degradation at all times. Let us say

> My strength is as the strength of ten,
> Because my heart is pure!

. . . without the pure heart, nothing can be done worthy of us." Nor was Ruskin's teaching without influence upon the Preraphaelites' moralistic conceptions of art. "Believe that there is that in the fact of truth," wrote Stephens, "though it be only in the character of a single leaf earnestly studied, which may do its share in the great labour of the world." The dissent of Brown from Hunt's theories however, is clearly revealed in his article on *The Mechanism of a Historical Picture*. For there, although exhorting artists to accuracy of detail, Brown showed a wider and juster conception of art when he wrote: "Who shall settle the claims between thought and beauty? But art has beauties of its own, which neither impair nor contradict the beauties of nature."

Thus, even as Preraphaelite propaganda *The Germ* had little value. The rambling aesthetic articles made little or no direct appeal on behalf of Preraphaelitism. William's clumsy sonnet on the cover,[1] intended as a statement of principle, a nailing of Preraphaelite colours to the mast, William Bell Scott, not unjustly, dismissed as unintelligible. So too was the explanatory advertisement on the back of each number. Of this there were two versions which appeared alternately, one better than the other only because shorter. Illiterate, ungrammatical, obscure, they rouse in the reader only suspicion and distrust of the principles they fail to clarify. Such was *The Germ*, the commonplace and dreary setting for the earliest jewels of Christina and the good paste gems of Gabriel.

Short as the life of *The Germ* was, it attracted the attention of literary critics. There were favourable comments in *The Dispatch*, *John Bull*, *The Guardian*, *The Critic*, and *The Morning Chronicle*. *The Spectator* was unfriendly, while "Shirt-Collar Hall," despite his encouraging letter to the Brotherhood, disappointed them by a lukewarm and patronizing notice in the *Art Journal*. But for the Preraphaelites the ill-starred *Germ* was not all loss. As its last hours approached, William Rossetti, its editor, was preparing, butterfly-like, to burst from the chrysalis of *The Germ* into the full sunshine of general literary journalism. For the editor of the *Critic* had invited him, if the *Germ* failed, to undertake honorary art-criticism for his own paper, or to induce one of the Brotherhood to do so. Upon the refusal of his colleagues, William, rightly foreseeing the assistance such a position might give the Preraphaelites by enabling him to influence public opinion, accepted the offer.

[1] *v. supra*, p. 81.

97   D

The Germ had also introduced Gabriel's *Blessed Damozel* to the public. Soon William heard it highly praised by Westland Marston, the dramatist, and by Hervey, editor of the *Athenaeum*. Patmore on first seeing it had also spoken of it with enthusiasm. Thus the reception of *The Germ* in literary circles had augured a happier destiny than it was actually to experience. It may be that if political and religious controversy had not been definitely excluded from the magazine, if even the note of aesthetic revolt had been clearly, unanimously and confidently sounded, its career would have been longer and more prosperous. But youthful idealism is a frail foundation for journalistic ventures, and the Preraphaelites' contemporaries showed an almost complete natural immunity to the contagion of *The Germ*.

For the Brotherhood the experiment began a process of disillusion which the following months were to develop, not without bitterness. Hitherto the rebel society had been ignored because unknown. *The Germ* attracted the attention of the enemy. Already a storm was brewing which would severely test the sincerity and endurance of the P.R.B.

Whatever disappointment the failure of the *Germ* caused Gabriel at the moment, he was far, in later years, from regarding the magazine with a sentimental eye, and when "Lewis Carroll" fourteen years later enquired about a copy, Rossetti returned an elaborately detached reply— too elaborate perhaps for absolute conviction—saying: "I really have not the least idea where that precious publication could be obtained, and if I had, should feel no irresistible impulse to put anyone on the scent of it. An exhaustive enquiry among some of the trades class—Buttermen for instance—might I fancy have produced some results in the year 1850."[1]

---

[1] Lizzie Siddal, whom Rossetti married, is said to have first become acquainted with Tennyson's poetry through finding one of his poems on the paper in which she had brought home a pound of butter.

VI

THE PRERAPHAELITE STRUGGLE
1850–1852

One could hardly have thought that mere eccentricity in young
artists could have excited an hostility so determined and so cruel.

Preraphaelitism J. RUSKIN

THE ROYAL ACADEMY EXHIBITION of 1850 marked the opening
of a two years' campaign against the Preraphaelite Brotherhood
in which the rebels were almost overwhelmed. The secret
meaning of "P.R.B." confided by Gabriel to Munro the
sculptor, by Munro to a journalist and by the journalist to the
British public had aroused bitter hostility against those who
would overthrow Raphael and the tradition of contemporary
British art. Such men were felt to be subversive, capable of
attacking even the British Constitution itself. "A school of
Artists," stormed the *Athenaeum*, "whose younger members
unconsciously write its condemnation in the very title which
they adopt—that of Preraphaelite. . . . Their ambition is an
unhealthy thirst, which seeks notoriety by means of mere
conceit. Abruptness, singularity, uncouthness are the counters
with which they play for fame. Their trick is, to defy the
principles of beauty and the recognized axioms of taste."

Simultaneously, *The Times* bewailed the actions of "Mr.
Millais and his imitators who are attempting to engraft themselves on the wildest and most uncouth productions of the early
German school with a marked affectation of indifference to
everything we are accustomed to seek and to admire." *Blackwood's Magazine*, meanwhile, was sneering at "Messrs. Millais,
Hunt, Rossetti and Co." for imitating the painters who preceded
Raphael, "not only in the earnestness of purpose visible in
their productions, but in their errors, crudities and imperfections—renouncing in fact, the progress that since then has
been made; rejecting the experience of centuries, to revert for
models, not to art in its prime, but to art in its uncultivated
infancy. And," it concluded, "a nice business they make of it!

99

Regardless of anatomy and drawing they delight in ugliness and revel in diseased aspects." Dickens vulgarly attacked them in *Household Words*.

Millais's *Christ in the House of His Parents* particularly drew their fire. Its mild Preraphaelite realism in association with a "sacred subject" made it, for the average spectator as for the *Athenaeum*, "a pictorial blasphemy" from which all must "recoil with loathing and disgust." "Plainly revolting," moaned *The Times*: "To attempt to associate the Holy Family with the meanest details of a carpenter's shop, with no conceivable omission of misery, of dirt and even disease, all finished with the same loathsome minuteness, is disgusting." *Blackwood* could "hardly imagine anything more ugly, graceless and unpleasant. . . Such a collection of splay feet, puffed joints, and misshapen limbs was assuredly never before made within so small a compass." The *Athenaeum*, finally relapsing into hysterical incoherence, babbled of "disgusting incidents of unwashed bodies . . . presented in loathsome reality," and of "flesh with its accidents of putridity . . . made the affected medium of religious sentiment in tasteless revelation!"

"Mr. Dante Rossetti, one of the high-priests of this retrograde school, exhibits at the Portland Gallery," announced *Blackwood's*, and it was because of this comparative isolation that Gabriel so largely escaped the censures generously bestowed upon Millais and Hunt. Rossetti had in fact again exhibited with the Society of Artists, who were responsible for the Free Exhibition in the Chinese Gallery at Hyde Park Corner in the preceding year, but this year they had changed the name of their Society to "National Institution," and the place of their exhibition, no longer entitled "Free," to the Portland Gallery, opposite the Polytechnic in Regent Street. There, Rossetti's picture, *Ecce Ancilla Domini*, attracted little of the unwelcome notoriety given at the Academy to the works of his friends. Actually praised by *The Times* as "the work of a poet," it was lamented by the *Athenaeum* as "an example of the perversion of talent which has been recently making too much way in our school of Art and wasting the energies of some of our most promising aspirants. . . . Here a certain amount of talent is distorted from its legitimate course by a prominent crotchet. Ignoring all that has made the art great in the works of the greatest masters, the school to which Mr. Rossetti belongs would begin the work anew, and accompany the faltering steps of its earliest explorers. This is archaeology turned from its legitimate uses, and made into a mere pedant. Setting at nought all the advanced principles of light and shade, colour and composition—these men, professing to look only to Nature in its truth and simplicity, are the slavish imitators of artistic inefficiency." And the writer went on to ridicule "such puerilities as the one before us, which, with the affectation of having done a great thing is weakness itself. An unintelligent imitation of the mere technicalities of old Art—golden glories, fanciful scribblings on the frames, and other infantile absurdities—constitutes all its claims. A certain expression in the eyes of the ill-drawn face of the Virgin affords a gleam of something high in intention—but it is still not the true inspiration. The face of the angel is insipidity itself. . . ." Nevertheless, some five weeks later, the same journal in an article on the Academy Exhibition, after denouncing the Preraphaelites, remarked: "In point of religious sentiment Mr. Rossetti stands the chief of this little band." Gabriel's resentment of these criticisms was extreme. So bitter was his retort to the *Athenaeum's* strictures, that the editor refused it publication, and Rossetti vowed never to exhibit to the general public again.

Instead of presenting a solid front to the enemy, the Brotherhood gradually disintegrated under the shock. The first, almost immediate defection was the usually somnolent Collinson. To be engaged to Christina Rossetti, who refused to marry a Catholic, Collinson had first turned Protestant, then recanted and renounced his love upon the altar of the older faith. Upon the same altar he laid this new, lesser renunciation, pleading a sudden moral illumination which revealed that he must not, "consciously as a Catholic, assist in spreading the artistic opinions of those who are not," and that to remain in the Brotherhood would "dishonour God's faith" and the "Holy Saints." The Brotherhood was, in fact, at this time, being publicly assailed in various extremist quarters for its supposed "popery," which these religious paintings were believed to have revealed. Indeed a year or two later, Gabriel changed the title of his

Ecce Ancilla Domini to *The Annunciation*, in order to avoid the imputation of "popery" apparently associated with an acquaintance with the Latin tongue. It was, ironically enough, at this very time, that the Brotherhood was in fact rejected by its only "papist."

It was upon the "foreigner" Rossetti, that the angry and alarmed Brethren vented their exasperation and dismay. Twice, they said, he had evaded the Academy Exhibition in order to be first in the field and steal a march on them. In this way too, he had, whether by accident or design, evaded most of the strictures showered upon his friends. And it was he who, by revealing the secret significance of the "P.R.B." they had painted on their pictures, had roused their enemies to this attack. Such were the whispered complaints and suspicions against Rossetti that went round amongst the Brotherhood. Millais's father, desolated by his son's fall from favour, blamed Rossetti for refusing to show due respect to important Academicians. It had, he believed, prejudiced the art-world against the Brotherhood. "A sly Italian," cried Mrs. Millais, holding out the abusive journals in trembling hands, "I wish you had never had anything to do with that Rossetti!" The prejudice now formed against Gabriel by the Brotherhood was to increase as his rise to fame, success, and to reputed leadership of the Preraphaelites aroused their envy. Within a few months of its foundation the Preraphaelite Brotherhood had fallen into internal dissension while an angry and hostile world stormed and threatened without.

Nevertheless, the Brotherhood, saved by its social rather than by its vague aesthetic function, survived the attack. Patmore brought William Allingham, a young poetical customs officer of Ballyshannon with literary ambitions and a growing reputation, to the Brotherhood. "Capital fellows—artists and otherwise," wrote Patmore, "to whom I should beg to introduce you." Allingham, holidaying in London for a few weeks, and finding the Preraphaelite circle eminently congenial, passed most of his time in their company. By introducing to Gabriel the modest little American poet-painter Buchanan Read, then the object of one of Rossetti's temporary enthusiasms, Allingham won Gabriel's gratitude, and soon Rossetti and Allingham were close friends. They joked about Read's diminutive stature. "The miniature poet," said Woolner. "You might put him into a snuff box, then into a waistcoat pocket," said Allingham.

The presence of Allingham and Read no doubt partly accounts for the marked revival of social meetings amongst the Preraphaelites during this summer of 1850. Despite their poverty and the professional harm done to them by their opponents, there were laughter and gaiety, parties in one another's rooms and walking excursions as of old. Allingham particularly remembered one evening in Hunt's first-floor room with its pleasant outlook on the river: the broken chairs forcing the guests to take oriental postures on cushions on the floor: the happy discussions and disputes on painting and poetry: the crude, harmless jokes about the drunken man who asked when told to bring milk from the pantry, "Is it done up in paper, or lying about loose?" and about the painter who chose a super-subtle subject: "Gil Blas about to assume an air of unconcern while waiting on the robbers in their cave." He recalled how Gabriel, acknowledged leader in such nocturnal frolics, and already notorious for keeping late hours, presided, lolling amongst cushions and showing no intention to depart, not even when Hunt, due at the Academy early next morning, lay across three chairs to sleep, while the rest threatened to sit on him. It was just as in the old days when Hunt and Gabriel lived together in Fitzroy Square. Three o'clock had struck, dawn lay broad upon the river, barges showed clearly in the morning light when Gabriel at last rose and the party broke up.

Such gaiety, however, stood out for most of the Preraphaelites against a dark background of personal poverty and consequent embarrassment. To such misfortune Gabriel at this time was almost permanently a prey. The owner of the "dancing academy" or as Gabriel called it "hop-shop," below his rooms, defaulted, and Rossetti, involved as sub-tenant, had, like Hunt before him, to make a strategic retreat, in which most of his goods and even Read's luggage stored in the studio, were lost. His books were saved by the loyal William, who smuggled them to Brown's. For a time Gabriel seems to have lived the life of an outlaw, for Christina, recovering at Brighton from the shock

of Collinson's renunciation, wrote of her brother to William:
"If his whereabouts is [*sic*] to be kept secret, pray do not let
me have his address." But in such straits Rossetti invariably
found in generous Aunt Charlotte a *dea ex machina*. On this
occasion, however, it was Aunt Margaret, the "laughing
hyena," who came to his rescue. With unusual warmth he
thanked her for help in his "unlucky pickle," and before long
he was re-established in Newman Street, at No. 74, a house
next but one to his last—a gloomy place with a slanting skylight
on which the rain pattered dismally in the dark autumn days.
But he still slept at home in Charlotte Street.

From the early autumn of 1849 until the late spring of 1850,
Gabriel, sustained by his enthusiasm for new ventures—the
Brotherhood, the foreign tour, *The Germ*, verse and prose
composition, translation from the Italian poets, and the painting
of his *Annunciation*—had shown extraordinary energy. Now,
with the anti-climax of recent humiliations—the failure of *The
Germ* and the Brotherhood, the perpetual embarrassment of
poverty—reaction set in, and he sank into a lethargy, an indolence, the external sign of his inner frustration, as complete as
that he had shown at Sass's and the Academy Schools.

The difficulties of oil-painting he still chose to evade rather
than overcome. *Kate the Queen*, hitherto his most ambitious
attempt, begun at the opening of the year, he now abandoned
after months of struggle with an inadequate technique. From
his failure in painting he returned to poetry, writing *The
Burden of Nineveh*, his translations and other verses, going to the
theatre for distraction and finding Miss Glyn the actress
"godlike." To Aunt Charlotte he regretfully admitted his
incurable lassitude; "my laziness is so great as to account for
many things which it cannot excuse." The watching Brethren,
not perhaps without a secret twinge of satisfaction, remarked
his protracted idleness with apparent dismay, and prophesied
that he would have no picture to exhibit in the coming spring.
Brown foretold the Preraphaelites' ultimate triumph—"if
Rossetti will only work."

But Gabriel, instead of working, was writing love-verses. To
William, holidaying in Edinburgh—"just a place," wrote
Gabriel, "where people tell lies in Scotch," he sent a short poem,

later called *The Mirror*, with the brusque query: "Can you explain the following?" William long afterwards "explained" it as "a man is in love with a woman, without declaring himself, and without her appreciating the fact."

Was it some rejection by the unknown lady of *The Mirror*, or the sustained thirst for vengeance of his late landlord that, near the close of October sent Gabriel, "forced at last to bolt o' the sudden, with my tail between my legs," off in the drenching rain to Sevenoaks, with an enormous canvas over seven feet long? At any rate he had a new project. "From Nature" he would paint the background of a new picture, *The Meeting of Dante and Beatrice in the Garden of Eden*. It was just such a subject as a youthful, mystical, sentimental, rejected lover who wished to express his experience in Dantesque symbolism might choose.

At Sevenoaks, Hunt, painting in Knole Park his *Two Gentle-of Verona*, awaited with Stephens, Hunt's dilatory "pupil," Rossetti's arrival. But Knole Park in a wet and windy autumn was no Eden, as Gabriel, painting in the incessant downpour with an open umbrella tied to his button-hole and in saturated clothes, quickly found. Woolner who soon joined them should, Gabriel ironically suggested, design a statue of Gabriel in this guise. Quickly wearying of outdoor work in such weather, Rossetti soon abandoned painting, and shutting himself up in his room in the High Street, translated Italian *canzoni* "at a great rate," and added new stanzas to *Nineveh*. He also wrote a sonnet of vain longing, *Autumn Idleness*, which might be a pendant to *The Mirror* and certainly expresses the unquiet mood which now possessed him. Another day, in early November, "between Ightham and Sevenoaks," he wrote the two stanzas entitled *A Young Fir-wood*, an unconscious or semi-conscious expression of the growing sex-urge of his adolescence. That it was at least semi-conscious is suggested by the fact that a little later, in *Love's Nocturn*, he again, and consciously, used the fir-wood as a symbol of sexual desire.

For three weeks he remained at Sevenoaks while the rain poured down and the leaves he tried to paint were torn off and blown away by the wind, until, losing patience, unable one suspects, to remain longer apart from the woman who had inspired his verses, he returned to town as suddenly as he had come. The abandoned background for the *Meeting of Dante and Beatrice* he converted twenty years later into *The Bower Meadow*.

Back in London he fell again into the old frustration, repainting, despite his need of a new picture for the spring exhibition, the angel's head in his *Annunciation*. The increasing poverty of the Rossetti family forced them early in 1851 to leave Charlotte Street for 38 Arlington Street, Camden Town. There, indomitable Mrs. Rossetti opened a private school which did not pay, and old Gabriele, crawling painfully about the tiny garden, wished to die. Gabriel, about the same time, though still sleeping at home, left Newman Street and joined his Preraphaelite friend Deverell in his studio in Red Lion Square. Their models, the suspicious landlord stipulated, must be "kept under some gentlemanly restraint, as some artists sacrifice the dignity of art to the baseness of passion."

Once again relations between Gabriel and his father were strained, for old Gabriele thought his son's indolence and relapse into the writing of financially unprofitable verse, particularly amidst the family distress, unpardonable. But his remonstrances were unheeded. Gabriel continued to make translations, to borrow money from his mother, brother, aunts and uncles, from all indeed who could be cajoled into lending. He borrowed and spent royally, caring nothing, so long as money came to him, as to the manner of its acquisition. With urbanity, even magnanimity, he accepted Aunt Charlotte's largesse. "Indeed were I not to do so," he wrote, graciously acknowledging her cheque, "I think I should be guilty of injustice to myself as well as of ingratitude to you." Upon such occasions the delicacy of his moral sense was exquisite! Most cunningly, when need arose, could he bait the hook for Aunt Charlotte who was ambitious for her artist-nephew. The "ground I have already gained with the public," he wrote to her, early in 1851, "I may add without vanity, is much more than most young men have gained upon the strength of two small pictures. Thus I need not say of what incalculable value to me, at this juncture, will be the means of dispensing with further delay in my picture, nor with how much gratitude to you I shall accept them, from a sense of duty towards myself; seeing that they may probably be instrumental in enabling me before long to be of no further charge to anyone. I may add an assurance that I should consider all such sums strictly as a loan, to be returned when the sale of a picture enabled me to do so." And in less exalted but more veracious style he added a bald postscript—"I cashed the cheque as soon as it reached me, i.e. this morning."

Generous Aunt Charlotte would have been astonished, however, could she but have seen Brown's account of her nephew shortly after he had written this elaborate epistle to herself. "Rossetti," wrote Brown, "has just thrown up a *third* picture, and will have nothing" (in the Academy), "but he has a commission to illustrate Longfellow's poems along with Hunt, which will bring him in some tin.[1] His head and beard grow finer every day, and he has made some designs which are perfectly divine. I mean by that, finer than anything I have ever seen, but paint he *will not*. He is too idle. You know he lives in Red Lion Square along with Deverell, and purports to keep himself. I had thought for some time there had been some estrangement between Rossetti and his brother, and I asked Deverell who was sitting to me this morning. He said no. That he believed they were as good friends as ever, but that he supposed his brother did not call on him oftener than he could help because he was ordered peremptorily to hand over all the cash he had about him."

Once indeed, when the resources of both Gabriel and his family reached their lowest ebb, he momentarily considered an offer of employment as a railway telegraphist. He even went to Nine Elms Station to see what a telegraph looked like. On seeing it he of course disliked it, courteously explained that to work it was beyond him as he would never understand it—and departed. To William he left for many years the honour of supporting the Rossetti family, as well as, largely, Gabriel himself.

Yet during these months of apparent futility, Gabriel's reputation was advancing in the outer world. Not only did Brown praise his designs, Sir Theodore Martin, author of the

[1] This apparently was never executed.

popular *Bon Gaultier Ballads*, was in ecstasies over Gabriel's
sonnet on *The Girlhood of Mary Virgin* in the catalogue of the
Free Exhibition. Martin declared it "one of the finest sonnets
in the language," and distributed copies amongst his friends.
Nor was Rossetti backward in attempting to draw attention to
his verse. To Tennyson he sent his version of Dante's *Vita
Nuova*, and on December 1st, 1850, received the Poet-Laureate's
reply. Tennyson thought Gabriel's verses "very strong and
earnest" but disfigured by "cockney rhymes" such as "calm and
arm," and these Gabriel determined to correct before
attempting publication.

But when in the spring of 1851 the Academy Exhibition
opened, and the public gazed upon new works by Millais,
Hunt and Brown, Rossetti had no picture to show.

Yet even in this he was fortunate. For with the opening of the
exhibition, the attack on the Preraphaelites was resumed even
more bitterly than before. Their enemies in fact did not realize
how successful had been the earlier onslaught, how demoralized
it had left the Brethren.

Disgraced, isolated, without commissions, they had fallen
into poverty, ill-temper and despair. Hunt, reduced to his last
penny, was saved by the chance discovery of a half-crown in the
upholstery of his broken chair, and suspected Divine intervention. They began to contemplate emigration to Australia
which teemed with gold! They considered a Preraphaelite
crusade to Jerusalem where Hunt would fulfil his earlier dream
of painting a moving Biblical scene so realistically that all men
seeing it would kneel before the Christ in worship, accepting
Him—and Hunt's aesthetic creed!

Hunt, strong in the faith, was indeed prepared for martyrdom; but most of the Preraphaelites were weaker vessels.
Gabriel, in poor health, disillusioned, lethargic, moody,
largely frustrated, neither supported nor abjured the unpopular
cause; but that "Nature," whether in life or art, was no genuine
ruling passion with him, he had already shown in a humorous
rhyming letter written in 1850 to his friend John Tupper in
which he confessed:

> Though as to Nature, Jack,
> (Poor dear old hack!)

> Touching sky, sun, stone, stick and stack,
> I guess I'm half a quack;
> For whom ten lines of Browning whack
> The whole of the Zodiac . . .

Millais, never an enthusiastic Preraphaelite, quickly recanted. "It's all nonsense; of course nature's nature and art's art, isn't it? One could not live doing that!" was his sensible comment upon Hunt's photographic copying of "Nature." Stephens, abandoning painting to Hunt's relief, exemplified Pope's ironical dicta in his *Essay in Criticism*, by turning art-critic instead.

Seeing with dismay this disintegration of the Brotherhood, William Rossetti vainly encouraged attempts to stem it by means of rules, fines for absence, and ultimately by demanding a declaration of aesthetic principles which, significantly enough, he could never obtain. Since the Academy's attack in 1850, fear had been more conspicuous in the Brotherhood than revolt. They had precipitately abandoned the provocative "P.R.B.," and even unselfishly decided, in the interest of new sympathizers, not to admit them to so harmful a distinction as membership of the Brotherhood involved. Even William Rossetti in silent commune with his diary, reflecting: "I should certainly be glad to do for something and with better prospects, what I am now doing for nothing," accepted at the same salary as that of Goldsmith's parson in *The Deserted Village*, the post of art-critic to the *Spectator*, and found less time for purely Preraphaelite interests.

Such was the situation when in the spring of 1851 there fell upon the already tottering rebels this new and fiercer onslaught. Eastlake, President of the Academy, had privately sworn that never again should Preraphaelite paintings deface its walls. The Press burst into yet more violent accusations of blasphemy, tractarianism, popery, "French realism," false perspective, "antiquated style," "affected simplicity," "crude colour," mis-shapen figures, "caricatures," "eccentricity," and a hundred other mutually contradictory vices. The committee of the Academy Exhibition were exhorted to pluck the offending paintings of Hunt and Millais from its walls, while emotional Professors led the students of the Academy Schools in hissing the

unpopular painters and their works. *The Times* declared there
could be no quarter, the Preraphaelite rebels against law and
order must be destroyed. The *Daily News* and William Rossetti's
articles in the *Spectator* alone opposed the hysterical outcry.
And once again Hunt and Millais were the chief scapegoats.

It was now that the Brotherhood, despairing, sought new aid
in the unequal struggle. For some time their hopes had turned
to Ruskin whose *Modern Painters* showed, they thought, a
spirit kindred to their own. Millais, overwhelmed by *The Times'*
attack upon his work, begged Patmore to move Ruskin in their
defence. Thereupon Patmore, anxious to help his Preraphaelite
friends, sought Ruskin's aid.

During the three years which had passed since the Preraphaelites first found in *Modern Painters* fortuitous encouragement, Ruskin's light had blazed in *The Seven Lamps of Architecture*, his reputation risen on *The Stones of Venice*. Now, at the
age of thirty-two, he was a celebrity. As he passed along the
street people turned for a second glance at the simian face
framed in light hair and reddish whiskers, the dark blue coat
with velvet collar, the bright Oxford blue stock and black
trousers of this latest dictator in the domain of art. Although no
admirer of the Preraphaelites, Ruskin, to please Patmore,
wrote at his request two letters to *The Times* in their defence.
That these letters, which appeared in May 1851, were a study
in diplomacy rather than in art-criticism, is doubtless the
reason of their success. Giving a somewhat misleading suggestion of absolute detachment, Ruskin commended the Preraphaelites' "labour" and "fidelity to a certain order of truth,"
deprecated their supposed "Romanist and Tractarian tendencies," and amidst infantile jests at the "painted window and
idolatrous toilet-table" in Millais' *Mariana*, and the nun and
tadpole "rather too small for his age" in Collins's charming
Convent Thoughts, pleaded for patience and reserved judgment,
in place of the general condemnation. The Brethren were
young, he emphasized, "at a most critical period of their career
—at a turning-point from which they may either sink into
nothingness or rise to very real greatness."

Finally, Ruskin found for the Preraphaelites what they had
been unable to discover for themselves, a common aesthetic

principle justifying their name! They did not, said Ruskin, wish to imitate "antique paintings as such," were indeed anxious to utilize all that later art could give them; but they meant to paint "stern facts" rather than "fair pictures," to return not to "archaic art" but to "archaic honesty," As often with Ruskin, conviction came to him on the flood of his eloquence, and from the "very imperfect sympathy" with the Preraphaelites of his opening passage, he proceeded to deny the general not always unjustified charges against them of bad perspective and ill-painted drapery, asserting that "as studies both of drapery and of every minor detail, there has been nothing in art so earnest or so complete as these pictures since the days of Albert Dürer." The Preraphaelites, he declared in a typically rhetorical climax to his last letter, might "lay in our England the foundations of a school of art nobler than the world has seen for three hundred years."

The gratitude of the Brethren, transmitted to their new defender by Patmore, was unbounded. Ruskin in reply, mingled an expression of pleasure with sneers at Millais' detail. Could he not have got a real olive branch for model instead of "painting one on speculation?" Had he "ever in his life seen a bit of old painted glass, near?" And "what modern stuff" had he painted from? Millais had in fact painted the coloured glass of Mariana's window from the exquisite thirteenth-century glass in Merton College Chapel; but Ruskin, when he descended from imaginative interpretation into the realm of hard, unadaptable fact and artistic technique, was often unfortunate. "Oil or water-colour?" Cardinal Manning asked him twenty-five years later as they surveyed one of Burne-Jones's pictures. Kneeling down, Ruskin closely examined the work for some moments, then answered: "Pure water-colour, my Lord," so quietly but authoritatively that the painter's wife, who knew it was oil, did not dare to contradict him! Despite his literary talent, Ruskin had something of the charlatan's instinct never to admit ignorance or error. And this was to be exceedingly fortunate for the P.R.B.

In the spring of 1851, to please Patmore, Ruskin had defended the Preraphaelites. Autumn found him their spokesman and leader, a consequence he had neither anticipated nor desired. Throughout the summer the Preraphaelite battle had raged. *The Times'* critic, daring to pick up the glove Ruskin had thrown down, had made sly allusions to Ruskin's two rambling letters, had cited Ruskin's own principles as the best antidotes to Preraphaelitism, which was, he declared, at the opposite extreme from Ruskin's idol, Turner; "but—as extremes meet —they both find an apologist in the same critic." Ruskin's own admissions, he argued, were sufficient to damn the Brotherhood; nevertheless he hoped to see them, next year, "stand forth as the founders of the illustrious school our correspondent announces to the world." It was this neat retort which brought the hitherto lukewarm if not actually hostile Ruskin, headlong into the Preraphaelite band. Before a personal challenge Ruskin's former detachment vanished. Eager to retaliate upon his adversary if only to preserve his own prestige as critic, Ruskin henceforth made the Preraphaelite cause his own. But for that it would almost certainly have perished as quickly as it had arisen.

Besides, during these months, Ruskin's sympathy with the Preraphaelites had actually grown more sincere. Revising the first volume of *Modern Painters*, and remarking his own exhortations there to artists to "go to Nature," Ruskin had come to regard the Preraphaelites as largely attempting to carry out his commands, and as receiving, in consequence, general abuse and scorn. In this mood he had written his pamphlet *Preraphaelitism*, in which he developed the cautious approval of the movement already expressed in his letters to *The Times*, warned the Brethren of their faults, and pretended to refute the critic who had dared to oppose him.

Ruskin's intervention was decisive for the Preraphaelite Movement. If, argued the bewildered public, a famous English critic "saw something in it," Preraphaelitism could hardly be so bad as they had believed. The Brethren were after all merely harmless, eccentric artists. Thus the fears of insidious moral, religious and political revolt died away. Ruskin had also invested the Preraphaelites with the dignity of a new aesthetic theory and practice which he declared fundamentally moral, right and true. Above all, the Preraphaelite battle gave the movement an immediate importance it would otherwise never have attained. From a small, poor, obscure and largely irresponsible art-coterie of youthful aspirants, existing rather for its social than its aesthetic utility, the Brotherhood suddenly became, through Ruskin, the most prominent element in contemporary English painting. Brown, with exceptional acuteness, immediately detected this result, and foretold its consequences. "The amount of abuse," he wrote of the Preraphaelites, "that has been lavished on them, has been such as to impart dignity to a name which used to be looked on more as a subject of mirth than anything else. You will remember that with all of us, whatever used to be thought of Rossetti's, Hunt's and Millais's talents the words Preraphaelite Brotherhood, or the letters P.R.B. used to be looked upon as the childish or ridiculous part of the business. But now, I can assure you that I pronounce the words without hesitation as an ordinary term in the everyday of art. The term will now remain with them, and, in the course of time, gain a dignity which cannot fail to attach to whatever is connected with what they do."

For three years the Preraphaelite Brotherhood had existed in its own amorphous way, in a no man's land between a jest and an ideal, but free to act as it pleased and for itself alone. Now, Ruskin, like some spiritualistic medium, had suddenly transformed its dwindling ghost into an apparently substantial, corporeal reality. Yet inevitably he had confined it at the same time within the limitations of the reincarnate, which were in this case, those of formulated definition and principle. First seeing themselves in the beautifying mirror of Ruskin's eloquence, the Preraphaelites only with difficulty recognized themselves. But in time, some of them at least accepted the embellished image as an accurate reflection of the truth.

Meanwhile the effect of Ruskin's support was immediately visible. In October 1851, Hunt's *Two Gentlemen of Verona* was awarded a prize of £50 by the Liverpool Academy, and when in the spring of 1852 the London Academy opened, Millais's *Ophelia* and *Huguenot* and Hunt's *Hireling Shepherd* were actually "on the line"! The struggle, though bitter, had been short. Rossetti once again had no pictures to exhibit, and Brown's *Christ Washing Peter's Feet* (now in the National Gallery), was "skied." Ruskin, who disliked both Brown and his work, said no word in his favour, and the unfortunate painter, blamed by some as a Preraphaelite, by others as no member of the Brotherhood, fell between two stools. Brown's anger against Ruskin and the Academy was great. Turning his back on the President he strode out of the exhibition, vowing never to exhibit there again.

With popularity came not only a temporary revival of the Brotherhood's activities, but a remarkable reversal of the rebels' attitude. Hunt and Millais applied for membership of the despised Academy—"as a refutation," Hunt long afterwards explained, "to the provoked suspicion that our movement was essentially inimical to that institution!" But heedless of their altruistic motive the Academy passed them by. Hunt never repeated the attempt. Millais, in anger, renounced all future dealings with so contemptible a society, until, hearing that his rejection was due to his being under age, and that next year he would be accepted, he changed his mind!

The summer of 1852 brought another defection from the Brotherhood. Woolner, failing to extract a living from sculpture, and fired by the Preraphaelites' talk of emigration, joined his friends Bernhard Smith, a sculptor, and Edward Bateman, a decorative artist, in the Australian gold rush. Tennyson, who to Rossetti's amusement expected Woolner to return with at least £10,000 a year, declared that but for Mrs. Tennyson he would go with them. Hopes ran high, and Bell Scott's estimate of an income of £1,200 a year as a digger's largest fortune was generally scorned by the Brethren as a "paltry sum." Carlyle, who approved the Preraphaelites for "copying the thing as it is," opposed Woolner's plan, "seeming" said Gabriel ironically, "to espy in it some savour of the mammon of unrighteousness."

Woolner's preparations, based apparently upon the adventure-stories of boyhood, were spectacular. Bell Scott found him preparing his "cradle" and "kit" and buying revolvers to protect the inevitable gold. On July 16th, the party sailed for Sydney on the *Windsor*; "All of them," Gabriel maliciously reported, "plentifully stocked with corduroys, sou'westers, jerseys, fire-arms, and belts full of little bags to hold the expected nuggets." At Gravesend, Brown, Rossetti and Hunt bade them farewell.

BOOK II

'YOUTH AND CHANGE'
1850–1862

The fair woman that was his soul.

Hand and Soul D. G. ROSSETTI

I

"ART, FRIENDSHIP AND LOVE"
1850–1852

And he knew her hair to be the golden veil through which he
beheld his dreams.

Hand and Soul D. G. ROSSETTI

UNCERTAINTY, with a consequent development of the anxiety
tendencies inherited from his father, was the most obvious
cause of Rossetti's increasing morbidity, his alternations of
moodiness, restlessness and lethargy during the last two years.
In this, poverty, the rival claims of poetry and painting,
technical difficulties and doubts of ultimate success had all
played a part. But even more disturbing than these was a
profound emotional experience. Rossetti had fallen passionately in love.

Elizabeth Siddal's attraction for Gabriel was at first essentially physical. In later years, Lady Burne-Jones, speaking of
the two women who most influenced Rossetti's life, declared
that while Mrs. Morris's beauty was that of a statue, Lizzie's
was that of a painting. How strongly colour appealed to
Rossetti his pictures show, and in Lizzie's colour, in her milk-
and-rose complexion, and above all in her copper-gold hair
which satisfied the almost atavistic craving of this descendant
of the Rossettis, lay Lizzie's chief appeal to his sense of beauty.

It was Deverell, the Adonis of the Preraphaelites, whose
handsome face was said to have sent staid Victorian maidens
flying down back-streets to gain another glimpse of it, who had
found Lizzie. Shopping with his mother, he had discovered her
in a milliner's shop in Leicester Square and persuaded her to
sit to him as Viola in a scene from Shakespeare's *Twelfth Night*.
During the first sitting he had made two surprising discoveries;
one, that she behaved "like a real lady," the other, though
how he discovered it he did not say—that she knew "how to
keep people at a respectful distance." Bursting into Hunt and
Rossetti's studio with this exciting news one spring evening of

1850, Deverell brought Lizzie Siddal into Rossetti's life. For while Hunt characteristically refused to leave his painting, Gabriel arranged to go to Deverell's at the first opportunity to see the wonderful creature for himself.

Soon Lizzie was established as a favourite model of the Preraphaelite Brotherhood; and red-gold hair became, under Rossetti's influence, a Preraphaelite passion. Hunt painted her as Sylvia in his *Valentine rescuing Sylvia from Proteus*, the scene from Shakespeare's *Two Gentlemen of Verona*. He inserted her head in his *Christians pursued by Druids*, and her gold hair in his *Light of the World*. Millais painted her as the Ophelia of his famous picture, and this, according to William Rossetti, was a "close likeness." Deverell, having painted her as Viola with Gabriel as the jester in *Twelfth Night*, drew her again as Viola, in another scene from the play, which formed a but indifferent frontispiece to the April number of *The Germ*. Lizzie first appears in Rossetti's work as *Rossovestita* in 1850, and henceforth is omnipresent in it until her death in 1862.

Lizzie, some six years younger than Gabriel, was the daughter of a Sheffield cutler long established in London. Though meagrely educated she spoke and behaved correctly, was not socially "impossible." After her death her friends and acquaintances differed, some praising her beauty while others denied its existence. William Rossetti, who evidently did not like her but tried to be fair, described her as "truly a beautiful girl; tall, with a stately throat and fine carriage, pink and white complexion, and massive straight coppery-golden hair. Her large greenish-blue eyes, large lidded, were peculiarly noticeable. . . . One could not have seen a woman in whose whole demeanour maidenly and feminine purity was more markedly apparent. She maintained an attitude of reserve, self-controlling and alien from approach. Without being prudish, and along with a decided inclination to order her mode of life according to her own liking, whether conformable or not to the views of the British matron, she was certainly distant. Her talk was, in my experience, scanty; slight and scattered, with some amusing turns, and little to seize upon—little clue to her real self or to anything determinate. I never perceived her to have any religion; but a perusal of some of her few poems may fairly lead to the inference that she was not wanting in a devotional habit of feeling."

Allingham, who pitied Lizzie, finding her "sweet, gentle and kindly, and sympathetic to art and poetry," did not think her beautiful, but rather, with her "pale face, abundant red hair, and long thin limbs . . . strange and affecting." Contemporaries, moved by her lot, romanticized her. Ruskin's fulsome compliments to her—"a noble, glorious creature," "charming as the reflection of a golden mountain in a crystal lake"—reveal little more than his love of rhetoric and the wish to atone for his unintentional insults to her, made before he had met either her or Gabriel, or even knew of their existence. For Ruskin, criticizing Hunt's *Valentine rescuing Sylvia from Proteus*, had publicly deplored the "unfortunate type chosen for the face of Sylvia," and its "commonness of feature." Such a Sylvia, he declared, was "not a person whom Proteus or any one else would have been likely to fall in love with at first sight." As a result, Hunt repainted Sylvia's head, so depriving us of a probably good likeness of Lizzie at that time. Rossetti's innumerable portraits and drawings of Lizzie, though described by William Rossetti as essentially true portraits, are sometimes in fact, so "idealized" that they fail to dispel the uncertainty about the significant details of Lizzie's appearance. Varying according to the painter's mood and aim, these portraits of Lizzie show in some cases a strikingly handsome woman, in others not; and the latter seem to have been the better likeness.

Ruskin's father, striving to outdo his son in compliments to Lizzie, said that "by her look and manner she might have been a countess"; but Bessie Parkes, the clear-minded, sensible friend of Lizzie and Gabriel at this time, objected. "She was not of his rank in life," wrote Bessie, referring to Lizzie and Gabriel, "and I did not think her in the least like 'a countess,' but she had an unworldly simplicity and purity of aspect which Rossetti has recorded in his pencil drawings of her face. Millais has also given this look in his *Ophelia*, for which she was the model. The expression of Beatrice was not hers, and when I look at the famous Beatrice (*Beata Beatrix*) in the National Gallery, I feel puzzled by the manner in which the artist took the head and features of a remarkably retiring English girl, with whom I was perfectly familiar, and transfused them with an expression in which I could recognize nothing of the moral nature of Miss Siddal. She had the look of one who read her Bible and said her prayers every night, which she probably did." But from these and many more descriptions, often fulsome and sentimental, and despite many drawings and paintings, no clear and consistent picture of Lizzie emerges. She remains, like all the women who most influenced Rossetti, a somewhat vague and shadowy figure. Her true character, even her much advertised physical charm, are not easy to determine with exactness. Somehow, people never agreed about Lizzie, not even about her complexion, her eyes, her character, her talent, her health or her age.

Like most human beings Lizzie evidently showed to the sympathetic and the unsympathetic different aspects of herself. Amongst her new artist friends she sought in silence and reserve the defence of a proud, shy, sensitive, slightly bewildered girl. The Rossettis, ambitious for Gabriel and disappointed in his passion for Lizzie, were unsympathetic and, inevitably, in their presence Lizzie was not at her best. William thought she combined dignity and sweetness with "disdainful reserve"—the obvious reaction of her feeling of inferiority. Her character he found "somewhat singular—not quite easy to understand, and not at all on the surface." He regretted the rather ill-bred, "chaffy" sarcasm of the shop-girl, which was part of her defence, and failed to understand and pity this defensiveness which, under the pressure of events, became combativeness.

As for Gabriel, now in his twenty-third year, he was certainly very ready to fall in love. Hitherto moral and idealistic beliefs had controlled his actions. "No juvenile liaisons or flirtations" said William had marked his youth. It was then only, Hunt declared, "that the soul within had been truly seen in his face . . . his inner life was untainted in the poetic atmophere of sacred and spiritual dreams that then dwelt within him in embryo." A dreamy asceticism indeed marked his almost haggard face. Hunt long recalled his "Southern breed and aspect" at this time, his tawny-coloured eye-lids, delicate aquiline nose "with a depression from the frontal sinus shaping the bridge," and full nostrils. His general bearing was slack and careless, an effect intensified by exceptionally wide hips, giving him a slouching, rolling gait. With a touch of affectation, as an artist he wore his brown hair long, letting it reach down to his sloping, barely masculine shoulders. His brow was prominent and rounded, his jaw angular and obvious. In all he was a lightly built person, some five feet seven inches in height, with conspicuously delicate hands and feet, and although of sound constitution, "altogether unaffected by athletic exercise."

To the external world Gabriel at this time might present a somewhat "seedy" appearance, but to the inner world of his own romantic imagination he was a mediaeval knight, a *preux chevalier*, dedicated to the chivalric ideal. During the earlier years of his adolescence his idealistic dream, capturing his imagination, had gradually enwrapped him in all its delusive glamour, untouched as yet by disillusion, bitterness, decay. The world about him radiated a mystic splendour, was strong with the strength, bright with the gaiety, glad with the courtesy and grace of romanticized mediaeval chivalry. And ever, for him, at the heart of life, the focus and centre of the imaginative world in which he most truly lived, beckoned ideal woman and ideal love to whose service he was already self-dedicated. This was "the one dream alone" of which he spoke later, in *The Orchard Pit*, saying: "All my life I have dreamt one dream alone."

Hitherto this dreamy "poetic" idealism had combined with his mother's strict moral and religious training to control the powerful urge of his highly-sexed nature; but now, "youth and change"—as he later entitled one section of his sonnet sequence *The House of Life*—were, he felt, in the air, and the verse he was now writing clearly reflects his feeling. The sonnet *Idle Blessedness* is one of the first instinctive cries of his warm yet languorous Southern blood, in praise of that mood of apparent lethargy, trance-like yet saturated with thought and feeling, of those "lazy moods," "drowsy humours" for which he says he offers "no excuse," into which, throughout his life, amidst external and internal frustrations, he increasingly withdrew in neurotic flight from drab reality.

In both his poetry and painting the prostitute or mistress soon became a frequent unconscious symbol of his inner conflict, a symbol which satisfied both elements in his nature, for sex disguised as moral idealism could contemplate it with conscious sorrow concealing unconscious pleasure. In *Jenny*, the exhortation against lust is equally significant, but that the ostensible theme of the poem was as yet drawn from personal experience is disproved by his comment upon it in later years: "I felt it was quite beyond me then—a world I was then happy enough to be a stranger to." A similar note is struck in such early studies and paintings as *The Sun may Shine and we be Cold*, *Hesterna Rosa* and *Found*, while in a memorial poem to a young friend written when Gabriel was but nineteen, he precociously rejoiced that the dead youth had at least been spared sexual temptation and disillusion.

Amidst this strife of conflicting elements in his nature, of his powerful instincts and his mother's stern moral and religious training, Rossetti in adolescence came to resemble the demon-haunted victims of the diabolic tales he loved. His frustration produced emotional ambivalence and he enjoyed contradictory moods: the exaltation of the mystical and idealistic, the ecstasy of the passionate, the perfect blending of all in the contemplation of ideal love. There came a palpable increase of nervous tension. Yet his Latin sense of reality remained, and in moments of reaction he could laugh at his own intensity as at the general comedy of life. Most clearly is his mood reflected in the translation of a song from Victor Hugo's *Les Burgraves* which Rossetti made in 1847. Through it rings an undertone of reckless, almost hysterical gaiety, the suggestion of an attitude violently forced upon a deeper, silent protest within himself. The intensity of his translation is the intensity of his own mood. Unconsciously symbolic, the poem definitely rejects, as he too was soon to reject, the mother's influence, leaving the individual a prey, as he too would soon become a prey, to the instincts her training had restrained.

> Through the long winter the rough wind tears;
> With their white garment the hills look wan.
>   Love on: who cares?
>   Who cares? Love on.

My mother is dead; God's patience wears;
It seems my chaplain will not have done.
    Love on: who cares?
    Who cares? Love on.
The Devil, hobbling up the stairs,
Comes for me with his ugly throng.
    Love on: who cares?
    Who cares? Love on.

The stanzas are an expression of the unconscious which, says Jung, "always foreshadows future events." Their mutually antagonistic elements are eddies pointing the quarters from which the great winds of Rossetti's spirit will blow, bearing to us, indeed, what Rossetti himself claimed to find in Dante's *Vita Nuova*, "a strain like the first falling murmur which reaches the ear in some remote meadow, and prepares us to look upon the sea."

But above all, it is in *Hand and Soul*, the trance-woven tale of 1849, that we find most clearly the unconscious record of Rossetti's inner conflict. Chiaro's regret that his ambitious years of youth, dedicated to art, have held no place for woman is obviously Gabriel's; so too is his account of awakening passion and the general mood of disintegrating asceticism which broods over the story. Such was Rossetti's state when Elizabeth Siddal entered and quickly dominated his life. So, to Gabriel, Lizzie almost from the first appeared some such spirit of beauty as Chiaro saw and worshipped. Like Chiaro he found her "the fair woman that was his soul," and knew "her hair to be the golden veil through which he beheld his dreams." Lizzie seemed, in fact, his ideal of love and beauty granted him in the flesh. Through twelve years of passion and pain the drama of their love, his attempt to live his dream, played itself out. Then from his life she passed, like the "soul" of Chiaro, as suddenly, as strangely as she had come.

There were, then, many causes for Gabriel's unrest in this spring of 1851, but above all others was his growing passion for Lizzie. In that lay the secret of his spasmodic energy, his now prevailing lethargy, his inaction following those months of strenuous endeavour with his painting and with *The Germ*. Brown, who persuaded Gabriel in May to quit Red Lion Square for a share in his own large studio in Newman Street, soon regretted the interruption to his work thus occasioned. Gabriel, he lamented, kept him awake talking until four o'clock in the morning, "painting sometimes all night, making the whole place miserable . . . translating sonnets at breakfast, working very hard and doing nothing." Throughout the year Gabriel's low spirits, his indifference to Preraphaelitism and painting in general continued. To poetry he still gave precedence, spending much time and labour upon his translations from the Italian poets, and showing his verses to Patmore and others for criticism. From the Brethren he drifted away, incurring by his idleness and unsociability their severe though secret condemnation.

Lizzie no doubt explains the hopeless longing and dejection of his verses, his withdrawal from the Brotherhood, his frequent abandonment of all painting, his flight to Sevenoaks, conspicuous incidents of the first two years of their friendship. He obviously languished as only an Italian can languish when frustrated in love. Certainly Lizzie's attraction for Gabriel was immediate and profound. "Rossetti once told me," wrote Brown, "that when he first saw her, he felt his destiny was defined." His passion was at first largely the offspring of his romantic idealism and the tradition, as he interpreted it, of mediaeval chivalry. True, he had fallen in love with her at sight, as he would have fallen in love with a beautiful painting. He wished to paint her, to immortalize her mortal beauty. But Lizzie was not only beautiful; she was poor, obscure, ailing, lonely, in distress. He thought her greatly superior by nature to her humble lot, chafed at the sight of Beauty, his Mistress Absolute, in poverty, sickness and a vulgar setting. He wished to save her as he would a rose lying delicate and fragile in the mire, a prey to the accidents of the street. His conscious intention, generous, idealistic even, was to help her, protect her, and, less consciously—for we must not take too literally that late confession to Brown of his immediate sense of destiny defined; other things, as we shall see, conflict with it—to enjoy the pleasure of having her about him.

One is tempted to believe that Gabriel's growing passion for Lizzie found expression in the poem he was now writing, *A Last Confession*. Certainly several of Lizzie's physical traits were incorporated in the appearance of the "heroine" who

> had a mouth
> Made to bring death to life—the underlip
> Sucked in as if it strove to kiss itself,

a characteristic of Lizzie's not only remarked by William Rossetti—who, however, did not apparently observe its association with *A Last Confession*—but also shown in many of Gabriel's sketches of her, particularly in a nameless caricature he made about 1850 and entitled *Stunner No. 1*. It was surely Lizzie's eyes too—"greenish blue" according to William, "luminous grey-green," said Swinburne, "golden-brown, agate colour, and wonderfully luminous," wrote Lady Burne-Jones —that Gabriel described in *A Last Confession*,

> As of the sea and sky on a grey day.[1]

It is not strange then, that the personal note sounds so strongly in some passages of *A Last Confession*, particularly that in which Rossetti describes the man's gradual change of feeling from an almost parental affection to love, as he sees the child he has adopted grow into womanhood.

> For now, being always with her, the first love
> I had—the father's, brother's love—was changed,
> I think, in somewise; like a holy thought
> Which is a prayer before one knows of it.
> The first time I perceived this, I remember,
> Was once when after hunting I came home
> Weary, and she brought food and fruit for me,
> And sat down at my feet upon the floor
> Leaning against my side. But when I felt
> Her sweet head reach from that low seat of hers
> So high as to be laid upon my heart,
> I turned and looked upon my darling there
> And marked for the first time how tall she was;
> And my heart beat with so much violence
> Under her cheek, I thought she could not choose
> But wonder at it soon and ask me why;
> And so I bade her rise and eat with me.
> And when, remembering all and counting back
> The time, I made out fourteen years for her
> And told her so, she gazed at me with eyes
> As of the sky and sea on a grey day,

---

[1] *v. inf.* also the passage from Swinburne's *A Year's Letters*, quoted under page reference 274 in *Notes* at end of vol.

And drew her long hands through her hair, and asked me
If she was not a woman; and then laughed:
And as she stooped in laughing, I could see
Beneath the growing throat the breasts half-globed
Like folded lilies deepset in the stream.

*   *   *

In those hours, no doubt,
To the young girl my eyes were like my soul,—
Dark wells of death-in-life that yearned for day.

In a sonnet of 1852, *On the Vita Nuova of Dante*, Rossetti
summarizes an experience identical with that in the above
passage, and describes how Dante's *Vita Nuova*, the work
which so strongly influenced his adolescence, indeed his whole
life and art, taught him to curb passion through idealism.

As he that loves oft looks on the dear form
    And guesses how it grew to womanhood,
    And gladly would have watched the beauties bud
And the mild fire of precious life wax warm:
So I, long bound within the threefold charm
    Of Dante's love sublimed to heavenly mood,
    Had marvelled, touching his Beatitude,
How grew such presence from man's shameful swarm.

At length within this book I found pourtrayed
    Newborn that Paradisal Love of his,
And simple like a child; with whose clear aid
    I understood. To such a child as this,
Christ, charging well His chosen ones, forbade
Offence: "for lo! of such my kingdom is."

Already Dante Gabriel was identifying himself with his
mediaeval namesake, his own love with Dante's for Beatrice.
It was the beginning of that almost life-long process of
scarcely conscious identification, which led him to see his own
life as literature, through the eyes of Dante and Malory,
and, dominating so much of his poetry and painting, gives
his work so often a hidden, autobiographical significance.

William Rossetti "believed" that "perhaps" before the close
of 1851, or early in 1852, his brother and Lizzie were engaged.
. . . It is Bell Scott, in the spring of 1852, who gives us our first
actual glimpse of the lovers. Gabriel was then living at The
Hermitage, a charming cottage on West Hill, Highgate, with
his friend Bateman, who was about to accompany Woolner to

Australia. Scott, calling one evening unexpectedly, and directed by the servant to the studio in the garden, suddenly found himself, he said, "in the romantic dusk of the apartment face to face with Rossetti and a lady whom I did not recognize, and could hardly see. He did not introduce her; she rose to go. I made a little bow, which she did not acknowledge; and she left." Such was Scott's first meeting with Lizzie of whom at that time he had not heard. Surely if any engagement existed between Gabriel and Lizzie at this time, as William later "believed," it must have been very secret, otherwise Lizzie, as Gabriel's *fiancée*, would naturally have expected an introduction to so close a friend of Rossetti as Scott, rather than to be summarily dismissed or slink away.

Certainly by this time Gabriel's feeling for Lizzie was warmer than that of mere friendship. That summer an unwonted elation succeeded his earlier moodiness. To the absent Christina in August, he wrote of Lizzie in a tone of fond proprietorship, detailing amongst various articles left at The Hermitage and now returned to him at home, "a lock of hair, shorn from the beloved head of that dear, and radiant as the tresses of Aurora, a sight of which, perhaps, may dazzle you on your return. That love has lately made herself a grey dress, also a black silk one, the first bringing out her characteristics as a 'meek, unconscious dove,' while the second enhances her qualifications as a 'rara avis in terris' by rendering her, 'nigro simillima cygno'." For Gabriel must draw upon Tennyson's *In Memoriam* and Juvenal's *Sixth Satire* to describe the charm of Lizzie at this time. Her simplicity, her meekness, rare combination with beauty, delighted him. "Dove" was one of his pet names for her, and the outline of a dove in his letters stands for her name. Little wonder that he now wrote ecstatically to Woolner of Bateman, his former host at The Hermitage: "Hug that dear old fellow for me, and tell him that the time I spent with him this summer was one of the jolliest of my life. . . ." But already upon this brightness a shadow although as yet of the lightest, was falling; Lizzie's health was declining, and she was now at Hastings, hoping to recover, and awaiting Gabriel who was to join her there.*

* *v. Notes.*

Was it parental opposition to Lizzie, as well as an increasing
desire for liberty that drove Gabriel in November from the
family home in Arlington Street into rooms of his own? The
time chosen was strangely inopportune for he was very poor
and the rent must be paid. But such matters little troubled
him as William could always be relied upon at need. Still
under the spell of his nocturnal voyages with Hunt, Gabriel
found rooms beside the river. No. 14, Chatham Place was the
last house at the north-west corner of Blackfriars Bridge. The
situation was by no means the healthiest London offered, but
he liked the quaint, picturesquely distorted lines of the old
house which had settled down towards the water, the fine view
of the Thames below his windows, the hurry and bustle of the
quays, the constant passing of boats and barges.

His rooms, on the second floor, included a large studio, a
pleasant living-room and small bedroom. The Fleet Ditch lay
below, but he did not mind, except on those occasions when
its neighbourhood was too obvious. He was delighted with his
new home. "You cannot imagine what delightful rooms these
are for a party," he wrote to Woolner, "regularly built out
into the river, and with windows on all sides—also a large
balcony over the water, large enough to sit there with a model
and paint—a feat which I actually accomplished the other day
for several hours in the teeth of the elements." From the
French window opening upon the balcony, one saw Blackfriars
Bridge close on the left, curving across the river. The studio
had windows looking southwards, and on fine days was bright
with sunshine.

Freed from the restraints of home, Gabriel at twenty-four
now enjoyed complete liberty. Alone, he was as desultory as
ever. For hours he would stand at the window, fascinated by
the ceaseless ebb and flow of life over Blackfriars Bridge. He
wrote a poem on the Duke of Wellington, buried on November
18th with pomp and ceremony at St. Paul's. "I have done
summat on the Dook," he wrote flippantly to Brown; but the
poem was full of his pride in being counted an Englishman, the
pride he had so conspicuously shown during his continental
tour with Hunt three years before. Some months later, in
calmer mood, he described it as "something *de rigueur* on the

Duke of Wellington, which I keep as a monument of the universal influence of public frenzy even on the most apathetic."

At first rather lonely, he often invited or visited friends. The painter Boyce described a typical evening at Chatham Place, on December 30th. "Met there Wells,[1] J. P. Seddon, Clayton,[2] and Mr. Munro, Mr. Stephens and Mr. Hughes," he wrote. "Rossetti showed me his studio but none of his works (which is his way). He had for our entertainment a series of anastatic drawings designed and coloured by the Hon. Mrs. Boyle, some of which as beautiful in feeling, natural simplicity, and colour, and in poetical treatment as almost anything I have seen. They illustrate a nursery rhyme. Also a quantity of Gavarni's works, and a grand and most striking mask of Dante taken from a cast of his face in death; a tracing of his head in Giotto's fresco with the eye imperfect; a pen and ink sketch by Millais from Keats's *Isabella*. In the physical way, roast chestnuts and coffee, honey, and hot spirits. His room has a jolly balcony overhanging the river, the reflection of the lights on the bridge and quays, etc., were [sic] charming. Conversation throughout delightful, resulting methought from the happy and gentlemanly freedom of the company generally. There was only one of D. G. Rossetti's works to be seen in the room, and that was a sketch, study of a man, back view. Gabriel invited me to his studio next Thursday." And on that second visit Boyce found practically the same company with one or two additions, including Holman Hunt and Millais.

Ere long, however, Lizzie's visits to Chatham Place became so frequent, the lovers' mutual absorption such that Gabriel gave little or no attention to the rest of the world. Lizzie continually sat to him as model, and now, towards the close of 1852, inspired by his enthusiasm, she began to draw and paint under his guidance, and, turning poetess also, to write plaintive little lock-sick verses, all pathos and self-pity. So, united by a mutual passion and a common aim, the lovers, aloof from all other society, passed quiet days and evenings in Chatham Place, working at their painting and poetry. Into some of

---

[1] H. T. Wells, portrait painter.
[2] J. R. Clayton, who later helped to found the glass painting firm of Clayton & Bell.

Rossetti's sonnets of this time the atmosphere of those secluded evenings has entered, and there it still lives for those who care to find it. The ceaseless murmur of the city below, the vague sounds rising from wharves and river, served but to accentuate their isolation. Gabriel's friends, feeling themselves unwanted, no longer called, and even William, knowing that Lizzie would certainly be there and that his brother desired no other company, remained aloof.

As Gabriel watched Lizzie's sad little drawings improve, her sombre, sentimental little poems increase, he came to believe her a genius and her hold upon him grew. In a semi-private way he went about with her, not taking her to his home, but widely amongst his nearest friends. She remained essentially of the Preraphaelite circle to which she had been model, although now she sat to him alone. He invented pet names for her; foolish, affectionate names, unintentionally expressive, as pet names often are, of the unconscious quality of his love: "Gug-gums," "Guggum," "Gug." Light, playful, hardly suggestive, perhaps, of a profoundly serious passion nor entirely pleasing, they suggest something of the unwonted simplicity, childlike-ness even, he believed she had brought into his life—"the gentle dove." Her image distracted him as he worked, and at his easel he would murmur to himself over and over again: "Guggum, Guggum, Guggum." And Lizzie, occasionally, in her brighter, more original moods, would call Gabriel "Gug" too.

From the first their love was one of vicissitudes, of stress and strain, quarrels and reconciliations, emotional ambivalences in which love suddenly became hate and hate love. It had its phases, moved like the sea to the ebb and flow of tides, was chequered with storm and sunshine. To this rhythm their lives would be patterned for the next ten years, until the end. It is not difficult to divine the chief cause in this early period, of the emotional tension, of their quarrels and reconciliations, for in both his poetry and painting Rossetti has left significant hints, straws in the wind, pointing the direction of their unrest. That he passionately desired Lizzie is evident. That he wished to marry her is far less clear, engagement or no engagement. That Lizzie demanded marriage as the price of possession is

easily divined. Gabriel's sonnet on Dante's *Vita Nuova* was
followed, just before he moved into Chatham Place, by the
sonnet *Broken Music*, a complaint of division in love, a lament
over the

> . . . pang of unpermitted prayer,

which even the cautious William long afterwards interpreted as
"prayer for a boon not to be granted."[1]

Gabriel was now also busy painting Lizzie in water-colour as
Dante's Beatrice. In *Beatrice Denying her Salutation*, she is a
"haughty beauty with half-closed eyes and a pose of forbidding
drawing back" as one critic described her. A little later, in a
painting dated "September 1852," entitled *Giotto painting the
portrait of Dante*, she appears as one of a virginal band, moving
with lighted candles in a church procession, while she intently
reads a missal and ignores the longing eyes of Dante who
pauses in the act of cutting a pomegranate—the fruit of Adonis
and symbol of passion—to gaze ardently on her. This painting
was meant to represent, said Gabriel, "all the influences of
Dante's youth" (and he also meant of his own)—"Art, Friendship and Love." Was there too a personal reference in that
other painting of Beatrice he made in 1852, *Guardami ben; ben
son, ben son Beatrice*, the words with which Beatrice greets her
erring lover, in Paradise—

> Observe me well. I am, in sooth, I am
> Beatrice. What! and hast thou deign'd at last
> Approach the mountain? Knewest not, O man!
> Thy happiness is here?

After which she proceeds to lament Dante's temporary desertion of her to give himself to others.

Certainly, from the exaltations of the summer, Rossetti sank
during the autumn and winter of 1852–3 into a sombre mood.
Brown, observing his unrest, jestingly referred to "D. G.

---

[1] *cf.* the following omitted stanza from *Love's Nocturn* (1854):

> As, since man waxed deathly wise,
>   Secret somewhere on this earth
> Unpermitted Eden lies—
>   Thus within the world's wide girth
>   Hides she from my spirit's dearth
>   Paradise
>   Of a love that cries for death.

Quoted by Sharp in his *D. G. Rossetti*, p. 344.

Rossetti and heroic acts, and whose struggles with chaos at any rate may be said to be perpetual (seeing that his room is still the same chaos as wont, from which he is without intermission, seeking to separate some black-lead pencil or penknife), whatever remission his conflict with the devil may undergo. I am sorry to say that out of three or four pictures begun he has not finished any, but he has painted and sold three or four lovely Dantesque water-colour drawings and written some lovely verses." Baffled by both art and life, difficulties of technique in oils, the rival attraction of poetry, the increasing complexities of his love, Gabriel was gloomily yielding to a creeping paralysis of will. He could not concentrate his attention, and while Hunt, Millais and Brown were steadily working towards the attainment of their ambitions, Rossetti restlessly abandoned one project for another, or sank into the lethargy of despair. Occasionally he would turn from the bitter and futile contemplation of his wasted days to find relief in his friends' companionship; but for the most part, save for Lizzie, he was alone. It was thus, "in his innocent adolescence," as William Bell Scott long afterwards described it, that Gabriel fell in love.

II

CHANGE
1853–1854

Alas for hourly change! Alas for all
The loves that from his hand proud youth lets fall,
Even as the beads of a told rosary!

Pride of Youth D. G. ROSSETTI

THE NEW YEAR, 1853, found Gabriel still restless, dissatisfied, depressed. On New Year's Night, while William slumbered in his chair and the candle guttered in its socket, he wrote contemptuously to Woolner of "that spiritual image of himself which this unlucky devil has been setting before himself any time these four and twenty years," and alluded bitterly to "art—the last thing with me as usual." He well realized now that the year just ended, in which the perseverance of Hunt and Millais had laid foundations for their fame and fortune, had been for himself as futile as its predecessors. Before the close of January his dissatisfaction with his own futility, apparently in both art and life, had found expression in a sonnet *Work and Will* (later renamed *Known in Vain*), which, like his sonnet on Dante's *Vita Nuova*, gave comparatively little heed to its ostensible theme and much to its opening analogy between the dissociation of will and action he deplored, and a pair of frustrated lovers:

> . . . two whose love, first foolish, widening scope,
>   Knows suddenly, to music high and soft,
>   The Holy of Holies; who because they scoff'd
> Are now amazed with shame, nor dare to cope
> With the whole truth aloud, lest heaven should ope;
>   Yet, at their meetings, laugh not as they laugh'd
>   In speech; nor speak, at length; but sitting oft
> Together, within hopeless sight of hope
> For hours are silent . . .

"More or less autobiographical," said William, long afterwards, of this sonnet. Gabriel's frustration, his general uncer-

133

tainty and inertia approached indeed a mild form of *folie du doute*. Inviting himself to dine with Brown, yet not appearing, he later sent vague, incoherent excuses about "being completely set at nought by accursed shoe-strings and other domestic demons."[1] But Brown, he insisted, must come and see "dear G's drawings"—so wonderful, in his eyes, by this time, were Guggum's sketches.

There was too a new anxiety. Lizzie was unhappy at home. Gabriel had taken her out of the milliner's shop, William "presumed," about the time of the supposed engagement towards the close of 1851, and how he managed to support himself, much less Lizzie, is a mystery upon which William could doubtless have thrown a revealing light. That her family, in need, failed to appreciate the withdrawal of Lizzie from remunerative labour, and opposed her ambiguous association with artists, is not strange. Certainly Gabriel's responsibility for her, particularly now that her health was deteriorating, was a growing anxiety. His rooms were now Lizzie's chief shelter from an unsympathetic world.

In poverty, sickness, isolation, failure, their passion took a deeper tone, a more sombre hue, an added intensity. A common morbidity of spirit drew them still more closely together. Perhaps it is the influence of those "dream-dowered days apart," as Gabriel called them in a sonnet, in the remote chambers of Chatham Place, which unconsciously penetrates the painting and poetry of Rossetti during this and immediately succeeding years. In his sonnets it is unmistakable, and a similar constriction of space, crowding of ornament and detail, are very evident in the water-colours of this time: in *Dante Drawing an Angel on the Anniversary of Beatrice's Death* (1853), *Arthur's Tomb* (1854), *The Wedding of St. George* (1857), *Launcelot escaping from Guinevere's Chamber* (1857), *Tristan and Yseult drinking the Love Potion* (1862). About them all—and they are of his best work—lies an atmosphere of secrecy and mystery, of tensity and suspense, while beneath a louring fate brood waiting figures upon whom lies heavy the inertia nullifying Rossetti's own life. In all we feel the inexorable will of destiny threatening the slender flame of love, of love symbolized in

[1] cf. *infra.*, p. 192.

The Wedding of St. George by the tinkling of golden bells, upon which beat quaint, mediaeval, half-hidden, angelic beings, whose sweet but fragile music fails to dissipate the general air of despondency, of love's futility in the presence of a malign fate.

James Smetham, Gabriel's painter friend of later years, has described *The Wedding of St. George* in words which reveal his perception of many of these qualities. It was, he said, "One of the grandest things, like a golden, dim dream. Love 'credulous all gold,' gold armour, a sense of secret enclosures in 'palace-chambers far apart'; but quaint chambers in quaint palaces, where angels creep in through sliding panel doors, and stand behind rows of flowers, drumming on golden bells, with wings crimson and green." Were not these the forms into which Gabriel's pseudo-mediaeval imagination transmuted the quality and atmosphere of his love? Are they not an expression of his dream of a central harmony which, although amidst discordant circumstance, Destiny had brought into his life?

It was now that in two sonnets, *The Church Porches*, Rossetti bade a reluctant farewell to the devotional mood, the religious tradition, which had inspired so much of his early painting and poetry. Although, like his father, of rationalistic mentality, Gabriel, largely influenced by the strict religious training of his devout, High Anglican mother, particularly felt the gracious charm, the sensuous and spiritual attraction of the Catholic tradition, in which indeed his father had been reared. Millais, Hunt, Shields, Bell Scott, William Rossetti, all testified at various times to the innately religious bent in Gabriel. For two years now he had experienced something of the devotional phase of adolescence. The painter William Richmond, when a boy, often saw Rossetti with Millais at the ornate musical services of St. Andrew's Church, Wells Street, then famous for its music and "high" ritual.

Gabriel's uneasy suspicion that his religious attitude was chiefly aesthetic and emotional had found expression in *Hand and Soul*, in Chiaro's discovery "that much of the reverence which he had mistaken for faith, had been no more than the worship of beauty," and in his poem *Pax Vobis*, written in the church of St. Bavon, Ghent, in 1849, and published in *The*

Germ, he had dramatized this part of his conflict, in the person of a priest who, feeling only his wandering desires amidst the beauty and solemnity of the mass, thinks longingly: "There is the world outside." The poem appeared again, unchanged, in Rossetti's *Poems* of 1870, but, it is interesting, and perhaps significant to note, when republished in the last year of Rossetti's life, in *Poems* of 1881, it was entitled *World's Worth*, while the priest instead of rejecting the church for the world cries:

"O God, my world in Thee!"

The mood of the second sonnet of *The Church Porches* is that of *Pax Vobis*. Through it rings a note of valediction, of regretful but inevitable withdrawal from the calm shelter of the church into the heat, glare and dust of life outside. In the very rhythm as in the content of the verse we hear the slow, reluctant feet retreating, drawn inexorably to the hot, unlovely but living street without. The church threshold is crossed; a door closes— but a sense of exile will remain.

With the summer, Gabriel's internal conflict drove him from London in search of peace. In June, complaining to sympathetic Aunt Charlotte of "continually returning illness" and his need of sea air and sea bathing, he obtained £12 and her carpet bag, and set out with Bell Scott for Scott's home in Newcastle. It was there the self-satisfied Scott first remarked "some sort of fascination" about Gabriel, but, since Rossetti used it for his own advantage, it seemed to Scott "a dangerous gift." Although Scott reluctantly permitted Rossetti's domination, the differences between the two were plain. Gabriel loved to shock his provincial and rather stodgy friend with his opinions, while Scott secretly marvelled at Gabriel's indifference to science, that he neither knew nor cared whether or not the earth revolved about the sun." What Dante knew was enough for him," exclaimed Scott, more in sorrow than in anger. But to Gabriel, ere long, even pulling Scott's leg became wearisome, and his company was little compensation for the absence of London and the presence of Newcastle. After two days in "the dreary place," finding "the general stagnation too like the spirit of Banquo,"[1] Gabriel, forgetting his urgent need

[1] *v. inf.* p. 214.

of sea air and bathing emphasized in his appeal to Aunt Charlotte, persuaded Scott to join him in a short painting trip
through the neighbouring countryside.

Amid the beauty of the open country, with "the beastly
place" Newcastle now only a fading nightmare of memory,
Gabriel was happy. In Hexham, the friends found a singular
charm, as from the window-seat of the ancient, half-timbered
White Horse Inn they contemplated the quiet beauty of the
quaint old town. Gabriel tenderly recalled afterwards how he
and Scott "sat and looked at the market-place from the deep
window of an inn some centuries old and talked of friends for
one pleasant hour, while sun and air seemed whispering together, and the 'hovering pigeons' touched the street." At
Newcastle Gabriel had painted a small "water-colour of a
woman in yellow," a picture now identified with that of *A Girl
Singing to a Lute*. At Carlisle he painted another water-colour,
The Lovers, later known as *Carlisle Wall*. At Wetheral the friends
parted. Gabriel, determined upon a solitary walking-tour in
Warwickshire, returned to Newcastle and took train to Coventry. "Disgusting work," for he loathed railways, he laconically
described the journey, but soon, although alone, he was
"having great glory," as he tramped the pleasant Warwickshire
lanes. From Warwick and Kenilworth he passed to Stratford
where, moved by the sight of Shakespeare's house, he relieved
the tension with a damnatory sonnet on a clergyman who had
cut down Shakespeare's mulberry tree.

Gabriel's mood during this lonely pilgrimage, the only
solitary journey he ever made, was often sombre. His inner
conflict still persisted. From The Red Horse Inn, Stratford, he
sent Scott a curious sonnet written on the way—*On Plucking a
Honeysuckle*, a symbolical allusion to a subject recently dominating his thoughts as well as his discussions with Scott at
Newcastle: the moral justification of free love. William Sharp,
a friend of Gabriel's last years, significantly described this
sonnet as having "a deeper meaning than is at first appre-
hensible." The dreary poem *Rosabell* which Scott was then
writing and discussing with Rossetti was on this same theme,
and at Newcastle, Gabriel had denounced free love and all
"self-culture" endangering others' happiness, especially the

sacrifice of woman to man's passion. "The egotistical side of this popular English Goetheism of the day," said Scott, "was the only one he could see," and on this subject the two differed. At Newcastle, in this mood, Rossetti had made a sketch for an intended subject: *The Magdalene. On Plucking a Honeysuckle* describes how, taking a first solitary flower, he had pricked himself with thorns, "fouled his feet in quag-water," yet found this wind-nipped flower "sweet and fair," until coming later to richer clusters,

> All virgin lamps of scent and dew,

he had thrown away the plucked blossom and refused to take more.[1]

"Rossetti," Scott had noted at Newcastle, "was already beginning to revise his intention of marriage." This question of marriage with Lizzie, which indeed he was to debate for the next seven years, was doubtless the chief cause of his inner strife, his restlessness, idleness and indecision. In another poem of this year he somewhat similarly refused to encourage the growth of a real love, fearing the loved one's reproachful gaze—

> Because in June it should not mar
> My ways, at noon when fevers are.

Another sonnet of this tour, *The Hill Summit*, ostensibly a poem of sunset and twilight beauty, written one evening amidst the peaceful Warwickshire scenery, is also a symbolical expression of his unrest, a record of bitterness of spirit so deep

---

[1] *cf.* D. G. R.'s poem *Chimes*, stanzas 1 and 2, and W. M. R.'s note on them:—

> Honey-flowers to the honey-comb,
> And the honey-bee's from home.

> A honey-comb and a honey-flower,
> And a bee shall have his hour.

> A honeyed heart for the honey-comb,
> And the humming bee flies home.

> A heavy heart in the honey-flower,
> And the bee has had his hour.
>
> etc.

"Sections 1 and 2, about the bee and the honeysuckle, must adumbrate love-making followed by desertion," Note by W. M. R., *The Works of Dante Gabriel Rossetti*, London, 1911, p. 670.

that, bidding farewell to the sun, he finally takes the downward path into a permanently darkened future. As a chance remark of Gabriel to Allingham a year later shows indeed, his mind as he wrote this sonnet was, for neither the first nor last time, turned towards suicide as a way of escape, though as yet hardly seriously. The greyness of the flooded landscape round Alveston, its old chapel and churchyard islanded amidst the waters, its ancient graves standing out beneath a louring sky, harmonized with his sombre mood, soothed his restless spirit. His solitary pilgrimage long remained to him a gracious memory—a valediction perhaps to his earlier, unfettered life.

Back in Chatham Place Gabriel found Lizzie working hard at her own portrait, which William Rossetti long afterwards described as "the most competent piece of execution that she ever produced, an excellent and graceful likeness, and truly good; it is her very self." Gabriel thought it "a perfect wonder," fit for exhibition. Before leaving London with Scott, he had installed Lizzie in his rooms, duly cautioning William: "Do not therefore encourage any one to go near the place. I have told her to keep the doors locked, and she will probably sleep there sometimes." Unable to do more than meet the expenses of his holiday, Gabriel had also deputed to William the payment of the overdue rent for his studio! Lizzie, elated by Gabriel's praise, thought of painting a picture from Tennyson's poems, for the Academy. But—anxious perhaps as Gabriel himself— during his absence she had been very ill.

Gabriel, painting hard through the August days in a desperate effort to overcome his inertia, and depressed by his return to London with its distractions, found his thoughts still travelling the same, dismal, unescapable round. "One feels again within the accursed circle," he complained to Scott, in a letter, "the skulls and bones rattle, the goblins keep mumbling, and the owls beat their obscene wings round the casting of those bullets, among which is the Devil's Seventh"—Sloth. Cynically, he thought his metaphor "very fine. Something might be done with it—in charcoal." He returned to his former discussion with Scott in Newcastle on "self-culture," denouncing "the favourite doctrine that scoundrelism is a sacred probation of the soul," which he found "everywhere." He had just discovered it in *Wilhelm Meister*—"On one page, he is in despair about some girl he has been the death of; in the next you are delighted with his enlarged view of *Hamlet*." He had found the same attitude in St. Augustine's *Confessions*. "As soon as the saint is struck by the fact that he had been wallowing and inducing others to wallow," wrote Gabriel, "it is all horrible together, but involves no duty, except the comfortable self-appeasement of getting out of it himself. As for the women, no doubt they are nascent for hell." "Nothing plainly," he concluded, "is so fatal to the duty of self-culture as self-sacrifice, even to the measure of a grain of mustard seed." If he were not "very sick of reading," which, he declared, "bores me excessively," he would "hunt up as many instances of this noble theory as possible, and form them into an encyclopaedia for the benefit of self-cultivators."

Gabriel's sense of liberty was probably intensified at this time by the absence of his father, mother and Christina from London. For some months they had been living at Frome in Somerset, hoping to found there, with the help of a local clergyman, their friend, a school more successful than the one they had opened in Camden Town. Frome, however, proved equally disappointing, and when William, early in 1854, upon receiving a small increase in salary, took No. 45, Upper Albany Street, and invited the family to share his new home, all but Gabriel gladly accepted his offer, and March saw the Rossettis reunited in London. Boyce, calling on Gabriel in the middle of the month, "found him at home but unwell; he sleeps little at nights. . . ."

The old Professor was overjoyed to return. Almost blind and rapidly weakening under successive attacks of paralysis, he obviously could not, despite his amazing vitality, live long. At Frome, debarred from his study of Dante, he had written a verse-autobiography, childlike in its characteristic naïveté, and unintentionally revealing the restlessness of a mind divided between reason and faith. Self-persuaded of mystic vision, he combined in his own person patriarch and prophet, believing himself what by the title of one of his works he had long claimed to be: *The Seer in Solitude*. Now, at one moment inspired, exalted, he gloried in the certainty of a life beyond death; but the triumphant emotion, the assurance of immortality would pass, leaving only a doubting, trembling, weary old man, lamenting: "Oh what a wretched thing is life, ending always with the grave!"

Amidst growing desolation, his pride in Gabriel, whom he thought destined for the success denied himself, had been his chief joy. With patriarchal pride he recounted in his verse-autobiography his son's genius in two arts, rejoicing that—

> Though yours is the most early dawn of life,
> As able poet I hear you already hailed,
> Already as able painter see you admired.
> Now onward, and the double race-course win!
> You will be doing what I could not do.

Such was William's translation, for his father's autobiography was, of course, in Italian.

From Frome, old Gabriele had sent Gabriel similar exhortations in prose, to which his son had returned dutiful rather than intimate answers. He had also sent Gabriel his *Arpa Evangelica*, a book of hymns written to beguile the tedium of sickness. In Italy, he declared, it had been received, according to the political sympathies of the local states, with rapturous applause or abusive prohibition, "on account," wrote Gabriele, "of the author's name, which has become a veritable scarecrow to kings." And he begged Gabriel, if ever he should visit Italy, proudly to proclaim himself his father's son. The old vain-glory of which Frere had so often warned Gabriele, was to pass only with life itself.

And now, on April 26, 1854, life itself was passing. Near the end, the thoughts of the dying man wandered back, past the dull, meaningless, pedagogic years, to his earlier, impassioned life of political and personal ambitions, enthusiasms and ideals. He believed the general commanding the fatal Neapolitan revolution thirty-four years before was present. The climax of his glory, the cause of his fall, of the insignificant, poverty-stricken later life, still ran in the old man's troubled brain. With his last cry: "Ah Dio, ajutami tu!"—"O God, aid me!" —the long, fluctuating battle of faith and doubt ended. To the watching women the words brought solace. "I am happy to say," wrote Christina long afterwards, with unaccustomed pride, "I am a daughter of that Gabriele Rossetti who so truly loved his country, and who after long years of exile, died a patient Christian." With the passage of time, the spirit of irony which all secretly but exquisitely had shaped poor old Gabriele's life, was to fashion yet more triumphantly his legend.

The ravages of a long disease left little cause for sorrow when to old Gabriele came the final peace. "It has been a wearisome protracted state of dull suffering from which we cannot but feel in some sort happy at seeing him released," Gabriel told Allingham in a short note containing no expression of grief. The cosmopolitan, conspiratorial crowd about Gabriele wanted to give him a grand funeral. But Mrs. Rossetti would not hear of it, and on May 3rd, the patriot-professor was quietly buried at Highgate, in the family grave.

Recently, Gabriel had seen much more than he cared to see of death. Within the last few months both his grandparents, the Polidoris, as well as his friend Deverell had died. Gaetano Polidori's strong spirit Gabriel had much admired. "Our family," he had sadly declared, upon his death, "may wait long now for so stout a branch." Shortly afterwards he had written of Deverell's death with almost feminine tenderness. And now the father whose pride and fear for him had roused but little sympathy in Gabriel was gone too.* The moment the funeral ceremony was over, Gabriel escaped from the house of mourning, from the funeral-atmosphere he loathed, and set off for Hastings where Lizzie awaited him.

Following the doctor's advice, he had taken her to Hastings a few days before. Ambitious, overworking Lizzie was now definitely an invalid, needed medicines, sea air and rest. During Gabriel's absence from her, caused by his father's death, worse reports of her health had reached him, and in alarm he hastened back. Immediately on his return to Hastings, on the evening of his father's funeral, he took a room at an inn near Lizzie's lodgings. He was glad to find her better than he had feared.

Fortunately Lizzie was no longer without friends. Gabriel had often taken her to the home of good Mrs. Howitt, well-known writer and journalist, who with her daughters awaited

¹ *v. Notes* and *infra.*, p. 653.

at The Hermitage, on West Hill, Highgate—the house in which
Gabriel had lived for a time with Bateman—the return of
Mr. Howitt from Australia. Gabriel, very friendly with the
Howitts, especially with one daughter, Anna Mary, a young
art-student, was a constant visitor at The Hermitage. The old
garden-studio in which Scott had surprised Gabriel with Lizzie,
was now Anna Mary's "Nest." He noticed how "elegant and
habitable" it had become since the days of his own "savage
bivouac" there, and declared The Hermitage, "especially the
'Nest,' a perfect fairy palace!" In the "Nest" he had long talks
on art with Anna Mary, wrote letters, criticized her paintings;
sometimes he accompanied her on her walks. When the Howitts
fell under the spell of the newest fashion, "spiritualism," just
imported from America, Gabriel enjoyed inventing ghost
stories to frighten them. Soon, Anna Mary began to record
his visits in her diary.

Liking Lizzie, the Howitts had quickly become anxious about
her health, suspecting beneath her weakness some serious cause.
With difficulty they at last succeeded in persuading the
obstinate girl to visit Dr. Garth Wilkinson, a noted homoeo-
pathist, Swedenborgian and editor of Blake's lyrics, a physician
in whom they had great confidence. Wilkinson had diagnosed
"curvature of the spine," a "very anxious case," "but by no
means a hopeless one," and had forbidden painting. "But this,
of course, she must," Gabriel had calmly informed Brown,
while Lizzie sat beside him, "working at the most poetical
of all designs," for to both Gabriel and Lizzie the thought of
temporarily abandoning art seemed absurd. Both, as long as
possible, had tried to ignore Lizzie's illness and the incon-
veniences it would entail.

It was, in fact, Anna Mary and her friends Bessie Parkes
and Barbara Leigh Smith who had pushed the lovers into
active pursuit of remedies. Barbara, kind-hearted, energetic,
somewhat masculine, amateur artist, champion of women's
freedom and endowed with a handsome fortune, a house in
Blandford Square and a small estate in the country, was particularly active on Lizzie's behalf. Gabriel, who liked Barbara,
described her jocularly to Allingham as "a young lady blessed
with large rations of tin, fat, enthusiasm and golden hair, who

thinks nothing of climbing a mountain in breeches, or wading through a stream in none, in the sacred name of pigment," and, adopting Thackeray's designation of Patmore's sister-in-law, he called her "a jolly fellow."

The women, apparently not unattracted by Gabriel themselves, had quickly resolved to stimulate the affections of these seemingly sluggish lovers who would neither marry nor part. By praise of Lizzie and her paintings—almost the sole encouragement save Gabriel's Lizzie had yet known—they had stimulated his pride in her, which had lately, perhaps, at times, appeared to flag. Gabriel, who had not yet introduced Lizzie to his family, doubtless because they refused to know her, had recently induced a reluctant Christina to meet her, but she did not admire Lizzie as he wished, and between brother and sister a coldness, unknown before, had arisen. But Lizzie's new friends made great plans for her. Allingham praised her sad little verses and made a selection from them for her to illustrate and publish in a little volume—which, however, never appeared.

When in mid-April Lizzie grew worse, Barbara, "quite thick with her," said Gabriel, had found "cheap and nice" lodgings for her at Hastings which was near Scalands, Barbara's country estate. Barbara had first urged Lizzie to go into the Sussex Hospital and then, as she refused, had offered to secure her admission—through a relative, no doubt Florence Nightingale, not yet "The Lady with the Lamp"—into a "Sanatorium" in Harley Street, "where," so Barbara described it, "governesses and ladies of small means are taken in and cured." To neither suggestion, however, would Lizzie or Gabriel agree. The environment, he argued, would harm her, and, besides, he thought their fears exaggerated. For several years, he said, he had known her "in a state hardly less variable than now," and could therefore understand "that those who have not had so long a knowledge of her would naturally be more liable to sudden alarm on her account than I am."

So, for the next two months they remained at Hastings. After three days, Gabriel left his inn and took a room at Mrs. Elphick's, in the same house with Lizzie. It was, he carefully explained to his mother, "cheaper." It was certainly un-

pleasantly unconventional for his Victorian mother and sisters.
Their opinion of Lizzie who allowed it was certainly not
improved. William Rossetti, who saw in the close relationship
of the lovers, in Chatham Place and elsewhere, nothing more
than an innocent companionship chiefly due to their common
interest in art, considered Lizzie's increasing disregard of
Victorian convention was due to Gabriel's influence. Now, too,
independent Barbara, supported by Anna Mary, encouraged
the lovers, stilling conscientious Mrs. Elphick's qualms. All the
ladies, Gabriel explained to his mother, were "most attentive
to Lizzie and everyone adores the dear. No one thinks it at
all odd my going into the Gug's room to sit there; and Barbara
Smith said to the landlady how inadvisable it would be for
her to sit with me in a room without a fire." Mrs. Rossetti,
however, of more rigid mind and habit, was perhaps hardly
reassured.

At first Gabriel found life at Hastings agreeable. Restless,
he rose early, saw the sun rise over the sea—"the most wonderful of earthly sights!"—yet one he was seldom to witness.
Barbara, and Anna Mary her guest at Scalands, came to see
Lizzie and took walks with Gabriel in which Lizzie was soon
able to join. Twice Lizzie and Gabriel spent a happy day with
their friends at Scalands, which stood on a hill, in a wood,
looking out over hop fields. There, wandering about the neighbouring country lanes Gabriel was happy. On his first visit he
mistook the hop kilns for private chapels and marvelled at the
religious fervour of the locality! Barbara and Anna Mary were
"very jolly" that day, but Lizzie was very tired. The second
visit was quite merry. The two girls, still match-making, joined
with Gabriel in sketching Lizzie—making "sketches of her dear
head with iris stuck in her dear hair," as Gabriel told Brown—
and all wrote their monograms on the window panel to commemorate a jolly time. The two women plotters carefully fed
Gabriel's pride in poor Lizzie who had so seldom received
man's or woman's homage. For Gabriel it was a pleasant
antidote to the aloofness of his own family. "Everyone," he
wrote with obvious satisfaction, "adores and reveres Lizzie."

He made many sketches of her now; tender, intimate little
sketches showing her in the simple attitudes of daily life: sitting

or standing by a window, seated in her chair, reading, or working at her drawings. For the next two years he continually sketched her in such domestic scenes, and even when they went out with friends, Gabriel, suddenly struck by some new beauty of attitude or aspect, would often hold up the party until a sketch was made.

Despite illness, Lizzie, knowing their need of "tin," worked hard at a design for a ballad *Clerk Saunders*. It was intended for a volume which never in fact appeared, a collection of old Scottish ballads to be made by Allingham, that she and Gabriel were to illustrate. Rossetti, deeply fallen in his erotic illusion, thought her a great genius, failed to see how imitative of his own her work was, and loudly proclaimed her a better artist than himself. Unfortunately her example failed to rouse him to a similar effort. For a year now, Brown had watched him as he abandoned picture after picture, until of six begun not one was completed. Vainly struggling with oils, Gabriel regretted more bitterly than ever his contempt for Sass's and the Academy Schools, his desultory, self-opinionated, idle youth.

> . . . A most weary thing,

he had written in an early sonnet,

> It is within the perished heart to seek
> Pain, and not find it, but a clinging pall
> Like sleep upon the mind.

Into this neurotic, self-protective lethargy he now relapsed more deeply than ever before. Although he found at Hastings "most wonderful things to paint, I do not," he added, "mean to paint a single one, as the pursuit of art is a bore, except when followed in the dozing style." In this mood he wandered in a waking dream about the cliffs and sea-shore, or lay inert in the sunshine. Then, as he told Brown, "sometimes through the summer mists the sea and sky are one; and, if you half shut your eyes, as of course you do, there is no swearing to the distant sail as boat or bird, while just under one's feet the near boats stand together immovable, as if their shadows clogged them and they would not come in after all but loved to see the land. So one may lie and symbolize till one goes to sleep, and that be a symbol too perhaps."

146

For a time Lizzie left her work and wandered about with him, roaming the streets of the "old" town, the sea-shore and neighbouring hills. Once, seeing a dark gipsy girl romping with her baby sister, Gabriel, tied to his invalid love, enviously contemplated this "image of savage, active health," and made a sketch of her. The incident and his comment upon it suggest one element in his unrest. The lovers often carved their initials on ruins and rocks—in a dearth, apparently, of conversation. Lizzie, however, soon tired of their walks and returned to her drawings, while Gabriel, as Barbara and Anna Mary had gone back to town, was left to continue his wanderings alone.

He was terribly bored, had indeed within his first week found Hastings, like Newcastle, "rather slow." Scalands, too, although "a stunning crib" had also proved, on Gabriel's second visit, "rather slow," despite the gaiety with Lizzie crowned with iris. For Gabriel, London was the only possible environment; but lack of "tin" prevented his going to town. In the circumstances, he could only beg news from Allingham: What reception had Hunt's *Light of the World* met at the Academy Exhibition? How was Collins's picture hung? What were William's art criticisms like in the *Spectator*? Did Allingham still dine at the Belle Sauvage on Ludgate Hill to meet the dashing waitress named by Gabriel "the cordial stunner," who smiled on them there? "I shall have no chance against you now any more," he told his friend, ironically.

When the rent at Hastings was due he wrote to William: "Tin is no more; spout that pin of mine," reminding him at the same time: "that crib—Harrison's—in Wardour Street seems eligible," and, "if you could spout your own too, or by any means let me have a modicum of bullion" the addition to his own resources would be very welcome. Towards the end of June "tin" arrived. On a pretext of seeing patrons and selling pictures, Gabriel at once escaped from the shadows of the sick room to town, and at the Belle Sauvage was "smiled on by the cordial stunner, who came in on purpose in a lilac walking costume," as he told Allingham. "I am quite certain," he added, "she does not regret you at all!"

The few days in town raised his drooping spirits; but back in Hastings with Lizzie, he fell again into the old apathetic mood. He wrote to Allingham—almost as he had written to Brown a month before—"There are dense fogs of heat here now, through which sea and sky loom as one wall, with the webbed craft creeping on it like flies, or standing there as if they would drop off dead. I wander over the baked cliffs, seeking rest and finding none. . . . The crier is just going up this street and moaning out notices of sales. Why cannot one put all one's plagues and the skeletons of one's house into his hands and tell him to sell them 'without reserve?' " To Gabriel in his frustration the external world seemed to stagnate like his own mind in the lethargy of the inane. This same sense of uneasy stagnation marks one stanza of the poem *Even So*, with so close a resemblance to this description of Hastings that it is difficult to believe it was not jotted down in his notebook at this time and afterwards incorporated in the poem which is dated some five years later. It is a stanza, "scratched," said Patmore, "with an adamantine pen upon a slab of agate":

> But the sea stands spread
> As one wall with the flat skies,
> Where the lean black craft like flies
> Seem well-nigh stagnated,
> Soon to drop off dead.

Above all other anxieties was his dilemma with Lizzie. "I am melancholy enough here sometimes, and shall be glad to discuss our concerns with you in London as soon as possible," he told Allingham, his confidential friend. "Lizzie is a sweet companion, but the fear which the constant sight of her varying states suggests is much less pleasant to live with." But Allingham, now abandoning a short interlude as a London journalist to return to the Irish Customs Service, could not resolve Gabriel's perplexities. It was indeed a problem, this question of marriage now complicated by ill-health, which seemed most likely to be solved ere long by Lizzie's death; or so at least Gabriel began to believe.

Whatever his affection for Lizzie and whatever William might say about his being already "engaged," Gabriel was certainly reluctant to commit himself definitely to marriage. His moods were obviously variable. The evident tightening of the bond between them during their first days together at Mrs.

Elphick's had been quickly followed for Gabriel by a languor, even a boredom, as of waning desire. Besides, love's reality, especially such a reality, must ever prove disappointing against the transcendence of his love-ideal, and already, no doubt, Lizzie no longer seemed to him to be "the woman who was his soul." Did he now, or a little later, in *Love's Nocturn*, strike the first clear notes of disillusion? "The first conception of this poem," he wrote long afterwards, "was of a man not yet in love who dreams vaguely of a woman who, he thinks, must exist for him." Surely this poem, even in the later, revised form, the only form in which we have it, is a striking revelation of Rossetti's state at this critical time. There as in a mirror we see his trance-like lethargy, his moral temptations and remorse, his dependence upon an ideal love for salvation, his horror of death and of a drab, unemotionalized reality; all the darker content of his mind is revealed as overwhelming him in the absence of the sole counter-charm, ideal love. Whether in the original version or not we cannot say, but in *Love's Nocturn* we find those two mental and emotional polarities of love and death, that dependence upon an ideal to save him from his own lower nature, which are characteristic of Rossetti's verse.

> Reft of her, my dreams are all
>   Clammy trance that fears the sky:
> Changing footpaths shift and fall;
>   From polluted coverts nigh,
>   Miserable phantoms sigh;
>   Quakes the pall,
>   And the funeral goes by.

From this his ideal saves him, for:

> Suddenly her face is there:
>   So do mounting vapours wreathe
> Subtle-scented transports where
>   The black fir-wood sets its teeth.
>   Part the boughs and look beneath—
>   Lilies share
>   Secret waters there, and breathe.

Once again we have the symbolism of *A Young Fir-Wood*, "polluted coverts," and "the black fir-wood sets its teeth." Did he take it from that Italian word "frasca" meaning a

bough, a bush and also a wanton? One conclusion at least
Love's Nocturn forces upon us: that from the dilemma of unpropitious circumstance and deepening disillusion Rossetti was
escaping, beneath the shelter of his protective lethargy, into
the warmth and light of his own, inner dream-world, was there
resuming, perhaps at first almost unconsciously, his search for
that ideal *alter ego*, "the woman who was his soul. . . ."

Remote from the interests and distractions of his life in
London, Gabriel yielded at Hastings, as never before, to his
innate introvert tendencies. Throughout the remainder of his
visit, the external world became for him but a reflection of his
own moods, usually one of weariness, doubt, disillusion. Yet
his lethargy gave place at times to a fleeting renewal of the
lost rapture. A sudden revelation of some new beauty in Lizzie,
some unconscious grace of movement, of attitude or expression,
some turn of head or hand, would transiently rekindle the
dying flame. Then for an instant his disharmonies resolved
themselves in erotic mysticism, and Lizzie became once again
his soul's image, one with himself, the Platonic archetype, loved
with a passion that preceded earthly existence, survived earthly
discords and transcended death. That was "Sudden Light," as
he named one of the most charming and intimate of his lyrics,
embodying one such experience and permeated with that sense
of the timeless and repetitive which haunts the instinctive life.

> I have been here before,
>   But when or how I cannot tell:
> I know the grass beyond the door,
>   The sweet, keen smell,
> The sighing sound, the lights around the shore.
>
> You have been mine before—
>   How long ago I may not know:
> But just when at that swallow's soar
>   Your neck turned so,
> Some veil did fall—I knew it all of yore.
>
> Has this been thus before?
>   And shall not thus time's eddying flight
> Still with our lives our loves restore
>   In death's despite,
> And day and night yield one delight once more?

Before the close of July, Gabriel and Lizzie returned to town. The change was little likely to help Lizzie. It was a weary summer, with intense heat; cholera was sweeping through the city like a flame and the smell from the river was so bad that for a time it drove even Gabriel from his rooms. From the London barracks a constant stream of troops was leaving for the Crimea.

Lizzie, in intervals of comparative health, struggled to complete her designs while Gabriel, still idle, fearing the worst, watched her in sorrow and admiration. "It seems hard to me," he wrote to Allingham, of Lizzie—"Miss S," he called her—"when I look at her sometimes, working or too ill to work, and think how many without one tithe of her genius or greatness of spirit have granted them abundant health and opportunity to labour through the little they can do or will do, while perhaps her soul is never to bloom nor her bright hair to fade, but after hardly escaping from degradation and corruption, all she might have been must sink out again unprofitably in that dark house where she was born. How truly she may say: 'No man cares for my soul.' I do not mean to make myself an exception, for how long I have known her, and not thought of this till so late—perhaps too late. But it is no use writing more about this subject; and I fear, too, my writing at all about it must prevent your easily believing it to be as it is, by far the nearest thing to my heart. I will write to you something of my own doings soon, I hope; at present I could only speak of discomfitures." Pity was the prevalent note when Gabriel thought of Lizzie in connection with his "duty to her" by marriage. The last note that he wrote before marrying her, six years later, and on the point of leaving for the church, was identical in spirit with this one.

But although Gabriel for the present would not marry her, he could not do without her, and to prevent her going into a hospital, clutched at any straw. Dr. Wilkinson thought her health improved, so Gabriel gladly concluded that "to make a beginning and set her mind a little at ease about her pursuit of art," would be the best for her; and he set her to "paint quietly" in his rooms. She had just renewed his admiration by a "splendid" illustration for his poem *Sister Helen*. Perhaps she saw something in the poem peculiarly appropriate. At any rate, the old, ragged, Bohemian life both loved in Chatham Place was resumed, and in a jocular verse invitation to Brown at Finchley, Gabriel now described their mode of existence with almost Hogarthian realism and felicity.

> Dear Brown,
> > Are you never in town?
> > I should have come down,
> > But it costs half-a-crown—
> > > At least if it don't
> > > The rhyme must account)—
> > > And not painting anything,
> > > My work don't a penny bring.
>
> > *   *   *
>
> > So I wish you'd look in
> > When you come up for tin
> > > (Or with ticker to spout it),
> > And tell us all about it.
> > And if from these cads
> > You've superfluous brads,
> > To my crib you may lug 'em
> > > (Dear Lizzy's a Guggum),
> > Where limited bread
> > You shall find, and a bed,
> > Or for tea we will ring,
> > If to get it you'll bring
> > A bob or a tizzy.
> > (What a Guggum is Lizzy!)
> > If you come though, don't holler
> > At my evident squalor,
> > Nor cut me and run
> > At the sight of the dun,
> > Nor make for the door
> > At the sound of the bore,[1]
> > Nor suppose that the landlord
> > With lodging will stand board,
> > Nor as to my picture
> > Throw out any conjecture.
> > So now if you come
> > To where *ego sum*,
> > You know the condition
> > (Dear Lizzy's a pigeon)
> > > And now don't be witty
> > > Upon D. G. Rossetti.

[1] *cf. inf.*, p. 192.

Another, happier moment, of pride and joy in laughing, blushing, golden-haired Lizzie, as he watched her feeding her pet bullfinch, inspired a sonnet *Beauty and the Bird*, which pleasantly illuminates the usually ignored simplicities of their daily life.

In Rossetti's verse of this time we can clearly trace many of the moods which swept over him. For although he had told William shortly after entering Chatham Place: "I have abandoned poetry," he was unfitted for ultimate renunciations, and indeed, while the difficulties of painting drove him back to poetry, the charm of poetry was not the least of the causes leading to his temporary abandonment of serious painting. So, in *Sudden Light, Love's Nocturn, The Birth-Bond* and *Lost on Both Sides*, Gabriel now expressed as he had done before in *The Blessed Damozel*, his Platonist love-ideal. Other sonnets of this time similarly reveal his unrest, self-division, vacillation, reflect his sense of his failure to realize his ideal in the world of reality. Now, too, he began a significant pen-and-ink design, showing Hamlet scorning Ophelia; "deeply symbolical and far-sighted, of course," he described it with mock irony to Allingham.[1]

In this same letter to Allingham of August 1854, Gabriel included the sonnet *Birth-Bond*, just written, recalling the idealistic mood in which he had dreamed of love, a love which he had not yet discovered in the world of actuality. And this ideal was again Platonist, the lovers' souls sharing a secret harmony akin to the intuitive sympathies of the blood which some children inherit from their common parentage.

> Even so, when first I saw you, seemed it love,
>   That among souls allied to mine was yet
> One nearer kindred than I wotted of.
>   O born with me somewhere that men forget,
>   And though in years of sight and sound unmet,
> Known for my own life's sister well enough!

This mystical recognition of twin souls he evidently did not find in Lizzie now; somewhere, he dreamed, that elect, dedicated spirit awaited him. That thought doubtless was the chief cause of his indecision. Such was his mood in August; but in

[1] *v. inf.* p. 255.

the following October, it had undergone a surprising change if we may take a sonnet he then wrote, *The Landmark*, as a personal revelation, which it obviously is. For in *The Landmark*, Gabriel recognizes a tardy but sincere love for some humble person whose affection he has abused and betrayed in his expectation of a sincere passion for some more exalted lover who will appear in due time. The sonnet is too interesting not to quote in full:

> Was *that* the landmark? What—the foolish well
>   Whose wave, low down, I did not stoop to drink,
>   But sat and flung the pebbles from its brink
> In sport to send its imaged skies pell-mell,
> (And mine own image, had I noted well!)—
>   Was that my point of turning?—I had thought
>   The stations of my course should rise unsought,
> As altar-stone or ensigned citadel.
>
> But lo! the path is missed, I must go back,
>   And thirst to drink when next I reach the spring
> Which once I stained, which since may have grown black.
>   Yet though no light be left nor bird now sing
>   As here I turn, I'll thank God, hastening,
> That the same goal is still on the same track.

Was not Rossetti saying in his own way what Shakespeare had said more clearly when he wrote—

> This is my home of love; if I have ranged,
> Like him that travels I return again,
> Just to the time, not with the time exchanged,
> So that myself bring water for my stain . . .?

Through *The Landmark's* vagueness rings a note of determination ending a long period of doubt, a doubt which perhaps momentarily returns the following January in *A Dark Day*, when the poet asks himself whether his dark, regretful mood be the presage of new storms coming, of a new struggle with himself, or only the aftermath of the one just passed. The endless debate as to marriage we may reasonably associate with this sonnet, especially as the "marriage-bed" appears as a symbol in the poem.

As recently at Hastings, so now in London, Gabriel's thoughts turned much on poetry. Encouraged by Macmillan the book-

seller, with hopes of publication, he continued to revise and
copy his verse translations from mediaeval Italian poets, but
of his original verse he held only a low estimate. Allingham's
offer to review it if he would only publish, he modestly rejected
on the ground that "I think well of very little I have written,
and I am afraid of people agreeing with me, which I should
find a bore. I believe my poetry and painting prevented each
other from doing much good for a long while, and now I think
I could do better in either, but can't write for then I shan't
paint. However, one day I hope at least to finish the few rhymes
I have by me that I care for at all, and then there they'll be,
at any rate."

Gabriel in fact as much feared public criticism of his poems
as of his pictures. He doubtless knew also that this, his first
poetic period, which had begun with the awakening of his
passion for Lizzie, was now ending. His poetic faculty, vitalized
almost solely by physical passion, declined with its decay. Save
for an occasional sonnet on a picture, or a pseudo-ballad on
some historical theme, he was to remain almost silent until
fourteen years later the outbreak of a new and greater passion
moved his lips once more to song.

Poetry, as he said, certainly interrupted painting. Until in
the late autumn of 1854 he desultorily resumed *Found*, he continued as idle a painter in London as he had been in Hastings.
The presence of "the cordial stunner," this summer even more
cordial than before, assisted in this result. "I've done no good,
had better have cut work for the day, and must go out to that
meal which combines the sweets of an assignation." Such were
the occasional mischievous glimpses of himself he from time
to time sent to the absent Allingham.

With characteristically unconscious irony, Bell Scott associated the placid and benignant radiance of Hunt's *Light of the
World*, glimmering in the spring of 1854 on the walls of the
once despised Academy, with the commencement of Gabriel's
moral decline. "From the time of Hunt's success," he wrote,
"D. G. R. continued for years to be unknown to the public
as an artist, but to gain in the respect of the intelligent, while
the man himself gradually underwent a surprising development.
His curious materialistic piety disappeared, burst like a soap

bubble, and the superficial prismatic colours vanished into air. The early views of self-culture and self-sacrifice we have noticed, underwent a similar bouleversement." It was the first clear indication of a change which, Scott declared, began when Rossetti was "just getting out of boyhood and in transition."

This change in Gabriel was reflected in his art, in both poetry and painting. We see it particularly in *Jenny, Hesterna Rosa, Found, The Magdalene at the Door of Simon*, and in that pen-and-ink sketch of a siren entitled: *Lo Marinaio oblia che passa per tal via*—*The Passing Mariner Forgets*—from a poem by Jacopo da Lentino,* which Gabriel also translated.

> I am broken, as a ship
> Perishing of the song,
> Sweet, sweet and long, the songs the sirens know.
> The mariner forgets,
> Voyaging in those straits,
> And dies assuredly.

"Youth and Change!" How regretfully conscious of it Gabriel was when, looking back seventeen years later, he sang in *Pride of Youth*:

> There is a change in every hour's recall,
> And the last cowslip in the fields we see
> On the same day with the first corn-poppy.
> Alas for hourly change! Alas for all
> The loves that from his hand proud Youth lets fall,
> Even as the beads of a told rosary!

* *v. Notes.*

III

RUSKIN
1854–1855

If one could only find the "supreme" Carlylian Ignoramus, him who knows positively the least about Art of any living creature—and get *him* to write a pamphlet about one—what a fortune one might make!

Letter to T. Woolner D. G. ROSSETTI

ONE CONTRIBUTORY CAUSE of Rossetti's indolence and unrest was the continued indifference of art-patrons to his existence. Aunt Charlotte in 1849 had persuaded the Marchioness of Bath, her employer, to buy *The Girlhood of Mary Virgin* for eighty guineas, but not until three more years had passed did another solicitant of Gabriel's oil-painting appear. It was January 1853 when a Belfast shipping agent, MacCracken, already a patron of Brown and Hunt, bought at their instigation Rossetti's *Annunciation* for fifty guineas. Irritated by its imperfections and unsaleability, Gabriel had long since called it "the blessed white eyesore." For the sake of his reputation he extensively repainted it before delivery to MacCracken.

Rossetti's treatment of MacCracken was prophetic of his later dealings with almost all his patrons, business men chiefly, without cultivated aesthetic tastes or interests, who bought pictures merely for social snobbery or as commercial speculations. Contemptuous of them at heart, Gabriel rejoiced no less in unscrupulously despoiling these Philistines than in pocketing their gold. To him it was self-evident that the sole justification of a business man's existence was to support artists; and in his dealings with them, Gabriel quickly developed a natural Latin aptitude for bargaining into a fine art.

From the first he treated MacCracken as an enemy to be pillaged, rather than as a patron to be won. Amongst friends, Gabriel referred to him as the "Irish maniac"—because MacCracken was speculating in Rossetti's pictures—and regarded him as a joke. With all the dignity of a long established

painter, he sternly refused MacCracken's suggestion that
Ruskin's approval of the *Annunciation* be a condition of purchase
—and had his way. To Ruskin, however, MacCracken afterwards submitted it, and the critic's verdict was such that the
pleased patron immediately commissioned another oil painting
at £150, and also began to buy Rossetti's water-colours. Soon,
so skilfully did Gabriel manage him, MacCracken was gladly
paying fifty guineas each for water-colour sketches which
hitherto Rossetti had willingly sold for twelve. Characteristically, Gabriel showed his gratitude by ridiculing MacCracken
to friends in a sonnet parodying Tennyson's *Kraken*. As for the
oil painting he had commissioned, Gabriel, having obtained
the purchase money for the pictures already sold and an
advance deposit upon the others, did not for some time trouble
even to begin it. Nor was it, in fact, ever completed.

He early decided, however, that the picture should represent
a "town subject" he had long contemplated, that of a conscience-stricken prostitute shrinking from her former honourable lover, a countryman taking a calf to market in his cart
—obviously symbolical—and who has caught sight of her in
passing. The theme was partly influenced by Scott's dull poem
Rosabell, which, Gabriel had suggested, should include a meeting
of the erring woman with her former true lover. When Scott
declined this as beyond his powers, Gabriel, mindful of his
long contemplated "town subject" or "modern subject," replied
that he would express it in paint himself. At Newcastle, he
had also offered to illustrate *Rosabell*, and though the promised
etching never appeared, he did in fact, long afterwards, in the
water-colour *The Gate of Memory*, keep his word. Nevertheless
Scott believed Rossetti's "town subject" (*Found*, as it came to
be called) and his poem *Jenny*, plagiarisms of *Rosabell*, and
another interminable Preraphaelite squabble as to originality
and precedence began. . . .

Suddenly, in the autumn of 1854, Rossetti emerged from
his lethargy and began to paint *Found* with extraordinary
though spasmodic energy. He would paint it in Hunt's way,
"from Nature," and he had at last found a suitable "brick
wall" to copy, at Chiswick, "which," he jocularly remarked,
"consists chiefly, as I ought to have remembered before, of

that material!" There, during the chilly autumn days, while friends marvelled at his returning energy, he painted away, cheered by the proximity of the grave of Hogarth, whom he much admired. He thought it a good omen for his "modern picture." For the Preraphaelites' decision to paint "modern" or "town" subjects, a principle no more closely followed by them than any other of their theories, was due to a desire to be "realistic" and "practical" or useful, by choosing themes from contemporary life, illuminating, as Dickens and others were doing in their novels, the darker aspects of the world about them, with the moral purpose, which Hunt emphasized, of improving the conditions amidst which they lived.

But Gabriel's spasm of energy soon passed. Brown, now living at Finchley, called at Chatham Place early in October and found Lizzie there too, "looking thinner and more deathlike and more beautiful and more ragged than ever," he confided to his diary: "A real artist, a woman without parallel for many a long year. Gabriel as usual diffuse and inconsequent in his work. Drawing wonderful and lovely Guggums one after another, each one a fresh charm, each one stamped with immortality, and his picture never advancing. However, he is at the wall, and I am to get him a white calf and a cart to paint here; would he but study the *golden one* a little more. Poor Gabriello!"

"I've been long 'meaning' Finchley, and shall turn up there (in an increased ratio of seediness) one of these days, and make you crusty and get crusty myself, about art as usual," Gabriel wrote to Brown, and soon afterwards, on the last day of October, he was as good as his word. Opposite Brown's was a farm with a calf and cart suitable for *Found*. Gabriel had come to paint them.

His anticipation of "crustiness" was amply fulfilled. Gabriel was inconsiderate, while ill-fortune and hardship were affecting Brown's nerves, overlaying his natural benevolence with ungraciousness and irritability. Some years before, Brown, then a widower, had imprudently eloped with the pretty, penniless, fifteen-year-old daughter of a farmer, and had made her his wife. Since then, his life had been dogged beyond anything he had previously experienced of the kind, by poverty, illness, domestic difficulties and disappointed ambition. The time of Rossetti's advent was too, peculiarly unpropitious, for in their tiny, cramped cottage at Finchley, Brown's wife Emma was expecting in the near future a child.

Believing that Gabriel would quickly finish his painting and return to town, Brown gave him a mattress on the parlour floor, and played the courteous if slightly grumpy host. But there were endless delays. Rossetti preferred "jaw," as Brown called it, to painting, discussing poetry and art far into the night with his yawning friend, and when they fell to arguing, "he becomes," wrote Brown, "spiteful and crusty, denying everything, and when chaffed he at length grows bitterly sarcastic in his way, but never quite unpleasant nor ever unbearable." Late nights were followed for Rossetti by late and languid mornings with belated breakfasts eaten long after the rest of the household were about their tasks. Often Gabriel left his work and made hasty visits to town to see Lizzie or Woolner— now glad to return to the civilization he had despised, though without Australian gold.

Even when Gabriel managed to reach the farm and began to paint, obstacles multiplied. The calf kicked, tried to hang itself, he said, while the exasperated Brown, watching Gabriel and longing with increasing impatience for his departure, thought bitterly to himself: "like Albert Dürer, hair by hair!" It began to rain and snow, so Gabriel urbanely borrowed his disgusted host's coat and trousers, "besides", Brown grumbled, "food and an unlimited supply of turpentine." In December, when Brown thought Gabriel must surely be going at last, a gust of wind overturned the easel on to Rossetti's leg which gathered and began to trouble him. Speculating as to whether the birth of his baby, bankruptcy or Gabriel's departure would occur first, Brown, scarcely able to conceal his exasperation, was kept out of bed until five o'clock in the morning discussing Gabriel's favourite theme, suicide! But when mid-December had come and Rossetti, calmly ignoring all hints to expedite his departure, casually spoke of remaining "several days yet," Brown's self-control broke down. "Delicately"—the word is, delightfully, Brown's—he told Gabriel "he must go, or go home at night by the bus." To this Rossetti replied that he could not

PLATE IV

J. E. MILLAIS
c. 1870

W. HOLMAN HUNT
1856

PLATE V

FORD MADOX BROWN
BY D. G. ROSSETTI
1852

ELIZABETH ELEANOR SIDDAL
SELF PORTRAIT
1853-4

afford to ride and "would never think of" walking. So, after a six weeks' visit, Gabriel, leaving *Found* unfinished, returned home.

This interlude at Finchley withdrew Rossetti from his friends in town. "Rossetti is a myth and seldom visible to the naked eye," wrote the young painter Halliday to Allingham: "I suppose we are all painting pretty hard in the day and don't know where to find each other o' nights." Perhaps Gabriel's sudden retreat to Finchley was partly due to a determination to escape the fascination of "the cordial stunner," who now falls into oblivion. For a little later he told Allingham: "My *rapports* you ask of with that stunner, stopped some months ago, after a long stay away from Chatham Place, partly from a wish to narrow the circle of flirtations, in which she had begun to figure a little; but I often find myself sighing after her, now that 'roast beef, roast mutton, gooseberry tart,' have faded into the light of common day. O what is gone from them I fancied theirs?"

Poverty alone could rouse Gabriel from his lethargy into such effort as he had just shown, and his poverty after the return from Hastings was extreme. His earlier, lordly tone in borrowing had now dwindled to pitiful appeals to Aunt Charlotte who "must indeed be weary of applications like this from me." Vainly grappling with oils, he lost his former buoyancy, sent her forlorn epistles, describing himself as "almost hopeless of my ever making myself in an independent position." But, as he pointed out, if only he could complete the works on hand all might yet be well; for—thinking of his water-colours—"anything I finish now is almost, if not quite, certain of sale." And Aunt Charlotte's faith in him proved great as her generosity. Naturally, in the circumstances, he painted his life in dark colours when writing to her, and she would doubtless have been much surprised by the gay acceptance of his hard lot revealed in the verse invitation to Brown already quoted.[1]

Rossetti's claim to be able to sell his water-colours without difficulty was, however, no exaggeration. His work in this medium was winning for him a reputation amongst an inner

[1] *v. sup.* p. 152.

circle of buyers and critics. "I also find purchasers, and I can see before me, much more clearly than hitherto the path to success," he had told his father at the opening of 1853; yet now, almost a year later, restless, uncertain, dissatisfied, apathetic, he had made no advance with oils. It was Ruskin who now came upon him dilatory, discouraged, indolent, and tried to draw him from the Slough of Despair into which he had fallen.

For long the painter and the critic had remained unacquainted with each other. Ruskin had first seen Gabriel's works at the Winter Exhibition of water-colours in Pall Mall at the close of 1852, and shortly afterwards MacCracken had sent Ruskin the *Annunciation* for his verdict. The result had pleased Gabriel, for Ruskin had not only admired the oil-painting but had also spoken highly of Rossetti's three exhibited water-colours in Pall Mall, *Rossovestita* (sometimes called *Portrait in a Venetian Costume*), *Beatrice Denying her Salutation*, and *Giotto Painting the Portrait of Dante*.

From the first Gabriel had proudly sought to conceal his hypersensitiveness to criticism behind a disguise of indifference. These three water-colours, he declared, "excited a good deal of attention and unpalateable [*sic*] praise." On receiving Mac-Cracken's account of Ruskin's approval, Gabriel attempted to maintain his pose of superiority to the opinions of others. "Extravagant praises (though with obtuse accompaniments)," he told Brown, speaking of Ruskin's comments, and professing at the same time that he could not discover to which of his exhibited works Ruskin referred. In his comments to Woolner, however, Gabriel's secret elation broke through his pretence of indifference. "Ruskin," he wrote, "goes into raptures about the colour and grouping which he says are superior to anything in modern art; which I believe is almost as absurd as certain absurd objections which he makes to them. However, as he is only half informed about Art anything he says in favour of one's work is, of course, sure to prove invaluable in a professional way, and I only hope, for the sake of my rubbish, that he may have the honesty to say publicly in his new book what he has said privately, but I doubt this. Oh! Woolner, if one could only find the 'supreme' Carlylian Ignoramus, him who

knows positively the least about Art of any living creature—
and get *him* to write a pamphlet about one—what a fortune one
might make! It now seems that Ruskin had never seen any
work of mine before, though he never thought it necessary to
say this in writing about the P.R.B."

Another year had passed when MacCracken, receiving
Dante Drawing an Angel in Memory of Beatrice, one of the water-
colours he had commissioned from Gabriel, sent it to Ruskin who,
in his enthusiasm, wrote Rossetti "an incredible letter about
it," as Gabriel said. That letter, dated "Monday 10th April,
1854," marks the beginning of the curious relationship between
Rossetti and Ruskin which was to bring such benefit to the
artist, such disappointment to the critic. "My dear sir," wrote
Ruskin, "when I heard of Mr. MacCracken's intention to ask
you to send your drawing to me, I was ashamed to allow him
to do so—but permitted my shame to be conquered by the
strong desire I had to be allowed to have the drawing by me
for a day or two; I was quite sure that I should be able at once
to write to Mr. MacCracken that any work of yours was quite
above having opinions passed upon it; and I have now only to
thank you for your condescension in allowing it to be sent to
me on such terms—and still more—for the very great delight
I have had in keeping it by me for a day or two. I think it a
thoroughly glorious work—the most perfect piece of Italy, in
the accessory parts, I have ever seen in my life—nor of Italy
only—but of marvellous landscape painting. I might perhaps,
if we were talking about it, venture to point out one or two
little things that appear to me questionable—but I shall write
an unqualified expression of admiration to MacCracken—and
I can only to you—express my earnest hope that you will not
allow any feeling of dissatisfaction with your own work to prevent you at any time—from completing in such development as
may be possible—your noble thoughts. I shall call on you in a
day or two—hoping you will allow me the privilege of knowing
you—and remaining always most faithfully and respectfully
yours—J. Ruskin."

Three days later, Ruskin, in accordance with his promise,
appeared at Chatham Place. The meeting was less unpleasant
than Gabriel had anticipated. He was not drawn to Ruskin,

found him physically "hideous," and had no respect for a mere uncreative critic; but, aware of his influence, determined at once, especially for Lizzie's sake, to extract whatever profit he could from this new and powerful friendship. "He seems in a mood to make my fortune," Gabriel told Brown, and in this at least Rossetti did not wish to thwart him. A few days later, Ruskin had called again, and shortly afterwards Gabriel had lunched with him at Ruskin's wealthy home in Denmark Hill. He had seized the occasion to present Ruskin with a copy of Allingham's *Day and Night Songs*, and so skilfully praised Lizzie's artistic talent that Ruskin's interest in her was aroused, and, as Gabriel reported afterwards to a friend, "he yearneth!"

But just as the acquaintance between Rossetti and Ruskin was developing, various events had arisen to separate them during the following months. From that very lunch with Ruskin an urgent message had summoned Gabriel to his father's death-bed, and they had not yet met again. Ruskin, on hearing of Professor Rossetti's death, had at once sent Gabriel a note of sympathy, a consolatory piece of opal, all his own published works, and a commission for a small sketch at fifteen guineas. He also requested a small drawing in exchange, to seal their friendship. Ruskin at the same time had informed Rossetti that he was leaving England for a Continental holiday, and he begged Gabriel to write to him. He promised also to come and see Lizzie's drawings upon his return. "I am truly anxious," Ruskin concluded, "that no sorrow—still less undue distrust of yourself—may interfere with the exercise of your very noble powers, and I should deem it a great privilege if you would sometimes allow me to have friendship in your thoughts and sympathy with your purposes."

The secret reason of Ruskin's departure was already whispered in London society. He could be a husband only in name and his wife was leaving him. "We must live," he was said to have declared with bitter humour to his uncomprehending sixteen-year-old wife as they drove away after the wedding, "like two blessed angels," and gossips whispered that he had made her swear a great oath on the Bible, not to reveal for ten years, the meaning of the jest. His pretty, pleasure-loving wife, long estranged, had now fallen in love with her husband's handsome Preraphaelite protégé Millais, and had begun a legal suit for the annulment of her unconsummated marriage. She was now awaiting, with all possible decorum, her "freedom," which Millais with equal decorum also awaited, so that they might marry. Ruskin, who would not oppose the petition of his wife, preferred to escape from gossip, scandal and humiliation, to the peace and beauty of the Swiss mountains he loved. Ruskin's generosity, however, touched no corresponding chord in Gabriel, who, hearing in due course that Ruskin's marriage was annulled, nonchalantly remarked: "Ruskin seems to take his sell coolly."

Rossetti was less cool about himself. From Hastings he had sent Ruskin a letter contrasting his own lack of recognition with that given to Millais and Hunt, a letter also calculated to remind the critic that while he had praised Rossetti's companions he had not yet even mentioned Rossetti himself. Ruskin, revising for the press his recent *Lectures on Architecture and Painting*, thereupon inserted a complimentary reference to Rossetti's "exhaustless invention." A "slight though very friendly mention of me," Gabriel reported to Allingham appreciatively, and when, shortly afterwards, he heard that a leading picture-agent, Gambart, wanted his work, he said, with truth, "Ruskin is beginning to bear fruit!"

It was a time when "the subject" ruled in British art; "originality" of subject was more important than painting, and as the time of the Academy Exhibition approached, artists— as Whistler a few years later described with amusing exaggeration—locked themselves in their studios and avoided one another, so great was their fear of plagiarism! Rivalry was rife amongst the Brethren, and Gabriel complained bitterly to Ruskin that Hunt and Millais were stealing his ideas, particularly his "modern" or "town" subject—which was merely the mistress or prostitute theme of *Found*. This same subject had, in fact, already inspired Watts's *Found Drowned* painted four years before, and doubtless Watts's work had influenced both Gabriel's theme and title. Besides, Watts's pupil Stanhope had imitated his master two years later in *Thoughts of the Past*. Nevertheless Gabriel, seeing a "mistress" in Hunt's *Awakened Conscience*, and an old red-brick wall in Millais's *Huguenot*, accused them, as both appeared in his *Found*, of plagiarism. So stirred indeed was Rossetti that he gave vent to his feelings in a small, ironical playlet which he sent to Allingham and which still survives.

Ruskin, however, not wishing to play Paris to these three graces of the paint-brush, replied to Gabriel as dexterously as he had written to *The Times* three years before in the Preraphaelites' defence. Doubtless, he said, Gabriel *had* first discovered the "modern subject," but if he had not, Hunt and Millais must assuredly have done so. He approved the theme of *Found* and particularly that of *Mary Magdalene*, sent advice and criticism, asked to see Gabriel's verse translations from the mediaeval Italian poets, and urged the penniless artist to soothe his mind by going to Rouen and studying "thirteenth-century sculptures" in the cathedral there. But the hypersensitive Preraphaelites, ever squabbling, bitterly resented Ruskin's acceptance of Rossetti's claim to priority in invention. The ensuing quarrel destroyed what remnants of solidarity remained to the Brotherhood. Their acrimonious debate continued long after most of the original disputants were dead, and was maintained by Hunt and William Rossetti into extreme old age and far into the following century.

Gabriel meanwhile, behind a pretence of complete indifference, had almost certainly studied to please Ruskin. Shortly after the critic's public denunciation of Preraphaelite "mediaevalism," Gabriel with rare modesty had declared to William that his own "mediaevalisms *were* absurd." Soon, experiencing the practical benefits of Ruskin's approval, Gabriel had followed the critic's advice to the Preraphaelites, as well as the tendency of his own personal development, by abandoning Biblical themes which Ruskin might condemn as "popery," and substituting a "modern" subject in their place. In painting this subject "from Nature," he had also, no doubt, been influenced by Ruskin's praise of Hunt and Millais for their realistic detail. It was surely the practical principle of pleasing Ruskin, rather than, as Hunt believed, Gabriel's conversion to Hunt's "Preraphaelite" theory of "truth to Nature," which had sent Gabriel to Finchley to find realistic detail for *Found*, the only painting in which he ever attempted such detailed "realism," and which, in fact, so wearied him that it was never finished.

When in the autumn of 1854 Ruskin returned to England, he quickly resumed personal contact with Rossetti. The occasion was the foundation, in Red Lion Square, of a college for working men. This Working Men's College was the happy result of a difference of opinion between Frederick Denison Maurice, Professor of Theology at King's College, London, and the College authorities as to the nature of Hell. Claiming a more intimate acquaintance with the subject than the professor's, the authorities proved their pretensions by dismissing him from his chair, and Maurice, ever an advocate of education for the people, turned to establish the Working Men's College with himself as Principal.

To staff the new institution volunteers were needed. Ruskin offered his services as drawing instructor, and persuaded Gabriel to join in a similar capacity. The wisdom of pleasing Ruskin was doubtless a stronger influence upon Rossetti than social idealism. "You may soon expect to find everyman shoulder his hod, 'with upturned fervid face and hair put back,'"[1] he told Allingham, with genial scepticism as to the result. In January 1855, he took his first class, using Hunt's Preraphaelite method "from Nature" in a quite modern way. Unable to pay for professional models, he set the class to draw one another. "None of your Freehand Drawing Books used!" he told Scott: "The British mind is brought to bear on the British *mug* at once, and with results that would astonish you."

Amongst the students attending this class were James Smetham, afterwards Rossetti's personal friend, and Thomas Sulman, a student whose sole importance lies in the fact that, fifteen years after Gabriel's death, he published in a periodical his recollections of his experiences at the Working Men's College. Rossetti, whose evenings at the College alternated with Ruskin's, taught figure and water-colour painting. "He was very kind and sincere; he spoke little and with a mournful inflection of voice," Sulman recalled "Art was his religion; he never talked Mauriceism." Although. Gabriel as a rule spoke little when teaching, sometimes "he did so enthusiastically,"

[1] Quoted from Browning's *Sordello*.

and Sulman long remembered how "he came late one night and said he had been with the Brownings, and had played with their only child, 'a boy who did not know his parents were poets,' and that Mrs. Browning had read some pages from her new poem that would be immortal. It was to be called *Aurora Leigh*. Whereat someone asked what was Robert Browning as a poet like? Rossetti cried fiercely: 'Like? Why, in his lyrics, he is like Shelley, in his dramas he is like Shakespeare!' "

Gabriel's directness and unconventionality admirably suited his students. Very soon he had his class "quite on a family footing" and as a teacher was a great success. "He could inspire and thrill us," said Sulman, "we loved him so, and were happy to render him the smallest service. . . . He did not want our worship." Nevertheless Rossetti gave vanity or pomposity in a student short shrift. When, for example, a pretentious youth with more money than the very limited means of his fellows allowed them, ostentatiously demanded the names and addresses of the best colour shops, Gabriel squashed him with the brusque reply: "I don't know; I generally use the halfpenny colours from the oil shop myself!" Although surprised at this "unexpected flash of satire," Sulman thought it might well be the simple truth as he watched Rossetti with the "shabby box of fragments that he used to rattle amongst, rubbing with an almost dry brush on hard chips, but getting always the colour he wanted with surprising and harmonious effects."

Ruskin and Rossetti did not always agree about educational methods. The critic would remonstrate with the artist for beginning with colour, while the artist, disgusted with his colleague's debauches in Prussian blue, once removed the whole stock during Ruskin's absence, making at the same time forcible comments upon the methods Ruskin employed. Yet to others, Rossetti highly praised Ruskin's teaching, even approving its results as better than his own.

Regularity was certainly not one of Rossetti's virtues, and it is not surprising that he was often absent from the meetings of his class. "Someone asked Ruskin," wrote Sulman, "if Rossetti were industrious; Ruskin replied: 'If you call beginning work at nine o'clock at night and working impetuously till daybreak, industrious, he may be.' " Certainly with increasing intimacy,

Ruskin's admiration for Rossetti's talent was marred by a growing dislike of his untidy rooms, intermittent inertia, ambiguous relations with Lizzie, and generally easy, Bohemian way of life. He wrote begging Lizzie to rouse her lover to sustained endeavour. Gabriel, meanwhile, still intent upon securing Ruskin's aid for Lizzie, and smothering his dislike of being watched at work, allowed Ruskin to haunt his studio and even gave him a little casual instruction at times. In return, the critic installed Gabriel in Millais's vacant place as protégé, advertised his genius, persuaded one of his own female disciples to buy Rossetti's pictures, and determined to do so himself.

Gabriel—chiefly for the sake of Lizzie, who although ill was working hard at "two lovely water-colours," *We are Seven* and *La Belle Dame Sans Merci*, which Rossetti hoped Ruskin would buy—bent his proud and contemptuous spirit to accept Ruskin's well intentioned but often irritating generosity, criticism and advice, until in March 1855, on his showing Ruskin Lizzie's work, the desired dénouement came. Anxious to help Gabriel, Ruskin exaggerated whatever admiration Lizzie's quaint little works aroused. "Feminine likenesses of Rossetti's" declared Arthur Hughes the painter, but Ruskin, chiefly perhaps to spur Gabriel to renewed effort, praised them as better than Rossetti's or "any one's," and for thirty pounds, which was five pounds more than Gabriel had dared to ask for them, bought up all her designs on the spot. They should, he declared, be "splendidly mounted and bound together in gold"; but that was one of the few promises Ruskin failed to keep!

Lizzie appealed to Ruskin's chivalry. Above all, he wished to see Gabriel, freed from financial anxieties, doing the best work of which he was capable. Ruskin quickly invited the lovers to his home, where Lizzie received a most gracious welcome. It was now that, despite his earlier disapproval of her as she appeared in Hunt's *Valentine rescuing Sylvia from Proteus*, Ruskin found her "a noble, glorious creature," and Ruskin's father, to Gabriel's derisive joy, declared: "by her look and manner she might have been a countess." The pathos of golden-haired Lizzie's situation opened all hearts. Old Mrs. Ruskin took her aside and diagnosed her mysterious malady as "principally weakness, but needing the very greatest care."

"God send it may be only this," wrote Gabriel with unwonted devotion, "at any rate the cure will now I hope be possible." That, in his dealings with Ruskin, had ever been his chief aim.

The visit to Denmark Hill, Ruskin's home, was decisive. The next day, Ruskin reappeared at Gabriel's as *deus ex machina* indeed. Lizzie, Ruskin declared, must be freed from financial anxieties. He really meant Gabriel, but this Rossetti did not perceive. Ruskin's offer was generous. Fearing Lizzie's proud and independent spirit, so different in this from Gabriel's, Ruskin dare not offer her a pension; instead, he offered to buy all her pictures as she completed them; or, if she preferred, he would settle on her £150 a year in return for all her works. Whatever surplus her paintings realized—he well knew there would be none—he would return to her. Feeling the matter too delicate for his personal intervention, he asked Gabriel to convey his suggestion to Lizzie, and this he followed up by a persuasive letter to her, begging her to accept his offer, and also to take a holiday at his expense.

Gabriel, as remote from Ruskin's delicacy and sentimentality in such a matter as from Lizzie's pride, was crudely practical. He "jumped" at the offer, of course preferring the second alternative as "there may be goodish intervals when she cannot work and might run short of money"—like himself! But fearing, and rightly, that independent Lizzie would choose the first, he jocularly but determinedly declared: "she will be sternly coerced if necessary." "Meanwhile," he rejoiced to Brown, "I love him and her and everybody, and feel happier than I have felt for a long while." That, of course, was what Ruskin particularly wanted.

But Lizzie was obstinate as well as independent. Gabriel had to do much arguing, Ruskin much cajoling, before she would give way. Ruskin had to write her more delicately persuasive letters, to stress his own *selfishness* in the matter. He was, he pointed out, trying to save her "genius," to save her as he would "a beautiful tree from being cut down, or a bit of a Gothic cathedral whose strength was failing," and she must consider herself as such. He urged her to see a doctor, to go where the doctor ordered her, to the South of France, or to Wales, "in some sheltered Welsh valley," in a cottage, "if possible near a cattle shed"; for he shared the popular belief that the proximity of cattle benefited weak lungs. "You must try to make yourself as simple a milkmaid as you can, and only draw when you can't help it," he bade her, showing already to this gentle rose-leaf-and-gold invalid something of that sentimental, benevolent tyranny which had helped to drive his wife to flight. He sent Lizzie "ivory dust" to make jellies, which old Mrs. Ruskin declared would cure her, and, as she was wayward, he asked her to send him "a little signed promise, 'I will be good:'" —like Queen Victoria's on her accession. In short, he was very kind, very generous, very noble, very tender to Lizzie; and Lizzie, doubtless temporarily considering herself a tree or Gothic cathedral as bidden, at last accepted his offer to take her paintings for £150 a year, and give her whatever more he could get for them.

Upon Mrs. Rossetti, Ruskin's adoption as it were of Lizzie had an immediate and astonishing effect. On April 11th Gabriel and Lizzie had gone to the home of Ruskin, who then saw Lizzie for the first time. The next day, Ruskin had called on Gabriel to make his offer. The day after, April 13th, Rossetti writing to tell Brown of the marvellous happening, concluded: "Lizzie will take tea, perhaps dinner, at my mother's to-morrow." The next night, April 14th, Brown who had spent that day as often before, running about in a vain search for Rossetti, recorded in his diary, alluding to Gabriel: "to his mother's, where I slept. Miss Siddal's first interview with ditto. Late talk while Gabriel saw her home." At last Lizzie and Mrs. Rossetti had met! The veto of five years had vanished in a day! "She is a stunner and no mistake. . . . Why does he not marry her?" had been Brown's first thought on hearing of Ruskin's generosity. It was doubtless this same question, already discussed by Barbara, Anna Mary, and Bessie at Hastings, that Mrs. Rossetti and Brown debated during their "late talk" that night, while a happy Gabriel took Lizzie home.

Ruskin indeed was now asking Gabriel this same question, though very delicately. "I should be very grateful," he wrote, "if you thought it right to take me entirely into your confidence, and to tell me whether you have any plans or wishes, respecting Miss Siddal, which you are prevented from carrying out by want of a certain income, and if so what certain income would enable you to carry them out." It was an awkward question for Gabriel, who wanted Ruskin's money but did not want marriage. Did Ruskin indeed mean it (bluntly), as a bribe? In his dilemma, Gabriel astutely delayed his reply, and in the meantime, Ruskin, uneasy at his own temerity, wrote apologizing for "my somewhat blunt question in my last letter." He had thought, he said, Lizzie's projected travels for health "might perhaps be much better managed in another way, and your own powers of art be more healthily developed, and your own life made happier." But he was sure Gabriel would dislike incurring any "obligation to any one in carrying out any main purpose" of his life. Ruskin was to know Rossetti better ere long!

Gabriel, troubled by no such qualms as Ruskin feared, preferred the close of the letter to its beginning, for it ended with the declaration that of all the painters Ruskin knew, Rossetti had "the greatest genius," was "unhappy" and unable to develop it as he should, and the offer, as with Lizzie, to buy regularly whatever pictures Gabriel painted, up to a certain annual value. This deliverance of Gabriel, the artist, had evidently been from the first Ruskin's chief aim. He wanted Rossetti's drawings he now declared, as much as Turner's; "only"—a first playful scratch of the benevolent dictator—"I won't have them after they have been more than nine times rubbed entirely out, remember that." He made this offer, he said, to enable Rossetti "to paint properly and keep your room in order." Gabriel's reply, unlike Lizzie's, was of course an unhesitating and immediate acceptance. "He is the best friend I ever had, *out of my own family*," he told Aunt Charlotte, emphasizing with an underline this subtle tribute to her devotion.

Unfortunately Gabriel's actual reply to Ruskin's offer has not come down to us; but from Ruskin's answer, it is clear that Gabriel had skilfully left the question of marriage an indeterminate probability, by representing the decision as resting upon Lizzie, or even upon Ruskin himself! For Ruskin in return sent advice, "feeling at the first reading that it would be best for you to marry, for the sake of giving Miss Siddal complete protection and care, and putting an end to the peculiar sadness, and want of you hardly know what, that there is in both of you. I shall be able to send you before the end of the week, as much as will secure her comfort, with a companion, for a week or two at Jersey. Then, if she could make up her mind to take you, and go quietly away together to Vevey for the summer?"

Lizzie's affairs had suddenly, extraordinarily changed from medicine to marriage! That so signally unsuccessful a husband as Ruskin should offer marital advice must have appealed to Gabriel's ironic humour. But so artistically, if not artfully, had Rossetti told the tale of Lizzie's misfortunes, that he had even overshot the mark. Ruskin, kindly and sentimental, seeing in their situation only a frustrated idyllic love, could not do enough for them—yet to Gabriel it must have seemed he was already doing too much. At any rate, Ruskin's fussy devotion to Lizzie was extreme. He offered her the run of Denmark Hill and its garden, Albert Dürers and photographs for her room, and wished to discuss her with Gabriel, "because you seem to me to let her wear herself out with fancies, and she ought to be made to draw in a dull way sometimes from dull things."

But all this did not satisfy Ruskin. He next wrote on Lizzie's behalf to his old friend Dr. Acland, of Oxford, Reader in Anatomy, Fellow of Christchurch and All Souls, high in the academic hierarchy, and so eminent in his profession that local wits declared no one of any respectability thought of dying without consulting Dr. Acland first! Above all, Acland was famed for hospitality and benevolence. Casual patients entering his surgery for a bottle of medicine were forcibly detained for lunch; undergraduates and chimney-sweeps were exhorted to make his house their home; to the sick he offered it as a hospital, while undergraduates' relatives visiting Oxford, almost booked rooms there as at an hotel. So hospitable indeed was Dr. Acland, so many strangers from all quarters of the globe did he invite, that often he forgot their identity, and sometimes, a yet more embarrassing circumstance, forgot having invited them, an omission not easily concealed when they arrived.

To Acland, then, obviously destined by Providence to befriend Lizzie, Ruskin now showed her pictures and explained her state. She would, he had reason to fear, soon die. A fortnight before, he had learned, "a leading London physician—I know not which"—had found one side of her lungs "'seriously affected" and had "strongly recommended change of scene and air." She was, too, "uncomfortable in her family, who, though kind enough in other matters, set their faces steadily against all her artist's feelings—and have in no wise any sympathy with her, so that she goes up to her room without fire in winter to hide herself while she draws." And, chief reason of all for Ruskin's intervention, Gabriel's sorrow at Lizzie's failing health was preventing progress in his art. "I feel this sorrow will soon be sealed—and with what effect upon him, I cannot tell; I see that his attachment to her is very deep. But how far he is prepared for the loss I know not . . . I fear no good can be done, but at least it would put Rossetti's mind at peace if he knew she was in pure air—and at rest."

Gabriel had certainly played upon Ruskin's ready sympathy, sparing no colour to deepen the pathos of Lizzie's situation: the nameless, mysterious, "leading" pessimistic physician; the unsympathetic parents; the legend of Lizzie as the patient, dying, gentle dove, which became a tradition, all were obviously exploited by Gabriel to convince Ruskin of Lizzie's imminent death, and open his heart and purse. But a few months before, Gabriel had argued with Barbara that Lizzie was too well to need a hospital, and later, in the autumn, only a few weeks ago, Dr. Wilkinson had pronounced her "better"!

Gabriel had also convinced Ruskin that for her own sake he wished Lizzie to leave London, "was deeply anxious," as Ruskin told Acland, "to get her out of town and out of the element that grieves her, but at present he can find no companion for her." Did Acland know, Ruskin asked, amongst his Devonshire peasantry (for Acland had an estate in Devonshire), "a kind woman in some pretty place by the sea-shore who could take charge of her? I should not think," he innocently added, "she was wayward or troublesome; I have only seen her twice, but she has a perfectly gentle expression, and I don't think Rossetti would have given his soul to her unless she had been both gentle and good. She has more the look of a Florentine fifteenth-century lady than anything I ever saw out of a fresco. . . ." For Ruskin, despite his own recent bitter experience, still believed that a gentle face necessarily denoted a gentle heart, and that women were naturally nobler and better than men.

Into so moving, so noble a cause, good Dr. Acland at once flung himself with characteristic energy. There was much cogitation, much writing of Acland to Ruskin and explanation from Ruskin to Acland: "Rossetti first got her to sit to him for his higher female faces, and thus found out her talent for drawing, taught her, and got attached to her, and now she is dying unless the rest and change of scene can save her. She is five and twenty." (According to William she should at this time have been not more that twenty-two or three, but everything about Lizzie was indeterminate.) And, hiding even from Acland his own generosity, Ruskin represented Lizzie to him as having a sufficient private income to support herself in simple comfort.

For Acland there could of course, in the first place, be only one solution to the problem of Lizzie, the inevitable solution with Acland—she must come to him at Oxford. But obstinate, primitive, stupid Lizzie no more wished to go to Oxford than she had wished to accept a pension, and Ruskin had again to write exquisitely chivalrous, gently persuasive epistles to Lizzie as to a peevish child: "Only once put your tongue out and let him feel your pulse." And again, after a decent interval Lizzie capitulated.

There was however, a difficulty. A new and exquisite sense of social decorum as understood by the mid-Victorians had suddenly descended upon the once intrepid lovers who, but a year before, had defied convention by living in the same house at Hastings. Someone must accompany Lizzie to Oxford. Who should it be? Ruskin, who did not know them, suggested one of Lizzie's sisters. Gabriel, who probably had no wish for Lizzie's sisters to accompany her to Oxford, volunteered "to take charge" of Lizzie on the journey if no sister were available, and this, in the event, he did.

At Oxford, the poor, sick, beautiful, golden-haired model of Mr. Rossetti the artist, Ruskin's new protégé was, as she herself complained, almost smothered in kindness and sympathy. Even Gabriel, visiting her from time to time, and rejoicing far more than Lizzie herself in the courtesies shown her, thought people

"too kind, for they bothered her greatly with attentions."
Nevertheless, he observed with satisfaction that Dr. Acland, who
wished her to settle in Oxford, introduced her "into all the best
society." Gabriel also declared as he had done a year before at
Hastings: "All the women are immensely fond of her." The
men, however, were the most attentive, and Lizzie seems ever
to have been happier amongst men. With the Oxford dons as
with Ruskin, Lizzie produced an effect, and they excelled
themselves in gallantry. The Warden of New College—"a great
swell" said Gabriel—lavished attentions upon her, showed her
the finest manuscripts in the Bodleian, and (obviously in the
course of a discussion of Preraphaelite "truth to nature"),
compared, to Lizzie's intense disgust, a black beetle painted by
Albert Durer with a living beetle brought up from some
domestic supply in his own kitchen.

Meanwhile, Dr. Acland's medical attentions were constant
and gratuitous. His report was in strange contrast to that of the
nameless, distinguished pessimist in London, which had so
stimulated Ruskin to good deeds. Instead of extensive tuberculosis and imminent death, he doubted whether the lungs of
the supposedly dying Lizzie were unhealthy at all! The true
cause of her illness, he declared, was "mental power long pent
up and lately over-taxed!" It was a strange diagnosis. Perhaps
he meant that Lizzie was suffering from what we should now
call nervous or neurotic disease; if so, he was probably correct
despite the quaint form in which he expressed it. Lizzie must,
he declared, to avoid serious consequences, move at once to the
South of France before the cold weather came. But in all this
was no suggestion of imminent or remote death.

Dr. Acland thought Lizzie "a kindly, gentle, quiet person."
He was pleased to help her and equally pleased to mitigate
Rossetti's fears. She made the doctor accept one of her water-
colours, representing the churchyard among the mountains in
Wordsworth's *We are Seven*. "That a girl brought up in London,
within a street or two of the Elephant and Castle, should have
selected such a subject and executed it from pure imagination,"
made it, for the doctor, "most remarkable." So late as 1903
it still hung in his daughter's drawing-room, "a strange and
somewhat weird arrangement of colours," as Dr. Acland's

biographer remarked. Certainly upon good Dr. Acland Lizzie
made an enduring impression. "I often think of you," he wrote
to Rossetti, eleven years later, after Lizzie's death; "I look at
the photograph *she* gave me of some sheep, now so faded that
you can scarce see the outlines even of the flock." Mrs. Acland
was less enthusiastic than her husband about Lizzie. Indeed the
relations between the two women seem to have been less
pleasant. "I don't know exactly how that wilful Ida"—Ruskin
had given Lizzie the name of Tennyson's "Princess"— "has
behaved to you," Ruskin wrote to Mrs. Acland in reply to
some complaint. "As far as I can make out, she is not ungrateful but sick, and sickly headstrong—much better however for
what Henry (Dr. Acland) has done for her."

If Mrs. Acland thought more than she said about Lizzie,
Ruskin too was by this time revising his first opinion of Gabriel.
At first all had gone well. From Allingham, to whom he had
sent them for advice, Gabriel had next extracted his verse
translations from mediaeval Italian poetry, in order to send
them to Ruskin, who would, he hoped, persuade some publisher
"to shell out something for them in a lump," and so encourage
him to complete the volume. Ruskin, after reading them carefully, urged Gabriel to omit some of the love poems which he
thought wearisome through sameness, advised "entire clearness
of modern and unantiquated expression," and prophesied:
"the book will be an interesting and popular one, if you will
rid it from crudities." It was on May 10th that Gabriel,
lending the manuscripts of his poems to Ruskin, made a false
and precipitate move. Forgetting that less than a month before,
Ruskin had granted Lizzie a virtual pension of £150 a year,
that twelve days later Ruskin had acted similarly to Rossetti
himself, that he had paid them the first instalments and undertaken the expenses of Lizzie's holiday, Gabriel now calmly
asked Ruskin (as he had already asked MacCracken, and would
henceforth ask every patron, to the end of his life), for an
advance payment upon a picture.

The orderly Ruskin, expecting gratitude rather than a new
request, and depleted by his recent generosity which he had
hidden from his parents, was inconvenienced and annoyed by
the cool and unexpected demand. To Rossetti he sent a note

explaining his position, together with another enabling him to obtain the money, but requested him not to do so until his picture was finished, "unless it is really a question of sheriff's officers." To this Gabriel sent a reply which brought from Ruskin a slightly irritated consent to the demand-note's being used, and concluded, in reference to Rossetti's gloomy allusions to its being his birthday: "Now have done talking about efforts, and get up instead of down. I only wish it were *my* 27th birthday." The inevitable battle between the two egoists was already joined.

Already Ruskin was beginning to suspect that his two protégés would be a nuisance. He had wished to make their pathway smoother, to set their feet on the right road, to issue from time to time such directions as they needed, to be obeyed, and to have the satisfaction of witnessing Lizzie's restoration to health and Gabriel's artistic success. That their gratitude would inevitably follow he had not for a moment doubted. Unfortunately whatever gratitude they felt to him did not result in obedience to his wishes. Both Gabriel and Lizzie were obstinate and headstrong, both would go their own way. Even Lizzie, he found, was not to be managed as one might try to control a sick or tired child. Chivalrous speeches, gallantry, cajolery were all lost upon her where it was a question of her will against his own, and Gabriel in all attempts by Ruskin at advice or persuasion was quite impossible. It was all turning out quite differently from what Ruskin had anticipated. The last thing he desired was to burden himself with human relationships involving perpetual problems, especially sordid, squalid, unfamiliar problems caused by poverty and sickness. In his own life he had had no such experiences and they disgusted him. Worries of this kind hindered his work: the calm, detached love of art, the writing of books about it.

"I find trying to be of any use to people is the most wearying thing possible," he complained to Mrs. Acland. "The true secret of happiness would be to bolt one's gates, lie on the grass all day, take care not to eat too much dinner, and buy as many Turners as one could afford. These geniuses are all alike, little and big. I have known five of them—Turner, Watts, Millais, Rossetti, and this girl—and I don't know which was, or which is, wrong-headedest. I am with them like the old woman who lived in the shoe, only that I don't want to send them to bed, and can't whip them—or else that is what they all want. Poor Turner went to bed before I expected, and 'broth without bread' the rest are quite as likely to get, as with it, if that would do them any good." To Lizzie, to whom he had promised to send books, obviously to educate her a little, he wrote in similar though milder vein. "The difficulty is to keep you quiet and yet to give you means of passing the time with some degree of pleasure yourself. You inventive people pay dearly for your power— there is no knowing how to manage you. One thing is very certain, that Rossetti will never be happy or truly powerful till he gets over that habit of his of doing nothing but what 'interests him'—and you must also try and read the books I am going to send you, which you know are to be chosen from among the most uninteresting I can find."

But Lizzie, no more amenable than Rossetti, soon left Oxford; precipitately, one suspects, ignoring remonstrances. Even them anuscripts and black beetles could not detain her. The sudden propriety of her relations with Gabriel at the time of Ruskin's first interest in her as suddenly disappeared. In June she was taking a short holiday at Clevedon. There Gabriel joined her. Two or three days they passed together, which Gabriel found "very delightful." They visited Arthur Hallam's grave and thought of Tennyson's *In Memoriam*. They made long excursions into the surrounding country, and found it charming. They pulled golden water-flags. And Lizzie, perhaps as a relief from the strain of Oxford, had a donkey-ride. It was in short a classical pastoral, Daphnis and Chloe, with Victorian decorations. On June 25th they returned to town. They brought the golden water-flags with them, and Gabriel planted them on his balcony over the river. Lizzie, back in town, found herself rather better. But, following Dr. Acland's directions, she would leave again shortly, to winter in the South of France.

IV

STRIFE
1855–1856

Ope not thy lips, thou foolish one,
    Nor turn to me thy face:
The blasts of heaven shall strike me down
    Ere I will give thee grace.

Love and Hate E. SIDDAL

RUSKIN SOON WITNESSED the results of his benevolence with dismay. He had forgotten that freedom from poverty meant also freedom from its discipline. But Gabriel and Lizzie did not forget. Instead of painting better, as Ruskin had intended, they now hardly painted at all. Social distractions, theatres, circuses, gossips with friends, were to them a flowery pathway more alluring than the stony one of art. Gabriel in fact now behaved exactly as he had done in youth despite his father's remonstrances, on receiving payment for his first attempts in painting. Old friends, Woolner, Munro and the rest, having heard doubtless of Ruskin's generosity, suddenly reappeared at Chatham Place, and night after night throughout that summer of 1855 a little group would linger on Rossetti's balcony overhanging the river, talking—long after Gabriel's favourite refreshment of ices and strawberries had been consumed—until dawn.

Brown now remarked another change—Lizzie's clothes! "Beautifully dressed for about £3, altogether looking like a queen," he described her enthusiastically. Gabriel thought so too; was again held by Lizzie's physical attraction. At three o'clock one morning he showed Brown "a drawer full of 'Guggums,'" as Brown himself described them, "God knows how many, but not bad work, I should say, for the six years he has known her; it is like a monomania with him." It was in fact a monomania, and one which his friends must share or risk excommunication. He quarrelled with his nearest friends and relatives about Lizzie, was cold to Stephens on hearing that he had spoken "irreverentially"—Brown's word—of her, and to

Christina "because"—and again Brown—"she and 'Guggums' do not agree." Christina, though unapproving, would not actively oppose her brother's uncertain, fluctuating passion, but Brown, like Gabriel, noticed Christina's significant silence. "She works at worsted ever," wrote Brown, "and talks sparingly!"

Financially independent, admired by all, Lizzie was no longer obscure, submissive, as in the old days when, model for Millais's drowned Ophelia, she had lain, fully dressed, in a bath of water, remaining there without complaining even when the lamps heating it had gone out, and had caught cold rather than interrupt the painter who, of course, was unaware of what had happened. Now, her new importance, and above all perhaps, the influence of Emma Brown, Ford Madox Brown's wife, an old friend of Lizzie's family, were making her self-assertive. She began to resent more than ever Gabriel's long delay, to demand immediate marriage. The once "gentle dove" turned bitter, even violent towards her lover, and quarrels between them became common. Into these disputes the Browns were quickly drawn. Lizzie was always with Emma Brown now, her only woman friend; and Gabriel, not without reason, blamed Emma for the change in Lizzie; accusing her of "setting Lizzie against him." Brown and Lizzie rushed into the field to defend Emma, and the vulgar squabbles were intensified.

Whenever Ruskin called at Chatham Place now he found idleness and disorder. The Browns were always there too. Lizzie and Emma would be half-dressed or still in bed, late in the day. Emma's baby would be crying, Brown in shirt sleeves, smoking his pipe in Rossetti's studio while Gabriel held forth on art and poetry. Believing Brown a bad artist and his influence a bad one for Rossetti, Ruskin was rude to Brown, while Brown, unpraised and contemptuous of Ruskin as critic, would reply with equal rudeness and ostentatiously leave the room. Ruskin, Gabriel complained, would then begin "sticking pins" into Rossetti himself, "for a couple of hours every three days." Lizzie, under Emma's influence, Ruskin saw, would soon reduce Gabriel to complete frustration, as Emma was reducing Brown. His determination to separate Lizzie and Gabriel at all costs, as they would not marry, increased. Lizzie, he decided (ostensibly of course for the sake of her health), must set out on her travels without delay.

For once, Lizzie proved amenable to advice, and preparations for her departure were quickly completed. A cousin of Gabriel's, a Mrs. Kincaid, wife of a solicitor, was conveniently discovered, and agreed to become Lizzie's companion; "so this," wrote Gabriel, once more sensitive to social convention, "might render my joining the party possible." In the stress of impending departure, Gabriel paid his first visit to Lizzie's home, her "native crib" as he called it, which he remarked, "I was glad to find comfortable." There, however, only Lizzie's sister was visible. Gabriel invited his mother to join Lizzie, himself and Mrs. Kincaid at tea on Saturday, September 25th. The next morning at 7 o'clock, Lizzie and her companion set sail for Le Havre and—somewhat indeterminately—"the South."

Restless after Lizzie's departure, Gabriel would soon have joined her, despite Ruskin's strong opposition, but was too hard up. In the circumstances then, he proceeded to find other distractions. He took Brown and Emma out to dinners and theatres, examined Giotto tracings at the Crystal Palace, went to art exhibitions with his artist friend Lowes Dickinson. Erratic as ever, he would leave Brown vainly waiting for him at some unkept rendezvous, "because," as Brown crossly explained in his diary, "he must go again that night to see a certain stunner"—Miss Herbert the actress—"a discovery of D. G. Rossetti. She is lovely." Gabriel thought so too.

Rossetti called on the Brownings now in London. They would soon be returning to Florence, and he thought they might be useful to Lizzie if she went there. Four years had passed since in his early enthusiasm for the anonymous *Pauline*, Gabriel had written to Browning in Venice asking if he were not the author, and had received a short note in reply, confirming his belief. A year later, Allingham had introduced him to Browning who, before quitting London, had returned the call. Ruskin's praise of his new protégé was already having an effect. Gabriel was now known as "leader" of the Preraphaelites, a clever young man who had published a few striking poems in magazines and painted some beautiful water-colours. Browning received him well, even quoted, to Gabriel's pleased surprise, *The Blessed Damozel*, and a few days later appeared in Gabriel's studio. Rossetti made the most of his visit, tactfully showing him his unfinished *Kate the Queen* (borrowed from Aunt Charlotte for the occasion), and Lizzie's *Pippa Passes*, both of course, themes from Browning's own verse. He even began a water-colour portrait of the poet, which, however, Browning's departure for Paris soon interrupted. As Gabriel wished, Browning, before leaving, expressed a strong desire to meet the inimitable Lizzie herself.

At the Brownings', Gabriel on two successive evenings met Tennyson, who was spending a few days in town. They had not met, apparently, since Patmore had introduced them in the early days of the Brotherhood. Rossetti, despite a sincere appreciation of many qualities in Tennyson and in his poetry, was soon conscious of an unintentionally comic element. The first of the two meetings was on the evening of the Sunday, September 26th, on which Lizzie had set out on her journey; the next was on the following night. On this second occasion Tennyson read *Maud* "through from end to end" as Mrs. Browning, with a significant particularity of emphasis, informed her sister. Browning, not to be outdone, had followed with his own *Fra Lippo Lippi*. William Rossetti and one or two other persons were also present. It was an exhausting evening, and Gabriel early relapsed into making a surreptitious sketch of Tennyson as he read. For Gabriel on reading *Maud* had been disappointed; found it "very great of course but seems an odd De Balzackish sort of story for an Englishman at Tennyson's age," and, after reflection, "some very like rubbish."

Having opened his second bottle of port and claimed his special privilege of smoking his pipe in the drawing-room, Tennyson, like some short-sighted lion with massive mane, his book held close to his eyes, had sat on the sofa beside his fragile hostess with her whimsical, unlovely face framed in "curls like the pendent ears of a water-spaniel, and poor little hands, so thin that when she welcomed you she gave you something like the foot of a young bird," as the irrepressible Locker[1] once described her. And hour after hour Tennyson, in his

---

[1] Frederick Locker (1821–95), who became Locker-Lampson in 1885.

deep, sonorous, emotional voice had declaimed *Maud*, commenting from time to time: "There's a wonderful touch! That's very tender! How beautiful that is!" And as he read the lyrics and pathetic passages, he let the tears roll unchecked down his cheeks, in complete surrender to the beauty of sorrow, while Gabriel in his corner, quietly, secretly, made his sketch. Tennyson, fortunately, for he would have been much annoyed, never learned of its existence. Gabriel, however, made a copy of it for Lizzie and then gave the original to Browning.

Rossetti laughed at Tennyson's egotism and fear of criticism, at his endless "groanings and horrors over the reviews of *Maud*," at the resentment anonymous, depreciatory letters aroused in him. " 'And no name,' says Alfred, scoring the table with an indignant thumb, and glancing round with suspended pipe, while his auditors look as sympathetic as their view of the matter permits," wrote Gabriel, in a delightful account of the evening, an account which, however, the editor of Rossetti's letters to Allingham was obliged to omit because he was warned by Tennyson's son that publication would "be the death" of Tennyson's widow.

That night, certainly, comedy ruled to the end. Gabriel accompanied Tennyson on his homeward way, and on their passing the Holborn Casino, "What's that place?" asked Tennyson. On learning what it was, Tennyson suggested going in, but on the doorstep sorrowfully turned away, remembering that he might be seen by some Press reporter, and if his presence were mentioned in any of the daily journals, lose his reputation and clientèle in a night! Nevertheless, Rossetti found Tennyson "quite as glorious in his way as Browning, and perhaps of the two even more impressive on the whole personally." Mrs. Browning he admired for her gracious, self-sacrificing hospitality, and thought "delightfully unliterary." Mrs. Browning described to Mrs. Tennyson, in a characteristically gushing epistle, all superlatives and underlinings, the Laureate's visit as "an increase of joy and life for us ever"; and in another letter, to her own sister, "dearest dear Henrietta: I didn't get to bed . . . till three o'clock in the morning. So that altogether I nearly died of the joy of it!"

Shortly afterwards, Gabriel received from Lizzie an urgent

request for money. Instead of fleeing to the warm south as ordered, Lizzie—no better now than Gabriel—fascinated by the shops of Paris, had stayed there and was bankrupt. For once, Gabriel showed himself a man of action. He worked night and day, painted a *Paolo and Francesca* within a week, got thirty-five guineas for it from Ruskin on behalf of a Miss Heaton of Leeds, and ignoring Ruskin's angry remonstrances, and refusing a request to give six lectures on Italian Art at Owen's College, Manchester, set off with his sculptor friend Munro for Paris, on a pretext of seeing the Great Exhibition there, which was about to close.

To the exhibition, in fact, he devoted but one day; "my head," he explained, "not being a teetotum nor my mind an old clothes shop." Only the paintings there interested him. He found Millais and Hunt "marvels and omens," Delacroix, "one of the mighty ones of the earth, and Ingres misses being so creditably." Rossetti, who had done nothing in oils for years, must have felt out of the race.

Lizzie's fluctuating hold upon Gabriel seemed stronger again in Paris. Munro, feeling irritatingly supererogatory, described Gabriel there as "every day with his sweetheart of whom he is more foolishly fond than I ever saw lover. Great affection is ever so to the mere looker-on I suppose. Well! Well!" But Lizzie was ill again, unable to leave her lodgings.

So too was Mrs. Browning, "fallen" as she told her sister, "upon evil days and yellow satin sofas in the Rue de Grenelle —due east in aspect, and with draughts flying about like frantic birds." There was cholera in Florence, so the Brownings awaited in Paris a more propitious day. Unwell and unhappy, Mrs. Browning, who did not like the French capital, was avoiding society. "We have been lying *perdus* in our hole, hiding from the face of men and women," she wrote, "and seeing nobody except such as we fell upon by chance and couldn't help speaking to—Sir Edward Lytton for instance—and Rossetti; the chief of the pre-Raphaelites in England." Once started, Gabriel's reputation as "leader" was largely becoming established—to the growing indignation of the Brotherhood.

Unaware of the Brownings' anti-social mood, Gabriel assiduously frequented the Rue de Grenelle. At the Louvre,

Browning surprised him by his knowledge of early Italian art —"beyond that of any one I ever met—encyclopaedically beyond that of Ruskin himself." Gabriel completed Browning's portrait begun in London, and, having brought with him a copy of the poet's latest volume, *Men and Women*, he got Browning to autograph it. In the Rue de Grenelle he met Browning's father and "a miraculous French critic named Milsand." Lizzie as usual, remained outside the social scene; unwell, she stayed in her rooms, met Browning only once for a few minutes when he called, and did not meet Mrs. Browning at all.

But this happy interlude in Paris soon ended. The bright, sad autumn days in the beautiful city, with russet and gold leaves falling in the Luxembourg gardens and before the crowded "terrasses" of the restaurants on the "grands boulevards," quickly sped. November was near its close. Winter was coming. Lizzie must fly south—to Nice it was now decided. Gabriel saw her off at the Paris station, watched sorrowfully the red-gold hair that had ensnared his heart and his life fade away into the distance, then turned away, and a day or two later was back in London's soft greyness of late autumn fog and rain. He had returned in serious, even sombre mood, to judge by the sonnet, *Dawn on the Night Journey*, which William, no doubt correctly, believed Gabriel wrote while re-crossing the Channel:

> When the last
> Of the sun's hours to-day shall be fulfilled,
> There shall another breath of time be stilled
> For me, which now is to my senses cast
> As much beyond me as eternity,
> Unknown, kept secret. On the newborn air
> The moth quivers in silence. It is vast,
> Yea, even beyond the hills, upon the sea,
> The day whose end shall give this hour as sheer
> As chaos, to the irrevocable Past.

Alone in Chatham Place, he hung his portrait of Browning over the chimney-piece, then set off to convert the sceptical Ruskin into an ardent admirer of Browning's poetry.

But Ruskin was less friendly now. In six short months Gabriel and Lizzie had too often disappointed him. His romantic benevolence was rapidly cooling into a critical realism. Gabriel, idling with the Browns and with "stunners," far more eager to obtain advance payments than to finish pictures, had again vexed him by ignoring his requests to complete and send him a *Nativity*. Next, refusing to go to Wales and paint a picture for Ruskin, who offered to pay his expenses, he had asked to be given the money to join Lizzie in Paris instead, and when Ruskin refused he had turned sulky. To Rossetti's ill-mannered request Ruskin had returned a sharper reply than any before: "I am ill-tempered to-day," he wrote, "You are such absurd creatures both of you. I don't say you do wrong, because you don't seem to know what is wrong, but just to do whatever you like as far as possible, as puppies and tomtits do." And he had forbidden Gabriel to go to Paris at all, telling him to order Lizzie south immediately, as Acland had directed. "Paris," he cried, "will kill her, or ruin her, like Sir J. Paul's Bank"— a reference to a recent financial disaster.

He was now almost as angry with Lizzie as with Gabriel. She was proving as unreliable, as spendthrift as her lover. Instead of going south at once she had stayed in Paris and spent all her money in the Paris shops. Then, just as Gabriel had begun to settle down she had disturbed him with an urgent request for more funds. Shortly before her departure, certainly, Gabriel had borrowed from her all the money she had saved from Ruskin's pension. Immediately afterwards, however, to "set her dear mind at ease," he had worked frantically at a *Vision of Rachel and Leah*, a *Launcelot and Guinevere* and a third water-colour, all for Ruskin, and had thus been able to send her abroad with £40 in her purse, which should have been ample until Ruskin's next quarterly payment should reach her. Yet this was the result!

Ruskin, in his disgust, fled to the neurotic's refuge, illness; was "mighty poorly," as he told Gabriel, although it was "nothing serious," he declared, "but bed, feverish nights, toast and water and physic." He resumed the quarrel about the *Nativity*, ordering his protégé to "take all the green out of the flesh" and "try to get it a little less like worsted-work by Wednesday, when I will send for it." *The Passover* also must be sent to him at once, "in such state as it may be in." When

Gabriel retorted with an offer to terminate both his own and
Lizzie's agreement with Ruskin, the critic replied in a more
paternally reproachful vein—"You and Ida are a couple of
—never mind—but you know it's all *your own pride*—not a bit
of fine feeling, so don't think it. If you wanted to oblige *me*,
you would keep your room in order and go to bed at night.
All your fine speeches go for nothing till you do that."

The next occasion of dispute had been more serious; was,
in fact, a bit of sharp financial practice by Gabriel upon Miss
Heaton of Leeds and even on Ruskin himself. A *Beatrice Denies
Dante Her Salutation* which Miss Heaton had commissioned, so
appealed to Ruskin that with her consent he took it for himself.
But seeing that Gabriel's substitute, *Dante's Dream*, was much
inferior, he generously offered to pay more, on condition that
an equal deduction was made from the price of the *Dante's
Dream* for Miss Heaton. But soon he discovered that Gabriel
had accepted the increase without making any reduction to
Miss Heaton as agreed. Earlier disputes with Ruskin had ended
with the latter's carriage reappearing at Chatham Place to
take Gabriel and Lizzie to dine at Denmark Hill; but now,
in deeper disgust, he withdrew. "I am a good deal puzzled
about this matter in various ways," he replied to Gabriel's
unconvincing explanation, and, after cancelling his "lessons"
in painting, "Please apologise to William very heartily for this
rudeness," he added, to show that William was not implicated,
"but I shall enjoy you both so much more when this thing is
off my mind." Immediately afterwards, in response to Lizzie's
note, Gabriel, having raised the wind, had dashed off to join
his bankrupt love in Paris. On this, Ruskin's opinion of the
couple sank lower than before.

Already he was wearying of them; of their unreliability, their
chronic, irremediable poverty, their irregular ways, their continual requests for financial aid, and above all, perhaps, of their
unyielding independence. Since his rash offer to buy all they
had to sell, he had complained of increased haste, carelessness,
lack of finish, in Gabriel's paintings. Lizzie, it appeared, was
now too ill to paint at all, too foolish to follow the doctor's—
and Ruskin's—orders to go south, preferred to lose health and
money in Paris. And now, this last proof of Gabriel's unscrupu-

lousness made Ruskin fear that to bring Rossetti into contact
with patrons would endanger his own personal relations and
reputation.

Gabriel's short absence in Paris meant at least a break in
the bickering, and upon his return their relations, for a time,
improved. At Christmas, Gabriel sent for Ruskin's approval,
Lizzie's last letter—from Nice. There, so she said, the unwelcome attentions of "bores," had forced her to dine in her own
room for the last three weeks. "First-class," she wrote with her
habitual plaintive self-consciousness, "one can get to the end
of the world; but one can never be let alone or left at rest."
Attempting something like Gabriel's broad and boisterous
humour, she achieved only a lamentable exhibition of insular
and ill-bred wit, of which the *chef d'oeuvre* was a comparison
of a post office clerk behind his *guichet* in Nice to "an overdone
mutton chop sticking to a grid-iron." Without the embellishment of Lizzie's rose-leaf and gold, her letter is but melancholy
reading. Gabriel's wit often posed as vulgarity, but that is not
vulgarity posing as wit. Ruskin, on receiving the letter, could
and did say but little, dexterously evaded approval by concentrating in his note of acknowledgment upon the evils of
the continental passport system, of which, like all good
Englishmen of the time, he, Gabriel and Lizzie strongly
disapproved.

Ruskin's one source of satisfaction was that, as he had hoped,
separation from Lizzie had helped Rossetti to work. Lizzie's
need of money, Gabriel's comparative tranquillity and freedom
from interruptions, had led him before the close of 1855, to
concentrate upon his water colours. He had, he declared, done
more during that year than for long before, and believed his
work was improving. Brown, watching his progress, rejoiced.
"His forte," he said, "and he seems now to have found it out,
is to be a lyrical painter and poet and certainly a glorious one."
That was an idea, the conception of making a reputation as
a "poetic painter," a creator of painted poetry, which specially
appealed to Rossetti.

At the close of 1855 the needy Brown observed another result
of Ruskin's benevolence. Gabriel, he confided to his diary,
"such a swell as I never saw before, but looking really splendid,

everything about him in perfect taste except his *shoes*; it will be some time before he goes that length. Otherwise his brown suit was most in the fashion; he looked handsome and a gentleman, talking of buying a 'ticker,' but not of paying me back my £15, alas!" That same night Brown's chimney caught fire. Abandoning the unwonted luxury of a cigar, Brown climbed on to the roof to stuff a blanket down the chimney while Gabriel, not to be outdone in an emergency, raked the live coals out of Brown's grate and spread them over his new Kidderminster carpet. He was surprised and a little hurt to find Brown upon his return to the room less grateful than he had expected!

The new year, 1856, soon brought new occasions of dispute between Gabriel and Ruskin. Rossetti found Ruskin's attitude of half-playful criticism, as of an indulgent schoolmaster towards a clever, wayward child, irritating. Even Ruskin's exhibition of Gabriel's works to potential patrons could not reconcile him to the continuous stream of commands, criticisms, exhortations and advice which the critic poured over him. Thus, for example, Ruskin's peremptory order to Gabriel to put "a dab of Chinese white into the hole in the cheek" of Beatrice, coupled with a snub for Patmore's praise of it and some sneering criticisms by Ruskin himself, merely resulted in Rossetti's erasing the whole offending head. Ruskin, calling in Gabriel's absence and finding it, went into a real or pretended rage, carried off the *Passover*, lest Gabriel spoil that also, and demanded the return of the headless *Beatrice* on the ground that Rossetti would not be fit to touch it for some time. Then, when at last the *Beatrice* was finished, Ruskin grumbled, asked Gabriel to sell it if possible elsewhere, and, when Rossetti in turn grew angry, playfully, even paternally, admonished him for being "a conceited monkey, thinking your pictures right when I tell you positively they are wrong. What do you know about the matter, I should like to know?"

Ruskin also revenged himself by criticizing Rossetti's clumsy, ineffectual endeavours to paint another picture in oils, *St. Catherine*, and advised him to attempt one from his early design *The Magdalene*—commissioned by MacCracken three years before but not yet begun—which Ruskin now wanted for himself.

Unable to handle a brush, yet always much wiser than the artists, Ruskin really wanted to paint by proxy. "I never, so long as I live, will trust you to do anything out of my sight," he told Gabriel. For if Rossetti was blind to the limitations of the artist, Ruskin was certainly not less so to those of the critic.

Nor was Ruskin allowed to forget his protégés' financial need. Abroad, Lizzie showed a chronic impecuniosity worthy of her lover, who, penniless through assisting her, did not hesitate to appeal to Ruskin to help her also, and, by a species of black-mail—the threat of Lizzie's immediate return—forced Ruskin not only to send money himself, but even to appeal on Lizzie's behalf to Miss Heaton. Drawn upon for innumerable "advance payments," probably also for the settlement of Gabriel's debts as well as of Lizzie's, Ruskin at length jibbed, advising Rossetti to sell some of his paintings elsewhere and so raise money in other quarters. Besides, Ruskin was "almost certain Ida, or Ida's travelling incubus of a companion, will have more debts than they say. People are always afraid to say all at once," he declared, "hence it is best to be prepared for the worst." With such dependants, bluntness had long since, and neces-sarily, replaced Ruskin's earlier, exquisite courtesy. That was true also of Lizzie and her "travelling incubus of a companion," Mrs. Kincaid. Relations had become strained between them, and William Rossetti, recalling their journey in later years, believed they had separated before Lizzie left Nice.

With the coming of the spring of 1856, Gabriel's longing for the absent Lizzie increased, and he sent her a valentine which gives us the best glimpse left to us of life in Chatham Place during these years.

> Yesterday was St. Valentine.
> Thought you at all, dear love divine,
> Upon the beard in sorry trim
> And rueful countenance of him
> That Orson who's your Valentine?
>
> He daubed, you know, as usual.
> The stick would slip, the brush would fall:
> Yet daubed he till the lamplighter
> Set those two seedy flames astir;
> But growled all day at slow St. Paul.

The bore was heard ere noon; the dun
Was at the door by half-past one;[1]
At least 'tis thought so, but the clock—
No Lizzie there to help its stroke—
Struck work before the day begun.

At length he saw St. Paul's bright orb
Flash back—the serried tide absorb
That burning West which is sucked up
 Like wine poured in a water-cup;
And one more twilight tones his daub.

Some time over the fire he sat,
So lonely that he missed his cat;
Then wildly rushed to dine on tick—
Nine minutes swearing for his stick,
And thirteen minutes for his hat.

And now another day is gone;
Once more that intellectual one
Desists from high-minded pursuits,
And hungry, staring at his boots,
Has not the strength to pull them on.[2]

Come back, dear Liz, and looking wise
In that arm-chair which suits your size,
Through some fresh drawing scrape a hole.
Your Valentine and Orson's soul
Is sad for those two friendly eyes.

A few days earlier, Hunt, after two years' wandering in
Palestine, had arrived in London, eager for news of Rossetti.
Gabriel, Brown told him, "was in Oxford, where the University 'had thrown themselves at his feet,' in recognition of his
poetic and artistic accomplishments." He "was not," Brown
added, "as some people said, engaged to Miss Siddal, but . . .
she stood in the position of pupil to him . . . had done some
designs of the most poetic character; and . . . had recently
been entertained by Dr. and Mrs. Acland at Oxford."

In the meantime, Ruskin's devotion to Lizzie had con-
spicuously declined. A reply to her, begun at the end of
January, he left unfinished until April with the sole apology:
"You and Rossetti have infected me with your ways of going

[1] cf. sup., p. 152.   [2] v. sup., p. 134.

PLATE VI

BEATRICE DENYING HER SALUTATION TO DANTE
BY D. G. ROSSETTI
1851

DANTE DRAWING AN ANGEL
BY D. G. ROSSETTI
1853

PLATE VII

ELIZABETH ELEANOR SIDDAL
BY D. G. ROSSETTI
c. 1854

on. Never did I leave a letter so long in hand before!" Headstrong as Gabriel, Lizzie had spoiled all Ruskin's plans for her welfare. Commands, appeals, cajoleries, all were vain. She wished to return. She would not visit Genoa or Turin, was unmoved by Ruskin's alluring descriptions of the "red campaniles, green and white torrents, purple-grey and russet rocks, deep green pines, white snows and blue valley distance" of Susa. He failed also to lure her to Switzerland, "all soft and pure air, clear water, mossy rock, and infinite flowers—I suppose you like that? If you do, write me word directly, and I will without fail in answer send you a letter of accurate advice; but it's no use my tiring myself if you are going to come home as fast as you can. . . . Now do be a 'good girl' and try Switzerland."

But all was of no avail. Lizzie would not be a "good girl," was fascinated by the splendour of Paris and Nice, not by the peaceful beauty-spots Ruskin loved, and despite his remonstrances, in Paris and Nice she remained. Perhaps Gabriel's valentine helped to draw the little cockney back from the brightness and glitter of the south to the old, drab London life she loved. At any rate, in time, neither natural beauties nor continental life could hold her, and early in May she was back again. Ruskin, leaving for Switzerland, sent Gabriel much advice and a word for Lizzie. "I must see Ida; I want to tell her one or two things about her way of study. I can't bear to see her missing her mark only by a few inches, which she might as easily win as not."

There was, perhaps, another, deeper reason for Lizzie's return. She was no better for her foreign wanderings. Her health, her strength, so at least she believed, were steadily declining. The weariness of her state, poor neurotic Lizzie with her copious self-pity, her love of mournful self-dramatization, sentimentally described in her verses entitled—not very happily—*Worn Out.*

> I can but give a sinking heart
> And weary eyes of pain,

she cried to her lover,

> A faded mouth that cannot smile
> And may not laugh again.

Surely Lizzie (then Gabriel's "gentle dove"), had been the theme of Christina's poem *Listening*, in 1854 :

> She listened like a cushat dove
>   That listens to its mate alone;
> She listened like a cushat dove
>   That loves but only one.
>
> Not fair as men would reckon fair,
> Nor noble as they count the line:
> Only as graceful as a bough
>   And tendrils of the vine:
> Only as noble as sweet Eve
>   Your ancestress and mine.
>
> And downcast were her dovelike eyes,
> And downcast was her tender cheek;
> Her pulses fluttered like a dove
>   To hear him speak.

It was, however, a very different Lizzie who returned to England in the spring of 1856, bent upon marriage and the ending of her ambiguous relation to Gabriel. Perhaps her sudden return was due to her having heard that during her absence, Rossetti was devoting his almost exclusive attention to Hunt's model for *The Awakened Conscience*, pretty Annie Miller. Eight months of independent, continental life, perhaps even the glances of the "bores" she had affected to despise, had wrought upon Lizzie's sense of inferiority, strengthening the effect of Ruskin's benevolence and of Emma Brown's mischievous persuasions, in setting a higher value upon herself.

To this new self-assertion Annie Miller was a challenge. Hunt, meaning to educate and marry Annie later, had left her in Gabriel's charge on going East. Annie had solemnly promised Hunt to sit to no artist during his absence, without his permission, and this he had granted to Gabriel alone. In place of gratitude, however, Gabriel not only persuaded her to sit to other artists, but also spent all his time with Annie, dining and dancing in restaurants and at the notorious Cremorne Gardens, until the voice of scandal was raised.

Immediately upon her return, Lizzie threw down the gage of battle, and in a short but intensive and masterly campaign routed the enemy. More hysterical than ever, Lizzie revealed

hitherto unsuspected combative qualities, relying particularly
upon violent and noisy demonstrations of disapproval, deeply
tinted with the local colour of her native Kennington Oval.
For amidst the stress of battle, the higher mental and social
qualities she had acquired in her association with Gabriel and
his friends, unconsciously gave place to the more primitive
culture of the Old Kent Road.

Lizzie's chief instigator and ally in this was Emma Brown,
who dragged her reluctant husband into the fray. For some
obscure reason Lizzie's rapprochment with the Rossetti family
had ceased as soon as begun, and her relation with Gabriel
was again more or less outside the pale of family recognition.
Emma and her husband, in their loyalty to Lizzie, now refused
Mrs. Rossetti's invitations to tea, and Lizzie in her need of
support and consolation haunted Emma's home, to the increasing disgust of Gabriel. But independent Lizzie, now—
thanks doubtless to Ruskin's generosity—in her own rooms in
Weymouth Street, at the corner of Charlotte Street, the street
of Rossetti's infancy—paid no heed to his protests, and her
intimacy with Emma increased.

From the preliminary skirmish to the culminating crisis, the
battles between Lizzie and Gabriel followed one single line
of development. The ostensible causes of strife varied, the technique seldom if ever changed. Mischievous Emma, for example,
would lead Lizzie to plan a holiday with Emma herself at
Ramsgate, would induce Lizzie to borrow money for it from
Brown, and so throw Gabriel into a rage. Or Lizzie would
complain to Emma that Gabriel ecstatically praised Annie
Miller, even to herself. The consequent "scenes" would terminate in the flight of Lizzie to the Browns, pursued by the
enraged, almost insane Gabriel. Lizzie would shriek and roll
on the carpet; Emma would be brought into the dispute, and
finally poor Brown would be dragged away from his painting
and brought in as his wife's defender. Their reconciliations
were as sudden, as neurotic as their hysterical frenzies. Sometimes Lizzie was pacified by a peace offering. "Supped at
Guggums," Brown recorded after one of these outbreaks;
"Gabriel has given her three pounds for a superb India opera
cloak, and they are for the Princess's [Theatre] to sport her

and it on Saturday." The increasing infantilism of such an existence was very obvious. Poor Brown, failing of course to see how much his wife was instigator, wearied of both Lizzie and Gabriel, just as Ruskin had done; of their constant interruption of his work, their sudden descents upon his home, their endless claims upon his hospitality and purse; for like Gabriel, Lizzie had now learned to borrow. And Brown cooled towards Rossetti.

The neurotic intensities of these passionate scenes found relief in verse. Gabriel's *Woodspurge*, written at this time, doubtless describes the aftermath of some such occasion:

> I had walked on at the wind's will—
> I sat now, for the wind was still.
>
> Between my knees my forehead was—
> My lips, drawn in, said not "Alas!"
> My hair was over in the grass,
> My naked ears heard the day pass.
>
> *   *   *
>
> From perfect grief there need not be
> Wisdom or even memory:
> One thing then learnt remains to me—
> The woodspurge has a cup of three.

Lizzie, meanwhile, yet more self-consciously dramatized herself:

> Gazing through the gloom like one
> Whose life and hopes are also done,
> Frozen like a thing of stone,

or crying as she contrasted the unhappy present with an idealized past:

> Can God bring back the day when we two stood
> Beneath the clinging trees in that dark wood?

For these incessant occasions of strife merely intensified the passionate interludes of the temperamental, self-conscious lovers, linked and inspired by a common morbidity.

Nor were Gabriel's and Lizzie's the sole poems describing these oppositions. Although Christina, cool, critical, self-contained and hiding her own now fading hope of an ideal love,

apparently saw little of either Gabriel or Lizzie, their con-
tentions must have been known to her, and must surely have
inspired the verses she wrote in mid-July, during the height
of the crisis occasioned by Annie Miller: *Look on this Picture
and on this:*

> I wish we once were wedded—then I must be true:
> You should hold my will in yours to do or to undo:
> But I hate myself now, Eva, when I look at you.
>
> You have seen her hazel eyes, her warm dark skin,
> Dark hair—but oh those hazel eyes a devil is dancing in;
> You, my saint, lead up to heaven, she lures down to sin.
>
> She's so redundant, stately; in truth now have you seen
> Ever, anywhere such beauty, such a stature, such a mien?
> She may be queen of devils, but she's every inch a queen.

The subject must have interested Christina, for the poem
was very long, originally in fact of "forty-six triplets" of which
William Rossetti published only half. The poem describes the
perplexity of a man drawn by two loves, a spiritual and a
sensual passion. The "higher" love was named "Eva." "Were
it not for the name Eva," wrote the presumably puzzled
William, in a curiously ambiguous note, "I should be embarrassed to guess what could have directed my sister's pen to so
singular a subject and treatment; but that name satisfies me
that she was here recurring to a favourite romancist of her
girlhood, Maturin. In Maturin's novel *Women* there is a per-
sonage Eva, and a situation which must certainly have
prompted the present poem." To be "embarrassed to guess"
does not necessarily imply ignorance; it may indeed imply an
inconvenient certainty. Occasionally in his loyalty to his
brother's memory, William purposely employed ambiguous
forms of statement. That without any directive influence from
actual life, Christina at the age of twenty-five, should suddenly
look back and write an inordinately long and impetuous poem
on an incident in a melodramatic, long forgotten novel of her
early youth, would be no less strange than William's suggestion
that Gabriel's adolescent poems of self-conflict merely described
how he wrote poetry and how he hesitated between poetry and
painting. But even if we admit that Christina was inspired by

Maturin's mediocre novel rather than only slightly influenced by it, the obvious reference to actuality must have been present in her mind. To believe otherwise is to deprive a conspicuously gifted woman of even common intelligence.

The first stage of Lizzie's campaign closed with the attainment of its objective in September 1856, if the report was true which Mrs. Patmore then sent to a friend, that Gabriel, and also William Rossetti, were both engaged. She refused, however, to mention names, lest the rumour be false, incidentally showing that even after the long years of their association, and despite William Rossetti's talk of their having been engaged some four years before, Lizzie at this present time certainly enjoyed no general recognition as Rossetti's prospective wife.

By the early autumn, with another relapse in health, Lizzie actually brought Gabriel to contemplate marriage—much as he had once contemplated the railway telegraph at Nine Elms! He would marry her at once, he decided, and take her for a cure to Algeria, the latest health resort, where Barbara Smith was now nursing a sister. He told Brown, who wanted to go to bed, all about it at half-past three one morning, for he was much troubled. But Lizzie declined Algeria, and Gabriel declined marriage until money he awaited for a picture should arrive. And when the money did arrive he still evaded marriage. Lizzie, now a red-haired fury, thereupon fled to Bath, swearing to leave the worthless fellow for ever.

Once again they ran through the old, habitual circuit of emotions, and when early in December, Gabriel arrived in Bath, harmony was immediately though only temporarily restored. "Bath has been a mud-bath ever since I came," Gabriel genially informed Brown: "Lizzie, you will be glad to hear is rather better than when last in London, and not quite so thin." She "has been," he told Allingham, "most terribly ill a month or two ago, but is now somewhat better again."

Christina, who through disappointed romance had become a realist, was not blind to the contrast between her brother's early, radiant idealization of Lizzie and the fading, wearied, embittered woman now fighting desperately to be made his wife. On Christmas Eve, 1856, in a sonnet entitled *In an Artist's*

Studio, Christina expressed, delicately, yet truly, her sense of this contrast between a lost alluring vision and a stale reality:

> One face looks out from all his canvases,
>   One selfsame figure sits or walks or leans:
>   We found her hidden just behind those screens,
> That mirror gave back all her loveliness.
> A queen in opal or in ruby dress,
>   A nameless girl in freshest summer-greens,
>   A saint, an angel—every canvas means
> The same one meaning, neither more nor less.
>
> He feeds upon her face by day and night,
>   And she with true, kind eyes looks back on him,
> Fair as the moon and joyful as the light;
>   Not wan with waiting, nor with sorrow dim;
> Not as she is, but was when hope shone bright;
>   Not as she is, but as she fills his dream.

Gabriel now retreated, as ever before unhappy circumstance, into his habitual protective lethargy, a coma that was almost sleep. His frustration, his weariness in the presence of a still coldly angry Lizzie found unconscious expression in a letter to Allingham. "What sort of Xmas weather have you there?" he asked. "Is it any good wishing you merriment out of it? To-day here is neither a bright day nor a dark day, but a white smutty day—piebald—wherein, accordingly, life seems neither worth keeping nor getting rid of. The thick sky has a thin red sun stuck in the middle of it, like the specimen wafer stuck outside the box of them. Even if you turned back the lid, there would be nothing behind it, be sure, but a jumble of such flat dead suns. I am going to sleep." He had struck once again, automatically, the old wearied note, the baffled, frustrated tone which formed the burden of these perplexed, restless years, the weary, dreary years of an old romance which has turned stale, lost its early ecstasy, its once visionary delight, substituting problems for poetry.

NEW DISCIPLES
1856

There was a year in which I think it never rained, nor clouded, but was blue summer from Christmas to Christmas, and London streets glittered, and it was always morning, and the air sweet and full of bells.

Memorials of E. Burne-Jones E. BURNE-JONES

DURING THE FIVE YEARS which had passed since Ruskin in 1851 first defended the movement, the Preraphaelite Brotherhood had dwindled to little more than a name. Ruskin, lecturing on Preraphaelitism at Edinburgh in 1853, had again praised the Preraphaelites who, he asserted, "now enjoyed the most extensive popularity." But while Ruskin in Edinburgh proclaimed the Preraphaelite victory, the Brotherhood itself was dying. The cause of its decay was, precisely, its success, as well as its failure. Its epitaph was composed by Christina Rossetti at that time, in two mischievous but veracious sonnets written in Gabriel's jocular vein, touching upon the individual and corporate weaknesses of the Brethren, and finally, upon the disintegration of the Brotherhood—Woolner in Australia, Hunt longing to go East, Gabriel doing nothing, Stephens and William Rossetti of no account, while . . .

> . . . he at last the champion great Millais
>   Attaining academic opulence
> Winds up his signature with A.R.A.
> So rivers merge in the perpetual sea;
>   So luscious fruit must fall when over-ripe;
> And so the consummated P.R.B.

As Christina with her usual clarity saw, such was the state of Preraphaelitism in 1853. Ruskin's championship had carried the day. Could the correctness of Preraphaelite theories be disputed now that Ruskin had adopted—and adapted—them, and a professor of Botany was using Millais's *Ophelia* to illustrate his lectures? "Our position," wrote William Rossetti, on the last page of his *Preraphaelite Journal*, "is greatly altered; we have emerged from reckless abuse to a position of general and high recognition, just so much qualified by adverse criticism as suffices to keep our would-be annihilators in countenance." Yet, at this very moment of its consummation, the final disintegration of "the consummated P.R.B." had begun. As Gabriel, on hearing of Millais' defection to the enemy—the Academy—wrote:

So now the whole round table is dissolved.

Then Hunt, early in 1854, after long delays, had suddenly finished his *Awakened Conscience*, called a cab, paid a hurried round of farewells, and set off for Palestine, carrying with him as a parting gift from Gabriel, a photograph of *The Girlhood of Mary Virgin*, with a quotation from Taylor's *Philip van Artevelde* in Gabriel's handwriting, expressing eternal affection. Millais had gone with Hunt on that last wild dash to the station, had seized food from the buffet and flung it through the open window of the moving carriage on to Hunt's lap as the train gathered speed, running beside it to the end of the platform, shouting farewell. It was, though neither had suspected it, the end of a chapter. Never again would they meet in the old, careless, intimate way. And to these divisions of life was added the severance of death when a few weeks later the ill-fated, handsome Deverell died.

Such had been the dispersal of the Brotherhood. But there had also been a return. When Woolner came back late in 1854, without the expected gold but glad to resume life in the civilization he had formerly despised, Gabriel, delighted, dreamed of a revival of the Brotherhood. Hunt, returning in the spring of 1856, regretted its dissolution. Brown, although he had refused official membership, mourned its passing and even dreamed of forming a new Brotherhood which should become what the original had not been, a real force in art. But dissension had played a greater part than dispersal in the Brotherhood's decease, and now, when a partial revival occurred, it was a momentary revival of dissension rather than of unity, and quickly resulted in the Brotherhood's extinction. Save for William Rossetti who avoided disputes, internal quarrels had quickly exhausted all mathematical possibilities in permutation and combination of the Preraphaelite band. If, as even the loyal Brown complained, Gabriel was pre-eminent among his Brethren for damnatory criticism, it was owing to his surpassing them in self-expression rather than to their moral superiority. The subjects of dissension widely varied, ranging from Millais' vilification of Ruskin, in defence of his wife, to Rossetti's squabble with Hunt about the choice of themes for an illustrated edition of Tennyson's poems. The Brotherhood, in short, was honeycombed with tittle-tattle, often ill-tempered and foolish, which invariably came to the victim's ears, until comradeship was destroyed. And all united to attack Rossetti, because Ruskin had chosen him as favourite, pro-claimed him, Carlyle told Woolner, "the greatest genius of the age," advertised him as "leader" of the Preraphaelites, was in short, making his fortune.

For their resentment there was some excuse. Rossetti had never been conspicuous as a Preraphaelite, had in fact, whether by accident or design, escaped the hard knocks that fell to others, had failed miserably in oils, had hardly exhibited a picture anywhere, and, since his attachment to Lizzie, had wandered away from the Brethren, working or most often *not* working, "on his own." Nevertheless, Ruskin's claim for Gabriel of leadership was not without some justification. As he clearly saw, in Rossetti's creative imagination lay the Brotherhood's chief source of vitality. Millais and Hunt, like Lizzie, had once worked under his spell, and his absence had largely assisted the Brotherhood's decay. But now, as the original movement frittered away by internal discord, sank into desuetude, Pre-raphaelitism entered a new, widely different phase, and one of which Rossetti was the undoubted "leader."

This new phase and his relation to it was neither planned by Gabriel nor desired. It was the result of circumstances which, at the very moment when his own adolescent dream was yielding to the sluggish acceptances and complacences of middle age, set him to lead and inspire a new, eager, adolescent circle, to vitalize and be in turn revitalized by, the idealistic craving of youth.

Even in the earliest, darkest years, the Preraphaelites had found in Oxford sympathy and esteem. Millais and Ruskin, with friends there, had introduced Hunt and Rossetti respectively to University circles, and Mr. Combe of the Clarendon Press had been one of the first patrons of the movement. In Oxford Rossetti now found new disciples who, under his influence, carried Preraphaelitism into this new, far more important stage, although if by "Preraphaelitism" we mean the ideals of Hunt when founding the Brotherhood, we can hardly call this later development under Rossetti "Preraphaelitism" at all.

Chief of this new band of acolytes were two Oxford undergraduates of Exeter College, Edward Jones, son of a Birmingham carver and gilder, and William Morris, son of a London billbroker. (Morris's father was dead, but had left his family a comfortable independence.) The two undergraduates were close friends, bound by a common idealism, a common intention to "take orders," a common bewilderment caused by the conflict between dogma and science, a common love of daydreams and of romantic mediaevalism, and a common disgust for the dull, uninspiring examination grind of their studies, the coarse stupidity they remarked in most of their fellow students. For youthful, disappointed idealists are severe critics.

Taking "angry walks" about Oxford, where, as they mournfully remarked, even the odour of Newman's sanctity no longer lingered, lamenting the evil days upon which they were fallen, the two presented a curious contrast; Jones, thin, pale, fragile, visionary; Morris, robust, thick-set, energetic, of explosive temper and wide range of expletives, looking indeed in his later years like a sea captain, for which in fact he was once mistaken. Morris's exceptional strength led his friends to invent tales of his picking up coal scuttles in his teeth, twisting pokers into knots, letting children swing on his beard, and, when irritated at dinner parties where verbal relief was denied, leaving his forks bent and twisted as by lightning, in his dental efforts at self-control.

Yet in the characters, aspirations and ideals of the two friends lay a common basis for mutual appreciation. Beneath Jones's light-brown locks, lank as the tresses of an emergent mermaid, reigned the same tense, sentimental, dreamy idealism as that which was covered by the dark, flame-like curls of

Morris. Through both ran a strain of Celtic blood, of Celtic melancholy; both loved laughter, pranks, jests, boyish fun. Both had the nervous tensity and intensity which marked Rossetti himself.

Their interest in art and letters grew. Malory's *Morte d'Arthur* was their favourite reading, their favourite day dream a romanticized mediaevalism, all colour, splendour, vitality, passion, to which the streets, buildings, gardens of Oxford, the illuminated manuscripts in its libraries contributed. Jones, self-hypnotized by fancy, would wander out to Godstow Priory, meeting on the way monks, nuns, knights in flashing armour, fair Rosamond, all more real to him than life, until he beat himself back into a consciousness of external reality. He rejoiced in Tennyson's most languorous lyrics, which roused in him, he declared, "that unutterable feeling which comes on me like a seizure at certain times, and which Schlegel writes of under the term 'sighing after the Infinite.' " He especially enjoyed Tennyson's *Tears, idle tears*. "In some hot dreamy afternoons," he said, "I have thought upon it for hours, until I have been exquisitely miserable." Morris was different. His dreams were generally dreams of action—thwarted, paralysed, in some almost supernatural mist or miasma though it often was. "Tennyson's Sir Galahad," he remonstrated, "is rather a mild youth." But both friends united in praising that eminently "Preraphaelite" poem *The Lady of Shalott*. Morris would read it aloud in his own curious way, half chanting, stressing the lines, while Jones would lie and listen in a dreamy ecstasy.

Feeling the mystic's abstract love of all life, especially of his fellow men, Jones thought of founding in Oxford some pseudo-mediaeval, celibate, almost monastic brotherhood formed of souls finer than our common clay. But he succeeded, with Morris's aid, only in forming at Oxford a small, informal coterie of undergraduates, which, though without conventual life or aims of social service, became known as the *Oxford Brotherhood*, and consisted of Morris and Jones together with several friends, chiefly former schoolfellows of Jones at King Edward's School, Birmingham, who were now undergraduates at Oxford and Cambridge. Soon, artistic interests and ambitions superseded the two friends' earlier intention to take orders.

With relief Jones turned to making designs from *The Lady of Shalott*, and minute, elaborate studies *à la* Ruskin and Hunt, of flowers and foliage in Bagley Wood, while Morris tried, in both verse and prose, to give expression to his mediaeval dream-world.

It was then that Jones and Morris first became acquainted with Rossetti's work. Ruskin's lectures at Edinburgh drew their attention to the Preraphaelites, and on seeing in the window of an Oxford art shop Millais' *Return of the Dove to the Ark*, they became enthusiastic admirers of the movement. "Give me the *Light of the World* and the apse of Westminster!" cried Jones, in antagonistic ecstasy on seeing the Crystal Palace. They visited the Academy Exhibitions of 1854 and 1855, as well as Mr. Windus's famous Preraphaelite Collection at Tottenham, where Rossetti's water-colour, *Dante Drawing an Angel*, aroused their "greatest wonder and delight." "Until I saw Rossetti's work and Fra Angelico's," Jones once said, "I never supposed that I liked painting." Next, a chance encounter with a number of the ill-fated *Germ* containing *The Blessed Damozel* and *Hand and Soul*, led them to exalt Rossetti into the "chief figure in the Preraphaelite Brotherhood." Gabriel's poem and mediaeval tale they "read and re-read for ever." The story of Chiaro soon became a literary model for Morris himself. In Allingham's *Day and Night Songs* they found Rossetti's illustration to the *Maids of Elfinmere*, and worshipped. "I feel it is possible," wrote Lady Burne-Jones after her husband's death, "to lay one's finger on his earliest work and say: 'This was done before and this after he had seen *The Maids of Elfinmere*. . . .' "

Incited by *The Germ*, and financed by Morris, the Oxford Brotherhood now produced a shilling monthly, *The Oxford and Cambridge Magazine*, which appeared at the opening of 1856, was ignored like its predecessor, and, when Morris had lost some hundreds of pounds in it, ceased with the closing year. Its failure was as inevitable as *The Germ's*. As contributions must be unpaid and anonymous, it offered writers neither money nor reputation. Magnificently adhering to its declared intention to exclude all wit, it enshrines nothing of value save a few contributions by Rossetti and Morris, and, even amidst the incredible dullness of Victorian periodicals, is pre-eminently dull. But it offered Rossetti another means of publishing his poetry.

In the first number, *The Germ*, *The Blessed Damozel*, *Hand and Soul*, and Rossetti's illustration to Allingham's *Maids of Elfinmere* were all highly praised. "Why," asked the anonymous writer in conclusion, "is the author of *The Blessed Damozel* and the story of Chiaro so seldom on the lips of men? If only we could hear him oftener, live in the light of his power a little longer."

Gabriel, despairing at this time of more general recognition, sinking gradually into the lethargy of the ignored obscure, read the eulogy with delight. It was, he told Allingham, "the most gratifying thing by far that ever happened to me—being unmistakeably [*sic*] genuine. . . . It turns out to be a certain youthful Jones, who was in London the other day, and whom . . . I have now met. One of the nicest young fellows in— *Dreamland*. For there most of the writers in that miraculous piece of literature seem to be."

For Jones the meeting with Rossetti had been a tremendous experience, to be detailed in intimate letters to Morris at Oxford. Determined to see his idol, he had, on hearing Gabriel might be present, paid his threepence for a hunk of bread and butter and mug of tea at the Working Men's College one evening, and attended a general meeting of the students. There from afar he saw Rossetti, "his face satisfying all my worship." Refusing in his modesty an introduction that evening, Jones accepted an invitation from Vernon Lushington, one of the College Staff, to meet Rossetti a few nights later in Lushington's own rooms, and there Jones had his "first fearful talk" with Gabriel, gladly watched him dominate the general discussion, overwhelming opponents who dared to express a liking for metaphysics or to speak disrespectfully of Browning's *Men and Women*, and loudly declaring "he would have all men painters!" Rossetti, flattered by Jones's obvious hero-worship, invited him to call at his studio the next day—a visit which completed Jones's subjection—and began a permanent friendship between painter and disciple.

For Jones, henceforth Oxford and its studies lost all charm. Soon, abandoning all thought of a degree, he settled in London as Rossetti's "pupil." Although he received no tuition from

Gabriel beyond "a few mornings' work in his studio," Jones
was enduringly grateful, particularly for Rossetti's encouragement of originality. Upon Morris, who having graduated was
now articled to an Oxford architect, Gabriel exerted the same
fascination. Morris was writing poems too, now, and brought
them with him when he joined Jones and Gabriel in town at
week-ends.

Until her return from Continental wanderings in May 1856,
Lizzie's absence left Gabriel one or two months' freedom to
enjoy without domestic complications the society of his new
disciples, and thus for a time their friendship flourished. There
was also a revival of artistic and intellectual discussions, which
since Lizzie's advent had almost ceased. As Ruskin had
shrewdly anticipated, indeed, Lizzie's departure had inaugu-
rated for Gabriel an artistic and intellectual renaissance,
although of course, Rossetti himself did not observe this. There
were constant meetings now between Jones and Rossetti, and
often on Saturday nights, when Morris was with them, the three
would go together to some theatre. But Gabriel, who was restless, would often disappoint them by leaving the play in disgust, long before the end, taking them with him to finish the
evening with talk and reading in his own rooms. Far into the
small hours they would sit talking until Gabriel was at last
tired, or they would wander aimlessly about London's streets,
which still held for Gabriel the fascination they had exerted
upon him in boyhood. Often too on Sunday afternoons he
would drop in on the two friends, in Sloane Terrace, until
gradually, with pride and joy, they came to feel that their
hero really liked their company.

Their delight in Malory's *Morte d'Arthur* they hid until they
heard Gabriel praise it and the Bible as the "two greatest books
in the world." With humour, sarcasm, eloquence, sympathy,
and a man of the world's knowledge of life, Rossetti forged the
chains of their slavery. For Jones and Morris, Gabriel was not
only a fascinating human friend, but also an inspiration, a god.
Their submissiveness was almost abject. Jones "never wanted
to think, but as he thought." Morris, under Gabriel's influence,
began to paint as an aid to his architectural studies. "Rossetti
says I ought to paint," wrote Morris, "he says I shall be able.

Now as he is a very great man and speaks with authority and not as the scribes, I *must* try. I don't hope much, I must say, yet will try my best—he gave me practical advice on the subject." Yet at this time Rossetti himself, unable to paint well enough in oils to complete either *Kate the Queen* or *Found*, was still confined to water-colours.

In the autumn of the year, as Street the Oxford architect to whom Morris was articled had moved his headquarters to London, Morris joined Jones in town, and soon, again upon Gabriel's advice, the two friends were established in the rooms Rossetti had shared with Deverell five years before in Red Lion Square. That Rossetti had once lived there was sufficient for them, and there they remained until the spring of 1859.

Morris at once began to shape the interior of their rooms into harmony with their mediaeval dream; "rather doing the magnificent there," said Gabriel somewhat ironically, "having some intensely mediaeval furniture made—tables and chairs like incubi and succubi." All set to work decorating chairs and cabinets with painted figures of mediaeval knights and romantic ladies, while Gabriel designed for an enormous settle with three cupboards in it, and for some chairs, various themes from Dante and from Morris's own verse.

A drunken housekeeper was quickly replaced by the plain, shrewd, good-tempered, resourceful little Cockney immortalized as "Red Lion Mary," who was a great favourite with them all. She made drapery for their models, sat as model herself at times, wrote notes to their dictation, read the newspaper to them as they worked, made up "camp beds" for them when visitors stayed the night, and met with unshakable calm both Morris's sudden rages and the rejected suet puddings he flung downstairs. To their levity she retorted with her own Cockney wit, and she took her revenge for Morris's obloquy by secretly putting his watch an hour forward when he had to catch a train. Gabriel made her his model for one of the ladies accompanying Beatrice when she meets Dante in Florence; and the careful drawing he made of her head he presented to her when she married. He sent her upon strange, impossible errands, telling her to go and "smash a brute" whose name he did not know, "but his shop is dirty and full of account

books. This book was ordered ten days ago . . . AND WAS PAID
FOR—So sit on him hard to-morrow and dig a fork into his
eye, as I can't come that way to murder him myself."

Life at Red Lion Square in fact closely resembled that in
Chatham Place, and at one or the other house, Gabriel was
soon to be found with his new friends at all hours of the day
and night. Perhaps Hunt, dropping in on Gabriel and finding
Morris there, making drawings, and Jones painting, somewhat
resented their presence, regretted the old, lost intimacy; but
Gabriel sat down beside Hunt and played with Hunt's majestic
red beard, passing his paint brush through it, and talking continuously all the evening. "Most gloriously," thought Jones,
lost in adoration of the two Preraphaelite stars, "such talk as
I do not believe any man could talk beside him."

Morris, practically abandoning architecture, was, although
he never produced more than one oil painting, striking out in
other branches of decorative art, trying his hand at drawing,
clay-modelling, illuminating, carving wood and stone. "In all
illumination and work of that kind he is unrivalled by anything modern that I know," said Gabriel. "Both, I find, wonders after their kind. Jones is doing designs which quite put
one to shame, so full are they of everything. . . . He will take
the lead in no time. Morris, besides writing those capital tales,
writes poems which are really better than the tales." "Very
intimate friends of mine," Gabriel told Scott some months later,
early in 1857, "both are men of real genius."

But Morris was reluctant to write verse. Before meeting
Rossetti, he had decided that so exquisite was Tennyson, no
further development in English poetry was possible; a belief
akin to that of Rossetti, who regarded Keats as the ultimate
perfection of English poetry, and argued that therefore artists
should make painting, which was only in its beginning, their
medium of expression. "If any man has any poetry in him he
should paint it. The next Keats ought to be a painter," Gabriel
constantly exhorted them. This, his own ideal, and also Hunt's,
to be a "poetic painter," he had already expressed to Patmore
a year or two before. "The best one can hope as a painter
just now," he had written, "is to have a place of some kind
amongst those who are to do for painting, as far as possible,

what you and a very few more poets are doing now for poetry."
And it was from this point of view that Rossetti was most
acclaimed, as a "poetic-painter," upon his death.

Nevertheless, Morris's contributions to *The Oxford and Cambridge Magazine* had greatly impressed Rossetti. "Morris's
facility at poetizing," he told Allingham, "puts one in a rage.
He has only been writing at all for little more than a year
I believe, and has already poetry enough for a big book. You
know he is a millionaire, and buys pictures. He bought Hughes'
April Love, and lately several water-colours of mine, and a landscape by Brown—indeed seems as if he would never stop, as
I have three or four more commissions from him. To one of
my water-colours, called *The Blue Closet*, he has written a
stunning poem. You would think him one of the finest little
fellows alive—with a touch of the incoherent, but a real man."
That Morris's commissions were cleverly extracted from a
reluctant Morris by Gabriel himself is hardly in harmony with
Gabriel's character as a friend, and indeed Morris's own
daughter has flatly contradicted the caustic comment of Dr.
Mackail in his *Life* of Morris: "Morris, while he was under
Rossetti's guidance, had to buy pictures as well as paint them."
But, ever anxious to help his old friend, Gabriel had taken
Morris to Brown's studio, hoping not in vain, that he would
buy.

Upon Rossetti the influence of Jones and Morris was almost
as great as his upon them. In them he found all the qualities
the outer world denied him. The enthusiasm of imaginative,
idealistic adolescence revived his own fading adolescent dream.
From his new "realism," with its "modern subjects" and
painting "from nature" to suit the taste of the age, they called
him back, insistently, to that mediaeval dreamland which,
since his childhood in the shadow of Dante, had ever been his
spiritual home. Yet theirs was the mediaevalism not of Dante
but of Malory; of the Arthurian Legend. Love, his unfailing
theme, he had hitherto presented in the symbolism of Dante
and Beatrice. Now, he would express it more exclusively in
the terms of Malory—of Launcelot and Guinevere.

To Gabriel's youthful admirers, seeing life through the rose
and gold mist of adolescent dream, this year of 1856 was an

annus mirabilis, the year in which they had won the friendship of their hero. "We shall see the greatest man in Europe," said Jones, taking his friend Dixon to see Rossetti. The glamour of this wonderful year never left Jones. It assumed, in retrospect, that unearthly splendour which lay so near to his sentimental heart. "There was a year," he said, long afterwards describing it, with the far off gaze in his "very blue gentle-looking eyes," "in which I think it never rained, nor clouded, but was blue summer from Christmas to Christmas, and London streets glittered, and it was always morning, and the air sweet and full of bells."

VI

PRERAPHAELITISM "ARRIVES"
1856–1857

We all thought a great deal of the P.R.B. movement . . . and what a contempt we had for the sleepy old conventional school.

The Richmond Papers SIR W. RICHMOND

BY THIS TIME Jones and Morris were not alone in their Preraphaelite enthusiasms. Amongst the rising generation at least, Preraphaelitism was now popular, had become the symbol of modernity, of revolt against outworn traditions and conventions. "Of course," wrote Sir William Richmond, describing in later years his experiences as an Academy student and the new spirit abroad at this time, "we all thought a great deal of the P.R.B. Movement. We liked the anarchy of it; we liked the old dodderers to be vexed; and what a contempt we had for the sleepy old conventional school, so British in its narrow ways, so respectable in its entire absence of virile enthusiasm! . . . We all knew of Watts, and the dislike which followed him for the great efforts he was making to uplift English art from nursery rhyme to epic poetry, from a mere academic coldness of accuracy, a kind of slick convention of painting, admirable in its way, but dull and uninspired. Leighton had not yet risen, had not yet taken the walls of the Academy by storm; when he did, he instantly became a great influence and factor, he brought Italy into cold England, he brought enthusiasm where before there was none, and the young men clustered round his inspiring presence even if they did not fall before him as before Rossetti, Millais and Hunt."

In 1857, however, two years had passed since Leighton's *Cimabue's Madonna carried in procession through the streets of Florence*, evoked general applause. A year later, Leighton meeting Rossetti, "one of the originators of the Preraphaelite Movement," found him "apparently a remarkable and interesting man." So popular indeed, had Preraphaelite paintings become, that Hunt already complained of "young adventurers" doing "a roaring trade" in faked Preraphaelite pictures.

Rossetti, in fact, as Ruskin's influence increasingly bore fruit, was now definitely establishing his position. "He flourishes and holds his head above the crowd—lots and lots of commissions," Woolner told Allingham at the close of 1856. New patrons were appearing. A Leeds millionaire, one Marshall, who had just set up house in Eaton Square, declared Gabriel's prices "trifles" and began to buy. A Leeds stockbroker and dissenter, named Plint, doubtless Marshall's friend, came to Rossetti shortly afterwards and not only accepted his prices readily, but even insisted on paying in advance. Gabriel found it almost too good to be true. At any rate his lethargy vanished and he resumed work with such energy that a moralizing acquaintance rejoiced to find him no longer "lying on his back tossing his legs in the air and Mon-Dieu-ing," as before.

The first use to which Rossetti put his good fortune was, as usual, to try to help Brown. To Brown's he took Plint—as he had taken Morris and many others—and showed him *Work*, Brown's *magnum opus*, which Plint bought on the condition that the painter agreed to introduce into it "both Carlyle and Kingsley, and change one of the four *fashionable* young ladies into a *quiet, earnest, holy*-looking one, with a book or two and tracts." "I hope we may both, in God's mercy, be spared to see it happily finished," wrote Plint to Brown when the agreement was made. Plint's devout wish, however, was not to be granted, for he died two years before Brown finished *Work*. Brown's gratitude to Gabriel for his help was very sincere. "Really Gabriello seems bent upon making my fortune at one blow," he wrote in his diary. "Never did fellow, I think, so bestir himself for a rival before; it is very good and very great to act so. Ever since he felt he had hurt me some little time ago he has done nothing but keep making amends to me, one after another. As Carlyle says of Mirabeau, how much easier it is to note the flaws in a circle than to grasp the whole sweep of its circumference!" And now, a striking sign of Rossetti's prosperity, he actually repaid his and Lizzie's debts to Brown, some £42 in all. A few days later, Brown, to whom life gave few prizes, was awarded that of the Liverpool Exhibition, which Hunt and Millais had won several years before.

During the single year of its existence, *The Oxford and Cambridge Magazine*, having published Rossetti's *Burden of Nineveh*, *Blessed Damozel*, and *Staff and Scrip*, besides enthusiastic praise of both his painting and poetry, had assisted in enhancing his reputation. Although it never paid for contributions, which, as Gabriel once ruefully remarked, were all written "for love or spooniness," he regretted its passing and recalled the similarity of its fate to his own early venture. "It was too like the spirit of *Germ*. Down, down! and has vanished into the witches' cauldron,"[1] he said.

Perhaps more useful than *The Germ* or *Oxford and Cambridge Magazine* in bringing Rossetti to public notice, was the famous illustrated edition of Tennyson's poems which appeared a few months later, in 1857. Rossetti's relation to the volume was characteristic. Believing that illustration fettered originality, he was reluctant to accept Moxon the publisher's invitation to join the distinguished artists chosen to illustrate the volume, and agreed only on the understanding that he was free to choose such poems as *The Vision of Sin* and *The Palace of Art*, "those where one can allegorize on one's own hook," as he said. For each design £25 was to be paid. Although granted the first choice of subjects, to excuse his own delay he falsely accused Hunt of having taken the themes which Rossetti himself wanted, especially *The Lady of Shalott*. After extracting from the publisher £5 more for each design than his fellow-illustrators received, Rossetti condescended to complete the work—a year later than the rest—after long wrangling with Dalziel the engraver. "Ministers of wrath," he denounced the engravers. "Your drawing comes to them like Agag, delicately, and is hewn in pieces before the Lord Harry." When someone questioned the importance of his complaint that a block for *St. Cecilia* was one-sixteenth of an inch too short, he shouted: "Good God! What do you mean by that? I could get a whole city in there." On seeing the block finally, he grumbled about "Dalziel performing his cannibal jig in the corner," and groaned: "I have really felt like an invalid ever since." En-

[1] *v. sup.* p. 136.

gravers always disappointed him. "As yet I fare best with W. J. Linton," he declared. "He keeps stomach-aches for you, but Dalziel deals in fevers and agues."

Rossetti's designs so amply fulfilled his declared intention to "allegorize on one's own hook," that Tennyson, unable to see their relation to his verses, and regarding all illustrations to his works as supererogatory, could not discover what the *St. Cecilia* "meant," and labelled Rossetti's pseudo-mediaevalism "Wardour Street work." "Tennyson loathes mine," Gabriel admitted of his designs. Ruskin too was disappointed. "We P.R.B.s must do better for you than this some day," he told Tennyson, congratulating him, however, on several of the illustrations, including two of Gabriel's. Woolner told Mrs. Tennyson that Rossetti's *St. Cecilia* was "most lovely," and Brown thought so too. Plint ordered a drawing of it for forty guineas. Rossetti's own favourites in the volume were Hunt's *Oriana* and *Lady of Shalott*, "both masterpieces."

Upon the publication of this volume, which introduced Rossetti's work to a far wider public than before, his name, for almost the first time since the Preraphaelite battle of 1851, reappeared in the public Press. The illustrations as a whole did not entirely escape censure. *The Saturday Review*, particularly severe, after praising the designs of Hunt and Millais as "something to be studied and understood," continued: "to assert that, after any study, we can understand Rossetti, would be an hypocrisy beyond the homage which human intelligence may justifiably pay to pictorial incomprehensibility." Exemplifying this, the critic proceeded to ridicule *Sir Galahad before the Shrine* and *St. Cecilia*; and so unfamiliar was Rossetti's name to the public, he spelt it invariably with one "s."

A sense of generally favourable conditions now led the Preraphaelites, headed by Brown, to stage at a private house, No. 4, Russell Place, Fitzroy Square, a free Preraphaelite Exhibition of over seventy pictures, which included Lizzie's as well as Gabriel's designs. At the private view Hunt, summoned by Gabriel to see "the stunning drawings" of "the Sid," offended him by remarking that he would have taken them for "happy designs by Walter Deverell." "Deverell," exclaimed Gabriel, "they are a thousand times better than anything he ever did." And Hunt, jealous, saw in the remark only a pretext of Rossetti's to quarrel with and desert his old comrades.

The Preraphaelite Exhibition of 1857 clearly revealed how far the tide of enmity to the Brotherhood had receded since the days when Ruskin was called upon to defend it. Professional critics were now timidly cordial. "Singular and instructive," declared the *Saturday Review*, "especially interesting as showing what are the real views and aims of the people calling themselves Preraphaelites." Amid the exhibitors' diversity, the critic found a common quality, "resulting from the artist's simple and sincere endeavour to render his genuine and independent impressions of nature. From Seddon and John Brett, whose eyes are simple photographic lenses, to Gabriel Rossetti and Holman Hunt, who see things in 'the light that never was on sea or land,' but which is, for all that, a true and genuine light, everything, as a rule, and as far as it goes, is modest, veracious, and effective." "If the Academy will not do justice, they will not be shown justice," threatened the *Athenaeum*. "Preraphaelitism has taught us all to be exact and thorough, that everything is still unpainted, and that there is no finality in art." Time, it seemed to this critic, had toned down the harshness of the Preraphaelites' earlier revolt. "Its errors, eccentricities, and wilful aberrations are fast modifying and softening. Its large hands and feet, ugly, hard, mean faces, gaudy colours, and streaky stipplings have subsided into common sense, good taste, and discretion." Millais, the critic described as "the chief of the sect," Hunt as "the apostle of the order," and Rossetti as "the original founder of the three-lettered race [i.e. P.R.B.] who is generally spoken of by them in a low voice, and is supposed from the fertility of his allegorical sketches to be capable of doing anything, though he does not and will not exhibit in public."

To Rossetti the reviewers as a whole gave both first importance and greatest praise; partly because of his refusal to exhibit in public, of which much was made. His "somewhat numerous contributions unquestionably constituted the main interest of the exhibition," said the *Saturday Review*, and proceeded to praise their "profound thoughtfulness," "peculiar tenderness," and colouring which "neither follows nor violates

nature" but is used "as a symbolic commentary on his thought."
That Rossetti largely differed from, and was even in some
respects opposed to, the other leading Preraphaelites, the critic
also pointed out, but considered him "a true Preraphaelite—
nevertheless"; for if he sometimes avoided a literal representation of "nature," he was still expressing nature and truth by
means of the imaginative and ideal. "Probably," said the
critic, "there is no other artist living who demands so much
mental and moral culture for his appreciation, or who appeals
so little to the passive senses, by which alone ninety-nine spectators out of a hundred are to be won." The appeal of much of
Rossetti's best work, such as the *Mary Magdalene* and *The Blue
Closet*, he concluded, was too elusive for definite criticism, and
he doubted "whether the strange delight which these works
must afford to all imaginative minds is capable of being explained to the understanding."

The *Athenaeum* in its detailed criticism of Rossetti was as
vaguely laudatory as the *Saturday Review*. *Hesterna Rosa, Dante's
Dream* and *Dante Drawing an Angel* it considered to be "mystic"
designs, "full of thought and imagination." *The Blue Closet* and
Mary Magdalene it said, "attracted much attention. That he is
a poet and a thinker we are the last to doubt—but sketching is
deceptive and dangerous. It is the day-dream of painting."

By the *Saturday Review* the remainder of the exhibitors were
briefly considered and with but moderate enthusiasm. Millais
received a mere five lines; Hunt seven; Brown actually thirty.
The rest were included in one final paragraph which began
with Lizzie: "There was one lady contributor, Miss E. E.
Siddal, whose name was new to us. Her drawings display an
admiring adoption of all the most startling peculiarities of
Mr. Rossetti's style, but they have nevertheless qualities which
entitle them to high praise. Her *Study of a Head* is a very promising attempt, showing great care, considerable technical power,
and a high, pure and independent feeling for that much mis-
understood object, the human face divine. *We are Seven* and
Pippa Passes, by the same lady, deserve more notice than we
can stop to give them. Her *Clerk Saunders*, although we have
heard it highly praised by high authorities, did not please us
so much."

As usual, Brown was unfortunate. He financed the exhibition, bore the resulting loss, and a year later was still complaining that his fellow exhibitors had not yet paid their £10 shares. Even the praise given by the *Athenaeum* to his *Last of England* was diverted from himself, as the critic mistakenly imputed the picture to Hunt.

Yet this very period of the Preraphaelite Exhibition and of the Brotherhood's growing success, was marked by a powerful attack on Millais, and his final defection from the Preraphaelite party. At the Academy Exhibition of the year, Millais' "Preraphaelite" picture, *Sir Isumbras at the Ford*, had provoked much bitterly adverse criticism, including Ruskin's. The then obscure painter Frederick Sandys made an amusing and popular caricature of *Sir Isumbras*, showing the chief Preraphaelites, Millais, Rossetti and Holman Hunt crossing a ford on the back of a braying ass labelled "John Ruskin (Oxon)." Henceforth Millais openly turned from the Preraphaelites and their ways. His marriage had subordinated all artistic aims to financial success, so, abandoning his earlier manner of work, he began to follow the vulgar taste of the general public. "As I must live, they shall have what they want," he remarked bitterly, and henceforth his paintings were commercial products rather than art.

Unfortunately, Rossetti's improving professional prospects developed against a darkening background of personal unhappiness. Throughout the spring and summer of 1857, Lizzie renewed her attack upon Gabriel more violently, more determinedly than before. Jealous also of the attraction to Gabriel of Jones and Morris, she became more capricious, more hysterical than ever, indulged with greater frequency in "scenes" intended to make her will prevail. About Brown's project of a residential "College" near London, for both married and single Preraphaelites, to which Gabriel and Hunt as well as Jones and Morris had given their blessing, Lizzie fell into a state bordering on insanity, and provoked quarrels between Gabriel, Brown and Hunt in which Rossetti, much troubled by Lizzie's bitterness, complained in self-defence that Lizzie had long wished to keep their engagement private. So effective were her tactics that Rossetti actually began to economize for marriage, and fell, as he said, into "the state of sleepy worry," which was his habitual reaction to this permanent dilemma of his life.

Lizzie's reaction meanwhile was her habitual one of apparently neurotic illness. "She does not better in health," Gabriel lamented, "never eating anything to speak of, and I am most wretched about her. What to do I know not . . . I cannot trouble her about it or feel any anger at her, only constant pain at her sufferings. Kind and patient she has been with me many and many times, more than I have deserved; and I trust this trouble is over. It is but too natural that her mind should be anxious and disturbed. . . ." Gabriel was ever humble and contrite when Lizzie's mysterious malady overwhelmed her, as indeed Lizzie well knew. In that now lay her chief power over him; her best means of getting her own way. So, despite the suspiciously sympathetic ministrations of Emma Brown, she grew consistently worse; much worse in mid-March when Gabriel, having borrowed £10 from Brown to get married, returned shortly afterwards, explaining when questioned, that he had unhappily and inadvertently spent the money on other things, and indeed, now wished to borrow more.

The storm now burst in all its fury. Emma visited Lizzie daily, took her for three days into her own house, and, when she returned to her own rooms, Brown believed she was dying and told Gabriel so—as no doubt the two women intended he should. Yet still the storm raged. Brown wasted days consoling and advising the repentant Gabriel, while Emma gave Lizzie similar aid. Refusing to see Gabriel, Lizzie from her sick room overwhelmed him with reproaches and vilifications, dutifully brought to his ear by Brown through Emma who, like some typical lady's maid of Restoration Comedy, acted as naughty go-between to these quarrelsome lovers, instilling in Gabriel fears of a final dismissal and of Lizzie's impending death. Lizzie, meanwhile, in the seclusion of her sick room was writing such minatory verses as—

> Ope not thy lips, thou foolish one,
>   Nor turn to me thy face:
> The blasts of heaven shall strike me down
>   Ere I will give thee grace.

Lizzie evidently enjoyed it all, loved self-dramatization, a compensation for neglect, inferiority feeling, as well as a protest against her real wrongs. Gabriel, of different breeding and with other interests, liked it less.

Only when the desired degree of self-abasement and repentance had been induced, was Rossetti allowed, with Emma as his intercessor, a grudging interview with Lizzie, and even then only so that he might see for himself the havoc he had wrought, and suffer more. The concession moreover must proceed in delicately graduated stages. First Brown alone might see the invalid. Not until a day or two later, and then only because of Brown's pleadings, was the vanquished Gabriel admitted to her presence. Emma, of course, was the skilful "producer" of the farce every time. For both Lizzie and Gabriel, increasing weariness of spirit, degenerating nerves, were the inevitable, almost sole result.

During these crises Rossetti vented his irritation in new quarrels with his Preraphaelite friends. Excluded from Lizzie's presence, he found some relief for his feelings in declaring Ruskin "a sneak." Ruskin, he asserted, liked him, Rossetti, because he, Gabriel, was a sneak also, and he liked Munro and Hunt for the same reason. But Ruskin hated Woolner and Brown for being "manly and straightforward," and he adored Millais for being "Prince of sneaks, but Millais was too much so, for he sneaked away his wife, and so he is obliged to hate him for too much of his favourite quality." Such were Gabriel's comments (obviously the foolish words of a weary, nerve-racked man), after a meeting at the Working Men's College during which Ruskin had flattered Gabriel, praised Munro and ignored Woolner. Gabriel, Brown observed, "was in such a rage about Ruskin and Woolner, that he bullied poor Munro all the way home." There he found Emma awaiting him with a note from Lizzie, consenting to receive him the following day. But this time, as often, the renewal of love only meant a renewal of strife. When Gabriel, Lizzie and the Browns all dined together the next day, Lizzie began to scream her opinion of Gabriel until he went home. Brown too departed in search of peace, sending the baby to Emma who remained to calm the vociferous invalid. For both Brown and Rossetti these were unprofitable days.

Ruskin, had he heard Gabriel's opinion of him would have cared less now than formerly. Estranged by his protégés' emotional indifference to himself, by their intractability, disorderly life and general futility, he was gradually drifting away from them, growing remote. Long absences on the Continent assisted this transition. There, solitary, thoughtful, depressed, he increasingly brooded over the disappointments and evanescence of human life, saw his relation to Gabriel and Lizzie in truer perspective, clearly realizing that he had failed to win their affection by the benefits he had conferred, saw that he held them solely by his wealth and influence. Absent he was forgotten. They would not trouble to write to him—except when they needed money, which was not seldom. In August 1856 he had broken a long silence with an obviously perfunctory letter to Gabriel, expressing his disappointment at receiving none from them and giving his address for "if you like to send one now." This letter he sent to Miss Heaton who, abroad but about to return to England, would deliver it together with his cheque—"Ida's August money, with my love to you both. Tell me all about your pictures, and yourself and Ida; I don't care to hear about anything else," he added, fearing more laments about dearth of "tin."

Shortly afterwards, however, Ruskin's waning enthusiasm revived on his learning that Gabriel was author of *The Burden of Nineveh* published in the August number of *The Oxford and Cambridge Magazine*. Reading the anonymous poem without any suspicion of its origin, and, as he told Rossetti, "wild to know who is the author," he dashed off a note to Gabriel—"It is glorious. Please find out for me, and see if I can get acquainted with him." On learning the truth he was delighted. Yet the poem, in this first version especially, contained many crudities. Gabriel too was delighted. The incident revived his dying belief in his own poetic powers, his buried poetic ambitions. Upon Ruskin's return to England in October, Gabriel showed him his original verse. Whereupon, forming an even higher opinion than before of Rossetti's talents, and with intensified conviction, Ruskin continued to acclaim Gabriel as the Preraphaelites' "leader." Intimidating opposition and dominating the President, Ruskin prepared for Gabriel a smooth entry into the Old Water-Colour Society, and urged him to apply for membership. But as usual Rossetti disappointed him. Fearing rejection, as always, doubting also whether so public an entry into the ranks of the water-colourists might not "chance to bonnet my oil-painting for good," he refused to seek election. Despite failures and interminable delay, Gabriel still meant, as ten years before, to achieve the greater successes and rewards of the painter in oils.

Ruskin's renewed intimacy with Gabriel and Lizzie quickly declined. In June 1857 Lizzie suddenly gave up her pension; for what reason or reasons we can only guess. Most probably because from this time she did little painting, partly no doubt hindered by ill-health, partly also perhaps by her increasing alienation from Rossetti. Ruskin, now too weary to remonstrate, regretfully but nonchalantly received Lizzie's refusal to continue accepting his pension, preferring to allow the headstrong and independent protégée to have her way. "I don't know," he wrote to Gabriel, "when I have been more vexed at being out of town, as I have been since Saturday; as Ida's mind and yours must have been somewhat ill at ease *thinking* I was vexed, or something of that kind. I shall rejoice in Ida's success with her picture, as I shall in every opportunity of being useful either to you or her. The only feeling I have about the matter is of some shame at having allowed the arrangement between us to end as it did, and the chief pleasure I could have about it now would be her simply accepting it as she would have accepted a glass of water when she was thirsty, and never thinking of it any more. As for Thursday, just do as you and your sister and she feel it pleasant or find it convenient. I hope to see you and arrange to-morrow, if you can be at home about four o'clock. If I don't see you or hear from you I shall expect you to dinner at two if it be fine. If Ida can't come, it's no reason why Miss Rossetti shouldn't." A significant postscript followed: "If it would be more convenient to you to put it off a week, or even till full strawberry time, do. The garden is duller than I expected just now. I shall be at home these three weeks yet. . . ." From Ruskin it was a clear indication of growing estrangement; gallantry, the old paternal, persuasive eloquence no longer flowed.

Whatever the reasons, Ruskin's benevolent enthusiasm had obviously cooled. He did not know what to make of them, could not understand them, chose now to let them go their own way without remonstrance, and, doubtless bored by their constant perplexities, preferred to be left to do his own work in peace. He accepted Lizzie's decision calmly if regretfully. The letter is touched with the scent of decay in friendship, the first hint of that indifference which is more fatal than anger and reproach. And Lizzie? Was it above all a last desperate step to force Gabriel into marriage? Had she discovered that the "independence" Ruskin had given her to facilitate marriage had in fact retarded it? Did she think that by once again throwing herself upon Gabriel for support, her poverty, the need for economy, would force him to the marriage which her pension from Ruskin was making more remote? Gabriel at any rate, weary of the unending conflict, now suddenly broke away from Lizzie. More resolutely than ever before he reclaimed the wider freedom he was finding once again in the company of Morris and Jones.

THE JOVIAL CAMPAIGN
1857–1858

What fun we had in that Union! What jokes! What roars of laughter!

> *Memorials of E. Burne-Jones* VAL PRINSEP

SOME NEW CAUSE of vexation, or perhaps merely another desperate attempt to bring Gabriel to marriage, sent Lizzie in the spring of 1857 in headlong, angry flight to the shelter of relatives in Sheffield. There, in the home of her cousin William Ibbitt, silver chaser, alderman, amateur artist, she remained, working in the ladies' class at the local art-school, walking with burning heart and saddened face the mean, provincial streets. Once she visited her family's ancestral village, Hope, in Derbyshire. Nor was Rossetti entirely happy. "Very quiet and said little," remarked an Oxford undergraduate, George Birkbeck Hill, to his friends Jones and Morris, at this time, after meeting Rossetti at their house, and his friends explained that Rossetti was engaged to a lady who was "in a consumption."

Wishing no less than Lizzie to escape, Gabriel now set out on a venture which long afterwards he aptly named "The Jovial Campaign." It was the unexpected result of a day's visit to Oxford to see the new University Museum and Union Society Debating Hall, which the architect Woodward, with Ruskin's copious advice, was then building. Baffled by oils and probably incited by Watts's mural decoration of Lincoln's Inn then proceeding, Rossetti had for some time dreamed of founding in England a great school of mural painting. Seeing ten bays in the new bare walls of the Debating Hall—now the library—he offered on the spur of the moment, to decorate them with the help of friends, and without remuneration, if only all expenses were paid. It was the long vacation, and Woodward, eager for so mediaeval an embellishment of his pseudo-mediaeval building, not only persuaded the interim

committee of the Union to accept Gabriel's offer, but also
agreed that Rossetti should similarly decorate the Museum
when work at the Union was completed; a qualification
which in the event nullified the second project. It was thus,
during that tragic summer of 1857, while all England watched
the gradual extinction of the Indian Mutiny, that Rossetti,
gathering his friends and disciples about him, light-heartedly
set out with them on "the jovial campaign."

Brown, Hunt and Scott were too wary to accept Gabriel's
invitation to join him, but he persuaded Val Prinsep and
Roddam Spencer Stanhope, disciples of Watts the painter,
John Hungerford Pollen, a recent acquaintance, ex-proctor of
Oxford and now Professor of Fine Art in the University of
Dublin, Arthur Hughes, an old friend, Jones and Morris, to
give their aid, and Munro agreed to carve the stone shield
designed by Gabriel for the entrance. Their designs were of
course, from mediaeval themes in the *Morte d'Arthur* of Malory.
As usual, Rossetti chose a dramatization of his own situation,
i.e. in his own words: "Sir Lancelot prevented by his sin from
entering the chapel of the San Grail. He has fallen asleep before
the shrine full of angels, and, between him and it, rises in his
dream the image of Queen Guinevere, the cause of all. She
stands gazing at him with her arms extended in the branches
of an apple-tree."

Soon Morris, Jones and Gabriel were all in Oxford, living
together in a pleasant old house in the High, opposite Queen's
College, and working each day at the Union. Shortly afterwards the others arrived. By mid-August work was well begun,
and they hoped to finish within six weeks at the latest.

From the first, competent observers doubted their success.
But Gabriel as in the old Preraphaelite days, thought it "a
great lark," as his optimism brushed aside the fears of the
younger, unskilled painters. Watts sardonically encouraged the
hesitant Prinsep; Stanhope, knowing Gabriel's dilatory nature
and ignorance of fresco or other kind of mural painting, prophesied failure. Despite Stanhope's pessimism, Watts's, Brown's,
Ruskin's knowledge of the venture and of painting processes,
despite the presence of Pollen who had recently decorated the
roof of Merton College Chapel, and was, Gabriel declared in a

reckless moment, "the only man who has yet done good mural painting in England," they completely ignored the technical problems involved, and upon the unprepared, newly-built, whitewashed wall, began to paint their designs in tempera.

Under Rossetti's irresponsible leadership they were soon floundering in a sea of troubles. Morris, unable to paint the fourteen-feet-high figures of his designs, covered the foreground with sun-flowers from which only monstrous heads emerged. Thereupon Gabriel sarcastically suggested he should help one of the others in a similar plight, by filling *his* foreground with scarlet-runners. Unforeseen difficulties arose. The distemper sank into the unprepared wall or fell off in flakes. The brick-edges caught the dust; gas lights below damaged the paintings, the two circular windows and a ridge in the wall in each bay made painting difficult. The six weeks were soon eight, yet much remained to be done.

For Rossetti, whose youth in poverty-stricken Charlotte Street had known few social pleasures, whose early manhood, burdened with the responsibility for Lizzie so soon an invalid, had known little freedom, this escape to a new life in Oxford with young, congenial, enthusiastic and admiring friends was a unique and entirely agreeable experience. This departure from the old, narrow ways in Chatham Place he enjoyed to the utmost, breaking out into irresponsible gaiety as if, belatedly enough at twenty-nine, he were enjoying that undergraduate life which, unlike some of those about him, he had never known. For a time he was to be free from the atmosphere of sickness, seriousness, reproach, rancour, misunderstanding and lack of sympathy which was, one feels, the atmosphere that now enveloped his life with Lizzie. Now, for a short season, life for Gabriel was to echo as never before and seldom if ever afterwards with wit and laughter, talk of poetry, of art, of mutual interests, to be enriched by fellow spirits alive with imagination, feeling, satire and mischief—with so much that evaded him and Lizzie in Chatham Place.

Joviality even more perhaps than lack of skill prolonged the labours of Rossetti and his band at Oxford. His love of mischief, of practical jokes and fun soon infected the rest. While painting leisurely proceeded, the Debating Hall witnessed some of the strangest scenes in its history. Upon Jones, posing as a mediaeval knight, Stanhope from the gallery, once suddenly discharged a bucketful of dirty water, amidst general applause. Jones, taking a vicarious revenge one morning, on looking down from the gallery and seeing Gabriel clad in armour as he supposed, and reading the newspapers, emptied a bucket of water on him. Rossetti, however, instead of being protected by a suit of mail, was wearing only the helmet, and his language as he jumped up, drenched, to vent his feelings, was said to be indescribable. "Oh, that's nothing, we often do that," Rossetti cheerfully remarked from the top of a ladder, upon another occasion, after upsetting a pot of expensive lapis lazuli ground into real ultramarine. Nor was the emptying of paint pots over one another the sole diversion of the mural painters. Undergraduates reading in the adjoining library were disturbed by their songs, jokes, laughter and scuffles, as well as by the continual popping of corks from innumerable soda-water bottles ordered at the Union's expense from the Star Hotel near by. After the painters' departure, the Union treasurer, on receiving the Star Hotel's account for it, was amazed at the quantity of soda-water they had absorbed.

"What fun we had in that Union! What jokes! What roars of laughter!" wrote Prinsep in after years. Pollen, older, more serious, and with a reputation to sustain, was less pleased. "There is such a rattle of talk from surrounding worthies," he wrote in one of his daily letters at this time to his wife, "that I fear my wits will fail: Topsy[1] and Rossetti giving vent to most startling opinions with which I need not trouble *you*. . . . I have worked just double as fast as the fastest; but I greatly fear the disadvantage of appearing in such company! and to work up to so rich a key of colouring is more than can be done hastily. . . . Now I am approaching a very imperfect sort of completion, for I can give no more time to the thing." Yet, so infectious was Rossetti's mood, within a few days, Pollen, Professor, ex-clergyman, ex-proctor, almost forty years of age, had joined him in morning expeditions to twitch off the bedclothes, pillows and mattresses of the slumbering Morris and Jones, or, with the rest, was painting wombats on the white-

---

[1] Morris, *v. inf.* p. 228.

washed windows of the Debating Hall. For by this time the
wombat, a favourite of Gabriel's earliest visits to the Zoo—"a
delightful creature, the most comical little beast," as he still
declared—had been adopted by the rest almost as a badge of
loyalty to their leader.

Morris, the first to begin, the first to finish, turned next to
decorating the roof "with a vast pattern-work of grotesque
creatures" as Gabriel said. Mid-October brought a new
academic year. The painters, obliged to evacuate their rooms
in the High, moved to another picturesque "crib" at 13,
George Street. Amongst the returning undergraduates were
some of the "Oxford Brotherhood," and these helped Jones
and Morris to finish the roof.

Prinsep, looking back upon these days nearly half a century
later, particularly recalled the happy hours of camaraderie in
George Street, the discussions on art and letters, Gabriel inter-
rupting from the sofa on which he lay, to say: "It's all very
well talking, but if I could paint like"—some popular contemporary artist or other—"Why, by Jove, I should do it!"
Upon which Morris, aghast, would stop his restless stumping
about the room a moment, and Jones looking up from his
drawing would cry "Oh, Gabriel!" and burst into incredulous
laughter. But Gabriel, ever in straits for money, probably
spoke truth.

There were delightful breakfasts with Morris, Jones and the
rest; whist parties in Gabriel's rooms in the evenings. Many a
night "Topsy" or "Top," as they now called Morris after the
humorous character in *Uncle Tom's Cabin*, would read his
verses, while Gabriel as usual lay on the sofa, listening, and the
rest of the band assembled round. It was thus Val Prinsep had
found them on his arrival in Oxford. Ordering his cabman to
drive him to "The Union," he had first been taken to the
Oxford Workhouse, and only with some difficulty had discovered Rossetti at his rooms, 87, High Street, where he had
received Prinsep "with great cordiality." Soon Jones, "thin,
pale-faced . . . with high cheek bones and round, very blue
gentle-looking eyes . . . hair straight and without curl . . . apt
to stray over his forehead," as Prinsep described him, "slipped
into the room" in his almost furtive way, "opening the door

just sufficiently wide to allow of his passing," and, as Jones already knew Val, greeted him in his habitual nervously effusive manner. Then came "the sound of a heavy footstep outside. The door was opened with a bang, and Morris entered . . . a short, very square-built, spectacled man with a head that appeared too big from the length and thickness of his dark, matted locks." But Morris like Jones was very shy, and after the introduction stood "shifting his legs and twiddling with his watch chain which gave him somewhat of a grotesque appearance." So at least Prinsep thought.

Throughout the evening, even during dinner or conversation, Gabriel would fall at times into his habit of humming to himself, as he did when working at his easel. The dinner was typical of an English lodging—"simple" viands, "particularly badly cooked." Prinsep had noted the others' indifference to the quality of their food, their preference for "meat in cinders" and "soups flavoured principally with pepper!" But in their conversation he found more than compensation for a miserable meal. Fun, jokes, laughter mingled with chivalric allusions to King Arthur and his Knights, and with slang, especially Cockney slang which Gabriel loved, and which his disciples had, in turn, adopted, so that every beautiful girl, whether married or single, "lady or model," was a "stunner." After dinner Gabriel had curled himself up on the horse-hair sofa, crying: "I say, Top, read us one of your grinds." Whereupon Topsy, his modest reluctance overcome, began to read in "a kind of melodious growl with a considerable sing-song, resting his head on one hand, while with the other he ceaselessly twisted his watch-chain." Through realistic and lyrical mediaevalism Morris led them with such verse as:

> "They hammered out my basnet point
>   Into a round salade," he said,

and:

> Gold on her head and gold on her feet,
>   And gold where the hems of her kirtle meet,
> And a golden girdle round my sweet;
> Ah! qu'elle est belle La Marguerite,

both soon to appear in Morris's first volume: *The Defence of Guinevere and Other Poems*. Jones, meanwhile, worked away at a pen-and-ink sketch. From the sofa, Rossetti gazed at Morris with "large melancholy eyes," listening to the rise and fall of the chant. On that evening Prinsep discovered that in this society of pseudo-mediaevalists, "for a man not to know what was the difference between a basnet and a salade was shameful. And in all art there was to be an abundance of pattern. Golden ornamentation, from golden hair to golden slipper, was to be the decoration of every 'stunner' you chose to depict."

It was now two years since Morris had learned, with surprise, that he was a poet. He had, in the beginning, fallen to scribbling verses which his friends had delightedly—though according to the poet Bridges who saw them long afterwards, erroneously—declared were poetry. "Well, if this is poetry it is very easy to write," Morris had replied, and continuing his scribbling, had by this time so improved that he was now, with Rossetti's critical aid, preparing his verses for publication. Some of his poems had already appeared in *The Oxford and Cambridge Magazine*, where Rossetti had at once remarked Morris's talent. The forthcoming volume Gabriel much admired. "I would fain be worthy," he wrote with unusual chivalry, "to sit down at his feet."

Once again, as in his early days, Gabriel was king of a little court. At Oxford, but with greater prestige and greater intensity, he was to play once more the part of "leader" which he had played at the Academy Schools and in the original Preraphaelite circle. The unfailing fascination which Scott, four years earlier, had resented yet succumbed to, was still active, procuring for Gabriel an almost effortless domination over his disciples. "Rossetti's personality," wrote Prinsep in later years, "was most attractive. To his friends he was very lovable, so much so that his very eccentricities became objects of idolatry. Those who are beginning the art of painting, who have not yet started a line of their own, are too pleased to find a strong nature with most positive convictions, and are prone to fall down and worship one who can talk and think without any doubt of himself. So it was that no man had more convinced followers than Rossetti. We had such an admiration for him that we even talked as he talked and used his very intonations. He would sometimes turn and rend his followers, even as Sam Johnson would trample on poor Boswell; but he would allow no one else to do so, and he would put himself to any trouble or inconvenience to oblige them, even to insisting on his purchasers acquiring the pictures of his followers." And elsewhere Prinsep declared: "Rossetti was the planet around which we revolved . . . we sank our own individuality in the strong personality of our adored Gabriel."

Stanhope's testimony was almost identical with Prinsep's. "My uncle," wrote Stanhope's niece, "used to endorse the fact that among the banded talent of the Preraphaelites, Rossetti's was the master-mind which dominated the rest. No matter that all recognized him to be morally a man of lower ideals than themselves, the lure of his genius and his vivid personality conquered all who came in contact with it." To Jones, familiarity with Rossetti had brought no disillusion. "I was sensitive enough," he said long afterwards, speaking of this time, "to have suffered a shock to my worship if any jar had come, but I heard and saw none, and felt him perfect." The young enthusiasts adopted Gabriel's ideas and ideals, his mediaevalisms, his love of colour, passion, dream. They became learned in the books he loved: *The Morte d'Arthur, Sidonia the Sorceress*, the poetry of Browning. They imitated his habitual slang, his special vocabulary, the tones of his beautiful voice, and Jones even imitated his handwriting.

That Gabriel's voice charmed all who heard it, there is much evidence to prove. "Dante Gabriel Rossetti, according to one of his ardent admirers," said a writer in *Temple Bar* in 1899, "had an ideal voice for a poet. It was of such exceptional sweetness and melodiousness that, as the writer referred to happily expresses it, the birds might hear it with delight as having in it a music equal to their own." Of Rossetti and his voice, his friend Sir Sidney Colvin, in an essay, *Famous Voices I have Heard*, declared: "In reading or recitation, and not to a much less extent in daily talk, he was the greatest magician of them all. To hear him was to listen to a kind of chant, almost a monotone, but one which managed to express with little variation of pitch or inflection a surprising range and power of emotion. A kind of sustained musical drone or hum, rich and mellow and velvety, with which he used to dwell on and stress and prolong the rhyme words and sound-echoes, had a profound effect in stirring the senses and souls of his hearers. It is close upon fifty years since I first heard him read his poems . . . and the enchantment of the experience was such that I have never to this day been able to judge and criticize them as coolly as I might have done had I read them for the first time to myself." Sir Edmund Gosse, recalling his acquaintance with Rossetti would speak in similar vein.

It was Birkbeck Hill, now also fallen under Rossetti's spell, who brought another undergraduate, Algernon Charles Swinburne of Balliol, somewhat late into the circle at Oxford. Acquainted with the verse of Rossetti and his friends in *The Oxford and Cambridge Magazine*, Swinburne was already attracted by this phase of Preraphaelitism, by its sensuousness, imagery, symbolism, mystery, by a quality often cruel and melancholy in its pictures, poems and tales. For Swinburne the Preraphaelite mood was to be a definite stage in his advance beyond the Mid-Victorian standpoint. Rossetti's spontaneity, unconventionality, immediately captivated the strange, intense, nervous youth, so small of stature, with his flaming crest of hair. Temperamentally prone to self-surrender as to combativeness, Swinburne showed Gabriel a devotion as whole-hearted as that of Morris or Jones. He loved too the Preraphaelites' noisy, childish merriment, their jests, scuffles, outrageous vocabulary, their aversion to Victorianism, to a merely conventional religion and morality. In the society of Rossetti, Morris and Jones, he found a rare spiritual harmony. "Now we were four in company and not three," said Jones long afterwards, describing Swinburne's advent.

Upon the impressionable adolescence of these intense, sensitive, imaginative and sentimental youths Gabriel impressed not only his external boisterousness, humour and geniality, but also the rich, sombre, romantic *décor* of his darkened, inner world. Within the theatre of his imagination they learned to love, like Rossetti himself, a beauty remote from that of life and action, saddened with unreal sorrows, swept by passions existing for themselves alone, decorative agonies and ecstasies of the soul, yet real for them beyond any mundane reality. Only in a world so divorced from relief of passion in action could such emotional intensity be sustained. Like Rossetti they made a religion of woman's beauty. All beautiful women were "stunners" to them, and the "stunner" was their ideal, the Queen of Love and Beauty reigning over the dreams of these nineteenth-century knights. "Such a stunner!" Gabriel protested one day to his disciples, against the execution of a beautiful murderess, and when Hill ventured to suggest the supremacy of moral law even over feminine beauty, his shocked associates, really scandalized, overbore him with horrified cries of: "Oh Hill, you would never hang a stunner!"

It was now, as Preraphaelitism passed into this peculiarly "mediaeval" phase, in the hands of this new circle almost a generation younger than the original Brotherhood and remote from the moral aestheticism of Hunt, that the "stunner" became the basis of the Preraphaelite sense of beauty. Already a new mood, new forms of thought and feeling were "in the air," and amidst mutual encouragement akin to that provided by the original Brotherhood, this new Preraphaelite circle had begun to give them expression. Swinburne too was already writing verse. Morris read and praised his manuscript of *Rosamond*, afterwards burned and rewritten, and at this time Swinburne began his Tristram theme, not until long afterwards fully developed. Morris was now discovering the versatility of his own talent. It lay, he soon found, less in painting than in decoration, and he was already studying the forms and colours which he later used in his stained glass, tapestries, embroideries, fabrics, and furniture; meanwhile he made, with the help of the Oxford blacksmith, "antique" armour, which, when he tried it on, held him prisoner until he was dragged out of it by his friends.

This new phase of Preraphaelitism was indeed a "crystallization" of earlier elements such as *The Blessed Damozel*, *Hand and Soul*, Malory's *Morte d'Arthur*, chiefly created or modified by Rossetti. In passages of Swinburne's letters at this time, as in the tales of Morris, the influence of Gabriel's over-fine writing in *Hand and Soul* is clearly visible, and his disciples' efforts anticipate the prose of Pater. In such early verse as Swinburne's *Leper*, the direct influence of Rossetti's poems is equally evident, although more often Rossetti affected Swinburne through the work of his own disciple Morris, who was now proudly inscribing his first volume of verse: "To my friend Dante Gabriel Rossetti painter I dedicate these poems." Already these later "Preraphaelites" were planting the seeds of that "aestheticism" which was to dominate the last years of the century, touch the antipodes of Hunt's morality and mark the passing of "Victorianism."

How quickly yet unconsciously the change began, the Oxford circle clearly showed. An ill-balanced, intense coterie, they continually exploded in scenes of abnormal gaiety, irritability or depression. Jones, sickly, feeble, burned his lamp of life with a small, still, tense flame; Swinburne, highly temperamental, inspired like Jones with a passion for self-surrender, was a shrill mountain torrent of energy uncontrolled, while even Morris, though sturdy, energetic and bluff in appearance, carried within him the legacy of the "markedly neurotic family" from which he sprang. With concern or amusement, contemporaries began to remark their strangeness, the first suggestions of change. With a kindly, critical eye, Watts the artist watched the effect of Rossetti's influence upon Val Prinsep; "painting a picture at Oxford," said Watts, "fourteen feet long with figures ten feet high—'A muffin!'" And shortly afterwards he protested to Ruskin that under Gabriel's domination "the fine young baby" was drowning his individuality in a flood of mediaevalisms. Ruskin, in reply, promised to have "a serious talk" with Val, and expressed his own increasing disagreement with the Preraphaelites. "The worst of it is," he declared, "that all the fun of these fellows goes straight into their work, one can't get them to be quiet at it, or resist a fancy; if it strikes them ever so little a stroke on the bells of their soul, away they go to jingle, jingle, without ever caring what o'clock it is."

Ruskin, in fact, had been very critical of the Preraphaelites that year, condemning in his *Notes on the Academy*, Millais, whose present state he said, was "not merely Fall" but "Catastrophe"; and he advised them all to study Correggio, because in painting hair, they were "all under the strongest conviction that it is made of red sand"—a remark which Lizzie must have specially appreciated, and perhaps might have been better able than others to explain. Indeed, so caustic were Ruskin's criticisms, journals formerly condemnatory, such as the *Athenaeum*, now actually defended the Preraphaelites against these strictures of their former ally.

Rossetti, rejecting exhibitions, was as usual out of the strife. Enjoying at Oxford his new-found liberty, he still happily sustained with his followers the "campaign" that seemed too good to end. It was, indeed, too good to allow the outer world to enter, and the Preraphaelite circle in Oxford soon became as exclusive as the old Preraphaelite Brotherhood had been. Almost every attempt to bring them into relations with the social life of the town and University they evaded. To elude an undesired invitation Rossetti and Jones even dashed late one evening to London, reached the station hotel at 10 o'clock that night and returned to Oxford the next morning by the first train. To escape the dullness of conventional dinner-parties, teas and similar social amenities, they invented whatever excuses were available.

Good Dr. Acland was their chief bugbear. "The Rose of Brazil," as for some undiscoverable reason they named him, seemed to them the very prince of bores. His generous hospitality was almost unescapable. To avoid tea in a meadow with him and his children, they again fled to London. Once Morris, shamming illness to avoid one of Acland's dinners, was caught by the benevolent doctor (who left the dinner table in order to give prompt and gratuitous medical aid), playing cribbage with a friend. Forced to invent an almost miraculous recovery as an explanation, the disgusted Morris and his cribbage partner were whirled away in the doctor's carriage to their inevitable doom. Swinburne, once trapped into hearing Acland read an interminable paper on "Sewage," lost all self-control and made a "scene."

The painters' hatred of what they regarded as smug middle-class, mid-Victorian England, encouraged by Rossetti, was deep; their revolt instinctive, comprehensive and elemental. Morris, detesting idleness, empty urbanity and the mental and imaginative limitations implied in an entirely conventional outlook, adopted an opposite extreme. Wearing a workman's blouse, often covering himself unconsciously, as he worked, with dabs of paint and dye, he took little trouble to remove the traces of his labour, and Gabriel, who in some things had his highly conventional moments, repeatedly declared: "Topsy has the greatest capacity for producing and annexing dirt of any man I ever met with." Morris, painting the Union roof while drops of paint fell on his head and smock and ran down the brush handle onto his hands, was certainly no typical mid-Victorian "gentleman." Prinsep watched him standing on the floor of the Union gazing up at the roof with legs wide apart, paint-stained hands behind his back, hair and clothes smothered in paint, and thought how comic he looked. Once, it was said, a housemaid, fearing from his unkempt appearance that he meant to steal the silver, refused to admit him to an Oxford tea-party to which he had been invited.

In his antagonism to contemporary "culture," Morris even adopted a rough, boorish manner to those he thought mere conventional snobs. "My good man," said an Oxford don, entering the Union one day with some ladies, and taking him in his paint-stained blouse for a workman, "can you tell me the subjects of these pictures?" "Morte d'Arthur," roared Morris fiercely, glaring through paint-splashed spectacles as he dashed up a ladder to the scaffolding in the roof; and the next day Rossetti received from the indignant don a complaint of the extreme rudeness of one of his "workmen." It was Jones who made a caricature that evening, showing Morris, covered with paint and gazing at the Union roof, and with the inscription beneath: "O Tempera, O Morris!"

Sometimes Rossetti found Morris's informality trying, for it rivalled, at times even exceeded, his own. It was so, for example, when, on going to dine at Christchurch, he found that Morris had brought no dress clothes. Gabriel thereupon ordered him to don the bursting costume of Hughes who was thinner. Morris, in fact, preferred to stay at home, as Jones, afraid to dine at the high table, was doing. But Rossetti, in unusually serious mood, made Morris join him, and on the way even sternly reproved him for a spot of paint he detected in Morris's hair. It was Prinsep, a witness of this comedy, who suddenly noticed during dinner, that Rossetti himself, instead of the evening-dress which seemed to him so important for Morris, was absent-mindedly wearing his old, shabby, paint-stained, plum-coloured frock-coat, daily worn by him at that time in the studio.

Morris was, of course, an important element in The Jovial Campaign. To him, as plutocrat, was granted the privilege of financing the expedition whenever, as often, money was scarce. He also occupied the post of chief butt or target for wit, humour, practical jokes. Gabriel's affection for him expressed itself largely in continual attempts to irritate his explosive friend. They teased Morris about his increasing stoutness, painting into the decorations of the Union roof which Morris had begun, fat little figures of him among the flowers. Stanhope and Jones, rising to more exquisite inventions, secretly sewed up his waistcoat overnight, so that in the morning, on attempting to wear it as usual, Morris was said to have regarded his supposed increase of girth during the night with alarm. Declaring that Morris would never get Iseult's head right until he had taken "stunner Lipscombe" for his model, Gabriel sent him off with his sketch-book to her at the inn at Godstow which her father kept. But the "stunner's" mother, already irritated by the attention her eighteen-year-old daughter's good looks attracted from undergraduates and artists, sent Morris back crestfallen. On his return he found a derisory rhyming placard over his bedroom door:—

> Poor Topsy has gone
> To make a sketch of Miss Lipscombe,
> But he can't draw the head,
> And don't know where the hips come.

Before the Jovial Campaign ended, however, Morris surprised his friends by his sudden attachment to one of their models, Jane Burden. She was, according to her marriage entry in the church register afterwards, the daughter of an Oxford "groom." Gabriel, who had just introduced her to the Pre-raphaelite circle, had discovered Jane and her sisters, during the last days of the long vacation, some said "in a box" at the theatre, others while looking round for models in church. Drawn to Jane's dark, passionate, un-English beauty, Gabriel had persuaded her to sit to himself and his friends. Rumour afterwards whispered that Gabriel and Jane had fallen in love almost at sight and would have married if Gabriel had not felt morally bound to marry Lizzie should he ever bring himself to marry at all.[1]

Now at any rate, Jane replaced the absent Lizzie as model for Guinevere in his painting at the Union. Guinevere, the cause of Launcelot's exclusion from the chapel of the San Grael, is prominently portrayed, standing amidst the foliage of an apple tree. The somewhat crude symbolism is the same as that Rossetti employs in his poetic and prose approximations to this theme, entitled *The Orchard-Pit*, written twelve years later. The earlier studies for Guinevere in the Union painting, it is interesting to note, were from Lizzie, but later ones and the painting itself, are portraits of Jane Burden. Later, the cynical story spread that Gabriel, in his dilemma, ordered Morris and Jane to marry, so that Jane should at least be kept within the Preraphaelite circle.

Whatever the circumstances, certainly Morris fell deeply in love with Jane Burden. His feeling found early expression in a poem, *Praise of my Lady*, which Lady Burne-Jones afterwards declared a true likeness of Jane, and which first appeared in the volume of verse Morris was then preparing for the press: *The Defence of Guinevere and Other Poems*.

> My lady seems of ivory
> Forehead, straight nose, and cheeks that be
> Hollow'd a little mournfully.
>   *Beata mea Domina!*
>
> Her forehead, overshadow'd much
> By bows of hair, has a wave such
> As God was good to make for me.
>   *Beata mea Domina!*
>
> Not greatly long my lady's hair,
> Nor yet with yellow colour fair,
> But thick and crispèd wonderfully:
>   *Beata mea Domina!*
>
> Heavy to make the pale face sad,
> And dark, but dead as though it had
> Been forged by God most wonderfully,
>   *Beata mea Domina!*

[1] *v. inf.* pp. 369 and 649–50.

> Of some strange metal, thread by thread,
> To stand out from my lady's head,
> Not moving much to tangle me.
> *Beata mea Domina!*[1]

So the description runs on for twenty-two stanzas in all, and full of details of Jane's appearance, many of which we again find in Rossetti's *House of Life*, some twelve and more years later.

> All men that see her at any time,
> I charge you straightly in this rhyme,
> What, and wherever you may be,
> *Beata mea Domina!*
>
> To kneel before her; as for me,
> I choke and grow quite faint to see
> My lady moving graciously.
> *Beata mea Domina!*

So ended the poem. That final note of modesty, of self-abasement even, was essentially Morris. Some of his earlier writings in both poetry and prose, as well as his Union painting: *Sir Palomedes' jealousy of Sir Tristram*, by their insistence upon unhappy, despised and rejected love, might suggest some earlier, deep disappointment in love, on the part of the author. More truly perhaps, they reflect his innate tendency to self-surrender and self-denial rather than to passionate self-assertion. His shyness, chivalry and reverence for "stunners," if we may believe Prinsep, now marked Morris's courtship with a decorum (within its limits), as exacting as even the most extreme Victorian convention required, for whenever Prinsep invaded the upstairs sitting-room in George Street to which Morris and Janey resorted for privacy, he found Morris absorbed in an apparently interminable reading aloud of Dickens's *Barnaby Rudge*, to his bored companion. Jane's entry into the circle led to the substitution of dark hair as the ideal in place of Lizzie's golden locks. "As this lady had dark hair," wrote Prinsep, "the legendary 'stunner' with the auburn hair was in abeyance for a time."

Rossetti and his circle might ignore the outer world, but they did not escape external interest and criticism, which, at times,

[1] *v. inf.* pp. 371–6 and p. 401 and *Notes* to p. 401.

became embarrassing to the dilatory painter Gabriel had now become. Having postponed profitable commissions in order to carry on the "campaign," Rossetti, practically penniless, and obliged to refuse Brown's request for repayment of debts, excused himself on the score of "this work which I ought not to have undertaken at all, knowing myself." Although "very jolly work in itself," he said, "really one is mad to do such things." The delay he explained as usual by excessive care, but Prinsep in retrospect, gave another reason, declaring that while the rest worked hard at the Union, he never saw Rossetti do more than "one half-hour's work at his picture" during the time he was in Oxford, and that instead, Gabriel spent most of his time painting water-colours, including *The Tune of Seven Towers* and *The Blue Closet*.

There had also for a short time been strained relations with the Union Committee, which believed that the interim committee had exceeded its powers in sanctioning Rossetti's project. Finally, however, Woodward the architect had secured for the Preraphaelites unanimous approval of a loan of £350 to meet expenses, and their admission, as honorary members, to the Union Society.

As autumn advanced, critical acquaintances drifted to Oxford to see the results of their industry. Patmore in mid-October, specially impressed by Gabriel's colour, "so brilliant as to make the walls look like the margin of a highly illuminated manuscript," "sweet, bright and pure as that of the frailest waif of cloud in the sunrise," compared his painting to "a steam of rich distilled perfumes," to Mendelssohn's *Lieder Ohne Worte*, declared him "the only modern rival of Turner as a colourist," and approved his theme! At Christmas, Patmore's eulogies appeared publicly in the *Saturday Review*. Ruskin meanwhile, grew increasingly curious to see the decorations at Oxford. "Anxious to hear of Gabriel's doings," he even wrote to William Rossetti asking if there was any truth in "a malicious report" he had heard "from an envious person," stating that Gabriel "'was going to Florence and we should hear no more of him.'" But when, a fortnight after Patmore's visit Ruskin came to Oxford to see for himself, he ecstatically declared, despite his recent disappointment with the Preraphaelites, that

Gabriel's was "the finest piece of colour in the world," and offered to knock seventy guineas off Rossetti's debts to him, if he would fill another of the bays in the Union. The roof he thought "clever but not right." "The fact is," he told William, "they're all the least bit crazy and it's very difficult to manage them." Ruskin always felt instinctively that the artists he met needed "managing" by himself, whatever their own opinions on the matter might be. He obviously did not suspect, as he certainly should have done, that the work he so admired was already doomed by technical incompetence to early extinction.*

On the last night of October, Gabriel and Morris had just sat down to play whist with two others of the circle, when Brown walked in. He admired all he saw, liked all he did, except climbing 80-foot ladders at the Oxford Museum which made him "quite giddy," and he particularly appreciated the genial atmosphere created by the circle. "All very jolly here . . . lots of good fellows of all sorts here," he wrote to his wife, with unintentional but doubly significant emphasis of repetition, at one o'clock in the morning, and, as his biographer described it, "in a somewhat Bacchic hand." But like Hunt, who also paid the band a visit, Brown, too poor to abandon remunerative work for such delights, refused all cajoleries to stay and help them. As November dawned, Hill watched them "still working away hastily." "What other set of artists," he mused, "would work so hard for nothing except fair fame and love of art?" Gabriel's he thought "almost the most beautiful painting" he had ever seen.

Interested in his work and play, happy at Oxford as he had seldom been before, never was Gabriel nearer to breaking Lizzie's spell over him than now. Lizzie must have divined this, had probably heard in some way—Emma would certainly "pump" Brown on his return—of the new star Jane. So once again the unfailing trump card was played, and Jones, in mid-November, learned with "awe-stricken distress" that Lizzie, whom he had not yet seen, was "ill again," and trying a hydropathic "cure" at Matlock. Gabriel, on hearing of her illness left Oxford to join her, and on November 14th, Cormell Price, one of Jones and Morris's Oxford Brotherhood, recorded

* v. Notes.

in his diary: "Rossetti unhappily called away through Miss Siddal's illness at Matlock." Swinburne, who had known Rossetti for but a fortnight, was bitterly disappointed.

Having enjoyed this "experiment in a style of which I, for one, should like to devote the whole of my time better than to any other branch of the art," as he declared, Rossetti long intended to return to Oxford and complete his unfinished painting, even to decorate more bays. But the intention was never fulfilled. "His panel alone," wrote Prinsep, "remains uncovered, with nothing thereon but a vision of angels, and Lancelot lying asleep. . . . But there was a large gap of bare wall which Rossetti never took the slightest trouble to fill." What he had done, however, he had enjoyed—painting, free from the embarrassments of oils, figures larger than life. "There, is no work," he wrote, "like it for delightfulness in the doing and none I believe in which one might hope to delight others more according to his powers."

Upon Gabriel's departure the group rapidly dissolved. Morris finished quickly; Jones very slowly; Pollen like Gabriel left without finishing at all. Soon the genial sounds of jokes, scuffles, laughter, popping corks, ceased. By the spring of 1858 the last of the painters was gone. Silence once more descended upon the Oxford Union. The Jovial Campaign was over.

VIII

DEAD LOVE
1858–1860

O never weep for love that's dead,
Since love is seldom true!

Dead Love E. SIDDAL

"TIN," even more pressingly than usual, was Rossetti's chief problem during the later months of 1858. Early in May he had returned from Matlock where he had been painting water-colours, besides apparently joining Lizzie in her "water cure" there. The pleasant days in Red Lion Square too were ended, for Morris was now in Oxford, determined upon a speedy marriage to Jane, while Jones had moved into Fitzroy Square after some months in Little Holland House as the guest of the Prinseps who had nursed him through a bad fit of melancholia due to solitude. Gabriel, who described Jones to Boyce as "an angel on earth and too good for this world," had shown such an uncharacteristic anxiety about him as hitherto only Deverell in his last illness had aroused.

And now, towards the close of the year, one effect of the Jovial Campaign was but too evident—there was no "tin"! Plint, scattering advance payments and—after a delicate "screwing up" by Gabriel—new commissions amongst Rossetti and his friends, had for a time saved the situation. But by July Rossetti was at the end of his resources, could not even repay Brown his own and Lizzie's share of the cost of the Preraphaelite Exhibition of the preceding year. And of this, Brown, forced to borrow from Plint in order to bury his dead baby, bitterly complained. In this crisis, with Ruskin's philanthropic ardour towards himself and Lizzie rapidly waning, Gabriel's thoughts turned towards Ruskin's American friend Charles Eliot Norton as a possible substitute for Ruskin himself. Like Canning in a different emergency, Gabriel decided that the new world should be called in to redress the balance of the old.

Taken by Ruskin to the Preraphaelite Exhibition in 1857, Norton, an enthusiastic student of Dante, had been impressed by Gabriel's Dantesque paintings there, and when, shortly afterwards, Ruskin had introduced him to Rossetti, he had immediately commissioned a portrait of Ruskin and a water-colour. After a year's unbroken silence he had written from America to Gabriel, enquiring about the progress of his commissions, and now, having received no reply, had written again, to ask if his previous letter had gone astray.

It was this which now turned Gabriel's thoughts to Norton as a possible source of supply. So, in July 1858, Rossetti sent Norton an unusually long and informative letter in which he tried to excuse his remissness with the plea of pressure of work, and to achieve his real aim of selling Norton *Before the Battle*, an inferior picture painted at Matlock. This, he now pretended, was the first work to hand fit for Norton's acceptance—which also explained his delay! With characteristic effrontery he proceeded to set forth his demands: "Meanwhile (to be thoroughly impudent, all things considered) may I beg your answer at once, that I may know how to act in the matter? and (worst of all, to be thoroughly sordid) may I beg without mincing, that you will consider this drawing or another as ready to be delivered at once on your decision, and that you will let me have with your answer to this letter, by return of post if possible, the amount of the commission (50 guineas if I am not mistaken)? for, to tell the truth, my Oxford labours of love have resulted in leaving me a little aground." Norton agreed to take the picture and must have sent the advance payment demanded, for Gabriel seized upon Ruskin's objections to the work and to the sale of it to his friend, as an excuse for leaving it unfinished until four years had passed. Norton almost certainly complained to Ruskin, for who can doubt that the reference is to Gabriel and Lizzie when in the following December, in language curiously reminiscent of his remarks to Mrs. Acland three years before, Ruskin asked Norton: "*Questi poveri*—what are we to do with them? You don't mean to ask me that seriously? Make pets of them, to be sure—they were sent to be our dolls, like the little girls' wax ones—only we can't pet them until we get good floggings for some people, as well."

Yet the close of the year found Gabriel once again penniless. On the last day of 1858 he sent William an S O S quite in the old way. He needed "£10 for a fortnight." By that time he was sure "the Llandaff people" (the Cathedral Chapter, which three years before had commissioned an altar-piece), would have sent him some money. "I am trying my best to keep at work," he continued, "but am driven so mad with small Xmas duns that I can hardly stay in the place." On getting "the Llandaff money" he would repay the loan "most faithfully. £5 would be better than none—or anything indeed." For the moment Gabriel had lost something of the careless ease with which he would order William to disburse. Perhaps even William was showing signs of revolt at last!

His pretence of unremitting industry he continued into the new year, boasting to Aunt Charlotte of the Llandaff alter-piece, a triptych, *The Seed of David.* "The first design for a work of some importance and therefore more valuable," he explained. "I feel quite emancipated in getting to work of so large a size. I trust to have something done to show you when you are next in London." Yet ten months later he was still "setting to work" on it, nor was it completed until 1864.* Already his power of invention was failing, and he was falling into the vicious habit of making "replicas" of the designs and paintings made in his earlier, enthusiastic years. These replicas were an easy means of making money at need, and their ever increasing number as the years passed—particularly after he employed "assistants" and contributed, it is thought, little beyond his own signature to these replicas—is a revelation of the continual monetary embarrassment he suffered and the consequent decline in his artistic conscience.

Although two years before, Rossetti had refused Ruskin's offer of membership of the Water-Colour Society, lest, as he told Allingham, "it might chance to bonnet my oil painting for good," his reputation as a water-colourist was now being rapidly established. His works in that medium were already fetching good prices which saved him from further visits to the pawnshop—"avuncularism" as he called it.

His contempt for his increasing but still mercantile patrons

* *v. Notes.*

grew with their unconscious claims upon his gratitude. "O wondrous Plint," he exclaimed to Brown. "Did you see that glorious stroke of business—the joining together of a head and a landscape into one great work here? Plint bites already and will buy I suspect." Bell Scott brought Gabriel a new patron, a Newcastle lead merchant, Leathart, who in the summer bought some of Brown's works. Congratulating his friend, Gabriel expressed a hope that Leathart would become "a victim of Art in the future. Who knows that he may not even pair with Plint as a twin lamb on the altar of sacrifice! He already courts the unsparing knife of the Druid Jones." It was not all fun. Certainly the buccaneering spirit was growing in Gabriel. Increasingly in the future he was to take this half jocular, half contemptuous attitude both to his patrons and the works he often foisted upon them. It was a sign of his growing demoralization. Probably below all lay the conviction he frequently and quite sincerely admitted to his most intimate friends as his life neared its close, that as an artist he had failed, his growing realization of the fact that he would never master the technique of painting. His dissatisfaction with his own work and with the aesthetically ignorant patrons who bought it, led him increasingly to look upon his art as mere business, and to express his disappointment in a half cynical humour. To "fool" his patrons was a kind of revenge not only upon them but also upon himself.

On April 26th, 1859, a wedding took place at Oxford, in the little old church of St. Michael. The bride—to quote the church register—was "Jane Burden, minor, spinster, of 65, Holywell, daughter of Robert Burden, groom"; the bridegroom, "William Morris, aged 25, bachelor, gentleman, of 13, George Street, son of William Morris, gentleman, deceased." Local tradition asserted that Rossetti, being in love with Jane himself, was not present. Although but negative evidence, the omission of his name from the church register and from all references to the wedding in the Rossetti records confirms belief in his absence from the ceremony, an absence all the stranger because the rest of the Oxford brotherhood, including Jones, did attend.

Certainly Gabriel had not lost the admiration he felt for Janey during the Jovial Campaign. Shortly after his return from Matlock, he had made, while talking to Boyce, a rough sketch of her—"a 'stunner' at Oxford, which he tore in fragments, but which," wrote Boyce, "I recovered from the fire-grate." Three weeks later Boyce left London, but in mid-December 1858, immediately after his return, he noticed in Chatham Place "a most beautiful pen and ink study of Topsy's 'Stunner' at Oxford." Was the change in Gabriel from the time of Janey's marriage, his increasing cynicism, neglect of Lizzie, marked preoccupation with other women, and sudden, precipitate marriage to Lizzie, a reaction to a double disappointment and disillusion in love?

After a six weeks' honeymoon on the Continent, the Morrises returned to London to occupy furnished rooms until the house Morris was building in the country should be ready for them. "The Red House," as it was named from its red brick walls, high-pitched roof of red tiles, was almost severely plain. "More a poem than a house," wrote Gabriel, enthusiastically, "but an admirable place to live in too." He christened it "Hog's Hole," the name of a hollow near by which amused him. The Red House, Morris decided, must be a model of originality and good taste. The large drawing-room upstairs he vowed to make the most beautiful room in England. The furniture and decoration must be after his own designs. At one end they placed the great settle from Red Lion Square, with its three painted cupboards now turned into a "minstrels' gallery." Jones designed seven pictures from his favourite romance, Sir Degrevaunt, and began to paint them in tempera on the walls. Below them Morris painted bushy trees, parrots, and labels bearing the motto he had adopted: "If I can." Gabriel, finding many labels still blank, amused himself by painting on them: "As I can't. . . ." On doors, walls and furniture Morris and his friends painted their pictures. Rossetti painted in oil on two panels of a cabinet his early designs: *The Meeting of Dante and Beatrice in Florence, and in the Garden of Eden,* with *Dantis Amor,* showing Love standing between the sun and moon, joining the two panels. The decoration of the Red House followed the model of the Jovial Campaign, even to the untimely fate of the mural paintings which faded and flaked off as at Oxford. The decoration of the hall, which was to have been filled with scenes from

Troy and a great ship carrying Greek heroes, was left like the Oxford frescoes, incomplete.

The same high spirits also prevailed. There were bearfights in the drawing-room, scrimmages even in the "minstrels' gallery," "apple-battles" from which Morris emerged on one occasion with a black eye, and there was much ragging of Topsy as in the past. There were also less primitive amusements: bowls in the garden, and hide and seek about the house, which made Janey Morris and Jones's *fiancée* "Georgie" Macdonald, hiding in lonely rooms, deliciously afraid. In the evenings they sang old English and French songs, including their beloved *Echos du Temps Passé* which had formerly beguiled the nights in Red Lion Square.

With Janey married and Lizzie estranged, embittered and ill, Gabriel showed an increasing tendency to find compensations elsewhere. His old habit of nocturnal wandering about the London streets now intensified. Sometimes during these noctambulations he must have contrasted his own aimless journeying with the presumably happy domesticity of Janey and William Morris amidst the rural charm of their new home. But Rossetti, "the Italian in London," was ever an "outsider" at heart, something of a "buccaneer," preferring the interesting, the exceptional, to the merely conventional or the "good." Even in later years, when he held the *entrée* to London society, he comparatively seldom availed himself of it, preferring his own intimate circle or solitary wanderings and adventures in the London streets to the dinner tables of the wealthy and respected.

An occasional companion of Rossetti's on these nocturnal expeditions at this time was the Scottish barrister Skelton, who now, in 1859, made Gabriel's acquaintance. For several years afterwards, Skelton, kept in London by Scottish Appeal cases and other business, would call for Rossetti in the afternoon when the House of Lords had risen, and together they would ramble about the river, dine at some unpretentious restaurant in the City, then go to the theatre or play whist at a friend's. "Rossetti," said Skelton, "liked a rubber, though he was a poor player, and rather addicted to abstruse speculations on the reasons which had induced him to play the wrong card."

They would "finish the evening with whisky-and-soda and poetry over the fire."

Italian or not, Rossetti loved London above all other places. Absent, he was nearly always unhappy and anxious to return. "He was a thorough cockney in his tastes," wrote Prinsep: "Until the indolence natural to middle age rendered exercise irksome to him, he loved to wander through the streets of London. He delighted in the vulgarities of the London slang. Many a night during the years '58, '59, '60 have I been his companion during his wanderings. I once took him to a sparring benefit at the Rotunda Theatre in the Blackfriars Road. Rossetti was no sportsman and nothing of a bruiser, but he wished to see it and I took him. I recollect our being shown on to the stage, where we took our places among a lot of sporting 'bungs,' *en evidence* of about as low an audience as could be found even in London. Rossetti reclined on his chair and hummed to himself in his usual absent manner as he looked at the roughs around him. . . . Pair after pair of young fellows stood up, sparred, received more or less 'gruel' and retired after their three rounds. Presently there stepped forward a negro. After his round he sat in his corner and was attended to by his friends, who fanned and otherwise refreshed him. While he was being fanned the 'nigger' assumed a seraphic expression which was most comic. 'Look,' cried Rossetti in a loud voice, 'Uncle Tom aspiring to heaven, by Jove!' The whole house 'rose' with delight. One of the 'patrons' seated by us wanted to stand us a pint apiece."

"Change," which Rossetti was so to emphasize in his auto-biographical sonnet sequence *The House of Life*, became very evident now, in both his life and art as he entered his thirtieth year. From this time he saw less of Lizzie than before, and the reason for this was, William surmised, Lizzie's ill health and the advent of new models for his painting, particularly Janey Morris, Miss Herbert and Fanny Cornforth.

Despite Janey's dark locks and the fact that Lizzie's pink and gold had lost its spell, Rossetti's atavistic passion for gold hair still held him. At the close of May 1858, shortly after his return from Matlock, he had called on Boyce, and read to him "a lovely little MS. poem of Browning's about a portrait of a golden-haired beauty on a golden ground that he copied from some lady's album." A few days later he persuaded the actress, "Miss Herbert," whom he thought "perfectly beautiful," to sit to him. Her name, said Boyce, was "rightly Mrs. Crabb, though she doesn't live with her husband." "Not a good actress," said Ellen Terry, "but her appearance made up to many for her want of skill. . . . Very tall, with pale gold hair and the spiritual, ethereal look which the aesthetic movement loved."

Gabriel's enthusiasm for Miss Herbert at this time was extreme. For her he now made "a delicate little drawing of a loving couple on a sea beach on a windy day," as Boyce described it, and borrowed two of Boyce's sketches of the sea coast near Babbacombe to make the background. Boyce he carried off in a hansom to see the drawing as well as a large head of Miss Herbert in water-colour, and also, what Boyce thought "a splendid design of Mary Magdalen meeting and jeered at by a lot of gay women on her way to the house of Jesus who is looking earnestly and absorbingly at her. D. G. R.," he added, "intends painting the head of the Magdalen from Mrs. Crabb." To the delight of Ruskin, who also much admired her, Rossetti chose Miss Herbert for the Virgin of the Llandaff triptych, but on actually beginning the work in the autumn of 1859, he substituted Janey Morris. Lady Burne-Jones, too, remembered a small water-colour of Miss Herbert, by Rossetti. It was, she said, "radiant in golden hair—just the head and throat on an emerald-green background—and deeply did we feel the tribute rendered to her beauty when we read the names which he had written around the four sides of the little picture: 'Beatrice Helen Guinevere Herbert'." It is a striking instance of the way Rossetti tried to bring his world of romantic dream to life, or to turn life into poetry.

"I think we got to know Rossetti," Mrs. Gaskell wrote to Charles Eliot Norton, in October 1859, after a three weeks' visit to London. "I went three times to his studio, and met him at two evening parties—where I had a good deal of talk with him, always excepting the times when ladies with beautiful hair came in, when he was like the cat turned into a lady, who jumped out of bed and ran after a mouse. It did not signify what we were talking about or how agreeable I was; if a particular kind of reddish brown, crepe wavy hair came in, he was away in a moment struggling for an introduction to the owner of said head of hair. He is not as mad as a March hare, but hair-mad."

Fanny Cornforth too had the kind of hair that held Gabriel as by a spell. "A pre-eminently fine woman, with regular and sweet features, and a mass of the most lovely blonde hair, light golden or 'harvest yellow,' " said William Rossetti. Fanny's first recorded appearance is due to Brown who, calling on Jones and Morris in Red Lion Square in January 1858, saw there "Fanny their model." "Interesting face and jolly hair and engaging disposition," commented Boyce on first meeting her, the following December, when Gabriel took him to see her at 24 Dean Street, Soho. The next day Boyce called on Stanhope: "He was painting his picture of a gay woman in her room by the side of the Thames at her toilet. 'Fanny' was sitting to him. She afterwards went up to Rossetti and I followed."

Of the two dates, 1856 and 1859 that Fanny herself gave in her two mutually contradictory accounts of her first meeting with Rossetti, one is demonstrably a little late. A water-colour study of her for *Found* is entitled *A Farmer's Daughter*, which in fact she claimed to be, and it is of course possible that *Found*, Gabriel's never-finished picture of a country girl turned prostitute in London, is based upon Fanny's actual experience. That Stanhope was now also painting Fanny in the same rôle may not be without its significance.[1] Nor, perhaps, is the fact that we have no definite information at all about Fanny's situation at this time. That she was illiterate and of humble, even vulgar social status, there is ample evidence to prove.

Fanny herself claimed, of course, to be of good but impoverished family, and to have been born in 1824 at the village of Steyning in Sussex, which, however, she placed in Surrey. Others declared she was a blacksmith's daughter and born in the same year as Rossetti himself. In London, turned artists' model, she assumed the name of a grandmother and became "Fanny Cornforth."

Her real name was Sarah Cox. William Rossetti rejected Bell Scott's story that Fanny was standing in the Strand

[1] I incline to say "almost certainly had its significance." *v. Notes.*

"cracking nuts with her teeth and throwing the shells about" when Gabriel first saw her, and that she threw some nuts at him as an introduction which quickly ended in his "carrying her off to sit to him for her portrait." Fanny's account (at least *one* of her accounts), told how she, an innocent village maiden visiting an elderly, respectable London cousin, was promenading the Surrey Gardens with this relative, during a firework display in honour of the return of Florence Nightingale from the Crimea in 1856, when Rossetti, accompanied by Brown, Jones, and their friend Cormell Price, succeeded by a pretendedly accidental collision, in knocking down her mass of golden hair, and while profusely apologizing, won her promise to come next day to his studio—with, of course, the respectable cousin—where, said Fanny, "he put my head against the wall and drew it for the head in the calf picture"; an easily recognizable description of Fanny's own easily recognizable portrait in one of Gabriel's studies for *Found*. Certainly Fanny's description of Gabriel's method of introduction and its association with the "gold hair complex" that had so impressed Mrs. Gaskell, is entirely in harmony with his temperament and ways, especially if we believe such tales as his biographer A. C. Benson tells, of Gabriel's making the acquaintance of one model by running out of a confectioner's with a half-bitten tart in his hand, to stare in her face, of another, "a simple country girl" who, sitting in a restaurant, felt her hair suddenly seized and untied. "I wanted to see how it looked," was Rossetti's reply to her indignant remonstrance, and, such was his fascination, within a few minutes she had agreed to sit to him for a picture.[1]

To many who knew them, the spell Fanny cast over Gabriel was inexplicable. Bell Scott, constrained to admit that for Rossetti she "must have had some overpowering attractions," at the same time confessed: "I never could see what they were." William Rossetti, who in this again disagreed with Scott, admitted that she had "no charm of breeding, education or intellect." Swinburne, sacrificing politeness to accuracy and

---

[1] The two elements this tale has in common with Fanny's, i.e. "the simple country girl" and the upsetting of the hair as an opening gambit, suggest that this is but another version of Fanny's tale, differing slightly as is usual with an oral tradition, and that something of the kind did in fact happen; cf. also Rossetti's own account of his method of obtaining passers-by as models; *v. inf.* pp. 423–4.

brevity, described her as a "bitch." She was, he asserted, "at the other pole of the sex" from Lizzie. In this fact, no doubt lay the secret of her hold upon Rossetti. Vulgar, vital, primitive, the antithesis of the over-strained ideal of "The Blessed Damozel," Fanny was the simplest, the most real of all the women Gabriel knew; she asked for no romantic sentiments, no heroics. Like the gipsy-girl who had attracted Gabriel at Hastings five years before as he wandered about, somewhat disconsolately with the ailing Lizzie, Fanny was, for him, "the image of savage, active health," a revitalizing influence upon so imaginative, so morbid a temperament as his.

Boyce liked both Gabriel and Fanny, and from this time until Rossetti's marriage and again after Lizzie's death, Fanny continually appears and reappears in the pages of his diary. Indeed, the association of the three friends is particularly prominent during these earlier months of 1859, and Boyce gives us the most intimate glimpses we have of their way of life at this time: a night in mid-January for example, when Boyce accidentally meets Fanny in the Argyle Rooms and takes her to supper at Quinn's. "She was in considerable trepidation lest Rossetti should come in—and lo! he did so." Three weeks later Boyce gives her a sovereign to help the furnishing of the house in Tennyson Street, Battersea, to which she was removing. Probably Rossetti was responsible for the removal and its cost, wishing to take her out of the atmosphere of Dean Street.

Henceforth, Tennyson Street became a favourite resort of both Boyce and Rossetti. "Rossetti came and we went to Tennyson Street and picked up Fanny, and thence to Zoological Gardens, where he wanted to draw the fawn for his Magdalen drawing. We stayed there three or four hours, most amused by the brown bear, wombat and some owls," Boyce recorded on March 24th; and again on April 2nd: "To Tennyson Street to tea with Fanny and D. G. R. Took with me a little oil sketch done on Hambledon Heath as a present for the former." A few days later, Boyce called on her with a present of a silver thimble and "made a slight pencil sketch of her." An entry for July 23rd, shows Gabriel in a characteristic situation. "D. G. Rossetti," he wrote, "persuaded me into giving him £40 commission for an oil portrait of Fanny, and asked me for £20

down which I could not refuse. Gave him £2 for a pencil sketch
of Fanny which he is to finish for me. He pleaded being very
hard up, or I should hardly have let him have so much tin on
account." Unlike so many of Rossetti's prepaid commissions,
the portrait was actually made, even completed by the following
mid-October, when Boyce rejoiced: "He has painted a splendid
portrait of Fanny for me (according to commission) in late
16th century costume. He has devoted the last month to the painting of it. Stanhope came in and admired it as greatly as I did."

Boyce's portrait of Fanny was doubtless *Bocca Baciata*, the
"kissed mouth" of Boccaccio's sonnet, which "loses not its
fascination but renews itself as doth the moon." Gabriel signed
the picture with his monogram, and inscribed on the back
Boccaccio's words: "Bocca baciata non perde ventura, anzi
rinuova come fa la Luna." "Rossetti," wrote the painter
Hughes to Allingham in February 1860, when Gabriel had just
completed *Bocca Baciata*, "has lately painted a most beautiful
head, a marigold background, such a superb thing, so awfully
lovely. Boyce has bought it, and will I expect kiss the dear
thing's lips away before you come over to see it. Gabriel," he
added, "is certainly looking tremendously well not to say fat."

This portrait, in fact, preluded the remarkable change which
now revealed itself in Rossetti's painting. In the first place it
was his first completed work of any importance in oils since his
Annunciation of nine years before. From this time onwards
Rossetti concentrated his energy upon his original ambition
to establish a reputation as a painter in oils. Nor was the change
in his painting one of medium alone. From his former Dantesque
and Arthurian themes he now increasingly turned to subjects
such as the *Bocca Baciata*, portraits of beautiful, richly clad
women, often presented under fanciful or exotic titles. Bell
Scott, unconsciously confirming and enlarging William's tentative explanation,[1] remarked: "The paradoxical conclusion
that women and flowers were the only objects worth painting,
was brought about by the appearance of other ladies besides
Miss Siddal coming within his orbit," and Holman Hunt, also
observing the change in Gabriel with regret, declared: "His
Cardiff Cathedral altar-piece (the Llandaff triptych), was

[1] *v. sup.* p. 249.

executed at the turning point from his first severity of style to a more sensuous manner."

From this time forward, certainly, "women and flowers" dominated his work; Guinevere replaced Beatrice, "Body's Beauty" (or "Lilith") ousted "The Blessed Damozel." Yet the earlier, ascetic ideal was neither destroyed nor banished. Henceforth new and old, "Youth and Change," Beatrice and Guinevere the symbols of his inner conflict, appear in his work as his conflicting moods dictate, a spiritual antiphony. "Rossetti," said his friend John Henry Middleton, Cambridge Professor and Director of the South Kensington Museum, "was addicted to loves of the most material kind both before and after his marriage, with women, generally models, without other soul than their beauty. It was remorse at the contrast between his ideal and his real loves that preyed on him and destroyed his mind."*

Rossetti's mental failure was due, as we shall see later, to other, more material causes than "remorse," although remorse was closely associated with the basic cause of all. Yet his work at this time, in both poetry and painting, echoing as it does the complications of his life and loves, remarkably confirms the general truth of Middleton's assertion. Gabriel's growing alienation from Lizzie and his reaction to Janey's marriage, seem to have thrown him into the arms of Fanny, the model for *Bocca Baciata*, and others of her kind. Was there no inner significance in his sudden resurrection and completion of a design begun four years earlier,[1] during his first period of doubt and disillusion about Lizzie, a pen-and-ink sketch showing Ophelia returning the gifts of Hamlet who cries: "I did love you once. . . . What should such fellows as I do crawling between heaven and earth! We are arrant knaves all; believe none of us. Go thy ways to a nunnery?" The design was elaborate but effective. The carving on the seat occupied by Ophelia shows the Tree of Knowledge encircled by a crowned serpent between two angels with uplifted swords, while on the frame was carved Hamlet's words to Ophelia: "I did love you once."

* *v. Notes* to p. 343.
[1] *v. sup.* p. 153. In an unpublished letter to Edmund Bates, dated September 24, 1879, Rossetti remarked: "The Hamlet subject has a lot of accessory meanings. . . ."

Gabriel's frustration, his inner dissatisfaction with the various complications and entanglements of his present way of life, as well as the "remorse" of which Middleton spoke, lie heavily upon his writing in both verse and prose at this time. "Your Shady Hill," he had told Norton in his letter of July 1858, referring to Norton's home, "is a tempting address, where one would wish to be. It reminds one somehow of the *Pilgrim's Progress* where the pleasant names of heavenly places really make you feel as if you could get there if the journey could only be made in that very way—the pitfalls plain to the eye and all the wicked people with wicked names. I find no shady hill or vale, though, in these places and pursuits which I have to do with. It seems all glare and change, and nothing well done. Another man might do better, no doubt, and find the shade that he could work in. But I see it is always to be thus with me."

And in this same letter, speaking of his translations, he tried by means of a pretendedly casual reference, to explain away, on academic grounds, the note of personal emotion so obvious in his version of the mediaeval Italian verses he entitled: *Laments the Presumption and Incontinence of his Youth*, and ascribed, probably incorrectly, to Guido Cavalcanti, the Italian poet he admired most after Dante. How Rossetti vitalized his version with personal emotion the following stanza clearly shows.

> How fierce aforetime and how absolute
>   That wheel of flame which turned within my head,
>   May never quite be said,
>   Because there are not words to speak the whole.
> It slew my hope whereof I lack the fruit,
>   And stung the blood within my living flesh,
>   To be an intricate mesh
>   Of pain beyond endurance or control;
>   Withdrawing me from God, who gave my soul
> To know the sign where honour has its seat
>   From honour's counterfeit.
> So in its longing my heart finds not hope,
>   Nor knows what door to ope;
> Since, parting me from God, this foe took thought
> To shun those paths wherein He may be sought.

It was, in fact, the very personal cry to which Rossetti was now trying to give expression in a poem he was vainly attempting to write: *God's Graal*, lamenting Lancelot's sin and its punishment, the ban placed upon his finding of the Grail. It had already been Rossetti's theme in painting, at the Oxford Union, nor was this to be his last treatment of the almost obsessive subject. Now too he praised Allingham's sentimental and melodramatic poem on incontinence, *Mea Culpa*, and painted in similar mood, *Sir Galahad at the Shrine*.

The sonnet Rossetti now wrote in 1859, *After the French Liberation of Italy*, which, despite its ostensible theme as a political allegory, is really a vivid representation of a prostitute's embrace, is in harmony with the similar subjects he was now representing in both verse and prose, in *Mary Magdalene at the Door of Simon the Pharisee*, in *Found* and *Jenny*.* This last he was now revising, adding to his earlier version of the poem "the slight framework of incident" as he described it, that is the realistic setting in Jenny's chamber. "I felt," Rossetti remarked in these later years, alluding to his earlier version of *Jenny*, "it was quite beyond me then (a world I was then happy enough to be a stranger to)."

How bitterly must the fading, neglected Lizzie have regarded the bold, vulgar beauty of her vigorous, golden-haired rival, Fanny, *Bocca Baciata*, flaunting herself as if in conscious derision, on Gabriel's canvas in Chatham Place. But Rossetti's light loves could not banish his unhappy consciousness of Lizzie in the background. His reaction when passion was spent, was a melancholy bewilderment and regret which permeates the poems he was now writing in the last months of 1859.

Rossetti's poetic impulse was almost entirely the off-spring of passion, and since the waning of his first spontaneous passion for Lizzie after 1854, he had written very little original verse. Now, for a short period poetic inspiration returned. He resumed both original poetry and his verse translations from the Italian mediaeval poets, and requested critical comments on them from various friends, including Allingham and Patmore. Strangely intimate and tender is the spirit of the poems he was now writing, *Even so, A Little While, A New Year's Burden*, all mourning the passing of love, and unlike anything he had written since his first poetic period closed six years before.

In *Even so*, the sea reappears, dull, stagnant, infected with

* *v. Notes.*

the heaviness of his own spirit as in the days at Hastings when the melancholy fit would fall. But now he mourns the lost happiness, intensity, significance love once brought into their lives:—

> Could we be so now?
> Not if all beneath heaven's pall
>   Lay dead but I and thou,
> Could we be so now!

For these lovers all is now heart's anguish in the presence of some nameless, irresistible, intangible evil, some blight or malignant spell cast upon their former passion. *A Little While* is the cry of love's last phase, while yet the lovers dread to see and admit that despite their wills and desires love is dying.

> A little while a little love
>   May yet be ours who have not said
>   The word it makes our eyes afraid
> To know that each is thinking of.
> Not yet the end: be our lips dumb
>   In smiles a little season yet:
>   I'll tell thee, when the end is come,
> How we may best forget.

And as the withering year dies it brings *The New Year's Burden*, a burden of dead love; of ways that part and do not meet again—

> The branches cross above our eyes.
>   The skies are in a net:
> And what's the thing beneath the skies
>   We two would most forget?
>   Not birth my love, no no—
>   Not death my love, no, no—
> The love once ours, but ours long hours ago.

Meanwhile, Lizzie too was versifying; less subtly, with an unsophisticated woman's directness, but with much of Gabriel's self-conscious pathos, of pleasure in pain—

> O never weep for love that's dead
>   Since love is seldom true!

Amongst Gabriel's various embarrassments at this time was the "siren-like" Annie Miller, as Brown described her. "Went to see Fanny Cornforth, and took her some apples and walnuts," wrote Boyce on October 15th, 1859. "She told me Rossetti had had a call from Annie Miller, who had left a card. He is in the habit, she says, of sitting in a large chair o' nights reading Balzac's novels." Three days before Christmas came the dénouement. "Miss Annie Miller called on me in the evening in an excited state," wrote Boyce, "to ask me to recommend her someone to sit to. She was determined on sitting again in preference to doing anything else. All was broken off between her and Hunt. I pitied the poor girl very much, by reason of the distraction of her mind and heart. Called on Hunt in the evening to tell him of her visit and that, finding that she was resolved on sitting again, I should ask her to sit to me if she could do nothing else, for she rejected (naturally enough) all his efforts to find employment through friends. Finding he could not get her to do what he wanted to make her a desirable wife for him, nor to wean herself from her old objectionable habits, he had broken off the engagement; but the whole affair had preyed on his mind for years. The interview was friendly throughout." Six days later Boyce wrote: "Annie Miller came and sat to me. Rossetti came in and made a pencil study of her. She looked more beautiful than ever."

That Gabriel played some part, perhaps a major part in the breaking of Annie Miller's engagement seems certain. William Rossetti, probably unaware of the details of the affair, described his brother as "not very deeply censurable" in the matter; but Edward Clodd, the rationalist, to whom Hunt told the story after Rossetti's death, interpreted it as a serious moral lapse on Gabriel's part. But that Rossetti's conduct was, as Hunt declared, the sole cause of his rejection of Annie, is hardly suggested by Boyce's record. Hunt had, indeed, long contemplated this break, for early that year Brown had noted in his diary a change in Hunt's feelings towards Annie and his abandonment of his intention to marry her. In later years Hunt, accidentally meeting Annie, "a buxom matron with a carriage full of children, on Richmond Hill," and learning that she, like himself, was now happily married, forgave "the offence, which in fact," he said, "worked me good rather than harm." In real life, Annie was obviously no apt example of the moral she had illustrated in Hunt's painting, *The Awakened Conscience*.

By this time, Rossetti, like his mediaeval knights was, at least nominally, engaged in martial exercises. Fear of Louis Napoleon had led to a revival of the volunteer movement, and the Preraphaelites shared the general enthusiasm for self-defence. Woolner, congratulating Mrs. Tennyson on her husband's poem "Riflemen form," thought it "like a gun booming of danger fast coming upon us." The artists raised and organized the Artists' Rifle Corps, very smart in its grey and silver uniform. Brown, Morris, Jones, Hunt, Rossetti, Millais, Swinburne, Prinsep, Stanhope and G. F. Watts all joined the corps. William Richmond was Honorary Secretary and Ruskin held the unique position of "Honorary Member." It was Brown who brought Gabriel into this new and different Brotherhood. The duration of Rossetti's active assistance is indeterminate, but seems to have been of the shortest, for his name is not on the muster roll. Perhaps his inclination to argue with the drill sergeant accelerated his departure. "Why?" he would urbanely enquire in his beautiful voice, when the sergeant yelled "Right about face." Morris, it was said, on hearing the order "right" or "left turn," invariably turned the wrong way, and in his surprise, effusively begged pardon of the man facing him. Rossetti's first shot was said to have restored his prestige instantly, as it hit the bull's eye. But his triumph was short-lived, as never again could he even hit the target. Brown's first attempt if we may trust tradition, missed the target, but injured his dog which was observing his efforts with approval. Hunt, stolidly attempting to improve as a marksman, invariably filled his pockets with the screws when cleaning his rifle, and forgot where he had put them.

But the Preraphaelites' greatest moment as soldiers was in June 1860, when Queen Victoria reviewed 13,000 volunteers in Hyde Park amidst tremendous enthusiasm. Sala the journalist "noted the Artists' Corps, and the pleasant murmur that fluttered through a standful of ladies: 'There's Mr. Leighton; there's Mr. Millais!' 'Do all the poets do exercises with rifles and bet on Tom Sayers?'" Mrs. Browning wrote to Allingham from Rome. "Why, how you are all advancing in the 'national defence and in civilization quotha!' Draw a little of this 'muscular Christianity' into the field to help my Italians in

Sicily or Venice, instead of spending it in dreams of French invasion which won't turn up after all!"

But that Rossetti assisted in the Hyde Park Review is improbable; not only because his association with the Artists' Corps was of the slightest, but also because on the day when the Park was crammed with troops and spectators, he had only just returned to London after a three weeks' honeymoon in Paris.

IX

THE WOEFUL VICTORY
1860–1861

"How should I your true love know
From another one?"
By his cockle-hat and staff
And his sandal-shoon."

"For a token is there nought
Say, that he should bring?"
"He will bear a ring I gave
And another ring."

An Old Song Ended D. G. ROSSETTI

IN THE SPRING of 1860, Gabriel and Lizzie had married at last! It was no such ideal consummation of love as he had once dreamed of in the first, unclouded enthusiasm of youth. Ten long, aimless, desultory years had passed since he first saw and worshipped "the fair woman who was his soul." Upon both, the intervening years had worked changes, spiritual as well as physical. The once slender, gracious, dreamy youth was now a "short, squat, bull-doggish" man of thirty-two with "sallow face . . . massive and powerful." The once beautiful girl of seventeen was now a broken and embittered invalid of twenty-seven. The shadows of their long probation lay heavily upon both. Their marriage, delayed beyond the freshness of youth and early passion, borrowed inevitably the bitterness of the mocking years.

The marriage was, in fact, but the dreary culmination of a trying experience in the spring of 1860. Lizzie was again very ill, and once again, as in the earlier days of his passion for her, Gabriel had accompanied her to Hastings. Playing perhaps a last desperate card, refusing even the offered ministrations of Emma Brown, Lizzie had kept Gabriel alone by her bed to watch her sufferings. Believing her dying, torn by a sense of guilt, by fears and sympathy for her in her misery, Rossetti had been brought to marriage—a marriage which he must have believed, as he thought her dying, could not last long.

262

Thus by mid-April, to the astonishment of the Rossettis who evidently expected no such dénouement, Gabriel was making preparations for the event. "Like all the important things I ever meant to do," he wrote to his mother in a gloomy, conscience-stricken mood, "to fulfil duty or secure happiness —this one has been deferred almost beyond possibility. I have hardly deserved that Lizzy should still consent to it, but she has done so, and I trust I may still have time to prove my thankfulness to her. The constantly failing state of her health is a terrible anxiety indeed; but I must still hope for the best, and am at any rate at this moment in a better position to take the step, as regards money prospects, than I have ever been before." His "prospects" had certainly improved, but only his prospects! A few weeks before, penniless, he had tried to raise money in every possible quarter.

Once again, in his indecision, he fell into his accustomed lethargy, saw this marriage as destined and inescapable. For this must be the nameless evil that menaces the lovers in *The Song of the Bower* which he now wrote—a song of separation, of parting, written, Swinburne believed, "if with any direct reference," to Fanny. "In fact," wrote Swinburne, "I may almost say I know it, from Gabriel's own admission—implied when he and I were discussing that yet unpublished poem, which in the early days of *Bocca Baciata* may not have been so comically exaggerative as it seemed to me even when I first met the bitch."[1] Amidst exaggerative sentiment, self-conscious dramatization, associative and symbolical erotic imagery characteristic of Rossetti, *The Song of the Bower* expresses his helpless, hopeless, "fascinated" mood before the "omen" of impending marriage to this sick woman, an invalid, barely existing as it seemed, in the shadow of death. Like some super-

---

[1] *cf.* W. M. R.'s hardly convincing comment: "*The Song of the Bower* I regard as relating to Miss Siddal. Circumstances had kept him more apart from her than had been the case in earlier years, and he gave voice to his feelings in this poem. So at least I regard it." *Memoir*, p. 203. Swinburne, it is worth noting, had an extraordinarily good and accurate memory.

The Song of the Bower does not describe the physical type to which Miss Siddal belonged. *cf.* also the following:—"Large lovely arms and a neck like a tower . . ." *The Song of the Bower* (1860). "These women are given to us no less noble in body than in soul; large-eyed, and large-armed also; such as a man may love with all his life," Rossetti's *Essay on Blake* (1862). The personal note in the passages is obvious, and could hardly relate to the dying or dead Lizzie.

natural spell the marriage threatens him, a portent of evil, of separation from the vulgar, earthy woman who gave him physical and mental renewal. It was a swan song, a remembered riot of passion under the threat of separation, the cry of one inexorably drawn from the sunlight into the dark. It was thus, reluctantly, hypnotically almost, he yielded to the thought of marriage, fearing it as his sister Christina feared it, accepting it at last, in these unhappy circumstances, "for terror for pity"—

> Thinking "I stirred not and yet had the power!"
> Yearning, "Ah God if again it might be!"

For marriage would mean, he thought, that she than whom "the sun's kiss is colder," must be discarded for a waning moon. So he stood as ever, helpless in the heart of his dilemma, like the *Dantis Amor* he had recently painted—love, standing between the sun and moon!

He had actually got the marriage licence when Lizzie suddenly grew worse than before. Then, remorsefully, penitently, frantically, as if fearing Lizzie might die in mortal sin, Gabriel hastened the arrangements for the wedding. "If I were to lose her now," he told William, "I do not know what effect it might have on my mind, added to the responsibility of much work commissioned and already paid for, which still has to be done, and how to do it in such a case." It was a curious, unconsciously revelatory remark. Fearing Lizzie could not "enter the cold church with safety," he enquired about a special licence, but believed it would mean too great expense and delay. "I still trust to God, we may be enabled to use it," he wrote of the ordinary licence he had already obtained. "If not, I shall have so much to grieve for, and (what is worse), so much to reproach myself with, that I do not know how it might end for me." The thought of suicide as an escape from his life's ceaseless dilemmas ever came easily to him.

Days of the "most agonizing anxiety," said Gabriel, followed, during which Lizzie seemed "ready to die daily and more than once a day." As before, mysterious and increasing attacks of sickness seized her, nor could she retain even the lightest of food or drink. Then, equally "sudden and unaccountable," a slight improvement began. Soon, Lizzie would "get up and come downstairs," even eat a little without sickness. Nevertheless, throughout this severe attack, no mention appears in Rossetti's available letters, of doctor or nurse, of relatives or even of landlady, while Emma Brown's offer of help was definitely rejected because Lizzie's state—so said Gabriel, but evidently at the desire of Lizzie—"would be too painful for any one to witness. I assure you," he added, "it has been almost too much for me!" Fearing and hating death, relapsing into almost complete identification with Lizzie in her sufferings, Gabriel was thoroughly frightened, deeply moved, felt, he said—his scarcely conscious thoughts and feelings suggesting as usual when he was in an emotional state, associative imagery—"as if I had been dug out of a vault, so many times has it seemed to me that she would never lift her head again."

And once again his painting reflected his mood. From the sensuous *Bocca Baciata* he turned during these days of anxiety to a theme from the almost prophetic *St. Agnes of Intercession*, his adolescent tale, painting the scene in which the beloved woman dies while her artist-lover paints her portrait, and calling it *Bonifazio's Mistress*. Rossetti's marked tendency, in mental and emotional exhaustion, to relapse from the dominantly rational plane into auto-suggestion, self-hypnotism, superstition, had probably led him to believe now in the prophetic quality of his story and that the moment of Lizzie's death, so long expected, was come. But again Lizzie recovered. A new date, May 12th, Gabriel's birthday, was chosen for the wedding but had to be abandoned, for not until eleven days later did the simple ceremony take place.

St. Clement's Church, Hastings, can hardly have known a wedding more sombre than that of May 23rd, 1860, when, accompanied only by the clergyman, by a stranger and his wife (probably the caretakers), as witnesses, Gabriel and Lizzie married at last. "Lizzie and I are just back from Church," he wrote briefly and dispiritedly to his mother. "We are going to Folkestone to-day, hoping to get on to Paris if possible; but you will be grieved to hear her health is no better as yet. Love to all." Of Lizzie's feelings now that the long fight for legal possession of Gabriel was over we have no sign. As in defeat, in illness, so in the moment of victory she remains obscure, enigmatic as ever. How far was her strange, nervous malady the unconscious or conscious result of her baffled desire for marriage, and of her knowledge that only through illness now, through Gabriel's anxiety, remorse and fear could she attain her end? Was her illness caused by addiction to a drug (first doubtless taken as a medicine), by the enormous quantities of laudanum, in fact, she was now taking, and of which, a few months later, she openly boasted? The questions which hover about Lizzie are many and unanswerable.

It must have been Lizzie, enchanted with the French capital —which Gabriel did not like—who fixed the honeymoon in Paris. But the honeymoon was little brighter than its prelude. The couple spent a few days at Boulogne where Gabriel was glad to see his old friends the Maenzas, and thought of renting an old château near by. In Paris, they began as usual to live extravagantly, and within a week had to leave the Hotel Meurice in the Rue de Rivoli for "rather cheaper lodgings" let by an Englishwoman. Jones, long since converted from celibate ideals and now marrying in Manchester, was, with his wife "Georgie," to join the Rossettis in Paris. But Jones fell ill immediately after the wedding and they could not come as arranged. Alone together, Gabriel and Lizzie found life stale. The mere realization, long deferred, of an intense desire, can, it is said, produce severe neurotic illness, and Lizzie's victory certainly brought little healing in its train. While she lay sick in her room, Gabriel read to her *Pepys's Diary*, which he had brought, intending, he said, regretfully, to have "yelled over it in company" with the Joneses. He painted at *Found*, and in pen-and-ink copied his early gloomy design *How they met Themselves*, showing two lovers who, lost in a wood, meet their own wraiths, an omen of impending death, at least to the woman, who sinks in terror to the ground. It was as apropos, yet as untimely, as *Bonifazio's Mistress*, this drawing of the two lovers lost in a thicket of doubts and fears beneath the shadow of death!

For relaxation, Gabriel stole away at times to wander about the streets and picture-galleries of Paris. He bought Lizzie two dogs, one big, the other little and fat. The fat one they named "Punch" on reading in *Pepys's Diary*: "Lord how I did laugh to hear poor common persons call their fat child Punch, which name I do perceive to be good for all that is short and thick." They soon wearied of what Gabriel called "dragging about" in Paris, and if the climate had not seemed to be doing Lizzie good, they would have returned almost immediately. Debating whether to settle in Paris, in the château they had liked near Boulogne, or to go "South" for the winter, they remained in the French capital three weeks; then lack of means, boredom, and the call of London, brought them home. The close of their dreary honeymoon was in harmony with its beginning; for, reading in the first newspaper he bought on landing, that a journalist he had known had suddenly died leaving a widow and children in need, Gabriel, on reaching London, with almost empty pockets, drove straight to an only too familiar pawnbroker, pledged all the jewellery he had given Lizzie as a wedding present, went on to the widow's lodging, forced the money upon her and, after paying his cab-driver, entered Chatham Place with his bride, penniless. The honeymoon was over!

But it was not without repercussions elsewhere of which Rossetti must have been miserably conscious. "Called on Fanny Cornforth who, I heard . . . was ill," wrote Boyce on June 5th. "Found her so in bed. It appears she frets constantly about R(ossetti), who is with his wife in Paris, the latter very ill and in a deep decline. F(anny) was seeing a doctor and was in a very nervous, critical state."

The only thing Gabriel and Lizzie had definitely agreed upon when planning their future, in Paris, was that for the sake of Lizzie's health, she must never again live near the damp, foggy river. At first, in pursuance of this resolution, Gabriel tramped daily about Hampstead and Highgate vainly seeking a suitable house, and finally took rooms at Spring Cottage, Downshire Hill, Hampstead, whither, after each day's painting in Chatham Place, he nightly returned to Lizzie. It was by Rossetti's arrangement that with the Browns too for company, at "the wombat's lair" in the Zoo, Lizzie first met Jones and his wife "Georgie," who found Lizzie "as beautiful as imagination poor thing," and long recalled her "slender elegant figure, tall for those days . . . in a graceful and simple dress."

The Joneses returned with the Rossettis to Spring Cottage. Lizzie took Georgie upstairs, into the little bedroom with its lattice window, and there, as Lizzie took off her bonnet, Georgie admiringly gazed at "the mass of her deep red hair" which she wore "very loosely fastened up so that it fell in soft, heavy wings"; noted her delicate complexion, "as if a rose tint lay beneath the white skin." There, in the bedroom, the two women talked together. Lizzie showed Georgie her latest design, illustrating Gabriel's *Bride's Prelude*. It was a crude, stiff little drawing, bleak even, showing a lady with averted head giving to the knight who had slain her lover the conqueror's prize. With conscious pathos, in which she always took delight, Lizzie had named it *The Woeful Victory*.

Even at this first meeting, Georgie had an uneasy sense of something not well in the Rossetti home. She was puzzled by the long years of illness Lizzie had experienced "without ever developing a specific disease." Dr. Acland's diagnosis of "mental power long pent up and lately overtaxed" must, she thought, be right. Gabriel, she believed, had unwittingly "forced" poor Lizzie's mental development; for Lizzie, she saw, was not without "original power, but with her, too, art was a plant that grew in the garden of love." Georgie was no doubt recording her own, later, actual observations when she significantly added: "One sees in her black and white designs and beautiful little water-colours, Gabriel always looking over her shoulder and sometimes taking pencil and brush from her hand to complete the thing she had begun." Georgie's comment agrees well with Graham Robertson's description, made only recently of "small paintings purporting to be by Elizabeth Siddal (Mrs. D. G. Rossetti) and indeed drawn and tinted by a faltering and unskilful hand but quite obviously, in all save execution, fresh from the brain of her magician husband."

But stronger than Georgie's sense of a mutual affection between wife and husband was her immediate intuition of division between them. On that afternoon of her first meeting with Lizzie, Georgie "received an impression which never wore away, of romance and tragedy" between Lizzie and Gabriel. Georgie was puzzled, could not understand it; but Bell Scott could doubtless have enlightened her. "The auguries of happiness from his marriage, entertained by some of Rossetti's friends," wrote Scott, "were frightfully dispelled. For myself, knowing Gabriel better than his brother did, though from the outside, I knew marriage was not a tie he had become able to bear."

Boyce, at the end of July, making his first call on Gabriel since his marriage, found him working at the Llandaff triptych with an Italian male model sitting to him. Before Boyce left, "Morris and his wife (whom he familiarly addresses as Janey), came in . . . ."

Soon Lizzie, in search of health, went with her sister "Lyddy" to Brighton, where, as in the daytime at Hampstead, she was rather lonely and "lost." She was quiet now, ominously quiet; had lost all the old fury, yet was not exactly resigned; was rather, perhaps in silent, ultimate despair; felt herself, imagined herself perhaps, unwanted and "in the way." "Dear Gug," she wrote to Gabriel, "I am most sorry to have worried you about coming back when you have so many things to upset you. I shall therefore say no more about it . . . perhaps after all I am better here with Lyddy than quite alone at Hampstead. . . . I should like to have my water-colours sent down if possible, as I am quite destitute of all means of keeping myself alive. I have kept myself alive hitherto by going out to sea in the smallest boat I can find. [Was it a threat of suicide?] . . . I can do without money till next Thursday after which time £3 a week would be quite enough for all our wants—including rent of course."

Despite their resolution in Paris, October found Gabriel and Lizzie back in Chatham Place, settling down once more after another spell of vain house-hunting, to "weather out the winter" in the old, familiar rooms. Chatham Place was indeed destined to shelter their domestic life to its not distant end. The obliging landlord, by making a door into the second floor of the adjoining house, gave them an excellent suite of rooms. Boyce called again early in October, and Gabriel, who was working on a pen-and-ink drawing of *How they met Themselves*, showed him "some exquisite drawings" of Lizzie. "His wife," Boyce noted, "was in his studio, but he said she had been sleeping and was not in a state to see any visitors."

Rossetti showed a surprising aptitude for domesticity. Throughout the winter he devoted his leisure to domestic decoration, was busy collecting furniture, bric-à-brac, willow-pattern plates and whatever else he could get cheap, for times were hard. He covered the fireplace with old, blue, glazed Dutch tiles, designed a remarkable wall-paper all conventionalized trees, red and yellow oranges, black leaves, white circles and yellow stars! The effect, he thought, would be "rather sombre but rich also," and he painted doors and wainscot "summer-house green." Adopting, like many of his contemporaries, the florid colours and dusty confusion of a cheap bazaar as his ideal in domestic decoration, Gabriel hung up in corners the bunches of peacocks' feathers then popular, and covered the walls with photographs of friends. The sitting-room he "completely hung round with Lizzie's drawings" of which he was very proud, and in January 1861 he could complacently tell Allingham: "I should like you to see how nice the rooms are looking, and how many nice things we have got into them." "He is making his place very comfortable," wrote Boyce.

Apart from these few alterations, marriage brought little change into Gabriel's and Lizzie's way of life. They carried on in the old, haphazard, careless, bohemian way to which Lizzie was as accustomed as Gabriel himself. Untrammelled by formal calls or other demands of a conventional world, they would paint until dusk, then dine hastily at some restaurant. Lizzie's housekeeping was doubtless more original than efficient, and Gabriel would run on various errands when told to do so. It was the painters Simeon Solomon and Henry Holiday who, sitting one day in Gabriel's studio, awaiting his return, at last heard his step on the stairs and Lizzie's voice in the entrance as the door opened: "Well, Gabriel, have you got the teapot?" And his reply, with solid satisfaction: "Yes, I've got the teapot!"

At first, while his wife was still an invalid, Rossetti resented the new anxieties and responsibilities, the unaccustomed solitude to which he was now so often condemned. It had been so in Downshire Hill immediately after the honeymoon, when Lizzie's fits of vomiting returned, and he spent days running about after doctors, or shut up with her in the sick room. Save for her sister and Emma Brown, Lizzie had no friends nor wanted any. Gabriel found it "very provoking to be unable to take her to see so many kind friends, all so pressing and anxious, or even to let them come to us." "I wish you were in town to see you sometimes," he told Allingham later, "for I literally see no one now except Madox Brown pretty often, and even he is gone now to join Morris, who is out of reach at Upton, and with them is married Jones painting the inner walls of the house that Top built." At such times, to Gabriel, his home seemed but a hospital and prison in which, for comfort, he could only revive brighter memories of the past.

One consequence of his marriage, with its isolation, increased expenses and responsibilities, was that from now onwards to the end of his life, he worked at his painting as never before. "No place," he told Scott, "out of my studio must know me this autumn, in spite of various invitations, tempting to wife and self." Marriage had dissipated the lethargy of the long years of hesitation and doubt. "I am not so despairingly dilatory quite now, I think, as I used to be in those famous old days," he told Allingham at the close of 1860.

At Christmas he joined Lizzie who was staying with the Morrises at Upton, where he made a pencil sketch of Janey. In the following spring, "fat and flourishing," as a friend remarked, he was working hard at the long delayed triptych for the altar of Llandaff Cathedral, *The Seed of David*, was preparing his translations from Italian verse, contemplating a volume of original poetry, and painting Fanny as *Fair Rosamund*. The final separation bewailed in *The Song of the Bower* had not happened after all. By this time, indeed, Fanny was a married woman, had married a mechanic named Hughes the previous August, but Hughes was proving a drunken waster. The portrait of Hughes adorns the Llandaff triptych as he was model for the figure of David; but whether Gabriel discovered Hughes first and introduced him to Fanny or *vice versa* is not known.

The Llandaff authorities certainly found Rossetti a difficult person to deal with. At the time when Seddon obtained the commission for Rossetti, Gabriel was asked to make his treatment broad, light and decorative. Ignoring these instructions, and requested to give his own opinion about them, he blandly proposed as a preliminary that the Cathedral Chapter be requested to allow the end of the Cathedral to be painted black! Both the difficulty and the importance to him of the commission, however, are evident in the remark he is said to have made, that if ever another such commission came to him, he would spend ten years in a preparatory study of decorative art. Those who best knew Rossetti would regard this as expressive of the will rather than of any potential deed. Another tale of Gabriel and the Llandaff triptych at this time, which however, is at variance with the evidence of his renewed activity after his marriage, tells how the Dean and Chapter of Llandaff, weary of waiting for the arrival of Rossetti's paintings or even news of them, delegated the Bishop of Llandaff, who was going to town to take his place in the House of Lords, to call on Rossetti in Blackfriars to ask to see the paintings and discover the reason for their non-arrival and of Rossetti's silence. But Rossetti, the maid who opened the door told the Bishop, was out. Thereupon the Bishop briefly explained to her his errand. "Oh lor! sir," replied the astonished servant, "Mr. Rossetti don't paint now —he's married."

As Lizzie's health improved, domestic life in Chatham Place brightened and Rossetti's hopes of his wife's achieving fame as a painter returned. She had, he told Allingham, "real genius," and with good health would "paint such pictures as no woman has painted yet." Scott, like Hunt, looked sardonically upon Lizzie's efforts, saw in them only imitations, harmful to Rossetti, of Gabriel himself, and accused him of "immoderately" praising them.

Now, too, old and new friends appeared again at Chatham Place. The Joneses, the Morrises, Swinburne, George Meredith, Alexander Gilchrist (who was writing his *Life of Blake*), Brown, and a few others, were now constant visitors. In their company Gabriel's happiness at times found expression in various boyish ways. He would, for example, vie with Swinburne in composing impromptu nonsense verses about his friends, such as— with sublime unself-consciousness—his description of:

> a poor creature named Georgie
> Whose life is one profligate orgy . . .

or of

> the poor painter named Jones
> For whose conduct no genius atones . . .

Gabriel also invented two imaginary friends to whom he constantly referred in these jesting moods—"Athanasius Snoox, lecturer on cats" and "Ornithorhyncus Bug."

As during the Jovial Campaign, Gabriel was now once again the centre of attraction, of animation, of a circle to which Swinburne, Meredith, and Gilchrist were new recruits. Upon the departure of the "campaigners" from Oxford, Swinburne had fallen into reprobate habits, taking to republicanism, rebellion, and drink. And when his landlady explained to the proctors the reasons for her disillusion as to the characters of "them Balliol gentlemen," Swinburne was "sent down." Leaving the university with neither a degree nor a regret, he had immediately, like Jones and Morris before him, turned to Rossetti as the needle to the pole. Jowett, Master of Balliol, who disliked the Preraphaelites, said it was they who had ruined the youth.

Intent upon a literary career, and with a small pension from his father the admiral, Swinburne now settled near Jones and the British Museum. Rossetti, who had recently enjoyed Swinburne's hospitality at the family seat, Capheaton, Northumberland, introduced "my little Northumbrian friend" as he called him, to acquaintances who might be helpful, in particular to George Meredith, then a comparatively obscure journalist turning to fiction and poetry. With Gilchrist, to whom on request Rossetti had lent the Blake MSS. bought with William's ten shillings in his youth, Gabriel now dined regularly at the Cheshire Cheese in Fleet Street, for the two men had become firm friends.

Lizzie, too, actually made new friends. While Jones and Rossetti talked in the studio, Lizzie and Georgie chatted in the drawing-room, and in time, something of intimacy, of need on the one side and sympathy on the other, grew up. Alone with Georgie, Lizzie discarded some of her habitual reserve, became "excited and melancholy, though with much humour and tenderness as well," said sentimental Georgie long afterwards. "Gabriel's presence seemed needed," she thought, "to set her jarring nerves straight, for her whole manner changed when he came into the room." And with the eye of memory, in those long after-years, Georgie pictured them again, as Gabriel entered, "took his place by her on the sofa and her excitement sank back into peace." "For love" of Lizzie, Georgie preserved her childlike little notes of invitation, such as: "My dear little Georgie,—I hope you intend coming over with Ned to-morrow evening like a sweetmeat, it seems so long since I saw you dear. Janey will be here I hope to meet you. With a willow-pattern dish full of love to you and Ned,—Lizzie."

But greater far than this friendship was Lizzie's friendship with Swinburne who, in a kind of calf-love, idolized her. Long afterwards he described her as "a noble lady," whom he came "to regard with little less than a brother's affection." She lit all his adolescent idealism as ten years before she had Gabriel's. The notoriously blasphemous and obscene youth became mild and reverent in her presence. He delighted to read his beloved Elizabethan dramatists to her, carefully bowdlerizing the indecorous passages. Her sympathetic attention charmed him, for as once she had assimilated Gabriel's tastes, so now she absorbed Swinburne's. Only when she preferred Fletcher to Shakespeare did his approval fail! "I can hear the music of her laughter to this day," he declared thirty-five years later, and in the deeply emotional, hitherto unnoted but obviously personal description of her as Lady Cheyne which he now introduced into the novel he was writing, *A Year's Letters,** the intensity and sincerity of his admiration are manifest.

Swinburne admired both Lizzie's painting and poetry, found in them "the same note of originality in discipleship . . . Gabriel's influence and example not more perceptible than her own independence and freshness of inspiration." He doubtless knew of the shadow of Fanny, perhaps also of others, darkening their home, and pitied the young wife in her illness and dejection; but his loyalty to Gabriel was equally great, and he doubtless saw in their domestic life, in which love was a torment, one of those dilemmas of temperament and circumstance in which there can be no definite distribution of "blame."

* *v. Notes.*

To the end of his long life, Swinburne retained clear and deep and sadly happy memories of his short friendship with Gabriel's wife. "I hope I may now speak of her as I should of a sister," he wrote to William Rossetti in 1895, protesting that she had received less than justice in William's *Memoir* of his brother. "I won't enlarge on the deeper and sadder side of my brotherly affection for her," he wrote, "but I shall always be sorrowfully glad and proud to remember her regard for me— not undeserved, certainly, if the warmest admiration and the greatest delight in her company could deserve it. She was a wonderful as well as a most lovable creature."

And when, in these later years Scott's posthumously published autobiography appeared, and its author was accused, unfairly, of dishonouring Lizzie's memory, Swinburne wrote to the Press, violently, in her defence. Amidst the vulgar and virulent abuse Swinburne hurled at his dead friend Scott and Scott's editor Professor Minto, he turned aside for a moment to pay one last tribute to the woman who had obviously inspired in him a secret, adolescent passion.[1] "It is impossible," he wrote in angry alliterative ecstasy, "that even the reptile rancour, the omniverous malignity, of Iago himself could have dreamed of trying to cast a slur on the memory of that incomparable lady whose maiden name was Siddal and whose married name was Rossetti. To one at least who knew her better than most of her husband's friends, the memory of all her marvellous charms of mind and person—her matchless grace, loveliness, courage, endurance, wit, humour, heroism, and sweetness—is too dear and sacred to be profaned by any attempt at expression. The vilest of the vile could not have dreamed of trying 'to cast a slur on her memory.' " All of which tells us in fact more about Swinburne than about Lizzie.

But Lizzie, reciprocating Swinburne's so emphatically fraternal affection, was happy too. Her brooding, tragic mood gave place, at least in Swinburne's company, to outbursts of

---

[1] Ford Madox Ford's account of Miss Siddal and Swinburne's friendship, intended elopement, and the servants' gossip he repeats, although demonstrably inaccurate in many respects, shows that Swinburne was considered by at least some of his contemporaries, even if only those in the servants' hall, to be in love with Lizzie.

See *Mightier than the Sword*, by Ford Madox Ford, London, 1938, pp. 248–51.

such childish merriment as both enjoyed. Lizzie laughed especially at Swinburne's shock of red hair, which she pretended was like her own, and she declared that once when they were in a theatre, the attendant, on seeing her red poll at one end of a row of seats and then suddenly Swinburne's at the other end, started back exclaiming: "There's another of 'em." And Swinburne, who could enjoy with Lizzie the simplicities she loved, laughed also.

From the social circle that gathered at Chatham Place was one marked abstention, that of the Rossetti family. The temporary rapprochement following the bestowal of Ruskin's pensions and so quickly terminated, was never actually renewed. Bessy Parkes's testimony given long afterwards about Lizzie: "When, after years of a long dragging engagement she became Gabriel Rossetti's wife, the ladies of her husband's family received her with a sweet welcome which did honour to all parties," conflicts with other and more definite evidence. Not without reason did Mrs. Bell Scott write in a letter to her husband, shortly after Lizzie's return from her honeymoon: "Mrs. Gabriel Rossetti has not yet been seen in his mother's house, and has been invisible to every one." For this, it may be, Lizzie and her illness were most to blame. That, partly at least through resentment of the coolness shown her by the Rossettis during the long years of her "engagement," she now refused to visit them, seems also to be true. Old Mrs. Rossetti had in fact, at the end of October, invited her daughter-in-law to Albany Street, but Lizzie, despite Gabriel's distress at the thought of a family dispute, was now in no accommodating mood, and on the plea of her ill-health, Gabriel excused her to his mother.

Suddenly life for both Gabriel and Lizzie seemed happier. "So prettily full of his wife," wrote Mrs. Gaskell of Gabriel, after a call at Chatham Place. For that, and for their general brightness there was another reason now, a new hope. The Preraphaelites were not only growing domesticated and middle-aged; a new, as yet inarticulate posterity was already arising —their own. As ever, from the ashes of youth fresh youth was springing, a consolation and a mockery. One autumn morning of 1860, Georgie, visiting at The Red House, had noticed with pleased surprise that Janey was making baby-clothes, that the Morrises expected a child. So, too, now, did the Rossettis. So, too, shortly, would Georgie herself. "Lizzie is pretty well for her," Gabriel told Allingham early in 1861, "and we are in expectation (but this is quite in confidence, as such things are better waited for quietly) of a little accident which has just befallen Topsy and Mrs. T. who have become parents. Ours however will not be (if at all) for two or three months yet."

Shortly afterwards, The Red House was crowded with a gay and happy company, assembled to witness the christening of little Jane Alice Morris. The resources of the place were strained to the utmost, so many were the guests. Swinburne had to sleep that night on the drawing-room sofa, the rest of the men on improvised beds on the floor. But Rossetti did not share the general merriment. He remained silent; aloof. At dinner, Georgie, his neighbour, noticed his silence and abstraction. Abstemious as usual, he drank water only, and when the neglected Georgie asked him to pour some for her, "I beg your pardon, Georgie," he said, "I had forgotten that you, like myself, are a temperate person." Another guest also remarked Gabriel's reserve as, before dessert, he sat "in a royal manner . . . munching raisins from a dish in front of him." Rossetti, in fact, seemed the prey of unhappy thoughts. Were they recollections of the days at Oxford, only four years before, when Janey's beauty first flashed upon him, or his growing fears for the life of Lizzie and of their own, shortly expected child?

Gabriel, awaiting the event with increasing anxiety, took every precaution for his wife. "I feel all is being done for the best," he wrote. "She has too much courage to be in the least downcast herself; and this is one great point, nor is her strength unusually low. So we can but wait and trust for a happy termination." Soon, however, their fears proved to be too well founded. A short note to his mother on May 2nd revealed the disappointment of their hopes. "Lizzie has just been delivered of a dead child. She is doing pretty well, I trust. Do not encourage any one to come just now—I mean, of course, except yourselves." To Gilchrist he sent a similar message. "This morning my wife was confined. Our fears were correct in one respect, as the child was still-born. In all other respects she fares as yet, thank God, better than we had ventured to hope. Still, of course, anxiety cannot be at an end yet."

Amidst his sorrow and disappointment in the loss of his daughter, Gabriel's first thought was ever for his wife. On hearing of her safety he wrote to Georgie: "She herself is so far the most important, that I can feel nothing but thankfulness." To Allingham on May 10, 1861, he was able to report: "My wife is progressing very well, all things considered, and got over her confinement much better than we had ventured to hope. The child had been dead for 2 or 3 weeks before, and you may imagine that my forebodings were none of the brightest."

X

AN OLD SONG ENDED
1861–1862

> "How may I, when he shall ask,
>   Tell him who lies there?"
> "Nay, but leave my face unveiled
>   And unbound my hair."
>
> "Can you say to me some word
>   I shall say to him?"
> "Say I'm looking in his eyes
>   Though my eyes are dim."
>
> *An Old Song Ended* D. G. ROSSETTI

> Lost love-labour and lullaby,
>   And lowly let love lie,

wrote Gabriel in after years, in the cryptic verse-autobio-graphy he entitled *Chimes*; and indeed it was soon evident that with the birth of their dead child, the new-found happiness of Chatham Place had finally departed. Lizzie's natural morbidity deepened under the shock into definite hysteria akin to mental breakdown. For hours she would sit by the fire, brooding over the empty cradle. Sympathetic Georgie, finding her in this state, "sitting in a low chair with the childless cradle on the floor beside her," thought "she looked like Gabriel's *Ophelia* when she cried with a kind of soft wildness" as they entered, "Hush, Ned, you'll waken it!" From this mentally unbalanced state Lizzie seems never afterwards to have completely emerged.

Beneath his habitual reserve, Gabriel too was deeply moved by the loss of his child. "I ought to have had a little girl older than she is," he once wistfully remarked, looking at the seven-year-old daughter of a friend. And when in the autumn of 1861 Georgie herself was eagerly expecting her own first child, Gabriel begged her: "By the bye, Lizzie has been talking to me of parting with a certain small wardrobe to you. But don't let her, please. It looks such a bad omen for us." Upon Gabriel's poetry too the sad experience left its mark, particularly in the

sonnet *Death-in-Love*, dated by him "Dies Atra, 1 May [the
child's birthday was, in fact, May 2nd], 1869," in his frequent
imaging of Death as a little child, and in his intensified association of love with death, the two normal psychological polarities
which Rossetti's long experience with the ailing Lizzie had
already strongly developed.[1]

It is Graham Robertson who reveals in his charming
reminiscences, a hitherto unknown and illuminating incident
in the life of Gabriel and Lizzie at this time: that they wished
to adopt the little girl who later won popularity as the actress
Nellie Farren. "I was one day showing her a picture by Rossetti
which recalled an old and long-forgotten memory," wrote
Robertson. 'Rossetti,' she said slowly, 'it's a long time since
I heard that name. He used to be a clever sort of man. Did
he get on?' 'My dear,' I explained, 'he got off some time ago.
He has been dead for years.' 'Rossetti,' Nellie repeated the
name thoughtfully, evidently quite unaware of its claims to
immortality. 'I suppose it's the one I mean. A queer fellow
—was going to marry a red-haired girl.'

" 'That's it,' said I.

" 'They wanted to adopt me,' said Nellie.

" 'Good gracious,' I gasped.

" 'Yes, that's what father said,' she continued. 'He thought
it an odd way to start married life—especially as they seemed
to have no money. Of course, he wouldn't give me up, but I
often used to go with him and sit in the painting-room. Is the
red-haired girl dead, too?'

" 'Yes,' said I.

"What would have happened if father had given Nellie up
and she had gone to be a daughter to the morbid, over-wrought
'girl with red hair' and her wondrous husband; her clear-cut
common sense in that house of dreams and shadows, her matchless vitality thrown against that painted arras of mediaevalism
and mystery; above all, her delightful sense of humour allied
to Rossetti's delightful sense of humour? The result might have
been surprising."

Despite their loss, the simple social life in Chatham Place

---

[1] *cf. Stillborn Love, Transfigured Life, Newborn Death I & II, Death's Songsters.*
Also *v. inf.* pp. 389, 393–4.

was continued. Brown, Swinburne, Jones, Morris, Gilchrist, Meredith responded cordially to Gabriel's bluff invitations to join the "few blokes and coves" coming to "participate in oysters and obloquy" or, to more laconically worded notes such as: "nothing but oysters and of course the seediest of clothes." Meredith, observing Rossetti's delight in Lizzie's gold and rose colour, teased him about "green eyes and carrots." Meredith's friend Hardman (later Sir William Hardman, owner of the *Morning Post*) also came occasionally, but, shocked by Swinburne's boasted admiration of De Sade, inimically watched the highly strung poet with his "curious kind of nervous twitching" which reminded Hardman of St. Vitus's dance. Everyone, Hardman complained, treated Swinburne "like a spoiled child."

Gabriel, helping Gilchrist to edit the Blake MSS., worked in a shockingly unscholarly way, omitting, transposing, altering and inserting at his own sweet will or in what he deemed the interest of public decorum. Then suddenly Gilchrist caught scarlatina and died. Gabriel, shocked and shaken, absented himself from the funeral, fearing "it would be hardly safe." To Gilchrist's widow he sent heartfelt sympathy and offered to finish her husband's *Life of Blake* or to preface it with an appreciation of his dead friend. And in language strangely similar to that of his sonnet *Memorial Thresholds*, he voiced his tremulous hope of a future existence.*

Now, too, at the close of 1861, he at last published his translations under the title: *The Early Italian Poets together with Dante's Vita Nuova*. Although they won the approval of the critical journals they attracted little attention among the general public. Not until eight years later, when six hundred copies had been sold, did they repay Ruskin the hundred pounds he had advanced for their publication and leave Gabriel the handsome profit of nine pounds! Despite the years of revision, Gabriel was not yet satisfied with his versions. He wished them "more literal," but while frankly confessing, "cannot do it all again," he thought they nevertheless fulfilled his cardinal principle of translation: "that a good poem shall not be turned into a bad one." His literary friends were complimentary, finding, as

* *v. Notes.*

others have done since, that however loose or inaccurate in detail they may be at times, Rossetti's translations are not those of a schoolmaster but of a poet.

Rossetti worked also at his original poems, revising, selecting, preparing a volume of them for the press. He wrote little or no poetry now, and was modest about these early attempts. "I hope you will not fancy," he now told Mrs. Gaskell, who had bought one of his pictures, "that I neglect my painting for any literary attempts. My sins of the latter kind are all old ones, and only now call for confession, and, if it may be, absolution." But the general critical appreciation of his translations had stimulated his growing ambition publicly to figure, like Bell Scott, Morris, Meredith, Christina, and Swinburne, as an original poet. Meredith, greatly admiring, added his encouragement. To a friend he now wrote of Rossetti: "He sent me a book of MSS. original poetry the other day, and very fine are some of the things in it. He is a poet, without doubt. He would please you more than I do, or can, for he deals with essential poetry, and is not wild, and bluff, and coarse; but rich, refined, royal-robed! . . . Rossetti is going to illustrate my *Cassandra*, which pome [*sic*] has taken his heart." For like Jones, Morris, and Swinburne, Meredith had fallen under the spell of Rossetti's personality, even, like the rest, to imitating his jocular cockney mis-spellings and mis-pronunciations. Gabriel, however, now that his earlier, adolescent inspiration had failed, chiefly feared, and not without reason, lest he should have insufficient good verse to make an acceptable volume.

At last it seemed as if the long-frustrated years of Rossetti's life were ending. Despite Lizzie's ill-health, responsibilities of marriage were apparently impelling him to more regular ways, to greater, more sustained, more productive effort. Although, early in his married life he had expected to sink to "the due pitch of starvation" required to make him accept an offer from Gambart, the art-agent he most disliked, he was in fact now anxiously calculating to what extent he could safely increase his prices. He had persuaded his Newcastle patron Leathart to buy two pictures and commission the now unwanted, still unfinished and never-to-be-finished *Found*, and Morris bought *The Tune of Seven Towers* and *Blue Closet*—which, like Gabriel's

other painting, *Arthur's Tomb*, brought Morris poetic inspiration. The "replicas," too, were increasingly helpful.

Ruskin, who in recent years had criticized Rossetti and the
Preraphaelites more often than he praised them, was consequently in little favour, not only with his two protégés, but also
with the whole "Brotherhood." "The Preraphaelites," wrote
Stanhope, at the opening of the Jovial Campaign, "give such
accounts of Ruskin. He seems to be the most prejudiced,
cantankerous fellow, and I shall keep as clear as I can of him."
Yet from time to time Ruskin still publicly defended the
Preraphaelite cause, proclaiming "Rossetti, Millais, Hunt, John
Lewis" the "four leaders of Preraphaelitism," and prophesying
that the Preraphaelite "great ones" would "hold their own
with the most noble pictures of all time."

But the increasing laxity of Gabriel's ethics in love and
finance was not unobserved by Ruskin who began to fear that
such methods would soon lead to Rossetti's ruin. To Miss
Heaton and Norton he expressed his dissatisfaction with the
pictures Gabriel was painting for them, particularly *Before the
Battle*, which morally outraged Ruskin, who believed that in
this Rossetti was exploiting Norton as he had already exploited
Miss Heaton, Plint, and others. Above all he was angry about
his own portrait for Norton, accusing Rossetti of being dilatory,
and denying Gabriel's excuses that the delay was due to
Ruskin himself. But, for Ruskin, Gabriel's charm had not yet
quite lost its power, and there were still moods in which he
would describe "the P.R.B.s" as "the only figure painters of
the age," though he thought them "all gone crazy about the
Morte d'Arthur," and Rossetti himself "half lost in mediaevalism
and Dante."

Henceforth, the impartiality of Ruskin's criticisms of Rossetti
became increasingly open to question, as Ruskin himself, in the
throes of a mental, moral, and intellectual crisis, relapsed into
a state of grave neurasthenia. Upon the completion of *Modern
Painters* he had retired in the summer of 1860 to the Valley
of Chamonix for solitude, rest, and recuperation. Far from
realizing these desires, however, he had found his withdrawal
merely the prelude to a new and unhappy stage in his development, "the beginning," as he afterwards described it, "of the

days of reprobation." For looking, back from his mountain fastness, over the forty years of his life, he was overwhelmed by the emergence of thoughts and feelings long struggling towards consciousness—scientific conceptions, and resultant attitudes, which disintegrated his former orthodox faith and left him lost, disillusioned, but with a new objectivity. This new outlook, combining with his increasing awareness of a sense of futility haunting his comfortable, sheltered, detached existence, had turned his interests from purely aesthetic to social and economic questions. The result was a series of essays published in *The Cornhill Magazine* and later reissued as *Unto this Last*, in which he placed before a sceptical and irritated public, his new ideas and ideals.

"Who *could* read it, or anything about such bosh!" Gabriel, recently back from his honeymoon, had asked Allingham after reading the first essay. Ruskin's father the wine merchant, on reading it, felt sure that his son's liver was out of order, and reflected, tearfully, that the popularity John was winning as writer and critic, must now be doomed.

Thackeray, editor of *The Cornhill*, was soon forced by the hostility the articles aroused, to close his magazine to Ruskin, and Ruskin, hitherto the somewhat spoiled and pampered child of Fortune, began to realize the extent and power of average humanity's prejudice. "Wild with contempt and anger," as he declared, Ruskin now "sulked" alone amidst the lonely beauty of his mountain retreat. Incurably introspective, scornful both of himself and others, sunk in endless reverie, without faith, often without hope, rapidly sinking into melancholia, he truly described himself at this time to Norton, with a touch of his habitual slightly querulous humour, as "at present an entirely puzzled, helpless, and disgusted old gentleman."

Abroad when Gabriel and Lizzie married, Ruskin sent them no message of congratulation, included them, perhaps, if he thought of them at all, in his universal attitude of disgust. But on returning to England shortly afterwards, he called at Chatham Place, and, finding no one at home, sent them an affectionate letter explaining, though hardly convincingly, that he had purposely reserved his congratulations on their marriage until he could give them in person. It was a friendly note with an eminently friendly postscript: "I looked over all the book of sketches at Chatham Place yesterday. I think Ida should be very happy to see how much more beautifully, perfectly, and tenderly you draw when you are drawing her than when you draw anybody else. She cures you of all your worst faults when you only look at her."

It was little likely, however, in the circumstances, that such cordial relations between them could endure. To the warmth of Ruskin's fussy affection Gabriel's response had always seemed cold, and the widening of the distance between them had been assisted by Ruskin's resignation in May 1858 from the staff of the Working Men's College, followed shortly afterwards by that of Rossetti. Gabriel, on his side, was annoyed by Ruskin's criticisms of *Jenny* which, such was their ambiguous phrasing, might well suggest, and probably were so intended, a subtle condemnation of Gabriel's own moral lapses.[1] Nor was Ruskin's refusal to ask Thackeray to publish *Jenny* in *The Cornhill*, likely to make Gabriel better pleased with him.

Indeed, Rossetti, who thought *Jenny* "the most serious thing I have written," was really annoyed. None of these things, however, but the merest trifle, as usual in such cases of cumulative irritation, caused Ruskin to explode in a wrath of hurt affection. Calling one day at Chatham Place, and met only by the "housekeeper" with apologies for the non-appearance of Gabriel and Lizzie, Ruskin departed hurt and angry. The incident, deeply intensified by his own morbidity, strongly affected him in his irritable, hypersensitive state, acquired in his mind a preposterous significance. This couple, he bitterly reflected, so recently dependent upon his bounty, who owed to him their reputation and the promise of success, would not trouble to give him a personal welcome to their home. And when Gabriel's own note of apology arrived almost immediately, he replied accusing him of unintentional, habitual selfishness "in little things . . . thinking only of what you like to do or don't like; not of what would be kind." "I wish," he said, "Lizzie and you liked me enough to—say—put on a dressing-gown and run in for a minute rather than not see me; or paint

[1] *v. inf.* p. 413.

on a picture in an unsightly state, rather than not amuse me when I was ill. But you can't *make* yourselves like me, and you would only like me less if you tried." But he sent "Love to Lizzie," and added an inevitable, qualifying postscript: "I am afraid this note reads sulky—it is not that: I am generally depressed. Perhaps you both like me better than I suppose you do. I mean only, I did not misinterpret or take ill anything *yesterday*: but I have no power in general of believing much in people's caring for me. I've a little more faith in Lizzie than in you—because, though she didn't see me, her bride's kiss was so full and queenly-kind; but I fancy I gall *you* by my want of sympathy in many things, and so lose hold of you."

But at heart, Ruskin was bitterly angry, nursing this with other grievances, particularly Gabriel's delay in painting his portrait. This, it seemed to him, was but another sign of Gabriel's indifference. In fact, however, for the delay with the portrait both men were to blame. To Norton, Gabriel complained that Ruskin's frequent postponements and absences abroad were the cause of the delay, while Ruskin laid the blame on Rossetti. Actually, Ruskin, hypersensitive about his personal appearance, long postponed the sittings upon one pretext or another, giving Gabriel excuses for delay which he gladly seized upon. And as often when angry, Ruskin worked off his feelings in adverse criticism of Rossetti's work, complaining of his ever doing "absurd things in the midst of his beautiful ones," that he had just "painted a Madonna with black hair in ringlets, like a George the Second wig, and black complexion like a Mulatto—*nigra sum*—not that he meant that, but he took a fancy to the face."* And still the recent occasion of his anger rankled: Gabriel and Lizzie, for so he chose to interpret the incident, had turned him away. "I see hardly anybody now," he told Norton, in his misanthropy; "I've got so fastidious and exacting that I never praise anybody enough to please them—so they turn me out of their rooms in all haste."

Yet even now Ruskin could not break the spell Gabriel had thrown over him. To Norton as to Gabriel himself, Ruskin praised his portraits of Lizzie. Gabriel drew her, Ruskin

* *v. Notes.*

believed, better than any other model. "When he was merely in love with her he used to exaggerate all the faults of her face and think them beauties." (So much for Ruskin's compliments!) "But now that he's married he just draws her rightly, and so much more tenderly than other women that all his harshness and eccentricity vanish whenever she sits."

In mid-June 1861, Ruskin returned to his continental seclusion, and, save for an occasional short visit to England, remained abroad, self-exiled, for two and a half years. But, alert to defend the interests of his friend Norton, he kept a sharp eye on the growling, grumbling Gabriel, making him improve *Before the Battle* until at last in January 1862 Ruskin was able to tell Norton that the picture was at any rate "worthy of him" (Gabriel), and acceptable.

Even Ruskin's humour may well have irritated Rossetti during these months. When, for example, Plint died suddenly, in the summer of 1861, and his executors began to press Gabriel to produce either the promised paintings or the six hundred and eighty guineas he had received from Plint in advance, Ruskin, to whom he appealed, facetiously replied: "My dear Rossetti, I was very glad to hear from you and will certainly recommend Mr. Plint's executors—if I am referred to by them—to act for their own or the estate's interest as you propose. But I hope somebody will soon throw you into prison. We will have the cell made nice, airy, cheery, and tidy, and you'll get on with your work gloriously. Love to Ida. Ever affectionately yours, J. Ruskin." Gabriel who, having just settled with his more pressing creditors, had only twenty-five pounds in the world, was annoyed at the demands of Plint's executors. He even complained—but for the first time!—of Plint's thoughtless and selfish "habit of pressing money on one for work in progress (of which I naturally availed myself, being always hard up)."

In January 1862, Ruskin, temporarily in England again, began to sit to Gabriel for the portrait commissioned by Norton four years previously, and promised "to get it done as fast as may be." It was during these sittings that Ruskin privately confessed to Gabriel his loss of faith in revealed religion, his disgust with his own writings and his intention to keep silence for many years. Early in February, Rossetti despatched to Norton a copy of his *Early Italian Poets* and *Before the Battle*. But the portrait of Ruskin was never completed and Rossetti's sole portrait of the man to whom he owed so much, is a crayon study that he made about this time with the intention of using it for the greater work.

Early in June 1861, a few days before returning to his continental solitude, Ruskin had sent Norton more favourable news of Lizzie. "She was very ill for long before her marriage," he wrote, "but is getting stronger now, and is looking well." Lizzie's letters to her husband at this time, however, suggest if anything an increased morbidity. From the Morrises in The Red House, Upton, where this same June Lizzie was vainly attempting to divert her thoughts from her recent loss, by unsuccessful endeavours at mural decoration, she lamented · to Gabriel, "My dearest Gug," in a short note, the death of some acquaintance: "All people who are at all happy or useful seem to be taken away," and exhorted him: "If you can come down here on Saturday evening I shall be very glad indeed. I want you to do something to the figure I have been trying to paint on the wall. But I fear it must all come out for I am too blind and sick to see what I am about." Gabriel indeed was less satisfied than Ruskin with his wife's state. "I wish I were with you, to get the benefit of some sun," he replied a few days later to Gilchrist's invitation to join him in the country, "and should much better even like it for my wife, but we must see; she has been working very hard these few days, and made a beautiful water-colour sketch, but is none the better for it."

Nor was it only Lizzie's health that suffered. The shadow over the Rossetti's home that Georgie with a woman's intuition had at once divined, had not lifted. Christina, too, saw it, and so, William believed, now described it in her poem *Wife to Husband*:

> Pardon the faults in me
> For the love of years ago:
> Good-bye.
> I must drift across the sea,
> I must sink into the snow,
> I must die.

*　　　*　　　*

> Not a word for you,
>   Not a lock or kiss,
>   Good-bye.
> We, one, must part in two:
>   Verily death is this:
>   I must die.

About this time Christina was writing another poem, a short
lyric entitled *The Prince who arrived too late.*[1] She can hardly
have overlooked the fact that whether intended as such or not,
the poem might well be taken for an allegorical description of
the relations of Gabriel and Lizzie during the preceding ten
years. Some stanzas seemed particularly apposite:

> Ten years ago, five years ago,
>   One year ago,
> Even then you had arrived in time,
>   Though somewhat slow.
> The frozen fountain would have leaped,
>   The buds gone on to blow,
> The warm south wind would have awaked
>   To melt the snow,
> And life have been a cordial "Yes,"
>   Instead of dreary "No."

Or was Christina, now thirty-one years old and relapsing into
a sombre, loveless celibacy, thinking rather of herself, and of
Cayley, the shy, eccentric scholar for whom she was beginning
to entertain a warm feeling, but whom, when five years later
he proposed to her, she rejected, as before she had rejected
Collinson, on the ostensible ground of religious differences; for
while Collinson was a Catholic, Cayley was a free-thinker?
Most probably the poem was no conscious elaboration of
Gabriel and Lizzie's relations, nor of her own with Cayley, but
rather a generalized expression of her own emotional state
amidst the totality of these various circumstances.

The autumn of 1861 found Lizzie in a state of ever-deepening
depression and hysteria. In October, while Gabriel was in
Yorkshire painting the portrait of a patron Mrs. Heaton (no
relation of Ruskin's friend) as *Regina Cordium*, Lizzie again
found a refuge with the Morrises in The Red House, where a

---

[1] Acting on a suggestion of D.G.R. Christina in 1865 wrote a longer poem, *The
Prince's Progress*, in which this lyric was included as nucleus.

guest noticed her "appearing without a word at dinner, rising —gliding away silent and unobserved as she had come—a ghost in the house of the living." But before Gabriel's return from the north Lizzie left the Morrises with extraordinary abruptness, apparently departing without any warning or farewell to her host and hostess, exactly as shortly afterwards she did at the Browns.

So disturbed was Gabriel on hearing the news, that in an unintentionally revealing letter to his mother he for once, tentatively, even apologetically, begged her to come to his distraught wife's aid. "My dear Mamma," he wrote, "I am out here painting a portrait, and left Lizzie staying with the Morrises. Now she writes me that she had left them in a hurry, making me very uneasy, as I know there was not a halfpenny of money at Chatham Place. If at all possible, would you go there, and take her some few pounds, which I shall be able to repay you on my return immediately and will punctually do so? It was impossible to bring her here with me, both from her very delicate state and from the very reason that what money we had hardly sufficed for my own journey. On my return I shall have earned 50 guineas, and shall certainly be back in a week from to-day. If not convenient to call, you might send the tin by post. I would not trouble you, but know William is away. At present, of course, it makes me very uneasy."

Shortly afterward, when the faithful Emma Brown forced Lizzie to stay with her for a time, hoping to dispel her depression, Lizzie quitted the Browns' home in Fortess Terrace, Kentish Town, and returned to Chatham Place as suddenly, secretly, strangely as she had done at the Morrises'. "She tells me," Gabriel told Brown, apologetically, "she felt unwell after you left yesterday, and finding the noise rather too much for her, left before your return lest she should be feeling worse. Many thanks, all of you, for care of her during her illness. I hope if she comes again she may be better and give you less trouble. I write this word since her departure must have surprised you, as her return did me." To this distraught, wandering woman anything might happen, as Gabriel feared, and he seems at this time to have watched over her with exemplary care and patience.

Despite long delay, Gabriel still held his original intention to leave Chatham Place and make a new home, for Lizzie's sake, in some healthier spot. "I would move at once," he declared in January 1862, "if I found a nice place elsewhere, and hope to do so before long." Nothing less than Lizzie's health could have moved him, for he loved the old rooms, finding them "delightfully quaint and characteristic." But Lizzie's health was a great anxiety. Already his ambitions for her were fading. "Unhappily too confirmed an invalid to leave a hope now that she will ever be able to make the most of her genius," he told Norton. "Indeed, the strength to work at all is only rarely accorded her." Lizzie, sinking into deeper depths of morbidity than ever before, brooding yet more darkly upon disappointed love, now sang also, in Gabriel's simple ballad style, of death:

> And, mother, when the big tears fall,
>   (And fall, God knows they may),
> Tell him I died of my great love,
>   And my dying heart was gay.
>
> And, mother dear, when the sun has set,
>   And the pale church grass waves,
> Then carry me through the dim twilight
>   And hide me among the graves.

Longingly, she named her gloomy verses *At Last*.[1]

Surely it was in those days that Lizzie's most morbid and bitter poems were written, verses full of her own sad and sentimental and self-consciously pathetic broodings over her own past, the expression of a tense, overstrained spirit. Lizzie's morbidity was entering a new phase now. Disgust, dismay, anger, disillusion, and discontent were subsiding into a settled, perhaps more dangerous melancholy of desolate resignation—resignation even of life itself; life the ultimate deception as she now saw it, brightened only by some glimmering hope of a life beyond the grave, of reunion with her dead child, her parents and a brother, for the loss of all these had preyed upon her mind. To the hereafter poor Lizzie had forwarded her soul's sentimental desires—a kind of spiritual luggage in advance; but ominous perhaps too!

[1] *cf.* D.G.R.'s sonnet *At Last, v. inf.* p. 398.

O grieve not with thy bitter tears
　The life that passes fast:
The gates of heaven will open wide
　And take me in at last.

Then sit down meekly at my side,
　And watch my young life flee:
Then solemn peace of holy death
　Come quickly unto thee,

But, true love, seek me in the throng
　Of spirits floating past;
And I will take thee by the hands,
　And know thee mine at last.

A note of hysteria, something inconsequent in thought and imagery, is evident in such verses as these. The thought of death was now apparently beating in her brain as insistently as the thought of love; those two psychological polarities which, ere long, would dominate the thought of Rossetti also. In Lizzie, as in Gabriel, the two great compulsions of love and death were inextricably mingled.

Lizzie, in her mental and physical decline, in her disappointment and disillusion with life, was turning to Death the restorer to heal the wounds of Love. And still, as in the earliest days of their courtship, the innate morbidity Lizzie indulged and enjoyed, appealed to the similar qualities in Gabriel, although in him, up to this time, they were usually repressed. But he painted Lizzie now in water-colour as the kneeling Princess Sabra, holding the helmet of St. George as a basin so that the knight may wash his bloodstained hands, while outside the window a triumphant procession passes with the dragon's head. Was there in the painting any conscious or unconscious symbolism such as many of his pictures admittedly contained, some reflection of the state of Lizzie and Gabriel with the temptations ever threatening their happiness while Fanny and her like were undismissed? He made several portraits of Lizzie now, in pencil, and one, which he named (like Mrs. Heaton's), *Regina Cordium*, in oil.

But whether the slain dragon of Gabriel's picture represented some transient victory for Lizzie over her rivals or not was now of little moment. For Lizzie all this would soon be of no account.

This was in fact her last sitting as model. The Woeful Victory was nearing its climax, would soon prove a Pyrrhic Victory indeed. . . .

The evening of February 10, 1862, was a festive occasion for Gabriel, Lizzie and Swinburne, who dined together at the Sablonière restaurant in Leicester Square. Lizzie, who was to leave town in a day or two for a holiday, and had bought herself a new "mantle" the day before, was in exceptionally high spirits, joking with Swinburne in her usual way. At eight o'clock the party broke up. Gabriel and Lizzie went straight home. Later, Rossetti went out again, leaving his wife about to go to bed.

*   *   *

Returning at half-past eleven, Rossetti, on entering his wife's room found her lying in bed unconscious and breathing heavily. The room reeked of laudanum and on the small table at her bedside stood an empty laudanum phial. Her doctor, Francis Hutchinson, who had attended her in her confinement nine months before, was summoned immediately. His efforts to rouse her, the stomach-pump, the various antidotes for laudanum poisoning, had no effect. She lay as if sleeping save for her cold, pallid face and strangled breathing. At three o'clock in the dark and chilly winter morning her sister Clara Siddal came from her home in the Old Kent Road, answering an urgent summons, to join the watchers round Lizzie's bed. At five, Brown at Fortess Terrace, Kentish Town, woke to find Gabriel at his door. With broken sobs and tears Rossetti told him of the tragedy then passing in Chatham Place, whither they at once set off together.

At six, Gabriel's old medical friend, John Marshall, already eminent in surgery, arrived, and Dr. Hutchinson left Lizzie in his care. Gabriel and Brown had no doubt returned when at seven twenty, without recovering consciousness, Lizzie died. Rossetti, it is said, unable to believe that his wife was really dead, brought in three more doctors before he would accept their verdict as true. Was it now that he scribbled in his note-book the poignant couplet:

> As much as in a hundred years she's dead,
> Yet is to-day the day on which she died.

It was Red Lion Mary who carried the news to the Joneses in Great Russell Street. Jones was too ill to go out, but Georgie went instead, to Blackfriars where everything seemed, she wrote later, "all a dreadful dream" and "saw her poor body laid in the very bed where I have seen her lie and laugh in the midst of illness." Gabriel she did not see, but the faithful Brown was there making the necessary arrangements. "Pray God to comfort Gabriel" wrote Georgie to her sister.

William Rossetti, plodding through his dreary official duties at Somerset House that morning, was surprised about twelve-thirty by the entrance of Mrs. Birrell, housekeeper to the various sets of rooms in Chatham Place, bearing, belatedly enough, the sad tale of Lizzie's death. William immediately set off for Blackfriars, and there from Brown he learned the whole truth. "The poor thing looks wonderfully calm now and beautiful," William thought, regarding Lizzie more sympathetically than usual, and a couplet of Dante, slightly misquoted, came into his mind:

> Ed avea in se umiltà si verace
> Che parea che dicesse, "Io sono in pace."

"And with her was humility so true that methought she said: 'I am in peace.'"

Swinburne, ignorant of all that had happened since the break-up of their dinner-party in Leicester Square the night before, arrived at Chatham Place as arranged, to sit for his portrait, which Gabriel was painting. Walking into the tragic scene without warning, he found that the woman he loved at least "as a sister," was dead . . .

During the week of nightmare into which Gabriel's life collapsed between the tragedy and the funeral, his mother and sisters were constantly with him, besides Lizzie's sister Clara, and Brown who, with habitual unselfishness, devoted the whole of his time to Gabriel. The news quickly spread. Hardman, the genial lawyer who had often accompanied Meredith to Rossetti's, soon heard of it and passed the news on to friends. So, too, did Browning, sorrowing for the recent death of his own wife. Gabriel was, of course, anxious to keep all reference to the tragedy out of the newspapers, and as he was still comparatively obscure, succeeded so well that only one notice of the matter appeared, in a single paper, and that was very brief.

An inquest, however, despite his efforts to prevent it, had to be faced. At one-thirty on the afternoon of Wednesday, February 12th, in Bridewell Hospital, the witnesses attended, including Gabriel himself, Francis Hutchinson the doctor, Sarah Birrell the caretaker, Clara Siddal and Swinburne. Their evidence was brief and threw no light on the tragedy. Nevertheless, some curious facts emerged. Lizzie, it was established, suffered much from sleeplessness, and was, at least during this last year, much addicted to drugging herself with laudanum. She often took it on going to bed, in order to secure sleep. So said both Sarah Birrell and Clara Siddal.

"I saw her on Saturday evening last, she seemed in tolerably good spirits then," said Clara: "she had no family alive.[1] I knew of no harm to her. I don't suspect any."[2] Katherine Birrell, apparently the caretaker's daughter, testified that the empty phial had been "about half-full. They lived very happily together," she asserted, while Sarah Birrell declared in the simple phraseology of the illiterate Londoner: "I knew of no hurt to her, nor don't suspect any; her husband and herself lived very comfortable together."[2] Good cockney charity perhaps, rather than ignorance of the Rossettis' domestic life influenced this declaration, for an entry in William Rossetti's diary, made long afterwards, includes a significant comment by Gabriel upon the domestic felicity of poets, a comment more in harmony with what we know of his life with Lizzie. "Gabriel's view of the subject-matter of my lectures *The Wives of Poets*," wrote William, "is that those poets who have been happy with their wives were, although truly poets in performance, personally of an unpoetic character. . . ."

Ellen MacIntire, a neighbour, who lived at 14, Chatham Place, also gave evidence at the inquest. She said: "I was with the deceased on Monday evening about half-past eight. She seemed cheerful then. I did not see her again till Mr. Rossetti called me up at half-past eleven. She told me once that she

---

[1] She had a weak-minded brother, Henry, living. *v. inf.* p. 342, and *Rossetti Papers*, pp. 270–1.
[2] Murder evidently had to be considered. *v. also* pp. 296–7.

had taken quarts of laudanum in her time. I have seen the phial with laudanum in it." Algernon Swinburne, "16, Grafton Street, Fitzroy Square, at present," said: "I have known the deceased and her husband. They dined with me on Monday. I saw nothing particular in the deceased except that she appeared a little weaker than usual." He had no more to say. Gabriel's evidence ran thus: "On Monday afternoon she was perfectly well. About six or seven we went out to dinner, but before we started she appeared drowsy and when we got half-way in the cab I proposed going home again. She wished to go on and we dined at the Sablonière in Leicester Square with a friend. She seemed somewhat between flightiness and drowsiness, a little excited. We left there at eight and came straight home. I went out again after nine leaving her just going to bed. She seemed as right as before. She was in the habit of taking large doses of laudanum. I know that she has taken a hundred drops. I thought that she had the laudanum in brandy. I returned home again at half-past eleven and then she was in bed and snoring. I found her utterly without consciousness. I found a phial on a small table by her bedside. It was quite empty. The doctor was sent for and he attended her. She had not spoken of wishing to die. She had contemplated going out of town in a day or two and had bought a new mantle the day before. She was very nervous and had I believe a diseased heart. My impression is that she did not do it to injure herself but to quiet her nerves. She could not have lived without laudanum. She could not sleep at times nor take food."

The doctor's evidence settled the matter. The room smelt strongly of laudanum. The empty phial was "about a 2-oz. phial" labelled " 'Laudanum Poison'; 100 drops is a large dose." Her "child was born dead and had been dead for a fortnight before it was born." When he attended her previously "she was in a very nervous condition. . . . Her husband appeared very much attached to her."[1] The doctor believed "that she died from the effects of laudanum which must have been a very large dose." After which the jury decided that Lizzie "accidentally took an overdose of laudanum" and thus "accidentally, casually, and by misfortune came to her death."

[1] *v. footnote* 2, p. 295.

Such was the formal verdict. Yet for those most closely implicated the original question apparently remained. Had Lizzie met her death by accident or by her own design? That even at the inquest attendant circumstances were concealed is suggested by allusions to the tragedy made by some of those associated with Gabriel at this time. "I would rather not write you about what has happened," Swinburne informed his mother immediately after the inquest: "happily there was no difficulty in proving that illness had quite deranged her mind, so that the worst chance of all was escaped." Editorial discretion has obliterated the remainder of Swinburne's comment, but the suggestion is plain. Mental derangement—which in fact the records of the inquest do *not* affirm or even suggest—would have no relation to a purely accidental overdose of poison, at least in these particular circumstances. If Lizzie's death were, as the verdict asserted, accidental, why rejoice to prove mental derangement? Mental derangement would rather suggest suicide. And what was "the worst chance of all" which was escaped? Apparently a charge of murder or manslaughter against Rossetti himself!

"We heard of the death of Mrs. Gabriel," Bell Scott answered some letter of William's bearing news of his brother's loss, "with sincere sympathy and sorrow for him. The circumstance you mention, and which we hear from other sources, has been the cause of some notoriety, adding to the natural pain of such a parting." To what did William and Scott allude? Perhaps to some such incident as Oscar Wilde reported in later years—an incident bearing at least some obvious points of resemblance to the records of the inquest—when he declared the truth was that Lizzie under the influence of laudanum had acted so foolishly while dining in the Sablonière, that Gabriel, very angry at her behaviour in public, took her home, and when she demanded more laudanum despite his protests, thrust the bottle roughly into her hands, saying: "There, take the lot!" and then went out with Swinburne,[1] returning with the dawn to find her unconscious, and the empty laudanum phial beside her.

Nor, particularly in the light of Wilde's story, must we forget

[1] Tradition asserts to visit Fanny or some similar acquaintance.

those despairing verses of Lizzie's which William Rossetti later called "the final piece" and described as "written in a very shaky and straggling way. I surmise," he added, "that it must have been under the influence of laudanum, which she frequently took by medical orders as a palliative against tormenting neuralgia, and probably not long before her death." That, for the cautious William, is almost telling us. The verses themselves are too significant to omit:

> Life and night are falling from me,
> Death and day are opening on me.
> Wherever my footsteps come and go
> Life is a stony road of woe.
>   Lord, have I long to go?
> Hollow hearts are ever near me,
> Soulless eyes have ceased to cheer me:
>   Lord, may I come to Thee?
> Life and youth and summer weather
> To my heart no joy can gather:
> Lord, lift me from life's stony way.
> Loved eyes, long closed in death, watch o'er me—
> Holy Death is waiting for me—
>   Lord, may I come to-day?
> My outward life feels sad and still,
> Like lilies in a frozen rill.
>
> I am gazing upwards to the sun,
> Lord, Lord, remembering my lost one.
>   O Lord, remember me!
> How is it in the unknown land?
> Do the dead wander hand in hand?
> Do we clasp dead hands, and quiver
> With an endless joy for ever?
> Is the air filled with the sound
> Of spirits circling round and round?
> Are there lakes, of endless song,
> To rest our tired eyes upon?
> Do tall white angels gaze and wend
> Along the banks where lilies bend?
> Lord we know not how this may be;
> Good Lord, we put our faith in Thee—
>   O God, remember me.

If these despairing verses, "written in a very shaky and straggling way," that is, of course, as by one already under the influence of the laudanum or the accompanying brandy,

NOTE FOR PAGE 299

We now know from Mrs. Angeli's recently published work, *Dante Gabriel Rossetti: His Friends and Enemies*, which reached me only when the present volume was in the press, that there was such a message, and that it ran, "Take care of Harry"—a reference to Mrs. Rossetti's weak-minded brother. That this would *convince* such a person as Rossetti that his wife had committed suicide, when his hopes were opposed to conviction, is improbable, and does not, I think, exclude my suggestion that he endlessly debated the question, and particularly his own personal responsibility, especially as regards his last words to her before leaving her on the fatal night. The discovery of this message at the inquest was, however, doubtless "the worst chance of all" to which Swinburne referred (p. 297), not, as I suggested, the fear of a suspicion of murder against Rossetti.

were found near the dying woman when Gabriel entered her room that night, how they would emphasize the insoluble question of accident or suicide, and how they would suggest, without affirming, suicide rather than accident. From that, too, might easily have arisen the very doubtful tradition, denied by members of the Rossetti family, that she left a note pinned to her nightdress with some such message as—for accounts of course differ—"Perhaps you'll be sorry now!" That Georgie Jones believed Lizzie had committed suicide is surely implicit in her comment: "How often has it seemed to us that if the little baby had lived, she too might have done so, and Gabriel's terrible melancholy would never have mastered him." Nor is it perhaps without significance that when Bell Scott's *Autobiographical Notes* were published, deletions were made in his account of Lizzie's death which the present holder of the original MSS. refused to supply to the present writer, while a similar refusal came from the executors of Swinburne when asked for the full text of the letter previously quoted,[1] as also from Allingham's executors when the use of his unpublished MSS. was desired.

"Accident," then, hardly explains Lizzie's death and all its associated circumstances, nor is there any reliable authority for the melodramatic embellishments which have grown up about it in the intervening years and been greedily swallowed by the merely sensational type of "biographer." Most probably, indeed, as will appear from Rossetti's own writings and attitude in later years, the question of Lizzie's death remained permanently obscure, even for those most intimately acquainted with all the facts.

> Oh who knows the truth?
> How she perished in her youth,
> And like a queen went down
> Pale in her royal crown?

sang Christina a year later in *A Bird's Eye View*, a somewhat intriguing poem which, whether intentionally or not, but as Christina can hardly have failed to see, suggests in places Lizzie's story.

[1] *v. sup.* p. 297.

Doubt as to the actual cause and circumstance of Lizzie's fate, an endlessly reiterated, unanswerable question, seems to have been an important element in Gabriel's later anxiety neurosis and decline. How far had his own actions or words contributed to Lizzie's death? Many of his later verses suggest that this question haunted his sleepless nights in after years of conscience-stricken, morbid regret, while "Might-have-been," "No-more, Too-late, Farewell," mocked him, declaring:

> Unto thine ear I hold the dead-sea shell
> Cast up thy Life's foam-fretted feet between:
> Unto thine eyes the glass where that is seen
> Which had Life's form and Love's, but by my spell
> Is now *a shaken shadow intolerable*
> *Of ultimate things unuttered* the frail screen.

The lines I have italicized—by no means the only ones in Rossetti's *House of Life* suggesting a doubt about his wife's death—may well refer to a haunting anxiety as to the actual manner of Lizzie's death, this "intolerable" ghost haunting his mind, raising the unanswered, unanswerable question and the vision of his dead wife who had left him with these "ultimate things unuttered," although *these* unuttered ultimates were not, perhaps the only ones he had in mind.[1]

Indeed, the next lines of this sonnet, *A Superscription*, drive home this interpretation, for the haunting spirit warns Gabriel of its unrelenting persecution as the very voice of conscience, of the super-ego, which, says Freud, can in its tyranny drive the individual to suicide—as indeed it was to drive Rossetti.

> Mark me, how still I am! But should there dart
> One moment through thy soul the soft surprise
> Of that winged Peace which lulls the breath of sighs—
> Then shalt thou see me smile, and turn apart
> Thy visage to mine ambush at thy heart[2]
> Sleepless with cold commemorative eyes.

For that "winged Peace" is Love, Dante's "pace d'amore," and although the full significance of this and many another later sonnet of Rossetti's will not be evident at this period of his life, it is sufficient to support the suggestion of his ultimate, gnawing doubt as to the real cause of his wife's death. The

[1] *v. inf.* pp. 347–9, 520–1 and footnotes.   [2] *v. inf.* p. 385.

memory of his first great love's unhappy fate, of Lizzie's tragedy, is to lie like some dormant curse upon him, wakening only in the presence of some new possibility of love.

Probably as much of "the truth" as Gabriel knew or thought he knew, found expression in a play he wrote at some time, *The Wife's Tragedy*, but which has unfortunately disappeared. All we know of it is a comment by a young friend of Gabriel's later life, Sharp, who described the play as "lost or destroyed —a mature production called *The Wife's Tragedy*, which only a very few have seen, and which was based upon a fact of the author's acquaintance." All the evidence in fact suggests that it was this uncertainty about his wife's death, along with other disappointments and uncertainties of Gabriel's later life, acting upon so "anxious," so unstable a temperament as his, that ultimately led him, by the path of mental, moral and emotional decay, to attempt suicide by means of the very drug which had destroyed his wife.

In one other way the evidence at the inquest was noteworthy. No mention seems to have been made of the illness, tuberculosis, from which Lizzie was said to have been suffering for very many years, which some doctors had found and some had not, for which she had been sent to Hastings, Oxford and abroad. All that Gabriel had to say of his wife's health apparently, at the inquest, was that he "believed"—a strange detachment, surely, this uncertainty implies—that she had "a diseased heart," a weakness nowhere else mentioned in the records of either Gabriel or his friends. Yet even long after both Lizzie and Gabriel were dead, William asserted that Lizzie's "consumptive malady, accompanied by wearing neuralgia continued its fatal course, and her days could at best, to all appearance, have only been prolonged for some very few years." There we must, for the present at least, leave the problem of Lizzie's death. Lizzie was to be enigmatic to the end. . . .

Gabriel, overwrought and hypersensitive, in the grief and pain of an as yet incredible loss, experienced a common reaction of the neurotic temper. Falling deeply into a mood of self-reproach and self-abasement, he bitterly accused himself of both real and imaginary and exaggerated wrongs against his dead wife, blamed himself unstintedly for her death.[1] To his mother's home he fled for refuge, and there, as Swinburne described it, "with sobs and broken speech he protested that he had never really loved or cared for any woman but the wife he had lost; with bitter self-reproach he referred to former professions not ostensibly consistent with this assertion: he appealed to my friendship, in the name of her regard for me—such regard, he assured me, as she had felt for no other of his friends—to cleave to him in this time of sorrow, to come and keep house with him as soon as a residence could be found."

Nevertheless Gabriel's mind, as William noticed, remained clear even in his anguish, nor did he lose self-control. But William long recalled one moment of despair when Gabriel stood weeping by the dead body of his wife, beseeching: "Oh Lizzie, Lizzie, come back to me." It is William, too, who describes how, on the second or third day after Lizzie's death, so life-like was her appearance—owing it is said, but probably wrongly, to some preservative quality in the drug—Gabriel refused to believe her dead and insisted upon Marshall's coming again to give a last opinion, before he would finally accept the bitter truth. It was William also, not Gabriel, who received Ruskin when he called on hearing the news. Ruskin was shocked, sympathetic, more baffled than ever by life and death, now that his "Ida" had come to so sad an end. Here was another experience flouting belief in a comfortable Providence, and so emphasizing Ruskin's new views. He enlarged upon the change in his beliefs to William, who now first discovered with surprise that Ruskin's views were, like his own, sceptical.

The funeral was on February 17th, a week to the day since that last dinner in Leicester Square. While the few mourners were gathered together in one of the rooms, Gabriel quietly went away to where his wife lay. Alone, and unseen by the others, he placed in the coffin, together with a Bible which someone had laid there, his red-edged manuscript book of original verses, bound in rough grey calf, the sole complete copy of the original poems he had intended so soon to publish. Was Gabriel once again following as in youth, an instinct for

[1] *v. inf.* p. 348.

self-dramatization? Did he unconsciously or consciously recall that twelve years before, Christina, in her overstrained, gloomy little moral tale *Maude*, not published until after her own death, had described just such an action? Or did Christina, plagiarizing from her brother's life, insert the incident later?

On rejoining his friends Gabriel told Brown of what he had done, saying: "I have often been writing at those poems when Lizzie was ill and suffering, and I might have been attending to her, and now they shall go." Brown, knowing that of some of the most important of these poems there were no other copies, and that of many there were but imperfect ones, appealed to Gabriel and William against this reckless decision to make but a vain, sentimental and uncalled-for sacrifice. But even the calm, clear-headed William was now sufficiently moved to sympathize with Gabriel's heroics. He knew that Gabriel, who had already in his *Early Italian Poets* advertised the forthcoming publication of his original poems, was now rendering their appearance impossible, renouncing apparently for ever, his long-cherished ambition of poetic fame. "Well," William replied to Brown's protests, "the feeling does him honour, and let him do as he likes." (William's reply was the same seven years later when Gabriel wished to recover his poems again!) Immediately afterwards the little procession set out for Highgate Cemetery.

They buried Lizzie after all in the grave of old Gabriele, the family grave, the only family institution the Rossettis seem to have allowed her, with Gabriel's penitential-poetic manuscript burning in the flame of her red-gold hair, that hair which was so largely the source of her woes—and his!

Fourteen years later—the fact prepares us for Gabriel's next period of "change"—in the mistaken expectation of imminent death, Rossetti expressly stipulated that he should not be buried near his wife, and ordered William: "Let me not on any account be buried at Highgate, but my remains burnt as I say." When, however, after Gabriel's death, old Mrs. Rossetti, and Christina, too, lay in the family grave, William added to the epitaphs of Gabriele and Lizzie, inscriptions in honour of his mother's and sister's memory, plentifully adorned with biblical and other texts of a pious and optimistic nature. "A line in Dante's

Purgatorio," wrote William, complacently, at the time, "I put on Christina's tombstone as suggesting (but not with such a degree of definiteness as I do not personally believe), the reunion of the other tenants of that grave with Christina in the spiritual world." Lizzie's epitaph, however, bears no pious or edifying commentary, only:

> Also to the memory of
> ELIZABETH ELEANOR,
> wife of their elder son
> DANTE GABRIEL ROSSETTI,
> who died Feb. 11th, 1862
> aged 30 years

Even Lizzie's age was in doubt. Her sister said she was twenty-eight, Gabriel believed she was twenty-nine, and her tombstone said she was thirty! . . .

To Gabriel, turning away when all was over, leaving behind him, in the earth, all the passion, idealism, ecstasy of his youth, death must have seemed no such ineffable consummation of love as he had dreamed of in the days of *Love's Nocturn* and *The Blessed Damozel*. Not for him, now, the visionary consolations of Platonism or Christianity, but only, in his heart, the bitter cry of Dante:

> Morta e la donna tua, ch'era si bella!
> —Thy lady that was so beautiful, is dead!

BOOK III

"CHANGE AND FATE"
1862–1874

The sunrise blooms and withers on the hill
Like any hillflower. . . .

True Woman D. G. ROSSETTI

I

DISILLUSION
1862–1864

Lost love-morrow and love-fellow
And love's life lying low.
Lovelorn labour and life laid by,
And lowly let love lie.

Chimes D. G. ROSSETTI

CHATHAM PLACE, haunted by bitter-sweet memories, became uninhabitable for Gabriel from the moment of his wife's death. Refusing his brother's generous offer of a permanent home with the Rossettis in Albany Street, he now returned, after ten years' absence, to once familiar Newman Street, taking rooms this time at No. 77. But quickly wearying of them, he was established by the end of April at 59 Lincoln's Inn Fields.

As soon as the first shock of Lizzie's death passed, he continued his usual way of life with little outward sign of grief. Painting hard and also helping Mrs. Gilchrist to complete her late husband's biography of William Blake, he found in art and letters the best anodyne. As a critic of Blake, he rightly followed his aesthetic intuition beyond the limits of conscious intellectual analysis. "The truth is," he told Mrs. Gilchrist, "that as regards such a poem as *My Spectre* I do not understand it a bit better than anybody else, only I know better than some may know, that it has claims as poetry apart from the question of understanding it, and is therefore worth printing." In some respects, however, his editorial methods were almost incredibly bad. Even Mrs. Gilchrist remonstrated when in destroying a "residuum" of Blake's MSS., Rossetti destroyed the best passages in *The French Revolution*; but the excitement of making bonfires of Blake's MSS. proved so contagious that soon she too was enjoying the experience of making similar holocausts. When after these exploits she received a copy of the *Life* with Rossetti's supplementary chapter on Blake's Poetry and Art, she expressed to him her heart-felt gratitude for "the magnitude and *rare quality* of your own and your brother's services to it—

pious service truly, for which I believe the dead as well as the
living bless you both." And Rossetti assured her: "I would
have done it gladly for Blake's or gladly for your husband's
or gladly for your sake, and, moreover, had always a great wish
of my own to do something in this direction."

Nor was work Gabriel's sole defence against his gnawing
misery. Amidst the distractions of the outer world he could for
a time forget. Two months after the tragedy, he was dining
at Hardman's club with Hardman the gourmet as his host,
Meredith as a fellow guest, and contemplating such a menu
as these degenerate days can seldom if ever show. The food
was excellent, the wines exquisite, and they "kept it up," said
Hardman, till half-past two in the morning. Returning home,
Hardman laughingly complained of their difficulty in piloting
Meredith through the Haymarket, "he was so very *rampant*."[1]

Boyce, abroad for some months, returned in April, took over
Rossetti's rooms in Chatham Place, and resumed the old association with him and his friends. The entries in Boyce's diary
at this time give us interesting glimpses of Rossetti attempting
by various activities in these early days of his widowerhood, to
escape from haunting, intolerable memories. On Easter Monday (April 21, 1862), Gabriel, William and Boyce went by
cab to Greenwich. Gabriel, now an enthusiastic "collector,"
picked up an old Indian basket on the way. They looked at
the pictures in the Hospital, especially a Turner, then "strolled
about the park. Gabriel, catching sight of a girl with a paint-
able face, made up to her and got her address." After dining
at a neighbouring inn, the party returned to the park, to find
"kiss in the ring and out of the ring and larking generally
going on,"[2] as Boyce described it. Then they returned for tea
to Boyce's rooms, where Gabriel and William remained until
nearly three o'clock the next morning. Such, increasingly at
this time, became Rossetti's way of life.

"Better, still somewhat shaken," was Meredith's description
of Gabriel in mid-June. Meredith and Swinburne were much
with him now. Early in July, Swinburne, who had taken over
Rossetti's rooms in Newman Street, gave a house-warming

---

[1] Italics are Hardman's.
[2] Greenwich Park on Easter Monday was a recognized Victorian saturnalia.

party there, which Gabriel attended. Boyce, who was also present, noted "the frantic delight" of the guests at Swinburne's extensive recitations from his own poems. A few days later, Rossetti and Swinburne, having refused an invitation from William Rossetti and Bell Scott to join them in an Italian tour, visited Meredith at Copsham. Allingham, recently transferred to the London Customs, was often with Gabriel now, and one evening they spent lying together on the grass in Lincoln's Inn, discussing Christina's poems. Since Lizzie's death, the old, intimate relations between Gabriel and his sister had been largely restored. Boyce, entering Swinburne's room in mid-August, found that enthusiastic disciple of De Sade showing Rossetti a copy of *Justine* which he had just bought. The three friends "then went on to the International Exhibition. Had some ices at a stall near the Egyptian things where there was a very lovely girl of whom Gabriel obtained a promise to sit to him."

But, for Rossetti, the companionship of others could not finally banish remorse, uncertainty, disillusion. Alone, sombrely surveying his frustrated past, he found little consolation in the spectacle of those barren, often sordid years separating him from his lost, idealistic adolescence—that adolescence from which he could never entirely escape. And the woman who had once been its inspiration, the symbol, as he had mistakenly believed, of his own soul, was now dead—perhaps through his fault. With that thought, the seed of a new, a life-long anxiety was planted, an anxiety which was to find somewhat cryptic expression in much of his verse, verse in which he vainly sought the resolution of his internal strife.

In a retrospective mood of regret for his wasted past, he now wrote his bitter sonnet *Lost Days*—days once so lightly discarded, but now seen as "ears of wheat sown once for food but trodden into clay," as "golden coins squandered and still to pay," "drops of blood dabbling the guilty feet," precious water spilt amidst the agonizing thirst of Hell. These, he said, would confront him after death, crying:

> "I am thyself—what hast thou done to me?
> And I—and I—thyself," (lo! each one saith,)
> "And thou thyself to all eternity!"

309

It was the earlier mental attitude of *How they met themselves*, finding a new form of poetic expression. But it was also ominous of the future; the paranoiac process of the "guilty conscience" had begun.

The bitterness of spirit in which the sonnet was written remained in Rossetti's memory to the end of his life; was too painful an experience, even in retrospect, for allusion. "Pardon an egotistic sentence (in answer to what you say so generously of *Lost Days*)," he wrote to an acquaintance in 1880, discussing *The House of Life*, "if I express an opinion that *Known in Vain* and *Still-born Love* may perhaps be said to head the series in value, though *Lost Days* might be equally a favourite with me if I did not remember in what but too opportune juncture it was wrung out of me."

On October 24, 1862, Rossetti moved into "Tudor House," 16 Cheyne Walk, Chelsea, which was henceforth to be his home. The fascination of the Thames which had drawn him to Chatham Place, had again drawn him to a house by the river, this pleasant old red-brick building with a large garden behind. The house had something of a history, and its alternative names of "Tudor House" and "The Queen's House" were doubtless survivals from its half-forgotten past. Reputed the residence at various times of Sir Thomas More and of Queen Elizabeth, described by Thackeray in *Esmond* as the house of the Dowager Viscountess Castlewood, it was certainly a part of the mansion to which Queen Catherine Parr retired on the death of Henry VIII, and there too the Lord High Admiral Seymour had courted her. With such a past it was, of course, haunted. "A strange, quaint, grand old place, with an immense garden, magnificent panelled staircases and rooms, a palace," wrote Meredith enthusiastically, at this time, while William, thirty years later described it less romantically as "a fine old solid edifice without anything peculiar or showy in external aspect," and within, as "old-fashioned, many-roomed, homelike and comfortable." Near by was old wooden Battersea Bridge, soon to be immortalized by the rising artist Whistler.

Still further to lighten the not heavy burden of the rent, and more particularly perhaps to avoid complete solitude, Rossetti took Swinburne as joint tenant, while Meredith and William

Rossetti, sleeping there regularly for one and three nights a week respectively, also paid their share. But the mutual combativeness of all save William, eliminated both Swinburne and Meredith within a year. They were indeed a strange household. Meredith, long separated from his wife, and now a cynical widower, so irritated Gabriel at times that one morning at breakfast, in the summer of 1863, he threw a cup of tea in Meredith's face, and immediately afterwards Meredith departed. Swinburne, a recently disappointed lover, made the house unbearable by indulging in nude corybantic exercises about the rooms and corridors whenever he had had a drink (which immediately affected him), by sliding naked down the handrail of the staircase, making drunken scenes and falling into ungovernable rages. Sometimes ex-proctor Pollen of the Jovial Campaign, who now lived near by, was brought in to quieten the "pandemonium" as he described it. "Dancing all over the studio like a wild cat," was Gabriel's description of Swinburne, later; it used, he said, "to drive me crazy." Soon, Swinburne's excesses brought on a nervous breakdown. He retired into the country to recuperate, and when early in 1864 he wished to return to Cheyne Walk, Gabriel, although in the friendliest way, closed the door against him.

The reason clearly was that, alone in Cheyne Walk, Gabriel, "a martyr to unsatisfactory servants," as he complained, had already allowed Fanny to instal herself as housekeeper to help him to run the place and keep solitude at bay. In work he found the best antidote to his unhappiness, and for the first time he now blessed the debts that kept him constantly at his easel. Nevertheless he chafed at the slavery of making potboilers and replicas to which he was often reduced. To lighten the burden he took an art assistant, Knewstub, who, having come under his influence at the Working Men's College, had abandoned his studies at the Royal Academy Schools at the close of 1862 and paid Gabriel a premium in order to become his unpaid pupil and helper.

Once again it is Boyce who gives us intimate little glimpses of Rossetti during these early months in Cheyne Walk. Calling in mid-November, Boyce "found Fanny there. He (Rossetti) had furnished his house most picturesquely, mostly with fine old Renaissance furniture bought of a man at 8 Buckingham Street." A few days later Rossetti and Allingham brought Browning to Boyce's studio, and Boyce was pleased to be introduced to so distinguished a contemporary. Calling on Gabriel early in December, Boyce "found him and Fanny at home. Stayed and dined. He gave me a pencil sketch of her as she lay on a couch, hair outspread, and her right hand under her head." The next day Rossetti went to Newcastle to paint a portrait of Mrs. Leathart. In mid-March, 1863, he was painting a portrait of Annie Miller "which he has converted into Helen of Troy," wrote Boyce; "ships burning in the background. He has also made several beautiful studies from divers women."

Throughout the months of that spring and summer of 1863, Boyce's pages are studded with the names of Gabriel and his circle of friends, patrons and models as they make their continual calls, excursions, or attend occasional formal dinner parties, like that Gabriel gave on April 30th in honour of Leathart. The other guests were William Rossetti, Swinburne, Meredith, Chapman the portrait painter, Marshall the surgeon, Jones, Gabriel's patron Anderson Rose (a solicitor), and Boyce. "We dined," wrote Boyce, "in the long drawing-room, which has been most exquisitely fitted by Gabriel with chintz hangings, pictures, porcelain and old furniture. . . ."

In September, Gabriel took a week's holiday with William in Belgium, following a route which, except that they did not visit Paris, resembled that taken with Hunt fourteen years before. For Gabriel at least it was a somewhat dreary excursion —the first and the last the two brothers ever made together. Through Calais, Brussels, Antwerp, Ghent, Bruges they passed, seeing Rubens's famous *Descent from the Cross*—which had been removed for cleaning at the time of Gabriel's former visit— patronizing dance halls—surely not at William's desire—buying old junk for Cheyne Walk, Chinese and Japanese *objets d'art*, and watching the animals in the Antwerp zoo.

Back in Tudor House, Gabriel quickly yielded to the old lethargy which, since his wife's death, again threatened him. Few disturbed his solitude. Swinburne, Jones, Morris, Brown often came, and so, occasionally, did Ruskin and Browning when in England; but Gabriel had fewer relations now with the outer world. Unable to afford holidays, he worked hard, overworked indeed, dreamed at times of going abroad again, to Venice in the autumn perhaps—"but I suppose it will not be"—or to see Allingham at Lymington whither his friend, soon wearying of London's docks, had now gone as customs officer. But when the moment for action came, Gabriel could do nothing, seemed paralysed, as so often in the days of his adolescence. Again and again he arranged to visit Allingham —even choosing his train and informing Allingham of the time of his impending arrival—yet at the last moment, irresolute, he could not break away. It was an early sign of the neurotic state into which he was gradually sinking, of that ultimate loss of interest in life which many years later was to mark the final stage of his decline. His short Continental tour had improved both his physical and mental health, but upon his return he was forced to resume "the very nauseous job I ran away from," the making of "pot-boilers" and "replicas," "for filthy lucre's sake," and was soon "quite as bad again as before I went."

Already Tudor House, offering him in his frustration the peace, the refuge from reality he unconsciously craved, was gradually weaving its fatal spell about him. Years later, when he made protracted but characteristically futile attempts to quit the house, he seems to have begun to realize that it was, in a very real sense, a part of his destiny. For distraction, he turned more insistently to collecting "old pots," curios, bric-à brac of every description, following his own freakish fancy rather than good or informed taste. He constantly employed a leading London agent, Murray Marks, to attend sales and secure for him expensive acquisitions, and in all this he showed the keen business instinct his patrons already knew so well. To Marks he introduced such important collectors as Mr. Huth the American millionaire and the London surgeon Sir Henry Thompson; but only on the condition that Marks should give him special consideration in return. "But I must have the first pick," was his characteristic stipulation when sending Marks a "good buyer" of blue china. Gabriel's own collection of blue china was due, said Prinsep, to his telling Whistler he would beat his collection within a week, which he did by buying up the whole collection of another person—the Marquis d'Azeglio, Prinsep believed. "The china mania did not last very long," wrote Prinsep. "He sold all his 'long Elizas' about four years after he bought them." At any rate, while the "mania" lasted, Rossetti showed great ardour in the pursuit of particular pieces he desired, and the story of his suddenly seizing a dish on which food was being served during a dinner party at which he was a guest, of his thoughtlessly turning it over and upsetting the contents on the table in his anxiety to see if it was a plate he had recently seen in a shop near by and intended to purchase, has been told by many different writers of reminiscences and described as happening in many different places. If not true in the letter, we may well take it as true in the spirit.

Nor did Rossetti confine himself to the collecting of china. Indeed the many and widely different objects he acquired, ranging from old oak, Dutch tiles, mirrors of all shapes and sizes and times, to jewels, robes, brocade, made a medley of Cheyne Walk which, in an interesting sketch, Sir John Gilbert, R.A., has well suggested. Many of these objects appear as accessories in Gabriel's paintings, and his exploration of junk shops, to find them, gave his love of solitary wandering about London a new direction and aim.

The anti-social tendency born of unhappiness and disappointment, a tendency which was ultimately to master his strong social instinct and drive him into almost complete solitude, already found expression in the creation of a domestic zoo. From the self-consciousness of men and women which, he declared, made them in a general way uninteresting, he now turned to the companionship of the animal world, which brought him relief and pleasure. At Cheyne Walk he assembled a strange, often disturbing menagerie of animal pets, ranging from kangaroos, wombats and salamanders to gazelles and even an Indian bull—"bought," said Ellen Terry, "because it had 'eyes like Janie Morris' "—which chased him round his own garden. The tales of what happened to Gabriel's animals are even more numerous and perhaps even more dubious than those told of his china, but his own letters prove that only too often they suffered extraordinary experiences and came to strange ends. His armadillos had a habit of suddenly appearing amongst his neighbours; his peacocks so disturbed them by their raucous cries that "Lord Cadogan, the ground-landlord, afterwards introduced into all Cheyne Walk leases . . . a clause to the effect that the tenants were not to keep any peacocks," and when Mrs. Tebbs, after sitting to Rossetti, found that the wombat had eaten her new hat, all that Gabriel could say was, "Oh, poor wombat! It is so indigestible!"

Inevitably, as Rossetti's interest in the external world declined, his morbidity increased. With the almost prophetic intuition of his adolescence, he now stamped upon his note-paper a design he had made from an old seal of his father's, representing a tree bearing the motto: *Frangas non Flectas*. That was indeed to be his own future; unable to bend, he must in time break. It was in a dark mood that he took the motto for himself. The supply of paper on which he had had it printed would, he declared, "last half my life-time—or indeed perhaps head the news of my death when that occurs, before the black-edged paper has arrived." The melancholia which was to dominate him later, was already revealing itself. Henceforth the thought of death appealed to him with growing insistence, often as a comforter—in the form of a little child, his own dead daughter, or as "Beata Beatrix," his dead wife.

Against the spell of Tudor House he would seek amongst his models or in Cremorne Gardens near-by, or in his street wanderings on nights of revolt and adventure, the amusements, excitements, "compensations" his senses craved. For although he did not know it, his romanticism was more Byronic than Shelleian. In other moods he found his compensations, his romantic thrill, in reverie or fancy. The river always held him under its spell, and on summer evenings he loved to watch the hayboats passing, their brick-red sails lit up by the sunset or the moonlight. On at least one occasion he extended a night's hospitality to a disreputable stowaway from one of them, who had been forced to swim ashore, and his humble acquaintance's candid account of his shameless way of life amused Rossetti. Like so many of the romantics Gabriel retained in his composition a primitive, intensely individualistic strain which resented the adaptations increasingly demanded by "civilization," and his sympathies with social rebels of all kinds increasingly revealed themselves.[1]

In reaction against his earlier disappointed idealism, he relapsed for a time to the levels of the almost purely instinctive life. In the summer of 1864, alone for the most part with Fanny in the great, empty house, he painted hard to meet his debts, tried to forget in light distractions, the dead, passionate past. Long afterwards, Allingham described to Graham Robertson the attitude of Gabriel to Fanny at this time. "I cannot," wrote Robertson, "recall much of that talk, but remember a quaint description of Rossetti's carefully explaining to him the points of his favourite model, Fanny Cornforth, in that lady's presence and with almost embarrassing minuteness. 'Her lips, you see' following their curve with an indicating finger—'are just the red a woman's lips always should be—not really red at all, but with the bluish pink bloom that you find in a rose petal.' Miss Cornforth the while spread her ample charms upon a couch and throwing in an occasional giggle or 'Oh, go along, Rissetty!'" Gabriel, in his present cynical mood, found a bitter amusement even in Fanny's vulgarities, in the contrast she presented to his earlier ideal. Here was his "Blessed Damozel" indeed!

He painted her now and often as once he used to paint Lizzie; but as an alluring symbol of purely animal beauty and desire, not as a Blessed Damozel or Beatrice. Even before Lizzie's death he had begun to paint Fanny thus: as *Bocca Baciata* in 1859, *Fair Rosamund* in 1861, as herself, Fanny Hughes in 1862, as *Fazio's Mistress* (not to be confused with the *Bonifazio's Mistress*) in 1863. This last, which showed Fanny plaiting her long, golden locks before a mirror, was praised as a particularly fine portrait of Fanny at this time. It was begun, people said, before Lizzie's death, was painted in part at Chatham Place, while Lizzie lay almost dying in the next room. Although repainted ten years later and renamed *Aurelia*,

[1] Freud's suggestive essay, *Civilization and its Discontents*, with which I was unacquainted until after the completion of this work, might almost have been written about Rossetti (though of course it was not), so applicable is it to his situation and development, and the reader who desires an insight into the deeper causes of Rossetti's decline would do well to refer to it.

the face was fortunately left untouched. . . . And now, in 1864, Gabriel was painting Fanny again; this time as a *Lady in a White Dress Combing her Hair*, and also as *Lady Lilith*—Lilith, Adam's beautiful witch-wife before Eve. Gabriel had probably learned from his father, so deeply read in such matters, that Lilith was supposed to have a baneful influence upon newly born children.

In the intervals of his incessant painting to pay his debts, throughout that summer of 1864, Rossetti would relapse into his characteristic lethargy. Lying on the grass beside Fanny in the neglected garden, he would watch the glittering peacocks spread their plumage bright as the ideal visions that had once gleamed before his own eyes. Or alone, wrapped in reverie, haunted by the face of his dead wife, he would sit dark and silent, brooding over all the vanished brightness, pain, passion and broken promise of the past. To the misery, the turbulence of their jarring loves, the discords of their life together, had now succeeded this great yet bitter peace, a peace no longer broken by active conflict of wills, but mocked by the agony of unforgettable, irreplaceable loss. So at least in this mood it appeared to Rossetti. Like the great house he had taken, his life now lay empty; quiet yet haunted—a wilderness of sorrow in which he wandered alone.

Allingham, penetrating his retreat in June, was quickly conscious of the change in him. He found him "painting a very large woman, almost a giantess, as *Venus Verticordia*"—Venus, the Turner of Hearts.* The model was a cook, recently discovered by Gabriel. Before dinner the two friends chatted of old Preraphaelite days, until with Fanny's entry the conversation immediately and entirely changed. Fanny grew lyrical over Bell Scott, whose thick, dark hair, recently destroyed by illness, had been replaced by a wig. "O my! Mr. Scott *is* changed!" she cried. "He ain't got a hye-brow or a hye-lash— not a 'air on his 'ead!" Gabriel laughed so heartily that Fanny pouted. "Well, I know I don't say it right." To avert the impending storm, Allingham stayed Gabriel's mocking laughter. . . . As he was leaving, Rossetti invited him to breakfast with them the next day.

* *v. Notes.*

Before half-past eight the next morning, Allingham re-appeared. Fanny, in white, joined them, and they all break-fasted together in the small but lofty breakfast room on the first floor, overlooking the garden. Afterwards they lay on the lawn, eating strawberries as in the old days on the little balcony at Chatham Place, and watching the peacocks. Then Fanny went to feed the "chicking" as she called the fowls. Soon Swinburne dropped in and recited his latest verses. Whistler came next, to talk of his pictures. So the morning passed. . . . One evening, Allingham and Gabriel dined together in Leicester Square, at the Hotel de Provence, and then went on to the opera. But Gabriel, caring nothing for music, soon left, doubt-less to go wandering about the London streets, and Allingham finished the evening alone. Allingham noticed the development of Rossetti's anti-social attitude, his rejection of his offer to bring Tennyson to Cheyne Walk, with the confession: "I have no finished work to show at present, and have moreover so fallen out of the habit of seeing any but intimates that I feel like a fool with others." To Allingham, Gabriel's way of life presented a sad contrast to the apparent domestic felicity of the Morrises at The Red House—"in its rose-garden," as Allingham described it in his diary, with "William Morris, and his queenly wife, crowned with her own black hair."

Early in November, a momentarily replenished purse allowed Gabriel to break the spell of Tudor House, and with Fanny he set off for Paris. It was his first visit since his honeymoon. As before, he first went to an hotel so expensive that within a few days he was forced to leave it for a cheaper one. In Paris he saw much of painters and painting, met Fantin-Latour and Manet, and just missed meeting Baudelaire, already famous and infamous amongst contemporaries for his *Fleurs du Mal*. As before, Rossetti showed extraordinary lack of insight into the excellences of French painting and painters. Delacroix he thought "worth the journey with all his faults"; "old Ingres . . . done for"; Gerôme not really a painter "though a stunner of a sort," and Millet who painted "really glorious things," "the best going by far." For the French Impressionists—"this incredible new French school—people painted with two eyes in one socket through merely being too lazy to efface the first and what not," he had neither understanding nor sympathy. He thought Manet's works "for the most part mere scrawls," and Courbet's "not much better." His attitude to French art in general was as prejudiced, hostile and unenlightened as when, fifteen years before, with Hunt, he first visited Paris. "A beastly slop and really makes one sick," was the description of French painting he sent to Swinburne; and to his mother, he wrote: "simply putrescence and decomposition." "It is well worth while," he said, "for English painters to try and do something now."

Despite Fanny's presence, he did not forget the companion of his last visit. To Georgie Jones he sent two photographs of Lizzie, explaining that they were photographs from two of his sketches of her, because all her actual photographs were bad and had been destroyed. He asked Georgie to choose one of them and to give the other, as he had once promised, to the nurse who had attended both Georgie and Lizzie in childbirth. Georgie thought the one she chose, which was of Lizzie after her marriage, "extremely like her and gives the peculiar lustre of her downcast eyes." Although he had brought work with him to Paris, Rossetti remained as restless yet lethargic as ever, and after three weeks, unable to paint, tiring of buying European and Oriental bric-à-brac, he returned with Fanny to London. He brought with him little presents for the Rossetti family: a tortoise-shell purse for his mother, a fan for Christina, and for Maria a dress which he hoped would not be "an abomination to her." For Maria's tastes were severe. Christina on seeing him, rejoiced to find him "looking perhaps less stout and so far better." Boyce, calling with Whistler at Cheyne Walk on November 25th, found that "He and 'Lumpses' had just come back from Paris where they had been staying for some weeks," and Gabriel showed them *Venus Verticordia*.

And once again, far from the lightness and brightness of Paris, back with Fanny in the gaunt, gloomy house amidst the river mists and winter fogs of Cheyne Walk, Gabriel watched the short November days, vaporous and dim as his own existence, fade and pass with the dying year.

II

SUCCESS
1865–1866

My prospects promise to improve very much just now.
Letter to H. F. Polydore[1] D. G. ROSSETTI

"The evening went off comfortably, though Mrs. Birrell told me afterwards that on this very evening three years ago, Mrs. Rossetti was taken so ill and died here," wrote Boyce, after entertaining the two Rossettis and a few other friends, in Chatham Place, on February 10, 1865. On this third anniversary of Lizzie's death, the housekeeper at least had remembered her.

By the irony of fate, those three empty intervening years of widowerhood had brought Gabriel the realization of his ambition, an established reputation as a painter. Increasing signs of growing prestige were now appearing in various quarters. Philip Hamerton, a well-known English art critic in Paris, eager to acclaim Rossetti's leadership of the Preraphaelites in the *Revue des deux Mondes*, had begun a correspondence with Gabriel which was but the prelude to the cordial reception given Rossetti by leading French painters during his recent visit to the French capital. Already, at thirty-seven, Gabriel began to feel himself on the threshold of "Success."

That this was at least as much due to Ruskin's generous praise as to Rossetti's actual achievement, can hardly be doubted. Three years before, at the time of Lizzie's death, he had, despite his ardent, youthful ambitions, but little to show for the spent years: a volume of translations, a few original verses in odd corners of one or two obscure magazines, some striking compositions in water-colour, a long, unsuccessful struggle to paint in oils. Nor had his artistic development followed a straight road. He had, as Ford Madox Ford remarked, "a habit of indulging himself in all emotions that he, and more particularly his friends liked," and this, by drawing him into the ways of his associates, had at times diverted him

[1] Henry Polidori had changed his name to Polydore.

320

PLATE VIII

ARTHUR'S TOMB
BY D. G. ROSSETTI
1854

WEDDING OF ST. GEORGE AND THE PRINCESS SABRA
BY D. G. ROSSETTI
1857

PLATE IX

ELIZABETH ELEANOR SIDDAL
BY D. G. ROSSETTI
c. 1855

ELIZABETH ELEANOR SIDDAL
BY D. G. ROSSETTI
1856

from his own path. Brown's "Early Christian" and historic styles he had soon discarded—through lack of patrons—for that of Hunt and the Preraphaelite Brotherhood and the "modern subject" *Found*. Next, the "Florentine" and "Dantesque" manner approved for a time by Ruskin, had claimed his allegiance in water-colour until, with Jones and Morris, he turned, still in water-colour, to "mediaevalism" of the Arthurian in place of the Dantesque kind. Only in 1859 with *Bocca Baciata* had his re-emergence as a painter in oils begun, though Ruskin had long urged what Gabriel well knew, that oils brought more money and fame than water-colours. Now, however, Rossetti was at last acquiring something of the necessary technical skill in the medium which he had abandoned twelve years before, after painting *The Girlhood of Mary Virgin* and *The Annunciation*. "At about the end of 1862," wrote Madox Ford, "Rossetti may be said to have been beginning to 'find himself'—to find himself as he then was, not as he ought to have been had he not fallen under the sway of various influences, of various entourages and of various demands."

The pictures and poems he was now producing reflected in their themes the change in himself. In poetry he had turned from *The Blessed Damozel* to *Jenny*;[1] in painting, from *The Girlhood of Mary Virgin* and *The Annunciation*, to *Bocca Baciata* and *Lady Lilith*. And *Bocca Baciata*, the first result of his newly acquired improvement in oils, was also the first clear promise of his own new manner, of those "imaginative, sumptuous, single figures" of women, as one critic described them, which he was henceforth to go on painting, until, in his final phase, broken by mental, moral and physical decay, he painted them sombre, deathly-hued, sinister, as if in revolt against his earlier adoration of the flesh. But woman, flaunting and vital or sad and deathlike, was to be his soul's symbol to the end.

Since his wife's death, however, and particularly during 1863–64, Rossetti's production of important oil-paintings had significantly and most markedly increased. In June 1864 he completed the Llandaff triptych, and now, in 1865–66, straining every nerve, he consolidated his position by continuing to produce his new type of picture, in oils.

[1] Begun in 1848 but mostly written 1858–69.

Various circumstances, in fact, were now combining to create in Rossetti an unusual mood of self-complacency. There were rumours that his pictures were fetching high prices, that Gambart the art agent was selling them at double the price he paid, had even sold *The Blue Bower*—a portrait of Fanny—for fifteen hundred guineas. New agreements with the rogue should, Gabriel decided, be stiffer than before, and he charged him five hundred guineas for a single head. New commissions, too, from old and new patrons, were also plentiful, and Rossetti employed his usual skill in making the most of his opportunity. A Yorkshire business-man, Dunlop, he persuaded to accept the hitherto unparalleled price of two thousand guineas for a work to be called *The Boat of Love*, and Dunlop's friend Heugh to agree to similarly profitable commissions. "I have quantities of commissions now, and never was nearly so prosperous before," he proudly told Aunt Charlotte: "I trust . . . henceforward to do almost exclusively large works in oil. Small things and water-colours I never should have done at all except for the long continuance of a necessity for pot-boilers."

To Uncle Polydore, who had lent Gabriel money, he now offered, in his elation, to increase the interest he was (presumably) paying, from 3½ per cent to 10 per cent, assuring him: "My prospects promise to improve very much just now, through the high prices which some of my pictures have fetched in the market." To pay his expenses in Paris with Fanny, he hastily painted *King René's Honeymoon*, and, when it was ready for his patron, a Brighton wine merchant named Trist, boasted to Brown: "I finished Trist's pot-boiler to-day, and lo! the pot shall boil for a season. For him, may his mirth, when he sees it, not be even as the crackling of thorns under a pot. He will face it on Saturday." When a few days later the despised Trist took his picture away, Gabriel reported—he "liked it very much, and paid for it. I have been at work on it exactly eight days, so it pays better than most things, though cheap."

Disappointments, however, quickly dashed Rossetti's premature assurance. Gambart denied the truth of the rumours, swore that *The Blue Bower* had sold for only a third of the sum reported, and declared that Gabriel's increased prices threatened "an end to the possibility of business." Next,

Rossetti had to "stroke down" a Bradford manufacturer, Mitchell, clamouring for the long since commissioned *Venus Verticordia*. Worst of all, Dunlop and Heugh, who had agreed to the highest prices, revolted after long delay and silence on Rossetti's part, refusing to confirm their commissions, "not to speak of a cheque," as the disgusted Gabriel informed Brown. With the two delinquents, however, Rossetti carried on a vigorous epistolary battle, until, finally worsted, he haughtily withdrew. "I know," was his final retort to Dunlop, "that there are those who applaud themselves when misconduct bears them no worse fruit than the expression of deserved contempt. To such species of success I make you welcome." Heugh, he dismissed with an even sterner reprimand: "There is nothing of a kind to surprise me in your present letter; for not one word of it is true. Enough for me that, in spite of your solemn tone, you know as well as I do that you are untruthful." Then, too, at the sale of Plint's pictures in June 1865, Rossetti's *Burd Alane* sold for only seventy-one pounds, thirteen less than Plint had paid for it. Gabriel, disgusted, accused Gambart of rigging the market against him.

Nor were these Gabriel's only quarrels and disappointments. Success, jealousy, rival interests had during recent years gradually withdrawn many of his former companions—including Millais, Hunt and Woolner—had even loosened the ties binding him to his later disciples of the Jovial Campaign. "Alas!" wrote Prinsep, long afterwards, "as time progressed, and each one of that faithful band had to strike out a line for himself, the bond of fellowship seemed loosened. It was not that any one of us loved our friend the less. The glamour of his personality became a little dimmed; the individuality of each man, as is ever the case when a man has anything in him, began to form his character and art; the Gabriel we admired was there, but, like the dread Jehovah of the Israelites, he was a jealous God, and, from the moment he was not all in all to us, a gradually widening rift established itself. Other young fellows took our place, though it must be owned that in later life these young fellows were more literary than artistic." Not until some years later, however, did these new, literary disciples arrive to replace the earlier admirers now drifting away.

It was now, in the dawn of Gabriel's success, that Ruskin too passed from the circle of Gabriel's friends, and indeed out of Rossetti's life. That in his first hour of triumph Gabriel broke or allowed to be broken, his bond with the one person to whom above all others his triumph was due is not really surprising. The basic significance of the rupture, though probably unnoticed by either, was very real. Rossetti, so independent in spirit, now making over two thousand pounds a year, no longer needed a supporter. Ruskin, benevolent but unconsciously tyrannical, resented, without knowing it, Gabriel's newly acquired independence. Between these two men, the undersexed and the oversexed, there were, below the surface, deep unconscious oppositions, just as within each were individual oppositions producing internal conflict and frustration.

Disappointed with the small return in affection his benevolence had won from Gabriel and Lizzie, Ruskin, shortly before Lizzie's death, had installed in Gabriel's place the docile Jones, "whose life," Ruskin significantly declared, "is as pure as an archangel's, whose genius is as strange and high[1] as that of Albert Dürer or Hans Memling, who loves me with a love as of a brother." But this, the factitious counter-passion to a genuine but unrequited love, failed to drive out the old affection for Gabriel, and on hearing of Lizzie's death, Ruskin's suppressed feelings had found relief in a letter of commiseration containing an almost abject plea for a resumption of mutual sympathy and a timid suggestion, apparently ignored by Gabriel, that they should travel together to Italy and live together afterwards in Tudor House. In revolt at that time against his parents' benevolent tyranny, largely the source of Ruskin's own emotional unbalance, and seeking a scapegoat for the division between Gabriel and himself, Ruskin had found one, conveniently, in his own father, who, doubtless aware of his son's generosity to needy artists, had sought to protect him from them. "He hates all my friends (except you)," Ruskin

---

[1] Ruskin's unconscious or semiconscious mental background when writing this throws a revealing light upon his transference of love from Gabriel to Jones. For that background was evidently Andrew Marvell's poem *The Definition of Love*:—

> My love is of a birth as rare
> As 'tis for object strange and high;
> *It was begotten by Despair,*
> *Upon Impossibility.*

told Lady Trevelyan, "and I have had to keep them all out of the house—and have lost all the best of Rossetti—and of his poor dead wife who was a creature of ten thousand. . . ."

Since then, three years had passed, spent chiefly, by Ruskin, abroad, alone in his house near Mornex, high on the Salève. There, he dreamed for a moment of building a châlet which should be decorated by Rossetti and Jones. But instead, he remained there, solitary as before, in a state of mental and emotional tension, raised at times above the confines of the rational, battling for certainty and sanity amidst the debris of a world which experience and thought had laid in ruins about him. Haunted by bitter memories of love and loyalty betrayed, of benevolence flouted, of the hostility his passion for humanity had evoked, of the inconceivable cruelty of man to man, of the overthrow of his own Christian faith by scientific knowledge, he had stood helpless, bewildered, frustrated amidst chaos.

Such thoughts became obsessive as day after day he sat, alone, melancholy, beneath his vines and fig trees, amidst the roses and convolvuli of his little garden, gazing southwards over the spreading landscape to where Môle, Brezon and Reposoir reared their "jagged chain of crests" against the light, or wandered on the Salève "amongst the gentians," or watched "quiet sunsets on the *aiguille*," before returning to the lonely, darkening house, there to fall into "a little dreaming by the fire and so to sleep." Solitude, disappointment, intense thought, overwork, repression, were bringing on neurasthenia, an anxiety neurosis. He was very ill yet did not know it. At times he lost all power to distinguish between the internal and external worlds. Out on the Salève he saw pagan deities about him, fell on his knees on the grass, weeping, and prayed to the Christian god in whom he had lost faith. Over the American Civil War then raging, he agonized, until he seemed to himself buried "in a tuft of grass on a battlefield wet with blood."

In sheer, instinctive self-protection he tried to harden his own too gentle, too affectionate, too generous nature, developing in reaction a bitter, sceptical, misanthropic attitude and a temper not easy of control. "The folly and horror of humanity enlarge to my eyes daily," he cried, in the presence of his first absolute vision of reality, and he refused to see friends because "to talk is impossible to me, owing to the state of quiet rage and wonder at everything people say and do, in which I habitually live." Almost his sole link with humanity at that time was the lock of hair he carried about him, shorn from the head of the little girl with whom, in the growing infantilism of his repressions, he was now falling in love.*

It was unfortunate that, during his visits to England, Ruskin in this overwrought state should have attempted to restore and indeed intensify his former friendship with Gabriel. His feeling for Ruskin Gabriel now characteristically expressed to Allingham—"Him I saw the other day, and pitched into, he talked such awful rubbish, but he is a dear old chap too, and as soon as he was gone I wrote my sorrows to him." This ambivalent attitude made a quarrel almost inevitable if, for any length of time, Ruskin in his present condition and Rossetti should meet. And soon a quarrel, their bitterest and last, broke out.

Although as late as February 1863, Ruskin from Geneva had written to some paper a letter declaring: "I believe at this moment the Preraphaelite school of painting (centred in England but with branches in other countries) to be the only vital and true school of painting in Europe; and its English leader, Dante G. Rossetti, to be, without any compare, the greatest of English painters now living," Gabriel's newest, "sensuous" phase in painting, his *Venus Verticordia* and her like, drove Ruskin to resume his fussy interference with Rossetti's patrons. Warning Miss Heaton that Gabriel was "in a state of transitional and enfeebled powers," he begged her to authorize him to remove from Gabriel's studio one of her Rossettis which Gabriel was retouching, and pestered Gabriel himself about it until he growled: "It wasn't going to be touched." Ruskin, his condition aggravated by his father's recent death, now bitterly complained of the Preraphaelite's ingratitude. "One generally sucks all the praise," he told Browning, "and throws the blame back in the critic's face with a 'and be damned to you,' for all thanks—at least that's the way the P.R.B.s serve me."

When a month later the impending storm broke, its course

* *v. Notes.*

was as surprising as ridiculous. Gabriel's contribution can only be guessed, but the general development of the dispute and even its petty details are preserved in Ruskin's correspondence. From a complaint by Rossetti that he heard Ruskin was selling his and Lizzie's drawings—which Ruskin denied—the contention passed to Ruskin's disapproval of Rossetti's recent work—with a thinly veiled implication that it included his present mode of life[1]—his "coarse painting" and "conditions of non-sentiment," to use Ruskin's words, and the critic added a final mischievous allusion to Correggio, whom Gabriel did not admire, in order, as Ruskin said, "to stir you up."

Hitherto the dispute had been half playful in appearance, but there were hidden fires barely suspected by either combatant behind, and it was Ruskin not Gabriel who was shortly afterwards "stirred up" as the bickering correspondence proceeded, by the quite irrelevant memory of a photograph which he had intensely disliked, taken two years before, showing Gabriel, Scott and himself in the garden of Tudor House.* At the time he had written "to scold" Gabriel, gently, for letting it be made public, and had sent it to Miss Heaton for her opinion, telling her, naïvely: "I dislike my face on entirely simple and certain laws—because it is bad in colour and form," yet at the same time he had insisted that the photograph was "scandalous." Miss Heaton had been consolatory; but now, a significant indication of the deeper, unconscious and semi-conscious psychological forces energizing this dispute, Ruskin suddenly referred to the photograph, attacking the well-known and respected photographer responsible, Downey, and reproaching Gabriel "for the entirely blameable introduction you gave to a mere blackguard, to me, has been the cause of such a visible libel upon me going about England as I hold worse than all the scandals and lies ever uttered about me."

Such were the two phases of the quarrel. The third was final. Although Ruskin, quickly repenting of his irrational outburst, had offered an olive branch to Gabriel with "we won't have rows," and an invitation to call, Rossetti in his turn, taking offence at Ruskin's dislike of *Venus Verticordia*, rejected the invitation. And once again, after some more foolish bickering,

[1] *v. inf.* p. 413.   * *v. Notes.*

Ruskin's now uncontrollable temper flared up into rage when Gabriel described one of Ruskin's protégés as "a mistakenly transplanted carpenter." Aware of his own neurotic state, "out of health and irritable" as he described himself, and—in reply to some assurance from Gabriel of affection—"nearly sick of being loved—as of being hated," wanting only "understanding," Ruskin now swept Rossetti out of the circle of his friends.

The peroration in which Ruskin outlawed the friend he loved is an unintended witness to Ruskin's overwrought state at this time, a lamentable revelation of wounded egotism, unjustified inferiority-feeling and mental and emotional overstrain. While in many things, he declared, he acknowledged Gabriel's superiority, there were others, he added, in which he, Ruskin, was superior. In the past he had not cared whether or not Gabriel knew or admitted this; "but now (being, as I say, irritable and ill) I do care, and I will associate with no man who does not more or less accept my own estimate of myself. . . . You know nothing of me," Ruskin passionately cried in conclusion, as the deeper, suppressed causes of the quarrel finally emerged, "nor of my knowledge—nor of my thoughts—nor of the sort of grasp of things I have in directions in which you are utterly powerless; and that I do not choose any more to talk to you until you recognize my superiorities as *I* can yours. . . . You simply do not see certain characters in me, and cannot see them . . . a day may come when you will be able. Then—without apology—without restraint, merely as *being* different from what you are now—come back to me, and we will be as we used to be. It is not the affair of the drawings —not this sentence—[a reference to some remark of Gabriel's which had hurt him] but the ways and thoughts I have seen in you ever since I knew you, coupled with this change of health in myself, which render this necessary—complicated also by the change in your own methods of work with which I have no sympathy, and which renders it impossible for me to give you the kind of praise which would give you pleasure. Though you cannot now refer to me as in any way helpful to you by expression of judgement to the public, my inability is no result of any offence taken with you. And I would give much to see you doing as you have done—and to be able to say what I once said."

Such was the end of their friendship, which, as Ruskin's final letter admitted, had never rested upon a solid foundation of mutual sympathy. Gabriel had hurt Ruskin not only by failure to respond to his excessive affection, but by not painting as he wished, and also by direct criticism. For when Gabriel rightly enough exclaimed: "I do not call John Ruskin's work criticism, but rather brilliant poetic rhapsody," no doubt this or similar harsher comments came to Ruskin's ears. Ruskin had evidently discerned in Rossetti the creative artist's inevitable, slightly amused tolerance for the "mere critic," had also inevitably if unconsciously envied Gabriel's creative power. In that lay the ultimate cause of their separation. Yet had Ruskin but known it, Gabriel's opinion of his art-criticism was higher than Ruskin believed. Only two years before, when a Royal Commission was investigating the state of the Academy, Rossetti had told Allingham: "The only evidence of the lot which is worth reading as original thought and insight, is Ruskin's." If Gabriel had sometimes said such things to Ruskin himself, the severance of their friendship might never have occurred.

Nor, in all probability, was Gabriel aware that shortly before, when painting Ruskin's portrait, he had hurt his friend's feelings as deeply as the photographer Downey had done. "I sat to Rossetti several times," Ruskin had complained, "and he made the horriblest face I ever saw of a human being. I will never let him touch it more." Instead, Ruskin commissioned two portraits from Jones, who, foreseeing no doubt the danger which had beset Gabriel, abandoned the first one, pleading mysterious difficulties, and never began the second.

The rupture between Ruskin and Rossetti was final, but that was not Ruskin's fault. When later, relenting, Ruskin attempted through William Rossetti a renewal of the old friendship, it was Gabriel's indifference which prevented Ruskin's return. . . .

Friends, patrons, might pass, but others remained, like Leathart, and new ones came, like Rae, a Birkenhead banker (both beginning to form their ultimately large collections of Rossetti's works), Leyland, a wealthy Liverpool shipowner, once an office-boy, and Craven, a new patron from Manchester, "a fish sure to bite," said Gabriel, "a very good paymaster, and not a haggler at all—a grave and (let us say in a whisper) rather stupid enthusiast of the inarticulate business type, with a mystic reverence for the English water-colour school."

It was unfortunate for Rossetti's own development that nearly all his patrons were Philistines whom he despised. The knowledge of this combined with his continual debts to undermine his artistic integrity and lead him to the making of "pot-boilers," "replicas," and much inferior work. With relief and genuine appreciation he hailed the advent of one patron of a different type, William Cowper-Temple, stepson of Lord Palmerston and recently chief commissioner of the Board of Works. "Very gratifying," Gabriel described Cowper-Temple's request for a painting, and "an exceptional pleasure to be asked for work by those who like it for its own sake. It is pleasanter," he added, "sending a poetic work where it will be seen by cultivated folks, than to a cotton-spinner or a dealer." He offered Cowper-Temple *Beata Beatrix* for three hundred guineas, and when the offer was accepted, rejoiced. Although, he told a friend, he could have got more for it elsewhere, he preferred to sell it more cheaply to a man of taste like Cowper-Temple, "not at present a very rich man."

Gabriel was not the man to leave success entirely to the gods. We may reasonably suspect that the occasional puffs of his work now beginning to appear in the Press owed something to his personal instigation. With Stephens of the old Brotherhood, now art-critic to the *Athenaeum*, Gabriel was still friendly, and it was the *Athenaeum* which anonymously, but in Stephens' grandiose, rhetorical vein and with an air of conscious advertisement, spoke in October 1865 of Rossetti's refusal to exhibit in public, and informed the world that he had now "resumed the practice of oil-painting," before proceeding to an ecstatic and flowery description of *The Blue Bower*, *Venus Verticordia*, and *The Bride*, all, according to the critic, "lyrical poems" in a descending scale of lyricism. Above all, *The Blue Bower* was exalted for "the marvellous fleshliness of the flesh" (praise that was to return boomerang-like with deadly effect upon Rossetti later), and "the fascinating sensuousness of the expression . . . refined if not elevated, by the influence of music." These pictures, the writer concluded, showed Rossetti "in the rare character of an original designer of merit, who has made an unfrequented path of Art his own."

Despite his ten years' struggle to master the technique of oil-painting, Gabriel at once seized the opportunity provided by this article, to assure readers, in a letter to the *Athenaeum*, as to his practice in that medium. "I never abandoned such practice," he somewhat misleadingly declared, "or considered myself otherwise than as an oil-painter, in which character only I first became known. Commissions for water-colour drawings have since induced me sometimes to adopt that material; but now, for a good many years past, all my chief works have been again in oil. As the proper understanding of this point is of great professional importance to me, will you oblige me by publishing this letter?"

It was doubtless again Stephens who, three weeks later, and again in the *Athenaeum*, puffed Rossetti's *Bellae Buona* (renamed *Il Ramoscello*), as a study of "cool-eyed chastity," asserting (a noteworthy comment as indicating Gabriel's conscious use of symbolism) the symbolical character of the silver casket introduced, and also describing *The Head of Medusa* upon which Rossetti was then engaged.

New friends as well as new patrons had also been gathering about the rising star. Whistler, Legros, the French painter recently settled in England, "that Scotch Mr. Skelton," as Gabriel called the literary lawyer of that name, Marks the dealer in curios, Sandys the eccentric, ever-impecunious artist who had ridiculed the Preraphaelites in his parody of Millais's *Sir Isumbras at the Ford*, Charles Augustus Howell renowned for wit, knavery and brazenness, Shields the strict Calvinist painter, Smetham the Methodist exalté painter, Conway the American Unitarian minister of the wealthy, "intellectual" South Place Chapel, London, all these and more had now entered Rossetti's circle of acquaintance. With them, in varying degrees of intimacy, Rossetti at times found distraction from unhappy memories and morbid thoughts. Now, too, his circle was increased by the return to London of Bell Scott and his wife, who in 1864 had left Newcastle for Notting Hill, and by the removal of Morris and his family from their beloved Red House at Upton to Queen's Square, Bloomsbury.

Success, money, friends meant, even for the recluse in Tudor House, an inevitably increased participation in social life. But the demands of society were ever irksome to Rossetti, who cared only for the unconventional, witty, semi-bohemian circle of his own more intimate friends. Thus, although this increased participation was still chiefly limited to this circle, and was never wide, Rossetti in these years played a greater part, socially, than ever before or after. For a time he was actually a member of several art clubs, despite a previous disappointment with the quarrelsome and short-lived Hogarth, which he had joined upon its foundation in 1859. For the year or two of its existence, the Hogarth's occasional exhibitions had, in fact, helped to increase both Rossetti's public and his reputation, and this no doubt was a chief reason for his joining early in 1865, the Garrick Club, and shortly afterwards, the Arundel. Upon its foundation early in 1866 he also joined the Burlington Fine Arts Club. The same spirit of independence as that he had shown at the Hogarth, led him in 1867 to resign from the Burlington as a protest against its expulsion of Whistler for having pushed another member of the club (Whistler's brother-in-law) through a plate-glass window during a heated encounter in a Paris street. Gabriel's membership of the remaining clubs ceased, as increasing debts, illness, and melancholia gradually withdrew him from the outer world.

For the present, however, he enjoyed occasional social relaxations. There were actually evenings such as that of April 12, 1865, when the dark and silent house in Cheyne Walk radiated light and laughter. On that occasion the whole Preraphaelite circle were there: Brown with his wife and two daughters (all rather tired after half a day in railway trains, following some involved, economical route of Brown's from Kentish Town to Tudor House by way of Kew and Clapham Junction!), the Morrises, Joneses, Munro the sculptor, Arthur Hughes, Swinburne and Legros with his "pale, handsome English wife," as Georgie Jones thought her. But Georgie was rather sad that evening, had bidden good-bye that day to her sister Mrs. Kipling, leaving with her husband for India, where that very year their son Rudyard would be born. Slipping away from the crowd in the studio, Georgie crept upstairs to the drawing-room, to look with a pang of pity at Lizzie's sketches on the walls. From the windows of the deserted room she watched the wide, placid river flowing softly beneath a full moon down to the sea, and thought of the past. That night, too, for the first time, Georgie noticed that Brown's thick hair was turning grey, that the first threat of autumn was lightly touching the Preraphaelite band. Georgie was particularly sensitive just now to the passage of time. Recently, with growing means, the Joneses had left their rooms opposite the British Museum for a house of their own in Kensington Square; but Georgie, although rejoicing in the change, was acutely conscious that "something was gone, something had been left behind—and it was our first youth."

A few days later there was a similar reception at Brown's in Kentish Town. Most of the same "set" were present: Christina ("gently caustic of tongue," thought Georgie), Swinburne, a fiery vision, Legros, unable to speak English, Whistler (looking, thought Georgie, more like a Frenchman than Legros) staring through "an angry eyeglass" at the outer world. There too was Howell, Ruskin's new Anglo-Portuguese secretary, rascally, plausible, magnificently gracing the occasion with his urbane presence and sparkling wit. Precocious little Oliver Madox Brown came in, and asked Gabriel "what he thought Pompeii must have looked like!" For Brown it was a great evening. . . .

Despite the vicissitudes of their friendship, Brown, still the same good fellow, still somewhat explosive, still saying "togam" for "toga" and "seriatim" for "seriously," still forgetting names, calling Miss Evans ("George Eliot"), "Miss Atkinson," Morris's housekeeper Mrs. Button, "Mrs. Penny," and confusing the name of Dr. Johnson's famous biographer with that of the Scottish lover of Mary Queen of Scots, was still Rossetti's chief friend. It was now that Brown made a bid for fame and fortune by holding a "one-man show" of his works. He advertised the exhibition in the Press and elsewhere, amidst a running fire of facetious suggestions from Rossetti, which, in fact, merely anticipated some of the imbecilities of later professional advertisement. Gabriel also gave Brown practical help in arranging his pictures, and when the exhibition won public praise, patrons and commissions for the exhibitor, Rossetti was delighted. Indeed, one of the first uses to which Gabriel turned his own success was that of helping his less fortunate friend. He also attempted to secure Brown's election to one of the art clubs, but so scandalized were the members by Brown's audacity and vulgarity, as it then seemed to them, in holding a one-man exhibition, that to prevent Brown's being black-balled his name had to be withdrawn!

Gabriel was more successful, however, in his attempt to persuade Brown to leave his remote abode in Grove Terrace, Kentish Town (to which he had moved from Fortess Terrace in 1862), and, if only for business reasons, to settle nearer the centre of London and nearer to Rossetti himself. So, at the close of 1865, Brown, reluctantly persuaded, took No. 37 Fitzroy Square, a large, somewhat gloomy, old-fashioned house, described only a few months before by Thackeray, as Colonel Newcome's; "vast, but it must be owned, melancholy . . . with a funeral urn in the centre of the entry." For Brown, however, in 37, Fitzroy Square, began and ended the most prosperous period of his thwarted, chequered life. For, with the help of his wife Emma, who suddenly blossomed into a leading hostess, he made their home a social centre of intellectual and artistic distinction. During the next ten years there regularly assembled in Fitzroy Square all who figured prominently in the Preraphaelite world of art and letters, and the Browns' receptions were soon famous.

Conway, a frequent visitor, whose theological unorthodoxy quickly won Brown's friendship, described them as "the weekly salon of unconventional artists and writers," and recalled meeting there, on one "single evening, Turgenev, the Rossettis, Holman Hunt, the Alma Tademas, Arthur Hughes, Woolner, Garnett, the Joneses, Whistler, Allingham, Swinburne, young Edmund Gosse, Westland Marston, and many others, including William Morris and his wife Janey, 'divinely tall,' not less remarkable for grace than for height, with heavy, dark hair and full, sensitive red lips." To this rendezvous of contemporary poets and artists came also O'Shaughnessy, John Payne, Theodore Marzials, and Joachim Miller the American cowboy poet in his usual dress of bright cowboy's shirt, wide-awake hat, and muddy riding-boots. There too came Val Prinsep, and

Brown's future son-in-law Hueffer, the clever, genial, music-critic of *The Times*.

Although two years later Gabriel not only sneered at the origins of the Preraphaelite movement, but also categorically denied (and in the deepest sense truly) that he had ever been a Preraphaelite at all, it was nominally at least as a "Preraphaelite" that he won success. Ruskin's early acclamation of him as the Preraphaelites' "leader" had permanently identified Rossetti with Preraphaelitism in the mind of the public, and therefore, as Preraphaelitism itself was now in the ascendant, it and Gabriel stood in a relationship of mutual benefit. In this high, Preraphaelite summer, Rossetti as "leader" was proportionately advanced.

The movement, already turning "aesthetic," had become for the average Victorian, partly indeed through its adherence to "nature" in an artificial age, strange, exciting, "modern," if not positively Bohemian, in spirit! Mrs. Howitt, Gabriel's early friend, attending "a great Preraphaelite crush" at this time, was overwhelmingly conscious of this. The Preraphaelites' pictures covered the walls, their sketch books (including a 'huge" one of Gabriel's), the tables. "The uncrinolined women with their wild hair," which Mrs Howitt thought "very beautiful, their picturesque dresses and rich colouring," seemed to her "like figures out of the Preraphaelite pictures," and looking back afterwards, it all seemed to her "very curious, like some hot, struggling dream, in which the gorgeous and fantastic forms moved slowly about!"

By this time, Gabriel and his way of life were beginning to arouse public interest, even curiosity. Hamerton, the English art-critic in Paris who had previously written to Rossetti about his work, now called in person at Cheyne Walk, and reported: "He lives in a magnificent house, furnished with very great taste, but in the most extraordinary manner. His drawing-room is very large indeed, and most curious; the general effect is very good. He was very kind in receiving me, and I saw his pictures, which are splendid in colour, and very quaint and strange in sentiment. His own manners are singularly soft and pleasant. . . ."

Hunt and other of the "Brethren," jealous of Rossetti's

335

"success," loudly declared it was merely the result of his isolation, his avoidance of public exhibitions, which, they said, by sharpening public curiosity, had brought him only cheap, unworthy notoriety, not the honourable recognition of true merit. Gabriel meanwhile privately pretended to deplore his own early abstention from exhibitions. "It has come right with me—more so, perhaps, than I could expect," he declared, "but I think that competition and appreciation are among an artist's best privileges." Protesting against "pigheaded or antagonistic notions, as to the natural ways of coming before the public," he attempted to excuse his own continued avoidance of public criticism with the declaration: "In after life I have adhered to my plan of non-exhibition, because I think it is well to adopt a plan of life, and not lose time afterwards in giving second thoughts to it." The excuse was hardly convincing; and, in fact, his early fear of public opinion, his original reluctance to exhibit, had, during the intervening years, actually increased. "So much so," said Skelton, who saw much of Gabriel at that time, "that the mere rumour that one of his pictures was being exhibited would make him uneasy for days. He had grown morbidly sensitive to praise or blame."

It would, on the other hand, be a mistake to think that Rossetti never exhibited his work in public. He had already done so at the small "Preraphaelite Exhibition" in 1857, in the following year at the annual exhibition of the Liverpool Academy, which was friendly to the Preraphaelites, at several of the exhibitions of the Hogarth Club, at the exhibition of the Royal Scottish Academy in Edinburgh in 1862, and would in the future, exhibit at Edinburgh in 1877, at Glasgow in 1878 and 1879, and in the last year of his life, 1882, at Manchester. To this great Loan Exhibition in Manchester, Rossetti sent nine of his works, the greatest number he ever exhibited together. These exhibitions, with possibly one or two more, are all to which Rossetti contributed.

Skelton, remarking that Gabriel "had grown morbidly sensitive to praise or blame," unconsciously indicated his hidden tension, his repressed but increasing anxiety state, which any stress such as that even of an exhibition could aggravate. Indeed, the satisfaction success brought him was often overshadowed by his growing melancholy. His sadness, his mental and spiritual isolation, did not escape the eyes of those about him, nor even in public could he entirely conceal his inner desolation. Locker, dining at Lord Houghton's at this time, with Rossetti and other distinguished guests including Thackeray's daughter and George Eliot, remarked that "Rossetti seemed moody enough," and "every now and then, after dinner, . . . sat with his face buried in his hands."

The mental and emotional strife he vainly tried to hide from all was already working towards his ultimate undoing. Of this inner waste the world knew little or nothing yet, but already, intuitively, it began to sense something strange, uncanny, about this remote, inaccessible painter shut up in his dark and silent house, and with an intriguing reputation for wonderful "poetic" pictures and poems which few were allowed to see, for a strange, unhappy, romantic past, a solitary, darkly Bohemian present, and a misanthropy, a contempt for public opinion so great that he would condescend to show neither pictures nor poems to the world. Already, in this first hour of triumph, the sinister but useful legend of Tudor House was taking shape.

Although Rossetti did not perceive it, his work was in harmony with a period no longer early Preraphaelite but in transition. Five years had passed since Whistler first appeared in the Royal Academy as the stormy petrel of French Impressionism, bringing with him from Paris an enthusiasm for Manet, Courbet, and the whole French school Rossetti despised, as well as an affection, shared by Gabriel, for Chinese and Japanese art. Whistler, like his French masters, ridiculed the anecdotal, "literary" subject and microscopic detail of the Preraphaelites, exalting in their place form, colour, design, technique in painting. The recent oil-paintings of Rossetti, exhibiting Preraphaelite richness of detail certainly, yet rejecting "anecdote" or "subject," and relying in some degree upon design, however unconsciously, showed affinities with both old and new. To this, largely, no doubt his success was due. If he were a "leader" of English art, he was not too far ahead of public taste to win contemporary fame and fortune.

From the height he had reached, Gabriel turned to look back complacently upon his "old first picture" as he now called *The Girlhood of Mary Virgin*, painted seventeen years before, and recently lent by its owner for repainting. He thought it "painted timidly"; could "look at it a long way off now as the work of quite another 'crittur,'" as he told Brown, "and find it to be a long way better than I thought." He wished indeed to keep it, but the owner refused to part with it; so, after repainting the white wings of the angel "deep pink," and the Virgin's yellow sleeves brown, and making other alterations, he returned it in the summer of 1866.

With new and good commissions arriving, Rossetti's hopes, damped by the defections of "the demon Dunlop" and of Heugh, again soared. Although the year 1866 was a particularly bad year for business in England, so bad that a commercial panic caused the suspension of the Bank Charter on "Black Friday," May 11th, Rossetti at the close of the year, had no complaints. "This panic year, strange to say," he wrote, "promises to be much my best as yet," and he dreamed of opening a bank account, for the first time!

III

WILLOW-WOOD (I)
1866–1867

O ye, all ye that walk in Willow-wood,
  That walk with hollow faces burning white;
What fathom-depth of soul-struck widowhood,*
  What long, what longer hours, one lifelong night,
Ere ye again, who so in vain have wooed
  Your last hope lost, who so in vain invite
Your lips to that their unforgotten food,
  Ere ye, ere ye again shall see the light!

Willow-wood D. G. ROSSETT

THE LONG YEARS of Lizzie's illness had burdened Rossetti's youth, blighted his first passion with the apparently ever-present menace of decay and death. From the desolation into which his life had fallen, he had turned to concentrate the energy of his single, intense nature, upon the realization of his artistic ambitions. But now, upon the very threshold of success, Gabriel's own health, undermined by his way of life, rapidly declined. In five months, he admitted at the close of 1865, he had been absent from his easel only twelve days in all, and boasted: "I have completely missed all exercise and change of air this year, yet have no reason to complain as regards health." His next reference to his health, however, six months later, was less confident, for although "pretty well," he added: "any imperfections in this respect I may pretty safely attribute more to a confirmed habit of life and work than to any defect of constitution." Two months later he was receiving medical treatment for hydrocele which necessitated medical aid at intervals for the rest of his life.

Nor was overwork the sole cause of Rossetti's declining health. Seeking forgetfulness and compensations after long hours in the studio, often in melancholy mood, he would spend many an evening in hard living amongst his more bohemian friends, with cards, drink and talk, until daylight summoned them to bed. The glimpses Boyce gives us of Gabriel amongst his friends at this time, clearly reveal his increasing demoralization.

* v. Notes.

On Whit Monday, 1866, for example, Gabriel and Boyce made an excursion to the Rye House in Hertfordshire, which Boyce thus describes: "May 21 (Whit Monday). Gabriel Rossetti came by appointment for our trip to the Rye House. . . . We chartered a hansom to take us to Rye House and back for 25s. It being a brilliant day and the meadows thick with grass and buttercups and the trees gay with young green leaves we enjoyed the ride very much. Arrived at the Rye House about 5.15. . . . Got some grub with difficulty (N.B. Take it with us next time). Gabriel somehow or other, perhaps by taking whisky, etc., on an empty stomach, got rather drunk and quarrelsome and fell down in the dark passage leading to the dungeons and lost his overcoat. Fortunately I noticed his disappearance and pulled him up or he would have been trodden on by the streams of people. After some fuss the overcoat was regained, though torn." Such was the diversionary social background to Rossetti's painting of the picture of his dead wife as *Beata Beatrix*. "Beatrice in a death trance," as Boyce described it at this time, "with hands folded, a bird flying into her lap. In the street beyond are seen Dante and Love holding a burning heart."

To counteract the consequences of the life he was leading with its pressure of overwork and dissipation, its hidden melancholy and hysterical gaiety, its lack of regular meals and exercise, its mental and emotional overstrain, Rossetti set out in October on a fortnight's walking tour with the ever-impecunious artist Sandys, whom he had sheltered in Cheyne Walk since the spring of the preceding year. Winchelsea, with its old ivy-covered church sheltering ancient tombs and effigies, delighted him. Both Rossetti and Sandys were in holiday mood, and from the window of their inn they delightedly watched the opening of the Court Sessions, laughing at the imposing procession of some half-dozen civic dignitaries in their robes of office, including the local barber and carpenter, and, as they entered the town hall, the two friends accompanied by their landlord rushed in after them, "in a mob of three," said Gabriel, to hear the mayor, as there were no cases, "severely animadverting on an individual who had once been found drunk in the streets, about six months before." In this same spirit of boyish fun Gabriel tramped the country round with Sandys, visiting Northiam and Tenterden, noting the best spots for painting and ordering photographs of them to be made. He bought a box-tree shaped into an arm-chair which he got his landlord to dig up and send to Cheyne Walk where it promptly died, and, as often, he contemplated a repetition of his tour of Warwickshire in 1853. But autumn was far advanced; the weather broke, and they returned to town. "Gabriel back," wrote his brother William on October 23rd, "seeming a good deal brisker and fresher."

Pressed by debts and heavy expenses, Rossetti, upon his return, immediately resumed painting with increased energy. The new year 1867 brought neither diminution nor cessation of his toil. The well-tried patience of patrons was now nearly exhausted, and they began to clamour for the delivery of pictures long since paid for. Leathart, having waited six years for *Found*, now demanded its completion, and upon Gabriel's haughty offer of a refund showed a disconcerting readiness to accept it. Besides this, the sale at Christie's of Rossetti's works in the collection of the solicitor Rose had disappointed Gabriel's expectations of good resale prices. Gambart's protestations two years before against rumours of high sums received for Rossetti's paintings were perhaps nearer the truth than Gabriel had believed. Fortunately new patrons still came, including a hyperconscientious solicitor, Valpy, so afraid of the nude in art that even a pair of bare arms disquieted him, and a wealthy brewer, Matthews—"a queer character," said Gabriel—who commissioned *Aspecta Medusa* at one thousand five hundred guineas and then refused the work because of the Medusa's severed head. There were, too, other disappointments, such as that, for example, revealed in a brusque note of Gabriel's at this time: "X has turned a bad lot. Just as he was beginning to buy, he has got engaged to get married, and is done for."

To counter such slings and arrows of fortune, Rossetti employed a native astuteness with great skill. Every business opportunity he exploited to the utmost, even sending Howell early in 1868 to the sale of Windus's paintings, at Christie's, to run up the price of his *Lucrezia* to £70. By various means, including water-colour "replicas" largely painted, it is said, by his new "art-assistant," Dunn, who had recently replaced Knewstub, Rossetti in 1867 made some three thousand pounds and reduced his debts to a thousand. The money he earned, however great, was badly needed, for he made no attempt to economize, but added constantly to his collections of animals and china, new and expensive purchases, paid for with advance payments for paintings usually not even begun, while at the same time he had to accept Marks' offer to get a "friend" to discount his bills, so that he might buy the very necessities of his art—brushes, paints, canvas, and frames!

Nor was this all. William Rossetti must lend him fifty pounds to pay a "butterman." Brown must send him a loan. It came as a cheque to Gabriel's surprise. "How you manage to have a banking account, I don't know," he replied. "I never can." His good resolution of a few months earlier to open an account himself had obviously failed. So now, while Gabriel sent ten pounds to Lizzie's obscure brother, an occasional recipient of his charity, to Brown, embarrassed by the expenses of Fitzroy Square and clamouring for the return of his loan, Gabriel could only send a first instalment of fifteen pounds, excusing himself at the same time, on the ground that "cormorants, porpoises, and great sea-serpents are so rife in these latitudes."

Thus it happened that despite industry, haste, replicas, increasing prices, Gabriel by the midsummer of 1867 was more embarrassed than ever before; so deeply in debt that henceforth moneylenders, tradesmen, curio-dealers, animal-dealers, patrons of unfulfilled commissions whose money or goods had been advanced without result, all clamoured for the payment of claims ranging from small sums to hundreds of pounds. This ever-pressing burden wrought great harm to Rossetti. Consequent over-work, inevitably often inferior painting, mental and physical fatigue, financial worry itself, and lack of exercise, all gradually wore down his morale, encouraged the tendency towards neurotic anxiety previously induced by his natural disposition and unhappy past.

The change in Rossetti's art which revealed itself upon his resumption of oil-painting from the *Bocca Baciata* of 1859 and after, soon attracted the attention of contemporaries. Hunt uneasily remarked the "epicureanism" usurping as he thought, the place of Rossetti's early "stoicism," and mourned the yielding of his youthful austerities to "heads of women of voluptuous nature," painted "with such richness of ornamental trapping and decoration." He condemned it as "sensuous and hot-house fancifulness," neither "robust" nor true to "nature." Ruskin's dislike of this new, coarse style, of its main source of inspiration, and of the mood from which it sprang, had fired the train of long-rankling disgusts that had ultimately destroyed their friendship in a general conflagration. Bell Scott's opinion was clearly indicated in his blunt remark that Gabriel now thought "women and flowers were the only objects worth painting."

The influence of Fanny was revealing itself not only in Gabriel's painting, but also in the increasing coarseness of his nature. In the life of the senses he sought to forget the unfulfilled promise, the vain idealism of the past, the long dreary em-bittered "courtship," the brief, unhappy marriage, the sordid, enigmatic end. In his new cynicism he took a bitter pleasure in destroying whatever of his former idealization of woman remained. To substitute for the impossible perfection he had vainly sought, a degraded image of womanhood was in some sort to mitigate his loss. To Brown he quaintly apologized in 1866 for some real or fancied rudeness of which Emma com-plained, with the remark: "I regard all women, with com-paratively few exceptions, as being so entirely loose-tongued and unreliable that to suggest such qualities in one does not seem to me to interfere with any respect to which a member of the sex is likely to have any just pretension."

He now at least seems to have known women answering more or less to his unflattering generalization, the Fannies and Jennies of street encounters, met in his restless leisure hours, when, too weary to remain at his easel, or after daylight had failed, he perambulated London. For the streets with their variety offered distraction from the intensity of solitude, labour, and loneliness in Tudor House, and opportunities for erotic adventure. There too he would find new models, and, accord-ing to Rossetti's friend Middleton,* it was these models who

* v. Notes.

became Gabriel's mistresses. During his visit to Winchelsea, Rossetti's cynically amorous mood had found expression in the translation of an inscription scrawled in "ill-spelt French verse" on the window-pane of his inn—

A DOCTOR'S ADVICE

My doctor's issued his decree
That too much wine is killing me,
And furthermore his ban he hurls
Against my touching naked girls.

How then? must I no longer share
Good wine or beauties, dark and fair?
Doctor, good-bye, my sail's unfurled,
I'm off to try the other world.

For Gabriel, with a dietary from his friend Dr. Marshall in his pocket, ordering "thin wines or cider . . . with equal parts cold water," in summer, and in winter "with half as much hot water and nutmeg," the verses were, it would seem, peculiarly appropriate.

It was now that Gabriel formed a new and unusual friendship. Adah Isaacs Menken, a beautiful American Jewess, actress and equestrienne, had come to England in 1864 and had taken London by storm as "The Naked Lady," dashing round the ring at Astley's Amphitheatre in tights and leopard skin and bound to a horse's back, in a thrilling representation of Mazeppa's famous ride. Poets and writers, including Dickens, Charles Reade, Swinburne and Rossetti, thronged Adah Menken's reception-room in the imposing Westminster Palace Hotel facing the Abbey, for this tamer of men and horses, marrying innumerable husbands, smoking innumerable cigarettes, breaking out into violent fits of rage upon small provocation, was also a sentimental poetess who lamented in Whitmanesque free verse her failures to discover the perfect lover, or gloomily anticipated the poignancy and peace of her own ultimate loveless tomb!

Although Adah Menken had made Gabriel's acquaintance shortly after her arrival in England, it was not until now, after a short visit to Paris, during which Theophile Gautier had advised her to cultivate Rossetti, that, inviting him to make

344

use of her box at Astley's, she met him and Swinburne there, and developed friendly relations with them. With Swinburne, indeed, her intimacy soon became a public scandal, and his private references to her as his mistress belie his public denials. She was the "Dolores, our Lady of Pain" of Swinburne's *Poems and Ballads*, this whipper of horses and at times, in anger, of men, who called herself "Dolores." To those familiar with Swinburne's masochistic verses, his relations with Adah Menken at this time are not beyond conjecture; yet that this independent, high-spirited and in some ways even admirable woman, earning the then enormous salary of a hundred pounds a week on the stage, should, as rumour asserts, have accepted a cynical offer of ten pounds from Gabriel to seduce the inhibited Swinburne, and, failing in the attempt, have returned the money, is most improbable.

In Gabriel's liking for the woman who bravely rode horses and wrote sentimental verse, cynical amusement mingled with something of genuine appreciation. She provided a distraction amidst his listlessness, and doubtless her sentimental erotic idealism interested him as a somewhat crude and vulgar parallel to his own. Charles Reade, although once her devoted admirer, cynically declared after her death that her poetry was "as bad as other people's—and would have been worse if it could." Gabriel, more charitable, described as "really remarkable" her small volume of mediocre verse, *Infelicia*, published little more than a year later, shortly after she had died poor and friendless in Paris, where the elderly Dumas had figured prominently amongst her lovers. Rossetti even offered to make a selection from Menken's poems and to write a short appreciation of them for an anthology of American verse which William was preparing.

Towards Fanny, Gabriel's attitude was curiously ambivalent. That he really cared for her, felt a sense of responsibility for her, his later words and actions show. At the same time she was for him the embodiment of his cynical disillusion. Whatever of romance he had associated with Fanny as in *The Song of the Bower*, had now departed. Fanny's reign as Gabriel's chief model, which had lasted from about 1861, was now ending; closed in fact about 1868 or at latest by 1870, and Alexa

Wilding, who had appeared in Gabriel's work increasingly since 1866, was to share with Janey Morris the dominant place as Rossetti's model, until 1877, after which Mrs. Morris held it alone, save for Mrs. Stillman, who also appeared fairly frequently for several years, from 1874 onwards. "Five faces," wrote Graham Robertson, "had notable effect upon the art of Rossetti: first the face of his sister, Christina, followed by that of Elizabeth Siddal, his wife; then began to appear the faces of two professional models, Fanny Cornforth and Alice [*sic*] Wilding, and finally, like Aaron's rod swallowing up all the rest, came the face of Mrs. Morris, and so potent was its influence that it is now universally accepted as the 'Rossetti type,' the absolute invention and patent of the poet-painter."

Fearing younger rivals, Fanny was growing jealous, and there were, tradition reports, bitter and violent quarrels with the coarse and vulgar woman who shared Rossetti's home. The home itself was, according to Prinsep, dirty and ill-ordered, as, in the circumstances, we may easily believe. Gabriel's disgust and self-disgust found expression in bitter, sarcastic commentary upon himself, Fanny and their general way of life. For although Rossetti, since Lizzie's death, in spiritual and emotional revolt against his own past had apparently sought relief and forgetfulness in a life of sensation, his nature was too intense, his idealism too deeply rooted, his feelings too profound for him to find permanent satisfaction in the superficial amours of the mere erotic adventurer.

The inevitable revulsion brought something of moral revival. Painting Fanny as Lilith he expressed both on canvas and in his accompanying sonnet (later renamed *Body's Beauty*) the mingled fascination and repulsion she exerted upon him, his growing desire to escape from the snare of sense without soul, to break

> the bright web she can weave,
> Till heart and body and life are in its hold.

In reaction against this bondage to sense he also painted *Sibylla Palmifera*, and wrote for it an explanatory sonnet entitled *Soul's Beauty*. The title of the painting, he explained, was intended "to mark the leading place which I intend her to hold among my beauties"; and the model was the most

beautiful of all his models, Alexa Wilding, first met in a casual
street encounter two years before. Alexa Wilding, to whom
Gabriel paid a retaining fee, so anxious was he to keep her for
himself, remained a favourite model until the last years of his
life. He painted her as *Veronica Veronese, La Ghirlandata, Sea Spell,
The Blessed Damozel, The Roman Widow*, and *Monna Vanna*. I
have somewhat extended my idea of the picture," Rossetti
wrote of *Sibylla Palmifera* in May 1866, "and have written a
sonnet . . . to embody the conception—that of beauty the palm-
giver, i.e. the Principle of Beauty, which draws all high-toned
men to itself, whether with the aim of embodying it in art,
or only of attaining its enjoyment in life." To emphasize this
deeper conception, Gabriel indicated it in the sonnet, and pre-
fixed *Sibylla Palmifera* as title, to the painting.

   The essentially self-expressive quality of Rossetti's two sonnets
Soul's Beauty and *Body's Beauty* is thus tacitly revealed by his
introduction of details not found in the pictures to which they
refer. In *Soul's Beauty* there again gleams, as once before his
adolescent eye, that vision of Ideal Beauty which has made him
"The allotted bondman of her palm and wreath." From the
barrenness of the emotional desert in which he now wandered,
from the present emptiness, boredom, satiety of his existence,
his thoughts turned back to his passionate, tortured, beauty-
intoxicated past, giving to his song a new dignity, passion,
power, yet leaving it at the same time, tremulous with the sense
of loss, disintegration, decay.

> This is that Lady Beauty, in whose praise
>   Thy voice and hand shake still—long known to thee
>   By flying hair and fluttering hem—the beat
>   Following her daily of thy heart and feet,
>   How passionately and irretrievably,
> In what fond flight, how many ways and days!

Here certainly, was no note of turning. Even in the desert to
which Love had brought him, there was to be no abandonment
of the endless quest. His dream still held him: "Men tell me
that sleep has many dreams; but all my life I have dreamt one
dream alone."

   Gabriel's physical decline became increasingly obvious. To
the earlier trouble, hydrocele, was added in the summer of

1867 chronic insomnia. According to Rossetti's secretary in later years (the son of Gabriel's friend, Dr. Gordon Hake), who assisted Rossetti in later stages of his illness, "The insomnia produced fits of melancholia, an ailment, according to the skilled opinion of Dr. Hake, more difficult than all others to deal with; for when the nervous system has sunk to a certain state of depression, the mind roams over the universe, as it were, in quest of imaginary causes for the depression.¹ This accounts for the 'cock and bull' stories that were somewhat rife immediately after Rossetti's death, about his having expressed remorse on account of his ill-treatment of his wife. No one of his intimates took the least notice of these wild and whirling words. For he would express remorse on account of the most fantastic things when the fits of melancholia were upon him; and when these fits were past he would smile at the foolish things he had said."

Gabriel's day-dream might still hold him, but night-dreams, sleep itself, fled him now, left him tossing and turning through the dark hours, racked by bitter-sweet memories he could no longer hold at bay. For Lizzie, summoned by the recessive mentality developed during these years of solitude had, for a season, come back.² Not the later Lizzie, spoiled by an unhappy life, but the radiant, idealized creature of his first love. At first only casual remarks or allusions indicated her return as when at the close of 1866 Gabriel sent Allingham photographs of Lizzie's sketches, announcing at the same time that he intended to have all her water-colours photographed.³ "Short,

¹ This is a good anticipation of Freud's "anxiety complex," from which Rossetti undoubtedly suffered, like his father before him. William Rossetti definitely states (what the sonnets in *The House of Life* so clearly reveal also) one cause of his brother's anxiety: "Insomnia began in 1867. Why did it begin? I consider that painful thoughts, *partly but not wholly* connected with his wife *and her death*, were at the root of it." *Memoir* of D. G. R., p. 265. Italics mine. "Partly but not wholly," was doubtless due to William Rossetti's knowledge of the additional anxiety induced by a new passion; "and her death" no doubt meant "doubt and anxiety as to the manner of her death." Evidently the increase of nervous tension caused by the addition of the anxiety *re* Janey to that of the long-standing one about Lizzie, explains Rossetti's degeneration and gradual collapse at this time and later.

² William Rossetti wrote:—"Although Rossetti was, as I have already said, not plunged into monotonous gloom by the death of his wife, the idea of her was in these years very constantly present to him. Poignant memories and painful associations were his portion; and he was prone to think that *some secret might yet be wrested from the grave.*" *Memoir*, p. 255. Italics mine. Was not the "secret" the question of accident or suicide? *cf. inf.* pp. 479–80.   ³ *v. inf.* p. 389.

sad and strange her life," thought Allingham, looking at them, "it must have seemed to her like a troubled dream."

Soon Gabriel's thoughts of Lizzie were to find expression in his verses, verses recording his doubts and anxieties during these sleepless nights, obsessive self-questionings as to the actual manner of Lizzie's death. "Who," he cried, in 1873, when his insomnia had reached a definitely pathological stage:

> Who, sleepless, hath not anguished to appease
> Tragical shadow's realm of sound and sight
> Conjectured in the lamentable night?[1]

and again, in the sonnet he wrote in 1868, *Sleepless Dreams*,[2] he cried:

> O lonely night! art thou not known to me,
> A thicket hung with masks of mockery
> And watered with the wasteful warmth of tears?

The recovered past inevitably challenged Gabriel's present self, and in his notebook he jotted down words of self-condemnation:

> Could I have seen the thing I am to-day!
> The same (how strange), the same as I was then!

For he was keenly conscious of the fact that despite apparent change, his old, unchanged self still persisted beneath the surface. In another scribbled comment of this time, Rossetti reveals his consciousness of the harmful tendencies in his idealism. "Seek thine ideal," he wrote, "anywhere except in thyself. Once fix it there, and the ways of thy real self will matter nothing to thee, whose eyes can rest on the ideal already perfected."[3] That was as near as he ever came to emerging from his unconsciously narcissistic dream.

Thus it was that after the years of hope, love, strife, disillusion, inertia, followed by a phase of sensuous reaction yielding to surfeit, boredom, and physical decline, Gabriel was haunted by memories, regrets, imaginings, as he lay through the long, sleepless nights in his heavily curtained bed, gazing down the sombre corridors of his past. Vainly attempting to win sleep, he worked harder than before in the daytime, protracted to

---

[1] *The Soul's Sphere. cf. Life in Love, inf.* pp. 417–18, and *v. inf.* pp. 479–80.
[2] Originally entitled *Sleepless Love.*   [3] *v. inf.* p. 616.

a still later hour his nocturnal wanderings, extended yet further his nightly readings. But all was in vain. His nights became a deepening desolation. Haggard, miserable, melancholy, he turned in his distress to an unfortunate antidote, spirits, "for which," he declared two years later, "Heaven knows I have no taste," hoping by nightly dosing with whisky to win elusive sleep. And, yet more unfortunately, for a time this new remedy proved a success, although its ultimate influence on him was disastrous.

More than ever the spell of Tudor House bound him, despite his continual but ineffectual resolve to leave. His failure to do so he ever excused to himself on the ground that he was vainly seeking a suitable house elsewhere. His habits became increasingly reclusive. His wild, neglected garden was "Eden" to him in the summer of 1866, and in March 1867 he told Allingham, who was announcing the discovery of another house suitable for Gabriel: "I have been pot-boiling to an extent lately that does not hold out much hope of estate-buying or even renting. Moreover, as I haven't been outside my door for months in the daytime, I shouldn't have had much opportunity of enjoying pastime and pleasances. I have accordingly no news whatever, except of my easel, which is too mean a slave to small needs to be worth reporting on. I do not see a fellow of any sort really much oftener than you do, I imagine." It was Rossetti's first clear statement of his withdrawal from the world, the first definite indication that the outward urge of his youth and earlier manhood was now, at thirty-eight, already in retreat.

As yet, however, this withdrawal was incomplete. Despite ill-health and the debts keeping him ever at his easel, he did not entirely relinquish social activities. "Eighty folks came to see me last Wednesday," wrote Mrs. Procter, wife of the octogenarian poet "Barry Cornwall," to her friend Mrs. Lehmann, following a reception at her home, 32 Weymouth Street, Portland Place, in February 1867. "Dante Rossetti came early, and we had a nice long talk together. My husband was as bright as possible and chirped about amongst the young ladies. . . . Have you read Swinburne's poems? They are charming; a very few, perhaps six, not readable. One, a

Ballad of Burdens, is perhaps the finest, and a *Hymn to Proserpine*
beyond my powers of praise." Amongst those present at this
reception was Matthew Arnold, so that now, if not before, the
two poets probably met. Only on one other occasion, that of
a small dinner-party a few months later, have we any further
record, apparently, of any meeting of Arnold and Rossetti.[1]
Gabriel's more intimate friends were still welcomed to Tudor
House, and in some cases, particularly that of Whistler,
increasing intimacy was established. It was so too with Howell,
now freely hunting, on a pretext of autographs, amongst whatever of Gabriel's letters had escaped the holocaust which had
marked his departure from Chatham Place. There were still
occasional callers. One was "Barry Cornwall" who came at
Rossetti's request, to discuss Thomas Wainewright, essayist,
forger, poisoner, whose biography he had written. Another
was Tom Robertson, the dramatist, who came to read his new
play *Caste*, which was soon to bring him success and a permanent
academic reputation as one of the originators of "modern"
drama.

But such incursions into the retirement of 16 Cheyne Walk
were now few. Increasingly solitude claimed Rossetti, moulding
into a not unwelcome monotony the sombre pattern of his days.
Outside glowed all the brightness of spring. The great grey
river laughed and glittered in the sun; the very air vibrated
with life and energy; but within the silent house in Cheyne
Walk a sick and wearied man worked ever, day after day and
all day long while light lasted, and nearly always alone. Nor
was his need of money the only spur. Like Chiaro in Gabriel's
own clairvoyant, adolescent tale, he now "feared sloth: for
then his stealthy thoughts would begin to beat round and
round him, seeking a point for attack."

As the months passed the pictures on his easel changed
again and again. In February 1867 he finished *The Christmas
Carol* in oil, and offered "the first refusal" of it to Boyce. "But,"
wrote Boyce, "Fanny said it was hers and I couldn't have it.
She wanted to sell it to me." In March, Rossetti resumed work
on, and soon completed, *Lady Lilith*, begun three years before,
and repainted *Venus Verticordia*. The close of March saw two

[1] *v. inf.* p. 392.

"replicas" of *Lilith* in water-colour; mid-April found him duplicating in the same medium *Paola and Francesca*; a week later he had begun *The Loving Cup* in oils, and of this, before the year closed, three "replicas" had been made. At the close of May, the wife of his patron Leyland was sitting to him for her portrait, while mid-June was devoted to *The Rose*, a water-colour of a girl leaning on her arm out of a window. By the end of the year he had painted some twenty pictures, including, in addition to those mentioned, *Joli Coeur*, and *Monna Rosa* in oils, and in water-colour *The Return of Tibullus to Delia* and *Tristram and Yseult Drinking the Love Potion*.

All day long he would work at his easel until silence gradually enfolded streets and river, and shadows gathered about the corners of the room, veiling floor and ceiling, pictures and furniture as the light dwindled and the gas lamps in Cheyne Walk sent their pale flicker of flame into the falling dusk. Only then, when the hard outlines of day yielded to the softness of the growing obscurity, to the velvet texture of grey tints and shadowy steel blues he loved, at twilight, when the very colours of his palette faded into the advancing blur of darkness, did Rossetti steal out of the shadowy house to wander by the companioning river, restless, ever questioning, like himself, and, far from the brightness of its source, hastening through greyness and darkness to the unknown.

PLATE X

'UDY FOR THE HEAD OF THE WOMAN IN 'FOUND' (Fanny Cornforth)
BY D. G. ROSSETTI
c. 1855

FANNY CORNFORTH

PLATE XI

HOW THEY MET THEMSELVES
BY D. G. ROSSETTI
1851-1860

IV

WILLOW-WOOD (II)
1867–1868

Alas! the bitter banks in Willow-wood,
  With tear-spurge wan, with blood-wort burning red:
Alas! if ever such a pillow could
  Steep deep the soul in sleep till she were dead,—
Better all life forget her than this thing,
That Willow-wood should hold her wandering!
Willow-wood D. G. ROSSETTI

BY THIS TIME, inner change was clearly reflected in Rossetti's external appearance. The ascetic of Hunt's oil-painting and Bell Scott's etching, both of 1853, had long since given place to the "plump little man"[1] of Val Prinsep's description four years later, during the Jovial Campaign. "Bald for his age,"[2] with large mouth, sensual lips, and Shakespearian beard, said Prinsep, who, like many others, thought Gabriel at that time vaguely resembled Shakespeare, just as a few years before he had reminded people of Chaucer.[3] But his eyes were "Italian, grave and dark with the *bistre* tinge round them," which had made Lady Ashburton or some other notable say "they looked as if they had been put in with dirty fingers."

The once slender, ascetic-looking youth was now, in fact, a dominating, genially cynical, middle-ageing man. "Short, squat, bull-doggish," with a sallow, massive, powerful face, he reminded Skelton of "the sleek and well-fed citizen of Milan or Genoa." "He has rounded out like a big baby. Bravo!" wrote an Italian cousin who now met him, to William. Gabriel himself remarked his increasing girth with whimsical regret. "Getting awfully fat and torpid," he described himself to Brown in 1861, and some time later, when at one of Brown's receptions his dress trousers proving inadequate to the increasing strain, forced him to

[1] The height of Rossetti as given by Dunn (*inf.*, p. 354), and Forbes-Robertson (*inf.*, p. 423), seems in some ways to conflict with this impression.
[2] *v. inf.* p. 621.
[3] Rossetti was, in fact, in 1851, the model for Chaucer in Madox Brown's *Chaucer reading to the Court of Edward III the Legend of Custance.* W. M. R.'s *Memoir*, p. 170.

M

"bolt," as he told Brown, he added, satirizing a famous but fatuous contemporary "poet," "Might not Tupper say truly: 'Let no man, fattening, leave his dress trousers too long unworn, lest the worse thing come unto him.'"

Marks, the curio-dealer, much impressed by Gabriel's appearance, which reminded him, too, of Shakespeare, noticed his "slopperty" walk like a sailor's, his cheek-bones, his cheeks rosy with excitement, his quickly moving hands with long fingers, twisting and twining as he talked, his way of standing with legs rather wide apart, hands in pockets, tie sticking out from collar, hat pushed back on head, and also his complete indifference to the cut, colour, or style of his clothes. Conway, who found an expression of Rossetti's genius "in every least line of his countenance," also remarked its smoothness as if carved, the lights, shades, and shifting colours as it sometimes seemed, passing over it, and the eyes sometimes dropped, sometimes expanded.

Henry Treffry Dunn, Gabriel's new art-assistant, has left us an interesting description of Rossetti at this time, just before his physical and mental decline changed him. "His face," wrote Dunn, "conveyed to me the existence of underlying currents of strong passions impregnated with melancholy. His eyes were dark grey, and deeply set; the eyebrows dark, thick, and well arched; the forehead large and well rounded, and the strongly formed brows produced a remarkable fullness at the ridge of the nose, such as I have often noticed in men possessed of great individuality. A thick but not heavy moustache partly concealed a well-formed and somewhat sensuous mouth, and at this time he wore a trimmed beard of a deep chestnut brown, with the cheeks shaven; his hair was much darker in colour, curly, and inclined to thinness. He was about 5 feet 7½ inches in height[1]—his drawing-room door was a faithful recorder not only of his own stature but that of most of his intimate friends. Although there was a tendency to a rather too extensive form with him, this was not particularly noticeable, owing to his shapely figure and easy carriage. He possessed a voice which was peculiarly rich and musical in tone; and when, later, I had opportunities of hearing him read his poems, which he

[1] *v. inf.* p. 423 and footnotes.

did from time to time to some of his intimate friends, it was delightful to listen to him. His hands were small, and very white. Of jewellery he made no display; all that he wore was an old-fashioned gold chain attached to his watch. He was equally unassuming in dress. For studio use he generally wore a loose overcoat, with capacious pockets into which he could easily thrust a good-sized memorandum book, which was indispensable to him, as it was his custom to jot down his thoughts either for poetry or painting as they arose in his mind." Such was Gabriel at the age of thirty-nine.

Indeed, the inevitable effects of time were now revealing themselves within the whole Preraphaelite circle. "F. M. Brown (oldened) . . . Mrs. Madox Brown (looks young with back to the window)" Allingham recorded in his diary after one of the Morrises' dinners, unconsciously echoing the recent thoughts of Georgie Jones. To Brown himself, Time's passing was being painfully emphasized by recurrent attacks of gout. The first generation of Preraphaelites were in fact falling somewhat heavily into middle age, while even the romantic dreams of their successors, the second Preraphaelite generation, were fading. Jones, unable to bear life's disillusions, was even physically ill, suffering from depression and insomnia, and complaining to Watts the painter of "evil nights" sleepless or haunted by bad dreams of friends who turned unkind or died. "I am really at present at the very lowest ebb of hope," wrote Jones. "A little bit is overwork, a bit is weakness of body, but most by a thousand times is a clear certainty that I shall never do what I thought I had already done."

The dreaminess pervading the first generation of Pre-raphaelites, particularly the youthful Gabriel, was yet more deeply permeating their successors. The poetry and prose of Morris is generally a tapestry of dream. In pictorial art this influence lies heavy upon the languid, brooding figures of Jones and his imitators, while in life Janey Morris, also a morbid dreamer at this time, would discuss with Jones their nocturnal visions, Janey pouring into Jones's ear such tales as how she had seemed to be standing quite alone in the market-place of an unknown city, when suddenly an old-fashioned coach drew up before her, one door of which opened to allow a rickety flight of steps to be let down. Then from the coach had descended a little, white-haired old woman who proved to be Georgie Jones. There in the silent market-place the two exchanged doleful greetings. "They are all gone, Georgie," said Janey sadly in her dream, and then the two women mingled their tears! Then in turn, Jones described to Janey how in his dream he had seen "a shadowy girl who was by a well in that mournful twilight that is the sky of dreams. 'Now listen to the noise of my heart,' said the girl, and dropped a vast stone into the well—which boomed and boomed until it grew into a roar unbearable," and he awoke. Thus the two exchanged their dream confidences, guileless in that age of all Freudian significances concerning flights of steps and wells, but much charged with the particular atmosphere of their sentimental period.

But while Jones's romanticism was turning anaemic and threatening to die of exhaustion, that of his friend and contemporary Swinburne, heated in strange fires, was turning into a veritable *vinum daemonum*. In the spring of 1867 he became increasingly excitable and erratic. In April, burning with enthusiasm for the liberation of Italy, he fell down at Mazzini's feet in adoration, and three months later excelled this achievement by falling down in a kind of epileptic fit while breakfasting with a large party at the London residence of Lord Houghton. Thereupon he was promptly seized and carried off by his father into the country, away from London and the ways of life which were destroying his health and bringing nervous breakdown in their train. From his rural retreat, Swinburne, having quickly recovered, cheerfully sent "love to Ned and Gabriel and all friends."

Solitude aggravated Rossetti's neurasthenia, and as the summer of 1867 waned, a new symptom appeared. His sight failed. Both sunlight and artificial light made him sick and dizzy, and the pain in his eyes increased. Mindful of his father's blindness, and timid towards physical ills, Gabriel believed himself a victim of heredity and fell into panic. His painting would soon end, he feared, in darkness. Anxiety not less than insomnia sent him to the whisky bottle and he rapidly sank into deep neurotic depression. To prevent permanent melancholia or worse, he must, he now saw, find distraction in general society, avoid solitude and over-work. In short, for a time at least, he must quit the dangerous seclusion of Cheyne Walk.

In his need he thought of Allingham, and of the long-promised, long-delayed visit to him at Lymington, which he still owed his friend. Allingham had certainly cooled to Rossetti. Visiting London in the summer of 1866, he had not called on Gabriel until after five days, and after their meeting had confided to his diary: "My old regard for D. G. R. stirs within me, and would be as warm as ever *if he would let it*." Since then there had been little communication between the two. But when on September 2, 1867, he received Gabriel's letter asking: "Shall I come to you?" he at once answered: "Yes, by all means," and in his diary, to avoid apparently any revelation of private rancour, wrote the self-warning: "*Mem.*— Use him nobly while your guest."

After several days of postponements and hesitations, during which he could not even now make up his mind about the visit, Gabriel at last reached Lymington at nearly nine o'clock on the evening of a rainy Wednesday, September 11th. He wore, Allingham noticed, "a ventilating hat, something like a policeman's helmet."[1] For nine days of Rossetti's visit, the unspoken burden of their intercourse was that of Clough's *Qua Cursum Ventus*. The estranging years proved stronger than their former comradeship, and over their reunion brooded the dissatisfaction of alienated sympathies and consequent all-pervading ennui.

At first they wandered in the daytime about the woods and fields around Lymington, or lay in green shades beside pools, talking casually, indolently, finding in their lack of mutual response, only an empty, drowsy content, and in the evenings they sat up late, still talking as in the Preraphaelite days. But the unbridgeable gulf between the disillusioned, cynical, reclusive widower and the sheltered, sentimental, ageing bachelor, became only the more obvious. When Allingham pointed out to Gabriel nooks in the forest, declaring them

---

[1] Could it have been some such early and rather ridiculous specimen of the afterwards common "bowler" as Gabriel wears in one of Bell Scott's sketches of him a year or two later, as he lies in the cave at Penkill Castle, writing poetry?

"camping places" of "Forest Gipsies" and a fit stage for
A Midsummer-Night's Dream, his unresponsive friend merely
answered: "You ought to have been a landscape painter. You
notice everything." "Sometimes to the length of boredom,
perhaps he meant," ruminated Allingham!

Their moods, their attitudes, were in fact, like their experience
of life, on different planes. The old unity, the old confidence
between them was dead. Gabriel, melancholy, silent, tired,
dispirited, gave an unintentionally exaggerated impression of
aloofness and indifference, which accidental circumstances
increased. On Sunday morning came a letter from the intrusive
Howell, asking permission to join them, and although the scamp
did not come, Allingham, at last for a short time alone with his
old friend, must have resented Gabriel's answer: "Come if you
will." As they walked and talked together, Allingham critically
noted his friend's traits of character. He found Gabriel self-
assertive, for he refused to hurry when late, saying: "in a
conclusive tone, 'I never do anything I don't like.' " He took
no interest in the external world, not even, to Allingham's regret,
in the sea and ships. When Gabriel refused to meet anyone
during his visit, Allingham was annoyed. To call on Tennyson
at Farringford, Allingham by herculean efforts, coaxed Gabriel
as far as the Lymington pier; but the day was windy, and
fearing sea-sickness would be the inevitable result of a voyage
to the Isle of Wight, Gabriel categorically refused to go a step
further.

To Allingham it was soon obvious that his friend's early,
ideal world lay in ruins. Hope, faith, joy were gone. Gabriel's
religious indifference, as it seemed to Allingham, was shocking.
Sauntering in a churchyard they discussed immortality and
suicide. Allingham was horrified to find that his friend merely
thought suicide "silly." "There are traces of superstition
noticeable in him," wrote Allingham, "none of religion." And
he noticed with disapproval Gabriel's comment after meeting
an old woman whose cottage had recently been destroyed by
lightning: "What a damned world where such things can
happen!" They discussed the fashionable spiritualistic craze
which again revealed Gabriel's scepticism, and all the comfort
the somewhat hypercritical Allingham could find was: "D. G. R.

has at least a curiosity" about it! They differed too when they discussed literature. The romantic customs-officer thought Maggie Tulliver's lover Stephen in *The Mill on the Floss,* "too mean and commonplace"; but Gabriel, now a realist, would not agree.

Allingham was equally unsuccessful in his efforts to make Gabriel work. Despite his weak eyes Rossetti had brought painting materials and the unfinished *Venus Verticordia* with him, intending to paint a background of roses. Yet even when a neighbour of Allingham's gave him the "wonderful roses" he desired, and Allingham himself actually untied the fastenings of his unopened picture case, Rossetti remained inert, evasive, declaring that the roses provided were not, after all, the right kind, that only an unobtainable "fresh-coloured loose-leaved China rose" would do!

Henceforth, abandoning all plans for Gabriel's pleasure, Allingham left him to potter aimlessly about Lymington and its neighbourhood day after day, as indeed Rossetti obviously wished to do. But to his diary, in his disappointment and irritation, Allingham confided the results of his observation of his former friend. Tired, stale, after years of overwork and solitude, Gabriel lay ever lounging on sofas now. "Curls himself up like a cat," wrote Allingham, more and more critical. With similar disapproval he observed Gabriel's general air of indolence and, for his own edification described his ways; his manner of walking, "very characteristically, with a peculiar lounging gait, but still obstinately pushing on and making way, humming the while with closed teeth, in the intervals of talk, not a tune or anything like one but what sounds like a *sotto voce* note of defiance to the Universe. Then suddenly he will fling himself down somewhere, and refuse to stir an inch further. His favourite attitude—on his back, one knee raised, hands behind head."

From such externals, Allingham, made no more lenient perhaps by Gabriel's success in painting and his own apparent failure in literature, proceeded to an intellectual and moral stocktaking of his friend, obviously a summary of their talks and discussions at Lymington. Like Bell Scott fourteen years before, he lamented Gabriel's indifference to science, his obliviousness of particular details in his natural surroundings as he walked, his literary tastes and general eclecticism. "It is plain," wrote Allingham regretfully, "that the simple, the natural, the naïve are merely insipid in his mouth; he must have strong savours, in art, in literature, and in life. Colours, forms, sensations are required to be pungent, mordant. In poetry he desires spasmodic passion and emphatic, partly archaic, diction." True as Allingham's comments were, they suggest, by their acerbity, that Gabriel's preferences had also, either directly or indirectly, implied indifference to such smooth insipidities as inspired Allingham's own usually pedestrian muse.

Returning to town on September 20th, with, as usual after almost any visit, a declared but never fulfilled intention to return and settle there, Gabriel, finding that now even the flickering street lamps pained him, became gravely alarmed by his increasing eye-trouble, and observed also "confusion" in his head. He feared too that news of his condition might leak out and adversely affect the commissions he so needed to repay his debts. Needing companionship in his trouble, he wrote to Allingham: "Do by all means come up, not for a day, but for as long as you can," and, upon the advice of friends, consulted Sir William Bowman, a famous oculist of the day, who advised a month or so of rest from painting, and cold water baths, obviously believing the trouble to be nervous. But Gabriel, little satisfied, wrote to Allingham, now hourly expected, that "blokes are coming to-morrow to meet you at dinner at 7," and added: "I went to Bowman who gave me the information that if it did not get better it might get worse. . . ."

"Well received," wrote Allingham of his reception at Cheyne Walk the following afternoon. Nevertheless, the few days he now spent with Gabriel only widened the unspoken difference between them. From the first Allingham was uneasily conscious of the disorderly house, the often incongruous society, the increasing disintegration of Gabriel himself. As promised, the "blokes" assembled to do Allingham honour, and that night he dined with Gabriel, Brown, Howell and Fanny. But the atmosphere was not to Allingham's taste. Howell as usual told stories: "himself an actor in all ('actor' in the stage sense)" Allingham disparagingly noted, while Howell told of dining with drunken bishops in a convocation of clergy. "Queer stories such as Sir Robert Walpole used to encourage," wrote the disgusted guest, obviously thinking of Walpole's remark that he always talked "bawdy" over the port, as that was the only subject in which all the guests could join.

During the evening, Dunn, Gabriel's "assistant and copyist," as Allingham significantly, perhaps even a little maliciously, described him, joined them. All sat up late, and when at last supper was mentioned, Howell and Dunn went down to the kitchen and brought up meat. Fanny was obviously no model housekeeper, as Prinsep indeed revealed, and Howell, returning with food, reported that he had just seen "a mouse eating a haddock" downstairs. The session ended at three o'clock in the morning, with Gabriel's departure for bed. Howell and Dunn went out in the rain to find a cab, while Brown with Allingham waited in the hall until, on the cab's arrival, Brown departed. Alone in the hall, Allingham, reviewing his impressions of his first day as Gabriel's guest, was a little depressed.

Most of the evenings during Allingham's visit passed similarly, in what he called "lounging chats." Wherever they went, Allingham noted, "D. G. R. lounges." For him it was almost the symbol of his friend's degeneration, as it had been at Lymington. More and more he resented Gabriel's new, "loose" ways; his coloured expletives. When coming back one night from the Joneses they took a wrong turning and Gabriel exclaimed "this is bloody", Allingham did not like it.

Gabriel, he noticed, was always calling things "bloody" now, was "very fond of this expletive as well as other phrases." But even worse was Fanny's pretence of decorum, her laughing protests after Gabriel's lapses from propriety, with: "Rizetti, I shall leave the room!" or "I'll put you out in the scullery!" —reminders of her own high standard of manners and social amenities, which made poor Allingham's blood run cold.

Allingham was happier with the Joneses; spent much time with them indeed during this visit to Rossetti, and was glad to see old Mrs. Rossetti when he called on the Rossetti family which had recently moved from Albany Street to Euston Square. Obviously uneasy about her son's way of life, Mrs. Rossetti was glad that the stable Allingham was with him for a time.

Gabriel's "lounging"—"lolling about and behaving like a
seal on a sandbank," said Rossetti's friend Smetham—one of
Allingham's first observations on arrival, was also one of his last
before departure, after spending six days in Cheyne Walk.
"Pack up, R. lolling on the bed; cab to Waterloo—train to
Lymington," was his suggestive comment, together with
another of greater significance: "Cheyne Walk, D. G. R. and I
—not like old times." This change in his friend, Allingham must
have profoundly pondered in his solitude at Lymington, for
some five weeks later he confided to his diary his ultimate,
considered impressions. "My last visit to London," he wrote,
"was an unhappy one. In art, and still more in life, Rossetti
and I have discords not to be resolved. Should we ever have
been or supposed ourselves such friends in early days if we had
lived constantly near each other? Has he changed? If I have I
am not aware of it. 'I loathe and despise family life!' he said.
I long and pray for it—and O, how the years slip away! The
only comfort is, 'you might have made a mistake, an irremediable one—and it's not too late even yet!' "

Between Allingham the "sentimentalist" and the "realist"
Rossetti, developing a reaction psychology against all he had
believed, hoped and loved, there could now be little mutual
sympathy. To Rossetti change had certainly come, but the
change was less radical in many ways than Allingham believed.
The past, in such a nature as Rossetti's could not be completely
erased. Rather his new self was, like some geological deposit,
superimposed upon his earlier identity. Some intuitive knowledge of this must have added to Gabriel's inevitable, cynical
amusement at his friend's visible concern, at Allingham's
inviolable naïveté. But beneath the external squalor of Gabriel's
present way of life lay a deep misanthropy, the sign of his
ineradicable idealism. This misanthropy, leading him increasingly to withdrawal from all human contacts, revealed
itself in a letter Gabriel wrote at this time to his friend Shields,
a supersensitive artist, who, now recovering from a nervous
breakdown caused by overwork and by London's noise, was
about to withdraw, for the sake of quiet, to an old, remote
house in Manchester. "I congratulate you supremely," wrote
Gabriel in genial irony, "on having attained at last to complete

desolation as regards social propinquity. I suppose from what you say that you can even take good walks without seeing or hearing your kind. Nothing could suit me better, and I still hope to be an outcast from humanity one of these days!" Once again, as so often, Rossetti was sounding the note of unconscious prophecy. Of that however, he little dreamed—as yet certainly had no suspicion how near were the days when he too would become such an "outcast."

For a time, it seemed as if Bowman's treatment would speedily cure Gabriel's impaired sight. "His eyes," wrote William, near the close of the year 1867, "seem to be as well again as if nothing had been wrong with them." But Rossetti's fears, undiminished, soon found apparently renewed justification. In the spring and summer of 1868, eye-weakness and insomnia returned, and Gabriel still needed periodical surgical treatment for hydrocele. Now desperately afraid of blindness, and angry at the interruption of his painting when money was much needed, he went in panic from one distinguished oculist to another, consulting Bowman, Bader the German specialist at Guy's Hospital, and one Critchett, in turn, who all assured him, as also did a general practitioner and his own friend Marshall the surgeon, that the trouble was not organic, but due to over-work, over-strain and nervous degeneration.

Unable to paint for the present, Gabriel visited with Howell, in August, the Leylands at Speke Hall, and in September, he at last made again, this time with Dunn, the tour in Warwickshire he had first made in 1853 and so long intended to repeat. But restless, from each of these excursions he suddenly returned to town to make abortive attempts at painting. In this state he accepted an invitation from Bell Scott and Bell Scott's friend Miss Boyd, to visit them at her estate, Penkill Castle in Ayrshire, and set out, very quietly, near the close of September, visiting an art exhibition at Leeds on the way. At the exhibition he admired "splendid heads by Titian, Morone, Bellini and Velasquez," saw Brown's *Work* and *Last of England*, and might also have seen his own paintings but, probably fearing lest some of his slovenly "replicas" and pot-boilers should appear, he had prohibited his patrons from lending any of his own works.

Penkill Castle, he found, still preserved something of that

mediaeval glamour dear to the Preraphaelite heart. Despite seventeenth century additions and even modern restorations, its worn battlements, particularly on warm, autumn afternoons, invited the romantic dreamer looking out over the glen below, beyond the quiet farmlands to the distant sea, to play with idle fancies, invent stirring legends, recall in pleasant, imaginative retrospect, something of the pain and passion of the past. Christina Rossetti who also visited Penkill, even compared it to Naples, declaring that when "beyond the immediate greenness a gorgeous sunset glorifies the sea distance, one scarcely need desire aught more exquisite in this world." Such was Penkill, the home of Miss Alice Boyd—"perhaps . . . the prettiest handsome woman I ever met," said Christina. Alice Boyd, now "turned forty," had gone eleven years before, upon her mother's death, to Bell Scott in Newcastle, determined, as Scott declared, "to find a new interest in life," and hoping to find it in art. In Scott at any rate she found it. A lifelong friendship with him quickly developed, a friendship so close that soon, despite her relatives' objections, she lived with Scott and his wife during the winter months, and during the remainder of the year shared with them her own hereditary domain of Penkill Castle. Scott's reciprocation of her friendship is shown by his dedication of his amatory sonnets to her as "AB."

Gabriel thought Penkill "a delightful place," the surrounding country "paradise," his hostess's kindness "unbounded," and "Scotus a good companion though not over fond of locomotion." From Rossetti, this last was a strange criticism; but, unable to paint and tempted in the midst of exquisite scenery by perfect autumn weather, he was daily taking the exercise he needed, accompanied by Scott. To his mother, Gabriel described his daily round at Penkill: "I get up very late here, to give myself the utmost benefit of sleep, which continues in a vastly improved condition. I then simmer gradually to walking-heat, and walk accordingly. In the evening, after dinner, we read aloud and sometimes play whist." A visitor at Penkill, Miss Losh, an eccentric old lady who was Alice Boyd's cousin, made much of Gabriel, to the annoyance of the jealous Scott, and then and later secretly lent him considerable sums of money ultimately amounting to £500 in all, as was discovered after her death, when, by Alice Boyd's orders, the incriminating papers were burned. But Scott, despite a promise of silence, could not conquer the mean temptation to inform Gabriel of the discovery.

Meanwhile, at Penkill Gabriel continued in a wretched state of health. Tramping the country round in the daytime with a somewhat bored and acid Scott, he read to the ladies in the evenings Christina's poems, in the beautiful voice they loved to hear, and when they had retired, sat with the weary Scott, heavily drinking whisky as a sedative, through the long-drawn nights, vainly awaiting sleep which came only with the dawn as he stumbled fuddled and sleepy to bed. Alone with Scott on their walks and during these night watches, Rossetti fell into pathological obsessive brooding which quickly wearied his friend, "the fearful skeletons in his closet," as Scott wrote long afterwards, "that were every night, when the ladies had gone, brought out for his relief and my recreation. These skeletons, which were also made to dance along the mountain high-road during our long walks." Except for Gabriel's fear of blindness, Scott did not state what these "skeletons" were, but we may be sure they included those neurotic self-reproaches for Lizzie's death, described by Hake.[1]

Soon Gabriel wrote to Bader of worse symptoms, but Bader's opinion was unchanged. In his morbid mental state, Rossetti talked, as he had done at Lymington, of suicide, but no longer thought it "silly," declared indeed that if the worst happened and he lost his sight, he would put an end to his life. "Why, if blind," he asked, "should he live?" To which Scott and the ladies, trying to arouse in Gabriel a new interest as antidote to his morbid fears replied: "Live for your poetry." They persuaded him to recite whatever of his verses he could remember, and as they walked along a country road he declaimed *The Song of the Bower*, which deeply moved Alice Boyd. Scott too, affected doubtless by the beautiful voice, and, as he afterwards declared, "lifted to a rhetorical moment," paid Gabriel a characteristic compliment, assuring his brother artist of the brush that "the value of his paintings lay in their poetry, that he was a poet by birthright not a painter!"—and was surprised

[1] *v. sup.* p. 348.

that such encouragement failed of its anticipated joyous effect.

Meanwhile Rossetti, longing in his happier moods for gayer company than Scott, vainly urged Brown to join them at Penkill, in which case "we should be as jolly as possible. I would recite to you all the ignominious rhymes I have made on Scotus, and I would make some on you too." Although his eyes remained the same, his insomnia, general health and spirits improved, and for once, although unable to paint, he was not anxious to return to town. The autumn days were fine; "more splendid walking weather could not well be imagined," he said, and (as usual when a locality pleased him), he thought of remaining for six months or so, renting Penkill throughout the winter. But when October came and Scott and Alice Boyd began to yearn southwards, so too did Rossetti. He delayed, however, until the weather broke, returning at last with Scott on November 3rd.

That the thought of suicide or fear of death still lingered, Gabriel's first act upon his return showed. Shortly before leaving Penkill he had hoped to bilk his creditors by making a deed of gift of his whole estate to William. This was not in gratitude for William's devotion, but, as he explained, "so that whatever may befall myself," his brother could "do the best for all parties concerned"—including Fanny. This plan, upon his return from Penkill, he began to put into execution until warned by his patron Rose, a solicitor, that the registration involved would at once bring his creditors down upon him and prevent it. Another sign of his morbidity was his condemnation of any *posthumous* exhibitions of his works, on the ground that they failed to satisfy him. This dissatisfaction with his own painting remained with him to the end; nor was the thought of death henceforth remote.

Despite his condition Rossetti was now forced to resume painting, for months of compulsory idleness had brought his funds perilously low. But not for another month was it possible, and then only in short spells followed by intervals of rest. Although he now wore spectacles, near objects were only fairly visible, while distant ones he saw more completely, but as if through a film or veil which he described "as like a combination of the curling of smoke and the effervescing of champagne." During this month of enforced leisure, Gabriel busied himself in various ways. With the unscholarly, airy casualness he had shown towards Blake, he helped his brother to prepare an edition of Shelley's poems and wrote to the French art-critic, M. Chesneau, correcting various errors about Preraphaelitism in one of his works. It was now that he almost yielded to Browning's exhortations to visit Italy—but chiefly because at this time the continent particularly appealed to him as a refuge from creditors.

Lack of means and ill-health do not encourage travel, however, and instead of going abroad, Gabriel, still largely prevented by the state of his eyes from painting, turned once again to poetry. The advice Scott and Miss Boyd had given him at Penkill seemed now to be exercising a belated influence. At any rate, while Scott on November 30th was reminding William that his brother "is a poet as well as a painter, and was a poet before he was a painter; . . . it would be a great thing to get him to be a poet again," Gabriel himself was busy, said William, "looking up his poems of old days, with some floating idea of offering some of them to the *Fortnightly Review*, and at any rate with a degree of zest which looks promising for some result with them." And not only did Rossetti "look up" and revise old poems, he was once again writing new ones. "Gabriel," reported his watchful brother on December 18th, "has just written a series of four sonnets—*Willow-wood*—about the finest thing he has done. I see the poetical impulse is upon him again: he even says he ought never to have been a painter, but a poet instead." The next day, at Euston Square, Gabriel wrote a sonnet on death. Obviously this poetic renascence was the result of his recent experience and of the crowding memories from the past which his present comparative inactivity in painting had released. The intimately biographical, or to use his own description of his earlier writing, "autopsychological" nature of his verse was evident on both external and internal grounds.

With the coming of Christmas his thoughts turned again to Allingham more warmly perhaps than of late. "I have been looking up a few old sonnets, and writing a few new ones," he wrote, "to make a little bunch in a coming number of the

Fortnightly—not till March, however, as they are full till then.
. . . I suppose you heard that I have been queer with my eyes,
this has caused inaction and a looking up of ravelled rags of
verse. I am now at work again however." And in a P.S. he
enquired: "Isn't there a chance of your coming up this Xmas?
Come and stay with me."

Rossetti's letter must have surprised Allingham. Surely
Gabriel, forty years old now, lately so weary even of life itself,
was not launching out again on a new poetic tide after an
almost unbroken silence of fifteen years! Yet so it was. As
Rossetti himself wrote a few months later:—

> . . . many men are poets in their youth,
> But for one sweet-strung soul the wires prolong
> Even through all change the indomitable song.

V

REGENERATE RAPTURE
1868–1869

> Oh! What is this that knows the road I came,
> The flame turned cloud, the cloud returned to flame,
>   The lifted shifted steeps and all the way?—
> That draws round me at last this wind-warm space,
> And in regenerate rapture turns my face
>   Upon the devious coverts of dismay?
>
> *The Monochord* D. G. ROSSETTI

IT WAS NOW, at the moment of Gabriel's surprising poetic renascence, that Janey Morris, some ten years younger than he, and long claimed after her marriage by domestic duties of wife and mother, reappeared in Rossetti's life and work. Henceforth her association with Gabriel and her influence upon his art and poetry were to be conspicuous.

The rumour that Jane Burden and Gabriel had fallen in love during the Jovial Campaign, that Rossetti, feeling morally bound to Lizzie, had persuaded the reluctant Janey to look favourably upon the infatuated Morris is, whatever exaggeration of actual fact it may contain, not improbable in the light of later events, and indeed in Rossetti's projected but never painted picture *The Cup of Cold Water*, elaborately described in a prose tale of his, a closely similar theme was treated.[1] Gabriel's realization of Lizzie's degenerating health and possible early death may have played some unconscious or conscious part in his continual postponement of marriage, at least after he had met Janey, and it is perhaps not without significance that his own marriage closely followed hers. Only then had he at last yielded to Lizzie's reproaches and married her.

Since then, Gabriel's short married life and six long years of widowerhood had passed. During the last three years, however,

---

[1] That William Rossetti believed in his brother's passion for Jane Burden at Oxford in 1857 is I think suggested by his tentative dating of *The House of Life* sonnet *Known in Vain* as 1857 in *D. G. Rossetti as Designer and Writer.* "More or less autobiographical," he described it. Later, he discovered the actual date, in a MS. version, to be January 1853, and its alternative title to be *Work and Will.*

the Morrises, formerly distant at Upton, had lived in London within easy reach, in Bloomsbury, because of the increasing demands, it was said, upon Morris's time and energy, made by "The Firm"—Morris, Marshall, Faulkner and Co.—the development of which was now and henceforth Morris's chief occupation in life. "The Firm," which consisted of Morris, Madox Brown, Jones, Rossetti and three of their friends, had originated several years previously as a result of the disgust with contemporary taste which had led Morris long before to design the furniture and decorations for his rooms in Red Lion Square, and later for the Red House at Upton. But while the partnership of Morris's friends in "The Firm" was merely formal, being limited to the investment of some five pounds apiece and the making of an occasional design for a stained glass window,* Morris had made the foundation of "The Firm" possible by investing in it a considerable sum, and in consequence, had quickly identified himself with it, making its various interests, from the designing of windows, furniture, wall-papers and fabrics, to the perfecting of new dyes, his own. For the scope of "Morris, Marshall, Faulkner and Co.," was wide, including as their original prospectus of 1860 declared: "any species of decoration, mural or otherwise from pictures . . . down to the consideration of the smallest work susceptible of art beauty." From its original quarters in Red Lion Square, "The Firm" had by this time moved to more commodious premises in Queen Square, Bloomsbury. There, above "the Shop," as they jocularly termed the work-rooms in the fine old house they had taken, the Morrises upon their return to London in 1865 had made their home. Upon this renewal of proximity, the earlier intimacy of Gabriel and Janey, severed by the Morrises' departure for Upton, seems to have revived.

The personality of Janey Morris proves, at least for the modern enquirer, as elusive as, perhaps even more elusive than, that of Lizzie herself. The daughter of an Oxford groom, Janey was, like Lizzie, of humble birth, and, amongst her husband's circle at least, seems to have been similarly detached, enigmatic, defensive. People's opinions of her, as of Lizzie, were widely varied, even contradictory. Watts-Dunton, the friend of

* *v. Notes.*

Gabriel's last years, declared that though few knew it, Janey was "superior to Morris intellectually." Bernard Shaw, doubtless a better judge, conspicuously though tacitly denied her intellect. "She was not a talker; in fact she was the silentest woman I have ever met," he said, and the only remark of hers he could recall was, that once, at dinner, on passing him a second helping of pudding she assured him: "That will do you good. There is suet in it!"

Whatever men's opinion of her intellect, all found Janey Morris impressive, although the eulogies of her later admirers are often touched with a hint of amusement, even of mockery. Buxton Forman thought no other woman "so strangely lovely and majestic as Mrs. Morris." Watts-Dunton declared her "the most lovely woman I have ever known, her beauty was incredible." Swinburne, in 1858, hearing of her engagement to Morris, had marvelled "to think of Morris's having that wonderful and most perfect stunner of his to look at or speak to. The idea of his marrying her is insane. To kiss her feet is the utmost men should dream of doing." Henry James, meeting Mrs. Morris eleven years later, during a visit to England, gave a detailed description of her which hardly supports those who dwelt so rhapsodically upon her beauty. "Oh, *ma chère*, such a wife!" he told his sister. "*Je n'en reviens pas*—she haunts me still. A figure cut out of a missal—out of one of Rossetti's or Hunt's pictures—to say this gives but a faint idea of her, because when such an image puts on flesh and blood, it is an apparition of fearful and wonderful intensity. It's hard to say whether she's a grand synthesis of all the Preraphaelite pictures ever made—or they a 'keen analysis' of her—whether she's an original or a copy. In either case she is a wonder. Imagine a tall lean woman in a long dress of some dead purple stuff, guiltless of hoops (or of anything else I should say), with a mass of crisp black hair, heaped into great wavy projections on each of her temples, a thin pale face, a pair of strange, sad, deep, dark, Swinburnian eyes, with great thick black oblique brows, joined in the middle and tucking themselves away under her hair,[1] a mouth like the 'Oriana' in our illustrated Tennyson, a long neck, without any collar, and in lieu thereof some dozen

[1] *v. sup.* pp. 238–9.

strings of outlandish beads. In fine complete." Twelve years later, just before Gabriel's death, Henry James met Mrs. Morris again, in Italy, and described her with far less enthusiasm than before.[1]

George du Maurier, seeing Janey in 1885, sent a short but typically amused description of her to his daughter "Trixie." "Mummy, Sylvia and I," he wrote, "went to a rather weird and gropy but pleasant lawn-tennis and dinner and evening party at the Richmonds. Twenty-four people sat down to the table. I sat between Friedlander (the singer), and Miss Stillman, but was depressed by Mrs. Morris, Rossetti's famous model sitting opposite in an old Florentine costume and her old Florentine face above it." Not unlike this word-picture, indeed, was Evelyn de Morgan's bizarre painting of Mrs. Morris in later years, named *The Hour Glass*. "Her handsome sombre face with its haunting air of melancholy was well adapted to the subject depicted," wrote Evelyn de Morgan's sister, of Mrs. Morris. "In an ancient chair, inlaid with ivory, a woman is seen seated. Behind her on the wall are glowing tapestries; a golden lamp of mediaeval design is suspended above her head. Her draperies, in wonderful hues of yellow and russet-bronze, are thickly strewn with pearls, the delineation of which in correct perspective constituted a *tour de force*. Jewels of barbaric design accentuate the richness of her attire, and gleam again from her quaint head-dress, beneath which shows the first indication of age—her whitening locks. Meanwhile, with a brooding sorrow her gaze is fixed upon an hour-glass, clasped in her slender fingers, wherein the sands are swiftly running out; at her feet is a dying rose, and close to her lies a book on which are visible the words *Mors Janua Vitae* (Death is the portal of Life). So, too, unheeded by her, outside the open doorway stands the figure of Life the Immortal, piping, piping joyously in sunlight, in robes of azure among the blossoming flowers of spring." Like most of Evelyn de Morgan's Pre-raphaelitesque monstrosities, the painting, in fact, as even the word-picture just given shows, looks like some elaborate parody of all that was worst in the movement, a ghastly *reductio ad absurdum* of Gabriel's later style of work for which Janey Morris was so often the model!

[1] *v. inf.* p. 627.

Bernard Shaw, meeting Janey Morris at her husband's home on various occasions in the eighties and later, described her some years ago, in humorous language not unlike the description of *The Hour Glass*, though much shorter. "When she came into a room in her strangely beautiful garments," he said, "looking at least eight feet high, the effect was as if she had walked out of an Egyptian tomb at Luxor." Georgie Jones, from the first moment of their meeting, had silently contrasted Janey's dark hair, "colourless perfection" and general statuesque beauty with the colourful beauty of Lizzie. "Very shy and retiring, almost fearful in her attitude towards others," Watts-Dunton described her, and Shaw praised her "plain good sense which had preserved her sanity perfectly, under treatment that would have spoiled most women." To Rothenstein, meeting Mrs. Morris after Morris's death, she seemed "an almost legendary figure" like Laura or La Simonetta, or Vittoria Colonna. Although her hair was then grey, to Rothenstein it seemed "as full and as rich" as in Rossetti's paintings, and she still retained, he declared, "much of the beauty which Rossetti has immortalized." As she sat one afternoon autographing a Kelmscott Chaucer, she reminded him of "a splendid Sibyl from the Sistine Chapel," and although he had heard of her silence as she moved among the great figures of the past, he now found her "serene indeed, but interested in a thousand things; an admirable talker, wholly without self-consciousness, always gracious, and in her person beautifully dignified."

Richard le Gallienne, poet of the romantic "90's," passing Kelmscott a year or two after William Morris's death, which occurred in 1896, has told how: "The temptation to look upon the face of Jane Burden whose strange loveliness dreams out at us from the paintings of Rossetti, the very Muse of the Pre-raphaelite Brotherhood, was too great to be resisted, and presently I was seated with her, tall and stately and lovelier perhaps for a touch of the years on her splendid hair, taking tea at the foot of the old sunny orchard, where, I said to myself, Rossetti too had once sat and painted her on just such an afternoon. I remember that we had some particularly good quince jam with our tea, and, on remarking upon its goodness, 'I made it myself,' said the Blessed Damozel, 'and, as you like

373

it so much, you shall have a jar to take with you.' A jar of quince jam made by the beautiful lady whom Morris had loved and Rossetti had painted! It was like receiving it at the hands of Helen of Troy. But before I took it away with me, Mrs. Morris led me into the house, into his study, with his books as he had left them, the superb Kelmscott Chaucer, which he and Burne-Jones had made together, lying open on the table, and as I departed with my quince jam, it seemed to me that it must indeed have come to me in a dream. I cannot recall now what became of it. Perhaps it vanished back into dreamland, for it cannot be conceived that it was eaten in commonplace fashion, like other earthly jams."

Another amusing description of Mrs. Morris closely agrees with those of Le Gallienne and Shaw. It is by Graham Robertson, in his charming book of reminiscences, *Time Was*, and shows the same semi-humorous appreciation of Janey Morris as marks the reminiscences of so many of his predecessors. "I fancy," he wrote, "that her mystic beauty must sometimes have weighed rather heavily upon her. Her mind was not formed upon the same tragic lines as her face; she was very simple and could have enjoyed simple pleasures with simple people, but such delights were not for her. She looked like the Delphic Sibyl and had to behave as such. She was a Ladye in a Bower, an ensorcelled Princess, a Blessed Damozel, while I feel sure she would have preferred to be a 'bright, chatty little woman' in request for small theatre parties and afternoons up the river. Brightness might equally have been expected from Deirdre of the Sorrows, chattiness from the Sphinx. She was Venus Astarte, 'betwixt the sun and moon a Mystery,' and there she had to stay. She required appropriate setting and was perhaps at her wonderful best in her own house, standing in one of the tall windows against the grey river or lying on a low couch with beyond her the dim splendours of a great cabinet painted by Burne-Jones with the legend of Little Saint Hugh of Lincoln. There she seemed to melt from one picture into another, all by Rossetti and all incredibly beautiful. I can well understand that her type was too grand, too sombre to appeal to every eye. When she travelled in France, our light-hearted and often beauty-blind neighbours found her appearance frankly amusing and would giggle audibly when she passed by, to the astonishment and rage of Morris, who was with difficulty restrained from throwing down his gage in the cause of his Ladye. I always recommended would-be but wavering worshippers to start with Mrs. Stillman (Marie Spartali) who was, so to speak, Mrs. Morris for Beginners. The two marvels had many points in common: the same lofty stature, the same long sweep of limb, the 'neck like a tower,' the night-dark tresses and the eyes of mystery, yet Mrs. Stillman's loveliness conformed to the standard of ancient Greece and could at once be appreciated, while study of her trained the eye to understand the more esoteric beauty of Mrs. Morris and 'trace in Venus' eyes the gaze of Proserpine.'" As he foretold in a poem, those who would look on her now must come to Rossetti, and in the portrait in blue, holding a rose, in the *Mariana* and the *Proserpine* and in the chalk drawings, *Aurea Catena* and *The Prisoner's Daughter* (to quote a few out of many) they will find her exact presentment, set down without exaggeration."

Mrs. Bell Scott, first meeting Janey Morris in 1860, was worried to "think what country-woman Mrs. Morris is like . . . not an Englishwoman, certainly." In her obscurity, her strange, statuesque "beauty," her silence and her original loose, light, then unfashionable clothes, Janey seemed indeed to her contemporaries a being of no age or country. Nor, unfortunately, do Janey's few accessible letters illuminate her shadowy image. Too impersonal to resolve the questions raised by the marked divergence between Shaw's and Robertson's estimates of her intellect on the one hand, and Watts-Dunton's and Rothenstein's on the other, they offer nothing to judgment, and we are left to conjecture that Janey, like Lizzie, responded in widely different ways to the stimuli of occasion and environment, would readily seek the refuge of silence in a too exacting or unsympathetic society.

Such then, was the woman whose presence henceforth haunts the life and art of Rossetti, whose face—accurately portrayed not idealized, so Henry James, Watts-Dunton, William Rossetti and Graham Robertson all independently asserted—now displaced Lizzie's in Rossetti's studio as the predominant one that "looks out from all his canvases."

"It seemed," wrote William Rossetti, in a unique and surprising spasm of what was for him almost lyrical incantation, "a face created to fire his imagination, and to quicken his powers—a face of arcane and inexhaustible meaning. To realize its features was difficult; to transcend its suggestion, impossible. There was one fortunate circumstance—if you could but represent its *appearance*, you stood thereby already high in the region of the typical or symbolic. For idealizing there was but one process—to realize. I will not conceal my opinion that my brother succeeded where few painters would have done other than fail; he did some genuine justice to this astonishing countenance."

Upon Janey's return to London at the close of 1865, her presence quickly revealed itself in Gabriel's art, both pictorial and poetic. In June 1866, he began the famous oil portrait of her seated before a table with a glass of roses, and wearing a blue dress. It is now in the National Portrait Gallery. Long before its completion he had begun another portrait of her, this time (significantly?) as La Pia, Dante's ill-starred lady of Siena, condemned by a cruel husband to perish amidst the pestilential exhalations of the Maremma marshes. To sit to Gabriel for this painting, Janey, sometimes accompanied by her husband, was, in the spring of 1868, Gabriel's guest in Cheyne Walk. "With Mrs. Morris for model and Rossetti for the painter and such a subject," wrote Brown to a friend in April, "You can imagine some of the tragic, fearful beauty of the picture." As once with Lizzie, so now with Janey; throughout this spring and summer of 1868, Gabriel made many studies of her, including the pensive *Reverie*—suggestive of the later *Day-dream*—and *Aurea Catena* with its delicate bondage of the golden chain, a touch of symbolism upon which William Rossetti who gave the latter work its Latin title, consciously prided himself. Henceforth Gabriel painted Janey almost unceasingly until his last days.

Upon Rossetti's poetry Janey's influence is equally obvious. In the verses he now wrote, as in his paintings, a change of mood, a new mental and emotional orientation gradually revealed itself. The ostensible subjects of the two illustrative sonnets he wrote in 1866-67, comparing "body's beauty" with "soul's beauty," were his pictures *Lilith* and *Sibylla Palmifera*, each representing respectively Fanny and Alexa Wilding; but it was no doubt the revival of his earlier idealism caused by his renewed intimacy with Janey, that inspired their mood of revolt against a merely sensuous eroticism. There is no indication that Gabriel wrote any other verse in the year 1867, but in January of 1868, in his sonnet for *Venus Verticordia*, there is a hint of coming change as of one who turns hesitatingly, almost tearfully indeed, after profound disillusion, from the weariness of mere unhappy retrospect and stagnation to a new tremulous hope born of the first stirrings of a new or renewed but heartfelt passion. In this same year, at last completing the portrait of Janey begun two years before, Gabriel expressed in his illustrative sonnet, *The Portrait*, a passionate and intimate admiration for Janey, its subject, exulting:

> Lo it is done. Above the enthroning throat
>   The mouth's mould testifies of voice and kiss,
>   The shadowed eyes remember and foresee.
> Her face is made her shrine. Let all men note
>   That in all years (O Love, thy gift is this!)
>   They that would look on her must come to me.

It was doubtless with Swinburne's help, for Rossetti was no Latinist, that he composed the couplet akin in meaning to the last line of this sonnet, and appended it to Janey's portrait:—

> Conjuge clara poetâ, et praeclarissima vultu,
> Denique picturâ clara sit illa meâ.*

To a crayon drawing he made of Janey the following year, he similarly appended two lines of his sonnet, *The Portrait*, thus again definitely identifying Janey as the subject of the poem. Already doubt, ennui, listlessness, regret were yielding to a new ecstasy, to the "regenerate rapture" of which he sang some months later in *The Monochord*. Once again within the warmth and light of the idealizing erotic illusion, he was happy. Surely, in Janey he had found at last the incarnation of his ideal, one who, as it seemed to him, uniting in her own person both the physical and spiritual elements of his erotic dream, met all the demands of his long frustrated desire.

* *v. Notes.*

Here, apparently, lay the secret of his "indomitable song." At forty he was entering upon a poetic renascence which was to endure at the point of intensity for the next two or three years, and of which the main record is his passionate sonnet-sequence, *The House of Life*. That much of it deals with a clandestine passion is evident in many of the sonnets themselves, while the self-contradictions, inconsistencies and mystifications of Rossetti and his friends in their references to these sonnets would be quite incomprehensible if the poems were solely inspired by the poet's dead wife.

That Rossetti and his brother wished to prevent any interpretation of *The House of Life** as definitely autobiographical, is evident. Sometimes, indeed, in their anxiety they unwittingly contradicted themselves and one another. "These poems," wrote Gabriel in one of his note-books, "are in no sense 'occasional.' The 'Life' recorded (*alt.* involved) is neither *my* life nor *your* life, but life purely and simply (*alt.* representative) as tripled with Love and Death." Yet William Rossetti, obviously ignorant of this denial, publicly declared after his brother's death, "The sonnets are mostly of the kind which we call 'occasional'; some incident happened, or some emotion was dominant, and the author wrote a sonnet regarding it. When a good number had been written, they came to form, if considered collectively, a sort of record of his feelings and experiences, his reading of the problems of life—an inscribed tablet of his mind: then, but not before then, he began marshalling them together, and entitled them *The House of Life*." Nevertheless, William's statement is no such contradiction of his brother as at first appears, for William, in fact, meant by "occasional," "casual"; and by thus tacitly denying that the sonnets were the expression of a profound passion for a single individual, he attempted, like his brother, to minimize their autobiographic quality. Yet even William was forced to admit a certain continuity in the sonnets. "The first part of the series, named *Love* [*sic*] *and Change*," he wrote, "has clearly some considerable amount of interdependence; the second part, *Change and Fate*, is wider and more diversified in its range."

For Gabriel, however, "occasional" meant essentially the

* *v. Notes.*

expression of personal experience,[1] and in a note to a manuscript version of *The House of Life* (a similar but more detailed
attempt to repudiate the personal element), he clearly revealed
the meaning he attached to "occasional," and his desire to
convince the reader that the sonnets were genuinely impersonal.
"To speak in the first person," he declared, "is often to speak
most vividly; but these emotional poems are in no sense
'occasional.' The 'life' involved is life representative, as associated with love and death, with aspiration and foreboding, or
with ideal art and beauty. Whether the recorded moment exist
in the region of fact or of thought is a question indifferent to
the Muse, so long only as her touch can quicken it." In that
passage, Rossetti accurately but in general terms, described the
content of *The House of Life*, as I have come to understand it
in the light of his own biography. For in that light *The House of
Life* suggests a life "associated with love and death, with aspiration and foreboding, or with ideal art and beauty" exactly as
Rossetti said.

But when he turns, as here—quite unnecessarily, if as he
would have us believe, the sonnets are purely imaginative—to
vague, evasive comments as to their detachment from actuality,
he unintentionally arouses suspicions that they do in fact contain the biographic significance he half denies and obviously
wishes to hide. Even in the last months of his life, shortly
before the publication of his *Ballads and Sonnets* in 1881, the
volume in which he completed *The House of Life*, he was still
much perturbed about this question of personal self-revelation
in the sonnets. The result was a note, "a disavowal of personality in the sonnets," as he described it. But in his nervous
indecision as to its retention, he consulted his friend Watts-
Dunton who must have advised its withdrawal. Even then,
however, Rossetti hesitated once more, telling his friend:
"I am really much perplexed whether to restore that note
in front of *The House of Life* or not." In the event it did not
appear.

Nor was this Rossetti's sole anxiety of this kind. Not less
irksome was the question of the dating of the sonnets. To date
them in detail might be, incidentally, to suggest awkward

---

[1] *cf.* Rossetti's use of the word in the quotation on p. 475 *inf.*

questions that might in turn provoke yet more awkward revelations; to reveal, in fact, those personal relationships of his private life he was anxious to conceal. In the first of the two so-called "trial books" of Rossetti's poems, privately printed in 1869, he made some pretence of dating, which, vague though it is, does at least definitely describe the majority of the sonnets in *The House of Life* as "recent." "Most of these poems," so runs the prefatory note, "were written between 1847 and 1853; and are here printed, if not without revision, yet generally much in their original state. They are a few among a good many then written, but of the others I have now no complete copies. The 'Sonnets and Songs' are chiefly more recent work." A few months later, however, when Rossetti's *Poems* appeared, in 1870, this prefatory note had become even less informative than before: "Many poems in this volume were written between 1847 and 1853. Others are of recent date, and a few belong to the intervening period. It has been thought unnecessary to specify the earlier work, as nothing is included which the author believes to be immature."

The House of Life was by no means complete when the volume of 1870 appeared, and its still tentative nature was indicated in Rossetti's title to that section of the book, "SONNETS AND SONGS, *Towards a Work to be called* 'THE HOUSE OF LIFE.'" Then followed the reticent note: "(The first twenty-eight sonnets and the seven first songs treat of love. These and the others would belong to separate sections of the projected work)." Eleven years later, when at last the completed *House of Life* was about to appear, Rossetti, after two days of anxious debate and hesitation, inserted a prefatory note to the sonnet sequence which ran:—"The present full series of *The House of Life* consists of sonnets only. It will be evident that many among those now first added are still the work of earlier years." This note was not merely uninformative, it was definitely misleading in its suggestion that many of the new sonnets (as well as those previously published), were written in youth, and so would be interpreted, biographically, if at all, as inspired by the woman who became the poet's wife. Similarly, Rossetti, upon the publication of the sonnets, changed some of their titles, apparently for the same reason. Thus *The Love-Lamp* became *The Lamp's Shrine; Love's Antiphony* was changed to *Youth's Antiphony*, and the frequency with which William Rossetti misquotes the title to the first section of *The House of Life*, "*Youth and Change*" as "*Love and Change*," makes one suspect that William's misquotation was its original title, and that there too, before publication, "Youth" was substituted for "Love."* At any rate, the carefully considered note preceding the complete sonnet-sequence was apparently calculated to mislead. In fact, of the forty-seven sonnets which appear in *The House of Life* in 1881 but nowhere in the *Poems* of 1870, only two are early, the second and third of the sonnets entitled *Old and New Art*, which are not love poems and were written in 1848. All the remaining forty-five new sonnets date from this later period of "regenerate rapture"; one is of 1869, one of 1870, twenty-seven are of 1871, seven of 1873, two of 1875, one of 1879, two of 1880, and four of 1881. That these and most of the other sonnets in the series were inspired by Miss Siddal whom Rossetti had fallen in love with as long before as 1850, married in 1860 and who had died in 1862 is incredible.

Nor was William Rossetti more enlightening as to dates, occasions, biographical and poetical significance, despite his many references to these sonnets and his paraphrase and commentary on *The House of Life*. Indeed some of his assertions are mutually contradictory. Thus, in his edition of his brother's *Collected Works*, published in 1887, five years after Rossetti's death, William declared: "I am far from having a clear idea or definite information as to the true dates of the sonnets." Yet two years later he wrote in *Dante Gabriel Rossetti as Designer and Writer*, "Most of the sonnets of *The House of Life* have naturally been familiar to me from an early date after they were composed," and, becoming less secretive with the passage of time since his brother's death, he asserted in his edition of Rossetti's *Works* published in 1911, "I know a good deal as to the true dates of the sonnets, and in the table of contents I supply the requisite information." Despite demonstrable errors in several cases,* all the evidence suggests that the dating of the sonnets in the *Works* of 1911 is substantially correct, and

* *v. Notes.*

as such it is, save for the few exceptions indicated, accepted by the present writer. The light these dates throw upon the origin as well as the general and individual significance of these sonnets is very great.

That Rossetti, so averse to any public revelation of an artist's private life, should, especially in the circumstances in which he now apparently found himself, fear any public revelation of his own, was inevitable. Thus, his almost paradoxical aim was to reveal yet conceal the most personally significant because most deeply emotional phases of his experience. To do this, he pretended that the life presented was impersonal, "representative," and as we have seen, disavowed "personality" in the sonnets,[1] besides attempting to conceal the dates of their composition and the experiences which were their inspiration. At one time, so William declared, his brother had meant "to write and publish some sort of exposition of *The House of Life*," an intention which, like so many of Rossetti's but in this case with better reason, was never carried out.

William believed he had never discussed with his brother the meaning of the sonnets, since "He and I were wont to assume that there was between us a certain community of perception which would enable me to understand what he wrote, either immediately or without close scrutiny of the details, or at any rate in the event of my applying myself seriously to a consideration of the written page." And for William, the result of this scrutiny, made for the purpose of his own paraphrase, was "that several things which I had hitherto regarded with vague and inexpress acquiescence, neither analysing nor pausing over them, were in fact charged with some particular significance, be it valuable or the reverse; and on the whole I now see more clearly than I ever did before the purport of the sonnets, and whether their purport is important or unimportant." Many words, but little illumination, as so often with William's elucidations, but here, little illumination was intended.

Yet, despite all this mystification, Rossetti himself in several sonnets—the Introductory sonnet to *The House of Life*, *Transfigured Life*, and *The Song Throe*—openly asserted the evidently autobiographical quality of the series, which was, indeed,

[1] *v. inf.* pp. 400, 418, footnote 1; p. 544 and Note to p. 142.

later admitted by his nearest relatives and friends. In a prefatory note to these sonnets, in the Siddal edition of Rossetti's works, which appeared at the close of the century, William, speaking of his brother and *The House of Life*, declared it "embodies salient incidents and emotions in his own life. There are very few of the sonnets which are not strictly personal, and not one through which his individual feelings and views do not transpire."[1] "When he loved a woman," wrote Watts-Dunton, "it was because he must, not because he would: and there is not one love-sonnet in his book which is a merely literary production." William Sharp, the friend of Rossetti's last years, wrote in similar vein: "But the impression nevertheless remains that the series is, in the main, a record of individual emotions suggested by the presence and absence of embodied love and what such absence and presence individually entail, a record of such and little further—a House, not of Life, but of Love. . . . These sonnets are the record of what a poet-soul has felt, and we see that love meant with him a dream of happiness while present, a dream of regret and a sense of frustration when passed away. . . . His genius lived and had its being in the shadow of love." For Sharp, like William Rossetti, and all who touched upon the subject, used vague and general terms to describe the beloved woman, instead of such direct statement as we should expect had she been the poet's long dead wife.

Indeed the life which energizes these sonnets is not life "representative," but life essentially individual, individualistic and of a particular period, despite the largely generalized form of expression created by the omission of definite personal and local elements. Like so much of Rossetti's art, both poetic and pictorial, this sonnet-sequence is essentially what he called Dante's *Vita Nuova* and his own *St. Agnes of Intercession*—"autopsychology." From this arise both the biographical significance and general obscurity of *The House of Life* which for the most part expresses thoughts and feelings aroused and conditioned in Rossetti by personal experiences of which the reader is left wholly or partly ignorant. Hence it follows that *The House of Life* and Rossetti's biography are interdependent,

---

[1] *cf.* Rossetti's account of his sonnet-writing, *inf.* p. 475.

each in some degree illuminating the other. Thus it is that in these poems of Rossetti's renascence we may often glimpse, as in a darkened mirror, the general course of his emotional (and in some degree intellectual) experience and development, during this critical period of his life.[1]

The first verses of Gabriel's poetic revival, the *Willow-wood* sonnets, and their immediate successors, suggest Rossetti's state during this winter of 1868–69. The four *Willow-wood* sonnets surely celebrated, as a whole, the ending of the long years of silence, severance, disappointment, and frustration in the "Willow-wood" through which he had wandered, haunted by

The shades of those our days that had no tongue.

For the *Willow-wood* sonnets apparently record a belated but mutual admission of a long-suppressed passion, and the canonization of the two Lovers by Love himself. Gabriel, in fact, explained the theme of these *Willow-wood* sonnets as "a dream or trance of divided love momentarily reunited by the longing fancy"; a declaration which William afterwards cautiously but significantly qualified with the remark: "severance by untoward conditions on earth appears to be more particularly contemplated." Nevertheless, the sonnets are nearly always lightly misinterpreted by commentators as an expression of Rossetti's passionate longing for reunion with his dead wife. Indeed a few months later, when Christina Rossetti wrote another poem of severance, entitling it *An Echo from Willow-wood*, William long afterwards suggested that while her poem *might* refer to Gabriel and Lizzie, he thought it much more probable that a reference was intended to a "wholly different train of events"; by which he probably meant the relations between Janey Morris and Rossetti, the inspiration it would seem, of almost the whole of *The House of Life*, not to mention other poems written during these years.

Meanwhile, from the darkly expectant mood of *Willow-wood* with its vain regrets for the past, its tremulous hope for the immediate future, Rossetti passed through the passionless despair of *Newborn Death* to the somewhat uneasy mood in

[1] For a full appreciation of their significance, the poems named but not quoted (owing to the length of this work), should be read in conjunction with my own comments here. *Vide* also dated lists of poems in Notes to pp. 385, 434, and 475.

1869, of *A Superscription* where Rossetti's abstractions, "Might-have-been," "No More," "Too late," "Farewell," in short, Disappointment, Retrospect, Disillusion, Separation, mock with bitter memories of Love's unhappiness during his life with Lizzie, this growing hope of a new, completely happy love, holding maliciously before his eyes the mirror of his unhappy, frustrated past, reviving memories that "in ambush at his heart," are ever ready to leap forth in warning against any new, extravagant hope.[1] For this "superscription," to use the name of the sonnet, which he wrote on January 24, 1869, is surely a new love "superscribed" as it were, upon his heart as on a palimpsest; written, that is, upon the old love. The image must have been strongly present to Gabriel, for a few months later he projected a tale, *The Palimpsest*, which, however, was never written.[2]

Shortly afterwards, in the March number of the *Fortnightly Review*, Rossetti published sixteen sonnets* under the title *Of Life, Love and Death*, including, he said, "a few new ones." The three themes indicated in his title, becoming an obsessive trinity, henceforth haunted his imagination to the end. The "new" sonnets, apparently four in number,[3] evidently continued the themes of his recent sonnets, particularly we may suspect, personal experiences following Janey's visits to Cheyne Walk in the spring of 1868. Emotional strain, physical decline, the constant, uneasy oscillation of the poet's thought between the polarities of Love and Death form the significant content of these latest poems, which clearly suggest the revitalization by a new passion, of the victim of ennui, dejection, insomnia, losing all hold upon life, who had recently so disappointed Allingham at Lymington. Something of profound significance to Rossetti had surely occurred in the interval, something that had changed his former despairing lethargy into this uneasy ecstasy in which hope and doubt now strove for mastery. Since Janey had dwelt within its walls, even his dull, empty home

---

[1] *v. sup.* p. 300.

[2] The probability that my interpretation of *A Superscription* as *Palimpsest* is correct is increased by the fact that not until later did I learn of the projected tale, *The Palimpsest*.

[3] *Sleepless Dreams, Winged Hours, Inclusiveness, Run and Won* (later renamed *The Vase of Life*).

* *v. Notes.*

in Cheyne Walk had become for him a source of somewhat
conscience-striken inspiration. For William Rossetti, who dated
Gabriel's sonnet *Inclusiveness*, 1869, supposed the reference was
"to an actual room in Rossetti's old-fashioned house, 16 Cheyne
Walk, Chelsea," when the poet cried with almost hysterical
intensity:

> May not this ancient room thou sitt'st in dwell
>   In separate living souls for joy or pain?
>   Nay, all its corners may be painted plain
> Where Heaven shows pictures of some life spent well,
>   And may be stamped, a memory all in vain,
> Upon the sight of lidless eyes in Hell.

Such, at least in William Rossetti's opinion, were the
thoughts now aroused in Gabriel by his house in Cheyne Walk.
It is Henry James who gives us an interesting glimpse of Janey
and her husband at home, at the same period, March 1869,
the very time that Rossetti's sonnets were appearing in the
Fortnightly Review. "Morris," wrote James to his sister, "lives
on the same premises as his shop in Queen's Square, Bloomsbury, an antiquated ex-fashionable region, smelling strong of
the last century, with a hoary effigy of Queen Anne in the
middle. Morris's poetry, you see, is only his sub-trade. To
begin with, he is a manufacturer of stained-glass windows,
tiles, ecclesiastical and mediaeval tapestry, altar-cloths, and in
fine everything quaint, archaic, pre-Raphaelite—and I may
add, exquisite. Of course his business is small and may be
carried on in his house: the things he makes are so handsome,
rich and expensive (besides being articles of the very last
luxury) that his *fabrique* can't be on a very large scale. But
everything he has and does is superb and beautiful. But more
curious than anything is himself. He designs with his own head
and hands all the figures and patterns used in his glass and
tapestry, and furthermore works the latter, stitch by stitch, with
his own fingers—aided by those of his wife and little girls."
After which James entered upon the detailed personal description of Mrs. Morris already given,[1] before continuing with his
general account, thus: "On the wall was a large nearly full-
length portrait of her by Rossetti, so strange and unreal that

---

[1] *v. sup.* pp. 371–2.

if you hadn't seen her you'd pronounce it a distempered vision, but in fact an extremely good likeness. After dinner . . . Morris read us one of his unpublished poems, from the second series of his un-'Earthly Paradise,' and his wife, having a bad toothache, lay on the sofa, with her handkerchief to her face. There was something very quaint and remote from our actual life, it seemed to me, in the whole scene: Morris reading in his flowing antique numbers a legend of prodigies and terrors (the story of Bellerophon, it was), around us all the picturesque bric-à-brac of the apartment (every article of furniture literally a 'specimen' of something or other), and in the corner this dark silent mediaeval woman with her mediaeval toothache. Morris himself is extremely pleasant and quite different from his wife. . . ." Such is the only intimate picture of the Morris *ménage* which has come down to us. Probably "this dark silent mediaeval woman" found her environment as "quaint and remote from our actual life" as it seemed to James. From the sentimental unrealities of *The Earthly Paradise*, her visits to Cheyne Walk as Rossetti's model must have provided the relief of complete contrast.

As for Rossetti, a new interest, a new hope, a new anxiety, were evidently counteracting the earlier cynical indifference, were making him as in *Sleepless Dreams*, the uneasy victim of renewed desire crying:

> O night desirous as the nights of youth,[1]

yet darkened by painful memories; nights

> Girt in dark growths, yet glimmering with one star,

the star of a new hope, beckoning him onward, while sleep withdrew,

> . . . waved back by Joy and Ruth,

that is by the pity of the dark past and the joyous expectation brought into his dreary existence by this new promise.

But disappointment had made Gabriel cautious. He was reluctant to trust this new hope, to believe in the happy realiza-

---

[1] That the poet referred to a period of his later life and therefore to one comparatively recent is shown more clearly by the earlier version of this line as it appeared in the *Fortnightly Review* for March 1869:

> O vain night sweeter than the nights of youth.

The original title of the sonnet, *Sleepless Love*, intensifies its suggestion of immediacy.

tion of his desire. Those interminable, sleepless nights of *Willow-wood* were not, he feared, so quickly to pass. The doubts and fears he had described in *A Superscription*, mocking his new tremulous hope, his reawakened desire, found even fuller expression in *Sleepless Dreams*, a sonnet of intimate, half-uncon-scious symbolism which almost fuses the two images of the embracing darkness and the passionately desired body of his love.

> Nay, night deep-leaved. And would Love feign in thee [1]
> The shadowy palpitating grove that bears
> Rest for man's eyes and music for his ears?
> O lonely night! art thou not known to me,
> A thicket hung with masks of mockery
> And watered with the wasteful warmth of tears?

To these restless nights of longing and uncertainty succeed the stolen lovers' meetings of *Winged Hours*, long awaited, quickly passing, in which Love appears as the bird of Dante's exquisite symbolism in the *Paradiso*—evidently a favourite image with Rossetti who employs it several times—

> Come l'augello, intra l'amate fronde [2].

But over these lovers' meetings lies heavy the fear of impending separation, of the frustration of their love, just as it does in Christina's *Echo from Willow-wood*. And only a few days after the publication of these sonnets in the *Fortnightly Review*, Gabriel wrote another sonnet, *Vain Virtues*, of profound moral condemnation, obviously in some such conscience-stricken mood as had inspired *Inclusiveness*. Fair deeds, he declared in this sonnet, according to William Rossetti's interpretation, are like fair virgins who, had death come before sin, would have been saints, but whose virtues are damned, like their vices, by subsequent sin. This destruction of the good by evil was, he affirmed,

> . . . the sorriest thing that enters Hell.

---

[1] *Fortnightly Review* version:

> Nay, night! Would false Love counterfeit in thee . . .

[2] *cf.*

> Each hour until we meet is as a bird
> That wings from far his gradual way along
> The rustling covert of my soul, . . .   (*Winged Hours*).

and

> Like leaves through which a bird has flown . . . (*The Portrait*).

Such then, were the sonnets that appeared a few months after Rossetti's return from Penkill at the close of 1868, sick, nerve-racked, depressed, half-blind, and meditating suicide.* Had the effect of his unhappiness been to break down the restraint set upon some long-suppressed passion such as he and Janey were said to have felt at Oxford, eleven years before? Had it led the lovers from a mutual admission of their love to a complete surrender to its sway? That now as fifteen years before with Lizzie, Gabriel's poetic inspiration was primarily the intoxication of an intense physical and spiritual passion cannot be doubted. This revival of emotional significance in his life after the long, desolate years in "Willow-wood," was finding its almost inevitable sequel in a poetic revival. There, behind a screen of abstractions and Dantesque imagery, Rossetti surely opened the secret chambers of his own "House of Life," which was essentially a "House of Love."

May 1869 came with promise of summer. But Janey, too, suffered from ill-health, and Gabriel's moods were often anxious, his thoughts still often with the dead. "Dies atra," he dated his sonnet *Death-in-Love*, commemorating the "birthday" of his still-born child in imagery which—like that of *Sleepless Dreams* and other sonnets—bore apparently a double significance, expressing not only his sorrow for the loss of his child, but also, in his growing fatalism, his fears that this new passion, like that for Lizzie, was doomed to frustration. A few days later his own birthday, his forty-first, evoked his usual plaintive mood on those occasions, as he mourned "most good things gone, and others that will never come now."

Janey's illness, increasing, was doubtless a chief cause of Rossetti's depression. He painted her now as Beatrice, and in the sonnet *English May*[1] gave vent to impotent anguish on her behalf. He must have been reminded of those days at Hastings with poor Lizzie, fifteen years before, when to Allingham he had sent some such lament in prose as now, for Janey, found expression in *English May*. The memory of his dead wife was also very active at this time. No doubt his tendency to self-reproaches was reanimated by his new passion. He had Lizzie's mediocre works photographed;[2] vowed he would never have

---

[1] First entitled *May 1869*.   [2] *v. sup.* p. 348.   * *v. Notes.*

parted with them had he not believed them "but preludes to much greater ones," and from Norton, who at the Preraphaelite Exhibition of 1857 had bought Lizzie's early drawing *Clerk Saunders*, he now got it back, sending Norton one of Janey in exchange.

These, however, were but diversions. Rossetti's main interest throughout this spring and summer of 1869 was his painting of Janey as *Pandora*, the "all-gifted." It inspired in mid-March his sonnet on the picture, a sonnet full, surely, of hidden as well as literal meaning, an invocation to the woman who had freed his spirit from its despondent lethargy and preserved Hope. The sonnet is, indeed, no mere academic, pseudo-classical exercise, but quivers with a personal passion that at times breaks through the mythological pattern and ostensible theme.

> What of the end, Pandora? Was it thine,
>   The deed that set these fiery pinions free?
>
> *   *   *
>
> What of the end? These beat their wings at will,
> The ill-born things, the good things turned to ill,
>   Powers of the impassioned hours prohibited.

The material of the sonnet is very obvious: the fusion of the classical Pandora, of the picture and its symbolism with the living model, Janey, and the personal problems associated with her. Thus even the mythology assumes a more or less personal symbolism, the poet asking if this Pandora has been made half divine in order to anger Juno (Hera, the goddess of marriage and of women), bring a frown to the brow of Pallas (Athene) the goddess of wisdom, and infuse

> In Venus' eyes the gaze of Proserpine;

that is, her love must be perplexed by difficulties such as those of Proserpine, the unhappy wife doomed to divide her life between the brightness of the upper world of freedom and the sadness of her existence with an unloved husband below.

But through the conscious, intellectual structure of the poem the basic emotional stimulus breaks, with the poignant, personal cry of regret over

> the good things turned to ill,
> Powers of the impassioned hours prohibited.

For a moment the disguise of Pandora is dropped, and although immediately afterwards Rossetti remembers his picture and reassumes his classical costume, the content is still the basic anxiety that dictated the opening of the sonnet as it now does its close:

> Aye, clench the casket now! Whither they go
> Thou mayst not dare to think: nor canst thou know
> If Hope still pent there be alive or dead.

That the whole sonnet is intensely personal, is surely evident. Swinburne, who doubtless understood the underlying significance of the poem, praised it as the finest of all Rossetti's sonnets on his pictures, and also the painting itself as "amongst the mightiest in its godlike terror and imperial trouble of beauty," language which vaguely hints at a deeper meaning.[1]

Besides *Death in Love* and *English May*, Rossetti now wrote "several new sonnets," and, in the first days of June composed two Italian ones* which, suppressed by William Rossetti as by Gabriel himself, have only comparatively recently been published, and glorify a long-suppressed passion symbolized in a long-undeclared but now triumphant desire to kiss the mouth of the beloved:

> O mouth! that in the hour of reward
> So often I kissed,
> From which so often heard
> Words of divine acquiescence,
> Welcomed with a thousand vows;
> May the sacred incense of thy kisses
> Enfold in ever thickening clouds,
> The many old ghosts at last buried,
> And fill the heavens with the immensity of our love.

So we may translate a part of one of these sonnets which closes with a reference to Gabriel's now almost obsessive trinity of *The House of Life*, life, love, and death. This trinity in his own soul, he declared, adored this mouth alone. There can be little doubt that these two Italian sonnets found amongst Rossetti's papers in the possession at one time of William

---

[1] *cf.* the sonnet *Venus Victrix* (1871) in which the beloved is again compared to Juno and Pallas; also in this connection, *v. inf.* p. 400, footnote 1.

* *v. Notes.*

Rossetti but unpublished by him, were in fact the two Italian sonnets Gabriel now wrote. In another poem of this time, *Dark Lily*, later renamed *Love-lily*, he not only emphasized his love's intensity and sincerity, but also revealed his beloved's identity with "Pandora," the "One Hope" life had hitherto denied him, as well as the reintegrating quality of this love, reuniting "body and soul," or, as in another sonnet he termed them, "passion and worship," the reunion of the long-severed components of erotic instinct, of "higher" and "lower," whose separation since Lizzie's death, during the reign of Fanny and her like, were both cause and symptom of Rossetti's moral decline.

Soon, however, Janey was so ill that sittings had to be abandoned. Gabriel, his passion for the second time in his life dogged by illness, was deeply concerned and relapsed into morbid brooding. Then with an effort, he for a short time resumed social life "in the hope," he told his mother, "of shaking off ennui." Thus it was that one evening in June he again met Matthew Arnold, this time at a dinner party. "A rather pleasant evening," Arnold described it in his detached, colourless way. Seven years later Swinburne complained: "Those two admirable poets, to my life-long perplexity and disgust, can see nothing almost in each other's work to admire or enjoy." "I have become (for me) quite a diner-out," Gabriel informed Miss Losh in July, "and have gone among friends and acquaintances more this season than for some seasons past."

Meanwhile, as Janey's health grew worse, Gabriel's anxiety increased. In mid-July she was so ill that Morris took her to the then fashionable German spa Bad Ems for a "cure." Lonely and restless in Janey's absence, Gabriel worked at *Sibylla Palmifera* and *La Pia*, half-contemplating a visit to Italy, worrying about his own eyes and, above all, about Janey's health. She wrote to him regularly, and at first the news was encouraging. In mid-August, hearing that she hoped to be back in London within three weeks, Gabriel, in order to be present upon her return, decided to take his own long-delayed holiday immediately, and complaining of heat and over-work at once set off again for Penkill.

VI

PENKILL ONCE MORE
1869

What shall be said of this embattled day
  And armed occupation of this night
  By all thy foes beleaguered,—now when sight
Nor sound denotes the loved one far away?
Of these thy vanquished hours what shalt thou say,—
  As every sense to which she dealt delight
  Now labours lonely o'er the stark noon-height
To reach the sunset's desolate disarray?

Stand still, fond fettered wretch! while memory's art
  Parades the Past before thy face, and lures
  Thy spirit to her passionate portraitures:
Till the tempestuous tide-gates flung apart
Flood with wild will the hollows of thy heart,
  And thy heart rends thee, and thy body endures.

Parted Love D. G. ROSSETTI

THE FEW WEEKS Gabriel passed at Penkill were darkened by a mental and emotional crisis more intense than any he had known since Lizzie's death. Separated from Janey, from London, and his painting, worried and restricted by his failing sight, he was as never before thrown upon his own resources, delivered with little or no external counterpoise to his inner world of secret anxieties, of overwrought thought and emotion. In this empty present, Rossetti's imagination became the strained, anxious meeting point of an unhappy past and uncertain future. To the many frustrations which had beset him in life, love, and art, was now added the final frustration of his physical decline, and apparently of an overmastering, mutual but illicit passion which, long suppressed, had now found expression only to suffer irritation and debasement beneath the moral and social ban of Victorian England.

This mental strain, indeed, soon revealed itself in ominous ways to those about Rossetti. During the empty years following Lizzie's death, he had gradually sunk into a lethargy in which death seemed to him not only inevitable, but even at times desirable as a sole possibility of escape. It was thus in the sonnet *New-born Death*, in the now permanently associated imagery of death with his still-born daughter,[1] that he had recently welcomed death itself as

> . . . an infant child
> Which her worn mother Life upon my knee
> Has set to grow my friend and play with me.

It was a preparation for the euthanasia he was now steadily, largely unconsciously but increasingly turning to desire. Since then, however, reborn passion had revitalized him, and this new threat to it evoked no longer a passive but an active response. Suicide, a half-playful topic of his adolescence, more recently a vague, morbid suggestion, was now, if we may trust Scott, becoming a definitely dangerous impulse.

For standing one afternoon with Gabriel and Miss Boyd above "The Devil's Punch Bowl," a deep black whirlpool made by a waterfall near Penkill Castle, Scott suddenly saw, or thought he saw, in Gabriel's face as he peered over a ledge of rock at the top of the ravine and gazed down upon the swirling waters below, an intention of suicide, as if he were about to hurl himself down into them. Miss Boyd, said Scott, also remarked Gabriel's expression, and both rushed forward to prevent him. But losing courage Gabriel had already fallen back in panic from the brink, into the arms of the trembling Scott. The whirlpool almost certainly inspired a new symbolization of his passion, in the last line of a never-finished poem Gabriel was then writing, *The Orchard Pit*, for there, in words closely resembling Scott's description of the Penkill pool, he wrote:

> . . . I love her as in the maelstrom's cup
> The whirled stone loves the leaf inseparable
> That clings to it round all the circling swell,
> And that the same last eddy swallows up.[2]

A day or two later, Gabriel's growing hysteria, Scott declared, again revealed itself in his taking a surprisingly tame chaffinch that settled on his hand during a walk, for the

---

[1] *cf.* also stanzas 160 and 174 of *The Bride's Prelude*, revised until publication in 1881, and the sonnets *Death in Love* (*v. sup.* p. 389), and *Stillborn Love* (*v. inf.* p. 422).
[2] *cf.*   Poor handful of bright spring-water
Flung in the whirlpool's shrieking face. . . .
               Jenny, 1848, but "mostly 1858-69."

spirit of Lizzie prophesying misfortune.[1] So moved was he, that with Scott he returned in silence to the castle; and when on arrival he heard that during their absence the gate-bell had rung without apparent cause, he turned what Scott described as his "curiously ferocious look" upon him, meaningly. But even in recounting the incident of the chaffinch to Alice Boyd, Gabriel, again sceptical, lost confidence. It was probably now that he wrote those stray lines of verse:

> This little day, a bird that flew to me,
> Has swiftly flown out of my hand again.
> Ah! have I listened to its fugitive strain
> For what its tidings of the sky may be?

But did Scott, who loved the "supernatural" and the "dramatic," despite his boasted scepticism, exaggerate these two incidents? William Rossetti thought so, and they must, in the hand of such a recorder as Scott, have lost nothing in the telling.

For Scott was temperamentally far more superstitious than Rossetti, who, indeed, instead of accepting the fashionable "spiritualism" of the day, as most of his friends did, profanely ridiculed such famous mediums as Mrs. Marshall and the ineffable Mrs. Guppy, the latter, said Scott, comparing her with Fanny, "as uncultured and mentally unfurnished as the evil genius of D. G. R." Yet it was Mrs. Guppy who almost converted the angry and sceptical Browning himself! For a year or two now, Gabriel had, with Scott, William, and Janey, occasionally attended spiritualistic séances. But his amused scepticism was very evident. Once when flowers grew out of tables and eau-de-Cologne descended upon the company, he derisively addressed the spirits as "bogies," until in anger they squirted water over the experimenters and withdrew! "Nothing in it which could reasonably be called convincing—unless possibly the affair of the mysterious light seen by Mrs. Morris

[1] cf.   Ah sweet! Even now, in that bird's song,
>   Strove not her accents there,
>   Fain to be hearkened?

The Blessed Damozel, 1847, "seriously revised 1870." These lines, however, definitely existed three years before this incident, as they appear in the version of the poem published in The Oxford and Cambridge Magazine in 1856. Probably the incident with the bird at Penkill revived the original poetic idea which Rossetti in his nervous state transferred to actuality.

as well as others," he had agreed with William after a séance in April 1868. If as Scott asserted, Gabriel in 1866 had tried to raise the spirit of his dead wife by table-turning, the result had obviously been to strengthen his native scepticism, and it was probably William's naïve questioning of various "spirits" which William thought *might* be Lizzie's, that as Gabriel's health and stamina declined, restimulated whatever interest he had had in the occult, an interest apparently much weaker than that of many of his friends, including Scott, William Rossetti, Ruskin, the Joneses, the Brownings, Whistler, and Holman Hunt.

So strong now was the tension, that the sceptic of April 1868 was at this time, sixteen months later, at Penkill, in such a state of hysteria, if we may believe Scott, that his friend actually feared in Gabriel "the subversion of reason itself." Bored by Rossetti's anxiety state, by his fears for his sight and general health, Scott complained that Gabriel was "more hypochondriacal than ever," lamented his whisky-drinking—"their nightly sederunts more prolonged"—while Rossetti vainly wooed elusive sleep. But so far there was no sign of chloral, a drug still unknown to Rossetti.

Penkill, Gabriel described to Alice Boyd years afterwards as "the place so well-known to me, and where the letter-bag was so welcome," and indeed Janey's frequent letters to him were now, in her absence, his chief consolation. At first, written in fairly hopeful mood, they brought news of improving health. But soon they changed to a less cheerful vein. "The news from Ems is pretty well, but I could wish it much better," Rossetti told Howell at the end of August. "If this were well nothing could be very ill." Howell begged one of Gabriel's drawings of Janey, but he refused to part with it, and, greatly perturbed by the loss of another—things were always being "lost" when Howell was about—wrote to Howell, anxiously: "Have you found the Janey in a chair? Do, do, do, find it." As the days passed, his anxiety for Janey's recovery increased. "No worse than at her last writing when the news was very hopeful," he told Brown at the close of August, "but I can see by the tone of her letter, and indeed by much she says plainly, that she is discouraged at the slow progress made." "My last news from

Ems shows very gradual progress, but still some, I suppose,"
he told Brown again, five days later. "Miracles are evidently
not to be expected." By this time, however, he knew that within
about a fortnight the travellers would probably be home.

Thus it was that in the summer of 1869, amidst the peace of
Penkill, Gabriel, almost blind and unable to paint, seeking in
Janey's absence a respite from ennui, unrest, and pain, turned
again to poetry, to find in the expression of his passion, of this
"regenerate rapture," some relief from the anxieties and irrita-
tions that beset him. Revising recent verses and writing new
ones, he produced during his short stay at Penkill, some
twenty poems, chiefly sonnets, which evidently continued and
developed the themes of those he had recently written and
published in the *Fortnightly Review*. Like those, the verses he
now wrote were obviously a record of his own recent experience,
describing, indeed, all moods and phases of the regenerative
passion which was their inspiration, as well as the state of
frustration and almost suicidal despair from which it had
rescued him at a time when, as he sang, in *The Sun's Shame*,

> . . . the soul's death of bodily death is fain.

The horror of that morbid state, as well as the "redemptive"
Love to which he owed his deliverance, formed the themes of
The Morrow's Message, Lovesight, and *Love's Testament* first more
significantly named *Love's Redemption*.

At times he would turn from the mingled joy and bitterness
of proximate retrospect to the actuality about him, and the
pain of Janey's absence found poignant expression in *Parted
Love*.[1] There he sang the misery of those "vanquished hours"
he must endure while

> . . . sight
> Nor sound denotes the loved one far away,

the agony of vain longing which racked him

> As every sense to which she dealt delight
> Now labours lonely o'er the stark noon-height
> To reach the sunset's desolate disarray.

1 " . . . the new sonnet *Parted Love* . . ." D. G. R. in Letter to W. M. R., September 14, 1869. *Family Letters*, II, 216.

Much of *The House of Life*, indeed, suggests that from the first the lovers' sky was darkened by the cloud of threatened separation, and many a sonnet—such as *Bridal Birth*—describing the genesis of their love—breathes a heavy atmosphere of defensive secrecy, as in some clandestine passion constantly menaced by a hostile world. In *Love's Lovers* and elsewhere, Rossetti rejoiced in the realization at last of his own love-ideal, a harmony of physical passion crowned, he believed, by intellectual and spiritual affinities with his beloved, "that gracious goal," as he sang in *Love-Lily*,

> Whose speech Truth knows not from her thought
> Nor Love her body from her soul.

To this for him supreme happiness, he gave exultant expression in the unpublished sonnet he significantly entitled *At Last*:*

> Fate claimed hard toll from Love, and did not spare:
>   Are the dues paid, and is all Love's at last?
>   Cling round me, sacred sweetness, hold me fast;
> Oh! as I kneel, enfold mine eyes even there
> Within thy breast; and to Love's deepest lair
>   Of memory bid thy soul with mine retreat,
> And let our past years and our future meet
> In the warm darkness underneath thine hair.
>
> Say once for all: "Me Love accepts, and thee;
>   Nor takes he other count of bygone years
> Not his, than do the affranchised earth and sea
>   Of hours wherein the unyoked inordinate spheres
>   Hurtled tumultuous round Time's ringing ears
> Ere yet one Word gave light the victory."

There surely lies the record of the long-separated lovers' reunion after their mutual confession of baffled longing in *Willow-wood*.

This, for Gabriel at least, was a passion far transcending the old, unhappy, adolescent passion for Lizzie with

> . . . youth and hope in mockery caught

as in *The Sun's Shame* he described his earlier frustrations. Gone now were those lonely years of "Willow-wood," with their burning memories of

> . . . longed-for woman longing all in vain
> For lonely man with love's desire distraught,[1]

* *v. Notes.*   [1] *The Sun's Shame, I.*

those "bygone years" of which, as he now sang in *At Last*, this new, ideal love "takes no count." The contrast between his earlier delusive passion and its successor, now found clear and frequent expression in his verse. As he sang a few months later, in *Pride of Youth*:

> . . . the winged New Love smiles to receive
> Along his eddying plumes the auroral wind,
> Nor, forward glorying, casts one look behind
> Where night-rack shrouds the Old Love fugitive.

Even while attempting in *The Love Moon* to refute some inner suggestion of disloyalty to Lizzie's memory, he admitted that her image no longer moved him; that:

> . . . that dead face, bowered in the furthest years,
> Which once was all the life years held for thee,
>   Can now scarce bid the tides of memory
> Cast on thy soul a little spray of tears,

and in other sonnets of this time[1] he referred to the earlier passion as to something now dead. Occasional twinges of conscience he quietened by his idealization of Love as one all-absorbing unity, whatever its individual manifestions, and he answered Love's stern question in *The Love Moon*:

> How canst thou gaze into these eyes of hers
>   Whom now thy heart delights in, and not see
>   Within each orb Love's philtred euphrasy
> Make them of buried troth remembrancers?

with the reply:

> . . . well
> Thou knowest that in these twain I have confess'd
> Two very voices of thy summoning bell.

There was, he declared, no disloyalty to Love, for these two experiences would be justified in Love's full consummation, beyond death.

> Shall not Death make manifest,

he cried,

> In these the culminant changes which approve
> The love-moon that must light my soul to love?

[1] *cf. Love's Baubles, Life in Love, The Monochord.*

Indeed, this Dantesque conception of Love as a single, all-embracing entity annihilating individual distinctions, became so intimately associated with Rossetti's own psychological development that in painting he at times created a composite figure, combining with Janey's portrait the gold hair of Lizzie.* For the De Goncourts' comment on Flaubert is equally applicable to Rossetti: "Toutes les femmes qu'il a eues n'ont jamais été que les matelas d'une autre femme rêvée." This same combination of Janey's portrait with Lizzie's hair is even more evident in Rossetti's verse, for in many a sonnet of the *House of Life* portraying Janey alone in its original form, Lizzie's hair was substituted for Janey's before publication,[1] though probably to prevent identification with Janey.

Generally, however, Rossetti's new ecstasy ignored the past, and he sang with an abandon rare in English poetry of this realization of his love-ideal. *The Kiss, Placatâ Venere*—misleadingly renamed, in a vain effort to placate Victorian "respectability," *Nuptial Sleep*—both apparently written at Penkill, and *Supreme Surrender*, also written then or shortly afterwards, seem to commemorate three phases of their Love's consummation. So, too, apparently, does another outspoken sonnet, *First Fire*,† excluded like *At Last* and doubtless for the same reason from publication in Rossetti's works:

> This hour be her sweet body all my song,
>   Now the same heart-beat blends her gaze with mine,
>   One parted fire, Love's silent countersign:
> Her arms lie open, throbbing with their throng
> Of confluent pulses, bare and fair and strong:
>   And her deep-freighted lips expect me now,
>   Amid the clustering hair that shrines her brow
> Five kisses broad, her neck ten kisses long.

* *v. Note* to p. 401.
[1] Of the seven sonnets in *The House of Life* in which gold hair appears, in the published versions, the following four make no mention of gold hair in their original form, while those marked with an asterisk, at first definitely indicated dark hair: *Love Enthroned, Youth's Spring Tribute, Her Gifts, Venus Victrix*. The remaining three sonnets present no problem in interpretation, since *Body's Beauty* admittedly describes *Lilith*, the painting for which the golden-haired Fanny was model, *Love and Hope* merely describes an abstraction—"Love's golden head"—while *Life in Love*, as I interpret it (*v. inf*. pp. 417–18) is inspired by the exhumation of the golden-haired Lizzie.

Dark hair appears in the published versions of *Love's Lovers, The Portrait, The Love-letter* and *At Last*. See also *Note* to p. 401.
† *v. Note* to p. 398.

> Lo, Love! thy heaven of Beauty; where a sun
>   Thou shin'st; and art a white-winged moon to press
>   By hidden paths to every hushed recess;
> Yea, and with sinuous lightnings here anon
> Of passionate change, an instant seen and gone,
>   Shalt light the tumult of this loveliness.

Inevitably, despite the discretion imposed upon Gabriel by circumstances, poetry so frank and so sincere reflects details of the actuality inspiring it, and we can easily recognize the verisimilitude of qualities in the "atmosphere" of these lovers' passion, in its progress, and in traits of the beloved herself. The Penkill sonnet *Secret Parting* particularly reflects the atmosphere of secrecy and suspense which broods over nearly the whole of *The House of Life*. "The reader," wrote Rossetti's brother, explaining this sonnet after Gabriel's death, "should observe in this title the epithet 'secret.' The lovers have met in secret, and have parted in secret, with an incertain outlook as to their meeting anew. All the imagery of the sonnet is framed to correspond."

Similarly the unnamed beloved, in harmony with this clandestine courtship, is ever in a state of unhappy tension, of emotional strain, half-afraid, half-regretful, almost tearful, yet driven by passion. Her tears, kisses, smiles, mouth, are ever "tremulous"[1]—Conway noticed Janey's full, sensitive red lips, Henry James her "mouth like the 'Oriana' in our illustrated Tennyson"—and often a neurotic rather than an erotic intensity marks these lovers' meetings.

> Sometimes she is a child within mine arms,
>   Cowering beneath dark wings that love must chase—
>   With still tears showering and averted face,
> Inexplicably filled with faint alarms:

Rossetti described her in *Hearts' Haven*, the conscience-stricken mistress, haunted like himself, by bitter memories. An unconscious spiritual sadism, a love of self-torture, of pain, clearly visible in the Preraphaelite movement, evidently formed a conspicuous element in their passion.

Other traits of the beloved conspicuous in these sonnets, as in others of *The House of Life*, are her "Queenliness,"[2] the

---

[1] *cf. A Day of Love, Love Sweetness, Hearts' Haven, Winged Hours, The Morrow's Message, Secret Parting.*
[2] *cf.* sonnets—*Supreme Surrender, Genius in Beauty, Gracious Moonlight, Hearts' Haven, The Moonstar, Her Gifts, Equal Troth, Venus Victrix, The Soul's Sphere, Threefold Homage.*

beauty of her mouth, the charm of her voice, all qualities remarked in Janey by her friends.* Indeed, in one or two of the sonnets, Janey can be definitely identified as the subject. *The Portrait*, definitely, associated with Janey's picture, also describes her in words, and another, later sonnet, *Genius in Beauty*, demonstrably refers to this same painting, then hanging on Rossetti's studio wall at Kelmscott, praising:

> . . .This sovereign face whose love-spell breathes
> Even from its shadowed contour on the wall.

Janey is thus identified not only with the beloved, but also with the "queenly" or "sovereign" quality so often emphasized in Gabriel's sonnets, and so often praised in Janey by many of her friends. Similarly in the sonnet *Her Gifts*, is a clearly recognizable portrait of Janey for the later substitution of Lizzie's golden hair in place of Janey's dark locks.

In one other unpublished sonnet, *Threefold Homage*,† Gabriel again unwittingly established the identification of his beloved with Janey, in emphasizing the fact that his passion had exalted her by "threefold homage," i.e. by painting, poetry, and the reality of love itself. Into this sonnet as into many another, he breathed his own personal ecstasy, rhetorically asking:

> Was I most born to paint your soverign face
>   Or most to sing it, or most to love it, dear?
>   Full sweet the hope that unborn eye and ear
> Through me may guess the secret of your grace.
> Yet ah! 'neath every picture might I trace,
>   And note beside each song,—"Let none think here
>   To breathe indeed this beauty's atmosphere,
> To apprehend this body and soul's embrace."
> Faint shadow of you at last I weave; except
>   That innermost image all unseen, which still
> Proves me at heart your beauty's crowned adept.
>   Yet was this nought, our hope's high day to fill,
>   That o'er us while we kissed, with answering thrill,
> Two Muses held Love's hands, and smiled, and wept?

The two "Muses" were evidently those of painting (Gabriel's own invention) and of poetry: smiling for love, weeping for pity of Love "in chains," to use Rossetti's own expression in the sonnet *Love's Fatality*.

* *v. Notes.*   † *v. Note* to p. 398.

Certainly *The Stream's Secret*, the poem Rossetti now began at Penkill and completed the following year at Scalands,[1] supports Scott's belief in Rossetti's overwrought state at this time, for frustration is its form, content and inspiration. Instead of progressing, his thoughts merely rotate in a repetitive psychological rhythm of obsessive hopes and memories, the reflection of his own anxiety.

The theme of the poem—hitherto misinterpreted as the poet's sorrow for the loss of his dead wife and desire for reunion with her—is surely his unhappiness in the absence of the woman he now loves and his longing for her return,

> Making me rich with every tone
> And touch of the dear heaven so long unknown
> That filled my dreams with flame.

But ever his hope is dogged by painful memories of a time when this passion was condemned to suppression and silence; an allusion, probably, to the days of the Jovial Campaign, at Oxford, when, according to tradition, he fell in love with Janey but felt too deeply bound to Lizzie to change; an allusion also to Janey's marriage, followed by his own; her marriage which, if deferred for but three years, would have found him, as things had turned out, a "free" man, free to follow the dictates of their mutual love. Were not these "wrongs" which Love himself had done to the poet, wrongs for which atonement was now being made in this belated, mutual confession of their love? So runs Rossetti's thought as he cries:

> O learn and understand
> That 'gainst the wrongs himself did wreak,
> Love sought her aid;[2] until her shadowy cheek
> And eyes beseeching gave command;
> And compassed in her close compassionate hand
> My heart must burn and speak.
>
> For then at last we spoke
> What eyes so oft had told to eyes
> Through the long-lingering silence whose half-sighs
> Alone the buried secret broke,
> Which with snatched hands and lips' reverberate stroke
> Then from the heart did rise.

[1] *v. inf.* p. 433.   [2] *cf. inf.* p. 607.

Yet even in joyous anticipation of his beloved's return, those days of frustration in "Willow-wood" still haunt him:

> O passing sweet and dear
> Then, when the worshipped form and face
> Are felt at length in darkling close embrace;
> Round which so oft the sun shone clear,
> With mocking light and pitiless atmosphere,
> In many an hour and place.

This passion has evidently been secret, clandestine, like that inspiring so many of the sonnets in *The House of Life*; and like them, *The Stream's Secret* breathes an atmosphere of tension and mystery, suggests a love which may not be openly declared.

> Now speak: for in the silence is no fear,
> And I am all alone,

the poet vainly exhorts the unresponsive stream, which, however, maintains complete silence to the end. For the "plot" of the poem is the secret message which Rossetti believes Love has breathed into the river's source, to be carried down to him by the waters now vainly attempting to whisper it into his ears. And the message for which he longs is the assurance of the beloved's well-being, affection and hour of return. Thus both occasion and content of the poem point to the absent but almost hourly expected Janey as its inspiration. So too do such expressions as "her shadowy cheek," incompatible with the fair-complexioned Lizzie, but in harmony with many a description of the dark Janey, as of the beloved in many a sonnet of *The House of Life*—and "the worshipped form and face," which recalls the sonnet *Passion and Worship*.

That this passion is censurable is clear from Rossetti's appeal to the stream itself not to forbid it:

> Withhold, I pray, the vain behest
> That while the maze hath still its bower for quest
> My burning heart should cease to seek.
> Be sure that Love ordained for souls more meek
> His roadside dells of rest.

The stream, he continues, must not reproach him, or it will distort Love's message, just as its ripples distort Love's image. Does not the stream itself, he asks, burst through all restraints

when in flood? The second half of the analogy he leaves to be
understood, without a word of clarification. Surely this is not
the language of a poet longing for reunion with his dead wife;
yet so it is generally interpreted!

And again, as with the love recorded in *The House of Life*,
this love is not only physical but also a harmony of souls, the
realization of Rossetti's narcissistic dream of finding his *alter ego:*

> Each on the other gazing shall but see
> A self that has no need to speak:
> All things unsought, yet nothing more to seek,—
> One love in unity.

The beloved has also the same "tremulous" quality, and their
love seeks the same "passion of peace," Dante's "pace d'amore,"
as in the sonnet sequence.

As the hour of the beloved's return approaches and the
stream still remains silent, the poet's impatience and excitement increase. What spell, he asks, will open its lips? Must he
tell the sad tale of his love's frustrations, to move it?

> All the sad sum of wayworn days;—
> Heart's anguish in the impenetrable maze?

Besides, is the new hope itself merely delusive? Time at any rate
is passing, age is approaching, love must not be further delayed.
When is the hour of the beloved's return?

> O tell me, for my lips are cold,
> And in my veins the blood is waxing old
> Even while I beg the boon.

How reconcile such lines with the usual interpretation of the
poem? Age would assist not impede reunion with the dead.
Evidently this is an earthly passion of living lovers, not one of
the living in love with the dead.

But the increasing tension that marks the nearer approach of
"Love's Hour," finds expression in imagery almost identical
with that of the sonnet *Stillborn Love*, as the poet visions the
dawning day of his beloved's return, and traces the shadow on
the sundial as it approaches the critical moment. Yet even
then, the usual reaction follows, and the haunting memories of

Sleepless Dreams and *Willow-wood* transiently obscure the poet's happier imaginings.

> Stands it not by the door—
> Love's Hour—till she and I shall meet;
> With bodiless form and unapparent feet
> That cast no shadow yet before,
> Though round its head the dawn begins to pour
> The breath that makes day sweet?
>
> Its eyes invisible
> Watch till the dial's thin-thrown shade
> Be born—yea, till the journeying line be laid
> Upon the point that wakes the spell,
> And there in lovelier light than tongue can tell
> Its presence stand array'd.
>
> Its soul remembers yet
> Those sunless hours that passed it by;
> And still it hears the night's disconsolate cry,
> And feels the branches ringing wet
> Cast on its brow, that may not once forget,
> Dumb tears from the blind sky.
>
> But oh! when now her foot
> Draws near, for whose sake night and day
> Were long in weary longing sighed away—
> The Hour of Love, 'mid airs grown mute,
> Shall sing beside the door, and Love's own lute
> Thrill to the passionate lay.[1]

But the stream makes no reply, has no message, and as night falls, and the night wind rises, and mists veil the glen, the poet emerges from his dream, reawakens to consciousness of the world of reality around him and,—with a renewed, intenser realization of his misery,—of the beloved's absence. Upon this (as ever with Rossetti in erotic frustration—we find it again in *The Orchard Pit*, also written at this time, and so supporting Scott's belief in the suicidal impulse) the life instinct suddenly turns deathward, and the poet dreams of Love's final consummation, of the beloved's absorption by the lover, of complete spiritual unity beyond the gate of Death, a fusion of two souls, that perfect identification of the *alter ego* with himself, which

[1] *cf. Stillborn Love.*

being indivisible can never suffer the misery of separation, as
on earth.

> Ah! by a colder wave
> On deathlier airs the hour must come
> Which to thy heart, my love, shall call me home.
> Between the lips of the low cave
> Against that night the lapping waters lave,
> And the dark lips are dumb.
>
> But there Love's self doth stand,
> And with Life's weary wings far-flown,
> And with Death's eyes that make the water moan,
> Gathers the water in his hand:
> And they that drink know nought of sky or land
> But only love alone.
>
> O soul-sequestered face
> Far off,—O were that night but now!
> So even beside that stream even I and thou
> Through thirsting lips should draw Love's grace,
> And in the zone of that supreme embrace
> Bind aching breast and brow.

This desire for death as the consummation of love, this
physical and spiritual vampirism which in its narcissistic urge
would absorb, destroy the beloved and indeed the self, was in
fact a basic psychological attitude of Rossetti's which, often
expressed in *The House of Life*, a year or two later drove him to
attempt suicide. As a contemporary critic has well said: "A
love of love as an absolute, unrelated to human conditions, is
a love of death. It is the supreme egoism which desires not
liberation but annihilation." And this was now, in his anxiety
and frustration, Rossetti's state.

It is, presumably, these three stanzas just quoted, which have
led critics lightly to assume that the poem was an expression of
Rossetti's passionate desire for reunion with his dead wife,
despite the incompatibility of such an interpretation with the
whole weight of meaning of the preceding thirty-five stanzas,
which in such a case appear vague or meaningless to the point
of incomprehensibility.[1]

That indeed the absent Janey is still in Rossetti's thoughts is

[1] Probably memories of both Janey and Lizzie are here fused, as in *The Love-
Moon*. Scalands, where the poem was completed, inevitably brought memories of
Lizzie, and of death. *v. inf.* p. 428.

also suggested by the next stanza, which is also the last; for as he finally reawakens to the world of reality, to the night round him and the darkly murmuring stream, to the misery of her absence, to hysterical revolt against everything that destroys his erotic dream, he feels tears upon his cheek and wonders whether she too is not similarly reduced by misery to tears, like himself.

> O water whispering
> Still through the dark into mine ears,—
> As with mine eyes, is it not now with hers?—
> Mine eyes that add to thy cold spring,
> Wan water, wandering water weltering,
> This hidden tide of tears.

So ends this so largely unconsciously revelatory poem, in which a tremulous hope ceaselessly alternates with despair. It is in fact the record of a neurotic flight from the frustrations of the world of reality into that of erotic illusion and exaltation, followed by a descent into reality again, which in turn produces an hysterical, tearful revolt against it, and a flight to death as the only refuge and consummation of love. In short, *The Stream's Secret* is the expression of such a mood as leads hysterical lovers to form a suicide pact as the only way of escape from frustrated passion.

Thus day by day, at Penkill, Gabriel wrote the poem, curled up in a little cave by the side of the rushing Penwhapple, the little stream in the glen, pouring out all the restless, chaotic emotions of his tortured, fevered spirit, racked by misery and anxiety until the woman he loved should be restored to him.

In varying degrees of intensity, this same mood inspires other poems he was then writing at Penkill. *The Orchard Pit*, *Troy Town*, *Eden Bower*, and his prose outline for a never-written drama *The Doom of the Sirens*, all repeat Gabriel's ceaseless alternation between the thought of passion and of remorse, love, and death; all repeat or vary the same well-worn erotic symbols: the primeval Lilith, the classical Helen, the mediaeval Guinevere, the modern Jenny. *Troy Town*, we have recently learned from the publication of Browning's letters to Julia Wedgwood, was suggested to Gabriel by Browning. "In my last good days at Rome, the best in my life," Browning wrote in 1864, "I was meaning to do what I could 'next year' with a subject that struck me—Helen dedicating a goblet, which reproduced the perfection of what Virgil calls 'exsertae mammae,' and was deposited in the temple of Venus—a group of her, bidding farewell to the imperishable beauty, and a young priest receiving the same, and revolving other comparisons: on mentioning this to my friend Rossetti, 'I'll paint it,' said he—and there it is, archaically treated indeed."

Since Gabriel had painted Janey as Guinevere, on the walls of the Oxford Union, twelve years before, there had been little or no personal development. His thoughts and emotions, like those of Swinburne, followed but one now weary round from which there was no escape. His mind had built its own prison-house, and increasing ennui, frustration, hysteria were almost inevitable. The continual oscillation of his mind and emotions between his obsessive polarities of love and death—largely the result, not only of frustration, but also of Lizzie's early relapse into illness, of the strong unconscious association during Rossetti's impressionable adolescence of the two extremes of erotic ecstasy and physical decay—is very evident in *The House of Life*, which, indeed, he originally intended to call *Sonnets and Songs of Love, Life and Death*, almost the title he had chosen for the sonnets he had published in the *Fortnightly Review*. Perhaps his preference for the antithetic sonnet form was unconsciously directed by the fact that it enabled him to contrast and so intensify, the love-ecstasy of the octave with its emotional opposite, weariness, despair, foreboding, death, in the sestet. At any rate, of the eighty-seven sonnets of this later period in the final *House of Life*, sixty-five show this emotional polarity, the contrast of Love or Joy with Death or Pain.[1]

Such alternations reflect Rossetti's growing emotional ambivalence, from which he found it increasingly difficult to escape. More significantly even than in *The Stream's Secret* do these tendencies reveal themselves in the final passages of the prose and verse versions of *The Orchard Pit*, where he described the siren:

[1] William Rossetti, speaking of *The House of Life*, writes: "I find 42 sonnets the essential tone of which is happy; 35 the essential tone of which is unhappy; and 26 which, though certainly not unemotional, may be termed neutral in regard to happiness or unhappiness." D. G. R.'s *Works* (1911), p. 651.

> . . . her hair
> Crosses my lips and draws my burning breath;
> Her song spreads golden wings upon the air,
> Life's eyes are gleaming from her forehead fair,
> And from her breasts the ravishing eyes of Death.

Similarly in his prose version of the same theme, he wrote: "And now the Siren's song rose clearer as I went. At first she sang 'Come to Love'; and of the sweetness of Love she said many things. And next she sang, 'Come to Life'; and Life was sweet in her song. But long before I reached her, she knew that all her will was mine: and then her voice rose softer than ever, and her words were, 'Come to Death'; and Death's name in her mouth was the very swoon of all sweetest things that be." As in the days of *St. Agnes of Intercession*, Rossetti's writings were still "autopsychology" whether he knew it or not. In them, his erotic-deathward urge finds full expression, beyond which—for both the prose and verse renderings of *The Orchard Pit* here break off unfinished—he apparently could not go. Such was the nightmare into which his "one dream alone" was now turning.

By September 6th the Morrises were already on their homeward way. Neither Janey nor her husband had much enjoyed their stay at Ems, where, although the town was not yet made famous or infamous by Bismarck's fatal telegram, the King of Prussia was already receiving the French ambassador, amid uneasy rumours of impending war. "Miracles," Gabriel had told Brown, alluding to Janey, "are evidently not expected." Nor in fact had miracles occurred. Nevertheless, Janey had at last, to Gabriel's great relief, "benefited considerably." But he was most anxious for news of her, begged William when the Morrises had returned, although he himself was about to quit Penkill, to send him a full account of Janey if he had seen her, despite his expectation of hearing immediately from Janey herself. From this time, William, when after his brother's death he came to edit his correspondence, deleted nearly all references to Mrs. Morris.

Eager to be gone to meet Janey, Gabriel nevertheless stayed a day or two longer at Penkill, completing his poems, writing sonnets to the very end. The day before his departure, in a

final, melancholy, anxious sonnet he bade farewell to the glen
he had haunted while writing his verses, recalling how only

> . . . an hour ago
> Thine echoes had but one man's sighs to bear,
> And thy trees whispered what he feared to know.

"On reading it over at home I thought it very dismal," he told
Miss Losh a month later. It was always his habit thus to throw
a protective disguise of flippancy over his deepest feelings.

On September 20th Gabriel returned to town.* William,
seeing him, confided to his diary the following day: "He looks
to me well enough, but says he has been very weak, perspiring
excessively, losing sleep, and that his health is breaking up.
He has done a good deal of poetry—ballads of Helen and Lilith
(*Troy Town* and *Eden Bower*), both very fine (the latter not yet
finished), sonnets, etc. He seems more anxious just now to
achieve something permanent in poetry than in painting—in
which he considers that at any rate two living Englishmen,
Millais and Jones, show a higher innate executive power than
himself."

* *v. Notes.*

VII

PAST, PRESENT, AND POETRY
1869-1870

> ... that dead face, bowered in the furthest years,
> Which once was all the life years held for thee,
> Can now scarce bid the tides of memory
> Cast on thy soul a little spray of tears.
>
> *The Love Moon* D. G. ROSSETTI

WHAT HAD GABRIEL, writing his *Farewell to the Glen* during those last hours at Penkill, "feared to know"? That the sonnet, in its passionate intensity embodied a very definite, personal meaning is obvious. Was it an expression of fear for his own failing health and eyesight? Or for Janey's illness? Or for some new threat to his passion? If, as later circumstances vaguely suggest, it was this last, then the overstrained emotion, the tense anxiety dominating him at Penkill, his half-attempted suicide by the whirlpool in the glen, the neurotic despair of *The Stream's Secret*, all become comprehensible.

Or was it, in part at least, the fear of hearing that what he dreaded yet desired, the exhumation of his dead wife in order to recover the poems he had buried with her, had at last been accomplished? Anxiety about this had certainly played no small part in reducing him to the morbid condition he had revealed at Penkill. For on the eve of his departure for Scotland he had instructed Howell to recover, as quickly as possible, the manuscript of his poems placed seven years before in Lizzie's coffin.

Gabriel's reversal of attitude in this was less sudden than at first sight appears. Although, even from the days of his adolescence, his poetic ambitions had waxed and waned with his moods, had even from time to time been explicitly renounced, they had never been finally destroyed, and now rose like the phoenix, from their own ashes. In his earlier years poetry had yielded to economic necessity, pictorial ambitions and personal diffidence. He cared very little for what he had written, he told Allingham in 1854, and feared the public would agree with him in this. "There are," he told a friend a few months later, speaking of poets, "many such nowadays—a conviction which results with me, when a poem begins buzzing in my head, in an utter inadequacy to the job of writing it down. But I believe the other view is the rational one; and that one ought no more to do as I do than, on the death of one's father the nabob, to kick one's cheque book into the grate because all one's fourteen brothers and sisters had volumes of the same work." Indeed, the years of struggle for recognition as a painter and of strife with Lizzie were far from "poetical" as Gabriel understood "poetry." "Since I have given up poetry as a pursuit of my own," he told Allingham in 1856, "I really find my thoughts on the subject generally require a starting point from somebody else to bring them into activity."

The following autumn, however, when Jones and Morris had applauded his verses in *The Germ* and Ruskin his poem *Nineveh*, Gabriel's poetic ambitions revived so completely that he began to contemplate the publication of a volume of original poetry, once his translations had appeared. Ruskin, to whom he showed his verses, gave them warm but qualified approval. He had read them, he said, "with great admiration," believing that "in many of the highest qualities they are entirely great." But they needed revision, he thought, while *Jenny* he definitely disliked. The man in that poem he found "anomalous," "altogether a disorderly person"—a thinly veiled criticism of Rossetti's way of life which doubtless played no small part in the ultimate destruction of their friendship. It was for these reasons that Ruskin had refused Gabriel's request to persuade Thackeray as editor, to publish *Jenny* in *The Cornhill Magazine*. Ruskin also objected that "Jenny" did not rhyme with "guinea," a criticism which even the placid William dismissed as "the stricture of a Scotchman."

Annoyed by Ruskin's comments, Gabriel sent the poems to Allingham, declaring: "When I think how old most of these things are, it seems like a sort of mania to keep thinking of them still; but I suppose one's leaning still to them depends mainly on their having no trade associations, and being still a sort of thing of one's own. I have no definite ideas as to doing anything with them, but should like, even if they lie at rest, to make them as good as I can." And when later in 1861 *The Early Italian Poets* appeared, it bore on a back page an announcement of the forthcoming publication of Rossetti's original verse. Before the volume was ready, however, Lizzie's death and Gabriel's impetuous renunciation of poetic ambition, sealed by the burial of his poems in her coffin, brought all thoughts of publication and success in poetry, to an end.

But this hysterically penitential mood quickly passed, and Rossetti's poetic ambitions as quickly revived. At first, passing off his verse as the work of obscure or forgotten poets, he sought the criticism of friends, explaining, when finally forced to admit their authorship, that the complete copies were "lost"—an allusion to the buried MS. which was soon understood. From that time, as the buried poems seemed lost for ever, his friends began to compare notes and write out what they remembered of Rossetti's verse, much helped by the excellent memory of Swinburne. Within two years of his wife's death, Gabriel's first fine rapture of self-sacrifice had paled to a scarcely conscious regret for his impulsive and futile action in burying his poems. A few months later, he was discussing with Christina, quite as a matter of course, a projected volume of his original verse.

He still, however, lacked enough original poetry to make a respectable volume, nor was his emotionally arid life during the first few years of widowerhood poetically stimulating. Only with the coming of this "regenerate rapture," this new and sincere passion in 1868 or thereabouts, did poetic inspiration return. Gradually withdrawing for a time, under this new influence, from the grip of the past, he found Lizzie, although even then inextricably intertwined with his reawakened emotions, no longer the poignant memory she had once been. A new, more powerful source of inspiration was present, and under that influence he now resumed his "indomitable song" of idealized love.

Nor were these the sole influences leading to the eventual publication of Rossetti's poems in 1870. His sister Christina had already won high praise for her *Goblin Market and Other Poems*, published in 1862, and followed four years later by the *Prince's Progress and Other Poems*, while his nearest friends, Bell

Scott, Morris, Meredith and Swinburne had already given several volumes of poetry to the world, much of it in fact showing Rossetti's own influence. Then too, friends and relatives, Christina, William, Scott, Morris, Swinburne and others, had urged him at the close of 1868 to publish his sonnets in the *Fortnightly*, while Skelton in one of his articles had publicly clamoured for the appearance of the volume promised eight years before in *The Early Italian Poets*. Buxton Forman the critic, had also stimulated Gabriel in two anonymous articles which had led Rossetti to inform his mother: "After twenty years one stranger has discovered one's existence!" He now began to rate his poetry above his painting, describing it as the art "in which I have done no pot-boiling at any rate. So I am grateful to that art and nourish against the other that base grudge which we bear those whom we have treated shabbily."

Nevertheless, in his fear of public criticism, he had hesitated to publish his verse, and at Penkill in 1869 had compromised with his fears and ambitions, by printing his poetry in a private edition for friends, giving at the same time the excuse that "blundered transcripts of my old things were flying about and would at some time have got into print perhaps—a thing afflictive to one's bogie." But to his mother he admitted his intention was "to keep them by me as stock to be added to for a possible future volume." And from Penkill on the day after his arrival he had written to the absent Miss Losh: "I have got my proofs here, and am tattooing them in the usual agonized state which such things bring me to."

These privately printed poems Gabriel at first thought of dating, but, as we have seen, no doubt foreseeing that awkward questions might ensue, he again compromised, prefacing the poems with the vague note already quoted, stating: "Most of these poems were written between 1847 and 1853. . . . The Sonnets and Songs are chiefly more recent work." That last admission, relating to the sonnets later entitled *The House of Life*, is biographically important, corroborating as it does the evidence that most of those sonnets were inspired by his new passion for Janey Morris, not by his old passion for Lizzie. Gabriel's increasing desire to figure like his friends, publicly as a poet, had now overcome his fears of publicity to such an exten tthat only the painful slenderness of this privately printed version prevented a general publication, warning him indeed that he still lacked sufficient original verse to make a presentable volume. His desperate remedy of filling it out with his early prose tale *Hand and Soul* Scott had dismissed as an "exhibition of poverty not to be thought of."

Thus it was that Rossetti had at last yielded to his friends' persuasions and his own ambitions, and on leaving London for Penkill in 1869, had authorized the recovery of the manuscript buried in his wife's grave, hoping perhaps that the exhumation would be carried out during his absence in Scotland. The lengthy negotiations ensuing, he followed from Penkill with "real anxiety," as he told Howell, promising him at the same time, in a surprisingly buoyant letter, "the swellest drawing conceivable," or if he preferred it, a portrait of Howell's young wife, if only Howell succeeded in obtaining from the authorities the desired permission to open the grave. His decision once made, Gabriel had been anxious for its immediate execution. But legal formalities had caused delay, and at the end of August, at Penkill, he was still impatiently awaiting news that the exhumation had been carried out. Then, suddenly remembering that the Home Secretary was the Mr. Bruce—later Lord Aberdare—who had so amicably negotiated with him thirteen years before about the Llandaff triptych, he sent Howell a letter of introduction to him, with an urgent message to Howell himself to present it and get Bruce's permission to carry out the plan. But Bruce, although sympathetic, required the consent of Gabriel's mother as owner of the grave. Gabriel, knowing her consent would certainly be refused, and no doubt at heart somewhat ashamed of this reversal of sentiment, insisted on keeping the whole of his family in ignorance of his intentions, and finally persuaded the Home Secretary to waive this condition. Thereupon preparations for the recovery of the poems began in earnest. To Howell Rossetti had sent from Penkill detailed instructions enabling him not only to distinguish Lizzie's coffin from the others in the grave, but also the precious manuscript itself, "bound in rough grey calf," from the Bible which had also been placed there.

Not, however, until after Rossetti's return to town did the exhumation take place. It was not without recent literary precedents which may have assisted Gabriel in making up his mind, for literary influence was strong upon his life and character from beginning to end. Long before her brother's marriage, apparently,[1] Christina Rossetti, in her sombre little tale *Maude*, had described the burial of manuscript verses in a girl's coffin. Twenty years had passed since Armand Duval in Dumas' *Dame aux Camelias* had in his frustrated passion brought back the corpse of his dead love to the light of day. Similarly, Gautier's Father Serapion had exhumed the body of the ineffable Clerimonde. Exhumation of the passionately loved dead indeed had become quite a literary fashion, and Gabriel's whole existence was chiefly an unconscious attempt to realize literary fashions in life.

Perhaps he remembered these literary parallels as one early October evening of 1869 he sat in Howell's house in gloomy reverie, while in Highgate Cemetery a scene was enacted surely as strange and macabre as any of his own imaginings. For at that time, Howell, and Dr. Llewellyn Williams of Kennington, were standing beside Lizzie's open coffin, in the light of a great fire made beside the grave as apparently the best protection against infection that they could then devise. Howell, the romantic adventurer, the teller of strange tales, true or false, must have gazed with intense elation upon the form, the famed golden hair, of what had by that time become an almost legendary figure, source of so much Preraphaelite inspiration!

Lizzie, they said, was still wonderfully preserved, perhaps— so they speculated as at the time of Lizzie's death—by the drug which had destroyed her. It was surely Howell, the romantic liar, who spread the tale that went far afield, as news of the affair gradually leaked out, of Lizzie's hair having continued to grow after her death, to grow so long, so beautiful, so luxuriantly as to fill the coffin with its gold! It was surely Howell's description of this which inspired Gabriel's obvious reference to the exhumation in his sonnet *Life in Love*, written shortly afterwards.* In this sonnet, biographically one of the most interesting, Rossetti clearly reveals that a new passion is the

---

[1] But *v. supra.* pp. 302–3.   * *v. Notes.*

source of his "regenerate rapture," and contrasts his present
happiness with his recent misery; his sleepless nights haunted
by memories of Lizzie's death, by insistent self-questionings as
to its cause and his own responsibility, by fears of a loveless
future. Such, he declared, had been his state; that of a servant
of sorrow and a thrall to death, until this new, regenerative
passion had brought back life and hope.

> Not in thy[1] body is thy life at all,
>> But in this lady's lips and hands and eyes;
>> Through these she yields thee life that vivifies
> What else were sorrow's servant and death's thrall.
> Look on thyself without her, and recall
>> The waste remembrance and forlorn surmise
>> That lived but in a dead-drawn breath of sighs
> O'er vanished hours and hours eventual.
>
> Even so much life hath the poor tress of hair[2]
>> Which, stored apart, is all love hath to show
>> For heart-beats and for fire-heats long ago:
> Even so much life endures unknown, even where,[3]
> 'Mid change the changeless night environeth,
> Lies all that golden hair undimmed in death.

"Hair," wrote William Rossetti, long afterwards, paraphrasing
this sonnet, "from a different head once so dear to thee";
different, that is, from that of the woman who was now revitalizing the poet with a new love. . . . And there, too, though
stained, holed and discoloured, lay the coveted manuscript-
book of Rossetti's poems.

When all was over and the manuscript handed to Dr.
Williams to be drenched with disinfectants and dried leaf by
leaf, Rossetti's eagerness gave place to shame. After a week of
self-conflict he mastered his fears sufficiently to inform his
brother, apologetically, of what he had done. William, who
had indeed, already heard of the exhumation from Scott,

---

[1] "thy (my) body" in W. M. Rossetti's paraphrase in *D. G. Rossetti as Designer
and Writer* (1889), p. 206. "My Life" also must be presumed—a typical example
of Rossetti's depersonalizing process. *v. sup.* p. 382, 400, footnote 1; *inf.* p. 544 and
Note to p. 142.

[2] "Even so much life as that of thine has the poor tress, stored apart, of hair
from a different head once so dear to thee— . . ." *Ibid.*, p. 207.

[3] "in that grave wherein . . ." *Ibid.*, p. 207. William Rossetti's paraphrase
definitely supports my interpretation of the sonnet, made before the paraphrase
was seen. *cf. inf.* p. 422.

approved his action. "Under the pressure of a great sorrow," William replied, "you performed an act of self-sacrifice: it did you honour, but was clearly a work of supererogation. You have not retracted the self-sacrifice, for it has taken actual effect in your being bereaved of due poetic fame these seven and a half years past: but you now think—and I quite agree with you—that there is no reason why the self-sacrifice should have no term."

Perhaps William's blundering entry into the delicate art of casuistry proved less consolatory to Gabriel than was intended. At any rate, the reasons Gabriel now gave Swinburne for his recent action, differed widely from those to which William referred. "The truth is," Gabriel told Swinburne, alluding to Lizzie, "that no one so much as herself, would have approved of my doing this. Art was the only thing for which she felt very seriously. Had it been possible to her, I should have found the book on my pillow the night she was buried; and could she have opened the grave, no other hand would have been needed." By this clever "rationalization" or subterfuge, which he no doubt largely believed, as in a sense he might, Gabriel became as it were, the reluctant, sorrowing agent of the dead Lizzie, fulfilling an almost sacred duty, however regretfully, for Lizzie's sake, instead of the changeable widower rifling his dead wife's grave at the dictate of literary ambition. And even Swinburne, despite his adoration of Lizzie, not merely approved, but enthusiastically applauded Gabriel's recovery of the poems as "absolutely and admirably right."

Much appreciating Swinburne's reply, Gabriel sent him a grateful note admitting: "I have undergone so much mental disturbance about this matter." The strain, indeed, soon produced evident physical effects. So confused was he, that almost immediately after the event he could not be sure of the day of the week on which it occurred, and early in November he complained of a "constant shaking of the hand . . . with corresponding internal sensations," ominous, he feared, of paralysis.

Boyce, calling on him on November 26th, "was sorry to find him in a morbid and rather depressed state. He has been doing little work lately, but what he has done is very beautiful. He has been taking up the *Found* picture again and *The Death of*

Beatrice.[1] Mrs. Morris has been sitting to him again lately. He went during the summer to W. B. Scott's or Miss Boyd's place in Ayrshire, but it does not seem to have done him the same good as last year. He was much engaged on preparing a collection of the greater number of poems yet written for publication. He read me again (after an interval of many years) one of the most beautiful and impressive of them called *Jenny.*—"

Dr Marshall ordered iron and other tonics, but throughout the winter Rossetti remained in a low state, yet managing, as he said, "to rub on somehow." He also consulted Christina's doctor, Sir William Jenner, who advised him to take care, give up "spirit-drinking," go to bed before midnight, and, for the next six months at least, to take life easily in the country. To Shields Gabriel sent a detailed account of his condition. "Various queer states of health for some time past," he reported. "My visit to Scotland seemed to do me no good this time. I have just lately been calling on doctors and oculists again, and the latter still say my sight is not really affected; while the former say much the same as to my health, but speak most warningly as to hours, exercise and abstinence from spirits, for which Heaven knows I have no taste, but had for a year and a half past fallen into the constant habit of resorting to them at night to secure sleep. I have now relinquished them entirely, and take only at night a medicine prescribed by my last doctor (Sir W. Jenner)—not an opiate, against which he warned me in all forms—and have certainly not slept worse but rather better, since doing so. I also, when weather is fine take walks in Battersea Park; whereas my habit had long been to walk only at nights except when in the country. For many months I have done no painting nor drawing, but have just lately resumed work of this kind."

To Shields Gabriel also confessed his poetic ambitions now maturing. "I have been doing a good deal of work in poetry lately," he wrote, "and shall publish a volume in the spring. I have got 230 pages in print, and want perhaps to add about 100 more. This is hardly necessary as it is all very close and careful work; but I daresay it may be some time before I print again, if ever I should wish to do so. At any rate, so

[1] *Dante's Dream* or perhaps *Beata Beatrix.*

much will be off my mind when the thing comes out, and it is certainly the best work of my life, such as that has been." During the following months the preparation of his poems absorbed most of Gabriel's attention. "Pretty well, painting little and writing much poetry and pretty hard up in consequence," Brown now described him.

"In a disappointing state," Gabriel, speaking of the recovered manuscript, had told Brown, shortly after its recovery. "The things I have already seem mostly perfect," he had continued, "and there is a great hole right through all the leaves of *Jenny*, which was the thing I most wanted. A good deal is lost; but I have no doubt the things as they are will enable me, with a little rewriting and a good memory and the rough copies I have, to re-establish the whole in a perfect state." To William he described it as in "a disappointing but not hopeless state," making at the same time a promise—which he did not keep—to dedicate his poems to his brother. The poems he had most wanted were *Jenny* (particularly), *A Last Confession*, *Dante at Verona*, *The Portrait*, and *Bride Chamber Talk* (*The Bride's Prelude*).

Before the close of the year and shortly after the exhumation, Rossetti produced a second privately printed volume containing the poems which had appeared in its so recent predecessor, together with several additional poems some of which were written at Penkill or in London, too late for inclusion in the earlier volume, while others were from the recovered MS. The most recent of the sonnets repeated and varied the familiar love-themes of their immediate predecessors. The obsessive siren reappeared in *Death's Songsters*—which William Rossetti strangely interpreted later as a reference by Rossetti to the cultivation in his poetry of a "noble or degrading tone!"—*Hoarded Joy*[1] laments, like *Willow-wood*, a belated passion.

> Alas! our fruit hath wooed the sun
> Too long,—'tis fallen and floats adown the stream.
> Lo, the last clusters! Pluck them every one,
> And let us sup with summer; ere the gleam
> Of autumn set the year's pent sorrow free,
> And the woods wail like echoes from the sea.

---

[1] Originally entitled *Joy Delayed*; also significantly—surely.

Similarly obsessive memories of those lost years in "Willow-wood" apparently inspired two other of these recent sonnets, *Stillborn Love* (again the imagery was evidently inspired by the memory of his own dead daughter), and *Life in Love*, this last regretfully referring, in the passage previously quoted, to a "poor tress of hair"[1] as all that remains to him

> For heart-beats and for fire-heats long ago.

Now at any rate, the joy of his present mingled in his verse with the remembered sorrows of the past. In *Supreme Surrender* he exalted passion; in *Passion and Worship* he rejoiced in the two-fold harmony of flesh and spirit; in *Love's Baubles* he appraised his present love above that he had felt for the ailing Lizzie, and the mere animal attraction Fanny and her like exerted upon him.

> . . . from one hand the petal and the core
> Savoured of sleep; and cluster and curled shoot,
> Seemed from another hand like shame's salute—
> Gifts that I felt my cheek was blushing for.
> At last Love bade my Lady give the same:
> And as I looked, the dew was light thereon;
> And as I took them, at her touch they shone
> With inmost heaven-hue of the heart of flame.
> And then Love said: "Lo! when the hand is hers,
> Follies of love are love's true ministers."

Similarly, *The One Hope* recalled the portrait of Janey as *Pandora*, with its illustrative sonnet and expressed the belief in an after-life where, beyond time and place, true love should find its ultimate, perfect consummation with this newly beloved, "The One Hope's one name," which William Rossetti later interpreted as "the woman supremely beloved upon earth," for she, known at last in this earthly life, is also his ideal love in eternity. . . .

Despite his desertion of painting for poetry, Rossetti, impelled by financial difficulties and a feeling that "life wears short," worked at several commissions given him by a recent patron, William Graham, Member of Parliament for Glasgow, including *Dante's Dream*, in which Janey appeared as Beatrice, a water-colour replica of *Pandora* and of Janey's portrait, and

[1] *v. sup.* p. 418.

the completion of the never-to-be-completed *Found*. Gabriel's delays had exhausted Graham's patience, and he was now begging, pleasantly but insistently, for the delivery of some at least of the promised works. For Norton, in return for Lizzie's *Clerk Saunders*, which Norton had duly surrendered at Gabriel's request, Rossetti was at last making, as long before agreed, a portrait of Janey. "I like it," he declared, "on the whole the best of the drawings I have made of her, and never mean to let any more go out of my own possession. The charm of such a model is too precious for the ordinary market." Janey, unhappily, was ill again. Ems had brought her no permanent recovery.

A youth of sixteen who now sat to Gabriel for the head of Love in *Dante's Dream* and later won fame as Sir Johnston Forbes-Robertson, the actor, was so impressed by Rossetti at this time, that long afterwards he made a word-portrait of him. "Let me try," he wrote, "to describe him as I, a boy of 16 remember him at the age of 42. His face was pale, the colour of old ivory as it were, but it glowed under excitement. His forehead was high-domed and broad, the brown eyes deep-sunk, lambent and sad, with the skin about them of a much darker tone than the rest of the face. His beard was black and slightly forked,[1] and his hair was thick, black and curly. The lips were rather full and red, seen slightly through his moustache, which was not heavy. The face was very handsome, deeply striking, with its calm nobility and impressiveness—one of those rare faces, in short, that once seen are never forgotten. His voice was rich and deep, soft to ear as velvet to the touch. His frame was robust, thick-set and muscular. He stood, I should say, a little under 5 ft. 10 ins.[2] but his whole appearance expressed his powerful personality." Forbes-Robertson who sat three times to Gabriel for the *Dante's Dream*, was flattered to find that Rossetti—as always with children—treated him like a grown-up. The youth posed "over a cushion on a sofa," and at the first sitting Gabriel threw him into confusion by remarking: "My dear Johnston, I am sorry I have not a beautiful creature for you to kiss." Later, Forbes-Robertson repeated a story that went round of how Rossetti, on being asked how he

---

[1] *v. sup.* p. 354 and *inf.* p. 549.
[2] Dunn's estimate is much more probably correct. *v. sup.* p. 354.

managed to get such beautiful models for his pictures, replied "that sometimes on a day too dark for painting he would stand at the window and watch the passers-by, and, to use his own words, 'if a lovely creature passed, I used to rush out and say, "I'm a painter and I want to paint you." Sometimes they would scream, then I would rush in and slam the front door.'"

How much Gabriel's mind was exercised at this period upon feminine charm, is also shown in a little known story told by a journalistic acquaintance of Rossetti, Sutherland Edwards, in his *Personal Recollections*. "In those distant days," wrote Edwards in 1900, "Rossetti, who, poor fellow, was to be struck with melancholy in the closing years of his life, had fine spirits, an abundance of humour, and even a disposition to 'chaff' his friends when they laid themselves open to it. Frank Marshall (author of several plays), was complaining after dinner that he had put a thousand pounds into a certain theatre, on the understanding that a farce of his was to be played, but that, after a single performance—during which the audience in order to show their displeasure with the management, did nothing but hoot and stamp—the piece had to be withdrawn. 'After all,' said Rossetti, when Marshall had begun to tire the company with his lamentations, 'you got some amusement for your money. There are plenty of pretty girls at the theatre; you had an opportunity of making their acquaintance, and doubtless had some very interesting flirtations with them.' To the astonishment of everyone, Marshall flew into a blind rage, protested vehemently against the scandalous imputations cast upon his moral character, and ended by using the most approbrious language. The host at once interfered, and requested Frank Marshall to leave the house. The indignant farce-writer, unable to enter into the spirit of a joke directed against himself, now disappeared, leaving the company somewhat depressed. Knight (the host) was vexed for Rossetti's sake; Rossetti was sorry to have provoked, however unwittingly, so disagreeable a scene. Everyone was a little gloomy. Time went on, when suddenly a knock was heard at the street door. Then a servant came into the room, saying, 'Please, sir, Mr. Marshall wishes me to tell you that his brougham is ordered for eleven, and, as it is now only half-past ten, he would be glad if you

would let him have a chair outside on the pavement.' The
grotesque character of the message provoked roars of laughter.
The picture of the ejected guest, sitting on a chair outside the
house from which he had been asked to remove himself, was
irresistibly droll. Rossetti, always amiable, begged that he
might be called in. It seemed a pity to be seriously angry with
such a man, and amid general hilarity Frank Marshall returned."

One other glimpse we have of Gabriel at this time. In the
spring of 1870 his old friends Mrs. Howitt and her daughter
Anna Mary, preparing to leave England for a brief continental
tour—which for Mrs. Howitt lengthened into permanent
residence abroad—and visiting Rossetti just before their
departure, found him "painting beautiful women, it seemed to
me, and nothing else, in gardens of roses," wrote Mrs. Howitt,
recalling the occasion seventeen years later, in Rome. "His
rooms were piled up with heaps of blue and white china, heaps
and heaps of it on the tables, and even on the floor."

Swinburne was now Rossetti's chief helper. Never before or
after were the two in such intimate relation as now. Encouraged
by Swinburne's criticism—"such generous praise, at a moment
when I am woefully out of sorts in health and nerves," as
Gabriel gratefully told him—Rossetti continued throughout the
winter and spring of 1869–1870, to work with unflagging energy
at the preparation of his poems. "I never can feel clear on
uncertain points till I get your opinion," he told Swinburne,
while Swinburne declared to him: "of the sonnets gathered up
together in the book I can only say I am always in an equal
admiration and wonder at this overrunning wealth of impec-
cable and inevitable perfection of expressive form. . . . I am shy
of sending you a sonnet as I might be of sending Shakespeare a
play, or Shelley an ode." Gabriel at the same time repaid his
friend's assistance by helping Swinburne to prepare for publication his *Songs before Sunrise*.

As for his own volume, no detail of preparation was too
minute for Rossetti's attention. From the choice of a publisher
—he chose Ellis, a well-known London book-seller—to the
designing and supervision of the binding, and the issue of an
American edition, Gabriel carefully arranged and planned. No

evil that human care and foresight could prevent should happen to his book; on that he was determined. "Bad colours and most unpleasant texture" was his just comment upon the average book-binding of the time, as he made plans for his own book to be different. And by the close of January 1870 everything was arranged.

But the smallness of the volume, which he wished to bring up to at least three hundred pages, still troubled him. "Even freer printing," he mournfully declared, "would only make some 250 or 260 as yet." In mid-February, "going to press now with last corrections," and as, save for "a sonnet or two," he said, inspiration lagged and his doctor advised him for the sake of his health to leave town for country air, he had "serious thoughts of going into retreat for a few weeks almost immediately in the country, and trying if I can hammer anything out before the inevitable day of publication is at the door." He wished, he said, "to try if there is any marrow left in me that can be squeezed out in the form of rhyme before I go finally to press."

Unable to decide upon any place, however, Rossetti delayed, until Madame Bodichon—the Barbara Leigh Smith of earlier years—hearing of his need, offered him her country house "Scalands," near Robertsbridge, Hastings, where he, Lizzie, Bessie Parkes, and Anna Mary Howitt had visited her during Lizzie's illness, sixteen years before. It was many years since Barbara had seen Rossetti and she now found him so changed in appearance that only by his beautiful voice did she recognize him. She though his progress in painting "amazing," his latest pictures "wonderful." Always fond of Gabriel, Barbara, as she now told Allingham (who was leaving the Customs at Lymington to become sub-editor, in London, of *Fraser's Magazine*), felt "very sorry" for him.

It was early in March 1870 when Gabriel set out for Scalands accompanied by William Rossetti's friend, the American artist and journalist William James Stillman, recently American consul in Crete. "A very fine specimen of an American," Rossetti described him to Norton; "I have known him in a fragmentary way for many years, but am seeing more of him now and like him extremely." Norton too was an American, and

Gabriel's description of Stillman to Swinburne, just before their departure, was freer. "William's Yankee friend," he wrote, "is an entirely unobstructive man and will leave me quite to myself." In Gabriel's eyes, this quietude of Stillman, whose wife had recently died, was one of his chief charms.

At Scalands Gabriel intended to stay but a few weeks, writing the new poems he still needed to make a volume of presentable size. He meant to finish *The Orchard Pit* and *The Stream's Secret*, as well as to write three more poems, *The Doom of the Sirens*, *The Harrowing of Hell* and *God's Graal*. *The Harrowing of Hell*, William explained at the time, in his diary, "He means to treat from the point of view of love-passion—as if the redemption wrought by Christ were to be viewed as an elevation of the conception of love from pleasure into passion, hence entailing the redemption from Hell of Adam and Eve, David and Bathsheba, etc., etc." It is a pity, at least for Rossetti's biographers, that the poem was never written. William thought the ideas conflicting, and said so, but in relation to Gabriel's life they are peculiarly significant, especially, surely, the introduction of David's illicit passion for the wife of Uriah the Hittite.

God's Graal, Gabriel told Swinburne, was to deal with "the loss of the Sancgraal by Lancelot—a theme chosen to emphasize the marked superiority of Guinevere over God." Yet of all these projects only the completion of *The Stream's Secret* was achieved. *The Harrowing of Hell* apparently never passed beyond an abstract intention; *The Doom of the Sirens* remained but a prose outline; *God's Graal*, postponed until Tennyson's treatment of the same theme should be made public, was finally abandoned after the first few lines. "Recruiting and 'working off' my book with the conscientious decency of Mr. Dennis the hangman," Gabriel at Scalands described himself to Allingham, for he meant to "have it out before the end of April."

For Rossetti, inevitably in the circumstances, Scalands was haunted, in these first days at least, by memories of Lizzie, of the days so long dead, when in that very house he, Barbara and Anna Mary had sketched Lizzie's "dear head" with iris entwined amongst her golden hair, and all had scrawled their monograms on the window panel to commemorate a happy day. Everything about him at Scalands now spoke to him of his wasted, deluded youth, of the dull, lethargic, dream-laden days into which his adolescent ecstasy had dwindled. So his thoughts now ran, and onward to the later phase, to his sordid, belated marriage in the empty church at Hastings, to the embittered invalid his first love had by that time become, to the pitiful, enigmatic end. In his note-book he scribbled the self-question:

> Where is the man whose soul has never waked
> To sudden pity of the poor torn past?

It was probably during these early days at Scalands, while his dark mood of retrospect lay heavy upon him, that he wrote *Barren Spring*, a sonnet of this time, reflecting the sadness which seized upon him as he surveyed his past. Not for him, bound to these brooding memories, the joy and gladness of the season:—

> So Spring comes merry towards me here, but earns
> No answering smile from me, whose life is twin'd
> With the dead boughs that winter still must bind,
> And whom to-day the Spring no more concerns.

Such now for Gabriel was this "barren spring." In *He and I*, another sonnet of this time, Rossetti turned upon his own morbid retrospection and introspection, lamenting his increasing disintegration, the two selves now within himself, the old, happy earlier "He," and the later self-conscious, self-critical "I" so destructive of the earlier instinctive, unthinking delight in life, so creative of "this new self," which now

> . . . wanders round my field,
> With plaints for every flower, and for each tree
> A moan,

where before were only beauty and joy.[1]

Stillman, divining Gabriel's need of sympathy, drew his usually secretive friend—so at least Stillman himself afterwards asserted—into unwonted intimacy of talk, as together they tramped the woods and fields round Scalands. "One of the men most dependent on companionship I have ever known," Stillman declared. "When not at work he needed someone to talk with, and in our long walks he unfolded his life to me as

[1] *v. Notes.*

he probably never did to any other man, for he had a frank egotism which made him see everything and everybody purely in their relation to him. And in these circumstances he and I were, after a manner, the only people in our world." Of this Gabriel too was aware. "In this Sussex desert one tells all his secrets," he said, apologetically, to Stillman. Gabriel talked also of art and poetry. Art, said Stillman, was "the dominant interest of existence, not only of his own, but of existence *per se*, and he tolerated nothing that sacrificed it to material or purely intellectual subjects. The artist was to him, the ultimate ratio of humanity, and he used to say frankly that artists had nothing to do with morality, and practically, but in a gentle and benevolent way, he made that the guiding principle of his conduct." It was in this belief that he cried to Stillman on hearing of the death in child-birth of a woman painter: "A great artist sacrificed to bringing more kids into the world, as if there were no other women just fit for that."

With his own work Gabriel was as ever dissatisfied. Although to Stillman as to Shields he disguised with a pretence of indifference, his fear of public criticism and consequent refusal to exhibit, he admitted technical deficiencies. He had not, he said, yet learned "the true method of painting," regretted his inferiority to the great Venetians and his contemptuous rejection of formal teaching in his youth. If only he had been taught in "a great school," he said, he would have been a better painter. And he had, Stillman truly noted, a "higher opinion of his own natural abilities than of his actual achievement." Fallen under Gabriel's spell, Stillman, like Jones and Morris before him, thought Rossetti the most gifted of contemporary artists, not only in England but in all Europe.

For the first month at Scalands there was but little improvement in Gabriel's health. "Not very brilliant," he told his mother after a fortnight, and three weeks later he told Shields: "I need hardly say that my health brought me here, and that means that there is not much to boast of." Over-work by gaslight in Cheyne Walk had aggravated his eye-trouble and insomnia, and these were still his chief afflictions. Increasingly anxious, he went to town in the first days of April to consult an eye specialist who, like his predecessors on the case, declared that the eye-weakness was nervous and that there was no organic disease. At Scalands, as there was no gaslight, Gabriel was forced to adopt a healthier way of life, and soon began to improve. Brown, visiting him, found his sight almost completely restored. Stillman soon noticed that their simple mode of life, daily walks "and freedom from all causes of excitement, rapidly brought him back to his natural condition."

But Stillman too was a victim of insomnia, and it was Stillman who now first brought to Gabriel's notice, as a remedy, the new and popular drug chloral hydrate, which later was to have so disastrous an influence upon Rossetti. Stillman, who had greatly benefited by the drug, was in the habit of strongly recommending it as a sleeping draught to friends. One result was that Brown, who found it "a splendid sleeping potion," had in turn recommended it to Shields, who now and for four or five years afterwards, gradually became its victim, until by a great effort he mastered its hold upon himself. "Chloral," wrote Shields in later life, "gives only death-like stupefaction without restorative power. The suicidal despondency produced by chloral I knew too well—only a resolute severance from it saved myself. No friend had the same experimental sympathy with Gabriel as I had."

As yet ignorant of the dangers of chloral, personally benefited by it and suspecting no harm, Stillman now recommended it to Gabriel, whom he had thought in a "very precarious condition of nerves and brain." Over Rossetti as over Shields it gradually obtained a dangerous, and in Rossetti's case a permanent, ultimately fatal power. Nevertheless, Stillman, with apparent justification, gave in his *Autobiography* a detailed and circumstantial denial to William Rossetti's assertion that Stillman's introduction of the drug to Gabriel's notice was the unintentional cause of his surrender to its influence. Rossetti, Stillman declared, "was then in the beginning of the morbid attacks which some time later destroyed his health completely. He was sleepless, excitable and possessed by the monomania of persecution. His family had tried to induce him to go away for a change but the morbid condition made him unwilling to do so, and he never left his house until late in the evening, under the prepossession of being watched by enemies." In these circumstances, Stillman recommended "twenty grains dissolved in water to be taken at three doses, but, as he forgot it on the first two nights, he took the whole on the third, and complained . . . the next day that it made him sleep stupidly for a few hours, and then made him so wakeful that he was worse than without it." After this, said Stillman, Rossetti refused to touch chloral until later a doctor prescribed it; when "he fell into the habit of using it to his great injury, from the want of self-control in the employment of it."

Stillman's account of Gabriel's gradual subjection to chloral, whether literally accurate or not—and it seems to be correct— certainly exposes the inadequacy of our information, for only on reading it do we realize that the biographers of Rossetti fail to give us precise facts as to the time and progress and circumstances of Rossetti's domination by the drug.[1] "No doubt," wrote Stillman of Rossetti, "chloral was ultimately one of the agencies of his prostration, though not of his death, but he did not have recourse to it until his power of recuperation from overwork had begun to fail, and, when he had become accustomed to the effect of the chloral, he took it as the means of a form of intoxication, a form well understood by those who have had any experience personal or by observation, in the use of the drug. The craving for this intoxicant, once it became a habit, is, like the use of morphia, invincible, and Rossetti indulged in it to such an extent that he used to take the original prescription to several druggists to obtain a quantity that one would not have given him. The crisis came long after my personal relations with him had ceased, and I had become only an occasional correspondent, living in Italy. But to make his decline the consequence of the use of chloral, even when it was finally become habitual, as some do, is absurd."

Despite minor harmonies, at Scalands as at Cheyne Walk

---

[1] The most definite statement about the chloral is William Rossetti's in the following passage: "Constant insomnia (beginning towards 1867), and its counteraction by reckless drugging with chloral, co-operated, no doubt, to the same disastrous end [i.e. Rossetti's ultimate mental and physical decline]; indeed, I find it impossible to say whether the more potent factors in the case were insomnia and chloral which gave morbid virulence to outraged feelings, or outraged feelings which promoted the persistence of insomnia, and the consequent abuse of chloral. All three had their share in making my brother a changed man from 1872 onwards." (In reference to Buchanan's attack on Rossetti and its effects.) *Dante Gabriel Rossetti as Designer and Writer*, p. 157. Also: *v. Notes.*

with his fellow tenants eight years before, a conflict of temperaments soon left Gabriel in absolute possession—alone. Relying
upon Stillman's "unobtrusive personality," as he also described
it, Gabriel from the first, assumed a position of authority, of
superiority indeed. Rightly or wrongly, Stillman believed that
Madame Bodichon had first offered Scalands to himself, and
to Rossetti through Stillman only as an after-thought. Nevertheless, Gabriel behaved, said his friend, as "master of the
house, as if he had invited me, rather than the converse, going
through the rooms to select and saying, 'I will take this,' of
those which suited him best, and 'You may have that,' of those
he had no fancy for." One consequence of this attitude was, for
Stillman, a financial difficulty. The two had agreed to share
expenses equally but as the impecunious Stillman invited no
one to Scalands, Gabriel's hospitable reception of the Morrises,
Madox Brown and others was largely at Stillman's expense.
Gabriel himself, although claiming at this time, and no doubt
correctly, to be making three thousand pounds a year, was as
ever in debt, so deeply indeed that he was even considering
the sale of his Oriental china. Yet he showed, said Stillman,
"the most princely disregard of expenditure, spending large
sums on old furniture and oriental porcelains, denying himself
nothing that took his fancy." Gabriel meanwhile, obviously
unaware of Stillman's grievances, often described him in his
letters as a "very pleasant and kindly companion, never obtru-
sive and always helpful," or in similar complimentary terms.
Nor did he suspect the reason when Stillman, irritated by
Gabriel's unconscious tyranny, troubled by the expense yet
too peaceable to protest, quietly departed.

That Rossetti's faults sprang chiefly from thoughtlessness
Stillman clearly saw. "Generous," he said, "to the same
degree of extravagance that he was indifferent to the claims of
others, he made no more account of giving you a treasured coin
than he did of taking. His was a sublime and childlike egotism
which simply ignored obligations, until, by chance, they were
made legal, at which, when it happened, he protested like a
spoilt child. And he had been so spoilt by all his friends and
exercised such a fascination on all around him, that no one
rebelled at being treated in his princely way, for it was only

with his friends that he used it. He dominated all who had the least sympathy with him or his genius."

Meanwhile, Rossetti was rapidly completing his volume of poetry. Within a week of his arrival at Scalands he had finished *The Stream's Secret*, written several sonnets and begun *God's Graal*. "I have just wound up my book with two more sonnets to the *House of Life* (making fifty now) and shall add no more," he told Ellis on March 26th, and three days later informed Swinburne: "All is now at an end."

His first mood at Scalands had been retrospective and depressed; but as his health improved this passed. Ere long, the presence of Janey assisted his recovery. That in going to Scalands he would be near Janey he had known, for she was staying with the children at Hastings, in weak health and hoping to benefit from the sea air. Morris, busy with the affairs of "the firm," was generally in town. At Hastings Gabriel visited Janey whose health at first greatly improved; but near the close of March he regretfully told Ellis she was "far from well" again. He invited her and Morris, who was coming from town to see her, to dine with him at Scalands and spend a few days there, and this they did. "Top and Janey are here to-day," he wrote on March 27th, "the former insolently solid—the latter better than when I last saw her at Hastings."

The visit to which Gabriel had referred was by no means the last visit of the Morrises to Scalands. "Our friends are all well," he was soon writing again, "with the exception, I am most deeply grieved to say, of Mrs. Morris, who is still in a very delicate state. She and Morris have been in this neighbourhood lately, and are coming again; and I trust the change may prove eventually of some decided benefit to her, as signs of this have already become apparent." A week later Morris was back in town and Janey apparently installed at Scalands, where she seems to have remained almost until Gabriel's own departure. He made a crayon drawing of her, which he thought "the best thing I ever did." "Janey Morris is here," he told his mother on April 18th, "and benefiting greatly. Top comes from time to time."

With Janey's companionship, her health restored and the brightening weather of the spring, Gabriel's own state remarkably improved. "For the last few days," he now told his mother, after five weeks at Scalands, "this glorious weather seems to be doing me good in some ways at any rate. It is impossible not to feel a different being when such a change is going on all round one. . . ." The air he found "delicious" and the days "very hot just now while the sun lasts." His despondency seemed to have vanished. He went for walks, delighted in the countryside covered with spring flowers, and sent his mother primroses, violets, wild daffodils and wood anemones. The prancing lambs in the fields pleased him. "They and their mothers make various toy-noises," he wrote, "only the mothers' are penny noises and the lambs' half-penny ones."

He was indeed a different being from the poet of *Barren Spring* and *He and I*. The sonnets he now wrote,* such as *Youth's Spring Tribute*[1]—written too late for inclusion in his volume—revealed the change, as well as the *mise en scène* he was describing to his mother in his letters from Scalands—

> On this sweet bank your head thrice sweet and dear
>   I lay, and spread your hair on either side,
>   And see the newborn woodflowers bashful-eyed
> Look through the golden tresses here and there.[2]
> On these debateable borders of the year
>   Spring's foot half falters; scarce she yet may know
>   The leafless blackthorn-blossom from the snow;
> And through her bowers the wind's way still is clear.
> But April's sun strikes down the glades to-day;
>   So shut your eyes upturned, and feel my kiss
> Creep, as the Spring now thrills through every spray,
>   Up your warm throat to your warm lips; for this
>   Is even the hour of Love's sworn suitservice,
> With whom cold hearts are counted castaway.

For Gabriel evidently, life and love were now renewed. In a week or so he would be forty-two years old; but that was no matter. Emotionally he was adolescent still, still naïvely idealizing and sentimentalizing love. This he now clearly showed when on Stillman's becoming engaged to the woman who soon became his second wife, the beautiful Miss Spartali, daughter of the Greek Consul-General in London, Gabriel

---

* *v. Notes.*
[1] Probably originally *Love's Spring Tribute*, v. *Note* to p. 381.
[2] For "golden" the original version has "rippling." *cf.* the descriptions of Janey, *sup.* pp. 238-9, and *Note* to p. 401.

told Norton: "She is a noble girl—in beauty, in sweetness, and in artistic gifts, and the sky should seem very warm and calm above, and the road in front bright and clear, and all ill things left far behind for ever, to him who starts anew on his life-journey, foot to foot and hand in hand with her. . . . She is a pearl among women." That was what Gabriel had once believed and hoped on meeting Lizzie!

Stillman's good fortune emphasized for Gabriel the general loneliness of his own lot. "I am left," he continued, "to lonely letter-writing. Goodbye, my dear Norton, I am going for a walk now in a pleasing but not very sympathetic *entourage* of leafless woods and English associations which I have grown old in, but am never perhaps quite at home with. I envy you your Italian ones." That was an almost unique but very significant admission. At Scalands, with Stillman's companionship now largely withdrawn and Janey often at the call of others, the unhappy past returned at times to depress him. Norton had, in fact, recently invited Gabriel to Florence, and for a short time Rossetti was perhaps nearer acceptance, nearer to actual departure for Italy than ever before. He even went so far as to ask William to accompany him, and on William's agreement, dallied with the half-intention throughout the rest of his stay at Scalands. Probably Janey's movements had something to do with Gabriel's endless postponements of the project; at any rate he had come to no final decision when he left Scalands for Cheyne Walk, nor, in the event, did he ever visit the beautiful country of his ancestors.

He kept Fanny informed of his condition lest she be anxious; told her in mid-April of the studies for *Dante's Dream* and a drawing he had made at Scalands, all of which he is now offering to Graham for a hundred and fifty guineas. He wishes to stay as long as possible at Scalands, but if his money runs out he must come up to town. Madame Bodichon has friends coming to Scalands after May 7th. So if he is not in town before, he must come at the end of next week, as that is the day his poems are to appear. Such are the topics he discusses with Fanny.

And still he sang of love, in new sonnets, *The Love Letter* and *Love Sweetness*, this last describing a passionate tryst with his mistress of the "tremulous" smiling mouth. And in his note-book he scribbled occasional amorous couplets which have the immediacy of recent experience.

Most significant of the sonnets he was now writing was *The Monochord*, written during music which inspired the imagery rather than the theme. Long afterwards William Rossetti declared this sonnet the most "obscure" of all in *The House of Life*, and would have been "baffled," he said, to explain it if Watts-Dunton had not reminded him that music was its inspiration! Thus prompted, William, although still finding it "very difficult . . . in its particular images and form of expression," thought perhaps its theme might be briefly described as "the mutual response of music and of the human soul." In a sense which William probably intended but did not mean to be perceived, this summary, despite Gabriel's notorious dislike of music, was true. For to William, intimately acquainted with his brother's life, *The Monochord* should have presented little difficulty to understand. Certainly Christina understood it.* In that profoundly emotional sonnet, Gabriel, under the momentary stimulus of strong feeling and the music to which he was listening, obviously recalled, in symbolism confused rather than adapted of the pillar of cloud which by day led the Israelites through the wilderness to the promised land and the pillar of fire which guided them by night, the flame of his own love, gradually dimmed by a cloud of frustration until Lizzie's death, and now revitalized by this new and greater passion. The sestet of *The Monochord* is a cry of "regenerate rapture" after the disillusion of his earlier love and the promiscuous animality—"the devious coverts of dismay"—into which, in the cynical interregnum following Lizzie's death, he had fallen. So now, in the intoxication of this new, supreme passion he cried:—

> Oh! what is this that knows the road I came,
> The flame turned cloud, the cloud returned to flame,
> The lifted shifted steeps and all the way?
> That draws round me at last this wind-warm space,
> And in regenerate rapture turns my face
> Upon the devious coverts of dismay?

* *v. Notes.*

Once again Love's exile was happy within the warmth and
light, the heightened consciousness, tension, of the erotic
illusion, of a passion which satisfied, at least for the time, the
demands of both sense and spirit.

Near the close of April Gabriel went to London to autograph
copies of his forthcoming volume of poems. To avoid meeting
friends who would detain him, he went almost stealthily, and
returned in haste to Scalands after only a half-day in town.
But before leaving London he regaled Morris, whose review of
his forthcoming *Poems* was just completed, at a favourite resort
of Rossetti's, Rule's oyster bar, as Morris wrote to inform his
wife. May, Gabriel celebrated with unusually light-hearted
gallantry, in verses he entitled *Fior di Maggio*,[1] beginning—

> O, May sits crowned with hawthorn-flower,
>   And is Love's month they say;
> And Love's the fruit that is ripened best
>   By ladies' eyes in May.

"Top is coming down again to-day, and we shall make some
more excursions probably, as there are various things worth seeing," he told his mother on the fourth of the month, and three
days later he told Ellis: "Dear old Top is here—not very well."

By this time the three weeks he had originally fixed as the
extreme limit of his stay at Scalands had been extended to
almost two months. Barbara Bodichon now needed the house
herself, and Gabriel had reluctantly to face the necessity of
returning to Cheyne Walk. Hitherto he had been by no means
enamoured of a country life, but now he determined to find
some other place near Hastings to which he would almost
immediately return. "I believe," he told his mother, "nothing
would do me so much good, if I could make it convenient, as
to bring work down and spend the summer in this neighbourhood, so as to get out in good air whenever I pleased. There is
a lovely old mansion near here in which I could rent a set of
rooms which would do well to paint in, and I have serious
thoughts of it; but in any case I should have to return to London at present, to start fair with my painting and see what I
should be going on with. . . . I am wonderfully better within
the last month—specially last fortnight, and have no doubt I

---

[1] Sometimes incorrectly entitled *Fin di maggio*.

am really benefited in every way, but London might bring on a relapse for all that." The change was marked, for before he was ever reluctant to leave London, even when ordered by doctors to do so. But he was certainly better, and so too, he reported, was Janey. To Skelton, Gabriel outlined similar plans: "I have been out here for two months now, recruiting after a spell of queer health, and have benefited greatly. I shall return to town almost immediately, and get to my painting again; but it is possible that, after making a good start with a picture I am beginning, I may bring it to this neighbourhood, and go in for a summer's working and walking together, of which I still stand in much need."

Five days later, on Monday, May 9th, he returned to town.

VIII

"POEMS"
1870

My book will have brought me £300 in less than a month, which is not so bad for poetry, particularly if it goes on.

Letter to Mrs. Gabriele Rossetti D. G. ROSSETTI

FROM SCALANDS, Gabriel had returned to London a doubly famous man; famous now both as poet and painter. His two-fold ambition was now attained. In the last days of April, as he had planned, *Poems by D. G. Rossetti* (price 12s.) had appeared amidst general acclamation, giving the final touch to his reputation, placing him, for contemporaries, almost in a class apart with such men as Blake who had manifested their genius in two arts. Now, too, he was one with his literary friends and relations who had already given their poetry to the world. G. F. Watts, the artist, who knew Rossetti personally, on reading his poems thought him greater as a poet than as a painter, and placed him at once amongst the greatest of English poets. Shortly afterwards he asked Rossetti to give him sittings for a portrait (now well known, which Watts intended to present to the national collection), and Gabriel agreed to his request.

The comments of distinguished contemporaries reveal the nature of Rossetti's appeal and of the taste of the time. "I quite accept your epithets for Rossetti's sonnets," wrote Henry Sidgwick from Cambridge to F. W. H. Myers, shortly after Rossetti's poems appeared, "also they pleased me critically and classificatorily, as I discovered in him the 'missing link' between Swinburne and Christina Rossetti. They seem to me to combine so many qualities, Elizabethan pregnancy, a romantic phantasy which is—well, I do not know of what age but it has all the charm of the antique and a vibrating subtle passion which is very modern—or Italian (I do not know Italian); I wish he would write some more. . . ." Pondering the poems, Sidgwick informed his mother, a little later, and

439

with more restrained enthusiasm, "I do not think I have read anything else lately except Rossetti's poems. Some of these are splendid; but they require selecting, and I should not exactly recommend the whole book."

No doubt the "moral tone" of some of Gabriel's verses had estranged Mrs. Sidgwick, for shortly afterwards, in the summer of 1870, her son attempted a temperate defence. "Please let me know if Forman[1] seems frightened at *Jenny* or anything," the uneasy Gabriel had commanded Ellis, his publisher, shortly before publication; for *Jenny*, long before condemned by Ruskin and more recently by Shields and Smetham, seemed to him a test piece. Sidgwick however would not allow *Jenny* to be called in question. "You ask me," he told his mother, "what is the 'good' of such a poem as Rossetti's *Jenny*. I do not quite know whether you mean to suggest (1) that the subject is too disagreeable to be fit for poetry, or (2) that the moral effect is likely to be bad. The latter I should scarcely think myself, as there is not a particle of morbid imagination in it, no idealizing of vice. It seemed to me a perfectly truthful delineation of common-place fact—indeed the pathetic effect of the poem is intended to spring from its fidelity to common-place. As for the first objection I should be inclined perhaps to admit it—only one would limit the range of tragedy a good deal if one excluded all disagreeable subjects. One would cut off several of Shakespeare's plays, for example. I do not myself think that one can demand that all literature shall be adapted for young ladies' reading, though one rejoices that so much of our best literature is so adapted."

"I wonder what you think of Dante Rossetti's volume, if you happened to see it when you were in England," wrote John Morley, editor of the *Fortnightly Review*, in February 1871 to Robert Lytton, more widely known as writer and poet by his pen name Owen Meredith. "Nobody, I suppose, believes that it contains many elements of permanent quality, or that it can ever attract more than a few esoteric souls. Yet this school has a certain charm. It recalls old ideals of beauty and simplicity and homeliness which are rather fascinating in our time of barbarous ormulu, and its combination of sadness with full joy

[1] Buxton Forman, the literary critic and editor of Keats.

of the senses is perhaps wholesome by way of reaction against
the wordy optimism which has made Tennyson so popular in
the sentimental middle-class. Some writers talk of Rossetti
being Greek, which is the blockhead's name for all that is
nineteenth-century British. This is nonsensical enough, but he
is pagan, only after the mediaeval type, which is the older
paganism made mystic and sad, I suppose. I admit there is a
grain of childishness in it all, and I see very clearly that it is
only a poetic episode, or aside—the true master-current being
in that wide, far reaching, historic direction to which Hugo's
Légendes des Siècles and your own *Chronicles and Characters* point
the way. Still in poetry I am polytheistic, and I am particularly grateful for anything that helps me in any way to break
up the hideous clerico-bourgeois amalgam that rules at present.
It is true that you will never have high creative art, so long as
one is content to admire work on the ground of its being
effectively solvent!"

This letter, Robert Lytton sent to his father, Lord Lytton,
the famous author of *Harold* and *The Last of the Barons*, who
warmly replied: "Morley's letter to you about Rossetti serves
to explain much of the prevalent error in criticism, and the
prevalent vice of recent poets (only don't tell him so). There is
a prevalent notion among these critics and poets, that a poet is
to be like a radical member for a metropolitan borough—a
delegate to represent a special idea which his electors favour
and probably all the spirits of the age. Of course, he is to upset
a something that has gone before, he is to be an advanced
Liberal, in the way of upsetting; and the more he goes the
whole hog and rejects pearls for the last new hogwash, the
more he is declared to have the divine something in the afflatus
of his grunt. Thus just as Tennyson was idolized by these
critics while he was revolutionary, so now that his affectations
are no longer advanced Liberalism but milk and water re-
forms, the critics want an out-and-outer to upset him."

Froude, editor of *Fraser's Magazine*, was almost as unsympathetic. To Skelton, about to review Rossetti's *Poems* in
Fraser's, he wrote in February 1870: "You might put Morris's
last poem with Rossetti's volume . . . poetry like all else, is
going post-haste to the Devil just now, and Alfred's [Tenny-

son's] last volume is the most signal instance of it. You might say as much as this—much as I like and honour him."

Of all Gabriel's unprofessional critics none can have been more enthusiastically appreciative than Anne Gilchrist, who was thrown by Rossetti's presentation copy into ecstasies surpassing even those of Swinburne himself. So moved was she that, after expressing in one letter her appreciation of the gift, she wrote a second long and emotional epistle, all sentimental exaltation about *Jenny* and "the glory, the imperishable life of the book . . . the poems which treat of Love." That she mistakenly believed the poems were inspired by Lizzie accounts for the unconscious irony of her comment. "They make me sigh with happiness," she wrote, "to realize that the earth did bear on its bosom such sweet life for two human creatures. . . . Only a little pause, in that blended life! Only one of the two hidden for a few yards by a bend of the road, my friend! How could God spare the sight of such happiness out of His Universe?"

Nor was professional criticism of Gabriel's poems less flattering than such private opinions. To this desirable consummation indeed, Gabriel himself had largely contributed, for, as the hour of publication approached, his anxiety for the success of his volume had so greatly increased that no precaution to ensure it was neglected. His endless alterations would have reduced any publisher less good-natured than Ellis to despair. Printing, binding, lettering, advertising, Gabriel supervised all with the minutest care. Not only did he utilize old friends such as Morris, Swinburne, Westland Marston and Skelton who had long urged him to publish, more recent acquaintances like Gordon Hake the poetical doctor, Joseph Knight and Buxton Forman, but even new admirers from the rising generation such as Sidney Colvin, the young Cambridge don recently introduced into Rossetti's circle by Jones.

With the publication of *Poems*, it had seemed to Rossetti himself that his growing eminence would be at stake. So, organizing his army with consummate skill, in a two months' masterly campaign he seized in advance every attainable point of vantage. Thus, before the day of publication arrived, he had contrived that the critics appointed to review his volume in the various journals and magazines were almost entirely personal friends and supporters. Morris, although reluctant, he forced to review for the *Academy*; Swinburne was placed with the *Fortnightly*; Skelton with *Fraser's*; Knight with the *Globe* and *Sunday Times*; Hake with the *New Monthly*; Marston with the *Athenaeum*; Colvin with the *Pall Mall Gazette* and *Westminster Review*. Besides, Gabriel obtained favourable assurances from the *Standard, Graphic, Telegraph* and *Edinburgh Courant*. Yet even this was not enough. From some unguarded loophole, he feared, some "outside," "unattached" critic (as he called those not of his own army), might attack him!

In anticipation of these preparations Gabriel had replied to Skelton's exhortations to publish, "that if his friends would stand by him he would run the risk. He would consent to publish because his friends had assured him that his poems ought not to be hidden away; would we say to the world what we had said to him in the confidence of friendship?" So wrote Skelton long afterwards, giving, indeed, Rossetti's only valid excuse for his actions, a legitimate excuse perhaps since he did not attempt to extort praise from reluctant critics, but, at least as he saw it, merely demanded a public statement of what they had long said were their private opinions about his verse, and their helpful co-operation in the step he was now taking at *their* desire! "To this of course there could be only one reply," wrote Skelton; "we were eager to get them on any terms; and I cannot see that there was anything undignified, anything that reflects injuriously either on Rossetti or his friends, in the assurance that we would be early in the field. It is easy of course to say that Rossetti was unduly disquieted, and that no man should be so morbidly sensitive as he was; and I am quite willing to admit the validity of the reply." Rossetti's action indeed would not have been remarkable in his day, and even less perhaps in our own, but for the fact that he so thoroughly organized the widespread practice of securing friendly Press criticism before the event.

That his friends might be first in the field he sent them early proofs of his volume, followed by advance review copies in "provisional covers." Carefully synchronizing the appearance of his *Poems* with that of the friendly reviews, he arranged for publication at the close of April, and, just before the hour struck, ordered the waiting flood of eulogy to be released. Thus, he thought, it would "look a little less like conspiracy than if they had appeared the day the book comes out." But a binder's error caused some delay, and to Gabriel's great consternation—for he feared lest his organization of friendly criticism became known—several of the reviews actually appeared before *Poems*. Yet so anxious was he to forestall "outside" critics, he found even this "hardly to be regretted." Even then his fears were not stilled. Two of the leading critical journals, *The Spectator* and *Saturday Review*, had eluded his efforts, and he expected them to be "nasty." "An old foe of mine," he told Ellis, "will I know have his fling somewhere, and I think it will be in one of the two." With some relief he learned that Sir Noel Paton, Queen's Limner for Scotland, was "yearning to review it somewhere and should be duly encouraged" by means of a presentation copy.

By this time the organized paean of praise had begun, the well-drilled orchestra struck up. It was Knight, in the *Globe* and Colvin in the *Pall Mall Gazette*, who had accidentally anticipated by a day or two the actual appearance of the volume and the general chorus of friendly criticism. The May magazines brought their quota. Skelton's article in *Fraser's Magazine*, despite Gabriel's short note of thanks, gave him little satisfaction. "Nothing," he told Ellis, with pardonable irritation, "could be more inane. Fancy my songs being 'arch and lively!' But such a gift-horse (even if admitted of market value) does not tempt me to minute analysis either of its mouth or other self-asserting orifice. However, one ought no doubt to be duly grateful. Be it for foes to bring one to a sense of every friend's value. They do it yet I dare say." His sense of a vast conspiracy against himself was growing very strong.

The May *Fortnightly*, giving Swinburne's review to the world, received from Gabriel very different recognition. The article had been discussed by the two friends long before it appeared, and once Morley the editor had refused to accept Swinburne's caveat that as Rossetti's friend he could not be his critic, Swinburne had turned with intense enthusiasm to the task, seeing in Rossetti's volume a continuation of his own recent attack in *Poems and Ballads* upon the Philistinism and prudery of the day. Gabriel's chief fear of Swinburne as critic was indeed that he would overpraise, and against this he vainly cautioned his impetuous friend, who uncompromisingly replied: "Having got the chance I have waited ten years for, of speaking out what I see to be the truth as regards your poems, I am very particularly and especially well damned if I am going to let it slip. It is my devout intention to cut it fat—as fat as a carver can cut, and yet retain any grace of handling or skill of dissecting. I shall not say a word which is not the fact. You shall see what it is to fall into the hands of a fellow craftsman."

In the event Swinburne certainly did "cut it fat"! Above all, he rejoiced to treat of *The House of Life*, at least of as much of it as appeared in the volume of 1870. "I have summed up in a swift cursory way," he told Gabriel, "the bearings of your great cycle of love-sonnets for *The House of Life*, so as to give such summary analysis as may obviate the charge of obscurity of aim or purport, which to a cursory reader of them by fits and starts was perhaps more or less plausible, but drops off and dies out when they are read as here consecutively arranged by the light of a little thought. This is the only question I can anticipate as possible for 'human stupor' and malevolence to raise as regards the book; and as the cycle in question is, perhaps, for wealth and splendour of poetic body and raiment the most wonderful of your works, I have thought it well to tackle it first. The rest will be plainer sailing. I cannot tell you," he continued, "how ineffable in wealth of thought and word and every beauty possible to human work I see that set of sonnets to be in thus laboriously going over them for revision, or how brutally inadequate I feel the best and most delicate comment possible on them to be. You and the British public will have to excuse that. Only Dante could write a proper comment on the verse of the *Vita Nuova*. But I hope to say something more nearly adequate of the other poems."

"I am delighted," Rossetti replied, "to hear that you are battling with the British dragon on the subject of my 'obscurity' in the sonnets. . . . I cannot say how pleased I am that you should tackle the sonnets seriously, as these I suppose on the whole constitute my most distinctive work, and in that direction, if in no other, I am pretty likely to do something more in spite of other occupations." That was, biographically, a particularly interesting comment. "I hope and think," Swinburne answered, "you will like my manner of exposition thus far, as I certainly have spent more thought and work on it, and put more heart into it, than I ever before did in prose— as you may well believe." That in this Swinburne was as good as his word his review soon showed. Upon *The House of Life* he lavished "fine writing," the poetic prose in the manner of Rossetti's own *Hand and Soul*, which passed on from the Pre-raphaelites, through Pater to the later "Aesthetes" at the close of the century. "There seems no story in this sequence of sonnets, yet they hold in them all the action and passion of a spiritual history with tragic stages and elegiac pauses and lyric motions of the living soul," Swinburne wrote significantly, yet still obscurely as he was in the circumstances bound to do. "There has been no work of the same pitch attempted, since Dante sealed up his youth in the sacred leaves of the *Vita Nuova*; and this poem of his namechild and translator is a more varied and mature work of kindred genius and spirit." Nor did Swinburne forget to praise *Jenny* as "great among the few greatest works of the artist."

Only one sentence of Swinburne's panegyric, Gabriel asserted, had he seen or heard before its publication, and that was a concluding laudation of himself at the expense of leading contemporary poets, including Tennyson, Browning and Morris, which, as he feared it would arouse their enmity, he persuaded the reluctant Swinburne to delete. "A dear piece of friendship but an avalanche of praise which I hope will not overwhelm me altogether," Rossetti described Swinburne's article to Ellis, when it appeared, and to Brown he spoke of "Swinburne's wonderful article . . . dearly friendly, and full of splendid things of course, but too much so in all reason. The *Athenaeum*," he continued, "is a very nice article, and *Fraser's* liable to be useful. Now for my foes with a clear course. I expect the *Saturday* or *Spectator* or both, to tune up on that tack. . . ." To Swinburne himself Gabriel wrote: "After reading your more than brotherly review of my book, what can I say adequate to so good a gift? You know already how much my love must

feel the love, and my pride the praise, of so great a poet. . . ."
And even before Gabriel, William had sent Swinburne the
thanks of the whole Rossetti family "for so lavish an attestation
of intellectual and personal sympathy."

Simultaneously with the heavy fire of the monthlies had
come the lighter crackle of the weeklies and dailies: the *Sunday
Times* appreciatively vocal through Knight, the *Daily News*
briefly approving, and hinting at a full-dress review later
which never appeared, the *Telegraph* which so annoyed Gabriel
that if, as he suspected, it was the work of "Mr. McD." an
acquaintance, he determined it would be a good "pretext to
cut him." Next came a whole broadside at once: Knight's
article in the *Graphic*, Morris's in the *Academy*, and an anonymous article in the *Saturday Review*, "a bestial one—almost con-
fessedly incompetent, but not hurtful," Gabriel declared,
"which one soon learns in the sty of British Criticism, to think
the only point worth considering." He suspected its author was
"Palgrave—forced to be grudgingly civil."

It was the mid-May *Academy* which brought Morris's article
before the public. Morris would have avoided the task if he
had been able. "Gabriel's review . . . I must say rather terrifies
me," he had declared, reluctantly beginning to write it. His
uneasy praise of *The Stream's Secret* and *Jenny* was matched by
his cold, vague, awkward yet extreme appreciation of the
volume as a whole—"complete and satisfactory from end to
end." He praised also "the magnificent collection of sonnets
. . . which, though there are some among upwards of eighty
that are not free from obscurity, the besetting vice of sonnets,
are nevertheless unexampled in the English language since
Shakespeare's for depth of thought, and skill and felicity of
execution." "Direct and complete—an honour and a profit to
the book," was all Rossetti said of the article, to Ellis.

As the weeks passed new reviewers appeared, not all appreciated by Rossetti. The back of the binding of the first copies of
Poems issued, had, to Gabriel's extreme annoyance, been cut
too wide, and blank sheets had been inserted at the end of the
book to fill it out. When towards the end of May the *Daily News*
waxed ironical over these blank pages, Gabriel merely told
Ellis: "The blank leaf business is a lark"; but William urged

action, and his alarmed brother wrote a reply which he asked
Ellis to publish as his own. When Alfred Austin, later poet-
laureate, reviewed *Poems* in the *Standard*, Gabriel merely asked:
"Did you see the charming *Standard*? It is, I find, the notorious
Marsyas flayed lately in the *Pall Mall*—to wit, Alfred Austin."
Dr. Hake's article on Rossetti's verse, which appeared in the
June issue of the *New Monthly*, Gabriel thought "very good,"
but he regretted that it had forestalled an intended review of
his poems by Bell Scott. In the same month the *Contemporary
Review* published an appreciative article, while a few days
later the *Spectator* reviewed him, and, as he had feared, without
enthusiasm.

July brought another spate of criticism. The *Westminster
Review* and the *North British Review* he found "civil though
short." A review in the New York *Nation* appeared in mid-
July, and one in *Blackwood's Magazine* in August. By this time
the Franco-German War had broken out; Gabriel's comments
upon it were characteristic. "I suppose all poetry will be as
dead as ditch-water now with this blessed war," he wrote,
"*Blackwood* and the *Nation* have come too late to smash me, as
no doubt the war has been beforehand with them as regards
poetry in general." The probable effect of the war upon the
picture market also troubled him. "This truly atrocious and
insufferable war," he described it shortly afterwards to the
agonizing Shields, naïvely asking him at the same time whether
his sorrow was due "simply to what all must feel or to more
direct influence of a baleful kind in your own immediate
prospects. Such would doubtless be a possible result for any of
us, as there is no knowing the moment at which entrenchment
[retrenchment?] may be forced upon the wealthy classes of
this country by the state of affairs abroad, or even at home,
and naturally Art goes first to the wall."

His recent critic in the *Nation*, Gabriel suspected was "poetaster Lowell," while "the other genius," his critic in *Blackwood's*, he admitted, "I can't guess at. The number of editions
seems to stick in his gizzard." "Blackwood and Co.," he
recalled, "wanted to publish the book themselves! 'Illae lacry-
mae' (sive pedita) may be thus partly traceable." Although
fairly restrained in comment, he was not at heart indifferent,

and when rumour whispered that his adverse critic in *Black-wood's* was a personal friend, he was deeply stirred. "What do you think of the *Blackwood* article being written by an intimate of mine," he asked Ellis. "Perhaps Morris told you. It isn't certified yet, but looks suspicious. I've written to ask him if he did it."

His belief in a secret conspiracy against himself, the belief that had haunted and spoiled his father's life, the fear of lurking treachery, a paranoiac fear, though as time would show not without a basis of fact, was steadily increasing.

In his unease he wrote to ask Allingham: "Have you seen the latest *Blackwood*? If you have not and need a relish before dinner, try it instead of gin and bitters. What Brother Bard but must find an added zest in the meat dispensed by the hand of detected mediocrity." Perhaps it was some request of Gabriel's that he should answer *Blackwood* that led Colvin, who had so recently reviewed Gabriel's volume in the *Westminster Review*, to publish another laudatory article on the book in the same review for January 1871.

Amongst those to whom Gabriel had sent presentation copies of *Poems* were Ruskin (despite their estrangement), Patmore, Meredith, Tennyson and Browning. "I am flooded with letters about my book," he soon announced, when acknowledgments arrived, but he was hurt by "a rather shabby one, I must say, from Tennyson, and none from Brown-ing as yet." Tennyson's actual opinion is only to be conjec-tured, so contradictory is the evidence, but that he more or less unconsciously resented the rivalry of the younger poet, or at least his growing popularity, is by no means improbable. Buchanan, trying later to excuse his own disgraceful attack upon Rossetti, declared that Tennyson, when Rossetti's *Poems* first appeared, "avowed to me *viva voce*, that he considered Rossetti's sonnet *Nuptial Sleep* the 'filthiest thing he had ever read.' "[1] But Buchanan was a liar in grain, and Palgrave, in a comment he wrote for the official *Memoir* of Tennyson by the poet's son, declared: "The passion and imaginative power of the sonnet *Nuptial Sleep* impressed him deeply"—a statement not necessarily out of harmony with Buchanan's, if taken

[1] *v. inf.* p. 500.

literally, without the inevitable suggestion of approval! Tennyson's son himself testified of his father, "among modern sonnets he liked some of Rossetti's." Tennyson himself in his later years declared to one of Rossetti's biographers: "I have neither drawing nor picture by Rossetti. I am sorry for it, for some of his work which I have seen elsewhere I admired very much. Nor have I any letter from him, nor do I remember his being present when I was reading the proofs of *Maud*. Indeed, I would willingly have known so fine a spirit more intimately, but he kept himself so shut up that it was all but impossible to come at him. What you call 'intimacy' never advanced much beyond acquaintance."

By May 3rd, out of the thousand copies of *Poems* printed, two hundred and fifty had gone to America, while all but two hundred of the remaining seven hundred and fifty were already sold and a new edition was being prepared. "My book will have brought me £300 in less than a month, which is not so bad for poetry, particularly if it goes on," Rossetti said. The first English and American edition of five hundred copies each would bring him, he said, "£800, not so bad for poetry after all, even if the public find themselves glutted after the second thousand." But his hopes of America were bitterly disappointed. "You ask me about America," he wrote to Scott in October 1871. "My volume was printed there at once, and I received through the publishers many reviews, some enthusiastic, others sulky or disparaging. All the author's percentage they have sent me is a beggarly £20, and I don't believe the thing has had a popular success there." And when Scott asked Emerson if the Americans had not cared for Rossetti's poetry, the philosopher of the "Oversoul" replied: "Yes; we scarcely take to the Rossetti poetry; it does not come home to us, it is exotic; but we like Christina's religious pieces."

But whatever the Americans thought of Rossetti's verse, the English public was far from "glutted" as Gabriel had feared, and with his unfailing flair for "good business," he at once set about making the most of his opportunity. By the first of June, *Poems* had entered its third edition of five hundred copies each; in September its fourth, to be followed by a fifth and sixth before the end of the year. He also persuaded Ellis to agree to a new edition of his *Early Italian Poets*. "I mean to set about the job soon now—as soon as I get into the country which will be before long," he told Ellis early in September, adding: "I suppose if ready for the printers by the end of October, that would be time enough, to be out by end of year."

Back in London, his health restored, Rossetti returned to his easel with renewed zest. To complete his enormous painting, *Dante's Dream*, he even postponed his revision of *The Early Italian Poets*, which consequently did not appear for several years. "A big picture is glorious work," he rejoiced to Shields, in August, "really rousing to every faculty one has or even thought one might have, and I hope I am doing better in this than hitherto." Despite his intention to return to the country, he lingered throughout the summer in London, working at *Dante's Dream*, his solitude seldom broken save for occasional visits from his mother and sisters, who on fine days would sometimes dine with him in the tent, amidst the quiet desolation of his garden. The old lady loved to see the deer running up to them to eat out of their hands. She was glad, too, to see that Gabriel was thinner and apparently in better health and spirits now. Yet beyond the shelter of his solitary retreat in Cheyne Walk, the reputation of Rossetti and of the later Pre-raphaelite Movement which, almost despite himself, he had founded and led, was approaching its zenith. Previously re-puted a painter and poet of distinction indifferent to both pictorial exhibitions and poetical publications, Rossetti upon the appearance of *Poems* was henceforth acclaimed as greatest of the few contemporaries to practise both arts, that is, as the supreme English painter-poet of the day. The professional painter was now also a leading, professional poet.

"The celebrity that awaited Rossetti's poems among critics," wrote Dr. Hake, explaining his friend's success, after Gabriel's death, "was latent in his paintings which were already famous for their emotional colouring and fine portraiture of women; and being in intimate social relation with many leading members of the Press, his poetical pretensions were accepted by acclamation. Then he had a powerful clientele among buyers. Those who possessed his pictures were very ready to receive and admire the poems of their favourite artist, and to push them about in the fashionable and the wealthy world, as the works of the poet-painter. . . . It was this that at once secured him his deserved success." It was a time, said Sir Sidney Colvin, long afterwards, when lovers of poetry, weary of mid-Victorian decorum in letters, disappointed by the mildness of the *Idylls of the King* which Tennyson had just given them at the height of his fame and power, specially hungered after poetic passion and romance. "We found ourselves," said Colvin, "all the more thrilled and satisfied by the full-blooded splendour and passionate colouring and imagery of Rossetti's work." "We that were interested in the future of English letters," wrote the literary critic of the *Academy* in 1892, referring to this earlier time in an obituary notice on Tennyson's recent death, "had lost all hope in Tennyson; our eyes were turned to Rossetti and Mr. Swinburne. It became the fashion to think and speak slightingly of the great master." Here perhaps lies one explanation of Tennyson's aloofness from Rossetti and his friends, and Sir Edmund Gosse in his study of Swinburne in *Portraits and Sketches*, hinted as much when he wrote: ". . . Tennyson had published nothing since *The Holy Grail*, and it was understood that he was slightly startled by the arrival of Swinburne, Morris and the Rossettis on a stage which he, with Robert Browning still very much in the background, had hitherto sufficiently filled. But the vogue of these new-comers was confined to the elect."

Nor was Gabriel's success without influence upon his friends. The "Preraphaelites" and their associates, had indeed risen during recent years, in Rossetti's wake. Jones's growing prosperity had been marked by his removal to "The Grange," Fulham, at the close of 1867, and the opening of his first (and very small) bank account. The Preraphaelites' social occasions were taking a new, more luxurious tone. "A very swell affair," Brown had described the Joneses' house-warming party on their entering "The Grange," and all had admired the house, decorated by "The Firm." Holman Hunt (just back from another Eastern journey taken after his wife's death), had come to the Joneses' party, though worn and ill and suffering from ague. William Rossetti and Morris had also been present, but strangely, neither Janey nor Gabriel. Morris, who had originally intended to remain and sleep in the studio, fortunately changed his mind and so missed the seven hundred pounds of plaster which fell during the night, when the ceiling collapsed upon the sofa that would have been his bed.

Morris and his firm were also carried on the swelling wave, and the Morrises' home in Queen Square saw festive nights too. "To Queen Square," wrote Allingham in his diary on May 27, 1868, "to dine with Morris, and find, just alighting, Mrs. Ned (Jones) in a gorgeous yellow gown; 'tis a full dress party! and I in velveteen jacket. Morris, Ned J. (thin), D. G. R. (looking well), Webb, Howell, Mr. Wilfred Heeley, Publisher Ellis, and W. A. (Allingham himself), (ten men). Mrs. Morris, Miss Burden, Mrs. Ned (gay), Mrs. Howell, Mrs. Madox Brown (looks young with back to the window), Lucy Brown, Miss Faulkner (I between these), Mrs. Ellis, Miss Heeley. (Ten ladies.) Banquet.—'Earthly Paradise,' I suggest, and Ned writes this atop of the menu. A storm of talking. I away with D. G. R. about 1; walk first, then cab to Cheyne Walk, in and stay chatting and lounging till 3 in old fashion. 'Come to-morrow and we'll go up together to my mother's.' " Allingham's former disgust with Gabriel during the preceding year seemed largely to have passed, and now, in 1870, he was dining with Rossetti from time to time.

But nowhere was Preraphaelite popularity more conspicuous than at Brown's receptions at his great barrack of a house in Fitzroy Square, which now reached the zenith of their brilliance and fame. It was there, one evening late in 1870 or early in 1871 that Edmund Gosse, introduced to Brown by Scott, first met Swinburne. The memory of that momentous occasion remained with Gosse vividly throughout his life. Long afterwards describing the scene, he recalled how Janey Morris "in her ripest beauty, and dressed in a long, unfashionable gown of ivory velvet, occupied the painting-throne, and Dante Gabriel Rossetti, who, though still almost young, was yet too stout for elegance, squatted for some part of the evening at least—on a hassock at her feet," while Brown's son Nolly, following the latest Preraphaelite cult, "spontaneity of behaviour in society," carried white rats on his arms and shoulders, to the horror of the ladies.

453

Brown's earlier life on the Continent had left a permanent mark upon him, and he welcomed the consequent stream of continental artists and writers attracted to these receptions, a stream larger at that time than usual, because many such, as well as a crowd of professional models, had fled to London from the miseries of the Franco-German War and siege of Paris. For these Parisian models, Gabriel's freedom from insular and Philistine snobbery, happily distinguished him—and Brown too, we may be sure—from the majority of his fellow artists in England at that time. The Graeco-Italian organ grinder Gaetano Meo, who had been a painter's model in Paris, and ultimately became a fairly successful landscape painter, voiced the general opinion of these foreign models, when, expressing his disgust at the aloofness of London artists towards their models, whom he complained they treated as "dirt," he specially excepted Rossetti as "different." To Whistler, trained in the art schools of Paris, this foreign element at Brown's was no doubt an additional attraction. "There were always the most wonderful people," he declared, "anarchists, poets, and musicians, all kinds and sorts; in an inner room, Rossetti and Mrs. Morris sitting side by side in state, being worshipped, and, fluttering round them, Howell with a broad red ribbon across his shirt front, a Portuguese decoration hereditary in the family." Howell, the liar, inventing the "noble birth" of his Portuguese mother, and forgetting his English father, the poor drawing-master in Lisbon, had also invented this decoration which he always wore at receptions. Morris who well knew him, on being asked on one such occasion what the ribbon was, replied that he did not know, but as he knew Howell he was sure he had stolen it.

Another resort of the Preraphaelites in these later years, was the home of Dr. Westland Marston the dramatist, in Northumberland Terrace, Regents Park. Marston's Sunday evening receptions became as famous in their way as Brown's. To them, more frequently than their leaders Rossetti and Swinburne, came the crowd of younger disciples, Richard Garnett, O'Shaughnessy the poet (whose volume *An Epic of Women*, published about the time of Gabriel's *Poems*, had been highly praised by Rossetti and Swinburne), Knight, Francillon and the rest. "Fascinated by the glamour of Dante Gabriel Rossetti's poems," Francillon was delighted to find him sometimes at Marston's receptions, and thought he "*looked* his poetry, as Swinburne did not, and as William Morris certainly did not, whose comical figure with the mop head was also met there now and again. I cannot say," Francillon added, "that Rossetti's presence was enlivening. My most representative recollection of him is of his sitting beside Mrs. Morris, who looked as if she had stepped out of any one of his pictures, both wrapped in motionless silence as of a world where souls have no need of words. And silence, however poetically golden, was a sin in a poet whose voice in speech was so musical as his—hers I am sure I never heard." The various recollections by different observers at these Preraphaelite social gatherings, whether at Brown's, Marston's or elsewhere, all resemble one another in their association of Rossetti and Janey Morris. One, a cousin of William de Morgan, vividly recalled "seeing Rossetti at a party given by Mrs. Virtue Tebbs, seated in a corner feeding Mrs. William Morris with strawberries. He was carefully scraping off the cream, which was bad for her, and then solemnly presenting her with the strawberries in a spoon!"

That—at least within the Preraphaelite circle—Gabriel's devotion to Janey Morris was attracting attention and comment, is also shown by the tale Whistler preserved in his Journal, telling how "When Rossetti was painting Mrs. William Morris, she was at work embroidering a design of Rossetti's on some hangings. And there she sat, day after day, embroidering, until, at last, the curtain was finished and Howell—'the owl' as they called him—hung it up between Mrs. Morris's bed and Morris's. But it was too short, about a foot from the floor, and Howell came to tell Rossetti. What was to be done? It was a foot from the floor, and some night Morris would crawl under! 'He would not dare!' Rossetti declared, bringing his fist down on the table with a bang." So the intimacy of Gabriel and Janey and Morris's apparent acquiescence, was finding its reflection in foolish, cynical tales, obviously false but of equally obvious significance. . . .

"No doubt," wrote Frederic Harrison, long afterwards, looking back dispassionately upon this time, "the Brethren called Preraphaelites were over-rated as painters. Rossetti's pictures were rather poems than paintings; and Burne-Jones, with all his fascination, forgot that mystical odes to beauty are not paintings. But the moral and social influence of these reformers redeemed the age of the Queen from the 'early Victorian' *mesquinerie* into which their predecessors had plunged it after the dismal era of her uncles."

To Gabriel, however, success brought little joy. Despite his absorption in painting, he continually lamented the almost unbroken solitude of his usual daily round. "Hardly any one comes to my place now," he complained, "as I have so long been engaged on work which I decline to show, and people have got sick of my sulks." When Scott now settled near Rossetti at Bellevue House, Cheyne Walk, Gabriel rejoiced. "He is a great acquisition," he said, and soon the evenings of whist with Scott, begun in 1868 at Elgin Road and Tudor House, changed with this closer proximity, to a definite system of "regular evenings for alternate visits and whist." Of these evenings, Boyce's record for 1871 gives us an occasional interesting glimpse: "February 14. W. B. Scott and Miss Boyd, D. G. Rossetti, Henry Wallis and Rev. G. Blunt (the local rector) came to whist and supper.[1] Just as we were sitting down to supper Rossetti sent for his marmot which trotted about the floor for the rest of the evening. April 11. To the rectory. W. B. Scott and wife and Miss Boyd, D. G. Rossetti, Mr. Way, Mr. Daniell. Whist, at which R. swore so outrageously that I made a mental resolve not to sit down to cards with him again until he in some way expressed his regret at what he had said. May 12. After a month's delay, Rossetti wrote a full, frank and very friendly apology for his conduct towards us at the Rectory on the 11th of last month. I responded to it at once."

With his brother William, however, Gabriel's relations were less intimate than in earlier years, but he still borrowed money from him at need, in the old way, despite his own large income and his brother's narrow means and wide responsibilities. Perhaps William was showing a little more independence now, for Gabriel, still sharp-tongued and keenly aware of what

[1] Boyce was now Rossetti's neighbour in Chelsea.

seemed to him his excellent brother's aesthetic limitations, was forced to apologize to him for some derogatory comment which had reached William's ears.

This year Gabriel had actually contemplated a "public show," but postponed it, in intention, to the next year, and in fact, to eternity. Although *Dante's Dream* was nearly finished, he had now turned from it "to finish several other things long in hand—viz: *Beatrice, Sibylla Palmifera* and *Mariana* with a boy singing (*Measure for Measure*)" and also *Pandora* as he told Shields. How hard he worked, how weary he often was, he showed in a letter of April 27, 1871, apologising to his mother, who had called that afternoon, for having momentarily forgotten that it was her birthday, that of "the dearest and best of mothers. I must," he continued, "have seemed very neglectful lately in not coming to see you; but daily I find my work pushes the day on and leaves me so weary that I am unable to start out anywhere till too late to reach Euston Square before your bedtime. . . ." Two months later he was still writing to his mother in this vein: "I cannot say how sorry and vexed I am at never seeing you just now. But the fact is that my work at present is almost always standing-work, as I have to go back constantly to look at the effect; and I am so tired by dusk that, if I do not wait an hour or so to rest before going out, I am obliged to take a cab and sacrifice my walk—without which I am done for. Thus I seldom get out till after nine, or sometimes (as this evening) even after ten, and then it is no use coming to see you."

Within a few days, however, with the opening of July, he would fulfil his long delayed intention to return for a time to the country. Nor would he go, as he recently intended, to rooms which Dr. Hake at Roehampton had set apart for him. He would go to the remote country house he had recently taken with Morris, Kelmscott Manor, three miles by road from Lechlade—Lechlade, where Shelley had once written poetry —and thirty miles by river from Oxford. In 1871 the nearest railway station to Kelmscott was Faringdon, and from there, to reach it, one must take a long drive over the Berkshire hills.

IX

THE IDLE SINGER OF AN
EMPTY DAY
1865–1871

I believe I have a friend,
Of whom for love I may not be afeard.

The Earthly Paradise W. MORRIS

THE CIRCUMSTANCES in which Morris had taken Kelmscott in joint tenancy with Rossetti were somewhat curious. In the first place, for several years now the two friends had been gradually drifting apart, and soon all association between them was to cease. Indeed, throughout the years of Gabriel's part tenancy of Kelmscott, he and Morris were hardly ever in the house together, and the few occasions on which they were seem to have been almost if not quite confined to an occasional weekend at the beginning of their occupancy. Yet Janey lived there with Gabriel for many months at a time. Whatever the increasing distance between Morris and Rossetti, Gabriel's friendship for Mrs. Morris became only the more intimate and their association henceforth for several years almost continual.

Nor, in the light of immediately preceding and later events, is it without interest and possible significance to note that shortly before taking Kelmscott, Morris had been working for some months upon a novel which his chief biographer, MacKail long since described as "certainly the most singular of his writings, a novel of contemporary life," which "dealt with the love of two brothers for the same woman, and was evidently going to take a tragic turn" if Morris had not abandoned it after more than a third was written. This theme, however, of two brothers or friends in love with the same woman, haunted Morris's thought and art to the end. It forms the subject of the most intense and passionate of his stories in *The Earthly Paradise*, the version of the *Laxdale Saga* he entitled *The Lovers of Gudrun* —which Rossetti declared the best poem Morris had so far written—as well as of one of his very last poems, *The Pilgrims of Hope*, in which the "hero," betrayed by his best friend who secretly becomes his wife's lover, shows the greatest magnanimity to them both, instead of

> . . . wrath or reproaching or the chill of love-born hate.[1]

This magnanimous attitude of the husband betrayed by his friend but forgiving or at least non-resisting—the influence of Tennyson's King Arthur was then very great—was one which certainly Morris himself shared, at least in theory, and, as one is now forced to believe, also in practice. Very few of either Morris's or Mrs. Morris's letters are published or otherwise accessible, but one by Morris, written seventeen years later, and so, long after Rossetti's death, clearly reveals the passive chivalry of Morris's own code. Silent even to his most intimate friends about matters nearest his heart, he was led by some question of his correspondent to speak in the plainest terms of marriage and of his own ideal system, in which the married "couple will be *free*. Being free," he continued, "if unfortunately distaste arose between them they should make no pretence of its not having arisen. But I should hope that in most cases friendship would go along with desire and would *outlive* it, and the couple would still remain together, but always as free people." As for "legal rights" of marriage, Morris would acknowledge none unless sanctioned by reciprocal passion. Marriage without that, he denounced as "venal prostitution," and approvingly declared: "real society asserts itself in the teeth of authority by forming genuine unions."

This same theory of "free" love, provided it *was* love, Morris again expressed in *News from Nowhere*. Into that ideal world he introduced the young married couple who "lived together two years the first time; . . . both very young; and then she got it into her head that she was in love with somebody else. But it did not last long, only about a year." And so, in Morris's story, the lovers were again happily reunited. From the ideal world of Morris's dream in *News from Nowhere*, he banished

[1] *cf.* May Morris's remark—"Literary inspiration in my father's early life came upon him, as it seems to me, in two very different moods: one produced the nerve-racked prose tales and poems of bitter loves and clouded lives. . . ." *Collected Works*, vol. xvii, p. xvi.

divorce courts as futile and immoral, with: "Fancy a court for enforcing a contract of passion or sentiment! . . . We do not deceive ourselves, indeed," he said, "or believe that we can get rid of all the trouble that besets the dealings between the sexes. We know that we must face the unhappiness that comes of man and woman confusing the relations between natural passion and sentiment, and the friendship which, when things go well, softens the awakening from passing illusions: but we are not so mad as to pile up degradation on that unhappiness by engaging in sordid squabbles about livelihood and position, and the power of tyrannizing over the children who have been the result of love or lust. . . . If there must be sundering[1] betwixt those who meant never to sunder, so it must be: but there need be no pretext of unity when the reality of it is gone. . . ." Morris, who had evidently thought long and carefully over marriage and its problems, was obviously the antithesis of a Soames Forsyte, would claim no privileges not readily granted by love, and, whatever the sacrifice, would in practice follow the dictates of his moral theory.

Little less interesting than these comments of Morris, are those of his friends upon Morris himself. "He was the only man I ever came in contact with who seemed absolutely independent of sex considerations," wrote Compton Rickett. "Morris," said Bernard Shaw, "was a complete fatalist in his attitude towards the conduct of his children and of all human beings where sex was concerned. . . . As to any sort of coercive interference on his part it was inconceivable." "In his domestic life," wrote another friend, Wilfrid Scawen Blunt, vaguely suggestive, and after Morris's death, "Morris was too busy to be unhappy, and of too sanguine a temperament to worry himself much over past disappointments; yet disappointments cannot but have been his. He had a strong and affectionate heart, and had centred his home affections on his two children. . . . One thing only, I think, he did not know, much as he had written about it, the love of women, and that he never cared to discuss."

Nor was this all. From the time of Gabriel's poetic renascence

---

[1] *cf.* Morris's tale *The Sundering Flood*, and the last words of *The Water of the Wondrous Isles*—"their love never sundered," etc. Note too the unsympathetic wife in *The Wood Beyond the World*, Ch. I, and the Knight who slays a friend for the lady he loves, in *The Well at the World's End*, I, 22.

three years before, most of Morris's poems had emphasized a
vein of thought and feeling manifested in the novel he had just
abandoned—that of unhappiness in love. In this they presented
a striking contrast to Rossetti's recent verse. For while Gabriel's
poems suggested mental, moral and spiritual revival through
passion, Morris's increasingly betrayed a sadness and despair
due to rejected love. As Gabriel, emerging from the shades of
Willow-wood, sang ever more insistently, more ecstatically, of
love and passion restored, Morris, as in some strange emotional
antiphony, sang with deepening sorrow of love lost. For many
years, indeed, Morris's verse was to echo this same plaintive
note of brooding anguish over love slighted, despised, rejected;
dead in one heart, poignantly alive in another, of loyalty and
patience in love vainly wrestling with dying hope. For him,
henceforth, love is but

> . . . the loss of all I seemed to gain,

as he sang in *Hapless Love*, a poem which first appeared in
Good Words for April 1869. In many a poem of this time, it is as
if some hidden sorrow of Morris found a voice. Thus, for
example, he lamented in *The Doomed Ship*:—

> Thus sorrow, are we sitting side by side
> Amid this welter of the grey despair,
> Nor have we images of foul or fair
> To vex, save of thy kissed face of a bride,
> Thy scornful face of tears when I was tried,
> And failed 'neath pain I was not made to bear.

In similar vein was the significantly named *Near but Far Away*;
and in *What all men long for and What none shall have*, he sang
bitterly

> Of love well trusted turned to shame,

steeling his resolution with—

> Harden thine eyes, make smooth thy face!
> Wear the mask still. Lie down with ill!
> Rest wearily from hope and praise;

and finally, looking to the end, he cried:—

> Choose, choose the best, the pain, but pray,
> If thou hast breath to cast away
> For somewhat of a better day;

A rest with something good to gain
More than dead love and wasted pain;
   Cry bitterly, to draw anigh
One heart at least, and cry in vain.

It was indeed such a man as this that Morris described in 1867 in his explanatory prologue to *The Earthly Paradise*; one vainly striving—even in the writing of the poem—

   . . . to build a shadowy isle of bliss
Midmost the beating of the steely sea,
   Where tossed about all hearts of men must be.

From the time of his return to London in 1865 until the close of 1870, Morris had devoted whatever leisure he could obtain, to the writing of this long poem, *The Earthly Paradise*, in which his thwarted desires found imaginative satisfaction, and which he ultimately dedicated to his wife. Into this poem, as Mackail long since remarked, went much of Morris's own experience. "Shy and reserved in life," wrote his biographer, "he had all the instinct of the born man of letters for laying himself open in his books, and having no concealment from the widest circle of all. In the verses that framed the stories of *The Earthly Paradise*, there is an autobiography so delicate and so outspoken that it must needs be left to speak for itself."

Certainly many a lyrical passage of those ostensibly seasonal poems on the months, dividing the stories in *The Earthly Paradise*, thrills to the obviously personal sorrow of the poet in the loss of love. This for example is the mood of those for August, written in 1867, and of those for July, published in April 1868, while many of the tales themselves, such as *The Lovers of Gudrun* already mentioned, and *The Man who never laughed again*, are inspired by the same theme. It was as if the life of Morris, the

                idle singer of an empty day

as he now significantly described himself, were become an emotional void which only the distraction of ceaseless labour could fill. After long, exacting days at "the shop," designing, experimenting, directing, he would pass the nights in his study, composing *The Earthly Paradise*, until long after the rest of the household were asleep, and Gabriel in fact, genially

caricatured him as *Bard and Petty Tradesman*, showing him as
Orpheus at one time, charming the beasts of the field, and at
another as a shopman cajoling customers.

Most clearly is the contrast between Rossetti's and Morris's
love-songs revealed in May 1870; for while Gabriel with unwonted light-heartedness carolled in *Fior di Maggio*,

> Love's the fruit that is ripened best
> By ladies' eyes in May,

Morris, in a poem which, whether accidentally or not, carried
a title similar to Gabriel's but in English—*The End of May*—
sang in widely different mood—

> How the wind howls this morn
> About the end of May,
> And drives June on apace
> To mock the world forlorn
> And the world's joy passed away
> And my unlonged-for face!
> For no more may I deem
> That any folk are glad
> To see the dawn of day
> Sunder the tangled dream
> Wherein no grief they had.
> Ah, the tangled dream!
> Where others have no grief,
> Ever it fares with me
> That fears and treasons stream,
> And dumb sleep slays belief
> Whatso therein may be.
> Sleep slayeth all belief,
> Until the hopeless light
> Wakes at the birth of June,
> More lying tales to weave,
> More love in woe's despite,
> More hope to perish soon.

"Fears and treasons" and lost love which as 1870 neared its
close, became in *Pain and Time Strive Not*, a dirge of spiritual
parting and farewell, of the saddened soul painfully returning
to its isolation: such were his obsessive themes.

> What part of the dread eternity
> Are those strange minutes that I gain,
> Mazed with the doubt of love and pain,
> When I thy delicate face may see,
>   A little while before farewell?

463

What share of the world's yearning-tide
That flash, when new day bare and wide
Blots out my half-dream's faint delight,
And there is nothing by my side,
And well remembered is farewell?

What drop in the grey flood of tears
What time, when the long day toiled through,
Worn out, shows nought for me to do,
And nothing worth my labour bears
The longing of that last farewell?

What pity from the heavens above,
What heed from out eternity,
What word from the swift world for me?
Speak, heed, and pity, O tender love,
Who knew'st the days before farewell!

This same mood, finding expression in a dramatic touch rarely found in these verses of regret, inspires the lines to January in *The Earthly Paradise*, where, in a scene recalling that other contemporary, autobiographical poem on a kindred theme, Meredith's *Modern Love*, we see the man and woman together in their home but silently estranged by doubts and love's passing.

From this dull rainy undersky and low,
This murky ending of a leaden day,
That never knew the sun, this half-thawed snow,
    These tossing black boughs faint against the grey
Of gathering night, thou turnest, dear, away
Silent but with thy scarce-seen kindly smile
Sent through the dusk my longing to beguile.

There, the lights gleam, and all is dark without!
And in the sudden change our eyes meet dazed—
O look love, look again! the veil of doubt
Just for one flash, past counting, then was raised!
O eyes of heaven, as clear thy sweet soul blazed
On mine a moment! O come back again,
Strange rest and dear amid the long dull pain!

Nay, nay gone by! though there she sitteth still,
With wide, grey eyes so frank and fathomless—
Be patient, heart, thy days they yet shall fill
With utter rest—yea, now thy pain they bless,
And feed thy last hope of the world's redress—
O unseen hurrying rack! O wailing wind!
What rest and where go ye this night to find?

No paraphrase can adequately communicate the particular quality of Morris's emotion and suggestion in such verses, and it is best to let him speak here for himself, in his own plaintive, elusive tongue.

Throughout 1870, as *The Earthly Paradise* drew towards its close with the closing year, this undertone of sorrow for lost love grew in intensity. "Insolently solid" Rossetti had surprisingly but perhaps significantly described his once so genial, spontaneous friend, when Morris and Janey visited him at Scalands in the spring of the year. For such "solidity," however, Morris had prayed in *The Earthly Paradise*, some months before, as the year dawned, begging to

> . . . be like to men upon the sea
> Laid fast asleep in midst of their distress.

But the prayer was largely vain, for a few weeks later he lamented—

> Shalt thou not wonder that it liveth yet,
> The useless hope, the useless craving pain,
> That made thy face, that lonely noontide, wet
> With more than beating of the chilly rain?
> Shalt thou not hope for joy new born again,
> Since no grief ever born can ever die
> Through changeless change of seasons passing by?

For despite his efforts the old love-sorrow still held him:—

> Look long, O longing eyes, and look in vain!
> Strain idly, aching heart, and yet be wise,
> And hope no more for things to come again
> That thou beheldest once with careless eyes!
> Like a new wakened man thou art, who tries
> To dream again the dream that made him glad
> When in his arms his loving love he had.

When not busily employed, Morris was obviously the prey of unhappy retrospect, and the secret burden of his sorrow was always the same, the longing that found vent in his cry:—

> Fair day, fair night, O give me back
> The tide that all fair things did lack
> Except my love, except my sweet!

More and more deeply, to the very end of the poem, Morris's

465

personal passion and pain penetrated *The Earthly Paradise*, as he brooded over—

> Change, kindness lost, love left unloved alone,

to repeat his own words in the verses for December. Yet to the last he kept personal silence and, unable to condemn those who had destroyed his happiness, was also unable to relinquish the last glimmer of hope, telling himself:—

> Though no soul knows wherewith thine heart doth yearn,
> Yet, since thy weary lips no curse can learn,
> Cast no least thing thou lovedst once away,
> Since yet perchance thine eyes shall see the day.

It was thus, at the close of 1870, that Morris came with peculiar regret to the end of *The Earthly Paradise* which, during these unhappy years, had been a chief source of consolation to him, offering distraction, the relief of self-expression, and imaginative compensation to the man who, in actual life, kept silence about his private sorrows. In the *Epilogue* to the poem however—*On Love's Ending—Life's Ending*—he struck again the same personal note, while the *Envoi* yet more fully reflected the disillusion of this "poor singer of an empty day," as at the close of each stanza he described himself. And in the *Envoi* he openly proclaimed the solace he had found in fashioning *The Earthly Paradise*, for, as he apostrophized the poem itself:—

> Kind words and praise because of thee I won
> From those without whom were my world all gone,
> My hope fallen dead, my singing cast away,
> And I set soothly in an empty day.

It was also in this *Envoi* that surely for one moment his bitterness towards Rossetti overflowed in somewhat tremulous but ironical humour, for in the light of their relation, Morris could scarcely have been blind to the *double-entendre* in his exhortation to his book as he sends it forth on its pilgrimage, declaring:

> Surely no book of verse I ever knew
> But ever was the heart within him hot
> To gain the Land of Matters Unforgot—
> —There, now we both laugh—as the whole world may,
> At us poor singers of an empty day.

> Nay, let it pass, and hearken! Hast thou heard
> That therein I believe I have a friend,
> Of whom for love I may not be afeard?

For poor Morris it was a bitter jest! His poem and himself he described as "children . . . late made wise in love," and his final consolation, even if *The Earthly Paradise* should fail to reach The House of Fame was, that it was

> not ill done to strive to lay
> The ghosts that crowd about life's empty day—

surely a clear revelation of the *causa causans* of *The Earthly Paradise*.

Although in but vague and general terms, the best informed biographers of Morris have suggested the personal significance of *The Earthly Paradise*. "The book," wrote May Morris, "which had been in his thoughts for so many years had at last gone from him, the strain of the final moments was over, and he was left relaxed and lonesome, yearning after the companion that was no longer his. All this yearning, all the unwillingness to part with his book is gathered in the loving farewell of *L'Envoi*." "The pity," wrote Mackail of this same work, "with which he clung to it, and the forlornness in which it left him when the two had parted company, he has written down with absolute truth and sweetness in the words of the *Epilogue*. And the final words which he puts in the mouth of his book when he sends it forth to seek a place with Chaucer, are the plain truth about his own life so far as he understood it, as well as his deepest thought on the mystery of things." To his wife, then at Torquay, Morris himself wrote in similar vein in late November 1870. "I feel rather lost," he told her, "at having done my book: I find now I liked working at it better than I thought. I must try and get something serious to do as soon as may be. . . ." "For me," he wrote to her again, a few days later, "I don't think people really want to die because of mental pain, that is if they are imaginative people; they want to live to see the play played out fairly—they have hopes that they are not conscious of. Hillao! here's cheerful talk for you. I beg your pardon, dear, with all my heart."

Such then was the ever-recurrent theme of Morris's verse, of which but a few out of many examples are here given, during these and subsequent years. It was a strange theme, surely, to haunt the work of a middle-aged, "successful" artist, married and with a family, unless there were actual reasons in his own life for such an obsession. Probably Georgie Jones, now less friendly towards Janey but henceforth and increasingly the chief friend of Morris, needed no explanation of this personal element in Morris's verse. "People," wrote Mackail of Morris—again discreetly explanatory—"who have not this imaginative instinct, often wonder how a poet can bear to lay open his inmost feelings, and uncover the weaknesses of which man is made; still oftener the self-revelation passes clean over the heads of his audience, and so far are they from wondering that they do not even notice. It is the knowledge, no doubt, that all of his inmost heart, his love and hope and sorrow, which he pours into his verses is to the unsympathetic reader simply meaningless, which allows a poet to write fearlessly what, being a poet, he must write in any case."

One other distraction Morris had found during these years, an interest in Icelandic studies, and it was this—in part at least—which somewhat surprisingly, unless we consider these circumstances, took him to Iceland immediately after he and Rossetti had taken Kelmscott Manor. Nor, despite the powerful influence of his earlier friendship with Gabriel, did Morris speak of that friendship in later years. "He had a certain respect for Rossetti," wrote Shaw, "but he never spoke of his poetry and of his painting. Apparently what awed him about Rossetti was that the poet-painter positively liked writing letters . . . and was so clever in business and diplomacy that he sold his pictures for good prices long before he had any public reputation."

X

KELMSCOTT
1871

Some heavenly solstice hushed and halcyon.

Heart's Compass D. G. ROSSETTI

IT WAS MORRIS, "looking about," as he said, "for a house for the wife and kids, "who, one bright May morning in 1871, discovered Kelmscott Manor. "A heaven on earth; an old stone Elizabethan house . . . and such a garden!" he wrote: "Close down on the river, a boathouse and all things handy. I am going there again on Saturday with Rossetti and my wife: Rossetti because he thinks of sharing it with us if the thing looks likely." Thus it was that Rossetti and Morris took a joint lease of Kelmscott "Manor," as it was called—by courtesy, for the house carried no manorial rights. Soon its association with the later "Preraphaelites" was to make it one of the most famous houses in English literary history. "A house," wrote Morris later, "that I love; with a reasonable love I think." Although his friend Webb the architect, when questioned, would not commit himself further than to remark vaguely that it was "really later than it looked to be," Morris delightedly declared the house "Elizabethan," and it was to Kelmscott, at the close of his Utopian tale *News from Nowhere*, psychologically so significant, that he took his compensatory dream-love Ellen, and in the "tapestry room" sat with her as his dream faded away. For the Freudian wish-fulfilment dream, the imaginary, compensatory love for erotic frustration are present in *News from Nowhere* as in so much of Morris's verse—a natural development of his apparent situation.

Amidst the meadows of a Thames backwater, Kelmscott offered to the outer world but a door in an ivy-covered wall, and the side of a grey stone barn, behind which appeared the grey stone gables of the house, a rather low, three-storied building with mullioned windows, roofed with stone slates—

"the most lovely covering," said Morris, "which a roof can have." The most notable rooms of Kelmscott Manor were its white panelled "parlour" overlooking the quaint old garden with its yew hedges clipped to fantastic patterns, and the "tapestry-room" which gave glimpses of clover meadows and a pretty little elm-crowned hill.

As soon as he had settled Janey and his two daughters in Kelmscott, early in July, Morris returned immediately to London, whence on July 6th he set off with a Scandinavian friend for Iceland to explore the native environment of the sagas, to which he had recently turned his attention. At the very moment of departure he thought regretfully of his wife and children at Kelmscott. "How beautiful the place looked last Monday," he wrote; "I grudged going away so; but I am very happy to think of all of you happy there, and the children and you getting well. . . . Now I will say goodbye dear, for the present, with all blessings on you. Kiss the littles and give them my best love. I shall write a line from Edinburgh. Live well and happy. . . ."

Six days later, Gabriel, again complaining of insomnia and eye-weakness, joined Janey and her two daughters at Kelmscott. There he intended to remain for at least two months, hoping that quiet, and pleasant companionship, would heal the morbidity solitude encouraged, and restore both his physical and mental health.

Both Janey and Gabriel delighted in Kelmscott. "A haunt of ancient peace," said Gabriel, borrowing for once from Tennyson. He described the farm buildings as "of the thatched squatted order, which look settled down into a purring state of comfort," and Janey—whose wit on some occasions at least was dismally reminiscent of poor Lizzie's—added that they "seemed as if, were you to stroke them, they would move." Gabriel's love of the old place indeed rivalled Morris's. "The loveliest place in existence," he told his friend Marks the curio dealer. "A most lovely house," he described it to his eccentric uncle Henry Polydore, adding: "It still belongs to the family whose ancestors built it, and whose arms are still on some of the chimney breasts. The garden, and meadows leading to the river brink, are truly delicious—indeed the place is perfect;

and the riverside walks are most charming in their way, though I must say the flatness of the country renders it monotonous and uninspiring to me."

Like Morris, Gabriel delighted in the assumed antiquity of his new abode; in its garden, "a perfect paradise, full of fat cut hedges that seemed to purr and simmer in the sun." The "tapestry room" (which could only be entered through his adjoining bedroom), he made his studio;[1] but unlike Morris who thought the tapestry designs created "a pleasant background for the living people," and "an air of romance," Gabriel, though he found the tapestry room "delightful," was but ironically appreciative of the tapestry figures ("certainly," he declared, "not the liveliest of company"), which indeed so wearied him at first by tempting him to elucidate their "incredible passages of drawing," that he almost yielded to the temptation to pull them down, and even later when he attained comparative indifference he admitted that "the questions why a Philistine leader should have a panther's tail, or Delilah a spike sticking out of her head, or what Samson, standing upon a heap of slain, has done with the ass's jaw-bone, will obtrude themselves at times between more abstract speculations."[2]

These few weeks at Kelmscott, passed in a normal tranquil daily round of work and relaxation such as Gabriel had seldom known, were probably the happiest of his life. Mornings of painting in the studio were followed by a daily walk, and in the evenings he read to Janey. "I am getting in something like order here and to something like work, though of course work is not my chief aim in a country holiday," he told Marks. Yet he pleaded work as his excuse for declining to invite friends to Kelmscott, preferring to remain alone there with Janey and the children. The complete solitude Kelmscott afforded them was to Gabriel one of its chief charms. "The very essence of all that is peaceful and retired—the solitude almost absolute"; he described it to his uncle, adding: "Kelmscott is a hamlet, containing I am told, 117 people, and these even one may be said never to see, if one keeps, as I do, the field-paths rather than the highroad." "This place," he

---

[1] For the disposition of these rooms see Note to p. 343.
[2] cf. stanza 102 of *The Bride's Prelude* revised up to publication in 1881.

told Marks, "is a desert or an Eden, whichever you choose to term it."

The weather, though "provokingly changeable" at first, soon grew so hot that Gabriel gladly abandoned waistcoats, arraying himself in "a blouse indoors and a wrapper out." Little May Morris long remembered that hot, pleasant summer of 1871 at Kelmscott; those "glowing August mornings" when she and her sister Jenny "sat in the pleasant cool of the panelled room trying to learn things about the Roman Emperors, and outside the wide mullioned windows the blackbirds were chuckling and feasting among the gooseberries, golden stocks were growing roof high in the yard outside, and the huge barn was alive with busy men and women," until May, tempted beyond endurance, would run out into the sunshine, leaving the studious Jenny to listen to her mother's instruction alone.

As before, at Scalands, both Gabriel and Janey miraculously improved in health; so that Janey was able to accompany Gabriel on the "nice little riverside walks" he discovered by the Thames, even, he rejoiced, "taking five and six mile walks without the least difficulty." "She is benefiting wonderfully," he told his mother, "and takes long walks as easily as I do." He liked their solitude, "as absolute as at Penkill," and the pretty country churches, especially Kelmscott church, "with two bells hanging visibly on the roof at one end—looking just as one fancies chapels in the *Morte d'Arthur*." He decided to use it in a picture some day. And he liked Lechlade. In Lechlade churchyard, he remembered, Shelley had once written a poem. So rustic was he becoming that he happily, but vaguely, contemplated buying a trap, a pig, and from Miss Boyd at Penkill "a highly desirable Ayrshire cow." His sole complaint was that away from the river, the country round Kelmscott was flat and dull.

Never before had Gabriel known this easy, pleasant domestic life, so different from the short scrambling existence in the Blackfriars rooms with Lizzie. The presence of the children increased his happiness. He found them "dear little things— perfectly natural and intelligent, and able to amuse themselves all day long without needing to be thought about by their elders . . . the most darling little self-amusing machines that ever existed." He determined to make drawings of them before leaving Kelmscott. May, the younger child, a romp and little studious, was his favourite. "Quite a beauty the more one knows her," he said, "and will be a lovely woman." He thought her "very clever," and, if "less lazy," good at drawing. He made her his model for angels, played jokes on her, such as gravely asking her which she thought the uglier of two ladies they knew, earnestly listening to her reasons and finally agreeing: "I think you are right." "It was very naughty of Mr. Rossetti," Janey dutifully reproved her daughter on hearing of it. Gabriel thought May "lovelier every day" and vainly tried, with May's apparent approval, to persuade Janey to let him adopt her. May, for her part, fully reciprocated Rossetti's liking. She enjoyed posing to him in the studio while he chatted with her, and he seemed interested in her talk just as if she were a "grown-up." This, Rossetti's usual way with children, had won him young Forbes-Robertson's appreciation a few months before. May was, as Gabriel saw, especially observant, and in later life she recalled his ways—his late breakfasts of many eggs, his days passed in the studio without break or refreshment until, as dusk fell and painting was no longer possible, he emerged for his constitutional walk which he now took daily, wet or fine. She noticed too, his loneliness; watching "the rather broad figure tramping away doggedly over the flat green meadows, in search of exercise and air enough to keep in health for the day's work," seeing him "returning after dark with a burden of weariness upon him," and recalled particularly one occasion when, playing hide-and-seek with other children, including "a vivacious but rather bored model," she suddenly crept into the silent drawing-room and finding Rossetti sitting solitary before the fire, felt with a momentary pang, a sudden inexplicable atmosphere of loneliness and desolation about him.

But whatever the ever-present menace, the threatened incursions of the spirit of dejection, Kelmscott kept it at bay. The days passed happily in painting Janey against a Kelmscott background as *Water-Willow*. Gabriel had no idea who would buy it, he said, but was tired of trying to attract purchasers by intriguing titles. "I can't be bothered," he exclaimed, "to stick

idle names: a head is a head, and fools won't buy heads on
that footing." He made chalk drawings of "the kids and their
mamma," and worked half-heartedly at a "vile replica" as he
called it, of *Beata Beatrix*. "Dreary work enough . . . a beastly
job," he wrote, "but lucre was the lure." The nine hundred
guineas his generous patron William Graham had promised
for it, would be very welcome. Yet not until the following year
could he make himself settle down to it in earnest, and even
when completed it was much inferior to the original painting
bought six years before by Mr. Cowper-Temple. He worked
also on a second replica of it, in water-colour this time, commissioned at three hundred and fifty guineas by Craven of
Manchester.

To share, in the evenings, his intellectual pleasures with a
beautiful woman of apparently kindred tastes was for Gabriel
a rare joy. To the presumably appreciative Janey he read
Shakespeare and Plutarch, "just as the first builders of the
house might have done," he said, describing their own way of
life at Kelmscott as "on the whole Elizabethan enough." He
presented Janey with a complete set of the Waverley Novels,
and also ordered from Ellis, doubtless for the same purpose,
Pepys's Diary—which he and Lizzie had laughed over during
their honeymoon in Paris, eleven years before—and also Boswell's *Life of Johnson*. Scott's works "surprised" him, he declared, by "their usual melodramatic absurdities of plot and
their astounding command of character in the personages by
whom all those improbabilities are enacted"; and his final
comment upon them was: "wonderful works with all their
faults."

In a characteristic reaction, Gabriel again revolted from
painting to poetry. "I wish one could live by poetry," he
lamented, "I think I'd see painting damned if one could." To
this change his environment at Kelmscott contributed. "There
are two splendid riverside walks," he told Brown, "to be taken
alternatively [alternately?] every day, without a soul to be
seen on the road to disturb the cud of composition and at home
everything lends itself to poetic composition." (So Kelmscott
was what Gabriel seldom knew—"home.") There was, he told
Scott, "a funny little island midway in one walk, which can

be reached by a crazy bridge, and does very well as a half-way house to commit sonnets to paper going and coming. It may perhaps lead to further effusions. I got one sonnet out of it to-day." Yet he feared he might write but little at Kelmscott as his walks were "seldom taken alone, Janey having developed a most triumphant pedestrian faculty, which," he told Scott, "licks you hollow, I can tell you."

At any rate his fears that Janey's company on his walks would prevent poetic composition, were not fulfilled. "A little sonnet-writing gets done too," he declared shortly afterwards, "and a ballad—of the *Sister Helen* kind rather—(it was *Rose Mary*)—is floating paperwards on a slow brain-breeze enough." By the middle of August he had thirty new sonnets "for the *House of Life*," all written since the publication of his *Poems*; sonnets obviously continuing the love-theme of their predecessors. Four of them Gabriel now sent to Scott, and although apart from these four it is impossible to identify them individually, certainly the great majority, if not indeed all but one, are to be found amongst the one new sonnet of 1870 and the twenty-eight additional new sonnets of 1871 in the completed *House of Life* which appeared ten years later.*

"I hardly ever do produce a sonnet," he now told Scott, "except on some basis of special momentary emotion; but I think there is another class admissible also—and that is the only other I practise, viz. the class depending on a line or two clearly given you, you know not whence, and calling up a sequence of ideas. This also is a just *raison d'être* for a sonnet, and such are all mine when they do not in some sense belong to the 'occasional' class." That these sonnets for *The House of Life* are, like their predecessors, chiefly of the first kind, that is, based on "special momentary emotion," is obvious. The experiences, the moods expressed are also the same; Rossetti's thoughts and feelings were now, like Swinburne's repetitive, obsessional. Bound to his revolving wheel he did not develop with the years. For him—a characteristic of neurotics, if we believe Freud—life was but a series of emotional and intellectual cycles, of repetitions. And in time, when the wheel stopped, both Rossetti and Swinburne became static, fell away from

* *v. Notes.*

reality into retrospect, dream, disillusion, indifference, infantilism or despair. To any possibility of further significant development in poetry or painting, such a state was evidently fatal. The flaw in verses—whatever their intrinsic excellence—which merely repeat the moods of adolescence into maturity, needs no exposition. And it is the consequence of frustration.

So in these sonnets of Kelmscott, written in later 1871, as in their immediate predecessors of 1869–1870 and onwards, we find again the old themes, though treated in general with growing tranquillity, or, when evil threatens, often with some approach to resignation. The lovers now wander through summer's bye-ways beneath cloudless, sunlit skies, or meet secretly, strained and furtive, fear evil omens of separation, or look beyond death to Love's final consummation. But the influence of Nature's beauty, of Kelmscott, is now often evident, and as we have seen, one sonnet, *Genius in Beauty*[1] actually reveals its subject to be Janey (the "sovereign" and "queenly") and its provenance to be Kelmscott by its reference to Gabriel's best-known portrait of Mrs. Morris, which hung in the Kelmscott studio. To Scott, Gabriel revealed his method of work. "I do a deal of making up in my head before I put pen to paper," he wrote, describing doubtless the "fundamental brainwork," the importance of which he later emphasized to Hall Caine.

Now too, he composed and translated into English verse one of his rare Italian songs, *Youth and Lordship*, gay, amatory, in the manner of Neapolitan street songs, and continued to develop his "ballad of the *Sister Helen* kind," *Rose Mary*. The theme had suggested itself as he watched Lucy Brown—Madox Brown's daughter by his first wife—painting a picture of "the Earl of Surrey regarding the image of his mistress in a magic mirror." It was just the sort of theme that would have fascinated Gabriel at seventeen, and now, at forty-three, he was no less fascinated by it. "My mirror, however," he wrote, "is a crystal ball." Dunn's chatter of "dreaming stones" and "magic Beryls" had impressed him. "Beryl," he found "the very word I want . . . for the title of my poem . . . it is better than crystal in every way; it is more rhythmical, and has a greater seeming

[1] *v. sup.* pp. 401–2.

of mysticism in its sound. Moreover, it is one of the mystic stones named in Revelations."

Nothing better shows how unreal, how essentially theatrical and tawdry, was some of the so exaggerated "mystical" element in Rossetti's work. "He has been frequently termed a mystic," wrote William Rossetti of his brother, "but he was almost the last man to be a mystic in the sense of disregarding or setting at nought the plain and obvious meaning of his author [Dante is referred to], and transmuting it out of human passion, emotion and incident, into mere abstract speculation or doctrinal framework.[1] Into his idea of Beatrice he would condense as much spiritual as womanly motive force; but it would have been contrary to his very nature to contemplate her as any other than a woman once really living in Florence, and there really loved by Dante as woman is loved by man. . . . In fact, he hated any glosses of a rationalizing tendency; and was as much indisposed to shuffle concrete things into allegory as he was prone to invest with symbolic detail or suggestion things which are in themselves simply physical and substantial."

The Beryl Stone Gabriel often called his new poem at first, but finally decided that its title should be *Rose Mary*, "a compound name," he explained, "dedicated to the Virgin, quite possible enough and useful to any scheme";[2] for he had apparently learned—no doubt from the library or conversation of his father, the learned historian of mediaeval Platonic love, familiar with the mystical and occult—the hidden significance of such terms as "the mystic rose," the well, and the bowl or cup which became *The Holy Grail*. These Rossetti at times introduced into his poetry, and, as he now explained, *Rose Mary* is "a story of my own, good, I think, turning of course on the innocence required in the seer," that is in Rose Mary herself, who, debarred by her illicit amour from seeing the fateful image in the Beryl stone aright, is unwittingly the cause of her lover's death. *Rose Mary*, Gabriel thought, was "much more plain-sailing narrative" than any other of the poems he had yet written, and when near the close of September he finished it— except for the Beryl songs introduced eight years later—he told Scott: "I hope it's a good 'un. It ought to have been done at

[1] *cf.* Preface, p. 611.   [2] *v. inf.* p. 639.

Penkill being a sort of Scotch or Border Story." The prose outline he had first made for it enabled him, he said, to "get on with it easily," though Scott thought this had ruined his impulse and invention, as most probably it had.

Although Gabriel described *Rose Mary* as a "Ballad—of the *Sister Helen* kind," he wisely preferred *Sister Helen* to *Rose Mary*. "I hope it is a good thing," he told Scott when *Rose Mary* was completed, "but there is so much incident that it is necessarily much more of a narrative poem than is usual with me, and thus lacks the incisive concentration of such a piece as *Sister Helen*", while he found the theme, he said, "so consumedly tragic that I have been obliged to modify the intended course of the catastrophe to avoid an unmanageable heaping up of the agony." He feared also that the poem was too long. To write it, he had indeed still further delayed the long contemplated and never written poem *The Orchard Pit*. "I should like to do that," he now wrote, "and another as soon as may be—and then with smaller things might perhaps make a fair volume again."

Already then, within eighteen months of his first volume of original verse, Gabriel was meditating a second. Towards it he had composed a few other poems at Kelmscott besides *Rose Mary* and the sonnets for *The House of Life*. The melodramatic and feeble *River's Record*[1] he gave to a short-lived journal *The Dark Blue*, to help Brown, who had been commissioned to obtain from him a poem for that journal and to provide for it an illustration. The poem duly appeared with Brown's design, in October. But Rossetti was rightly critical of the quality of his poem, which dealt with the then popular theme of the betrayed woman, who in this case commits suicide by throwing herself and her baby into the river. "Rather out of my usual way," Gabriel apologetically explained, "rude aiming at the sort of popular view that Tennyson perhaps alone succeeds in taking." But, a rare thing for Rossetti, he proudly pointed out a technical finesse of the poem which to us seems rather humorous: "two epithets are interchanged in each stanza between the landscape and the emotion!"

From Kelmscott in mid-August, Gabriel sent Scott two of his best known poems *Sunset Wings* and *The Cloud Confines*, besides

[1] Entitled *Down Stream* in Rossetti's *Poems*, 1881.

three stanzas of the long cryptic verses finished much later and entitled *Soothsay*, a poem to which he attached considerable importance. *Sunset Wings* and *The Cloud Confines* present—with unwonted calm and resignation for Gabriel—the inevitable now obsessive themes of Love and Death, touched in *Sunset Wings* to an exceptional beauty against a stormy Kelmscott sunset through which homing doves, starlings and rooks swoop down to their nests. "Another little poem done from Nature," he told his mother when sending her the verses. Watching the birds in this calm, evening hour beneath a lurid but darkening and ominous sky, the poet mused upon his eternal problem of love and death, of the beloved beside him, and of time, stealing life away—

> Even thus Hope's hours, in ever-eddying flight,
> To many a refuge tend;
> With the first light she laughed, and the last light
> Glows round her still; who natheless in the night
> At length must make an end.

From the cry of the rooks, which sounds to him like a knell for the death of day, his thought turns again to Hope—which also dies, in the heart of man.[1]

The Cloud Confines expressed another obsessive mood of Gabriel, that mood of doubt or rather of wistful longing for knowledge about the elemental problems of man's existence, which indeed, henceforth increased its hold upon Rossetti's thought and imagination until his death. In this poem of five short stanzas, Rossetti debated the mysteries of the past, of death, of hate—this last suggested by the Franco-German war just ended—and of love. Each stanza of the poem suggests Rossetti's mental association of each general conception with some particular event exemplifying it in his own life; the past with Lizzie's death, and surely with the unsolved problem of its manner, when he cries:

> But no word comes from the dead;
> Whether at all they be,
> Or whether as bond or free,
> Or whether they too were we,
> Or by what spell they have sped.

[1] *v. inf.* pp. 536-7.

This last line, voicing a most unusual question, is surely almost inexplicable save on the assumption already made on other grounds, of Gabriel's uncertainty as to the facts of Lizzie's death.

Finally, in this poem, Rossetti sang of Love, and we may count that too a reflection of his present experience, like the rest, when he laments Love's

> Kisses snatched 'neath the ban
> Of fangs that mock them above,
> Thy bells prolonged into knells,
> Thy hope that a breath dispels,
> Thy bitter, forlorn farewells
> And the empty echoes thereof.

The answers to these sad questionings will, he says in the refrain—affecting the general attitude of the day which in actual fact he did not share—be given after death.

> Strange to think by the way,
> Whatever there is to know,
> That shall we know one day.

Indeed it almost seems from the verses he was now writing, as if some new shadow had fallen upon his love, some new menace of evil, of separation, some fear of the end. And this, other verses of this time were to echo, were perhaps already echoing, with greater intensity.

"I cannot suppose," Gabriel replied to some objection by Scott to *The Cloud Confines*, "that any particle of life is *extinguished*, though its permanent individuality may be more than questionable. Absorption is not annihilation; and it is even a real retributive future for the special atom of life to be re-embodied (if so it were) in a world which its own former ideality had helped to fashion for pain or pleasure. Such is the theory conjectured here." For the final refrain of this early version ran:

> Atoms that nought can sever,
> From one world-circling will,—
> To throb at its heart for ever,
> Yet never to know it still.

But he had to explain to Scott that in this clumsy, ambiguous final line "still" did "not mean *quiet*," and he remarked: "I

PLATE XII

MRS. WILLIAM MORRIS
BY D. G. ROSSETTI

MRS. WILLIAM MORRIS
c. 1866

ANNIE MILLER
BY D. G. ROSSETTI
1860

RUTH HERBERT
BY D. G. ROSSETTI
1858

ALEXA WILDING
c. 1880 (?)

PLATE XIII

THE BLUE BOWER
(Fanny Cornforth)
BY D. G. ROSSETTI
1865

SIBYLLA PALMIFERA (Alexa Wilding)
BY D. G. ROSSETTI
1866

believe I am of opinion with you, perhaps, that it is best not to try to squeeze the expression of it into so small a space, but rather to leave the question quite unanswered." Suggesting other lines, not included in the later published version, he feared: "Does this not seem as if it meant a personal God? I don't think it need do so." To William, early in September, he sent the poem, saying:—"One short thing I have done, not meant to be a trifle. I want your advice about the close." He had at first, he said, "meant to answer the question in a way, on the theory hardly of annihilation but of absorption." But had finally decided on the version he now sent William, closely resembling that afterwards published, leaving the question open, "as the safest course." It was rarely he discussed such matters.

Despite these poems, Gabriel chafed at the little done. "I wish I could get some serious verse-writing done here," he complained to Scott, "but begin to see that I shall not. In fact, I cannot carry it on with painting to do also, at any rate not unless I am quite alone; and I had some painting task-work to do, and have set about a little not task-work also; and these have kept me from the other Muse, who, I believe, after all is my true mistress . . ."—so uncertain even to the end were his loyalties in art.

"Top comes here to-night from Iceland," Gabriel wrote to his brother on September 10th. At first news of Morris had been slow in coming, but early in August, while Gabriel was writing to Scott, Janey had entered with her husband's first letter from Iceland, and upon the arrival of another shortly afterwards, Gabriel could report that Morris was "enjoying himself thoroughly." "Good-bye my dear, I have so often thought of the sweet fresh garden at Kelmscott and you and the little ones in it, and wished you happy," Morris wrote to Janey. But after six weeks of travel, despite all that the land of the sagas had meant to him, Morris returned to Reykjavik, riding straight to the post in "excitement" for letters, as he recorded in his journal. "Why," he asked himself, "doesn't one drop down or faint or do something of that sort?" For a great fear had been upon him that in his absence some relative or friend had died! The letters awaiting him however brought no such tragic news, and he read them, as he told his diary, "with no more than the usual amount of disappointment, wondering at people's calmness." Perhaps in that comment we may legitimately read between the lines.

Early on September 8th, Morris reached London, but did not arrive at Kelmscott until the night of the 10th, although he was anxious to see his wife and children again. Gabriel, like Jones, had laughed at Morris's expedition to so rugged a region, and had prophesied that he would bring back "wonderful tales of Iceland; for what," he asked, "is the use of going there if you are not allowed to make people stare well when you come back?" Morris "has brought a fund of anecdotes, of course the country seems pretty well barren of all else, as far as I can judge," Gabriel told Smetham shortly after Morris's return. But to Scott he admitted: "the stories are not so funny as I hoped." "Skald," an Icelandic paper had described Morris, to the delight of Gabriel, who declared: "He ought to go by no other name for the future, and 'The Bard' be reserved for Swinburne." And when a day or two after his return, Morris went on the river, fishing, Rossetti wrote:—

> Enter Skald, moored in a punt,
> And Jacks and Tenches exeunt.

Morris could not refrain from contrasting English with Icelandic scenery, yet admitted: "my own little house by Lechlade though is sweet and innocent enough, and though it has a sadness about it, which is not gloom but the melancholy born of beauty I suppose, it is very stimulating to the imagination." Nevertheless, Morris's stay at Kelmscott was of the shortest. Within four days he had gone again; but a few days later he made a second visit to Kelmscott and stayed a week.

Gabriel's neurotic boredom afflicted him even at Kelmscott with Janey, and from time to time he would complain. "These stagnant surroundings," he moaned after six weeks of painting there; "The place needs no Sunday to quiet it, so that I only identify the day by the trouble of having to send to the town for letters and papers." Their solitude was, as he said, "absolute." Nevertheless he refused to invite friends. For his moods greatly and quickly varied, and at the very time of his complainings he told Brown: "One might settle down into complete and most satisfactory habits of work here."

So at Kelmscott he lingered until far in the autumn despite his often repeated intention to return to town. For this delay he blamed the slow progress of alterations to his studio in Cheyne Walk—the enlargement of a window, chiefly necessitated by his huge *Dante's Dream*, now nearing completion; but his growing fear of solitude in Cheyne Walk, and of the unhappy memories solitude released, played a part. "I hope to see you soon," he wrote to Smetham in mid-September, "in a studio new swept and garnished, though a devil or two may be there yet." "I shall have to get back soon now," he told Scott, on finishing *Rose Mary* at the close of September, "with less painting done than I hoped, as the poem clawed hold of me and had to be done." "My health," he told Smetham a few days before, "is not brilliant in any way, but I push on as yet."

October brought Gabriel to decision at last. "Morris," he told Scott on the second day of the month, "has been here twice since his return, for a few days at first and just now for a week again. He is now back in London and this place will be empty of all inmates by the end of this week, I think. Morris has set to work with a will on a sort of masque called *Love is Enough*, which he means to print as a moderate quarto, with woodcuts by Ned Jones and borders by himself, some of which he has done very beautifully. The poem is, I think," Gabriel imperturbably continued, "at a higher point of execution than anything he has done—having a passionate lyric quality such as one found in his earliest work, and of course much more mature balance in carrying out. It will be a very fine work." "The quest for a dream mistress" is one modern critic's description of *Love is Enough*, and in that it anticipates elements in *News from Nowhere*, and repeats a thousand conceptions and incidents in *The Earthly Paradise*. But it is more than such a quest. It is a poem of self-abnegation:—

> Because for love's sake, love he cast aside,

and of sublimation, of compensatory idealization of love when love in the real world was lost. "Beneath the charm of the new verse and the beauty of the pictures presented," wrote May

Morris, "there is something in the melancholy unrest of the opening episodes and the deeper note of faith and peace of the conclusion that must arrest the attention of any but the most casual and impatient reader of the poem. No glimpse of the inner life of Morris was ever vouchsafed even to his closest friends—*secretum meum mihi*. It was a subject on which he never spoke except in *Love is Enough*. But here he certainly does reveal much of himself, as a poet must in developing a story which expresses the passionate desire of the soul to come into contact with something utterly beyond worldly experience. . . . Pharamond the Freed, his dreams of another life where he is seeking to get nearer the ultimate freedom of the soul, and of Love the Lord of all, who guides him. . . . At the conclusion, Pharamond, reborn into a world of his own, sees the pageant of his old Kingship pass before him like a shadowed scene; the life of the spirit towards which Love leads him has become reality, and the real people recede and become faint images of a world that grows unimportant and vague. If love is enough it is not the world's love and contentment, but that final absorption in eternal good, that something-beyond-all for which the speech of man can find no defining words and towards which the thoughts of man travel down every path of belief."

Some hint of this new mood towards which he had long been struggling, Morris had given in some verses on *Winter*, published in *The Academy* early in 1871, in which he cried:—

> Ah! shall Winter mend your case?
> Set your teeth the wind to face.
> Beat the snow, tread down the frost!
> All is gained when all is lost.

Surely during his wanderings in Iceland, he had, like the heroes of the old sagas he loved, steeled his resolution to fight and win his spiritual battle, and so moved up to this new height of *Love is Enough*.

To Norton in this autumn of 1871, Jones described Morris at work on his new task. "He makes a poem these days," wrote Jones; "in dismal Queen Square in black old filthy London in dull end of October he makes a pretty poem that is to be wondrously happy; and it has four sets of lovers in it and THEY ARE ALL HAPPY and it ends well, and will come out some time next summer and I shall make little ornaments on it—such is Top in these days. As for Gabriel I have seen him but little, for he glooms much and dulls himself and gets ill and better and is restless, and wants and wants, and I can't amuse him. But he writes too, pretty constantly, sets of lovers, *un*happy —so Top and he are exhausting all poetry between them you see." Jones's words seem to echo with an inner meaning.

XI

THE FLESHLY SCHOOL OF POETRY
1871–1872

In our Contemptible Review
I struck the beggar through and through
(Oh! Robert-Thomas is dread to see).

The Brothers D. G. ROSSETTI

"HERE COMES my last Kelmscott letter," Gabriel had written to Scott on October 2nd; "Of course I'm leaving here just as I was getting into the poetic groove and I know were I to stay I should have a volume ready by the end of another three months. But it may not be . . . I see by advertisements I figure as the first victim in a series (I presume) under the title of the 'Fleshly School of Poetry,' in the *Contemporary Review* for October, but haven't seen it yet." Rossetti's tone was jocular, probably to hide his fear. But when upon his return to town he read the article, which bore the unfamiliar signature "Thomas Maitland," he saw that his own description of himself as the "victim" had been prophetic; that now, although delayed until all danger had seemed over, the attack he had so long anticipated, so persistently striven to prevent or forestall, had begun.

The attack was, indeed, deadly. For in describing the poetry of Rossetti as "fleshly," his unknown assailant had maliciously seized upon a word calculated to rouse all the prejudice and irrational emotion which the violation of a dominant taboo in any period inevitably excites. "Fleshly" for the mid-Victorians had all the mystic power of a word that embodies a contemporary complex, a word energized by all the repressions of the taboo, in this case the mid-Victorian taboo upon any unnecessary exposure of the body in actuality, and upon its counterpart in the world of art; the ban upon realism, upon nudity, upon passion, which Dickens so amusingly caricatured in the person of Mr. Podsnap and his obsessional fear lest anything in art should "bring a blush to the cheek of the young person."

486

Nothing indeed at that time could make an artist more un-popular with the middle-class in general, than an open recog-nition of the fact that human beings are made of flesh and blood. And this, Rossetti in his verse certainly had done.

With this taboo, carried to a now barely credible extreme, the painters of the time had seriously to reckon. It was thus that in 1854, over his figure of Christ—already clad from the waist down—in his now famous painting of Christ washing the feet of Peter, Madox Brown had mournfully pondered: "What to do with it, however, I scarce know. To suit the public taste, however, it should be clothed, to suit my taste, not." Gabriel's patron, the solicitor Valpy, "had," wrote William Rossetti, "a particular objection to nudity . . . and was disquieted even by a pair of bare arms." Henry Holiday's statue *Sleep* was rejected by the Royal Academy until draped, and only a year before that, Burne-Jones had resigned from the Old Water Colour Society because of its objection to one of his nudes.

Tennyson—who in middle age, during a private discussion of the all-absorbing question with Allingham confided, secretly and sentimentally, "naked model—the chastest thing I ever saw"—escaped the taboo by resorting in his poetry to classical and mediaeval legend, as in *Oenone* and *Godiva*. Ruskin, ponder-ing the matter at various times throughout his life, and swayed by the conflicting influences of his aesthetic sensibility and of contemporary prejudice, gradually changed from a surprisingly detached and objective attitude, to one in his later years of uncompromising and even irrational hostility. In 1872, as Slade Professor of Fine Art, at Oxford, he described the repre-sentation of the nude in art as having "been essentially destruc-tive to every school of art in which it has been practised," and not satisfied with this sweeping condemnation of such art throughout the ages, went on to denounce even the study of anatomy by art students as "not only a hindrance but a degra-dation."

Such was the state of contemporary taste, almost incompre-hensible to the modern world, when Rossetti's unknown assailant launched in *The Fleshly School of Poetry*, an attack which, if successful, would brand Rossetti, for contemporaries, almost as a criminal, would deprive him of patrons and his works of commercial value. Yet this charge of "fleshliness" had no doubt been suggested to his assailant in the first place by the eulogies of Gabriel's supporters, who in their anxiety to claim him as a leader of the anti-mid-Victorian revolt, had frequently emphasized the "fleshly" element in his work, with special approval. For several years these critics, in somewhat overstrained reaction against the popular taboo, had extravagantly acclaimed Rossetti's treatment of flesh in painting, a treatment which in actual fact was seldom if ever happy.

It was almost certainly the rhetorical Stephens, of the original Preraphaelite Brethren, but an entirely futile one, art critic to *The Athenaeum* since 1859, who, in that journal in 1865, had praised Rossetti's *Blue Bower* for "the marvellous fleshliness of the flesh," while Colvin, two years later, writing of Rossetti in the *Fortnightly Review*, had declared: "On the value and significance of flesh this painter insists to the utmost."

Swinburne, the following year, in *Notes on Some Pictures of 1868*, had similarly dwelt, in language of unrestrained rhetoric, alliteration and enthusiasm, upon "the sleepy splendour" of *Lilith* as "a fit raiment for the idea incarnate of faultless fleshly beauty," had praised *Sibylla Palmifera*, "as ripe and firm of flesh as her softer and splendid sister," and pointed out in tones of deep emotion that *La Pia* "presses the deadly marriage-ring into the flesh of her finger, so deep that the soft skin is bloodless and blanched from the intense imprint of it." So stirred indeed was he, that he likened *Lilith* with "those terrible tender lips," to Theophile Gautier's creation, "the hero of the most perfect and exquisite book of modern times—*Mademoiselle de Maupin*." And quite recently, in his review of Rossetti's *Poems* in the *Fortnightly Review* for May 1870, Swinburne had written: "No nakedness could be more harmonious, more consummate in its fleshly sculpture, than the imperial array and ornament of this august poetry."

Gabriel's friends might scathingly condemn or ridicule the mid-Victorian taboo upon "fleshliness," but it was not to be lightly overthrown. Such indeed was its intensity and persistence that as late as 1880, Shields, the puritanical Calvinist, who had himself, ten years before, organized a public protest against a painting in the nude, profoundly shocked his life-long friend Christina Rossetti by showing her a popular lady artist's designs for child fairies, and, four years later, provoked the headmistress of Cheltenham School, by introducing into his design for a memorial window there, a diminutive, undraped Cupid, and refusing the outraged lady's suggestion that it be girt with roses. To the sympathetic Miss Thomson, creator of the child-fairies which had deprived Christina of a night's sleep, the angry Shields expressed his bitter disgust. "As soon as you undertake any other, or almost any other, subjects but water-babies," he cried, "you will find yourself strangled by calicoes and flannels, or burnt by them like the shirt of Nessus, till you wish the whole race had remained in Adamite innocence, if only for the cost to your brains of dressing them with propriety."

By this time, indeed, the influence of the new, uninhibited generation, which had evidently modified Shields's own attitude, was gradually winning its way. Thus, in 1885, when an indignant, dominating and loquacious "British Matron" wrote a "public remonstrance" to *The Times* "against the display of nudity at the two principal galleries of modern art in London," despite the approval she won from Ruskin and from a hyperconscientious and worried Royal Academician named Horsley, new and flippant voices of revolt filled the air, and Whistler attached to his *Note in Green and Violet* (a small pastel of a nude he was exhibiting), the derisive motto: "Horsley soit qui mal y pense!"

In 1871, however, those days were still in the future, and taste was as Ruskin, already preparing his Slade lectures denouncing even the study of anatomy, represented it. Yet even so, it would have been difficult to justify this attack upon Rossetti, who had never been more than a moderate rebel, avoiding nudity in his art, partly no doubt lest the industrialist patrons he depended on but despised should be frightened away, partly also, it may be, because of inadequate technique.* He shared too, despite his bohemianism, the contemporary cult of "respectability," and had been as outraged as Ruskin would have been, and even more perhaps, when Swinburne had taken to nudist descents of the stair-rail at Cheyne Walk.

* *v. Notes.*

Indeed, although associated in "Thomas Maitland's" article *The Fleshly School of Poetry* with Swinburne, as a leader of the rebels against contemporary moral standards in art, Gabriel had in fact jeopardized his friendship with Swinburne by his objections to the more extreme violations of mid-Victorian prudery in Swinburne's works. In this way Gabriel had warned his friend not to publish various passages in *Poems and Ballads*, declaring: "The public will not be able to digest them, and . . . the paternal purse will have to stand the additional expense of an emetic presented gratis with each copy, to relieve the outraged British nature." And upon Swinburne's refusal of his advice, Gabriel admitted to a friend that Swinburne's genius certainly did not benefit "by its association with certain accessory tendencies." When *Poems and Ballads* was withdrawn by the publishers, in face of the storm its contempt for current prudery aroused, Rossetti, although assisting in the negotiations for its republication, had soon lapsed into indifference, declaring: "my own occupations have prevented me from meddling further in the matter, or from becoming the reporter, apologist or antagonist, of those who do or do not" approve it. For although Gabriel considered the publishers had withdrawn the volume "unjustifiably from a business point of view," he regretted that it would reappear "unaltered." "The attack in the Press," he had written in reference to *Poems and Ballads*, "has been stupid, for the most part, and though with some good grounds, shamefully one-sided."

Even Ruskin had supported *Poems and Ballads* more enthusiastically than Rossetti, for although timid about their publication which would, he said to Swinburne, "win you a dark reputation," he had, on their appearance, ecstatically but privately applauded the poet with: "I consent to much—I blame, or reject, nothing. I should as soon think of finding fault with you as with a thundercloud or a nightshade blossom. All I can say of you, or them, is that God made you, and that you are very wonderful and beautiful. To me it may be dreadful or deadly—it may be in a deeper sense or in certain relations, helpful or medicinal."

Nor was it only over *Poems and Ballads* that Gabriel had opposed Swinburne's reckless defiance of convention. In 1870, when Swinburne was preparing his *Songs before Sunrise*, Gabriel had warned him that to include two recent sonnets ridiculing Napoleon III as *The Saviour of Society*, a burlesque counterpart to Christ, would bring unpleasant consequences. "Saviour of Society," was in fact the popular designation in France for Napoleon III, and Browning employed it as sub-title for his own ironical poem on the French Emperor, *Prince Hohenstiel Schwangau*, written ten years before. But as this poem had not yet appeared, Gabriel must have believed the title to be Swinburne's own invention. So, while praising the sonnets themselves as "glorious pieces of poetic wisdom," he nevertheless deprecated, courteously yet firmly, the title and its ironical implications. "You know," he declared, "how free I am myself from any dogmatic belief; but I can most sincerely say that (except as a joke admitted and necessarily restricted to such hearers as well know it to be a joke only), I do myself feel that the supreme nobility of Christ's character should exempt it from being used—not as a symbolic parallel to other noble things and persons in relation with which dogmatists might object to its use—but certainly in contact of this kind with anything so utterly ignoble as this. I should myself," he continued, "feel to breathe more freely in the splendid atmosphere of your genius if this little cloud were cleared away from it." And he begged Swinburne to withdraw the sonnets or at least restrict them to private circulation. "After all," he told Ellis, "what is to be done when (to enlarge the old saying) 'Poeta nascitur non fit for publication?'" The result was that Swinburne withdrew the sonnets from *Songs before Sunrise*, but two years later included them in *Songs of Two Nations*.

Nevertheless, Rossetti was an easily vulnerable target for attack by this unknown enemy, in *The Fleshly School of Poetry*. Gabriel's association with Swinburne, emphasized in the article, made him, as the elder of the two, as well as through his reputed "leadership" of the Preraphaelites, appear to the general public as one of the influences responsible for Swinburne's flouting of contemporary standards. Yet whatever poetic influence of Rossetti's appeared in Swinburne's *Poems and Ballads* was chiefly indirect, through the work of William Morris, who had at one time so completely yielded to Gabriel's domination. Whatever direct influence Rossetti had exerted upon his friend's work was mostly confined to Swinburne's earliest verses, and in *Poems and Ballads* revealed itself chiefly in such sonnets as *Hermaphroditus*, *Love and Sleep*, and *A Cameo*. Later, indeed, Swinburne in *Sonnet for a Picture*, in his *Heptalogia*, cleverly parodied characteristic mannerisms of Gabriel's sonnets.

In one other respect also Gabriel had influenced Swinburne's *Poems and Ballads*. To Swinburne he had enthusiastically introduced FitzGerald's *Omar Khayyam*, whence Swinburne in turn had derived formal elements incorporated in his *Laus Veneris* which to many contemporaries was one of the most scandalous of Swinburne's poems. *Omar Khayyam*, written in 1857 at the time of Gabriel's "Jovial Campaign," rejected by *Fraser's Magazine* and ignored in a small, anonymous, five shilling edition, was "discovered" in the "penny box" of its publisher Quaritch, in 1861, by some unnamed friend of Rossetti. Gabriel, delighted with it, rushed off to buy a copy for himself, and quickly spread its reputation amongst his friends. Not until later was the author's identity discovered, upon which Fitz-Gerald became one of the Preraphaelite idols. It was an admiration which FitzGerald, however, far from reciprocated. "I wonder," he told Lord Houghton in 1872, "Messrs. Browning, Morris, Rossetti, etc., can read Keats's hastiest doggerel and not be ashamed at being trumpeted as great poets in the *Athenaeum* and elsewhere." He rated them far below Tennyson, and two years later ironically told Mrs. Tennyson: "When I look at the *Athenaeum*, I see there are at least four poets scarce inferior to Dante, Shakespeare, etc.: Browning, Morris, D. G. Rossetti, Miss Do. They will have their day."

The reasons for the attack upon Rossetti were in fact remote from those so speciously but unconvincingly presented in *The Fleshly School of Poetry*. Indeed, in the origins of the quarrel in which he was now so disastrously involved, Rossetti had played little or no part. It had begun almost five years before, when Swinburne, at the request of a publisher, and with the approval of William Rossetti, had withdrawn from the inept editorial clutches of a Scotch journalist and poetaster Robert Buchanan, a projected edition of Keats's poems, and edited it himself.

Buchanan in revenge, upon the appearance of Swinburne's *Poems and Ballads* shortly afterwards, compared the author, in the *Athenaeum*, to the Gito of Petronius, and in the *Spectator* for September 15, 1866, published his own comic verses, *The Session of the Poets*, in which Swinburne and other contemporary poets, including Buchanan himself, were mildly burlesqued over the *nom de guerre* of "Caliban." A reference in the poem to Swinburne's being "tipsy," struck home, and William Rossetti, usually so pacific, was stung to unwonted fury in his friend's cause. Shortly afterwards, defending *Poems and Ballads* in a pamphlet, William retaliated by describing Buchanan— accurately enough—as "so poor and pretentious a poetaster." Upon this Buchanan, in the *Athenaeum*, anonymously attacked Willam Rossetti's badly edited edition of Shelley's poems when it appeared at the close of 1869.

Upon Gabriel the effects of this squabble were most unfortunate. Anticipating an attack upon his *Poems* similar to that his brother had experienced, he had desperately attempted to defend himself by every means in his power, principally by "cornering" the literary journals for his friends' criticisms. His anxiety had aggravated his paranoid tendencies, had kept him constantly on guard, so that, as he wrote: "certain spite which I judge to be brewing in at least one quarter, might find itself at fault." He fell a prey to suspicion, saw secret enemies everywhere and schemed against them. He suspected the editor of the *Athenaeum*, Sir Charles Dilke, and ¦cried, during the defensive operations preceding the publication of his poems, "Dilke may perhaps be bilked yet!" How unfounded were his suspicions in this case was soon shown, for Dilke not only allowed Gabriel's friend, P. B. Marston, to review *Poems* favourably, in his journal, but was also denounced by the angry Buchanan, as editor of "the leading organ of the Fleshly School . . . as peculiar in its notions of literary decency as Sir Charles Dilke himself in his notions of political propriety."

By this time Rossetti was personally involved in the quarrel. Irritated by Buchanan's attacks upon his brother and Swinburne, he had spoken of the Scotsman in the language of unrestrained vulgarity which was now, in anger, his habitual mode of expression. The anal imagery to which he almost invariably resorted when speaking of Buchanan, would probably be related by the Freudian to the incipient paranoia from which he already seemed to be suffering.[1] To Gabriel, at any rate, it brought emotional relief. Spurred by fear, as he continued his preparations for the publication and defence of his poems, he had intensified his personal but private denunciations of Buchanan, as well as the coarse invective in which they found expression. But so complete had been Gabriel's defence, so widespread the paean of praise raised by his friends when *Poems* appeared, that for eighteen months Buchanan had been held at bay. Only now, and from behind the shelter of his pseudonym "Thomas Maitland," had he dared to strike.

On reading *The Fleshly School of Poetry—D. G. Rossetti*, in the October number of the *Contemporary Review* of 1871, Gabriel was at first merely contemptuous. "Have you seen our contemptuous *Contemporary*?" he asked Ellis: "What fools we must be! For it seems that we are greater fools than the writer, and even I can see what a fool he is. For once abuse comes in a form that even a bard can manage to grin at without grimacing." But when a few days later he heard from Ellis that the unknown "Thomas Maitland" was almost certainly Buchanan, Rossetti's real or assumed indifference changed to almost hysterical rage. "Can it be!" he replied. "Do tell me your authority. I won't show it. By God if it is, I'll give myself a treat and write and print a *Letter on Literary Lying* (to Thos. Buchanan, Esq.)." Gabriel was indeed almost beside himself with anger, obviously abnormal if we may believe Scott, who said that in the evening of this same day when Buchanan was discovered to be the enemy, Gabriel, arriving late at a dinner-party at Scott's, startled and disconcerted the waiting guests by angrily and impatiently knocking on the door and ringing the bell, rushing noisily upstairs, and bursting into the room shouting out Buchanan's name. "He was," wrote Scott, "too excited to observe or care who were present, and all the evening he continued unable to contain himself, or to avoid shouting out the name of his enemy. I was glad when the sitting came to an end, and one after another left with a private word of

[1] See the *Letters of D. G. Rossetti to his Publisher, F. S. Ellis*. Ed. O. Doughty, London, 1928.

enquiry regarding Rossetti.[1] From this time he occupied himself in composing a long reply, which he read over a hundred
times, till the lives of his friends became too heavy to bear."

How unbalanced the attack left Gabriel the intensity and
persistence of his attempt to verify Buchanan's authorship
showed. Nor was the ever pugnacious Swinburne less eager
than Rossetti to find and chastise the enemy. It was Swinburne
who discovered, and informed Gabriel, that "Caliban" whose
signature had footed the derisive *Session of the Poets*, was certainly Buchanan, who, to divert suspicion and advertise himself, had even introduced himself into the poem, by name. It
was, said the disgusted Gabriel, "a dodge" that "would just be
up to the skunk's mark and looks like him," and he compared
the trick with "Thomas Maitland's" false suggestion in *The
Fleshly School of Poetry*, that *Jenny* was plagiarized from some of
Buchanan's verses. William Rossetti, rising to the occasion,
turned literary detective and subjected *The Fleshly School of
Poetry* to a kind of Higher Criticism, the sole result of which
was his hopeful declaration: "The phrases *weird—solemn league
and covenant—*have a Scotch sound"; but on recollecting that so
had the name "Maitland," he despaired. So keen indeed was
the hunt, that even young Nolly Brown was set to extract an
admission from wary elders suspected of knowing and concealing the true authorship of the attack.

October, for Gabriel, passed, amidst these diversions, in the
writing of a reply entitled *The Stealthy School of Criticism*, and,
also to relieve his feelings, of such occasional verse as this:—

> As a critic the poet Buchanan
> Thinks "Pseudo" much safer than "Anon";
> Into Maitland he's shrunk,
> Yet the smell of the skunk
> Guides the shuddering nose to Buchanan.

For perhaps above all else, Buchanan's pseudonymity angered
him. "No skunk," he declared, "can get rid of his own name
by giving it to another." All such comments, however, were
fulsome flattery compared with his frequent, physically nause-

---

[1] W. M. Rossetti considers Scott's account of this incident greatly exaggerated,
and points out Scott's error in dating the party towards "midsummer 1872" in
Memoir, p. 297.

ating references to Buchanan in various letters of this time to his closest friends. The Preraphaelite sense of beauty, outraged, reacted violently, and without restraint. Swinburne, not only attacked in *The Fleshly School of Poetry*, but also in a recent novel, *Two Plunges for a Pearl* (written in fact by an obscure and drunken journalist, Mortimer Collins), delightedly girded himself for the fray. Reluctantly yielding to Gabriel's persuasions not to inflict upon Collins personal chastisement, Swinburne happily sat down to write a pamphlet, *Under the Microscope*, which should overwhelm their common foe. Hearing that Knowles, editor of the erring *Contemporary*, had admitted to the artist Simeon Solomon, that "Maitland" *was* Buchanan, Swinburne relieved his feelings in an outburst of pornographic invective chiefly expressed in pseudo-Biblical phraseology. And when shortly afterwards Solomon wrongly denied Buchanan's authorship, Swinburne was disappointed. His pamphlet, he explained, would have "made insipid by comparison the highest flavours of Juvenal's, Swift's and Landor's satire combined," would have even been worthy of the great de Sade.

"Maitland's" identity was said to be known also to Locker. So to Locker, Gabriel now wrote, asking for Solomon's "grounds of recantation." And before the end of October he completed *The Stealthy School of Criticism*, his reply to Buchanan's attack. In mid-November, Locker confirmed the report that it was Buchanan, while Colvin about the same time also learned it from Knowles. So, Gabriel told Swinburne, both author and editor were trying to place responsibility each on the other's shoulders.

Gabriel's reply, *The Stealthy School of Criticism*, published in mid-December, 1871, in the *Athenaeum*, over his own signature, was but a pale replica of the angry and passionate original, which, yielding to strong legal advice, he had largely toned down. "Here," he declared of his poetry, answering Buchanan's charge of "fleshliness," "all the passionate and just delights of the body are declared—somewhat figuratively it is true, but unmistakable—to be as naught if not ennobled by the concurrence of the soul at all times." And he castigated both editor and author for breaking the *Contemporary's* rule against pseudonymity, and blinding readers to the fact that behind a mask of pretended morality, one merely would-be poet was unfairly attacking a successful rival. To this, the publishers of the *Contemporary* returned a weak reply in the *Athenaeum* of December 30th. "Maitland," declared the liar and hypocrite Buchanan, was appended to the article entirely by "inadvertence." To which Rossetti replied—but in Ellis's name!—that Buchanan's excuse was proved false by his having carefully referred to himself, Buchanan, as if to a third person other than either the writer of the article or Rossetti, and that in *The Session of the Poets*, he had played the same trick before.

In fact, besides jealousy, journalistic motives of self-advertisement and monetary gain had led Buchanan to this attack. Without adequate means he had settled down in Scotland to the life of a country gentleman, now badly needed money, and was ready to use any journalistic trick to divert attention from the fame or notoriety of Rossetti and his friends to his own comparatively obscure self. A love of luxury beyond his means had repeatedly led this ascetic moralist into financial speculations and consequent vicissitudes, and already the abandonment of his house and way of life at Oban, which soon occurred, seemed inevitable. And as Buchanan had a contract at this time to supply Strahan, the publisher of a journal named *The Argosy*, with monthly copy, to start a moral-literary controversy might be in every way profitable to himself.

At first, indeed, Buchanan's plan seemed assured of success, as other journals followed where he had led, particularly *The Quarterly Review*, which in January 1872, attacked Rossetti and Swinburne in an article reputedly written by Courthope. Largely concentrating his criticism upon *The House of Life*, the critic complained of its obscurity, described the sonnets as vain "endeavours to attach a spiritual meaning to the animal passions," and summarized the sonnet sequence as "emasculated obscenity." *Jenny*, with its "descriptions repulsively realistic," was also disapproved of and Rossetti's conception of love dismissed as "pious sensuality." "The whole spirit of Mr. Rossetti's poetry," the critic concluded, "is of the earth, earthy." The following month Buxton Forman in *Tinsley's Magazine*, defended Rossetti at great length and in great detail, in a dull, anonymous article entitled *The 'Fleshly School' Scandal*, attacked Buchanan for his motives and methods in *The Fleshly School of Poetry*, and asserted the essential morality and dignity of the attitude which refused to regard physical passion as opposed or inferior to the so-called "higher" elements in love.

In May, Buchanan, despite the exposure of his identity, his falsehoods and devious ways, repeated his offence by reprinting in pamphlet form an extended version of his original attack. He declared Rossetti a sensualist, and that sensualism was making London "a great Sodom and Gomorrah waiting for doom." Projected through Buchanan's vulgar and prurient mind, both life and literature were contaminated, and he complacently inveighed against the books "on the drawing-room table, shamelessly naked and dangerously fair," against the streets "full" of "fleshliness," the shop windows crammed with "photographs of nude, indecent and hideous harlots in every possible attitude that vice can devise," while even the sweet-shops, he complained, displayed "models of the female leg, the whole definite and elegant article as far as the thigh, with a fringe of paper cut in imitation of the female drawers and embroidered in the female fashion."

We are hardly surprised, after the obvious zest of such writing, to find through Buchanan's quotations, delivered with a similarly obvious gusto, an intimate acquaintance with the most pornographic passages of seventeenth and eighteenth century verse, nor does it seem strange that he perverted the most passionate of Gabriel's poems to a similar quality, even describing *The Germ* as "an unwholesome periodical"! Nothing, indeed, could more clearly demonstrate Buchanan's hypocrisy and insincerity, than this renewed attack upon Rossetti, for everywhere it reveals his vulgar delight in "discovering," that is, in creating—what he called "nastiness." To what extent this "nastiness" was of his own invention, is shown in such comments as he makes on *Parted Love*: "the lady has retired to get breath and arrange her clothes." In the same vein is Buchanan's unconsciously revelatory ejaculation: "We get nothing very spicy till we come to Sonnet XXXIX"—that is, to *Vain Virtues*! So, through Rossetti's *House of Life* the vulgar hypocrite ranged, until he finally concluded that *The House of Life* was "probably the identical one where the writer found Jenny"—in short, a brothel!

Buchanan, in fact, whatever his professions of high moral aims, had a mind which touched nothing it did not contaminate. Low in mind, low in taste, low in breeding, and, as an apostle of morality, evidently insincere; such was Buchanan. He even complained of "fleshliness" in Rossetti's *Ave*, before concluding with a Pecksniffian peroration in which, while emphasizing his fears for public morals, he also, to show his broadmindedness, praised the works of Paul de Kock! For Buchanan was not only a hypocrite, but a clumsy hypocrite; and not through any element of honesty, but through sheer stupidity perhaps the most contemptible figure in English literary history. Beside him, Collier denouncing Dryden appears, despite his crudity and stupidity and arrogance, an embodiment of good taste.

But at last, even Buchanan, finding that the boasted purity of his moral motives placed too great a strain upon human credulity, admitted that a personal element was present in his attack upon Rossetti and his friends. It was not, of course, mere jealousy of a successful rival; that was impossible for Buchanan! Even if personal, the motive could only be noble, and was, he now asserted—contradicting his earlier profession of entire moral disinterestedness—to avenge the memory of his early friend, David Gray, a youth of poetic ambitions who, many years before, had fled to London about the same time as Buchanan, hoping to live by his pen, but only to die shortly afterwards of consumption aggravated by the privations of poverty. On Gray's death, his verses, of no great merit, in truth, had been published by subscription, and Swinburne, reviewing the volume, had adversely but not unkindly criticized them. Although Gray, being dead, could hardly be affected, the sensitive Buchanan, it now appeared, had received from Swinburne's review a permanent wound, and had dedicated himself henceforth to vengeance. Such at least was Buchanan's latest, pathetic excuse for his attack on Rossetti.

What all this had to do with Rossetti was certainly obscure; but the false pathos Buchanan invented about David Gray and his own self-dedication to his memory had already on more

499

than one occasion served his journalistic ambitions, and might now, he thought, be used to disarm those who, as he noted with growing dismay, had begun to doubt the sincerity of the high moral motives by which he sought to justify his base attack upon a leading contemporary poet, and the self-contradictions and inconsistencies into which it had led him.

Illness was soon to prevent Rossetti's further participation in the quarrel; but first he wrote on the hypocritical Buchanan-Maitland, a poem, *The Brothers*, an ironical pseudo-ballad, closely imitative in form of Tennyson's *The Sisters*, in which Buchanan is supposed to gloat over his miserable conduct, exclaiming:—

> In our Contemptible Review
> I struck the beggar through and through
> (Oh Robert-Thomas is dread to see).

The quarrel, however, went on. Soon Swinburne's satire, *Under the Microscope*—said to have been bought in large quantities by unsuspecting German scientists!—appeared, and in August 1872 Buchanan's feeble reply, *The Monkey and the Microscope*, was published in *St. Paul's Magazine*.

But already Buchanan's courage was failing. Before launching his cowardly attack he had, he believed, made certain of overwhelming support. Not only would the vast Philistine and conventionally moral section of the country be with him, but even such leaders of poetry as Tennyson and Browning, despite references in Buchanan's article to both poets, probably designed to prevent any suspicion of their having the slightest association with it. Tennyson, William Rossetti said later, "was one of the first to object to the attack," and no doubt Buchanan's vulgarity must have repelled Tennyson. Yet there seems to have been some truth in Buchanan's assertion that he received encouragement from the two poets, whom he probably canvassed beforehand to ensure, as he thought, his own safety.

Shortly after the appearance of *The Fleshly School of Poetry*, Tennyson, so Buchanan long afterwards asserted, told him in conversation that he thought Rossetti's sonnet *Nuptial Sleep*, the "filthiest thing he had ever read,"[1] while Browning (though not averse to a *risqué* jest with a lady himself), had, according

[1] *v. sup.* p. 449.

to Buchanan, been no less emphatic than Tennyson in disapproval of Rossetti's verse. To Browning, indeed, shortly before the publication of his article, Buchanan had written a characteristically false letter, informing him that *The Fleshly School of Poetry* was "just ready, and be its literary merit what it may, I am convinced that it will do good—most good of all to the men criticized, perhaps even saving them from going headlong to Hell. You will see," he continued, "the whole matter there put in its perfect form of simple and out-spoken truth, and you will moreover see other allusions to yourself. In this matter of the Fleshly School I know every great-hearted and honest man will stand by my side; and, come what may, a Snake is scotched effectually, and his entire scheme ruined." This, and the allusion to David Gray which followed, could hardly have been addressed to an openly unsympathetic correspondent. Besides these, Buchanan's private supporters included Cardinal Manning, who sent him a message of good cheer, and the Hon. Leicester Warren (better known later as the somewhat anaemic poet Lord de Tabley) who sent him drawings of wayside flowers for the floral designs on the paper covers of the pamphlet, "so pointing," said Buchanan, "the moral of the diatribe."

But unfortunately for the Galahad who had challenged the powers of darkness in the mistaken belief that the big battalions were with himself, these supporters were timid; at least they kept their approval strictly private, and seemed averse to any public appearance in Buchanan's company. Thus, as he soon bitterly complained, he found himself left alone to fight a losing battle against a host of brilliant and outraged foes. For nearly all the rising *literati* who counted, both poets and critics, ranged themselves behind Rossetti and Swinburne, whom they admired as literary leaders of the "modern" movement, and regarded Buchanan as the most contemptible of vulgar and Philistine outsiders.

The battle indeed somewhat resembled that in the seventeenth century between Dryden and the "wits" against Sir Richard Blackmore and the "cits," and the result was the same. Reputation, brilliance, wit, sarcasm, all were at the service of Buchanan's enemies. Even when a few of Buchanan's supporters attempted to hide defeat by giving him a public dinner with music and song, the "Comic Spirit," as Meredith would have said, outraged by the Scots moralist, introduced *Love-Lily*, one of Gabriel's recent love lyrics, into the programme, and it was sung, apparently in all innocence, by Malcolm Lawson. Thereupon the young, enthusiastic and indignant Edmund Gosse, already writing poetry and literary criticism, ridiculed Buchanan in a witty triolet:—

> "Who wrote that song?" Buchanan said.
> They answered with one voice, "Rossetti."
>   Embarrassed, shuffling, pale and red,
> "Who wrote that song?" Buchanan said.
>   They laughed till they were nearly dead.
>   This affectation seemed so petty.
> "Who wrote that song?" Buchanan said.
> They answered with one voice, "Rossetti."

Only now did Buchanan begin to appreciate the Nemesis he had brought upon himself. For years afterwards, he complained in later life, he was openly insulted in criticisms and reviews, and for long was forced to publish his works anonymously in order to escape immediate damnation by the literary critics.

To retrieve as far as possible the false step he had taken, to extricate himself from his unhappy position, Buchanan took an even more ignominious step than any preceding, embraced the final humiliation of a public recantation of his charges against Rossetti, or rather, as Gabriel's reputation increased, a series of recantations, servile, sweeping, and as insincere as his original challenge had been. Retracting his criticisms in a fulsome apology as nauseating in its insincerity as the original attack, Buchanan in 1881, shortly before Rossetti's death, and when Gabriel was at the height of his fame, dedicated to him, as "An Old Enemy," a romance he had written, entitled *God and Man*, in the following unctuous and sycophantic verses, really designed like the original attack, to give himself a portion of Rossetti's eminence or notoriety:—

> I would have snatch'd a bay leaf from thy brow,
>   Wronging the chaplet on an honoured head;
> In peace and charity I bring thee now,
>   A lily-flower instead.

> Pure as thy purpose, blameless as thy song,
>   Sweet as thy spirit, may this offering be:
> Forget the bitter blame that did thee wrong,
>   And take the gift from me!

The motive, however, or at least one of the motives, was less to placate an uneasy conscience than the angry reviewers who prevented Buchanan from publishing his works under his own name. Gabriel, his health by that time fatally affected, and largely through Buchanan's foulness, must have felt in every word of the dedication the sentimental falsity of the fellow, and no doubt his private response to these overtures was the contemptuous couplet he scribbled in his notebook,

> Aye, we'll shake hands, though scarce for love, we two;
>   But I hate hatred worse than I hate you.

How insincere were both Buchanan's attacks and recantations his own explanations and apologies clearly show. The odium long attaching to his name, and revived upon Rossetti's death in 1882, Buchanan then sought to allay by a new series of abject protestations. "Mr. Rossetti, I freely admit now," he wrote in the *Academy* for July 1, 1882, "never was a Fleshly Poet at all," and about the same time, writing to Hall Caine in similar terms, Buchanan unconsciously revealed that jealousy of Rossetti's fame was the basic incentive for the attack. "The newspapers," Buchanan now admitted, speaking of the time of publication of Rossetti's *Poems*, "were full of panegyric. Mine was a mere drop of gall in an ocean of *eau sucrée*"; and in the preface to his novel *The Martyrdom of Madeline*, Buchanan was careful to point out that it was not intended as a satire upon the Preraphaelites. Four years later in *A Look Round Literature*, Buchanan included a section entitled *A Note on Dante Rossetti*, which was indeed another recantation of his attack, and written in fact, immediately after Rossetti's death. But these various recantations appear to have served their conscious or unconscious purpose, which was apparently to associate himself publicly with greatness as Hall Caine was to do later. For Buchanan seems to have been one of those who, like Boswell on a higher plane, would rather be remembered through some pitiful, or farcical, or contemptible or scurrilous association with greatness than not be associated with the great, or even than not be remembered at all.

For his own satisfaction—or perhaps rather for that of his biographer, who later inserted it in her *Life of Buchanan*—the Scottish writer composed a record of the incident, which openly reveals how false his supposed moral reasons for the attack were. "Not consciously dishonest," he now described it. "I really believed then that Rossetti was an affected, immoral and over-praised writer. I was not alone in that opinon, absurd as I consider it now." Could he but have seen it, Buchanan might indeed have found a little consolation in a letter Cardinal Newman sent to Edmund Gosse, shortly before Rossetti's death. "As regards Swinburne and Rossetti," he wrote, "their poems are soaked in an ethical quality, whatever it is to be called, which would have made it impossible in the last generation for a brother to read them to a sister." In this, doubtless many of Newman's older contemporaries would have agreed with him. It was especially the younger generation, weary of mid-Victorian inhibitions and hypocrisies, who hailed the new "Preraphaelite" poetry with delight, realizing, as Ruskin in his more enlightened moments had realized, that "purity" and "impurity" in art depended far less upon subject or form than upon the quality of the artist's imagination.

XII

CRISIS
1871–1872

A land of darkness as darkness itself
And of the shadow of death.

Job x. 22, and D. G. ROSSETTI'S
The Card Dealer.

FOR ROSSETTI, Buchanan's attack had been particularly ill-timed. The blow struck him at the height of his career, in the full enjoyment of his "success." Not satisfied with the simple reputation of painter and poet, Gabriel had desired recognition of the "poetic" quality with which, as he believed, he invested his painting, and the general approval given to his poems now emphasized the pre-eminence accorded him as a "poetic" painter. Already, too, he began to be widely and not unjustly regarded as "leader" of the rising "aesthetic school" in letters. Very different in many ways from the later "aesthetes," whose extravagance, indeed, disgusted Gabriel, and despite his adverse criticism of their principle—which was indeed his own unexpressed standard in art—of "Art for Art's sake" as "two-thirds absolutely right and one third so essentially wrong" as to invalidate the whole of it, Rossetti's deepest tendencies were evidently towards "aestheticism."

How instinctive this was he unconsciously revealed when in 1865, warning the self-depreciatory religious mystic Smetham, he remarked: "What you lack is simply ambition, i.e. the feeling of pure rage and self-hatred when anyone else does better than you do. This in an ambitious mind leads not to envy in the least, but to self-scrutiny on all sides, and that to something if anything can. You comfort yourself with other things, whereas art must be its own comforter or else comfort-less." That was also Gabriel's mature comment upon his own earlier struggles. "Rossetti," complained Hunt, "never strictly adhered to the original character of our movement," and in fact it was Rossetti who unconsciously led art from the simple,

505

moral Preraphaelite precepts of Hunt, to the obvious aestheticism of the later Preraphaelites, and thus, ultimately, to those faerie or satanic regions inhabited later by the more ecstatic devotees of "Art for Art's sake."

Success had also improved Gabriel's fortunes. "I make lots of money (for a poor painter)," he had recently remarked, adding characteristically, for he was improvident as ever, "and never have a penny to play with." Indeed, but for his incurable extravagance, the sums he squandered on curios, china and animals, he might now have become a wealthy man. Above all he was apparently happy in a reciprocated passion which, in its blending of physical and spiritual elements, realized his love's ideal.

Until Buchanan's attack, Rossetti's star had certainly seemed to be in the ascendant. Even from his long-dead father he was receiving a reflected glory, for now, by a last irony of fate, to old Gabriele was posthumously granted that renown as poet-patriot which, to his immense chagrin, life had consistently denied. Italy now rang with the dead Professor's name, while his admiring compatriots vainly sought Mrs. Rossetti's permission to bear his body from its obscure resting place in High-gate Cemetery to the public monument erected in his honour in Santa Croce, Florence. Rossetti, who got William to advertise his father's new importance in the *Athenaeum*, alone of the family regretted his mother's interdict. The rest, less partial than Gabriel to exhumations, whole-heartedly supported her.

Even the suspicions and dislikes excited in some quarters by Gabriel's works and ways had only served to intensify and extend his appeal to many admirers. For in the mid-Victorian desert, as Sidney Colvin said,[1] it was a time when lovers of poetry, weary of the pedestrian, moralistic and "improving," and longing for the passionate, elemental and romantic, believed that in Rossetti they had found the qualities they desired. Thus, perhaps the majority of Rossetti's devotees were largely attracted by the popular legend of him, now developing, as a mysterious, romantic, even sinister figure with a strange, dubious, tragic past.

For Colvin certainly, this "strange" and "sinister" reputa-

[1] *v. sup.* p. 452.

tion was a part of the attraction which had led him in 1868 to extract from Jones an introduction to Rossetti. Nor was he disappointed on acquaintance, finding "the man himself and his surroundings and way of life . . . irresistibly, if somewhat weirdly impressive." It was thus, too, the following year, with Henry James, who nearly half-a-century later recalled, vividly but with a maddening reticence, "that day of the early spring of 1869" when Charles Eliot Norton took him to Cheyne Walk to meet "the great (if great!) and strange and more or less sinister D. G. Rossetti, whom Charles was in good relation with, difficult as that appeared already then to have become for most people." Similar, though with much darker shadows, was the picture that Hall Caine, particularly attracted by the morbid and macabre, drew of Rossetti upon their meeting twelve years later, in 1881, when this last phase of Rossetti's existence, now beginning, was nearing its culmination in death.

Upon an innate rebel against the age, Buchanan's indictment would have had little or no effect save the provocation of such amused contempt as Meredith expressed for it. "It would certainly have been entertaining to me," Meredith told William Rossetti, "to read the opinion formed by the North of the South—by Scotch mists of Southern Sunshine—if the onslaught had not been made on my friend. But the victim in such a case might really enjoy it. Our sweet English and Scotch are always very suspicious of colour. Warmth of colour makes them huddle together and take a common oath that they will be virtuous. Eccentricity they have a general instinct to lapidate—as boys have a bird." But Rossetti, largely subservient at heart to the conventional standards of the time, if not even approving them in considerable degree, though probably unconsciously, was but too sensitive to the easy plausibility Buchanan's charges must assume when directed against the subject of such a "legend" as that which was already growing up about himself, nor did he by any means overlook the damage it could inflict upon his reputation (with consequent decline in profits), amongst his so largely Puritanical and Philistine patrons. Thus, instead of ignoring or being amused by Buchanan's antics, he took them tragically, saw himself as one put to open shame, believed his fall the deeper because of the height to which he had risen.

Before Buchanan's attack, and even for a short time afterwards, Rossetti had believed that the personal indifference to criticism he desired was at his command. "I have been surprised (and pleasantly)," he told Shields in August 1870, when *Blackwood's* depreciated his *Poems*, "to find such things producing a much more transient and momentary impression of unpleasantness than I should have expected—indeed I might almost say none at all." But after the publication of Buchanan's article in the *Contemporary*, this immunity, which he had largely attributed to his absorption in completing *Dante's Dream*, proved illusory, despite all his attempts to appear indifferent in the eyes of the world. To his note-book he confided, as time passed, the bitter truth:

> An ant-sting's prickly at first,
> But the pain soon dies away;
> A gnat-sting's worse the next day;
> But a wasp 'tis stings the worst.

And in truth invulnerability was hardly to be expected in one who had all his life avoided public exhibition through fear of criticism, and who, but a few months before, had taken measures of such meticulous completeness to defend his poems from possibility of attack.

Weak health now made him a peculiarly vulnerable target for his enemies. Exhausted by disappointment and overstrain, his nervous system, never robust, had for the last four years shown increasing symptoms of obscure disorder: insomnia, depression, hypersensitiveness, failing sight, loss of self-control, neurasthenic tendencies in short, while his remedies, chloral and spirits, had but intensified the evil. Quite recently at Kelmscott and again since his return to town, he had been spitting blood. A victim of drug, drink and passion, he was increasingly succumbing to paranoid tendencies, towards anxiety and persecution complexes, such as his father had shown in a mild form from comparatively early years. At times he relapsed into fits of eccentricity, became increasingly introvert and regressive, preferring solitude and brooding again over his own painful past. In fact, at forty-three, Gabriel was falling into a morbid mental state closely resembling in many ways that of Ruskin at the same age, nine years before. Upon one in this condition, the almost immediate consequence of Buchanan's attack was an alarming decline in both physical and mental stability. Scott remarked that from this time, Rossetti's "vigour in all things, painting, poetry and letter-writing . . . he had left never to find again." They attempted to continue their customary games of whist at each other's houses that winter, "but the article in the *Contemporary* . . . was to him like a slow poison, till at last he could not follow the game, and used to throw down his cards."

However exaggerated Rossetti's reaction to the *Contemporary's* criticism while it remained anonymous, it enormously increased when, upon the discovery of its authorship, the emotions generated could be focused upon Buchanan. How excited Rossetti became, Scott's account of his eccentricities at the dinner-party suggests, while William declared that from the time of Buchanan's pamphlet and the identification of him as its author, Rossetti was "a changed man, and so continued till the close of his life." For long, Gabriel's anger found vent in continual and repetitive paroxysms of rage, foul speech and nervous excitement, all manifestations of growing hysteria. For a time Buchanan replaced the former obsessive themes of "Life, Love and Death," and when *The Echo*, referring to Rossetti and the "Fleshly Scandal," used the word "coward," Gabriel—"possibly without the least reason," said William—imputed the article to Buchanan, and, greatly peturbed—"so over-strained," said William, "was the balance of his mind"—consulted his brother as to whether or not he should challenge Buchanan to a duel.

These agitations intensifying his insomnia, Gabriel increasingly resorted to chloral and spirits as sedatives. The result was that the painful obsession of Buchanan gained yet a stronger hold on him. Each new edition of his *Poems*, Gabriel now valued chiefly as showing "we have advanced so far into the bowels of Robert Thomas," as, combining Buchanan's real and assumed Christian names, Gabriel now called him.

Amidst the world of enemies into which his diseased imagination now transformed or exaggerated reality, Rossetti preserved a defensive aloofness that misled and repelled strangers. Samuel Butler, who had recently published *Erewhon*, spending an evening in the early spring of 1872 with Rossetti, Scott and the painter Wallis, in Wallis's rooms, was deceived in this way by Gabriel's manner and appearance. He thought Gabriel "horrid," and complained of having been "oppressed by the sultry reticence of Rossetti's manner, which seemed to me assumed in order to conceal that he had nothing worth saying to say. I dislike his face and his manner and his work," wrote the crotchety Butler, "and I hate his poetry and his friends. He is wrapped up in self-conceit and lives upon adulation." Perhaps there was something of unconscious jealousy of Gabriel's success in this condemnation by a contemporary and in some ways a rival artist who, however brilliant, was then still far from obtaining Gabriel's rewards in reputation and financial profit. The irritation of that first and last meeting of Gabriel and Butler long remained with the author of *Erewhon*, who even fifteen years later growled: "This silence trick is common with people who would get a reputation cheaply. Rossetti, the painter, played it when I met him in Wallis's rooms shortly after *Erewhon* appeared; he sat still, moody, impenetrable." Even at this later date, apparently, Butler did not know that at that time Rossetti had been on the threshold of a mental collapse. Gabriel for his part, apparently left no hint of what impression Butler made on him, unless it is to be found in his cold words to William two years afterwards, when Christina wrote and projected publishing *Nowhere*. "Christina's title," he said, "seems unlucky because of that free-thinking book called *Erewhon*, which is 'Nowhere' inverted . . . I should change it." And Christina, doubtless shocked at the suggestion of even the remotest association with free-thought, as Gabriel—himself in fact a "free-thinker"—must have known, changed the title.

Buchanan's attack seemed to bring long-forming mental and emotional tendencies in Rossetti to a head. His gradual withdrawal from social intercourse was, like Ruskin's, largely the result of disappointment in friendship as well as in love, and of his consequent scepticism about human nature and the value of ostensible "friends." Gabriel's generosity had—like Ruskin's to Rossetti in the past—often evoked little beyond ingratitude or treachery. Jealousy, dogging his career ever since those now distant days when Ruskin first offended Rossetti's Preraphaelite companions by publicly acclaiming him as their "leader," had laid waste nearly all those early friendships, an almost inevitable part of the price paid for "success." Since then, his early confidence undermined, Rossetti had lost the desire to make new friends or even, if trouble arose, to retain the old. Looking back upon these friendships—to which Henry James (unfairly imputing their rupture in every case to Gabriel), had referred when recalling their first meeting—Rossetti found little cause for satisfaction, and in their passing, little to regret. Especially generous in helping brother artists in need of any kind, he had, according to Whistler, deeply resented Millais' failure, in the early days of the Brotherhood, to nominate him for membership of the despised and denigrated Royal Academy when an opportunity to do so with ease had occurred. This, if true, was doubtless due to the jealousy towards Gabriel which Millais and Hunt had soon shown, and until the end of their lives continued to show; was perhaps the first rift in the lute, leading later to their separation.

Gabriel, uneasily aware that the progress of his own reputation increased the animus against him, had remained uncompromisingly aloof, and in recent years, Sandys, vainly trying to heal the breach, had only managed to bring the former friends together by inviting both Millais and Rossetti to his rooms, and leaving Gabriel in ignorance of his expectation of a second guest. On that occasion, good form preserved urbanity, and, as the guests walking homewards together reached Millais', Gabriel accepted his friend's urgent invitation to enter and see his latest work. On leaving, Gabriel had returned the compliment by inviting Millais to call at Cheyne Walk; but later Millais complained that although he had twice called there in consequence, he had both times been refused admittance, nor had any explanation or apology been forthcoming from Gabriel. It was, Millais concluded—and the conclusion was unintentionally significant of Millais's state at least—another sign of Gabriel's "jealous temper"!

In fact, Gabriel's nature was far from such a petty and uncouth revenge. As he rigidly excluded callers during working

hours, he was probably quite unaware of Millais' visit. On
several occasions at least, Millais' fate befell other visitors to
Cheyne Walk, including even prospective patrons who called
unexpectedly. It was thus with Mr. and Mrs. Cowper-Temple,
to whom, on hearing by chance of the incident, Gabriel sent a
note of regret. Indeed some years later Rossetti was reported
to have denied admittance to the Princess Louise and was
forced to contradict the rumour in a letter to *The Times* of
December 28, 1878. Perhaps it reminded him of his refusal
twenty-three years before, under Brown's influence, of Lady
Waterford's request to him to teach herself painting.

As for Rossetti's reputed desire to become a Royal Academician, Hunt long afterwards declared that in 1867, he, Rossetti,
Brown, Jones and several others refused an invitation from the
newly-reformed Academy to join their ranks; but as William
Rossetti makes no reference to this it is improbable that Gabriel
at any time was included.

More recently, Rossetti had been ungratefully treated by
Sandys himself. To that ever-impecunious painter, whose
caricature of Rossetti and the other Preraphaelites had done
them so much harm in early days, Gabriel had been particularly kind, not only lending him considerable sums of which
only a small part was ever repaid, but even keeping him, in
Cheyne Walk, from the spring of 1866 until the end of the
following year. Yet in the spring of 1869, in the midst of those
days of "regenerate rapture," Gabriel heard that Sandys was
spreading much scandal about him, and when before the close
of the following May, Gabriel courteously but firmly objected
to Sandys's repeated imitations of his pictorial subjects and
style, the ungrateful painter, although still heavily in debt to
Rossetti, refused his attempts at pacification, and broke off all
relations with him. It was, too, in that same month of May
1869 that Gabriel learned to his extreme anger that Hunt and
Woolner, long estranged, had just made, "Hunt especially—a
virulent attack" on some water-colours he had recently done
for Craven. And only a few months since, in the autumn of
1871, he had withdrawn from Howell, not for any personal
reason, but because Jones, believing himself injured by Howell,
was "so extremely hurt and even irritated" at Rossetti's con-

PLATE XIV

WILLIAM BELL SCOTT, JOHN RUSKIN, DANTE GABRIEL ROSSETTI
1863

PLATE XV

**DANTE GABRIEL, CHRISTINA, WILLIAM MICHAEL ROSSETTI
AND THEIR MOTHER**
in Rossetti's garden at 16 Cheyne. Walk,Chelsea
1863

**DANTE GABRIEL ROSSETTI, WILLIAM MICHAEL ROSSETTI,
A. C. SWINBURNE, FANNY CORNFORTH**
in Rossetti's garden at 16 Cheyne Walk, Chelsea
c. 1863

tinuing Howell's acquaintance that Gabriel for a time reluctantly withdrew from him, "Jones," he explained, "being
so much the older and more valued friend." Similarly, although
there was no open breach, the old intimacy with Allingham
was dead, despite their occasional dinners together. Nor in fact
were his relations with Jones really intimate now.

Psychologically, Rossetti was caught in a vicious circle.
Now that his original confidence in human nature had been
undermined by experience, his hypersensitive reaction had
created suspicions which rapidly developed with his growing
morbidity and fame. Thus, hiding his wounds behind a proud
mask of indifference, he rejected all overtures and, appearing
such an essentially anti-social person as was in fact remote
from his temperament, seemed to insist upon isolation. It was
thus he complained that Lady Ashburton, patron of artistic
and literary "lions," had long but vainly pestered him "from
at least six different parts of the British Islands, to come down
instantly and meet a sympathizing circle," a suggestion he
promptly dismissed as "quite impossible to me at the pitch of
brutal bogyism at which I have arrived." Similarly when
Hunt's second wife, hoping to heal the breach between her
husband and Rossetti, sent him an invitation, he coldly replied:—"My dear Mrs. Hunt, I'm afraid I must admit
complete abrogation of all my duties as a social being of the
festive order and can only thank you for your kindness in
asking me." Success, he felt, had brought him enemies, and
enemies were everywhere; worst of all, they were disguised as
friends. Jottings in verse and prose, in his note-books, suggest
the depth of his smothered resentment of disloyalty in friendship.

> "Was it a friend or foe that spread these lies?"
> "Nay, who but infants question in such wise?
> 'Twas one of my most intimate enemies,"

he ironically answered his own self-questioning, or lamented
the period of life he had arrived at,

> The bitter stage of life
> Where friend and foe are parts alternated,

as he wrote; and in two stanzas of *Soothsay*, he clearly traced the
decline of his early faith in friends:—

> Let thy soul strive that still the same
> Be early friendship's sacred flame.
> The affinities have strongest part
> In youth, and draw men heart to heart:
> As life wears on and finds no rest,
> The individual in each breast
> Is tyrannous to sunder them.
>
> In the life-drama's stern cue-call,
> A friend's a part well-prized by all:
> And if thou meet an enemy,
> What art thou that none such should be?
> Even so: but if the two parts run
> Into each other and grow one,
> Then comes the curtain's cue to fall.

And now, it seemed to Gabriel in this early summer of 1872,
that "the curtain's cue to fall" had come. Anxiety, insomnia,
chloral, spirits, disillusion and disappointment, had brought
him to the very boundaries of insanity. Suspicions of a conspiracy of envious enemies, confirmed as it seemed to him by
Buchanan's attack, began to dominate his reason, and brought
on a definite mental crisis.

Nor were his paranoid fears and suspicions without some
actual foundation in fact. As usually in such cases, despite
excessive emotional reactions unchecked by normal, rational
self-restraint, the fears and suspicions rising within him, were
the greatly exaggerated response to small realities actually,
even if unconsciously, observed, by abnormally refined sensi-
bilities; realities so slight or delicate as often to elude the
observation of normal, less sensitive minds. Certainly Gabriel's
belief that Strahan and Co.—the publishers of the *Contemporary
Review* and of Buchanan's pamphlet—purposely encouraged
the enemies of himself and his friends, was shared by Swinburne who, at the close of this same year denounced "the very
sweepings of Messrs. Strahan's refuse stock—of periodicals
which have for some time been persistently and consistently
devoted to the defamation of Rossetti and myself, not merely
by means of insult and reviling but by means also of flat false-
hood and calumny."

That even before the close of 1871 Rossetti had heard of Tennyson's private sympathy with Buchanan's indictment, but was far from suspecting Browning, is perhaps suggested by his remark to Ellis: "Strahan and Co. must be a nice firm for Tennyson to cotton to. Just think of them mixing up Browning's name in their lie." But not long afterwards Rossetti doubtless became convinced that Browning too had played him false— as at least it must have seemed to him. Yet the guileless William —who even when later he heard of Browning's association with Buchanan's article refused to believe it—thought that only illness could explain his brother's changed attitude to Browning in June 1872, at the time of Gabriel's nervous breakdown, since Browning had once been his poetic idol and personal friend.

Browning, in fact, despite his earlier praise of *The Blessed Damozel*, was at heart no admirer of the Preraphaelites' poetry, and, particularly in view of his own long unavailing struggle for public recognition, was perhaps, unconsciously, a little jealous of his brother poet's easy and early success. " 'Florid impotence' to my taste," Browning had wittily and privately described Swinburne's verse, in March 1870, "the minimum of thought and idea in the maximum of words and phraseology. Nothing said and done with, left to stand alone and trust to its effect in its own worth. What a way of writing," he added, "is that wherein, wanting to say that 'a man is sad' you express it as 'He looketh like to one, as one might say, who hath a sadness and is sad indeed, so that beholders think: "How sad is he!"'" And three months later, after acknowledging with praise Gabriel's gift copy of his *Poems*, Browning described them to the same friend as "scented with poetry, as it were—like trifles of various sorts you take out of a cedar or sandalwood box. You know," he continued, "I hate the effeminacy of his school: the men that dress up like women; that use obsolete forms too, and archaic accentuation—fancy a man calling it a lilý—liliés and so on. . . . Then how I hate Love, as a lubbery naked young man putting his arms here and his wings there, about a pair of lovers; a fellow they would kick away in reality. . . . I am getting ill-natured."

Whether some rumour of Browning's real opinion of Gabriel's

verses reached his ears or not, Gabriel shortly afterwards, and even before Buchanan's first article, became no less critical of Browning's latest poem *Balaustion's Adventure* which, he said, "consists chiefly of a translation of Euripides' *Alcestis*, interlarded with Browningian analysis to an extent beyond all reason or relation to things by any possibility Greek in any way," and Gabriel renamed it, "*Exhaustion's Imposture!*" It was, he thought, quite inconsistent with Browning's frequent denunciation of all translation, which had, ten years before, Gabriel now recalled, led Browning to omit all acknowledgment of the complimentary copy of *The Early Italian Poets* that Gabriel had sent him on its publication.

It was now, in June 1872, a month or so after Buchanan's attack had reappeared in extended, pamphlet form, and when Rossetti was on the point of nervous breakdown, that Browning's presentation copy of his latest poem, *Fifine at the Fair*, came for Gabriel. The reading of it brought Gabriel's suspicions of Browning, rightly or wrongly, to a head. He believed himself to be the original "Don Juan" of the poem, and was deeply offended. *Fifine*, Browning once declared, was intended "to show morally how a Don Juan might justify himself partly by truth, somewhat by sophistry"; and certain elements in the poem must have recalled to Gabriel's sensitive conscience, at least *Fanny* and his dead wife. At the moment, such associations were peculiarly irritating to him, sore as he was after Buchanan's attack, and vulnerable as he must have felt amidst the complexities of his present passion.

No doubt, too, Gabriel remarked how habitually Browning based his work upon actual facts, upon real incidents, situations and individuals of the past or present. Besides, in *Fifine*, the problem raised, that of "sense and soul," was particularly Rossetti's. Several allusions might well relate to Rossetti's own past—although, of course, they might equally well bear no conscious relation to it—and some of the ideas Gabriel favoured were ridiculed, especially that of "sense" being sanctified by "soul," an argument which in fact Rossetti had just used against Buchanan. That in some degree, though not entirely without sympathy, Browning had consciously or unconsciously drawn upon his acquaintance with Gabriel for inspiration, is certainly possible, perhaps even probable. In these circumstances, Gabriel, almost inevitably, in his over-wrought state, believed himself implicated, and was particularly annoyed by some lines near the close of *Fifine*, which William cautiously refrained from indicating in detail, but said Gabriel believed them "intended as an attack upon him, or as a spiteful reference to something which had occurred or might be alleged to have occurred at his house." Perhaps the passage to which he objected seemed to him a veiled allusion to the rumour that on the night of Lizzie's death he had left her for some clandestine assignation, returning only to find her unconscious and dying; for I find no other remotely possible allusion to Gabriel's life in the poem's close.

How little William Rossetti knew of the actual circumstances of his brother's and Browning's separation is shown by his belief that Browning, unaware of Gabriel's changed attitude, was baffled by his withdrawal from his company, and only wished, if allowed, to call again on Rossetti and resume intimacy. Holman Hunt knew better; for once, when Hunt mentioned Gabriel's name to Browning, he "suddenly flamed up, saying: 'That is a man I will never forgive; he is unpardonable,' adding that 'he had no patience with him and would never overlook his insolence.' " Reluctant to question Browning further, Hunt imputed his anger to a remark by Gabriel of which Hunt had already heard. Was it Gabriel's reputed comment on *Balaustion's Adventure*, to the effect that "Browning and poetry had parted company for ever?"

But whatever may have been the slender basis of fact in Gabriel's suspicions of Browning, delusions were certainly by this time gaining control over Rossetti's mind. Shortly after this, he found in the recently published *Hunting of the Snark*, the work of "Lewis Carroll," (or to give him his own name, C. L. Dodgson,) another acquaintance, new personal injury. Again the vicious circle was complete. Ill-health sowed suspicions and the suspicions increased the ill-health. *Fifine*, said Scott, "greatly aggravated Rossetti's state of mind; he believed it was entirely written about him, and against him, all the innuendos and insinuations being aimed at him! . . . This confirmed [Browning] to be among the enemies. What did the book mean if it did not mean what Rossetti said?" Henceforth, for Gabriel, both Browning and Dodgson as well as Buchanan, were members of the secret "conspiracy" against himself, which now haunted his mind, exactly as those secret conspirators of the mysterious "sect" and the jealous rivals in Naples, had once haunted his father's.

By this time, Gabriel's state was indeed alarming. "All this past cursed state of things began on my birthday," he declared a few months later, when, recovering, he dared to look back for a moment over his immediate past. If, as he thus indicated, this definite illness began on May 12th, it was not, according to William, until three weeks later that the externally obvious crisis came. For it was apparently on June 2nd—a day or two *before* he received Browning's *Fifine* according to Scott, a day or two *after* William believed—that Gabriel obviously passed the bounds of sanity, astounding William by talking wildly about a conspiracy against himself, of which Browning was the leader! Rossetti was evidently, as his brother said, "not entirely sane," "an actual monomaniac." "It was," said William, "one of the most miserable days of my life, not to speak of his." This temporary insanity William attributed to chloral and alcohol and consequent hypochondria, behind which, however, were, he believed—and certainly rightly—other causes of anxiety and unrest.

Gabriel's "seizure," as we may call it, began with the sale on this day of his painting *The Meeting of Dante and Beatrice in the Garden of Eden*, which he had begun to paint at Sevenoaks, twenty-two years before, and having then only painted in part of the background, had now at last resumed and converted into *The Bower Meadow*. Messrs. Pilgeram and Lefevre, who had by this time replaced the detested Gambart as Rossetti's agents, bought it for the high price of £735; yet Mr. Lefevre, on entering the house in Cheyne Walk in order to complete the transaction, found Gabriel greatly agitated, obsessed with the belief that all sorts of people were inimical to him and trying to undervalue him. He protested—most uncharacteristically—that if the dealer, who was in fact well satisfied with the price, suspected he was being overcharged, the agreement must be cancelled. The paranoiac conscience or "super-ego" was evidently active on this occasion, in contrast to Gabriel's normal business negotiations.

William, unable to control his brother, went early in the morning for Scott, and soon Professor Marshall and Dr. Hake were called in for medical advice. Rossetti's condition was obviously paranoid, with irrational ideas and auditory delusions. Marshall, seeing the seriousness of his state, called in an eminent specialist, Dr. Maudsley, whom Gabriel at sight insanely charged with falsely posing as a doctor in order to do him harm. A change of scene was ordered, and good Dr. Hake took Gabriel into his own house at Roehampton, overlooking the Robin Hood Gate of Richmond Park. William never forgot "that dismal cab journey," with his brother and Brown, to Dr. Hake's. The drive was not without incidents. Gabriel insisted again and again that a bell was being rung on the roof of the cab to annoy him, and on alighting at Hake's door surprised the Cheyne Walk cabman, who had often driven him about London, by sharply asking: "Why did you ring that bell?" It was ten o'clock when the weary party reached Dr. Hake's and too late to do more than settle down for the night; but Gabriel was comparatively happy for a short time in Hake's drawing-room, finding what his own solitary abode, haunted by memories, had so long denied him—"peace."

But his strange behaviour continued. The next day, the Saturday before Whitsunday, walking with Hake along the high road crowded with gipsies' vans and all the paraphernalia of a fair, he was moved by the general excitement to reject Hake's explanation of the unusual activity about them, and, insisting that it was a hostile demonstration of his enemies against himself, he tried to run after some of the vehicles and begin a quarrel with their drivers, so that the walk had to be abandoned. Throughout the day he was quiet, but after dinner, as William read aloud for their entertainment Merivale's *Roman Empire*, Gabriel again became excited, being reminded by some passages of his own persecution as he believed it, and the reading had to be abandoned. Until late, he talked to William of family affairs,[1] and, on retiring, had the worst night he had ever known, troubled by delusions,

[1] Probably of Lizzie's death.

519

including a voice which, said William, "twice called out at him a term of gross and unbearable obloquy!"[1] In desperation he swallowed the contents of a bottle of laudanum which he had secreted amongst his belongings, and dropped the empty bottle in a drawer. How he obtained the laudanum William never knew, but in fact Gabriel had sometimes taken Lizzie's drug, laudanum, instead of chloral, as an opiate.

Ignorant of Gabriel's attempted suicide, and mistaking the coma consequent upon his secret self-poisoning for healthy, recuperative sleep, Hake and William watched Gabriel with satisfaction for hours, and not until four o'clock on the Sunday afternoon did Dr. Hake suspect some hidden, sinister reason for so prolonged a slumber. A neighbouring doctor, on being summoned, decided the cause was an "effusion of serum on the brain," and William, who had thoughtfully kept his mother and sisters in complete ignorance of Gabriel's breakdown, hurriedly brought his mother and Maria—Christina, bedridden for months, with exophthalmic bronchocele, could not be moved—to be present at what all expected to be Gabriel's last hours. Hake, meanwhile, resting a moment from his task of holding ammonia under Gabriel's nose, found the empty laudanum bottle, and so learned the truth.

Once again for William, too, history was repeating itself. Ten years before, he had seen the dead woman and an empty laudanum bottle, in Chatham Place; and now this new, yet familiar scene—this time certainly attempted suicide—or was it again to find sleep? But surely this was no coincidence. "Chance" does not thus repeat its grotesque patterns so exactly, within the narrow limits of a single life. Had not the paranoiac's super-ego, the too sensitive "conscience" of Gabriel, admittedly so active in other relations, hounded him on to the death he believed in his heart he had brought on his dead wife, however mistaken that belief might be? Was the influence of Lizzie, which William in his foresight had always regretted, secretly still active, even ten years after Lizzie's death? Was this the

---

[1] Probably the term was "murderer"—a projection of his anxiety complex and self-accusation *re* Lizzie's death. Hence, too, his attempted suicide afterwards and by the same means. Apparently the possibility of murder had to be considered at the inquest and must have deeply affected so sensitive and imaginative a person as D. G. R. *v. sup.* pp. 295–7 and footnotes.

consummation of long-standing, secret fears, a consummation
almost prophetically indicated by Gabriel four years previously
in *A Superscription*?[1]

Beneath the shock, even William for a time was overwhelmed,
and abandoned the placid entries of commonplace in his
diary. But that his brother had attempted suicide he so well
hid from the rest of the family, representing Gabriel's illness as
a kind of "fit," that to the end of their lives neither his mother
nor his sisters ever knew, or even suspected, the truth.

It was late at night when Mrs. Rossetti, Maria and William
reached Roehampton, and shortly afterwards Dr. Marshall,
also hastily summoned, arrived. He ordered strong coffee,
which the poetical Dr. Hake seems not to have thought of, gave
other directions to keep Gabriel's circulation and respiration
active, and before leaving saw signs of recovery. But not until
the Monday did Rossetti fully awaken from his two days'
trance. For two or three days Mrs. Rossetti and Maria remained with him at Dr. Hake's, and a few days after their
departure, Gabriel, still restless but afraid of the solitude of
Cheyne Walk, went to stay with Brown in Fitzroy Square.
Boyce, hearing of Rossetti's illness on June 12th, was profoundly
disturbed. "W. B. Scott called," he recorded, "and told me, to
my very great regret, that poor Gabriel Rossetti was seriously
unwell, in fact had for the time quite lost his head. The symptoms became obvious about a week ago when he became
possessed by the idea that people were lying in wait for him
and wished to destroy him, This so increased on him that Dr.
Hake who had been called in induced him to come to his
house. On Monday he showed some signs of violence, irritated
by noises of merrymakers with brass bands in the streets, after
which he sank into a state of lethargy. Waking up from this he
became greatly excited, and rather worse than better. The
opinion is that even if he recovers it may be months before he
does so. Very shocking and lamentable, this!" The following
day Boyce "Went to W. B. Scott's and heard Rossetti was
much better."

Since his attempted suicide, Gabriel's physical condition had
deteriorated, for on awakening from his coma, he was found to

[1] *v. sup.* p. 300.

be suffering from hemiplegia or partial paralysis around the hip joint—a weakness often associated with paranoia. Consequently, lame in one leg, he was obliged to walk with a stick, a condition very obvious for some five or six months, and not entirely overcome for another year or so; but afterwards cured —or so nearly cured as to escape notice.

Dejected, unable to work, but easily controlled now, and apparently normal, Gabriel remained for about a week at Brown's until, by June 20th, he was sufficiently recovered to go for change of air and scene to Scotland. Accompanied by the faithful Brown and by Dr. Hake's son George, whose undergraduate studies at Oxford eye-strain had temporarily suspended, Gabriel went to Urrard House, in Perthshire, placed at his service by his kindly patron Graham. Restless, he moved a week later to another Perthshire seat of Graham's, Stobhall, which two centuries before had been the home of the historic Drummonds, whose head, the Duke of Perth as the Jacobites called him, had lost everything in the revolt of 1715. As before, country air and exercise soon improved Gabriel's health; his insomnia, lameness and chloral dosing declined, although his dejection, delusions of conspiracy and apparent indifference to the external world did not pass. Scott came and relieved Brown, and soon, in his turn, Dr. Hake came to relieve Scott. At last, in mid-July, Dr. Hake was able to encourage Brown with "the first letter of a really hopeful kind," believing that within three or four months Rossetti would be well and at work again.

But even the delightful gardens and charming views of Stobhall, with its outlook over the Tay, could not curb Rossetti's restlessness, and he was soon established at a farmhouse, named Trowan, near Crieff, which Dr. Hake found for him, beautifully situated by a river-side, near a lake, amidst pine-clad mountains and waterfalls. The house was kept by a lady farmer, "whose manner and person," said urbane Dr. Hake, "had every agreeable trait." Still mentally remote, but, with the aid of a stick, stumping along by-roads, pathways and the riverside, Rossetti continued to improve. Dr. Hake marvelled, as others had long since done before him, at the huge breakfasts of bacon and eggs Gabriel consumed, and also, apparently, at

his fondness for whisky—despite his vow of years before to give
it up—for Hake drily remarked that Rossetti at Trowan "did
not regard tea as possessing the attributes of Totality." Less
imperious than before his illness, Gabriel expressed gratitude
for his friends' aid. The "goodness" of the Hakes, he said, was
"quite unwearying." Late in the summer evenings Dr. Hake
would read to him, or tell travellers' tales—for he had seen
much of the world—until Gabriel fell asleep.

Soon, urged by Brown, Rossetti summoned his art-assistant
Dunn to Trowan with his paints, and, resuming work, felt
happier. He made a chalk drawing of Dr. Hake—which later
appeared as frontispiece in *New Day*, Hake's volume of sonnets
—and also one of George Hake, and completed the long-
delayed *Beata Beatrix* for Graham, which he had abandoned as
"hopeless." But even when it was finished, he could say nothing
better of this replica than "*tant bien que mal* or *plus mal que bien*."
The nine hundred guineas Graham had long since advanced
for *Beata Beatrix*, were of course all spent, but the predella
would bring Gabriel another hundred and fifty pounds, and so
almost cover his expenses in Scotland.

For, as ever, Gabriel's chief incentive for painting was an
urgent need of money to meet the rising flood of debts which,
since his illness, had alarmingly increased. During this illness,
and without his knowledge, William had placated the most
pressing of Gabriel's creditors with £650 raised by the sale of
Rossetti's china, and additional funds realized by the sale of
some of his paintings. And at the same time the private zoo
was also disposed of.[1] The loss of his collection of china, said
Scott, not only troubled Rossetti more than anything else, but
also (as he still insisted that the conspiracy was real, and not
he but his sceptical friends the deluded ones), it most brought
home to him the reality of his illness. Indeed, William's zeal
for settling his brother's debts seemed to Gabriel supererroga-
tory, and as soon as he was well enough to do so, he reproved
William for his folly in settling accounts at midsummer with
various tradesmen to whom he had himself sent small token
payments only six months before!

With this reproof, indeed, was associated one of Gabriel's

[1] *v. inf.* pp. 652–3.

chief anxieties during his illness, the position of Fanny, whose affairs were becoming as involved as his own. It was because of this that he now cautioned William: "Pay away as little as possible. . . . Should I be going to the deuce, I am much less anxious to square accounts with the rapacious harpies who have been flaying me for years than to do what may be for Fanny's maintenance; and the only question would be whether the sum in hand at such juncture would be of more or less service to her than the proceeds of my furniture and remaining drawings if saved by payment to creditors from the danger of a forced sale."

Never before, probably, had the reality of his affection for Fanny, his sense of responsibility, been so clearly revealed. He did not forget her in absence, and his letters to her from Kelmscott, shortly before his breakdown, often show a playful tenderness.

It was thus in September 1871, when gently reproving Fanny for taking no holiday, he wrote: "I am sorry you have been so little away, as I fear your health will suffer for it, but I suppose your funny old head could not rest while there was so much opportunity of making messes at home. . . ." For small domestic tragedies of Fanny's as well as for her little ailments, Gabriel would express unusual sympathy. Indeed in this same letter of September 1871 and the letter following, he attempted to console her for one such misfortune. Some venison—or as Rossetti called it, "a fawn"—had come for him, Dunn reported, in Cheyne Walk. It was, Dunn believed, a present from Graham, who also sent some grouse. So "high" was it, however, that Dunn, considering it uneatable, buried it in the garden of Cheyne Walk, instead of forwarding it to Rossetti at Kelmscott. When Gabriel informed Fanny of this, casually, in a letter, Fanny took it tragically. Declaring, truly or not, that the buried "fawn" was not a present from Graham but from herself, she so bitterly condemned and lamented Dunn's action that Gabriel, usually rather callous about others' minor misfortunes, replied in a surprisingly consolatory strain. "My dear Fanny," he wrote, "your poor dear letter has almost made me cry. It comes at a moment when I happen to feel in very low spirits, and I cannot tell you how grieved I feel to think

that your affectionate remembrance of me in sending the poor
fawn should only have brought you disappointment and
vexation. I wish I was with you at this moment, poor kind Fan,
to kiss you and tell you how much I feel about it. Of course I
had no idea till now that the fawn was your present, but
thought it came from Graham with the grouse, otherwise I
should have written much more seriously about it in my last
letter to you, and should have expressed to Dunn at the time
my great regret that he had not sent it on. I cannot understand
how opinions should differ so as to its condition, as Dunn
assured me it was so far gone as to render it no use at all to
send it on. I am not surprised at your great annoyance at his
conduct, and can only beg you to overlook it, as no doubt he
did for the best as far as he thought, and I believe he was
under the impression certainly that the fawn came from
Graham. But I am sure he has the most friendly feeling towards
you and deserves that you should pardon him this oversight. . . .
It seems poor Dunn is going to Croydon—I suppose with the
intention of flying from your wrath." For any outrage upon
Fanny's finer sentiments produced exhibitions of vulgar violence, far more energetic, if we may trust both tradition and
probability, than even those of his dead wife.

Gabriel's letters to Fanny, skilfully adapted to his correspondent's mentality, were simple, factual, childish. His
passion spent, he treated her as he might some old nurse of his
childhood, who was to be humoured, cared for, laughed at,
and at times even conciliated. A year later, for example, in
September 1872, just after his breakdown, he wrote to her
from Trowan, sympathetically deploring the twinges of rheu-
matism of which she complained, fearing she did not get
sufficiently good food in her own home, and discussing the
complaints of lack of money which she now, if not before,
frequently made. "What you tell me about Brown and William
telling you that you ought to let your rooms, was, I think, on
the whole, the best step to take at present, particularly as you
seem to have found a quiet lodger. You say that they have
given you no money, but you do not tell me positively that you
have been in want of any, or I should send a cheque with this.
At present, however, as you of course know, it is advisable to

be very careful, and I know you always are so. I am anxious that you should not begin spending that £100 you had laid by, and sooner than you should do that, I would send money at once, though I am obliged to spend as little as I can. You must not suppose that either William or Brown are anything but true friends to you; and as for myself, you are the only person whom it is my duty to provide for, and you may be sure I should do my utmost as long as there was a breath in my body or a penny in my purse." To no other, throughout his whole life, did Gabriel, ever so ready to transfer his own financial responsibilities to others, and also, of course, equally reluctant to assume those of any other person, write in this vein. Nor is it less obvious that Fanny must have been largely responsible for Gabriel's increasing solitude; Gabriel's less bohemian friends were as little likely to please Fanny as Fanny was to please them.

From Urrard House, Gabriel had even begged William to help Fanny, fearing, as he said, that her drunken "incubus" of a husband, or her husband's creditors, would seize the furniture at 36 Royal Avenue, Chelsea, where Gabriel had installed her. To prevent this he made William a "gift" of the furniture in Fanny's house, "in consideration of divers sums of money lent to me by you on various occasions, and which I have never repaid." The last clause was true enough, but the bogus "gift" was merely to preserve the things for Fanny, not a belated recognition of his debt to his brother. Gabriel's patron Valpy was, he suggested, to draw up the deed of gift, as he was a solicitor, but Howell too must be consulted, especially "as to whether Valpy, who is a desperately religious man, can be employed, or whether it may be better in that case to go to Tebbs or some other lawyer." Finally, Gabriel petitioned, would William rent Fanny's house for Gabriel, but in William's own name?—but this William categorically refused to do.

From Stobhall Gabriel had again begged the demurring William's acquiescence, explaining: "the suggestions came from Brown. . . . Of course I would not ask you to do what seemed to you objectionable, but if Brown and the lawyer can remove your objections, poor F's mind would no doubt be greatly relieved, and I fear it must be much harassed at present." He was also troubled by suspicions of carelessness or dishonesty amongst the servants left in Cheyne Walk, never dreaming that the worst if not the only culprit was apparently Fanny herself, unless tradition and the testimony of Rossetti's friends do her wrong. How far Gabriel was from suspecting her is shown by the fact that he innocently sent her, from Trowan, directions to lock up his studio and keep the key. "I hope," he told William, "you manage to see poor Fanny now and then," and proceeded calmly to suggest that William, the highly respectable civil servant, should invite Fanny to call on him occasionally in his room in Somerset House!

Brown, meanwhile, anxiously awaiting news of Gabriel's recovery, was able to rejoice to Shields on September 6th: "He is perfectly recovered and at work again. . . . For at least a fortnight Hake's letters have invariably given the same information—total recovery." With Hake, however, the wish seems to have fathered the thought, for on the preceding day Rossetti himself had complained to William: "My lameness continues the same and I have little doubt will be permanent. An utter sleeplessness, except some two or three hours about once a fortnight, is the state of things in spite of heavy narcotics. I go out daily for a six miles or so of walk, unless the weather is very bad, in which case my walk is shorter." Although the laudanum poisoning had been eliminated, the hemiplegia and mental unrest stimulated by insomnia, chloral and spirits increased his distress, and now the hydrocele so troubled him that Marshall was summoned to Scotland to relieve him. A local surgeon, however, was found, who performed the small operation so well that Marshall was able to remain in town. Inevitably in such a state, Gabriel's opinion of his condition varied with his moods. "One must hope for the best," he wrote to his mother, dejectedly, in mid-September, "even if the worst is all one gets by it."

The Joneses, who had heard of Gabriel's collapse with profound sorrow, followed the fluctuations of his "recovery" with increasing disquietude. "Utterly broken down," Jones described Gabriel to Norton shortly after Rossetti's departure for Scotland, "fluctuations of better or worse from day to day I believe are little guide in his case, and we must wait. It has been the saddest sight I have had in my days, and seems to tinge everything with melancholy and foreboding. There is more than any tenderness of friendship in what I feel for him —he is the beginning of everything in me that I care for, and it is quite dreadful."

At first, like a wounded animal, Gabriel on leaving for Scotland had sought only solitude. But with returning health came increasing weariness of his environment, an increasing desire to return, not to Cheyne Walk but to Kelmscott, the happiest place he had ever known. When at last Dr. Hake departed, Gabriel became lonelier than ever. Gloomily from the windows of Trowan, he watched the slow, silent procession of sad autumn days pass. Each day now, despite the many pleasant walks at his disposal, he mechanically took the same road. And he thought that if only he could be back at Kelmscott he would paint a new picture. To rejoin Janey and the children at Kelmscott was indeed his first passionate desire as the mental cloud lifted. As early as September 11th, he had tactfully hinted at it even to Fanny, saying: "I do not expect now to be staying very much longer here, but am not inclined to return to London if I can help it. Perhaps I may go for awhile to Kelmscott, where I should be living at much less expense than here." And as September neared its close, although he was still lame, and aware of his "somewhat morbid state of mind," as he described it, he insisted upon return. Refusing both Alice Boyd's and Howell's invitations to visit them, and rejecting William's offer to keep him company at Kelmscott, he nevertheless prepared to return there, and from that moment his health, spirits, powers of painting, all wonderfully improved. "Wherever I can be at peace," he wrote, "there I shall assuredly work. But all, I now find by experience, depends primarily on my not being deprived of the prospect of the society of the one necessary person." That, for the biographer, is obviously a most suggestive and intriguing remark, the possible implications of which will be considered later.

Shortly afterwards, before the close of September indeed, reserving a third-class carriage for himself and young George Hake—he was momentarily too poor for luxury—and leaving Dunn to settle his affairs in Scotland, he set off in high spirits for Kelmscott and, surely, "the one necessary person" to be found there. Refusing even an hour's delay to visit his family in London, and particularly forbidding William to tell Fanny of his passing through, he tried to prevent any interruption on the direct road to the house he loved. Nevertheless, either William's entreaties or the exigencies of the railway timetable, brought him to the Rossetti home in Euston Square for an hour or two, "the first happy ones," he declared, that he had known for months. A few hours later he was back at Kelmscott with Janey.

XIII

RETROSPECT
1871

> . . . remote from the world's throng,
> Work, contest, fame, all life's confederate pleas,—
> What while Love breathed in sighs and silences
> Through two blent souls one rapturous undersong.
>
> *Love's Antiphony* D. G. ROSSETTI
> (Later renamed *Youth's Antiphony*.)

WHAT, ONE WONDERS, were the underlying causes of Rossetti's collapse in the summer of 1872? The attendant circumstances, even when all possible credit (or discredit), is given to the effects of alcohol and chloral, hardly allow us to regard Buchanan's article as more than the "last straw" in a series of events that so undermined Rossetti's morale as to culminate in attempted suicide. Not only do these alone seem inadequate to account for so severe a crisis, we should surely expect the shock of Buchanan's onslaught to be greatest when first made in the November *Contemporary*, rather than upon its repetition in pamphlet form eight months later.

Even William Rossetti, while apparently imputing his brother's breakdown to Buchanan, declared that but for the chloral, his attack would have had little or no effect, and once at least William admitted that behind alcohol, chloral, insomnia and Buchanan were other, deeper causes of anxiety. Scott, indeed, like Stillman, denied that chloral was to any extent the cause of "either the mental or bodily peculiarities" Rossetti now showed, and was also assured by Dr. Marshall "that the chloral was merely a desperate attempt to cure his evils, not the cause of them," "These evils," Scott asserted, "were in fitful activity very long ago, and were really the cause of his resorting to chloral—not the effect of that in any way." Nor when we remember how closely Rossetti's attempt at suicide resembled the circumstances of his wife's death, need we entirely reject the unsupported testimony of the largely unreliable and melo-dramatic Hall Caine, that amongst the delusions haunting

Rossetti in his illness "were some that related to the exhumation of his wife's body, and the curse that was supposed to have followed him for that desecration." For in Gabriel reason and imaginative sympathy were often at strife, and superstitions which his reason rejected even with contempt would master his imagination and emotions. This, indeed, was one of the many resemblances between Rossetti and his father.

How vivid his imagination was his friends well knew. Ruskin spoke of Rossetti "whose mind a thousand living imaginations haunt." Watts-Dunton, his closest friend in later years, described him as "the slave of his own imagination—an imagination of a power and dominance such as I have never seen equalled. Of its vividness," Watts-Dunton added, "no artistic expression of his can give any notion. He had not the smallest command over it. And let it not be supposed this was a slight affliction . . . having lost the governance of the most powerful of all the human faculties he suffered much misery. . . . This I say was Rossetti's curse . . . the tremulous flame of his soul was disturbed by every breath. To tell him anything of a specially pathetic or tragic nature was cruel, so vividly did he realize every situation." And Watts-Dunton went on to tell of how when at Kelmscott he had amused Rossetti by inventing stories during their walks, "so powerful (that is to say, so childlike), was Rossetti's imagination, so entirely did it dominate an intellect of unusual subtlety, that these stories interested him just as much as real adventures, and though he knew them to be gossamer fictions woven at the moment of telling, he would be as much affected by an unhappy catastrophe as though they had been incidents of his real life, and would sometimes beg for the catastrophe to be altered." To-day we should regard such a quality as empathy, self-identification with imaginary situations rather than as a true and powerful imaginative faculty.

Nor was Rossetti's intellect, subtle rather than powerful, a sufficient corrective to so dominating an "imagination." Rossetti's "intellectual force," wrote Dr. Hake "was not of a striking order, but it was adequate; his charm lay in the artistic colouring of his mind, arrayed as it was in the fascinations of a Provencal attire." "He was," said Watts-Dunton, "an idealist . . . if ever there was one: he paid the penalty for living in the idealist's world of beautiful dreams, if ever that penalty was paid by man." And Watts-Dunton went on to describe how on one occasion, when he invented for Rossetti a parable of the idealist's mingled sense of joy and exile, in the guise of Eve's daughter wrapt in mystic visions of the Paradise she had never known and which her parents had forgotten, Rossetti took the allegory to himself and wept. . . .

Unless we realize this dominance of Rossetti's imagination, the basic fact that both his life and art were dominated by dream, that he was trying to live his myth, his "one dream alone" (for him, almost the sole important reality), both his art and life must be scarcely comprehensible. And at Kelmscott with Janey, life and dream had more closely approximated, more happily harmonized than ever before. In Gabriel's sonnets of that period, this happiness, this harmony, clearly reveals itself. Gabriel's remark upon his recovery, in obvious reference to the cause of his illness, needs therefore no interpreter: "Wherever I can be at peace, there I shall assuredly work, but all, I now find by experience, depends primarily on my not being deprived of the prospect of the society of the one necessary person." His headlong flight afterwards to Kelmscott and Janey was therefore to be expected rather than explained.

What, therefore, one wonders, had brought the happy existence of Gabriel and Janey at Kelmscott so suddenly to an end in the late autumn of 1871? Was it external pressure from friends? From Morris himself we know pressure would never have come. Did Janey, from choice or necessity, insist upon returning to town for the winter? Was Rossetti forced to return by the need of new commissions—or rather of money?—for he had more commissions (paid for) than he ever tried to fulfil. Or did the ultimate threat of separation come later, about the time of Buchanan's renewed attack and Gabriel's collapse, in May 1872? Was it due to some prohibition of an intention to resume their life together at Kelmscott in the spring or summer of 1872? By that time seven months had passed since they left Kelmscott, and Rossetti's nostalgia must have greatly intensified. In Buchanan, probably, the anger of Gabriel's frustrated passion largely found a convenient excuse, his neurotic exhaustion a plausible disguise.

Certainly, if we may take the sonnets of 1871 as evidence—
and they obviously continue the love-story of 1869–70—Janey
and Gabriel were supremely happy together during that
secluded summer at Kelmscott. Rossetti—so he told Scott in
mid-August 1871—had just completed thirty new sonnets for
The House of Life;[1] and of these "thirty," we may reasonably
assume, are the twenty-eight sonnets, or most of them, dated
"1871" by William Rossetti in the 1911 edition of his brother's
literary works. These sonnets, which surely reflect the atmosphere of Kelmscott during the lovers' residence there in 1871,
voice many moods of love: sometimes even contradictory
moods—regret for Love's evanescence and uncertainty, as in
Pride of Youth, the bitter-sweet emotions of secret love-trysts to
which a fascinated but sad and tearful and apparently conscience-stricken woman comes as in some illicit passion, in
Heart's Haven, yet offering her lover a refuge from his own
despondency. Other sonnets of that year, such as *The Lovers'*
Walk, *Youth's Antiphony* (originally named *Love's Antiphony*),
Beauty's Pageant and *Silent Noon*, are a record of physical passion
amidst some such rustic environment as Kelmscott:

> What while Love breathed in sighs and silences
> Through two blent souls one rapturous undersong.

A similar note of immediacy sounds in *Beauty's Pageant*, which
records the thoughts of the lover, alone, reliving some recent
passionate meeting with his mistress:

> What glory of change by Nature's hand amass'd
> Can vie with all those moods of varying grace
> Which o'er one loveliest woman's form and face
> Within this hour, within this room have passed?

A similar intensity of passion inspires these sonnets of a lover
rejoicing as in *Soul Light*,[2] that

> After the fulness of all rapture, still,
> As at the end of some deep avenue
> A tender glamour of day—there comes to view
> Far in your eyes a yet more hungering thrill—
> Such fire as Love's soul-winnowing hands distil
> Even from his inmost arc of light and dew.

---

[1] *v. sup.* p. 475 and Note.   [2] Originally entitled *Lovelight*.

Nor are the calmer moments of their love less precious, for:—

> . . . as the traveller triumphs with the sun,
>   Glorying in heat's mid-height, yet startide brings
>   Wonder new-born, and still fresh transport springs
> From limpid lambent hours of day begun;—
> Even so, through eyes and voice, your soul doth move
> My soul with changeful light of infinite love.

Such, then, are these sonnets of 1871—reflections of the varied moods of Love, from such simple praise of the beloved as *The Moonstar, Equal Troth* and *The Lamp's Shrine*[1] express, from praise of Love itself, as in *The Dark Glass* and *Love's Last Gift*, to such mystical illuminations of Love as that in *Heart's Compass*, in which the beloved appears to him

> . . . not as thyself alone,
> But as the meaning of all things that are;
> A breathless wonder, shadowing forth afar
> Some heavenly solstice hushed and halcyon . . .

It was in this mood that Gabriel had painted Janey as *Water-Willow*, during those halcyon days at Kelmscott in 1871. "There is little to say as to any 'subject' in the *Water-Willow* picture," he wrote: "The figure is meant to be, as it were, speaking to you, and embodying in her expression the penetrating sweetness of the scene and season."

Nor is the identification of Janey as Rossetti's chief source of inspiration at that time restricted to painting. Occasional references in the sonnets or chance turns of phrase there, more or less definitely suggest that Janey's image was before his mind's eye as he wrote. This, as already stated,[2] is particularly evident in the sonnet *Genius in Beauty*, which is also demonstrably associated with Kelmscott, where, on the wall of Gabriel's studio, Janey's portrait hung. In *Venus Victrix* and *Her Gifts*,[3] Janey is evidently the original source of his descriptions, even to her dark hair, as we have seen.[4] The final couplet of *Her Gifts* closely resembles the short prose outline Gabriel made in one of his notebooks for a never-completed poem to be called

---

[1] Originally *The Love-Lamp*.   [2] *v. sup.* pp. 401–2.
[3] Originally entitled *My Lady's Gifts*.   [4] *v. sup.* p. 400 and footnote 1.

My Lady, and this resemblance is too close not to be significant.

> These are her gifts, as tongue may tell them o'er.
> Breathe low her name, my soul: for that means more,

is the final couplet of *Her Gifts*, and in his short prose outline for the never-written poem *My Lady*, Gabriel wrote: "She is full of incidents like all beautiful Nature," adding, "Then follow descriptive lines about her different attitudes, expressions, etc. Perhaps to wind up by saying that nothing one can say is so expressive of her as her own name, which means herself only: and that cannot be said for others to hear." Is it too Philistine an interpretation to suggest that both here and in the final line of *Her Gifts*, Rossetti's secrecy is dictated, even if unconsciously, less by reverence than by discretion? And if we seek autobiographical references in these sonnets, what can more strongly suggest Rossetti's sense of the contrast between this love for Janey and the old love for Lizzie than his assertion in *The Dark Glass*, that he

>   . . . cannot weigh
> To-morrow's dower by gage of yesterday?

And is there no reference to Gabriel's choice of an illicit love against an opposing world when, in *Heart's Compass*,[1] worshipping Love in the person of the beloved, he cries:

> Yea, by thy hand the Love-god rends apart
> All gathering clouds of Night's ambiguous art;
> Flings them far down, and sets thine eyes above;
> And simply, as some gage of flower or glove,
> Stakes with a smile the world against thy heart?

So from its first intensity of passion their love passes in *Mid-Rapture* and similar sonnets into the more tranquil region of love's maturity; and this quieter, deeper note dominates such sonnets as *Last Fire*, in which Rossetti gives expression to the harmony of sense and spirit, of the two lovers, with the natural beauty around them:

> Love, through your spirit and mine what summer eve
> Now glows with glory of all things possess'd,
> Since this day's sun of rapture filled the west
> And the light sweetened as the fire took leave?

---

[1] Originally entitled *Love's Compass*.

Yet over their summer's happiness lies a darkening shadow, the threat of approaching Autumn and Winter and, as Rossetti sang in *Heart's Compass*:—

> . . . gathering clouds of Night's ambiguous art.

That this shadow was the fear, perhaps even the growing threat of separation when summer ended, many passages in Rossetti's sonnets, and even an occasional remark in his letters, strongly suggest. Certainly this shadow of impending severance had gradually darkened the paradise of the lovers at Kelmscott, as with the approach of Autumn, the time of departure drew near—

> all sweet blooms of love
> To thee I gave while Spring and Summer sang;
> But Autumn stops to listen, with some pang
> From those worse things the wind is moaning of—

as he wrote in *Love's Last Gift*; while in *Last Fire*, he more passionately feels the happy present because—

> Many the days that Winter keeps in store,
>   Sunless throughout, or whose brief sun-glimpses
>   Scarce shed the heaped snow through the naked trees;
> This day at least was Summer's paramour,
> Sun-coloured to the imperishable core
>   With sweet well-being of love and full heart's ease.

Indeed in the sonnets of this time the fear of separation slowly deepens into the bitterness of love's frustration. As we pass from the unalloyed ecstasy of *The Lover's Walk*, *Silent Noon*, and similar sonnets, to the clouded content of *Last Fire*, and finally to the despair of the lover left alone with only memories for companionship in *Without Her*, we seem to trace the course of Gabriel's experience during that crucial summer and autumn of 1871. Even by mid-August Rossetti was lamenting in *Cloud Confines*, the inevitable conflict, as he saw it, between man's love and fate—

> . . . kisses snatched 'neath the ban
> Of fangs that mock them above,

bewailing "Hope that a breath dispels" and "bitter, forlorn farewells" already looming for them in the near distance. On this same note of sorrowful, despairing questioning, *Sunset Wings*, written at that same time, had ended:

> Is Hope not plumed, as 'twere a fiery dart?
>   And oh! thou dying day,
> Even as thou goest must she too depart,
> And Sorrow fold such pinions on the heart
>   As will not fly away?

Similarly ominous of impending calamity was the sequence of sonnets Rossetti had also written at that time, shortly before leaving Kelmscott in the late autumn of 1871, sonnets which now appear as Nos. XL–XLIV in *The House of Life*. An almost hysterical confusion and anxiety suggests the images and atmosphere of *Through Death to Love*[1] and *The Dark Glass*, both written by mid-August, while in *Hope Overtaken*, this hysteria rises, or sinks almost to despair:

> O Hope of mine whose eyes are living hope,
>   No eyes but hers—O Love and Hope the same!—
>   Lean close to me, for now the sinking sun
> That warmed our feet scarce gilds her hair above.
> O hers thy voice and very hers thy name!
>   Alas, cling round me, for the day is done!

As that bitter-sweet summer at Kelmscott neared its end, and the time of parting drew nearer, while

> . . . Autumn stops to listen, with some pang
> From those worse things the wind is moaning of,

the signs of mental and emotional strain in Gabriel's verses deepen; the old oscillation between the two polarities of love and death returns; the thought of death as an escape from frustration reappears. It lurks in *Love and Hope*,[2] grows in *Cloud*

---

[1] My interpretation is strengthened by my later remarking that in the Bancroft MS. the 3rd line of this sonnet is—

> Like multiform *malifluence* manifold,

not as when published, *circumfluence*.

[2] Instead of—"Bless love and hope. Full many a withered year," etc., the Bancroft MS. reads, significantly:—"Kiss once again. Even now the withered year," etc.

And in place of line 8 as published—"Bless love and hope, true soul; for we are here," the Bancroft MS. reads—"Kiss once again my love; for we are here."

And again, line 13, in place of:—"Or but discern, through night's unfeatured scope," Rossetti first wrote two alternative lines, thus:—

> Or but discern, where 'mid dark night we grope. . . .
> Or but discern, where deep in night we grope. . . .

and Wind, rises almost to hysteria in *Through Death to Love.* And then, it would seem, when the long-dreaded calamity of their parting has fallen upon them, Rossetti emerges for a moment from his confusion and anxiety into the despairing certainty and clarity of actual loss, in the sonnet *Without Her,* a sonnet filled with the overwhelming sense of an immediate physical and spiritual desolation—

> What of her glass without her? the blank grey
>   There where the pool is blind of the moon's face.
>   Her dress without her? The tossed empty space
> Of cloud-rack whence the moon has passed away.[1]
> Her paths without her?[2] Day's appointed sway
>   Usurped by desolate night. Her pillowed place
> Without her? Tears, Ah me! for love's good grace,
> And cold forgetfulness of night or day.
> What of the heart without her? Nay, poor heart,
>   Of thee what word remains ere speech be still?
>   A wayfarer by barren ways and chill,
> Steep ways and weary, without her thou art,
> Where the long cloud, the long wood's counterpart,
>   Sheds doubled darkness up the labouring hill.

It was surely thus that Gabriel and Janey's residence at Kelmscott had ended in the autumn of 1871. Janey, it would seem, for some reason, whether voluntarily or involuntarily, had left Gabriel alone at Kelmscott, and the sonnet is in fact the poetic counterpart of Gabriel's first cry upon recovery from the ensuing illness: "All, I now find by experience, depends primarily on my not being deprived of the society of the one necessary person." Nothing else can be the inspiration of that sonnet, through which, one suspects, glimmers the scenery of Kelmscott itself, in the background of misty landscape with its pool and wooded hill environing Gabriel's despair.[3] "I cannot tell you," murmured Rossetti in a voice choked with sobs when ten years later he read this sonnet to Hall Caine: "I cannot tell you at what terrible moment it was wrung from me."[4] It may

---

[1] For "moon" = Janey, *vide Gracious Moonlight, The Moonstone, The Soul's Sphere* and *inf.* pp. 552–3.

[2] *cf. sup.* p. 475.   [3] See Rossetti's painting *Water-Willow,* and *sup.* p. 470.

[4] Sharp's comment on *Without Her,* is also significant: "The sonnet in question was the outcome of the poet's own most bitter personal sorrow, and it has hence an added significance and pathos." *D. G. Rossetti,* p. 425. If the sonnet had related to the loss of Rossetti's wife, surely Sharp would have said so.

well be also that in this sonnet as in many another, Rossetti was using his old symbolism in his old way, that the "cloud," the "counterpart" of "the long wood" at Kelmscott, was also, for him the symbolical "cloud" of impending severance, a "counterpart" to "the long wood" that was "Willow-wood," the lost years of their earlier separation following the conclusion of the Jovial Campaign and Janey's marriage to Morris. Thus the "doubled darkness" would represent the doubled misery of the destroyed promise of the future and the absence of the beloved, a darkness deeper than that of "Willow-wood" which had known no such promise, while "the labouring hill" would be the road of life over which this "doubled darkness" broods as the poet painfully journeys in mental, emotional and physical suffering towards death.

Certainly, as many an allusion in *The House of Life* shows, that earlier separation was much in Rossetti's thought, and even William Rossetti's cautiously impersonal comment upon *Hope Overtaken*, explicitly alludes, like that upon *Willow-wood*, to some such experience when it states: "The Lover, now united to his Lady, refers here to the untoward delay which took place before the union was effected. He speaks of his 'Hope' which may at starting be understood as meaning the hope that he entertained for union with the lady." That "Hope" was surely the *Pandora* of his painting—Janey Morris. William's English was never a model of concision and propriety of diction, but its clumsiness and vagueness here are largely due to the difficulty of his position in pretending to give the meaning of sonnets whose full significance he was at the same time attempting to conceal. Unable to write "Lizzie" or "wife," and unwilling to write "Janey," William falls back upon such impersonal terms as "lover" and "lady." Usually misinterpreted, like so many of Rossetti's poems, as a reference to his dead wife, *Without Her* is almost certainly inspired by Janey Morris, and is most probably Rossetti's cry of despair upon her departure from Kelmscott in the late autumn of 1871. If so, it gives us almost our last glimpse of Rossetti before his nervous breakdown and attempted suicide some six months later; for those intervening months, the record is curiously silent.

One other of these sonnets of 1871 offers a special interest as it appears immediately to follow *Without Her*. The sonnet is *Severed Selves*, which describes Rossetti's misery at the separation and his but faint hope of their reunion:—

> Two separate, divided silences,
>   Which, brought together, would find loving voice;
>   Two glances which together would rejoice
> In love, now lost like stars beyond dark trees;
> Two hands apart whose touch alone gives ease;
> Two bosoms which, heart-shrined with mutual flame,
>   Would, meeting in one clasp, be made the same;
> Two souls, the shores wave-mocked of sundering seas:—
>
> Such are we now. Ah! may our hope forecast
>   Indeed, one hour again, when on this stream
>   Of darkened love once more the light shall gleam?—
> An hour how slow to come, how quickly past—
> Which blooms and fades, and only leaves at last,
>   Faint as shed flowers, the attenuated dream.

The climax of their love's frustration however, seems to be marked by the sonnet which immediately follows *Without Her*, in *The House of Life*, the sonnet Rossetti entitled *Love's Fatality*. There, Rossetti seems to give a backward glance as it were, over the recent catastrophe of the lovers' separation.

> Sweet Love,—but oh! most dread Desire of Love,
> Life-thwarted. Linked in gyves I saw them stand,
>   Love shackled with Vain-longing, hand to hand . . .

"The leading idea of this sonnet," wrote William Rossetti, "appears to be as follows. Love is in himself free and happy. But Loving Desire enchained by the necessities and prohibitions of Life, is a dismal captive, and brings Love himself into the same fetters and the same misery."

Was it pure accident that led Rossetti in this sonnet to the imagery of just such an ill-sorted marriage as Janey's to William Morris? Such a marriage at least is suggested by his representation of frustrated Love whose

>   . . . lips, two writhen flakes of flame,
> Made moan: "Alas O Love, thus leashed with me!
> Wing-footed thou, wing-shouldered, once born free:
> And I, thy cowering self, in chains grown tame—
> Bound to thy body and soul, named with thy name—
>   Life's iron heart, even Love's Fatality!

"Love's Fatality!"—was not that, rather than a belated repetition of a contemptible literary criticism, the basic cause of Rossetti's breakdown, and the explanation of his first spontaneous cry upon recovery?

Last of all these sonnets, perhaps, comes another sonnet of 1871, *Love Enthroned*, in which the intensity of frustrated passion sinks to a calmer note while the lover, attempting to sublimate his emotion, exalts love high above the world of sense, as Morris too was doing at that time in *Love is Enough*, in a similar state of compensatory fantasy. In this mood Rossetti turned to contemplate Love as a remote abstraction, seeing it high above Truth, Hope, Fame, Youth or even

> Life, still wreathing flowers for Death to wear.

So, still striving to attain an unattainable peace, he came at last to see Love far beyond the pangs of severance—

> far above
> All passionate wind of welcome and farewell.

XIV

THE RETURN TO KELMSCOTT
1872–1874

Ah! may our hope forecast
Indeed one hour again, when on this stream
Of darkened love once more the light shall gleam?

Severed Selves D. G. ROSSETTI

BUT NOW, AFTER THOSE MONTHS OF DARKNESS, once more the light gleamed. It was September 1872, and Gabriel was back at Kelmscott with Janey and the children, had resumed the old, happy, tranquil existence with immense content, had refound the "peace" he sought. "Here all is happiness again, and I feel completely myself," he told William. "Such charming and lovable children," he thought, watching Jenny and May romping with young George Hake, while Kelmscott, brightened by Janey's presence, seemed to him "a perfect Paradise." And there he remained, generally with Janey and the children, for the next two years.

"As well as ever I was in my life," he declared before the close of September. "I am determined now to make every effort not to go under again, and feel at this moment as if such a thing were impossible." Only once did the old paranoid suspicions reveal themselves, when he found one of the letters that came to him, open. Not until he had examined the postman and sent the letter back to London for detailed investigation, was he satisfied that "no suspicious symptoms seemed discoverable." Under Dr. Marshall's guidance, the morphia recently prescribed was now given up, while attempts were also made to abolish the chloral.

Early in October "wonderfully well now" save for the "slight lameness," as he described himself, he invited William to visit them at Kelmscott, warning him, however, "Janey will be sitting to me for the greater part of the day, and I shall not be very much at liberty during the light hours." "Very bad colds" which both he and Janey contracted in November,

542

delayed work on the *Proserpine*, but during Janey's illness he made "a very careful" chalk drawing of May Morris which he valued at a hundred guineas. "George and I are alone here now," he wrote on the 25th to William who had long since returned to town.

So, steadily painting to pay his debts, Rossetti spent the autumn and winter of 1872 at Kelmscott. He completed the predella to Graham's *Beata Beatrix*, and then concentrated his attention upon the portrait of Janey as *Proserpine*.[1] But uncertainty, hesitation, dissatisfaction now marked his work as never before. At least seven *Proserpines* were begun on canvas, besides many studies, before it was completed to his satisfaction and sold to a Mr. Turner for eight hundred guineas.

That *Proserpine* stood in some intimate emotional relation to himself, drawing probably upon memories or hallucinations haunting him during his recent illness, both the Italian and English versions of his illustrative sonnet to the picture suggest. This sonnet, said William Rossetti, who received the Italian version on November 7th, 1872, was Gabriel's first attempt at verse since his breakdown three months before. Indeed the sonnet, like some he was soon to write in the following year, is closely in harmony with the present interpretation of Rossetti's nervous collapse, for it is a poem of frustrated passion, of parted love lamenting

> . . . how far away
> The nights that shall be from the days that were,

while the sestet surely describes his own recent state of anxiety and melancholia, when he cries:

> Afar from mine own self I seem, and wing
>   Strange ways in thought, and listen for a sign;
>   And still some heart unto some soul doth pine,
>   (Whose sounds mine inner sense is fain to bring
> Continually together, murmuring
>   "Woe's me for thee, unhappy Proserpine!"

The Proserpine motive, so applicable to his own situation, is equally emphasized in Rossetti's painting. Janey, as Proserpine,

---

[1] "The subject was originally intended for Eve holding the apple: it was converted by afterthought into Proserpine holding the pomegranate." *D. G. R. as Designer and Writer*, p. 80.

stands, a sad, cold figure, holding almost ostentatiously the bitten pomegranate which, according to the legend, binds her as by marriage to remain with her husband Pluto in his world of shades, whence she may escape for short periods only. Beside her is an incense burner, "the attribute of a goddess," Rossetti explained; and that he definitely used other symbolism in the painting is shown by his explanation of the ivy-branch in the background as "a symbol of clinging memory." And surely the weak expressions "some heart" and "some soul" in the sonnet, were originally "my heart" and "thy soul."[1]

Gabriel had returned to Kelmscott with the intention of painting two other pictures of Janey, *Monna Primavera*—which became ultimately *The Daydream*,—and a full length *Pandora* which he apparently never achieved. *The Suicide of Paetus and Arria*, he contemplated but never painted.[2] Already Dunn in Scotland had made studies for the background of *The Daydream*, but Rossetti did not begin work on it until some seven years later. Gabriel also painted Janey in water-colour as *A Lady in a Blue Dress*, probably a study for another *Salutation to Beatrice* painted eight years later. On a scroll painted on the back of this water-colour he inserted Dante's sonnet from the *Vita Nuova*:

Tanto gentile e tanto onesta pare . . .

which in his *Early Italian poets* he had translated:

My lady looks so gentle and so pure . . .

Sitting to him daily in the tapestry room, Janey was now almost his sole model. When one of his drawings of her was slightly damaged during its transit from Scotland, Gabriel, greatly concerned, had all his drawings of Janey brought to Kelmscott.

William's visit during Janey's stay at Kelmscott was quite exceptional, and probably due to the need of receiving an account of his stewardship during Gabriel's recent illness; for seldom if ever again did Rossetti receive visitors when Janey was with him. During her now frequent absences, however, he

---

[1] *v. sup.* pp. 382, 400 and footnote 1, 418 (footnote 1) and Note to p. 142.

[2] When the Emperor Claudius ordered Caecina Paetus to put an end to his life, in A.D. 42, and Paetus hesitated, his wife Arria stabbed herself, and handing the dagger to her husband, said: "Paetus, it does not hurt me." Again the suicide theme that appears in D. G. R. from youth to age. He made a pencil sketch of *Paetus and Arria* in 1872.

brought a constant stream of his more intimate friends to stay with him, as if to counteract the dreariness of Janey's absence and of rustic solitude. So, early in December, Bell Scott and Dr. Hake came to Kelmscott as his guests, a visit which Hake sentimentally commemorated in several mediocre poems.[1]

Less happy in Janey's absence, Rossetti, while concentrating upon his painting during the winter and autumn of 1872, for exercise tramped the higher meadows around Kelmscott to avoid the floods, saw a winter gale uproot trees round the house, and was driven from the "tapestry room" by the cold. With the aid of a Lechlade carpenter, who stopped draughts and made double windows, he turned the drawing-room into a temporary studio, and used the room with the tiled fireplace as his drawing-room instead. But the chimney smoked. Left with but a housekeeper and one servant as the other had gone away with Janey, he admitted to William on December 11th, "I get on well with work, though much inconvenienced till Janey's return." Christmas he spent with the Rossetti family in London.

Thanks to William's management of his brother's affairs during Gabriel's illness, to the salesmanship of Howell, now an art-agent in partnership with a Mr. Parsons, and to Rossetti's own industry, the close of 1872 found him with all his debts paid and a thousand pounds in the bank. Upon his recovery, Gabriel had immediately resumed possession of the £540 recently deposited with William and Brown in order to be beyond the reach of creditors, as well as of the paintings housed for the same reason at Scott's. Some six months later, as his financial position still improved, he contentedly observed: "I shall soon be much better stocked with tin than my wont." William's advice to economize by quitting Cheyne Walk, however, he rejected, unless, as he explained, he could discover some "suitable" place in or near London. With Howell at this time he was particularly pleased, thinking him the most fitted to overcome the difficulty of his own remoteness from picture-buyers.

Hitherto, Rossetti's carelessness about money had been as conspicuous as his talent for keen bargaining over the sale of

---

[1] *Reminiscence* in Hake's volume *New Symbols* and the first three sonnets in his volume *New Day*.

his pictures. Only recently had he opened a bank account, and Val Prinsep largely attributed Gabriel's chronic impecuniosity to his long delay in having a banker and his consequent cashing of cheques received; for the gold or notes he left in an open drawer, accessible to Fanny, and perhaps also to the servants. But recent experiences during his illness had taught him something of prudence, and part of his Christmas visit to London he spent in making an inventory of his unfinished works at Cheyne Walk, works which could, he said, quickly be "made presentable" at need, and so might provide "many hundreds of pounds."

He was still completing these unfinished works, at the close of January 1873, at Kelmscott, and the reason for his new foresight he confided at the time to Fanny, when he wrote: "I have got some old drawings of mine which were knocking about at Chelsea, mounted and sent down here to touch up, and think of getting all the old drawings on strainers sent down to work on. There is a very large value lying idle there, which might bring good money now; whereas, if one waits till a moment when one needs money in a hurry, the only result is that all those who call themselves one's best friends gather round one to try and get one's best things for as few shillings as they can manage to get them for. When I needed money in the summer, not one friend who had capital came forward to offer to lend me any, though I would have done so in a like case not only for my intimate friends but for any friend who needed it. All they did was to stand aloof while I sold my property much under its value. Therefore the best thing I can do is to turn everything that will sell into money while they know they must give the full value to get it."

Nor was Rossetti's financial anxiety solely for himself. For Fanny, whose drunken husband Hughes had died recently, he now felt an increased sense of responsibility. Casually, on November 25th, 1872, he had informed William of Fanny's widowhood with: "By the bye, I suppose you know that F. has got rid of her incubus who died just lately?" One effect of Hughes' death and Rossetti's absence at Kelmscott was to make Fanny more than ever before the resident mistress of 16 Cheyne Walk, despite the house in Royal Avenue, near-by, which

Gabriel rented for her. Although he had deliberately avoided Fanny when passing through London in September, on his headlong flight to Kelmscott, he had since maintained a regular correspondence with her, and at Christmas, on re-visiting Chelsea, had of course seen her again.

Rossetti's Christmas visit had however, been brief. Two days before the close of the year he had returned to Kelmscott and there continued his efforts for Fanny's welfare, getting Howell to value and try to sell some £500 worth of pictures he had given her, and so help him to buy her a house. Almost every letter he sent Fanny now contained either a cheque, the promise of one, or an excuse or apology when one was not forthcoming. Fanny, naturally enough now anxious about her future since her husband was dead and Rossetti ill, was not the person to allow any remissness in the despatch of money to pass without comment, and the beginnings of some of Gabriel's letters to her strongly suggest that her own last letter had included a vigorous protest at the omission of some expected cheque.

Perhaps prejudice rather than proof led Rossetti's relatives and friends to accuse Fanny of stealing his property, for there were servants at Cheyne Walk. But upon his recovery Gabriel had often to complain that various articles, including a coat, a "blue pot," a roll of Utrecht velvet, had "unaccountably disappeared." That she occasionally took possession of various articles she fancied, Fanny made no attempt to conceal, but this, especially after so long a domestic association, was not "stealing." Sometimes Gabriel was merely amused by her methods of acquisition, and even when they inconvenienced him to the point of demanding their return, he did so tactfully, sending her little comic drawings of an elephant burying its booty in a hole in the ground or similar hiding place, while underneath he wrote such exhortations as "Hullo Elephant! Just you find that pot for I can't do without it!" And if Fanny proved recalcitrant, there followed sterner demands for restoration. But despite all vicissitudes, many a playful passage in the letters he sent her, his apostrophes to her to "take care of your funny old self," his wishes to see "your good old face," which remind us of his epistolary invocations to his mother as "Good Antique," "Teaksicunculum," and advice to her also to "take care of your funny old self," "the dear Ancient," leave no doubt as to the warmth and sincerity of his affection, and largely contradict the traditional account that his life with Fanny in Cheyne Walk was one of unrelieved misery.

The opening of 1873 found Gabriel working hard at *Proserpine*, for which Janey seems to have made frequent visits of a week or so at a time to Kelmscott. She was there early in January, but in the middle of the month Gabriel, again inviting William, said that except for George Hake he was now alone. A female model, brought by Dunn at Rossetti's request, came to sit for *Ligeia Siren*, originally one of Gabriel's rare nudes, but later draped in obedience to the contemporary taboo. And throughout that spring and summer came the beautiful Alexa Wilding, to sit for *La Ghirlandata*.

La Ghirlandata, in fact, showed that Rossetti's old imperiousness towards patrons had lost nothing with the years. Objecting to Leyland's wish to see the picture before purchase, he sold it to Graham, and a week later rejoiced to Fanny: "Leyland is ready to bite his head off with vexation at having missed my present picture from Miss Wilding, and old Graham has sent me a cheque for the price in full. It will teach Leyland not to miss another chance." "Putting the last touches" to it in mid-September, he thought it, as ever with his latest work, "about my best." "Little May Morris," he told his mother, "appears twice in the picture as a couple of angels. She has become a most lovely model."

Now too, Gabriel's thoughts were again turning to fresh literary projects—a translation of Michelangelo's poems, never realized, and a "small original volume" of his own verse, when sufficient material had been accumulated—a condition not attained until nine years later. A new edition of his *Early Italian Poets*, renamed *Dante and his Circle*, was about to appear with a dedication to his mother in place of the original one to his wife. "The first," he told his mother, "was dedicated to poor Lizzie, and I had some thought of retaining the dedication with date; but, this seeming perhaps rather forced, I shall substitute your dear name in the second edition." Doubtless he realized that, in the present circumstances, re-dedication to Lizzie or the substitution of Janey was impossible. In the *Fortnightly*

Review for April there also appeared one of Gabriel's rare critical articles, a review done, for the sake of friendship, of Dr. Hake's poetical *Parables and Tales*.

In mid-April, Boyce, William, Fanny and young Hake dined with Gabriel, who had come to Chelsea for one day. "Looking extraordinarily well and stout, and younger than a year or two ago," thought Boyce, on seeing Gabriel. "He has let the whole of his beard grow (instead of only moustache and chin hair), and it has a good deal changed his aspect." This development was doubtless the result of declining energy and a rustic environment. "Whiskers and beard all round," was the description William gave of it, adding with a fine impersonality, "as some people thought to the detriment of his appearance." Gabriel at any rate retained this fashion to the end.[1]

Another, happier example of rustic influence upon Gabriel was the sonnet *Spring*, which he wrote in May, a naturalistic description of the season in the country, almost unique in his poetry. Only in its last line, and then somewhat irrelevantly, as a simile—but with Rossetti love could not be excluded—does the obsessive theme appear:—

> Chill are the gusts to which the pastures cower,
>   And chill the current where the young reeds stand,
>   As green and close as the young wheat on land:
> Yet here the cuckoo and the cuckoo-flower
> Plight to the heart Spring's perfect imminent hour
> Whose breath shall soothe you like your dear one's hand.

"A sonnet resulting from these Kelmscott ruralities," he described it when at the close of the year he sent a copy of it to his friend Davies. Now too he published in the *Athenaeum* his poem *Sunset Wings*, written at Kelmscott two years before.

With the coming of spring, indeed, something of the old poetic impulse had returned, and in several of the few sonnets he wrote this year the influence of the season finds definite expression. These sonnets of 1873, later included in *The House of Life*, have perhaps a greater biographical than aesthetic interest, not only because Rossetti's poetic power had, like his pictorial, failed since his illness, but also because they so obviously exemplify the principle he now laid down in one of them,[2] that

[1] *cf. sup.* pp. 354 and 423.   [2] *Transfigured Life.*

true poetry must be in essence autobiographical, the "trans-figured life" of the poet, that is, an imaginative realization of his experience. That amidst the peace of this spring at Kelmscott his mind should turn retrospectively to such an imaginative realization of his recent illness and misery was almost inevitable. Indeed, *Proserpine* and its accompanying sonnet were already manifestations of the fact, which becomes yet more evident in the remaining sonnets of this time. Some of these indeed, may have preceded the sonnet on Spring. If so, the immediacy of emotion and depths of despair in *Heart of the Night* and *The Soul's Sphere* point to their being in all probability the earliest, quite apart from the fact that of the remaining three, *The Sun's Shame* (II) and *Life the Beloved* both allude to the spring itself in ways that suggest they were being written during that season, while the last of the sonnets, *Memorial Thresholds*, does not deal with Rossetti's recent illness and has a general atmosphere of remoteness from it in both thought and time.

Thus it is that in these few sonnets we can clearly distinguish the obsessive thoughts and feelings and underlying anxiety which had caused through the consequent insomnia, chloral habit and addiction to spirits, Rossetti's recent breakdown. And these causes are identical with those which had so gravely undermined his health in 1869, and continued throughout the intervening years to increase their evil influence upon him. Now, as before, everything suggests that Rossetti's hereditary tendency to anxiety was chiefly exacerbated by two obsessive uncertainties. The first of these was as to whether his wife's death was accidental, or suicidal and so, as he would interpret it, caused by himself. For eleven years the thought of Lizzie had haunted him, and the fear of losing Janey had apparently pursued him for the last five. Now, energized by his morbid tendency the two fears had become obsessions. As like causes yield like effects, it is not surprising that the themes and imagery of these sonnets of 1873 closely resemble those of the preceding period. Indeed the repetitive, obsessive tendency of Rossetti revealed in both his poetry and painting is also suggested by his periods of almost exclusive concentration upon Dantesque, as afterwards upon Malorian, themes even before Lizzie or Janey had brought their particular problems into his life.

Even the discreet William described Gabriel's recent sonnet *Heart of the Night* (its title an obvious reference to his late illness and its causes) as an "evidently intense personal utterance." This "intense personal utterance" is phrased like so many of Rossetti's sonnets, ambiguously—as in the circumstances we should expect. Yet it, too, surely suggests that his illness is due to these two obsessions, especially that of a feared separation from Mrs. Morris. For in this sonnet Gabriel summarized his life up to the moment of his breakdown as a series of emotional phases, culminating in one that advances "from doubt to dread; from dread to bale and ban" (as he first wrote it), that is from uncertainty to fear, anxiety, from fear to "evil, calamity, sorrow" and to "a curse bringing evil, an authoritative prohibition" as the dictionary interprets "bale" and "ban," words which of course can apply to both his illness and a factual cause of it in some such "authoritative prohibition" of his association with Janey as earlier evidence has suggested and later evidence will tend to support. Rossetti had, in fact, used this same word "ban" in *The Cloud Confines*, written in the despairing mood that had marked the close of his life at Kelmscott with Janey in 1871.*

Indeed all the most significant, most deeply emotional experiences of Rossetti's life had been seized under the threat of dispossession. His early, adolescent passion for Lizzie had been throughout (so at least he believed) a fight with death, while that for Janey had always been menaced by the fact of her marriage, the stress of social convention and opinion and the strain of secrecy. Love and anxiety became for Rossetti inextricably associated, an additional strain instead of a release and renewal, though unconsciously he enjoyed the added intensity, or rather tensity, that in both cases the fear of dispossession gave to his passion. "Tense rather than intense," said Patmore, truly enough of Rossetti, probing more deeply than he knew. Gabriel indeed, at the end of his life, well summarized his experience in the third poem of his short sonnet sequence in *The House of Life* entitled *True Woman*, proclaiming:

> This test for love:—in every kiss sealed fast
> To feel the first kiss and forebode the last.

* *v. sup.* pp. 480 and 536.

Nor, perhaps, as we shall see later, was his experience with Janey not without its influence upon that suggestion of the "mulier semper mutabile" which the couplet almost inevitably suggests, in addition to purely circumstantial sources of frustration.

It is this threat of dispossession, this endless frustration, that finds expression in the next of these sonnets, *The Soul's Sphere*, a vivid glimpse of Rossetti's troubled spirit and tortured imagination during his recent illness.

> Some prisoned moon in steep cloud-fastnesses,—
>   Throned queen and thralled; some dying sun whose pyre
>   Blazed with momentous, memorable fire:
> Who hath not yearned and fed his heart with these?
> Who, sleepless, hath not anguished to appease
>   Tragical shadow's realm of sound and sight
>   Conjectured in the lamentable night?
> Lo! the soul's sphere of infinite images!

The images, with Rossetti, are unfortunately far from "infinite," indeed they are, like his own circle of obsessive thoughts and emotions, monotonously repetitive. But biographically they are significant. Again and again in *The House of Life* Janey is, as we have seen, "queenly" and "moon,"[1] and here she appears, throned queen by Gabriel, yet held in thrall by marriage. The moon-image suggests the sun-metaphor for Rossetti himself that follows, the sun dying in splendour, an inapt image for the man who had hysterically sought death as an escape from unkind reality. But doubtless Rossetti in some romantic moods saw himself as a grand, heroic figure, dying like Tristram for frustrated passion. And in the train of this had come, in now almost inevitable sequence, the image of his other obsessive anxiety, the memory of those sleepless nights haunted by the unanswerable question raised by Lizzie's death, the torturing question that knew no appeasement.

How true for Rossetti, beyond his own consciousness of its truth, was his assertion seven years later,

> A sonnet is a coin: its face reveals
>   The soul,—its converse, to what Power 'tis due . . .

---

[1] *v. sup.* pp. 538 and footnote 1.

Here, in the octave of *The Soul's Sphere*, he had revealed the soul through its images. In the sestet the anxiety motivating them, finds as a climax powerful expression, energized by the memory of his own recent escape from self-destruction, the climax it still anticipates if, instead of a happy future, his love is doomed to the dispossession he fears.

> What sense shall count them? Whether it forecast
>   The rose-winged hours that flutter in the van
>   Of love's unquestioning unrevealed span,—
> Visions of golden futures: or that last
> Wild pageant of the accumulated past
>   That clangs and flashes for a drowning man.

How strong the impressions of his recent illness still were is again shown in the imagery of another of these sonnets, *Life the Beloved*, whose title indicates his present revulsion, in retrospect, from his late suicidal impulse. Its opening lines reveal the horror of the melanacholia which had held him, and was only gradually relaxing its hold, and once again the obsessive memory of Lizzie in death returns, a tendency no doubt strengthened at this time by her association with the dedication to her of his *Early Italian Poets*, that dedication which as we have seen, he was now discarding in order to substitute one to his mother, also probably in part an act of unconscious symbolism.

> As thy friend's face with shadow of soul o'erspread,[1]
>   Somewhile unto thy sight perchance hath[2] been
>   Ghastly and strange, yet never so is seen
> In thought, but to all fortunate favour wed;
> As thy love's death-bound features never dead
>   To memory's glass return, but contravene
>   Frail, fugitive days, and always keep, I ween,
> Than all new life a livelier lovelihead:—
>
> So Life herself, thy spirit's friend and love
>   Even still as Spring's authentic harbinger
>   Glows with fresh hours for hope to glorify;
> Though pale she lay when in the winter grove
>   Her funeral flowers were snow-flakes shed on her,
>   And the red wings of frost-fire rent the sky.

There again the sonnet is an expression of his recent abnormal state, but although Rossetti still looks back to his melancholia

---

[1] Bancroft MS.—*in shadow of pain or dread.*   [2] Ibid.—*needs must have.*

of the previous winter, under the influence of returning health
and spring the shadow is lifting. Here in place of the despair
that marks *The Soul's Sphere*, or Gabriel's cry in *The Sun's
Shame* (II) —

> Woe's me, for whom
> Inveteracy of ill portends the doom,

a new-born hope reveals itself.

From Dawn to Noon, in its comparatively unemotional
rationality and absence of the provocative obsessive imagery,
even of all reference to Rossetti's recent illness, bears tacit
witness to his improving health and increasing emotional and
mental stability, though less effective as verse. But with
Memorial Thresholds, which may of course have preceded it,
definite autobiographical references and their related emotion
return. This sonnet (which bears a close general resemblance in
theme and mood to *Inclusiveness*, as William Rossetti noted)
may, as he believed, refer to the same house, in that case
Rossetti's house in Cheyne Walk, and to the same circumstances,
presumably Janey's visits. But more remote experiences seem to
be the inspiration of *Memorial Thresholds* with its references to
"passion of surprise" and "frost-bound, fire-girt scenes of long
ago," which William actually paraphrased as "scenes reminiscent of anguish and passion."[1] "Anguish" indeed is neither
mentioned nor suggested in the passage; the only anguish in
the sonnet arises from the poet's later contemplation of his lost
happiness, as he looks back in memory at the "single, simple
door" which, recreated and "with one lost figure filled as once
of yore," must be his "life-porch in eternity." This reference to
the "lost figure" (changed before publication to "one
presence"), strongly suggests that the references are to Lizzie,
not Janey, and this impression is strengthened by his placing
the doorway "'Mid hurrying crowds," a description far more
applicable to Chatham Place than to Cheyne Walk. Probably
during one of his occasional visits to London, chance or a mood

---

[1] *cf.* the following stanza from Elizabeth Siddal's poem *Worn Out*:—

> I cannot give to thee the love
>   I gave so long ago—
> The love that turned and struck me down
>   Amid the blinding snow.

of reminiscence about Lizzie who was, as we have seen, much in Gabriel's mind at this time, took him past the house in Chatham Place and this sonnet was the result.*

To fill, so far as possible, the void of Janey's absences, the stream of visitors to Kelmscott was constantly renewed. The helpful Howell, genial German Dr. Hueffer, music-critic to *The Times*, who had just married Brown's daughter Cathy, Brown himself, sometimes with the inimitable Emma, and a new, also helpful acquaintance, Theodore Watts, a solicitor with literary ambitions who had recently settled an awkward little affair caused by the forging of Gabriel's name to a cheque by the daughter of one of old Gabriele's Italian friends: all came to Kelmscott during this spring and summer. Madox Brown unfortunately had fallen upon evil times; was now forced to accept an occasional loan from Gabriel, and growing bitter and suspicious was ready like Rossetti himself to believe in conspiracies of jealous enemies.

Doubtless Janey was again at Kelmscott but preparing for departure when Rossetti on May 20th invited his mother and any others of the family who cared, to visit him, explaining as usual: "The house is not free but will be so soon I believe." So at the end of June, Gabriel's mother, now in her 75th year, came with Christina, who had been reduced to a physical wreck by exophthalmic bronchocele. Their quiet enjoyment of the garden and peaceful country life delighted him. Before their departure exciting family news arrived. William, who had gone on a tour of Italy with Scott, Alice Boyd and Madox Brown's daughter Lucy, had got engaged to Lucy.† Gabriel had been "greatly tempted" to go with them, but, he told William, I "fancy May will be just the time when I am most detained here," and he could not, he explained, leave Kelmscott "just when this place had most attractions," a typically ambiguous reference to Janey's expected visit as well as to the season. No doubt Janey was explicitly mentioned in the letter, for there are the usual deletions made by William as editor of his brother's correspondence, whenever her name appears.

Two other Preraphaelites, at least, were also exploring Italy during that spring of 1873, William Morris and Jones. A few

* *v. Notes* to p. 281.   † *v. Notes.*

months before, Morris had published his passionately lyrical work *Love is Enough*, its theme the sublimation of unhappy love into "higher" emotions and ideals:—

> Love is enough: ho ye who seek saving,
> Go no further; come hither! there have been who have found it,
> And these know the House of Fulfilment of Craving;
>   These know the Cup with the roses around it;
> These know the World's wound and the balm that hath bound it:
> Cry out, the World heedeth not, "Love, lead us home!"

As late as March 1873—to take the dates on the printer's copies—Morris had written *Spring's Bedfellow*, and that double-edged poem, *Echoes of Love's House*, in which joyous love-lines, such as:

> Love turns life to joy till naught is left to gain,

alternate with such disillusioned "echoes" as:

> Love turns life to woe till hope is naught and vain.

Morris had certainly been in low mood throughout that late autumn of 1872 and the earlier months of the following year. Late in 1872 he was still singing, in his now habitually plaintive manner, of unhappy love, particularly in *Love's Gleaning Tide*:—

> Ah when the summer comes again
> How shall we say, we sowed in vain?
> The root was joy, the stem was pain,
> The ear a nameless blending.
>
> The root is dead and gone, my love,
> The stem's a rod our truth to prove;
> The ear is stored for nought to move
> Till heaven and earth have ending.

So, ever, insistently, and with a strange delight in pain, Morris continued to sound the note of bitter disillusion. The few glimpses we gain of Morris in the social world at this time, accord with the mood of the verse he was then writing. Dining with the Nortons shortly before his departure for Italy, and meeting for the first time Sir Leslie Stephen, a fellow guest,

Morris, who would be thirty-nine in a day or two, "complained of feeling old" and that his hair "was turning grey." Jones, his sole companion on the Italian journey, found Morris "rather exacting," "a little disposed to make the worst of things," and little interested in what he saw. From Florence, early in April, Morris wrote to Janey, promising to bring her a bottle of scent and toys for the children. Evidently very restless, shortly after his return he set out early in July on a second visit to Iceland, which, more than any other place, seemed to give him moral and spiritual strength.

On July 18th, two days after Gabriel had, as usual when Janey was expected, emptied Kelmscott of all its visitors, and when, presumably, the strenuous preparations he had made for Janey's reception, were practically complete, Janey herself reappeared with Jenny and May. Janey looked "wonderfully well" Rossetti told his mother, but not "over strong," and Janey sent to old Mrs. Rossetti her "kindest regards." On the very day of Janey's arrival at Kelmscott, her husband, who had just arrived at Reykjavik, and was still suffering from a stormy crossing, wrote to his wife: "My dear how I wish I was back, and how wild and strange everything here is. I am so anxious for you too, it was a grievous parting for us the other day— and this shabby letter! But how can I help it, not knowing whether I am on my head or my heels? With all love to you and the dear good little ones, I am, your loving W. M."

With Janey's return, all was bustle and preparation at Kelmscott. Gabriel's letter to his mother the following day, full of domestic details that would please her, reflects the new animation about him. "The window of the little drawing-room," he wrote, "at which I often used to see your darling head from the garden, now shows on inspection a dismantled room, everything having been removed—the furniture to the large drawing-room, my former studio, and the drawings to my present studio in the tapestry room, where they go along the whole of one wall, and look better than ever they looked before, with the fine dim tone of the tapestry behind them." So he continues his description of Kelmscott that summer, to interest the old lady: changes in ornaments, "the white lily in the garden" grown "divinely lovely"; "St. Swithin should be called St. Swindler this year, for he has beneficently cheated us. There has not been a drop of rain since his ominous downfall." "Pleasantness," he told Hueffer, at the end of July, "is mostly the order of these summer days." So strong, indeed, was his feeling of revitalization, he was for once happy about his painting. Two days after one of Janey's arrivals, painting his "large picture" *Dante's Dream*, he told Sandys: "I feel for the first time in my life something like a sense of *style* in my work, a quality quite deficient before with me." It was probably during this short period of rare happiness and peace that he scribbled in his note-book the never completed lines beginning:

"My world, my work, my woman, all my own . . ."

The effect of his country environment as well as of the other gracious influences of this summer at Kelmscott revealed itself even more clearly in his letters than in his verse. To his nature-loving mother he often described sights which would please her —apple blossom in the orchard, flowers in the garden, and to her as to Fanny he would send flowers, both wild and garden ones, with descriptive comments. How surprisingly domesticated Gabriel became at Kelmscott, how whole-heartedly he would give himself up to romping with the children and dogs, or reading aloud to Janey, or to a country walk, his letters clearly show, although seldom, for neither in correspondence nor in conversation did he generally care to reveal his more intimate life, internal or external. Nevertheless we get an occasional revealing glimpse of him at Kelmscott, see him pleasing the children by placing lumps of sugar on stringed instruments to attract one or other of the five dogs in the house which, on touching the strings, ran away frightened at the noise they made. Sometimes the long-suffering animals retaliated, and in February 1874 Gabriel, "going about with a black patch over my nose," as he said, described how "Last night Jenny *fille* and I agreed to shriek at the same moment (one 'Creepy' and the other 'Crawly') in Dizzy's two ears while May beat a tattoo on the top of his head. The instant result was that he turned round howling, and bit me (fortunately not Jenny) across the nose; at which I am not surprised." And, a week later, to his mother, by way of sequel: "Dizzy has had a green velvet coat made for him, and walked about the dinner-table to-day like dog Toby. Perhaps William told you of his biting me, but it was quite my own fault, as I was teasing him past bearing. The bite is all right now." Then too there was "Mossy," the captured baby owl that lived in the attic and came down to sit on the dining table and share their meals.

But Kelmscott, however "remote from the world's throng," as he sang in *Youth's Antiphony*, could not be entirely detached from the external mundane. One inconvenient reminder of this was Fanny, increasingly resentful of Gabriel's absence, jealous of Alexa Wilding's visits, if of no other, and threatening a descent upon Kelmscott in person. At first, Rossetti peacefully diverted all occasions of strife by extreme tact, courtesy and consideration towards Fanny in his letters, which contained cheques, excuses, regrets and apologies. But when she continued to insist upon sharing the amenities of Kelmscott with himself and his friends, he replied with a friendly but firm and definite refusal. "I am very sorry to disappoint you," he wrote, "indeed it gives me great pain to do so, as I should like to see you here, but the thing is quite impossible. Please don't ever press the matter again, as it is very distressing to me to refuse, but as long as I remain here it is out of the question." After which he promised Fanny money for her "hoard."

Fanny's relations with Gabriel's servants and helpers in Cheyne Walk were also a source of discomfort to him as well as to herself. Her sense of inferiority, her jealousy and consequent harshness, only intensified the servants' dislike of being controlled by a woman they doubtless despised on both social and moral grounds (and perhaps also in some ways envied), and although Rossetti reluctantly yielded to her demand to dismiss an old servant, he reacted sharply a few days later to her complaint of rudeness from his new friend and helper, the solicitor Watts,[1] and brusquely defended him. To Fanny, however, he confidently turned for sympathy on hearing that his sister Maria had entered an Anglican Sisterhood. She "has turned what is called Sister of Mercy," he told Fanny, "one of those old things that you see going about in a sort of coal-

---

[1] In 1896 he took the name of "Watts-Dunton"; which led Whistler to ask him: "Watts! What's Dunton?"

scuttle and umbrella costume." To his mother he wrote: "She will indeed be a great loss, being much the healthiest in mind and cheeriest of us all, except yourself. William comes next and Christina and I are nowhere." But when a few weeks later he received from William a sufficiently dismal account of Maria's new environment, his dislike of the step she had taken found fuller expression. "I have really felt very sincerely anxious about Maria since what you tell me of no fires in this blessed place," he replied. "I simply could not exist on such terms—it would be a novitiate for another world; and I view the matter as most serious for her."

Certainly no one familiar with Rossetti could imagine for a moment his existence "on such terms" as Maria had chosen, but neither would the normal person have approved the terms of Gabriel's present existence at Kelmscott, where he still kept late hours as in London, dining at ten o'clock at night, going to bed at any time from three to five o'clock in the morning, and again dosing himself with chloral and whisky to get sleep. In general however, the chloral was now taken according to Marshall's directions, and was sometimes secretly diluted to half its normal strength.

Preparing the Tauchnitz edition of his poems, Rossetti would have composed more verses now, including a poetic version of *The Cup of Cold Water*, written three years before, but, as he now remarked, "the Crust of Bread has to be secured and that can only be done by painting." "Work," he told his mother on September 13th, "thickens round one, wherever one is," and he was very busy, not only completing the *Ghirlandata* for Graham eagerly awaiting its arrival, but also at work on a new *Dante's Dream*, a smaller version of the embarrassingly large original which Graham had not been allowed to see before completion, and had then found too large to hang in any room. From the wall of a staircase which alone would accommodate it, Graham had returned it to Rossetti for sale, commissioning at the same time a smaller replica at the same price, but with the addition of a double predella which was to cost an extra £300. From the original now back in Gabriel's studio at Cheyne Walk, Dunn was outlining the subject and laying in the background for the replica which was to be completed in eighteen months, but was in fact not finished until seven years later. Nevertheless, shortly before the close of the year, Gabriel agreed to paint another work for Graham, a *Blessed Damozel*, or *Blowed Damozel* as in his cynicism he now referred to the idealization of his romantic youth. And that too, was not completed until nearly five years had passed.

Despite unreliability, endless delays, artistic decline, Gabriel's reputation continued to grow, at least amongst the general public. In mid-September, the anonymous author—probably Stephens again—of a series of articles in the *Athenaeum* on *The Private Collections of England*, drew attention to Leathart's collection and particularly praised Rossetti. Rightly emphasizing the dissimilarities of the Preraphaelites, he went on to lament Rossetti's aloofness and to demand from him "an end to what is simply reticence, not whimsical concealment." Gabriel's works of later date than those in Leathart's collection were, he asserted, "larger and more laboured," but none showed "a more exalted imagination, finer design and richer colour," or displayed more clearly "his powers and genius." About this time another art-critic, J. Comyns Carr, having undertaken to write for the *Globe* a series of articles on contemporary painters, obtained through George Hake a personal introduction to Rossetti. Writing to Carr from Kelmscott, in November, Rossetti admitted: "As a painter, and I am ashamed at my age to say it, I have never even approached satisfaction with my own progress until within the last five years. My youth was spent chiefly in planning and designing, and whether I shall still have time to do anything I cannot tell." Yet by this time Rossetti had produced most of the work by which he is remembered.

Thus, amidst plans for commissions, to obtain the money he again so badly needed, Gabriel came to the close of the year. He wrote often now to Brown, "extremely numerous letters during the year 1873," said Ford Madox Hueffer, "nearly all coupled with business matters, schemes for cajoling purchasers—in which it must be confessed, D. G. Rossetti succeeded infinitely better than Madox Brown." Christmas came. The Joneses at The Grange held their seasonal festivities; Morris and Jones were there, while "Mrs. Morris placed safely out of the way watched everything from her sofa," wrote Georgie. Little

Rudyard Kipling was there too, playing with his cousins Philip and Margaret Jones; the early promise of a new generation that was to be widely different from that of the Preraphaelites. Gabriel, who spent Christmas in London with his family, seems to have been absent from the Jones's festivities.

"I have done nothing but my daily painting all my time here," Rossetti declared at Kelmscott, at the end of the year, nor did his habits change in 1874. Graham, fascinated by Gabriel, bought in a sale room his early *Annunciation*, which Rossetti now drastically revised. Graham also bought *The Bower Maiden*, just completed. Leyland bought *Proserpine* and *The Roman Widow*, and for Craven Gabriel painted in water-colour *Rosa Triplex*, "three heads of lovely little May Morris," as he described it. In February he wrote *Winter*, a companion sonnet to his *Spring*—and published both in the *Athenaeum* in May.

On the last day of March, William and Lucy Brown married very quietly, for as both were agnostics the ceremony was not held in church, and Gabriel had made his own attendance conditional upon a minimum of guests. Indeed the event clearly revealed the extent to which his remoteness had increased. Combating the suggestion of more extensive celebrations he remarked: "I should not feel equal to coming unless the party were strictly confined to old friends without admixture of new acquaintance." When at Lucy's insistence a larger party to consist of many relatives was again proposed, Gabriel refused to attend it. "I am most loth, even to great regret," he told William, "to be away from the party on the eve of your wedding; but the fact is that, at such a gathering as you indicate, every bore I know and don't know would sweep down on me after these two years' absence, and I am not equal to it, now that solitude is the habit of my life. I cannot say that a breakfast of unknown relations smiles on me either, any more than on you; but that is unavoidable, so there's an end. I cannot see what is the object of Brown's getting together all the relations he never sees." The party was held as planned, but Gabriel's defection from the breakfast could not be permitted, so to it came only the bride and bridegroom, old Mrs. Rossetti, Christina, Gabriel, the Madox Browns and William and Janey Morris.

With the coming of this spring of 1874, guests again began to arrive at Kelmscott. Genial Dr. Hueffer came for a week-end of cards and gossip, accompanied by his brother-in-law, young "Nolly" Brown, Madox Brown's precocious son, who, only seventeen years old, had produced a very immature novel which all his friends acclaimed as a work of almost transcendent genius. Nolly stayed longer than Hueffer, and Gabriel discussed literature with him, stigmatizing George Eliot as "vulgarity personified," dismissing Thackeray as of no account, describing Balzac as "melodramatic in plot, wishy-washy and dull," startlingly original criticisms then, and largely so even now, but not without considerable acumen. In Dumas, he found, no doubt exaggerating to shock Nolly, "the one great and supreme man, the sole descendant of Shakespeare!" In June came Madox Brown and Emma, together with William and Lucy just back from their Italian honeymoon, and on following week-ends, Howell, and Watts the solicitor now rapidly becoming as indispensable to Gabriel as Howell appeared to be. Before June ended, old Mrs. Rossetti came with the still ailing Christina.

Since his own illness Gabriel had become more openly responsive to family ties, was now even furnishing a little room in the Rossetti home in Euston Square, so that he might some-times, when in town, stay the night with the family. Towards his mother he was demonstrative, thinking during the dark February days, as he told her, of "her dear beautiful old face," whenever he passed the window of the little drawing-room where she had loved to sit and read and look out on the garden. He got Jenny and May Morris to pluck for her what flowers still remained there, "no very choice gleaning," as he said, but "better than nothing to your flower-loving heart."

Was it the strain of his relations with Janey, the uncertainty, perhaps, as to her presence or absence at Kelmscott, even it may be a new uncertainty as to his hold upon her, which caused Rossetti's increasing signs of renewed mental unrest? Despite his almost miraculous recovery upon his return to Kelmscott, he had never been the man he was before his breakdown, and William, although finding him afterwards "extremely well," had also thought him "a little beset—hardly perturbed," by suspicions of enemies secretly conspiring his ruin. Hake, during his visit in December 1872, believed that already Rossetti's recent illness was "dwindling into a dream," and noticed that he would never allude to so painful a theme—a bad symptom, had Hake but known it. Scott however, in this more penetrating than the doctor, disagreed, believing that despite his silence, his illness was very present in Gabriel's mind, that his recent delusions were "still to him realities," even if only in the sense that they *had* existed as delusions. That Scott was correct in this, the *Proserpine* picture and sonnet, and the sonnets of 1873, strongly suggest.

Nor were other of Gabriel's friends more confident than Scott of the reality of his recovery, despite appearances. The Joneses, for example, found their fears for Rossetti increasingly justified. Never again was he to them the Rossetti of old. Indifference towards all but a few intimates replaced the warmth of his earlier feelings, and from the time of his breakdown even Jones and Swinburne were rejected. "A sad inertia slowly changed him," wrote Georgie, sorrowfully, "and soon Edward had to realize that all joy in their intercourse belonged to the past. I never remember Rossetti again under our roof," she declared, "but Edward continued to go to him: sometimes wondering almost bitterly whether if he ceased doing so it would be noticed." As for Swinburne, who had so valiantly wrestled with the arch-enemy Buchanan, Gabriel, even during his illness, refused to see him, and William was forced to warn Swinburne, anxious to see his sick friend, not to do so. Swinburne agreed, deeply regretting being thus prevented from giving his friend "the same attention and affection as friends who can hardly love him better—as indeed I think no man can love his friend more than I love Gabriel—but I know it can be from no doubt of my attachment that he shrinks from seeing me as yet." For long Swinburne continued, as occasion offered, to send his love to Rossetti, which Rossetti, who never spoke of Swinburne without kindness, gratefully acknowledged, and not until several years had passed without any lowering of the barriers did Swinburne turn upon his former friend and idol with all the bitterness of a deep but disappointed affection.

By this time, such was the effect of Rossetti's isolation and general condition of mental heath, any departure from his

usual, secluded, daily round completely unnerved him. There
had been a summons to serve on a grand jury in 1872, which had
so alarmed him that to evade it he had obtained legal advice
and a certificate of physical unfitness from Marshall. The year
following there had been his alarm on again receiving an
opened letter, probably from Janey—an incident which had
revived his suspicions of conspiracies against himself to such an
extent, indeed, that early in 1873 he had even warned Fanny to
buy a seal and not seal her letters with a thimble.

How dominant, despite constant suppression, or rather no
doubt because of constant repression, were his anxieties and
fears is shown by his refusal, upon the publication of *Dante and
his Circle*, to see any reviews of it. "The dirt of dogs," he said, in
that habitual nauseating language of invective which marks
these later years and seems to be associated in some subtle way
with his mental and moral malady, "the dirt of dogs is quite out
of sight and scent with me here and perhaps it is hardly among
the things for which one turns the sod or snuffs the zephyr."
"It seems," he had however remarked some months before,
drawing bitter consolation from a damnatory review of another
writer, "I am no more blackguarded than other people!" And
when the New York *Catholic World* very belatedly reviewed his
poems this year, he was greatly heartened by what he considered
the justice and subtlety of the article.

Gradually, signs increased that Rossetti's tendency towards
hysterical anxiety was again asserting itself. It was ominously
evident during Nolly Brown's visit, when Nolly failed to return
one evening from a solitary boating excursion in time for the
ten o'clock dinner. In uncontrollable alarm, Gabriel had nervously paced from room to room, unable to eat, imagining
every possible fatality. Equally significant had been his unrestrained anger and reproaches upon Nolly's ultimate re-
appearance, upon which Nolly, coolly insolent, had returned
home, leaving behind him a damaged boat (Gabriel's property)
and a book Rossetti had lent him, spoiled by rain. The sequel
clearly reveals Gabriel's nature. Discovering the harm done
to his property by his late inconsiderate and insolent guest, he
wrote about it to Nolly, who, fearing lest his father should hear
of it, and also fearing the cost of repairs, pleaded ignorance of

the damage as well as personal poverty, and begged that his father should not be told. It was a humiliating descent from the heights of impertinence he had recently scaled in order to avert well-deserved reproof, but Rossetti was far too magnanimous to take advantage of the situation. "To preach to you," he replied, "was one thing (and that was only on the spur of the moment) but to peach to your dad would be quite another thing, and no moment will spur me to that fiendish act. . . . Of course no assault will be made on your purse. . . ." But Rossetti took advantage of the occasion to offer Nolly £20 for a picture he had, by some other painter, probably a portrait of Janey. "My wish to possess it," he declared, "is solely as an early portrait of its original, of whom I have made many studies myself—thus as long as there is any question of the work becoming mine, please don't touch the figure on any account in the least." With this request Nolly complied, whereupon Gabriel protested that a chalk head or such, inferior to it in value, was all he could give in return!

From the late spring of 1874, Rossetti, his brother noticed, became "over-strained and fanciful" owing to insomnia and chloral, and as spring passed into summer these disturbing signs increased and intensified. In May, George Hake remarked that after walks or any other exertion, Rossetti turned faint; and towards the end of June, William and Lucy, visiting Kelmscott, observed with dismay his suspicions of servants and others about him. Scott, in mid-April, had thought Gabriel mentally disordered when a cheque for £200 he had sent at Rossetti's urgent request was at once returned with thanks and an explanation—which Scott did not believe—that he had "just received some money." It was a trick, said Scott, to discover whether Scott was a genuine friend or one of his enemies. William Rossetti, accepting his brother's explanation as genuine, vigorously challenged Scott's interpretation of the incident in later years, but Scott's suspicions now reveal themselves as closely in harmony with the attitude Rossetti had shown almost two years before to Fanny, when complaining of the lack of help from "friends" during his illness.

Perhaps Janey's departure at the end of July, when she set out with her husband and family to tour Belgium, was not without its influence upon Gabriel's marked decline that summer. Was it accident or a revival of sentiment that led the Morrises at Bruges to occupy the rooms they had taken there during their honeymoon, some fifteen years before? And what part did Janey play in all this? Was she temperamental, changeable, sentimental, tired of her "romance" with Rossetti, or growing afraid of him since his mental breakdown? Did her feelings towards husband and friend vary inversely with the square of the distance, like the intensity of light? Had Rossetti's growing eccentricities frightened or repelled her? Had she already decided that (as she declared after Gabriel's death) he was "mad"?

Whatever the explanation, Gabriel, at the close of July, about the time of Janey's departure abroad, left Kelmscott for ever. The circumstances of his going were unfortunate, and, as they gradually leaked out, caused among his friends and relatives renewed concern. According to Scott, he had "got into a foundationless quarrel with some anglers by the river" at Kelmscott. In fact, the auditory hallucinations and persecution mania of paranoia had returned. Strolling one day by the river with George Hake, Rossetti passed a party of three or four anglers when, fancying that they had called out some insult to him in passing, he suddenly turned and attacked them with reproaches and abuse for the supposed outrage. Hake ran up and parted the disputants, apologizing and explaining as well as he could, to the astonished anglers. Rumours of this outbreak quickly spread about the neighbourhood, and finding Kelmscott impossible Rossetti, before the month was over, returned to Cheyne Walk.

His departure from Kelmscott was indeed final. At the same time he relinquished his share in the tenancy, "not a little," wrote Mackail, "to Morris's relief for many reasons." Early the following year came Morris's insistence upon taking sole control of "The Firm," and, in an atmosphere of acute discord, his payment of compensation to the sleeping partners and co-founders he was now ejecting, including Rossetti. Henceforth the breach between Morris and Rossetti was complete. "From this time forward," wrote Mackail, "Morris was no longer to be seen in Rossetti's house at Cheyne Walk, and the estrangement between the powerful and self-centred personalities was final."

During these Kelmscott years, Rossetti's introvert, introspective tendencies were being counteracted, extraverted as never before. All around him were new interests—human, animal, scenic—floral, all the many sights, sounds, relationships of country life, creating in the life-long townsman a new awareness which was evidently a new source of strength and joy. In leaving Kelmscott Rossetti lost all this wide variety of life he was learning to love. From these bright influences of earth and human companionship he now returned to the gloomy, silent house in Cheyne Walk, with its coarse, grasping mistress, to deliver himself up once more to the dark internal gods. . . .

With this change, his life in the truest sense was over. Only its melancholy epilogue remained.

BOOK IV

THE LAST PHASE
1874–1882

When vain desire at last and vain regret
  Go hand in hand to death, and all is vain,
  What shall assuage the unforgotten pain,
And teach the unforgetful to forget?

The One Hope D. G. ROSETTI

I

DECLINE
1874–1876

Lo! this new self now wanders round my field,
With plaints for every flower, and for each tree
A moan, the sighing wind's auxiliary:
  And o'er sweet waters of my life, that yield
  Unto his lips no draught but tears unseal'd,
    Even in my place he weeps. Even I, not he.

He and I D. G. ROSSETTI

THE EIGHT YEARS that lay before Rossetti upon his return
from Kelmscott in 1874 were to be years of slow decline,
chequered by a middle period of temporary recuperation, and
terminating in the short, sharp struggle of the end. Over these
painful "chloralized years," as William Rossetti once called
them, there is no need to linger, for they offer little beyond a
monotonous alternation of uninspired work necessitated by
debts, and of increasing illness. "What?" asked Matthew
Arnold, discussing his own poem *Empedocles on Aetna*, "What
are the situations, from the representation of which, though
accurate, no poetical enjoyment can be derived? They are
those," he continued, answering his own question, "in which
the suffering finds no vent in action; in which a continuous
state of mental distress is prolonged, unrelieved by incident,
hope, or resistance; in which there is everything to be endured,
nothing to be done. In such situations there is inevitably something morbid, in the description of them something monotonous. When they occur in actual life, they are painful, not
tragic. . . ." And such henceforth was to be the situation of
Rossetti. For him, these last years held little more than a
wearisome round of increasing personal perplexities, physical
ills and gradual exhaustion. Degeneration, physical, mental,
moral and artistic, in loneliness, anxiety and dejection, a continuous succession of chloral crises and financial embarrassments, the complications of an ill-starred passion, such are the
ever-recurring vicissitudes of Rossetti's last, sorrowful years.

Upon his return from Kelmscott friends quickly noticed a change in him, due rather to mental causes than to age. Scott found him "quiet and taciturn." Skelton, on seeing him, thought "the step was less elastic, the spirit more weary than of old." These must have been "the earlier days of the return of the malady," during which Stillman said he saw a great deal of Rossetti and witnessed his illusions that he was beset by enemies conspiring to attack him, and continually heard them plotting in an adjoining room. Buchanan, he thought, was one of the band. "No reassurance," wrote Stillman, "had any effect; he had heard, he declared, the voices of those who had combined to ruin his reputation discussing the measures they were going to take, and it was evident that it had become a mania closely resembling insanity."

Kindly Dr. Hake emphasized illness as the cause of Rossetti's deterioration. "It was no fault of his own making," he wrote: "His illness never subsided. . . . I can further say that when I saw Rossetti in his prime, a healthy man, he was the noblest of men, and had a heart so good that I have never known a better, seldom its equal. Illness changed him, but then he was no longer himself." Not all Gabriel's acquaintance were so kindly in their judgments, in these later days, as Hake. Rossetti's consciousness of the change in himself almost inevitably found expression at times in his verse, and in one of his notebooks he scribbled the unanswered, unanswerable question:—

> Who shall say what is said in me,
> With all that I might have been dead in me?

For a year after quitting Kelmscott, he remained working hard in the solitude of Tudor House. The chief result of these labours was *La Bella Mano*, a painting once particularly praised by critics for beauty of composition and colour, representing a lady washing her "beautiful hands" in a brass basin. Nevertheless, critics have also seen in the work premonitions of Rossetti's artistic decline, have indeed regarded it as marking the close of the intermediate period of his art which followed his earlier, fresher work, and as also foreshadowing the next period then beginning, characterized by an exaggerated portrayal of necks and lips, and a deteriorated sense of colour; the result, doubtless, of his failing eyesight and increasing morbidity. As before, he painted all day, dined when darkness forced him to leave his easel, and then often paced the London streets until the small hours, vainly endeavouring to obtain sleep. Sometimes Watts, George Hake or his assistant Dunn would set out with him upon these nocturnal excursions, but often, wearied out, they would return home, leaving him to continue his wanderings alone.

Illness sharpened, if possible, Rossetti's old commercial shrewdness. Fearing the effect upon his patrons and prices of rumours that his declining health was causing deterioration in his art, he exerted himself to counteract it by maintaining the high prices of his works in the saleroom. To this end he employed his friend and agent Murray Marks to run up the bidding, as Howell had long done and was still doing. Howell's supremacy, however, was now threatened by the tactful solicitor Watts, rapidly becoming indispensable to Rossetti. For Watts's range of activities far surpassed even Howell's. He would discuss the drains with plumbers, smooth Gabriel's distracted finances, put off duns, run errands, write sonnets himself or criticize Gabriel's, tell interesting tales or read stories to Rossetti during the long insomnia-haunted nights, or act as picture agent when required.

In mid-October, 1875, however, the cumulative effects of a long spell of solitary toil, of loneliness, over-work, restlessness, the demands of a landlord insisting upon an inspection of the dilapidation of the house during Gabriel's tenancy, and increasing debts now culminating in what Rossetti referred to as "a bloody writ," combined to persuade him to set off with George Hake for Bognor where he had just taken a lease of a house named Aldwick Lodge. "A large, fine house—oldish but without much character," was Rossetti's description of it, and Dr. Hake said, "near to the roughest bit of beach on the Sussex coast." At Aldwick Lodge Rossetti spent the next nine months, experiencing there, said Watts, "the most secluded life he ever led before or afterwards, suffering most of the time from ill-health."

It was Monday, October 18th, when Rossetti, in sombre

mood, set out with George Hake for Bognor, leaving Watts, who refused an invitation to accompany them, to grapple with a pile of unpaid bills that had long been accumulating in Tudor House. Rossetti also took with him the unfinished *Blessed Damozel* (begun two years before for Graham and not completed until two years later), as well as the canvas for a new painting, *Venus Astarte*, recently commissioned at two thousand guineas by a new patron, Clarence Fry, a well-known Bond Street photographer.

Aldwick Lodge, although conveniently situated within two minutes' walk of the sea, had its drawbacks in such stormy weather as Rossetti and George Hake now experienced. Gabriel at once complained that rain prevented walking, and that draughts flying through the rooms and shaking the unseasonable muslin curtains made him feel "like a ballet girl with a strong draught from the side scenes." The light, too, was bad, and at first he declared, to Fanny, then disporting herself at Margate, that the place was "almost impossible to paint in. Every window of any importance," he grumbled, "has a sort of hood which shuts the light out a good deal." Yet he grudgingly allowed: "I suppose I shall manage somehow if necessary," and described the house to his mother as "very agreeable and particularly sheltered and well suited for winter quarters." "This place," he told Watts, "is quite a pleasant sojourn, but weather is against us just now."

That in his letters to relatives and friends he should make the best of the place was natural, since in his weariness of solitude his first act was to try to induce them to come and keep him company in his new home. Nor can he have been long alone there with George Hake, for when Alexa Wilding arrived on November 3rd to sit for *The Blessed Damozel*, she found both Dr. Hake and Watts with Rossetti, and when she left on the 14th, Rossetti's mother and Christina had arrived several days before, and would not be leaving for another week or more.

Mrs. Rossetti and Christina had, in fact, postponed their visit for a week or two in order to attend the ceremony of Maria's formal admission to the religious sisterhood now that her novitiate was ended. As Gabriel succinctly rather than sympathetically reported it to Miss Boyd: "Poor Maggie is parting with her grey hair next Saturday and annexing the Kingdom of Heaven for good." Such devotional exercises made little appeal to Rossetti's now prevailingly rationalistic temper;[1] but as he avoided the discussion of religious topics on the one hand yet, unlike his brother, never made an open profession of rationalism on the other, his views on the subject are little known, and, indeed, after his death he was, for these reasons, claimed by various writers, according to their predilections, for both Christianity and agnosticism. Only once, so far as we know, did Rossetti ever "speak out" on this subject, and that was in 1865 when he was categorically examined by his friend Smetham, the religious enthusiast. In his sincere, urbane but reluctant reply, Rossetti firmly yet delicately revealed his dislike of such questioning, and equally clearly showed his sympathy with and respect for those who could accept orthodox Christian dogma, while at the same time he equally clearly expressed the impossibility of such an acceptance for himself. "I had better tell you frankly at once that I have no such faith as you have," he wrote. "Its default in me does not arise from want of natural impulse to believe nor of reflection whether what I should alone call belief in a full sense is possible to me. Thus I know that while discussion on such points with a believer is painful to me, it affords me no counterbalancing profit; and I abstain from it absolutely. I feel this plain statement due to such sincerity as yours, though I do not ordinarily feel bound to explain myself at all on the matter. As regards the pursuit of Art, which we have in common, I feel a pleasure in being so associated with you, as well as a true regard for yourself; and if you can be content to consider these the chief bonds between us, I do not think we need feel a want in such intercourse on account of what I have felt it my duty to say here; of which I neither wish to mitigate the significance, nor to declare myself thereby a confident denier—still less an apostle of opposition. This is all I feel able to say on the subject. . . ."

Yet that his agnosticism was unchanged six years later, he

---

[1] cf. "I myself was never gifted with implicit faith in things not undeniably proved." *D. G. R. to Edmund Bates*, October 1, 1879.

showed in a stanza of the verses entitled *Commandments* which
he sent to Scott in 1871 :—

> Let no priest tell you of any home
> Unseen above the sky's blue dome.
> To have played in childhood by the sea,
> Or to have been young in Italy,
> Or anywhere in the sun or rain,
> To have loved and been beloved again,
> Is nearer Heaven than he can come.[1]

This stanza, however, he omitted on publishing the *Commandments* with additional stanzas, as *Soothsay*, in 1881.[2]

The presence of Rossetti's friends and relatives at Bognor
failed, however, to prevent a continued decline in his health,
an increasing dejection of spirit. For this, in addition to all the
usual causes, was that of anxiety about Janey, again unwell,
and his frustrated desire for her companionship. She was to sit
to him for the *Venus Astarte*, but for some reason could not
come immediately, might not, indeed, be able to come at all.
The hope of resuming at Aldwick Lodge the old, happy way of
life he had enjoyed with Janey and the children at Kelmscott
was probably one of the incentives to his leaving London, for,
except at Kelmscott, he had never been happy for long out of
his native town, had always insisted upon returning to it after
a few days' absence. Now, certainly, Kelmscott was in his
thoughts. "After all," he now told Fanny, "the place cannot
compare for beauty with Kelmscott," although when in residence there he had often written with but lukewarm appreciation of its natural attractions. Now, however, as a contrast to
this dreary waiting at Bognor, those days passed with Janey
and the children there assumed the heightened beauty of
retrospect.

Bognor, he soon began to fear, could not be like Kelmscott.
"I suppose there is no chance of other inhabitants as yet," he
had told Watts, in a characteristically cautious allusion to
Janey and the children, a day or two before leaving town, and

---

[1] "I don't know what copy of my poems you have lent to the Revd. gentleman
. . . but apprehend there may be things here and there in the book which might
rather ruffle the nap of 'The Cloth,' though not a line that is vile, by God!"
D. G. R. to Bates. Christmas Eve 879. cf. inf. p. 587.

[2] *cf. Dante at Verona*, stanza 15. The poem was written 1848–50, revised 1869–70.

on the third day after his arrival at Bognor he told Fanny:
"Fry has sent the first £500 on the *Venus*, but I shall not be
able to get to the picture for two or three weeks yet, as I shall
not get my models till then at soonest—perhaps not at all."
And so, to fill the intolerable period of waiting and suspense,
he had invited his relatives and friends to Aldwick Lodge,
carefully arranging that their departure should precede Janey's
return. "Later," he had warned his mother, when urging her
and Christina to come to him at once, "I expect other visitors
to sit for a picture (*Venus Astarte*, which I now want to begin if
possible); but this prospect is, unfortunately, uncertain." It
was always thus with Janey's visits; never did he wish to share
her company with others.

Soon Hake and Watts reported Gabriel's condition to Scott
as "alarming," although, like many persons in such a state, he
showed, as Scott remarked, no sign in his letters of mental
abnormality. But to Fanny, (now the "elephant"), Gabriel admitted a fortnight later: "I am excessively out of spirits to-day,
and wish I had a good elephant to talk to." This mood of frustration in absence, of dejection even to despair, of sorrow in
separation, inspires Rossetti's few verses of this year, 1875, and
some at least, we may reasonably assume, were written at this
time, at Bognor.

> To-day your lips are afar,
>   Yet draw my lips to them, love.
> Around, beneath, and above,
>   Is frost to bind and to bar;[1]
> But where I am and you are,
>   Desire and the fire thereof.
> O kiss me, kiss me, my love!

So he sang, significantly enough in *Parted Presence*, of enforced
severance. At other times now he would look forward, but
hopelessly, to Death, as in *Hero's Lamp*, in which he described
love as

> Death's pallid neophyte,

explaining in a footnote to the poem: "After the deaths of
Leander and Hero, the signal lamp was dedicated to Anteros,

[1] The line suggests a loveless marriage *binding* the beloved to her husband
and *barring* her marriage or love to himself.

with the edict that no man should light it unless his love had proved fortunate." Rossetti intended to paint a picture on the theme but never did so.

How insistently his spirit oscillated now between the twin polarities of Love and Death his work clearly shows. The death of young Nolly Brown in the preceding year he had commemorated in a sonnet, *Untimely Lost*, written in the coach as he returned from the funeral, while Watts, sitting opposite, also composed a sonnet on the same theme. Gabriel also personified Nolly in the figure of the dying youth in a pencil sketch he now made, entitled *The Sphinx* or *The Question*, in which he gave expression to his own persistent questioning of inscrutable fate. "A sort of painted *Cloud Confines*," was his description of this sketch, or rather of the intended but never realized painting from it. Yet how long the thought of it remained in his mind is shown by his writing for it two very mediocre sonnets (so far only privately published), four days before his own death.

Increasingly Rossetti now saw himself as the victim not only of man's malevolence but also of Fate's. To small incidents he began to attach ominous significance. When a November gale now overturned an elm tree on the lawn at Aldwick Lodge, he recalled in detail similar incidents at Cheyne Walk and Kelmscott as omens of impending misfortune, and expressed these fears in a sonnet, *The Trees of the Garden*, in which he again gave rein to his obsessive questioning of destiny, asking:—

> . . . is it all a show,—
> A wisp that laughs upon the wall? decree
> Of some inexorable supremacy
>   Which ever, as man strains his blind surmise
> From depth to ominous depth, looks past his eyes,
>   Sphinx-faced with unabashed augury?

How much the storm which obviously inspired this sonnet with its reference to

> The storm-felled forest-trees moss-grown to-day
> Whose roots are hillocks where the children play,

had affected Rossetti's imagination is shown in the accounts he sent Fanny and Watts the following day, November 14th.

"There is such a gale of wind to-day, and all last night as I never knew in my life," he told Fanny, "and the sea is higher than at any time the last eighteen years. The noise is something tremendous, and the house absolutely shakes to and fro. The trees are broken down on the lawn and the cows are eating the leaves from the boughs as they trail along the grass." To Fanny, Gabriel merely expressed the physical effects of the storm, but in describing it to Watts he allowed a suggestion of his own personal interpretation of it as an evil omen for himself to peep out for a moment from the concluding associations. "The gale here last night," he told Watts, "has been something appalling and without cessation—havoc on all hands and the sea higher than it has been known to come for eighteen years. The fine elm-tree in the centre of the lawn is uprooted and the cows are feeding on its prostrate branches. To-morrow it will be cleared away and leave a blank. When I took my house at Chelsea, a large tree—one of the finest in the walk—(in front of my gate) fell after I had been there a month or two. When I settled at Kelmscott, three of the tercentenary trees of the avenue toppled over one another and lay headlong —I think you were there at the time; and now this tree here, the feature of the view, is gone as soon as I arrive!" Evidently in his depression and anxiety he was sinking below his dominant rational mood into a primitive world of superstitions, of supernatural, personal symbolism in which the stricken trees overwhelmed by the storm represented himself overwhelmed by an evil destiny and hastening to a similar fate.

By this time, however, Rossetti had heard that Janey would come. He had already begun, as before at Kelmscott, to make elaborate preparations for her reception, involving the removal of furniture as well as of his present guests. "My mother and Christina are here now," he told Watts on November 14th. "They will leave, I think, on Thursday, when George will accompany them to London, making his way on Friday morning to Kelmscott where he will meet a van to convey the necessary furniture, and will be back here, I suppose, early on Saturday. The van following (presumably by rail) and the furniture reaching here on Monday, by which day or Tuesday, I expect Mrs. M. and children if all goes well. Far from well she still is, and will not, I judge, be able to sit at first, but I trust the air may really benefit her." Three days later, after informing Fanny of his dejection he added: "In about a week I expect my other visitors." Hake, however, for some reason, instead of accompanying Mrs. Rossetti and Christina to London as intended, set out for Kelmscott alone, and on his return to Bognor on the 21st, found the two ladies still there. A week later, however, they were back in town, and Janey and the children were installed in Aldwick Lodge. Christina at the close of the month sent her own and her mother's greetings to them: "All cordial regards from us both, please, to Mrs. Morris."

The sea air of Bognor quickly improved Janey's health, and *Venus Astarte* began to progress. But the picture became another symbol of Gabriel's mood. Love for him, now, was no longer the fair Greek Aphrodite, but that more ancient Venus of Assyria and Babylon, fatal, stern, cruel, mysterious, "that face," as he described it in his illustrative sonnet to the picture,

> That face of Love's all-penetrative spell,
> Amulet, talisman and oracle—
> Betwixt the sun and moon a mystery . . .

Yet for a time, as the painting advanced, something of the old happy existence at Kelmscott was resumed at Aldwick Lodge, with mornings of painting in the studio, afternoon walks and evening readings, as before. At Gabriel's request, his mother and Christina sent him *Walpole's Letters*, and Janey sent back friendly greetings in return for their "cordial regards."

Then all too soon Janey departed. Gabriel, bored, restless, anxiously awaiting her return, gave a Christmas party at Aldwick Lodge to which came his mother, Christina, aunts Eliza and Charlotte Polidori, Dr. Hake, his three sons, and Watts. By the time of the party, however, Gabriel had fallen into his former depression, and was in no mood for entertaining guests. "I am now once more alone with George here," he told William on December 15th, and the next day, writing to Fanny, remarked: "My spirits are not very high, I assure you." "That holiday," wrote Dr. Hake, long afterwards recalling this Christmas at Aldwick Lodge, "was made cheerful less perhaps by the host himself than by his guests." He saw that Rossetti was "much unstrung," noticed his silence as, between Watts and himself Gabriel stumbled along on their daily walk over the boulders of Selsey Bay amidst a wilderness of seaweed, stones and ruined wooden groynes, dismal, depressing as his own mood—as life unillumined by love.

That Rossetti's anxiety-state was finding everywhere material to feed upon, even among the simplest details of domestic life is very evident in the account he sent Fanny of the dinner on Christmas Day. It was, he wrote, "a great failure. The fact is," he continued, "George had put all the comfortable chairs on one side of the table backing the fire, and on these the four ladies were deposited with the four gentlemen (Watts had not then come down) grimly facing them on the opposite side and I at the top. It looked as if I were going to preach a funeral sermon: but as it so happened that I came in last when the others were already seated, I thought it better not to make a fuss. Then Charles carved everything single-handed in the room, so that there was at least a couple of minutes between each plate being handed, and then the vegetables and sauces followed after it all when the plates were nearly finished. Moreover nobody got more than a bit of fish and a bit of beef *or* turkey, since Charles like a fool went round to every one asking whether they would take beef or turkey: so by the time they had taken a plate of either one or the other, everything was out of the room again. The plum-pudding was not a good one—indeed Mrs. G. is bad at pastry altogether. On the following day I took matters into my own hands—placed people properly at the table—got Mary to help in serving—and made them carve everything in the kitchen and hand it round. Thus the following dinners were all successful, but I was extremely mortified and irritated at the stupid mess on Xmas Day. . . ." Hake—and doubtless the other guests also—soon saw that Rossetti had "got tired of his visitors," and after a day or two the party broke up. Nevertheless, in his small volume of sentimental poems entitled *New Day*, Hake commemorated this Christmas party of 1875, while Watts in a sonnet entitled *Two Christmases* carried poetic licence to its limit by describing Gabriel as moving amongst his guests "with peace upon his brow."

Not until the following March did Janey reappear at Ald-wick Lodge, and only to leave again a fortnight later. Wearying of country life in solitude, Rossetti would have returned to town, but, as there was still a possibility of Janey's return and the *Venus Astarte* was unfinished, he remained throughout the spring and summer at Bognor, in a state of ever-increasing tension. Solitude and anxiety had their usual effect upon him, and morbid symptoms increased. "A train of untoward cir-cumstances, viewed through the fumes of chloral," was William Rossetti's explanation of his brother's decline, and in a passage too important for paraphrase he described the chloral itself as having "little or no power over that part of his mind which was purely intellectual or inventive, but only over that other part which was emotional, and was applied to the construing of himself and his surroundings."

So it now was with Rossetti. His dejection and paranoiac suspicions returned. He read the posthumously published works of Nolly Brown, and, as Nolly admittedly used his friends as "material" for his writings, was probably not entirely mistaken in believing some parts of these stories to have been uninten-tionally inspired by himself. But only a sick man would have so taken it to heart. Interpreting the passages as an attack upon himself, he put the volumes aside, too pained to continue reading. Believing, too, that his correspondence was again being spied upon—and perhaps Fanny or Howell could have enlightened him—he sealed all his letters and warned Watts to do the same.

Rossetti was now, in fact, reaching the "peak period" of his consumption of chloral. With the emotional ambivalence and exhibitionism of the confirmed drug addict, he would even boast at times, to intimates, that his dose had now risen to 180 grains, while in another mood he would bitterly lament the hold chloral had gained upon him. William believed his brother was deceived in this high estimate, on the ground that by order of the doctor, Marshall, the drug was purposely diluted without Rossetti's knowledge. Thus, said William, the dose perhaps never rose above ninety or perhaps even sixty grains. But not until after Gabriel's death did he learn that with the cunning of the drug addict, Gabriel, despite chemists' regulations, had managed to obtain large quantities of chloral from other sources. Nor was the harm entirely due to chloral, for Rossetti still washed the drug down with alcohol, and that too increased its hold upon him.

So greatly and rapidly did his health now deteriorate that towards the close of April, George Hake was forced to beg Watts to come to his aid. "Your advice and above all your influence with Rossetti," he wrote, "would be invaluable at this critical juncture. I need hardly say I do not feel equal to cope with it alone. The mental ease of your presence would be a great boon to me. I cannot give you any better report. Spirits fearfully low and no abatement of suspicions." Believing death near, perhaps again meditating suicide, Rossetti wrote out instructions for his cremation, and—a sign that Lizzie was still in his mind—strictly forbade burial at Highgate, and also the taking of any cast of his face or head. This last prohibition, if still in force at his death, was certainly ignored. He also parti-cularly ordered that in the event of his death, letters at Aldwick Lodge and at Cheyne Walk (obviously Janey's), should be destroyed, and that William should inform the writer of them that this had been done.

Nineteen days later, George Hake again summoned Watts to his assistance. "Although," he wrote, "there is a certain irksomeness and inconvenience attending a visit, I hope to make it in some way agreeable to you. . . . We can count upon the morning and part of the afternoon to ourselves as Rossetti *never* breakfasts now *before one*." The lateness of Gabriel's rising was of course a sign of his insomnia. "Although," Hake con-tinued, "I said yesterday that things were quiet it was only that I was temporarily deceived. I have been obliged to-day to see about hiring a man to keep off birds and such noises from the studio so as to enable him to work. He is very depressed." Evidently the auditory and emotional irritability of paranoia were again developing.

To Fanny at this time Rossetti sent an account of himself, pathetic in its simple, unconscious revelation of his unhappi-ness. "I should certainly be returning now," he told her, "for I have reason to think the air is no longer benefiting me, and I wish for a change; but the visitor whom I was expecting some time back has since been very ill and prevented from coming, and is now again thinking of being able to come. This keeps me here, though whether I shall be well enough to work successfully at the picture I do not know. I have lately felt so extremely weak as to be quite distressing, and feel so little interest in anything that I can hardly push on my work at all. I do not think I have ever before felt so depressed. I should have been much pleased to see you here for a time, but you will perceive that my own staying on has been so uncertain, and I so worried, that it has not been in my power to settle anything of the kind. I must hope to get better when my work is proceeding successfully. It has hung back sadly, from one cause or another, ever since I have been here. I am of course again getting anxious about money matters, and do not see my way to raising further supplies from Fry till I can get his picture forward." And in a postscript he added: "You must not be anxious about what I say above with respect to my health. I dare say I shall soon be feeling better again, particularly when I am able to leave this place which is so very lonely." In Mid-June, Gabriel was forced to write apologetically to Watts for some impatient outburst, declaring: "I am truly and greatly concerned to think that when you were last here I must have tried your patience in various ways. The fact is I have gradually got so completely out of health that I need more indulgence from my friends than I have any right to expect. What are your views as to my best course at present? Is London really the best place for me? I feel greatly exhausted here, but must be where something like rest can be had. Please *seal* letters if possible."

The effect of this degeneration upon Rossetti's intellectual life was, in fact, much greater than William realized. Carried as on a refluent wave from his former ecstatic affirmations of love, life and beauty, Gabriel was now sinking into the final negation, moving deathward from light to darkness, from desire to satiety, from his "one hope" to his ultimate despair. Exhaustion was following frustration. The wearied ego now vainly revolved in its cage, following the primitive repetitional rhythm of mental life, driving him merely to repeat in many a picture and poem, and generally through the old, too familiar symbols, the themes of his earlier, still creative years, themes which now produced but replicas of past experience or of anticipated death. Uneasily aware of this, Rossetti now complained of "finding myself as I grow older, more than ever at the mercy of my first sources of inspiration." In poetry too inspiration was failing. The first rapture of that strange poetic renascence of middle-age had waned, and he wrote little verse now. Besides, painting hard to pay his debts, he could give little time to verse. "As for poetry," he told Miss Boyd, "it seems to have fled afar from me; and indeed it has no such nourishing savour about it as painting can boast, but is rather a hungry affair to follow. Nevertheless," he added, "I mean to write some more poems yet, and good ones too." But poetry henceforth clearly would not come to him (in Keats's phrase), "as the leaves to the tree." Indeed, it never had done.

Yet Rossetti's misery still found occasional expression in verse. Of the three published poems by him, dated this year, 1876, one, *Three Shadows*, is of a man's love for a woman, while the other two, *A Death Parting* and *Adieu*, are expressive of the poet's suffering in love-in-absence, of his spiritual weariness unto death.

> Leaves and rain and the days of the year,
>   (Water-willow and wellaway),
> All these fall, and my soul gives ear,
> And she is hence who once was here.
>   (With a wind blown night and day).
>
> Ah! but now, for a secret sign,
>   (The willow's wan and the water white),
> In the held breath of the day's decline
> Her very face seemed pressed to mine.
>   (With a wind blown day and night).
>
> *   *   *
>
> Leaves and rain and the days of the year,
>   (Water-willow and wellaway),
> All still fall, and I still give ear,
> And she is hence, and I am here.
>   (With a wind blown night and day).

Such was Rossetti's cry in *A Death Parting*, the expression of his intolerable agony in the loss of a companionship which was for him, almost literally, his life. "Water-willow," how the words must have recalled Janey sitting to him in the happy Kelmscott days for the picture he so named. And now, he must find inspiration only in the compensatory phantasies created by his imagination, those phantasies which so significantly appear in the poem. In *Adieu*, his misery again turns deathwards: —

> Sinking suffering heart
> That know'st how weary thou art,—
> Soul so fain for a flight,—
> Aye, spread your wings to depart,
> Sad soul and sorrowing heart,—
> Adieu, Farewell, Good-night.

Losing all hope of Janey's return, Gabriel would have gone back to town, but feared the too familiar solitude of Cheyne Walk. He had many troubles now. His "chronic impecuniousness," as he called his extravagance, had brought him to the humiliation of re-borrowing almost the whole of the thousand pounds he had settled on Janey upon receiving it from Morris as compensation for waiving his rights as a member of *The Firm*, during its recent reorganization by which Morris assumed sole control. Fanny, too, in dire straits apparently, was pressing him as never before, wanted him to pay arrears of rent for the house he had taken for her in Chelsea. "Delicious is the prosperous elephant," wrote Christina on one occasion, to her brother, thanking him for an "elephant book" he had sent her. "I wish," she added drily, with an almost audible sigh for her incorrigible brother, "all Elephants were prosperous."

Even when Rossetti was at last brave enough to face his difficulties in London, he was unexpectedly frightened into remaining at Aldwick Lodge by the threat of a subpoena to appear as witness in a libel action brought by the incredible Buchanan against the proprietors of *The Examiner*, as publishers of Swinburne's attack on him in *The Devil's Due*. Terrified at the thought of a public appearance, particularly in relation to the loathsome Buchanan, Gabriel lay low at Bognor until the absurd trial, which evoked much abuse of Rossetti and his friends, ended in the award to Buchanan of £150. Only then, when all was over, in the first days of July, did Rossetti venture to return to Cheyne Walk.

There, solitude and over-work almost immediately brought on a relapse of chloral, followed again by persecutory, paranoiac symptoms. As on a previous occasion when William found him enraged with a thrush, believing it had been trained to insult him in its song, or as with the anglers at Kelmscott, Rossetti now again found an irrational cause for anger in the exercises of a distinguished musician living near-by. The music he took for mocking voices, and to evade them had his studio sound-proofed. And he became so weak, physically, that even when "cushioned round in his chair," he complained, weakness in his back prevented painting.

Soon, persuaded by Watts, he accepted an invitation of his kindly patrons Mr. and Mrs. Cowper-Temple, to visit them at their magnificent Hampshire seat, "Broadlands," and set out with George Hake as companion, intending to spend August there. This visit, in Rossetti's voluntarily retired existence, was a unique experience. He liked "Broadlands," the great house, the park, the surrounding country, and above all his host and hostess, so well, that even a clerical conference which was also enjoying the Cowper-Temple's hospitality did not unduly disturb him. "The utmost toleration," he ironically remarked of his clerical fellow-guests, "is shown towards me as an entirely foreign substance." But his "most womanly and most queenly hostess," so different from his usual commercial patrons, particularly aroused his enthusiasm, and in letters to his mother he enlarged upon "the noble beauty" of "her Christ-like character." Gladly he seized the opportunity to make a chalk drawing of her, having "long wished to draw her most noble face."

In his present desperate need—for insomnia still held him, "utter unrest" and much bodily pain, so that despite chloral he would often pass three days and nights without sleep—he found Mrs. Cowper-Temple "simply an angel on earth." At "Broadlands," aloof for the most part in his own private rooms, "a very quiet corner," he saw little or nothing of the fifty or sixty guests who came and went during his visit, but painted away at *The Blessed Damozel* as well as his health allowed, though little to his own satisfaction. Sometimes, in the evenings, to his host, hostess and a few privileged guests, "all true enthusiasts for their beauty," as he said, he read Christina's poems. "My spirits have gained much," he wrote, "through the intercourse with these most sympathetic people, but my physical weakness has of course been a great disadvantage." It was a rare, a gracious interlude in his life.

Growing ever more afraid of the solitude of Cheyne Walk, he lingered at "Broadlands" until almost the last summer visitor had gone; then, abandoning an intention to take a cold water cure at Malvern, he returned at the close of August to London, where for the next twelve months he remained, a prey to chloral, old anxieties, sorrows and fears. For a time he resorted to a lady mesmerist with, he believed, some slight, temporary benefit. But his existence during this year was an almost unrelieved horror. Yet only very occasionally in his letters do we gain some sudden, poignant glimpse of the tragedy gradually playing itself out in the life of the sick, solitary man in the silent, neglected, gloomy house in Cheyne Walk. As if casually he refers to "the awful ordeal of two nights entirely without chloral" urged upon him by Sir William Jenner, the doctor who had now taken him in hand. Cautiously, behind a mask of pretended humour, he postpones at another time the visits of his mother and sister, when suffering through attempts to conquer his craving for the drug, "since what sort of a bogie I may be under the new night system I can't tell," and, most distressing of all, on another occasion, the same ineffective disguise of crudely jovial speech in his message to William— illuminating as in a lightning-flash the horrors of those black night-hours of misery when the drugged and drunken man, stumbling alone about the dark house of bitter, passionate memories, of frustrated hopes and dreams, staggers and falls:— "You will find my mug in rather a sorry state as I tumbled down and hurt myself in the night. I fear the mark on my cheek will be permanent. You had better not mention this at home." Nevertheless, Mrs. Rossetti and Christina were not without their suspicions, seeing at times similar signs on him. More and more his friends became aware of the gravity of his condition. "Rossetti," Brown reported, "has had distinct hallucinations, but . . . I believe them to be the product of chloral."

In October, Janey returned, was sitting to Gabriel for *Venus Astarte*, in Cheyne Walk. . . .

This autumn of 1876 was indeed a time of change and sorrow for the whole Rossetti family. Since William's marriage and the entry of Lucy Brown into the family life as his wife, all had not gone smoothly, and in October matters came to a head with the departure of old Mrs. Rossetti and Christina from William's home in Euston Square, to live at 30 Torrington Square, near-by. Aunts Eliza and Charlotte Polidori, who had left the Rossetti home for Bloomsbury Square at the time of William's marriage, now joined the two women in their new home. A few weeks later, Gabriel's sister Maria died in her convent, in a rapture of heavenly anticipation like some mediaeval saint.

HEART OF THE NIGHT
1877

"Woe's me, for whom
Inveteracy of ill portends the doom,——"

The Sun's Shame. II D. G. ROSSETTI

THE NEXT YEAR, 1877, was for Rossetti but a weary continuation of the unhappiness of its predecessor; an alternation of associated miseries due to surrenders to chloral followed by spasmodic attempts to check his craving for the drug. Besides, there were new anxieties about Janey. Some months before, her eldest daughter, Jenny, had had a nervous breakdown, which left permanent mental effects, and at the time Gabriel was painting at "Broadlands," Janey was at Deal with her daughter, who was being nursed there through her convalescence. Perhaps it was to this that Gabriel in obvious anxiety referred in a note to Watts in February 1877, when the Morrises were living near Turnham Green. "Bad news from Turnham Green," he wrote, "is worrying me, but must hope for the best," and it was surely in reference to this same anxiety that two months later he told the same friend: "To-day I have been feeling very low. You know how much anxiety I expressed as to getting no news from the anxious quarter. To-night I have written asking when I can go there, and if silence should still be the result, I shall be quite at a loss. It is making me quite ill and unable to attend to work."

It was indeed at this very time, in the spring, that Rossetti's condition again gravely deteriorated. In May a relapse occurred, so severe that it brought him in mid-June to his bed, extremely ill, while shortly afterwards the old trouble of the hydrocele developed such symptoms that William feared for his brother's life, and Marshall had to perform an operation much more serious than the previous tappings. Marshall also cut down the "chloral with its accompanying whisky," declaring that while a few months' abstinence from them could work wonders, "he could not survive many months" of his present way of life. Intimidated, Rossetti reluctantly accepted the supervision of a nurse, Mrs. Mitchell, by day, and of a man-servant, Albert, by night, to "enforce," said Christina, "that moderation which his very life requires." Yet his depression increased, passing beyond all relief or cure. All the attempts of Brown, Dunn, and others to interest him failed, and Christina found him "so dreadfully depressed" that she despaired of his recovery.

Ordered by Marshall, in this crisis, to leave London or die, he reluctantly set out with Brown, in mid-August, for Herne Bay near Margate. After a false start with a "vixen" of a landlady, as Brown described her, they moved to "a pretty cottage with a pleasant garden in front, and a kitchen garden behind," at Hunter's Forestall, near-by. There for the next two months they remained. Christina described her brother, shortly after his arrival, as in a pitiable state, sitting in semi-darkness, in deepest dejection, and—so greatly now did his hand tremble—desperately afraid that his painting days were over. From this misery his sole means of escape was the forbidden drug and spirits, and to prevent his obtaining these, a constant succession of relatives and friends, his mother, Christina, Brown, Shields and Watts, came and went continually.

Although he bitterly complained of Brown's watch upon him as "bullying," he managed to evade his guards and secure so much of the drug, in secrecy, that before leaving Hunter's Forestall, he experienced several more crises. Enforced idleness, "rotting my life away hour by hour" he chafed in growing irritation, and boredom increased the temptation of the forbidden relief. By the end of August, however, with his dose of chloral reduced to thirty or forty grains, he had sufficiently improved to allow his rooms to be no longer darkened, and had ceased, as Christina remarked, to sit "in that attitude of dreadful dejection with drooping head," perspired less, felt less pain in his limbs, and occasionally, as his sister gladly noted, "a shadow of the old fun breaks out and lights all up for the moment." Gradually his interest in life revived. At times he would listen to those reading to him, even play whist in the evenings, and, as his hands regained firmness, he rejoiced with renewed confidence in his ability to resume painting. "The worst of it is," Brown told his wife, evidently alluding to causes of the depression below chloral, "the whole matter is so involved that stronger wills than ours would fail to see a way out of it now."

There was, indeed, by this time no way out save the final one five years later. Apart from other aspects of his illness, Rossetti was now a hopeless victim of anxiety, and new causes for anxiety now crowded upon him from every quarter. Chief amongst these were his debts and fears that illness might prevent his painting to meet them, and associated with them was Fanny, rapidly becoming a chief anxiety to him for various reasons now coming to a head.

Since his entry into Tudor House, indeed, Fanny, domiciled in Royal Avenue near-by, had become almost indispensable to Rossetti, as the continuous stream of little notes he sent her almost to the end of his life clearly shows. Some require her services for his pictures—will she go to Covent Garden at once, get a rose-tree and bring it back in a cab? Will she get "some common white fringe" and "sew it on that towel I am painting?" Domestic exigencies would lead to affectionate notes in the baby language that bridged the gap of their social and educational difference:—"Good Elephant—An old Rhinoceros wants you to come down at once. The woman is going and has to be paid and the new servants are coming sooner than they were expected." Cheques frequently accompanied the notes.

On other occasions Fanny would be summoned, or if in unaccommodating mood implored, to lighten the burden of solitude. "Dear Fan," he would write, "it is half past seven. I have put off the dinner to eight, hoping to see you. Do come. George is not here. Your affec. R." When guests who would object to Fanny's company arrived, Gabriel would send her some more or less tactful hint to keep out of the way, such as:— "Dear Fan—I find Smetham would like to stay to dinner, so, as I am uncertain of your coming in any case, I will not expect you. I hope to see you to-morrow." How anxious he was for her return as soon as such visitors had gone, many notes testify. "Good Elephant," he writes, for example, "Webb and Watts have gone. The surveyor is coming back to-day but nothing will be in the way of your coming whenever you please, so I hope to see you."

At times, differences and tensions developed between Gabriel and Fanny, but, as we should expect, little of the surviving correspondence throws light upon Fanny's reputed jealousies and the consequent violent quarrels which oral tradition asserts. There certainly were times when Fanny would not come to Gabriel's summons, when, angered by some real or fancied slight or anxious to extract more money from him or to dominate him in some way, she remained coyly aloof, ignoring his blandishments. "Good elephant," he would then write, "Do come down. Old Rhinoceros is unhappy. Do come to old Rhinoceros." But if "Fan" remained unmoved by such pathetic appeals, Gabriel's notes would take a mature, sterner tone, such as: "Dear Good Fan, I do not wish to interfere with your going out and amusing yourself to-day if you have any engagement; but if you are only staying away because of any uncomfortable feeling, do come, my dear Fan, for I have been in very low spirits about what happened yesterday, and the only thing which would make me feel like myself again would be to see your good cheerful face with two funny holes in it. So do come if you can, my dear, but not if you really wish to be anywhere else. In case you are pushed for expenses at the moment, I enclose a trifle, owing to something you said yesterday."

No doubt in anger Fanny reproached Rossetti for their chronic impecuniosity, either disbelieving in its genuineness in the case of a man obtaining such high prices and so many commissions as he was doing, or irritated by his spendthrift habits. But if Fanny remained deaf to the sterner form of appeal, Gabriel would address her in a quaint tone of moral reproof mingled with entreaty: "My dear Fan,—You are really trifling with me in a very unfair way, and behaving with a want of sense which is not worthy of you if you reflect for a moment. I hope you will let me see you here to-morrow, and you may be sure of being received as affectionately as usual. . . . Do come round to-morrow and recover your usual spirits, like a good old friend." Whenever any little ailment afflicted Fanny, Gabriel's anxiety and attentions were as marked as ever, and George Hake would be despatched to Royal Avenue to take messages of condolence and bring back news.

Such were the normal relations of the two when Gabriel was in London. But now, during his residence at Hunter's Forestall, a crisis developed between them. Fanny, who some months before had extracted from Rossetti an I.O.U. for £300, was now especially active. Probably still fearing that Gabriel's life might soon come to an end, and that she must begin to consider her own future, she constantly begged for money which, through illness and declining patronage, Rossetti was less able than ever before to supply. Throughout September the contention between them continued in a series of notes from Hunter's Forestall with occasional voluble replies from Fanny in London. Believing that his painting days were over, and probably influenced by his relatives about him, he informed Fanny: "I am most anxious on your account, and can only advise you to take the best step in life that you can for your own advantage, and quite to forget me. It is most probable that I shall have to give up all thoughts of work and settle down in the quietest and cheapest way with my mother and sister. Still, this is not yet certain, but I grieve deeply to say that it is impossible to reckon on me in any way at the present moment."

Fanny must have suspected that Gabriel's pessimism and advice were largely due to the influence of his mother and Christina, who were then attending him at Hunter's Forestall without other company than the paid nurse. That Rossetti was less decided about leaving Fanny than he tried to appear, his next note showed; for after describing "some decided improvement in my hands," he continued: "I now look forward to the future more hopefully. Nevertheless, if you can get on for the present without my help, it will be a great assistance to me, and will greatly increase the chances of my being able before very long to return to work and to help you as before." And he went on to emphasize the impossibility of his giving her, for the present, financial aid. In his anxiety, Rossetti got Watts to keep an eye on Fanny, as well as on his letters, which were again mysteriously disappearing. The effect of all this upon Fanny was startling. Angered by Gabriel's defection, by the removal of the keys of Tudor House from her care, by the insistent demands of her landlord for two quarters' rent which Rossetti was unable to supply, and by the opposition towards herself she suspected in the Rossetti family, as well as amongst Gabriel's own friends, she suddenly decamped to an unknown destination, sending Rossetti at the same time an illiterate and reproachful letter of farewell.

The result was an agitated reply from Rossetti, in which he surveyed some of the difficulties in which he was now involved. "Your letter," he wrote, "has upset me extremely, and is a great discouragement to me. To be uncertain of your whereabouts and well-being is greatly to add to my anxieties. I did think that, while I was living on borrowed money, you might have managed to draw on your own resources, as you have sometimes done before; particularly as I told you that I had now some real hopes of improvement. Added to this, I had understood from you that what Mr. Schott [Fanny's lodger], paid you was near meeting the rent of your house. It is very painful to me to be kept in ignorance of your plans and of where you are gone to and how situated. If I return to Chelsea I shall be just as much in want of your help as before—perhaps more so. I do not think that, in case I am able to work as I now hope, it would do to live with my mother and sister. My ways are not theirs, and they would get anxious and uneasy If you had told me that you meant to take such a step as leaving your house at once, I would much rather have sent you money, difficult as it is for me to do so at this moment. Dunn has chosen the present time to begin talking about his arrears of salary. Of course I cannot be paying him anything now. He has gone out of town so that my discomfort on returning will be greatly increased if I am quite alone in the house. I know what you say of your willingness to give me all is perfectly true, for you have sometimes proved it; but it will not do to desert me and leave me in utter solitude."

Rossetti's letters, indeed, reveal Fanny in a better light than the almost inevitably prejudiced accounts of her given by Gabriel's friends and relatives would lead us to expect. His belief that she had made sacrifices for him must have been based upon definite knowledge, he had certainly claimed her almost as his property for many, and her best, years, obviously liked her companionship, preferred her company to any other available person's, and that a real affection existed between this strange couple is evident from their correspondence. Fanny was, in short, the only woman Gabriel knew with whom he could *live* in any sort of comfort. One reason was that his relations with the two women he respected, idolized and idealized were impossibly sentimental for a life in common with its commonplace demands, while his relation to Fanny was essentially real; another is that their free relationship kept Fanny's feminine possessiveness within bounds. Rossetti could never be anyone's property, and marriage to Fanny (or probably to any other person) would have quickly ended in separation.

Their present crisis no doubt chiefly depended upon the fact that Fanny now had a lodger in her house in Royal Avenue, a Mr. Schott, said to be the son of a bandmaster in the Grenadier Guards. He had been divorced, and was now a widower with two children. Our first knowledge of Mr. Schott's existence is a note of Rossetti's, undated, but probably written early in this year, 1877, inviting him to call and see the *Venus Astarte*. Soon Schott had been pressed into Gabriel's service, like so many others, and was running errands for him, trying to find purchasers for his pictures, even secretly obtaining from chemists in Oxford Street and Bond Street the large quantities of chloral which Gabriel feared would be refused to himself if he went in person to ask for them. Schott also acted as Fanny's ambassador when she was ill or coy, and Rossetti was glad to see him so as to have news of her. But whatever the temporary convenience, the presence of Schott was a disturbing influence between Gabriel and Fanny, who soon gained Schott's allegiance to such an extent that two years later she became his wife. Schott, when strategy demanded, could now be played off against Rossetti, and but for the knowledge that she had Schott to fall back upon, it is unlikely that Fanny would now have played her trump card by running away.

It was, at any rate, effective. Rossetti, alarmed, sent his

henchmen Watts and Dunn in pursuit of her. It was almost as in the old days with Lizzie! At length Dunn ran her to earth in "The Rose Tavern," 96 Jermyn Street, where Fanny was already installed, apparently as part-proprietress since some of the contents of the "Elephant's Hoard" seem to have been invested in it, a first step towards the later marriage with Schott the proprietor.

Already Fanny boasted in true Moll Flanders style of having "three servants and an accountant." From the sanctuary of the Rose Tavern, she now complained to Gabriel, in a voluble epistle, of her wrongs. "You surely cannot be angry with me for doing what I have done," she wrote, "after receving [sic] such a letter from you telling me I must forget you and get my own living, you could not expect me to remain in the neighbourhood after what had tak [sic] place." Not satisfied with working upon Gabriel, the Rossetti family seem to have taken advantage of his illness and absence to attempt at Cheyne Walk to break the connection with Fanny. Dunn, she complained, had passed her house, sneering, "rejoicing at my downfall." As for Gabriel himself, "your letters led me to suppose you were tired of me, you shall never say that I forsook you although I felt it very much when another woman was put in my place when not wanted the key taken away from me and that is the way I was treated for taking your part. I hope I shall see you soon again and be with you as before but I never wish to meet any of your friends after the cruel way in which I have been treated." And referring to the romance of the Rose Tavern with its "three servants and an accountant," ("and Mr. Schott interests himself for me"), she declared: "It is better than a lodging house where I should often be cheated out of the rent and get people I did not like. I must impress your mind that I have *none of your* pictures in any part of the house excepting my bedroom and private sittingroom." "I took this step," she said, "thinking I should never be with you again and thought it a certainty." "Your aff. Fanny," as she signed herself, certainly made out a strong case.

Gabriel meanwhile, oscillated between the advisability of seizing so good an opportunity to get a superannuated "stunner" off his hands and the equally selfish fear of having no one to

run Tudor House on his return. "The matter," he had told
Watts when sending him in pursuit of the errant Fanny, "may
prove an annoyance on my return to London." But by this
time he had begun to feel that the convenience of ridding
himself of responsibility for Fanny was perhaps greater than
any drawback, and his reply to her letter reflected this change.
"If," he wrote, "you have embarked *all* your savings in this
venture, it would indeed be a serious responsibility for me to
interfere in any way with the course you have taken. How you
have managed the matter I cannot understand. At any rate I
am truly thankful to know that you have secured such real
friends as Mr. Schott and his family have proved themselves
to be. I am very anxious about the house in Cheyne Walk. . . ."
And after detailing these domestic anxieties he concluded with
obvious relief: "When I see you we can speak further of our
affairs. I judge you are comfortable in your present arrangement, so that I have no need for anxiety on that score at
present. You will perceive by the writing of this letter that I
am improving in the use of my hands. Indeed I now look forward much more hopefully as regards work and income." If
Fanny (the woman who, when her days as a "stunner" were
over, had guarded Tudor House, sometimes for months, even
years, alone), hoped to extract from Rossetti some sign of
jealousy, of unhappiness in separation, she had dismally failed.
Evidently Fanny was not the inspiration of the recent poems
of sorrow in severance that Gabriel was writing and would yet
write.

Christina, too, shared the weariness of spirit experienced by
Gabriel as she wandered about the autumn garden at Hunter's
Forestall in a mood of saddened resignation to her own frustrated existence, a mood which now found expression in her
verses *An October Garden*: —

> In my autumn garden I was fain
>   To mourn among my scattered roses;
>   Alas for that last rosebud which uncloses
> To Autumn's languid sun and rain
>   When all the world is on the wane . . .

So the time passed, drearily, with Gabriel again a victim to
insomnia, so that even his guardians, to give him sleep, were

forced to allow large doses of the drug once more. "God help us," sighed Christina. "In general health he is wonderfully recovered, but this sleeplessness saps hope and spirits."

Weary of Hunter's Forestall, but afraid as ever to return to the solitude of his home, Gabriel still lingered, would have accepted his mother's and sister's offer to come and live with him in Cheyne Walk, but, as he told Watts: "I have some misgivings as to whether my habits as regards exercise, etc., might not scare them; and then there is the difficulty of Fanny, who, although she need not of course be always there, is at times almost necessary to me. Still, as I should of course give them the drawing-room—indeed the whole first floor—entirely to themselves, it might not perhaps present difficulty. Have you," he added, "any news of Fanny?" Later, upon receiving Watts's reply, Gabriel continued the theme: "The situation is in every way a perplexing one, as regards the points referred to in your last letter. Utter solitude, if I return to such in London, may be well nigh fatal: and F(anny)'s society mitigates it only in a slight degree, even if still to be reckoned on. Besides, if it should chance that she has really embarked on something of an advantageous kind, it would indeed be a serious responsibility for me to break it up, considering the uncertainty of my own prospects of permanently assisting her." Even the arrival of "a cheerful letter from Fanny," as he described it, did not change his belief that Fanny should not lightly abandon her new way of life.

As November approached, there came rain and omens of winter, despite days "still divinely sunny and enjoyable." "Tin," he groaned, "just upon run out here." But above all other incentives to return to Town was the impending departure of Janey for Italy on November 15th. "I don't want to miss seeing her," Gabriel told Watts. So, after a month's indecision and delay, he at last prepared to leave. He invited Brown to come again, because, as he naïvely told Watts, he "would be very useful in packing." But Brown, angry at Gabriel's opposition to his attempts to cut down the choral, refused; "assuming," Rossetti complained, "a tone of dictation as regards the endless chloral question. These people," he added, with rising indignation, "seem really to think that they have some control over my actions. The reduction in the drug has been very great, sometimes amounting to less than a third of what I started with here, but when at work again, more sleep than I get here must be secured again, or work will be impossible. The fact is," he told Brown, summing up his tragic dilemma, "that any man in my case must either do as I do, or cease from necessary occupation, which cannot be pursued in the day when the night is stripped of its rest."

Again and again during October Gabriel made plans for return, only to abandon them when the moment for action arrived, just as when in past years he remained inert, in the grip of the lethargy that at times beset him. It was only the impending departure of Janey that at last roused him, in the first days of November, to put his plans for return into effect. "I suppose," he told Watts, on November 2nd, "on the whole I must stay here till Wednesday next, though much averse to doing so, being quite worn out with the place at last. . . . Later than Wednesday next I could not well be staying, as it might put it out of my power to see Mrs. M. before her leaving for Italy."

So, on November 9th, as a wintry afternoon faded into twilight, Gabriel re-entered the gloomy portals of No. 16 Cheyne Walk. . . . But a day or two before his arrival he had written to Watts: "If you do find the latchkey in the handkerchief drawer, I should like it to be sent to Fanny if you can do so without inconvenience, as I know she has none." Habit and necessity are often stronger ties than "love," and the public house in Jermyn Street, even the egregrious Schott, were not to disrupt the ménage in Cheyne Walk.

III

CHEYNE WALK AGAIN
1877–1879

> . . . when flown
> All joys, and through dark forest-boughs in flight
> The wind swoops onward brandishing the light,
> Even yet the rose tree's verdure left alone
> Will flush all ruddy though the rose be gone;
> With ditties and with dirges infinite.
>
> *Ardour and Memory* D. G. ROSSETTI

UPON HIS RETURN to Chelsea, Gabriel withdrew ever farther into his own dreary world of silence, obscurity and solitude. Even the few friends remaining to him were yet further reduced in number. Patmore's attempts, after long withdrawal, to resume relations, Gabriel had rejected two years before. George Hake he had recently dismissed after a quarrel. Howell, too, he had banished, in annoyance, upon discovering himself to be the victim of that sharp dealing which, when practised upon others, had merely amused him. But Rossetti's indignation, even in this, was not moral. He was too fond of a "clever" deal himself, for that. "It is commonsense," he said of Howell's gross overcharges for models' dresses bought on Rossetti's behalf, when he discovered the fraud, "but why not tell the truth about it?" And even after Howell's banishment, Gabriel found excuses and a good word for him. Nor was Rossetti himself blameless in regard to the incidents which caused Howell's dismissal. "Weary," he described himself, of being pestered by people to whom Howell as Rossetti's agent had promised his paintings. Yet they had made Gabriel payments in advance, only to find that it was impossible to extract from him the promised work. And these were commissions which Gabriel had authorized Howell to accept. Most probably the chief though perhaps unconscious reason for Howell's dismissal was that Watts, having proved more useful in many ways than Howell, had made Gabriel's former agent supererogatory, and in his momentary annoyance, Rossetti conveniently got rid of him.

Swinburne, too, despite William Rossetti's continued assur-

ance of his brother's esteem for him, was still avoided by Gabriel.
The hot-tempered little poet's affection for Rossetti now turned
to bitterness, and he ironically contrasted his own stoicism
with Rossetti's fears of "a public conspiracy against his name—
a confederacy of enemies on the staff of the leading journals—
to swamp and stifle all mention of it anywhere." Even William,
since his marriage, seldom visited Cheyne Walk. Gabriel does
not appear to have "taken to" his brother's wife, and this was
probably the chief cause of William's aloofness, from this
time. Brown too, annoyed by Gabriel's quarrel with him at
Hunter's Forestall, kept away for the next two years, and the
appearances in Cheyne Walk of old Mrs. Rossetti and the ailing
Christina were inevitably rare. Henceforth Watts and Shields
(again resident in London) were almost the sole regular visitors
until near the close of Rossetti's life. Not even his art-assistant
Dunn remained, for Dunn, vainly demanding his arrears of
salary, now went away for long spells of painting, heedless of
Gabriel's peremptory orders to return, and retorting that as
Rossetti could not afford to pay him, he must obtain money by
painting for himself.

Amidst all these trials the indefatigable, ever patient, ever
resourceful Watts remained Gabriel's surest shield and stay.
Day and night Watts combined the functions of faithful steward,
sick nurse and literary friend. To run errands, pay bills, put
off duns, sell pictures, give legal or other advice, smooth away
difficulties, soothe sleepless nights with anecdotes, readings,
conversations, sonneteerings, all came with equal facility and
felicity to Watts. For Watts, who was now less accommodating
to Fanny, Gabriel now sometimes put off "the Elephant," who
was again much in evidence at Cheyne Walk.

Above all other trials, however, was the increasing inacces-
sibility of Janey. Her absence must have darkened still further
for Gabriel that already dark winter of 1877–8. A few weeks
after his return from Hunter's Forestall, a new chloral crisis
developed, during which he lost all self-control. On Christmas
Day he begged his mother and Christina to come and dine
with him, vowing that he would view their refusal as ";a bad
omen for the coming year." Since his return to London he
limited his walks to his own garden save for an occasional visit

to his mother. A "good deal drearying lately," he described himself in the Spring, and he even dreamed of visiting Italy if he could find a congenial companion.

Janey was still in Italy. Whatever the reason, Janey was certainly more elusive than of old. Almost on the day that Rossetti had set out for Herne Bay, Morris had written to her at Kelmscott, promising to come to her there on the following day, and that the Joneses would join them a day or two later. There was more social life at Kelmscott now, apparently, than in Rossetti's time, and Morris went there oftener than before. And now, for the sake of Janey's health, it was said, she must remain with her daughters in the Italian Riviera, in a charming corner on the Corniche Road, near to her friends Mr. and Mrs. George Howard (later Lord and Lady Carlisle), and in the spring Morris, despite his dislike of Italy, would join his wife and children at Oneglia. But with the summer of 1878, Janey was back again at Kelmscott, while her husband, momentarily detained in town, was writing to her: "I confess I sigh for Kelmscott."

Gabriel, who had awaited that summer "with apprehension," declaring "for several years it has been my worst season, but must hope for the best," was now in fact fairly well. Indeed from the time of his return from Hunter's Forestall until the autumn of 1881, he remained in Cheyne Walk, painting hard to stem the tide of debt threatening to overwhelm him. It was this unremitting toil, Meredith declared later, that fatally undermined his weak health and wrecked all hope of ultimate recovery. The need for energetic action was certainly great. Patrons, their patience finally exhausted after years of vain waiting for pictures on which they had advanced large sums, now fearing that as the painter's health declined his work would deteriorate or be abandoned, clamoured ever more insistently for the delivery of their commissions. At the same time new commissions ceased, and new patrons were shy of appearing as Rossetti's reputation for bilking them and exaggerated rumours about his illness spread.

Ever since his breakdown in 1872, he had particularly feared the harm that reports of his illness might do him, and in 1875, after declining an invitation to exhibit at the newly established

Grosvenor Gallery, he had seized the opportunity to deny, in a letter to *The Times*, that his refusal—which was in fact due to his ineradicable fear of criticism—was owing to ill-health. "I never painted," he declared, "so many pictures of the same size and study as within the last few years and up to this writing," and in a private letter to the secretary of the Gallery, after objecting to the admission of works by Royal Academicians, he declared, significantly, that the reason for his refusal to exhibit was "simply that life-long feeling of dissatisfaction which I have experienced from the disparity of aim and attainment in which I have all my life produced as best I could." Nevertheless in the spring of 1878, persuaded by the importance of the cause and perhaps also by the need of some personal advertisement in the dearth of commissions, he reluctantly allowed one of his *Proserpines* to be shown at Manchester in an exhibition to help the Art-Schools Building Fund.

Henceforth, to counteract rumours of declining powers, Rossetti lost no opportunity of asserting the continued and ever progressive quality of his art, especially as he believed his popularity was in decline. "My power of work," he had written to Shields from Hunter's Forestall, "is not essentially impaired at present I believe, but I must confess that enthusiasm no less than encouragement seems other than it was," and when Shields in reply suggested that chloral, by destroying Gabriel's passion for painting, was the real source of his dejection, Rossetti declared: "As to the eternal drug, my dear Shields, if I suffer at times from morbidity, it is also possible for others to take a morbid view of the question. I am quite certain that I have, as an artist should have, made solid progress in the merit of my work such as it is, and this chiefly within the last five years, during which I have supplied by application, some serious qualities which had always been deficient in practice, and produced, I will venture to say, at least a dozen works (among those covering the time) which are unquestionably the best I ever did. . . . To reduce the drug as far as possibility admits, is most desirable (at present it *is* reduced to less than a third of what I started with here); but if an opinion were to get abroad that my works were subject to derogatory influences which reduced their beauty and value, it would be most injurious to me and would in reality be founded on a foregone conclusion as to the necessary results of such a medicine, and not on anything really provable from the work itself. I find that I have written more than enough in a vein which I hope does not seem too egotistical."

No longer did Gabriel haughtily reject his patrons' demands. Reduced, before leaving Hunter's Forestall, to a bank balance of but £400, and with eyes, as he said, "fully open to the evanescent character of £400," he had been forced to resort to thinly disguised touting to sell his works, getting Watts to send his former patron Rae, *Water-Willow*, unsolicited, and marked down to three hundred guineas. He also advised Watts that Rae, being "a banker and a very nice old friend, might be the person to pawn pictures if that course is adopted." "I shall do my best to meet the emergency as far as in me lies," he wrote dolefully to Watts, "but alas! it seems to me that the world of patronage is crumbling so far as I am concerned." It was in this state, and with his landlord threatening distraint for arrears of rent, that Rossetti had returned to Cheyne Walk in the late autumn of 1877.

Continuing his painting, he had completed before the close of that year, under pressure from the impatient Fry, the *Venus Astarte* that Fry had commissioned. Fry's cheque for two thousand guineas, the greatest sum Rossetti ever obtained for a painting, though helpful, had failed to stem the flood of debts. That same autumn he had begun to paint the beautiful Mrs. Stillman as *A Vision of Fiammetta*, and now, a year later, was finishing it and beginning *Desdemona's Death Song*, which never made much progress, although he returned to it in the last summer of his life.

Soon he complained of being "bedevilled by Valpy," who in this autumn of 1878 became "Valpy the Vampyre, greatly grieved," said Gabriel, "by my commercial obliquities." And far from repaying the money he had given and then reborrowed from Janey, Gabriel could now no longer even pay the interest on it which he had formerly insisted upon doing. Yet on September 1st, 1878, he boasted to his mother: "I have £500 now in the bank, with other prospects: so at last things look a little better than usual." In fact, the "prospects" for artists at this time were far from encouraging. Trade was bad, money and commissions were consequently scarce. Anxiously watching the trend of business, so important for his once despised commercial patrons and hence for himself, not until the close of 1879 could Gabriel heave a sigh of relief over "a decided improvement in trade," and begin to hope for a share of the benefits it must bring. Shortly before this, indeed, when things were at their worst and banks on all sides crashing, he had so feared for his own slender store that, in the spirit of the Italian peasantry from which he sprang, he had regretted not having hidden his money in some safe corner at home.

Rossetti was also aware that taste in England was changing, and that the French Impressionism he hated was threatening the Preraphaelites' popularity. In the new Grosvenor Gallery to which he refused to contribute, old and new fashions in painting were hanging side by side. It was there that Ruskin first saw Whistler's impressionist sketch of fireworks at Cremorne Gardens, entitled *Nocturne in Black and Gold*, and stimulated by the contrast between old and new to renewed enthusiasm for the Preraphaelites, indulged in such violent criticism of Whistler's painting that, in November 1878, even a prejudiced jury was reluctantly forced to award damages to Whistler —contemptuously assessing them at a farthing. Gabriel, once the friend of both contestants, saw little in the famous trial beyond a "lark." Although scornful of "Impressionism," he was not without appreciation of Whistler's work, and was well disposed, during the trial, towards his witty and gallant American friend. "I must say he shone in the box," Rossetti admitted, "the fool of an Attorney-General was nowhere." But when the verdict was given, Gabriel (mischievously parodying Whistler's use of the words "arrangement" and "nocturne" as titles for his paintings, and with a disguised reference to Whistler's insolvency), merely declared: "Alas for Jimmy Whistler! What harbour of refuge now, unless he turn Fire-King at Cremorne? And Cremorne itself is no more![1] A *nocturne andante* in the direction of the Sandwich Islands, or some country where tattooing pure and simple is the natural School of Art can now only avert the long impending Arrangement in Black and White!"

[1] Cremorne Gardens were closed down in 1877.

In 1879, while Janey again sat to him, Rossetti began to develop in oils studies he had made of her in 1870, for *La Donna della Finestra—The Lady of the Window*, or as he also named it, *The Lady of Pity*. As was now his practice, he modified Janey's face to obtain the conventional "idealization" he desired. This *Lady of the Window* or *of Pity* was the young, beautiful and pitying lady of Dante's *Vita Nuova* who, finding the poet weeping for Beatrice his dead love—as Gabriel had wept for Lizzie —inspired in Dante a counterpart of his passion for Beatrice— such as Gabriel had described in his sonnet *The Love Moon*—so that he pondered: "perchance Love himself set her in my path, so that my life might find peace."[1] As usual, Gabriel at first thought this, as his latest painting, his best, and declared with renewed confidence: "It looks as if I were not dead yet." But towards the close of the year, as it neared completion, he came to value it only for Janey's sake, saying: "I had written it down a thing, but I won't because of the sitter, to whom I owe the best of my art such as it is."

Besides this and other paintings, including a *Mnemosyne* for Leyland, Rossetti had recourse increasingly to "replicas" (still chiefly, it is said, the work of Dunn), to raise money quickly. "Times are very bad," he complained, hoping that his *Lady of the Window* and another *Blessed Damozel* would "bring grist to the mill." Unable in June 1879 to pay his wine-merchant's bill, he plodded through the drudgery of two such "replicas": a *Dante's Dream* for Graham—"a dreary job," he said—a *Blessed Damozel* for Leyland, "not a triumph but good hap for all that." But in spite of his toil his income sank that year from the usual £3,000 of the last two or three years to a mere £1,030.

Debt and general demoralization had brought Rossetti far from the aims of the young idealistic painter Chiaro in *Hand and Soul*, were indeed bringing him to mere, unconscientious pot-boiling. His creative power was almost extinct, his work little more than inferior repetition of old themes, the reflection of a mind caught inescapably in the closed circle of his own past, instead of developing to maturity, a mind permanently imprisoned in the ideals and ideas of adolescence, amongst symbols once significant to him, even inspiring, but now, after

[1] *v. sup.* p. 403.

the years of disillusion, only pale, devitalized but haunting ghosts. For with the fading of his human and aesthetic ideals, Gabriel's respect for his art, for his work, even for himself, had died. *The Blessed Damozel*, once the symbol of his moralistic-erotic idealism, he now habitually referred to in the crude speech he defensively affected in these later years, as the "Blasted Damozel," or, more emphatically, as the "Bdy Dam"! That was the measure of his disillusion.

Towards the close of 1879, however, he began to work on a new theme, *Monna Primavera*, which he soon renamed *The Daydream*. It showed Janey sitting in the fork of the sycamore tree in his garden, with a book on her knee and a sprig of honeysuckle in her hand. Of all the portraits Gabriel had made of Janey he liked this best.

It was this sycamore tree of *The Daydream*, growing near his studio window, that Rossetti was painting one day late in 1879, when Mrs. Gilchrist and her son Herbert called to discuss plans for a second edition of Alexander Gilchrist's *Life of Blake*, in which Rossetti had been concerned at the time of its publication and of Gilchrist's death nearly twenty years before. Herbert Gilchrist, who had not met Rossetti before, was charmed by his "easy winning manner," by his interest in the projected edition, and in Herbert Gilchrist's own designs, as well as by his courtesy in showing his visitors *Dante's Dream*, which was in the studio, and in reading to them from the *Vita Nuova*—that symbol of Gabriel's secret adolescent dream which experience had not been able entirely to destroy. Young Gilchrist remarked the poet's "pleasant but unusual inflection, musical in its ascending lisp," as he read. That Gabriel was not invariably so kind to callers Herbert learned later, for he would tell an amusing story of how on one occasion Rossetti, hearing at the door an insistent stranger armed with an introduction, intervened at the moment when the servant was about to yield to the visitor's pressure, and leaning over the banister of the staircase called in his "firm, mellifluous voice: 'Tell the gentleman that I am not at home.'" Before the Gilchrists' departure, Rossetti presented Anne Gilchrist with signed photographs of eight of his paintings. . . . Such was he still to the outer world. "A splendid fellow," said Gilchrist, "of generous nature, . . . possessed of the fullness of manhood that we associate with the genius of Samuel Johnson, and I may add, with Walt Whitman."

Throughout these months, despite his usual background of petty cares and anxieties: the extension of the expiring lease of Tudor House, troubles with servants, forgeries of his drawings (apparently made and disseminated by Howell and Howell's artist-friend, Rosa Corder), forgeries against which Gabriel publicly protested in letters to *The Times* and *Athenaeum*, and the departure of Brown to decorate the Manchester Town Hall with frescoes, Rossetti's health had remained fairly good. But the autumn of 1879 witnessed a sad decline. "As ill as ever I was in my life," he told Watts in mid-October, "and really don't know how it may end." Christina, visiting him with her mother, found him "less depressed than I was prepared for. But," she exclaimed, "what a state his mouth is in, and his voice was wretched." At the close of the same month Rossetti described himself. "I am getting a little out of the dumps," he declared. "I was very low last time." At the end of November, when even his chemists (protesting against his twelve bottles of chloral every eight or nine days, and two bottles on the preceding day) refused to supply henceforth more than one bottle daily, Rossetti was able to say that except for a cold he was "pretty much in my usual state now."

Did any new emotional complication lie behind this new crisis of insomnia and chloral? Had it any relation to a sonnet he now wrote—and verses were very rare with him now—entitled *Pleasure and Memory*—renamed before publication *Ardour and Memory*? He sent it to a friend, the minor painter-poet Davies, describing it somewhat bitterly as a poem "written just now, and which I fear has by no means a special Xmas flavour." Did Gabriel feel as the sonnet suggests, deserted, abandoned? Was he, like the symbolical rose-tree of the sonnet, left without the rose, to sing only of the past? Had that long sojourn in Italy of Janey's with the Howards, and later with Morris, and again those weeks in August when she had been the Howards' guest at Naworth—had all these combined with Gabriel's increasing age and illness to loosen the ties between them? . . . "Danced with Mrs. Morris . . . and with her daughter

May," wrote Henry Holiday, the painter, on returning from the Joneses' Christmas dance at The Grange. Janey's health seemed better too. No longer was she forced as in 1873 to lie and watch the Joneses' Christmas festivities from her sofa. Now Gabriel was the invalid, excluded from participation in Christmas revels. "My dear Gabriel," Christina was writing about the time of this dance, "We are quite grieved to hear of your continuing ill and weak, and fear that the many dark days we have had of late must have tried you in more ways than one; but we are glad to hear of friends who chase away loneliness." . . . Was it the contrast between his own present existence and Janey's that gave such poignancy to the sonnet he wrote for this Christmas of 1879, especially to its last desolate cry:—

> . . . when flown
> All joys, and through dark forest-boughs in flight
> The wind swoops onward brandishing the light,
> Even yet the rose tree's verdure left alone
> Will flush all ruddy though the rose be gone;
> With ditties and with dirges infinite?

IV

INDIAN SUMMER
1879–1881

Within the branching shade of Reverie
Dreams even may spring till autumn.

The Day Dream D. G. ROSSETTI

BY THIS TIME, Rossetti, although but fifty-one years of age, had already entered the autumn of his short, uneasy life. That autumn, however, was now to be tempered by somewhat improved health into an Indian summer that smoothed his passage almost to the end. From the opening of 1880 until late in the following year, Gabriel, his brother declared, was "about as well in health and spirits as he had been at any ordinary time since the summer of 1874." And with better health came something of an intellectual and artistic revival. He was, said William, "as diligent in his art-work as he had ever been" and now "produced some of his very best poetical work." For William, like so many of his time, overrated the pseudo-balladry of Rossetti, and thought his long, last poems, *Rose Mary*, *The White Ship* and *The King's Tragedy* his greatest works in verse.

Certainly Rossetti now turned again to poetry, completing his ballad *The White Ship*, begun two years before, and writing a number of sonnets which unexpectedly reveal a critical, objective, almost academic attitude in place of the passionate self-expression of his earlier work. One reason was that now, though late, he was painfully acquiring a more "realistic" attitude to life. The "reality principle" he had so long evaded was now forcing itself upon him, destroying amidst pain and disillusion his myth, his dream:—"All my life I have dreamt one dream alone." Yet at times, even now, he would fly to his dream as to a refuge from the harsh world of reality, would cry as he now cried in his sonnet to his picture *The Day Dream*:

Within the branching shade of Reverie
Dreams even may spring till autumn.

And now the autumn of his life was closing in; winter he knew
was near. In his notebook he scribbled a couplet that voiced his
new sense of reality, and of the illusions that had so long
sustained him:

> . . . the garlands of heaven were all laid by,
> And the daylight sucked at the breast of a Lie.

Despite the change of mood, the old erotic symbols were too
ingrained to be cast aside.

Yet the sonnets he now wrote were, beneath their external
objectivity, largely an unconscious dramatization of Rossetti's
own internal struggle to accept with resignation the bleak picture presented by reality. To that resignation he could not
attain. Through these sonnets runs a quiet but intense despair
—despair of this newly-perceived reality, despair of a universe
and a humanity which destroys beauty—spiritual, physical,
visionary—without and within the individual, leaving only the
intolerable unintelligence and cruelty of the "real." It was the
despair of an essentially aesthetic temperament, such despair
as Ruskin had known in his Alpine solitude, and which many
another, soon after Rossetti, would also know and portray.

The symbol of this cosmic cruelty he now found in London
itself, the city he had so loved—and now also hated. The
London he now contemplated was the London of *Found*, the
long-abandoned "modern painting" to which, in this mood,
he next year returned; the mood also of his illustrative sonnet
to that painting. This mood inspired in January 1881 another
sonnet, *Cleopatra's Needle in London* (later renamed *Tiber, Nile
and Thames*), in which he described the city as it now appeared
to him in the light, or rather darkness, of his new and sombre
vision—

> A city of sweet speech scorned—on whose chill stone
> Keats withered, Coleridge pined, and Chatterton
> Breadless, with poison froze the God-fired breath.

It was thus that Rossetti amidst the final frustrations of his
life saw the romantic dreamers he loved at strife, like himself,
with a base, unintelligent, insensitive "reality" endlessly frus-
trating the finer elements in humanity, thwarting, finally
destroying them. As for the romantic poets whose lives so
vividly exemplified this, Gabriel's interest in them was largely

due to the fact that with somewhat better health he had turned
to assisting Mrs. Gilchrist with the new edition of her husband's
Blake, and also to helping Buxton Forman with his edition of
Keats's Letters. To do this he had turned again to the great
romantics, reading and re-reading and commenting upon
Blake, Keats, Chatterton, Coleridge and Shelley. Upon each
of these he also wrote a commemorative sonnet, and into these
ostensibly impersonal poems he breathed the bitterness of his
own spirit, contrasting Blake's fiery soul with his mean
environment, picturing Coleridge dreaming regretfully of

Heaven, lost through spider-trammelled prison-bars,

Keats,

Weary with labour spurned and love found vain.

And in the same mood he meditated upon the unhappy destinies of Shelley and Chatterton. In all he found symbols of
himself, in their lives a counterpart of his own experience—the
decay of early ideals, of a romantic faith, a physical and moral
decline, the vain questioning of inevitable death. It was this
same mood that inspired his remaining sonnets of 1880, which
were suggested by pictures—Botticelli's *Spring*, Michelangelo's
Holy Family, his own *Day Dream*. The exquisite beauty of that
Italian spring which had once inspired Botticelli winter had
quickly destroyed; the joyous innocence of Michelangelo's
Christ-child had long since perished amidst age and death.

The apparent impersonality, the almost academic quality of
these sources of inspiration were no doubt partly due to the
increasing isolation and emptiness of Rossetti's life, and also to
the almost nightly discussions on literature with Watts during
the long hours when sleep refused to come to him, and he and
Watts beguiled the time by writing sonnets or talking of art
and letters. Watts, indeed, through Rossetti's influence, was
now blossoming into a recognized literary critic and bad but
much-appreciated sonneteer. Rossetti, glad of anything that
mitigated his loneliness and boredom, was also writing long
letters on similar literary matters to a young, astute and
ambitious youth in Liverpool, a builder's clerk named Hall
Caine, who had introduced himself to Rossetti's notice, by
letter, as an admirer, and now obtained poems and advice

from Gabriel, for an anthology of sonnets that he wished to publish. The influence of these, and other, chiefly youthful, poetic admirers, encouraged Rossetti's present interest in sonneteering, of which, however, Gabriel revealed another, darker side when in January 1881 he told Christina: "With me, sonnets mean insomnia."

By this time, the sonnet revival which Rossetti had largely inspired was in full career, and sonnet anthologies were rapidly appearing and becoming the order of the day. An article on *The Sonnet in England*, in *The Contemporary Review*, the very journal which had published Buchanan's attack, now recognized Rossetti as an eminent sonneteer, and Gabriel, particularly pleased, interpreted this as both a retraction of the past offence and the homage of a new generation. Having read the essay, he debated in letters to Caine, with rare, almost academic detachment, the evolution of the English sonnet from the time of Shakespeare to his own day, and it was to Caine he sent in February 1880—despite his own denunciation eleven years before of such poems as "intellectually incestuous —poetry seeking to beget its emotional offspring on its own identity"—the sonnet on The Sonnet, just written, to accompany a design on the same subject, both intended as a present for his mother on her forthcoming eightieth birthday. It was to be inserted in her copy of a recently published sonnet anthology compiled by a Glasgow bookseller, David Main. Later it became the introductory sonnet to *The House of Life*. Similarly, now, in another sonnet of *The House of Life*, entitled *The Song Throe*, he insisted that the sonnet should be essentially self-expression:

> By thine own tears thy song must tears beget . . .

"Fundamental brain-work," he also told Caine, "that is what makes the difference in all art. A Shakespeare sonnet is better than the most perfect in form because Shakespeare wrote it."

If material circumstances could have lightened Rossetti's discontent, he should have found much by this time to counteract his despondency. Since his *Poems* first appeared, ten years before, a new generation of poets and their supporters, the new "aesthetic school," had arisen, and these, rightly recognizing in Rossetti's intoxication with beauty and revolt against mid-Victorian Philistinism one source of their own movement, hailed him as leader or pioneer. Thus it was that to Rossetti, these young poets and writers, Pater, Wilde, Richard Garnett, O'Shaughnessy, Marzials, Gosse, John Payne, P. B. Marston and the rest paid ready homage. Young critics, too, were appreciative. Mrs. Meynell (who never saw Rossetti) pleased him by an article in *The Pen*; another critic won his approval with an appreciation in *Temple Bar*. Humbler admirers also appeared, including Ruskin's two protégés, Thomas Dixon, the cork-cutter of Sunderland, and Joseph Skipsey, the collier-poet whom Gabriel thought "a man of real genius." These two, now visiting London and being received by various celebrities, dined with Rossetti one evening in Cheyne Walk. Poor Dixon, on his return to Sunderland, "exhausted," wrote his biographer, "by the excitement and exaltation" of his recent experiences, collapsed and died, almost in the manner of Tennyson's too modest heroine in *The Lord of Burleigh*. "I feel truly concerned," replied the gentle Christina on receiving from the shocked Gabriel the news of Dixon's death, "though," she added, with pious but chastened optimism, "I earnestly hope he is the gainer."

Rossetti's popularity with the new "aesthetes" was not without its unconscious irony, for their movement, at least in its more extreme forms, he heartily disliked. Decidedly Francophobe from youth, he disliked the French influences largely inspiring English aestheticism, and ironically likened Flaubert and "the latest French Muse" to Nero. When in 1881 —long, of course, before opprobrium, or even, apparently, cause for opprobrium, had gathered about Wilde's name—he received from its author Wilde's first volume of poems, expressing (in *The Garden of Eros*) enthusiastic homage to himself, he was not only indifferent, but, bitterly resenting the association of his name with that of the leader of the aesthetes, he refrained from even meeting his admirer, and actually remonstrated with Jones, who was Wilde's friend, for supporting so prominent a figure in the aesthetic movement. Nor was Rossetti attracted to the leading aesthetic prose-writer, Pater, who, like Wilde, admired and admitted his indebtedness to Rossetti. "The most significant as well as the most fascinating of contemporaries," was Pater's description of Gabriel; "the greatest man we have among us, in point of influence upon poetry and perhaps painting." But Rossetti, meeting Pater, sensing his remoteness so different from his own remoteness, detecting his repressed, coldly contemplative spirit, "disliked him extremely" if we may trust Watts.

Whatever Rossetti's dislike of these admirers, they were not mistaken in recognizing him as the chief English source of their movement, in acclaiming him as of a mood kindred to their own. Even Swinburne, in October 1866, writing his political *Song of Italy*, in ecstatic adoration of Mazzini, and consequently in momentary revolt against "poetry for poetry's sake," had detected the essentially "aesthetic" attitude of Rossetti. "It is nice," he told Howell, "to have something to love and believe in as I do in Italy. It was only Gabriel and his followers in art (*l'art pour l'art*) who for a time frightened me from speaking out." Rossetti's spirit indeed, although he failed to perceive the fact, was identical with the aesthetic quality which, as one critic, Burdett, has remarked, ultimately revealed itself in the "aesthetic movement," the spirit of one who, having lost all convictions, can assert only the right of the ego, the sole remaining entity, to develop untrammelled by convention or tradition, can affirm only a personal, isolated individualism, and shows a tendency amidst the frustration of disappointed idealism, to relapse from exhaustion into self-destruction or into the arms of a paternal church. It was, indeed, in a momentary revolt against this same innate egoism that Rossetti had long since exhorted himself, in his private note-book,

> Than that beyond thy real self dost see
> A self ideal, bid thy heart beware.[1]

Upon Wilde's verse, certainly, the influence of Rossetti was real enough, and there is some truth in the assertion of one of Wilde's biographers, that the success of his volume of poems was largely due to the fact that "people who had heard of Rossetti and Swinburne but never read them, were able to recover their self-respect by purchasing Wilde."

From *Rossetti's* "Preraphaelitism," that is, from Gabriel and the little band of followers, Jones, Morris, Swinburne and the

---

[1] D. G. R.'s versified form of his self-exhortation in prose, quoted *sup.* p. 349.

PLATE XVI

DANTE GABRIEL ROSSETTI
1863

CHRISTINA ROSSETTI AND HER MOTHER
BY D. G. ROSSETTI
1877

PLATE XVII

110 HALLAM STREET,
PORTLAND PLACE

TUDOR HOUSE,
16 CHEYNE WALK, CHELSEA

rest whom he had drawn round him at Oxford in 1857, "aestheticism" had grown almost as from the seed the flower. Jealous, disappointed Holman Hunt watched this poisonous blossoming, as it seemed to him, with increasing dismay; this last strange metamorphosis of *his* "Preraphaelitism" into the very Satanic opposite of his own original Preraphaelite theory, and blamed Rossetti. That "Preraphaelitism" should be confused with "aestheticism," with the "utter School," "unutterably utter," the target of Gilbert's wit in *Patience*, that Rossetti's "mediaevalism" should also be confused with Preraphaelitism and similarly acclaimed, these things were henceforth amongst Hunt's bitterest sorrows. As for Rossetti, he had long recognized that "Preraphaelite theory" had been little more than Ruskin's invention, and that in Hunt's sense of the term he himself had never been a "Preraphaelite" at all. "What you call the movement," he now told Caine, "was serious enough, but the banding together under the title was all a joke. We had at that time a phenomenal antipathy to the Academy, and in sheer love of being outlawed signed our pictures with the well-known initials"; and, to Hunt's renewed indignation, he dismissed Preraphaelitism as "the mere affectation of a parcel of boys."

To the impartial observer, certainly, the future was now with "aestheticism"—so far at least as such a movement could have any future—not with Preraphaelitism, which, challenged by newer developments in both painting and poetry, was already in decay. For as their original hopes and ideals faded amidst the disenchantment of "reality," others of the Preraphaelites had fallen, like Gabriel himself, in varying degrees through disillusion into exhaustion. But the effects of this had widely varied with the individuals. Disillusion had drawn both Ruskin and Morris to active political idealism; Swinburne, incurably aesthetic despite his momentary revolts, had now sunk into futility, lamented his weariness of life, even of poetry, complaining that now verse itself was only "better than nothingness, or at least seeming better than nothingness," until the heroic Watts, yielding to the entreaties of Swinburne's mother, had descended upon him in 1879, and— to the amazement of the Town, for since the Rape of the

Sabines there had been nothing like it—triumphantly borne the excitable poet away from his follies to the peace of his own suburban, bachelor dwelling—specially taken for that purpose —there to linger, "the prisoner of Putney," a shadow of a shade, devoted to the reading of the Elizabethan dramatists and the occasional writing of a "poem" from which all inspiration had fled. So for the next thirty years the once rebellious poet lived, guarded by Watts-Dunton and gaining an increasing reputation for respectability, criticism and poetry, until, as the *doyen* of English writers, he died, in his seventy-third year, amidst nation-wide lamentation. Thus, to these late romantics, as to their greater predecessors, revolt against an uncomprehending or antagonistic environment brought its almost inevitable consequence of frustration, unhappiness and decline.

This same mood of scepticism and disillusion increasingly affected Rossetti's attitude to painting; an attitude also promoted by the fact that under the increasing burden of his debts he came more and more to regard his art from a commercial rather than a purely aesthetic point of view. His former contempt for mere technique had now, after years of often futile, even angry attempts to overcome technical difficulties, given place, at least in some moods, to an over-emphasis upon method beyond that which the once despised Reynolds would have endorsed, and a corresponding depreciation of the value of that "inspiration" or "genius" in which he had once (and those were his greatest days as a painter), so largely trusted. He now boasted that he taught Shields the use of colour by rules as definite as those of arithmetic and which anyone could learn. In painting, he now asserted, there was little originality save in "fundamental conception." The rest, he said, was chiefly "something of the craft of a superior carpenter, and the part of a picture that is not mechanical is often trivial enough." In this belief, he now derided the common, crudely romantic conception of a painter as one who comes "in a fine frenzy every morning to daub canvas." As he wrote to Caine when discussing the sonnet: "Conception, my boy, *fundamental brain-work*—that is what makes the difference in all art." Probably his over-emphasis of the formal, technical elements in art at this time, was not merely to counteract his neglect of them in earlier years, but also to reconcile himself to an uneasy consciousness that despite some improvement in technique, *something*, what he used to call "inspiration," was now largely absent from his work.

Anxiously complaining of low funds and few commissions, he plodded on at *The Day Dream* throughout the winter of 1879–80, nor did he desist, although hampered by a recurrence of his eye-weakness, until in the summer the picture was finished. Throughout these months Janey, his model for the work, was again a constant visitor at Cheyne Walk, and as Rossetti now avoided Morris, the ever useful Watts frequently arranged matters when Janey's silence or absence alarmed Gabriel, or the quarterly interest on the borrowed money (now apparently resumed), was to be paid to her.

In August, upon the completion of *The Day Dream*, Janey joined a family boating party on the Thames. Christina was thrilled at Janey's daring. "I might also gasp a moment," she wrote, "at the vision of beautiful Mrs. Morris with her family boating on the river Thames for a week; not only (I trust) with a cabin, but, I surmise, needing one." Shortly before, on seeing *The Day Dream* near completion, Christina had found Janey's portrait in it "so beautiful . . . that she fully sufficed me." Soon, to the relief of Gabriel who feared that no purchaser might appear, Constantine Ionides, a Greek acquaintance, bought it for £735. But Rossetti remarked with dismay that this, his favourite among all his paintings of Janey, had brought him considerably less than Graham's payments of £840 for *La Ghirlandata*, £1,102 for *Beata Beatrix*, and £1,207 for *The Blessed Damozel*. But, as he complained to Watts in the spring, both Graham and Leyland were "getting rather vicious" about their unfinished commissions, and from that quarter, for the present at least, nothing was to be expected. To placate Leyland, Gabriel turned, as soon as *The Day Dream* was finished, to resume work on *La Pia*, commissioned and doubtless partly paid for at least twelve years before. "Very fine and perfect," he proudly described it to his mother, when completed, shortly before the close of the year.

By this time, however, Rossetti's health was again showing signs of deterioration. The summer of 1880 had been the most solitary he had ever known. Seldom since his return from Hunter's Forestall, three years before, had he ventured beyond the confines of his house and garden, except for a very occasional almost furtive nocturnal visit to his mother and sister in Torrington Square. Now hardly one of his few remaining friends was accessible. Brown was in Manchester, William on holiday, Shields, for his health's sake in what Gabriel called "Hell's Aberdeen"; even the loyal Watts, now bound to Swinburne, was less available than before. No doubt some of Rossetti's undated, numerous appeals to "the Elephant" to come to him are of this time, for Fanny, despite her previous anger when leaving Rossetti, seems to have quickly resumed her old attendance on him in Cheyne Walk, almost as if Mr. Schott, whom she had married in 1879, did not exist. And of the few old friends who still visited Gabriel, one of the chief and oldest, Scott, was now at heart unfriendly. "Rossetti," wrote the jealous Scott, referring in his *Autobiographical Notes* to these years, and exaggerating both Rossetti's actual isolation and dependence upon him, "Rossetti had been the last of a succession of men I had loved and tried to make love me; for each of them I could have given all but life, and I was again defeated by destiny. Equal candour and confidence he never had to give, but now his singular manias made ordinary friendly intercourse impossible to him. After having been both his banker and nurse I could not depend upon him either in action or word. Still I remained faithful to the old tie, and Miss Boyd agreed in doing so also. We continued our occasional visits, either morning or evening, the only two of all his old circle."

William Rossetti, in his *Memoir* of his brother, spoke of his own weekly visits to Cheyne Walk, from the autumn of 1879 to that of 1881, and of a timetable by which friends so arranged their calls on Rossetti that he should never or seldom be alone. But Rossetti's own endless complaints of solitude during these last years, as well as his constant appeals to Watts and Shields, now almost his sole regular visitors, largely belie William's account. Amidst this isolation, Rossetti, bitterly resenting the disappearance of his former friends, endeavoured to attain indifference. "If an isolated life has any sting," he scribbled in his note-book, "it is felt in the absence of those friends who made for years unheeded avowals of obligation and gratitude. Still, this will come, in time, to pass and be forgotten, if not emphasized by momentary visits once or twice a year. Life is a coin which we once shared together, but which has now quite passed from my pocket into yours—doubtless rightly enough. Only I desire no half-farthing of its small change."

Solitude, over-work, lack of exercise again intensified Gabriel's insomnia as the autumn of 1880 passed, and throughout the following winter, spring and summer his mental health steadily declined. Jones, calling on him at Mrs. Rossetti's and Christina's request, found him greatly changed. "Change— enough for us all if it had been distributed amongst us, amongst any seven of us," Jones told the anxious Norton. "He has given it all up, and will try no more, nor cares how much it all goes. It's nine years since he came to The Grange—now he goes nowhere and will scarcely see anyone. Four or five times a year I go to spend a ghostly evening with him and come back heavy-hearted always, sometimes worse than that—it's all past hope or remedy, I think, and his best work has been done—and I don't know how it has all come about." Neither indeed did Gabriel, as during this very visit he remarked with secret pleasure that Jones, though five years his junior, was as bald as himself. Yet according to William, Rossetti was never in fact noticeably bald.[1]

As the year 1880 neared its end, Gabriel's depression deepened. Old patrons were ceasing to buy, new ones did not appear, and he was living beyond his income. "The discouragements of the year," he told his mother, "have only increased to its close. I will not despair however of improved times: it would not be the first occasion when something unexpected has brightened matters for me." Even depression could not entirely destroy the considerable Micawber element in his disposition. Nor, he reflected, were "worldly fortunes everything." Besides, he continued, his "bad luck" was not unique. "I should not forget that the times are bad for all, and that I am no absolute exception." "I see the usual friends and jog along," he told Davies in December. "My work is certainly no worse as days follow each other. That at least I can see and that at least

[1] But *cf. sup.* p. 353.

is satisfactory." In another note-book jotting he gloomily pondered the grey lethargy of his now almost mechanical existence. "As in a tract of lifeless land, the scattered pools of rain-water that for a moment catch the sky as the traveller passes, so are the far apart intervals of living labour in the life of an idle man. After death, if these intervals be worthy, will all be sky-brimmed water, or all a desert of sand?"

Yet even now, the old, stimulating illusions, though intellectually rejected, retained much of their emotional power over him. His response to the conception of ideal love, still active, now revealed itself in the enthusiasm with which at this time he almost nightly declaimed the *Marriage Song* in Stopford Brooke's recently published sentimental little lyrical "love drama," *Riquet of the Tuft*:

> Deep falls the dark, I cannot sleep, mine eyes
>   Are filled with night:
> Tell me, my maidens, in the eastern skies,
>   Is there no light?
> Cry to the moon to sink her lingering horn
> In the dim seas, and let the day be born
>   When love and I,
>   All ecstasy,
> Shall see him coming through the gates of morn.
>
> Bid him bring rosemary that ever keeps
>   Remembrance true:
> And myrtles gathered where warm Venus sleeps
>   In fragrant dew;
> And marigolds that wed the burning sun
> And close to tell desire the day is done;
>   And full blown roses,
>   Passion's posies,
> To deck the room where we shall be at one.
>
> Scatter the flowers, uplift the hymn, he comes;
>   O Paradise!
> Before him sound the pipes and merry drums,
>   And in his eyes
> The morning breaks, and elfin queens above
> Stoop to his smile, and hear, like me, the dove
>   Brood in his voice
>   And sing—"Rejoice,
> Come forth, my bride."—"I come, I come, my Love."

"It is," Rossetti declared, "one of the most beautiful lyrics I have read. Every night I repeat it to myself." So, to the end, Gabriel's imagination turned his insomnia-haunted nights into the sleepless lover's ecstasy . . .

> Within the branching shade of Reverie
> Dreams even may spring till autumn!

Christmas Day 1880 was ominous of the future. Too ill to leave Cheyne Walk, and in weather too bad for his mother and Christina to come to him, he would have been entirely alone but for a call by William and Lucy. Although he told his mother a day or two later his "bodily health" was "fair enough," he admitted: "I am often unfit to see anyone."

Yet to the outer world on the rare occasions when it penetrated into his fastness, he still maintained much of the impressive, debonair appearance of the past. Young Gilchrist who now occasionally dined with him declared: "It has seldom been my good fortune to dine with a more genial man." He found Gabriel "poignant, individual, grand, grandiose even, but not cosmic or of Olympian grandeur." Gilchrist's description of the first of these dinners, or rather of the later hours of that evening, is intimate and graphic. "At twelve," he wrote, "Theodore Watts came in. He threaded his way past easels, lay figures, and substantial pictures of the Sibyls which rested as pendants upon easel stands. . . . Everything was of the easiest, and after a hasty snack of something upon a side-table the poet and future author of *Aylwin* joined us. Rossetti, without the least discourtesy, remained in a reclining position, with his legs twisted up upon his comfortable lounge-sofa—large enough to accommodate Mr. Watts at the end. Rossetti's nickname amongst some of his intimates at that time was 'The Sultan.' For, as a mutual friend explained, everyone flies at the least sign to work for Rossetti. And there seemed to be a suggestion of the oriental in his inimitable air of easy indolence, his small, finely shaped hands, his supple diction, colloquial yet dignified, and always expressive. No one smoked; the conversation was rapid." When Watts suggested that Chatterton was *difficile*, Rossetti warmly replied: "Well, I suppose he was proud;—poets are proud—'And kin to Milton through his Satan's pride.'"

Gilchrist never forgot the charm of those conversations, and long afterwards recalled Gabriel's amusement at the Old Water Colour Society's rejection of Jones's *Phyllis and Demophoön* on the score of nudity (an action which led Jones to resign his membership in disgust); the "sympathetic reservation" with which he spoke of Millais; his appreciation of Whistler; and the way Gabriel shuddered when Gilchrist described to him Blake's water-colour of "The Pope burning in Hell." Like Watts, Gilchrist noticed the extraordinary hold of the supernatural upon Rossetti's imagination. He remarked also that Gabriel spoke "with Blake-like intolerance, or rather depreciation, of the painter pure and simple—the executant— as a man who might be and usually was possessed of little brains." And like other acquaintances of Rossetti he noticed that "he allowed, perhaps, his personal liking and good nature distinctly to influence his written opinion of contemporaries."

Closely similar to Gilchrist's account of those evenings at Cheyne Walk were the memories of Comyns Carr, the critic who had first made Rossetti's acquaintance in 1873. "Those never-to-be-forgotten evenings that I passed in his company," Carr recalled long afterwards, "became at the time a sort of enchantment. His talk assuredly more inspiring than that of any man I have ever known; most inspiring certainly to a youth who had ambitions of his own, for, although intolerant of any utterance that was merely conventional, and quick to detect the smallest lack of sincerity, he was ever patient with the expression of any enthusiasm however crude, and was as ready to listen as to reply. I can see him now," said Carr, "as he used to lie coiled up on the sofa in his studio after dinner, and can hear the deep tones of his rich voice as he ranged widely over the fields of literature and art, always trenchant, always earnest, yet now and again slipping with sudden wit and humour into a lighter vein."

With amusement Carr noted Rossetti's idiosyncrasies, particularly his "pathetic helplessness" in carving at dinner. "He would lunge at a joint," said Carr, "as though it were a hostile foe [Carr's ear for tautology was not sensitive!], driving it from one end of the dish to the other till he got it securely cornered in its well of gravy, and then plunge his knife into it with something of deadly ferocity." At these dinners, Carr, listening to Rossetti as he talked "with rare eloquence" of the poets of the romantic revival, especially of Keats, fell completely under his spell. At other times, Gabriel would interest and amuse Carr by his comments upon painters, describing Albert Moore's work as "sublimated café painting," Leighton as an artist who could do almost anything and do it well but with manners that were indescribable, and asserting that since painting began there had never been a man more greatly endowed with the painter's power than Millais. Carr also recalled one afternoon when Virtue Tebbs called to take Rossetti to see a picture of Turner's which had aroused Tebbs' enthusiasm. "What is it called?" asked Rossetti. "Girls surprised while bathing," answered Tebbs. "Umph," said Rossetti. "Yes, I should think devilish surprised to see what Turner has made of them!"

But as Rossetti's health declined, Carr, like most of Gabriel's friends, was gradually discarded. "Little by little," wrote Carr, "the invitations, once so freely extended to me, slackened in their warmth of hospitality, until the day came when I realized the fact that my visits to Cheyne Walk were no longer welcome. It was not until years afterwards that I learned the cause, and if I give it here, it is only because it curiously illustrates that almost morbid sensitiveness of character which lay side by side in his nature with the most masculine grasp of the problems of life and art. He had, it seems, as I had learned from the lips of a friend whose devotion to the poet endured until his death, a very high opinion of my judgment as an art critic, and he had conceived the belief, perhaps true at that time, that I thought more highly of the work of Burne-Jones than of his own. And although he himself had often said to me things of Burne-Jones's genius which no word of mine could outmeasure in generous praise, it fretted him, in the supersensitive condition in which suffering and ill-health had consigned him, to be reminded by my presence of a judgment that in his own person he would not have resented."

Another devotee of Rossetti at this time, a youthful literary aspirant, William Sharp, afterwards best known by his pen name of Fiona McLeod, also remarked Gabriel's graciousness and charm during his last years, and later protested against the Rossetti legend that represented him as sunk in a permanent melancholy. "Some accounts of Rossetti," he wrote, "have represented the poet-painter as a morbid dreamer, a curse to himself and a burden to his friends; a hater of the common interests of mankind, a selfish devotee at the shrine of abstract Beauty, an enemy to the widening of man's intellectual horizon. Others, who knew him intimately, and saw him continuously through several years of his least propitious period—can only say that they found him none of these things. In sweetness of temper, in graciousness of manner, in healthy and energetic, if not very comprehensive sympathy with the little things of life, in ready interest in everything intellectual, in quick willingness to see the humorous aspect of things, in urgent sympathy with and desire to share vicariously the troubles of his friends, in deep and broad insight into the fundamental principles and subtlest beauties of art and poetry —in one and all of these they found him the opposite of what he has sometimes been portrayed."

At the same time Sharp admitted the darker shades in the picture—Rossetti's melancholy, his temperamentality, emotional ambivalence, "the rapid transition whereby he would frequently pass from a mood of dire despondency into one of alert interest, his eyes glistening with keen appreciation, his mouth twitching sensitively. Friends would arrive on an afternoon (it would not heighten the effect to say 'on a dull,' or 'gloomy' or 'wintry' afternoon, for to summer and winter, gloomy and bright days, Rossetti was—save in so far as these interfered with or assisted him in the prosecution of his painting —mostly indifferent), and find him in the depths of fathomless despair. By dinner-time he would be in shallower seas of despondency; an hour or so later he would be on the high tide of conversational cheerfulness; and between the hours of ten and three—when he was at his best—many a jest and hearty laugh, keen criticism and pungent remark, recondite reminiscence and poetic quotation, would make the lurking blue devils depart altogether from the studio—to await their victim when, in the sleepless morning hours, he should be alone once more with his sufferings and unquiet thoughts."

As the new year dawned Rossetti's nervous depression markedly increased. "A menace of the most serious kind . . . absolute solitude," he complained to both Shields and Watts in January 1881 when the first snow threatened further isolation. "I have been almost entirely alone lately, and feeling a good deal depressed." Doubtless a chief cause of Rossetti's depression is unwittingly revealed by a chance remark of Henry James, the American novelist, now more sophisticated than on his first meeting with Janey twelve years before. "I called upon our friends the George Howards, who had been wintering at Bordighera, a few miles away," he wrote to Mrs. Fanny Kemble, from Milan, in March. "I didn't fall in love with Mrs. William Morris, the strange, pale, livid, gaunt, silent, and yet in a manner graceful and picturesque, wife of the poet and paper-maker, who is spending the winter with the Howards; though doubtless she too has her merits. She has, for instance, wonderful aesthetic hair."

Perhaps Henry James's opinion of Mrs. Morris was not uninfluenced by his attitude towards Rossetti and the whole Preraphaelite circle, an attitude of general dislike, as "Bohemians," according to Ford Madox Hueffer. Calling on Gabriel once at tea-time, and finding him in his long painting coat (which he mistook for a dressing-gown, "a very symbol, to James, at that time of day, of moral depravity"), he henceforth regarded Rossetti, said Hueffer, with a "sort of shuddering indignation," deducing from his unconventional attire that he was "disgusting in his habits, never took baths, and was insupportably lecherous!"

That the solitude of this winter of 1880–1881 was working havoc with him, Rossetti well knew. Shields, fearing for Gabriel's prospects in another world, made strenuous but unavailing efforts to convert his friend to his own stern Calvinistic creed. "To Rossetti's," he wrote in his diary on January 7th. "A serious talk with him. Lord give me faith and courage for more." "Very depressed," Shields found him four days later. Despite Rossetti's rejection of orthodox theology, the Christ-ideal appealed strongly to his imagination, and indeed, at this very time, when asked for advice by young William Sharp as to a poem about Christ, he refused to advise "on so

627

abstruse a point," adding: "Strange to say, I can conceive no higher ideal than the Christ we know; and I judge it to be very rash to lower in poetry (to the apprehension of many beautiful minds) that Ideal, by an assumption to decide a point respecting it which it is not possible to decide, whichever way belief or even conviction may tend. . . ."

So gravely had Rossetti's health deteriorated that by this time even the slight strain of unexpected visitors was too much for him, sometimes even the sudden arrival of intimate friends or relatives whom he was really glad to see. On such occasions, frightened into reserve or escape, he would later suffer tortures of anxiety and self-reproach, believing that his manner had sent his visitors hurt and angry away. In this mood he now wrote even to Christina: "I felt I did not show how much pleased I was to see you to-day. Don't answer on the point but feel sure I *was* pleased nevertheless." Yet a slight delay in his sister's reply upset him, and he sent her a second note describing himself as "seized with a sudden and unreasonable panic" as to the non-arrival of the first, adding: "you know how these things lay hold of one."

Other things too now "laid hold" of him: caricatures in *Punch* wrongly associating him with the ridiculed "aesthetes," a play, *The Colonel* (by Francis Burnand, already on the staff of *Punch*, and later to be its editor), Gilbert's *Patience*; both plays ridiculing the Aesthetic Movement. Convinced that all this meant a new attack upon him by his old enemies—did not the *dramatis personae* of *Patience* describe Bunthorne as "a Fleshly Poet"?—yet fearing to go and see the plays himself lest he lose self-control, he at last persuaded the reluctant Shields, who as a Calvinist identified plays with damnation, to attend a performance of *The Colonel* in order to verify or dissipate Gabriel's fears. Shields, conscience-stricken at his own wickedness as a playgoer, was however able to reassure Rossetti—despite a possible sinister allusion to "Hawthorne China"—that no reference to him was made in the play. Knowing and disliking Gilbert, Gabriel probably feared *Patience* even more than *The Colonel*, but Shields, now a hardened sinner, again reported that Rossetti had been spared. This was true enough, for although George Grossmith as Bunthorne was made up to suggest Swinburne, and Rutland Barrington as the rival poet was made up to suggest Wilde, the characters of the two poets as Gilbert created them were rather composites of the qualities of the various leading Preraphaelites and Aesthetes than any recognizable imitation of any one of them, and the fashion for collecting Oriental art was now too widespread for Bunthorne's description of himself as

> Such a judge of blue-and-white, and other kinds of pottery—
> From early Oriental, down to modern terra-cotta-ry,

to suggest Rossetti.

These were amongst Gabriel's major trials. Meanwhile the crowd of petty cares that dogged him throughout life was increasingly beyond all control. To the chronic disorder of his house, bad servants and their replacement, the evasion of summonses to serve on juries, and an avalanche of debts, were now added repairs to the drains necessitated by the making of the Chelsea Embankment, the impending expiration of the lease of his house and its renewal subject to the condition that he part with half of his beloved garden upon which the flats, later known as "Rossetti Mansions," were to be built. All this greatly aggravated Rossetti's nervous state, particularly what he now called "the bloody question as to the wall," the new boundary-wall to what remained of his garden. This necessitated such countless, agitated little notes to Watts that one might have mistaken it for The Great Wall of China.

Yet occasional touches of the old humour recalled the Gabriel of earlier years. When his old acquaintance Anna Mary Howitt, now a widow and a near neighbour in Cheyne Walk, lamented the felling of the trees in the lost part of his garden, he commented: "A most frantic note from my old and most sentimental friend Mrs. Howitt Watts, at No. 19, as to the unspeakable horrors of these trees in question coming down!" And shortly afterwards he remarked, apparently forgetful of the fears fallen trees had inspired in himself—"Several of the elm trees fell to-day, and Mrs. W. is doubtless a weeping willow."

In the spring came what was practically the final separation from his oldest and best friend, Madox Brown, who, to complete his frescoes in the Manchester Town Hall, upon which he had been working for the last year, was now leaving London to take up permanent residence in the northern city. London had denied Brown a living, and his house in Fitzroy Square, scene of so many happy Preraphaelite receptions, must be sold. "To see Brown at Fitzroy Square; all dismantled—a sad sight," wrote poor, lugubrious Shields, deeply moved, in his diary. To Brown and Emma—no other guest was invited—Gabriel gave a somewhat mournful farewell dinner at Cheyne Walk. Throughout the remainder of Rossetti's life, Brown was to see London only as a visitor, and both Brown and Rossetti would have cordially agreed with Dr. Johnson that "when one is tired of London one is tired of life."

At this time, too, another of Gabriel's oldest companions and disciples was, unknown to Rossetti, bidding him a private, sorrowing farewell. Ill-health probably as much as indifference had prevented Gabriel from visiting Swinburne, now permanently isolated with Watts and the Elizabethan dramatists in the Putney villa. On May 23rd, Swinburne's growing bitterness at his former friend's desertion found sorrowful, sentimental expression in verses that are the swansong of their friendship, verses hitherto only privately printed—

AFTER MANY DAYS

As though the billows of the breaking years
    Rolled back reversed,
And sounds and sights came back on eyes and ears
    Unknown since first
Youth quenched at fountains bright as angels' tears
    His great glad thirst,

Deep drinking down dreams of transfigured grief
    And figured joy,
And gave his heart up as a shaken leaf,
    The first wind's toy,
To the first wind of song, with all belief
    That fires a boy

Whom hope and passionate wonder and delight
    Thrill as they throng
Confused and consummated; so to-night
    Before the strong
Bright wind of memory wakening with the bright
    Keen sound of song

My spirit spreads full sail to take again
    That old sweet sense,
Which yet is strange and is not: now as then,
    For all the dense
Years interposed with change of times and men
    And things passed hence,

I know the joy known first when years were less
    By full a score,
And find the same song's very loveliness
    Beloved before
As bright and sweet and fit for praise to bless
    As then of yore.

No praise may give sweet song a blessing worth
    The gifts it gives,
Joy, passion, pity brighter-eyed than mirth,
    Whose heart forgives
The painless pain that seems not born of earth
    Where scarce it lives,

The soft swift pang that hurts not; these the years,
    Change not nor slay:
The same sense gathers what the same soul hears
    The same song say,
As though the day when first it thrilled our ears
    Were yesterday.

The old Round Table of Preraphaelite Knighthood was dissolved indeed! "A very uncheered one," Gabriel now described his life to Davies in Rome. "Yet I shall not sink, I trust, so long as the poetic life wells up in me at intervals (and with me it was always and by preference intermittent), and so long as my painting still interests me and still staves off the horror (against which I am not proof), of inability to meet indebtedness. At present I have no cause to complain on either ground. My work in painting rather betters than worsens, and the market shows good revival. Of poetry I have written a fair amount for a year past, and am about to print a new volume, besides reprinting the old, which after a good many editions has been some time out of print. Among other work I have written two historical ballads which will certainly find a much wider field of appreciation than anything I have yet done. Even if I did not paint, I should never be a redundant poet. To write as much as one can write leads either to meandering narrative, empty declamation, or mere jagged jargon." In this mood he worked away at another *Salutation of Beatrice* for Leyland. After some hesitation between the choice of Mrs. Stillman and Mrs. Morris as model he had finally chosen Janey. But when almost completed, the picture had to be abandoned beneath the stress of his increasing illness, and was never finished.

So long as he could paint, however, his debts forced him to do so. Hearing that Howell was about to pass through the bankruptcy court, he anxiously asked Watts about the rumour "as you will probably think it renders imperative the settlement of my affairs with him." In June, despite his former resolution (already broken in fact), to sell none of his portraits of Janey, he offered Fry two head studies of her at £150 each, and in August Janey was again regularly sitting to him for a new *Lady of Pity*, never completed by him, though Brown finished it after Rossetti's death. Whenever Janey came, Gabriel sent up a note to Hall Caine, now living with him in Cheyne Walk: "The lady I spoke about has arrived and will stay with me to dinner. In these circumstances I will ask you to be good enough to dine in your room to-night." Thus it was, if Caine is to be believed, that he never saw Janey Morris.

It was on August 7, 1881, that Caine, the young builder's clerk from Liverpool with journalistic ambitions, had come to live with Rossetti as a kind of attendant with bed and board free. Some months before, Caine had gained Rossetti's acquaintance and gratitude by sending him a copy of a local magazine containing an account of a lecture in which he had defended Rossetti from the charge of "aestheticism." Coming in one of Gabriel's spells of deep dejection the article had pleased him, and a correspondence had developed between the poet-painter and his new admirer. Despite the great difference between them in age, education and social position, Caine soon attained a certain intimacy with Rossetti, partly because of the poet's loneliness, partly because of a common bond of morbidity and sentimentality such as had drawn him to Lizzie in the distant past. Caine had sent Gabriel samples of his own bad verses, in the hope that so powerful a friend would help to launch him on a poetic career, but Gabriel had tactfully replied that he should restrict himself to "fervid and impassioned prose"—which in the novels Caine afterwards wrote he certainly did, and with no small financial success.

Caine had quickly followed up this correspondence with a personal call on Rossetti, and shortly afterwards, at Easter 1881, by a night's stay in Cheyne Walk. The sensation-loving provincial had been greatly impressed by the dark house and its lonely, distinguished, drug-intoxicated inmate, about whom clung rumours of a strange, tragic, even scandalous past. Nor was Rossetti so disinterested as he appeared. He had recently dismissed his "assistant," the elusive Dunn, who had remained in Truro since New Year's Day, replying as before to all Rossetti's protests that, as Gabriel could not pay him his arrears of salary, he must take whatever commissions he could get, and was now doing so in order to live. When at the close of July Dunn showed an inclination to return, Rossetti, very angry with him, sent him £50 with a promise of the balance of his unpaid salary at the rate of £3 a week, and curtly dismissed him. "He proposes to remove his goods (or d—d bads) next week. Meanwhile I shall clear the rooms," he told Watts on August 5th, amidst much violent denunciation of the erring Dunn. The secret of this unusual firmness Gabriel had revealed in a letter to his mother two days before, when, after informing her of Dunn's dismissal he continued: "You may have heard of a young man named Hall Caine who has shown himself very well disposed towards me. I am going to try the experiment of having him to live in the house, and so shall have more society. . . . Caine has tastes similar to my own, and is a reading man. He follows literature. He is likely to be coming here next Saturday."

Christina, after reading Caine's lecture which her brother had sent her, had shrewdly but ambiguously commented to Gabriel: "If you come to know him, I should like to know what he is like; conflicting images of him evolve themselves from my inner consciousness and he cannot be like both!" "I like him extremely," Rossetti told Brown after meeting Caine; "He seems modest, yet not likely to miss a chance that can be duly seized." Caine, on his side, had thus achieved his immediate aim, and was to profit by it. But the time of his entry into Cheyne Walk was far from propitious. With Rossetti in his present condition, Caine would need all his power of diplomacy, and many other qualities as well.

For Gabriel was now in the depths of a new chloral crisis. Increasingly throughout that summer of 1881 he had complained of ill-health and solitude, ever more insistently had appealed to Watts to come and lighten the burden of loneliness. "The amount of solitude I endure," he complained in mid-July, "must really have an avoirdupois weight if it could be computated" [*sic*]. "I am much more ill," he told Watts a few days later, repeating his plea for a visit; and on July 21st described his "physical condition" as "short of the absolutely gelatinous." The pitiful tremulousness of his handwriting, he told his mother on August 3rd, was shamefully emphasized by the firmness of her own. Deafness now troubled him, and he anxiously wondered what new development of his illness it might portend. Nevertheless, he could not give up the chloral. His friends observed his state with renewed anxiety. Shields, throughout August, contemplated him with despair. Deeply depressed, hypochondriacal and desperately needing change of air and scene, Rossetti was at length persuaded to leave London and try the effect of a visit to the English Lakes.

V

THE LAKES
1881

Plaintive days that haunt the haggard hills
With bleak unspoken woe. . . .

Fragments D. G. ROSSETTI

IT WAS TUESDAY EVENING, September 20th, when Rossetti, accompanied by Fanny and Caine, set off for the English Lakes, in a reserved railway carriage crowded with books and artists' materials—enough, thought Caine, for a year's holiday!

Upon Caine, with his natural bias towards the melodramatic and sensational, we are chiefly dependent for our knowledge of Rossetti's visit to the Lakes. That Caine was no reliable historian, the many discrepancies, inaccuracies, even self-contradictions in his three accounts of his relations with Rossetti show, and we may reasonably suspect that the marked increase of the sombre and macabre in Rossetti and his way of life at this time as described by Caine, is partly due to the temperament, in some cases even to the creative fancy, of Caine himself. Nevertheless, despite exaggeration, exploitation of the sensational and errors of fact, Caine's description of Rossetti is almost the only one we have of him written by a man with any literary skill.

If we believe Caine, the ill-advised journey to Cumberland was unpropitious from the start. Rossetti, dissatisfied with the dose of chloral given him on the train, secretly filched one of the phials of the drug in Caine's keeping and took some of it, so that, on arriving in the early morning at the Vale of St. John, he was still too stupefied to observe and admire the magnificent mountain scenery during their carriage-drive to their lodgings at the foot of Fisher Ghyll, and on arrival immediately stumbled upstairs to bed. But Caine, unexpectedly entering Rossetti's room shortly afterwards, found him surreptitiously drinking from the stolen phial. Such, apparently, was the demoralization to which, during this crisis, chloral had reduced Rossetti.

Making one of his extraordinary recoveries, he set out next day with Fanny and Caine to climb the neighbouring hill, Great How, some twelve hundred feet high, at the head of Thirlmere. On the summit he rested an hour, gazing out over the mountains and down on the lake below, in which was an island, he remembered, "on a stone of which Coleridge had carved his name." When descending, he slipped and rolled down some little distance, to the great amusement of all. The exuberant Fanny lay on the grass roaring with laughter, in which, at the sight of her, Caine joined, while Rossetti laughed at them both. He was proud of his climb, and, although his limbs were, he said, still affected by his illness, he contemplated yet more ambitious ascents. These, however, he never actually attempted, contenting himself henceforth with walks on level ground.

His lodgings in the Vale of St. John, he found "very comfortable with obliging people," and "the cookery splendid." Three years later, when the painter Henry Holiday and his wife chanced to stay in this same house, Mrs. Holiday was given by the landlady "a receipt for a savoury dish which Rossetti had taught her," and which the Holidays much appreciated.

The scenery Gabriel described in his letters as "grand in the extreme—mountains rising on all hands," but Caine noticed with dismay that in his present state, he was really indifferent to the natural beauty about him. To William, Gabriel brusquely excused himself from giving descriptions, with the remark: "Landscape-letters are things to me impossible; but I dare say you know the country, which is very beautiful and an absolute solitude." Financial need drove him to resume painting, "to drudge a little at an easy replica for Valpy," as he described it—a *Proserpine*. Caine, preparing his sonnet anthology and some lectures on English literature he was to give at Liverpool, admiringly watched the *Proserpine* grow, and thought (truly enough), "the painter's life had been a dream into which nothing entered that was not as impalpable as itself."

During these autumn days of 1881, while Rossetti in his secluded valley vainly strove to conquer his craving for chloral and to regain health and strength, his *Dante's Dream* was much in the public eye. Painted during 1870 and 1871 for Graham, transferred two years later to Valpy because of its inconveniently large size, and again, for the same reason, returned to Gabriel in 1878, it now awaited in his studio a new purchaser when Caine, who had much of Howell's cleverness, saw it and at once urged its purchase upon the Liverpool municipality. The negotiations, however, had proved delicate and difficult, chiefly because of Gabriel's refusal to admit to Cheyne Walk the chairman of the inspection committee, who had once publicly described Rossetti—in ironical allusion to the feminine, sensuous types represented in many of his works—as "the greatest animal-painter in England." But at last, through Caine's diplomacy, the meeting was accomplished, and Rossetti sufficiently relented towards the erring councillor to declare him a "really good fellow at bottom" but with the qualification that "he had better take care that the place at which he was a good fellow did not get kicked."

The result was that shortly before Rossetti's departure from town, the Liverpool municipality had bought *Dante's Dream* for their gallery (where it still holds an honoured place). Congratulations on the sale now reached Rossetti from Graham, Sir Noel Paton, and others. To Davies' enthusiastic praise of the picture Gabriel, much cheered, replied: "Its sale has been a stroke of luck for me—I was getting sick of its company." A day or two later he was much gladdened to hear of an excellent article about his work, in the *Manchester Courier*. His satisfaction was due, not only to the intrinsic pleasure of having his work approved, but also to whatever suggested the failure of those ever-active, imaginary plotters against his name and fame, of whom he now lived in perpetual dread.

Since the spring, he had been hard at work on a new volume of verse which now appeared as *Ballads and Sonnets*, dedicated to the indispensable Watts, because, as Gabriel told Christina, Watts had "set his heart" upon it. "So good a friend," Christina replied, was worthy of "even the honour of a Dedication from you." For this volume Rossetti had completed early in

1881, the long poem *Rose Mary* (begun ten years before), and a little later, in March, *The King's Tragedy* (or *Kate Barlass*, as it was then named). It was only then that his former vague intention to produce a new volume of verse, thwarted almost on the eve of fulfilment by his breakdown in 1872, had come back to a definite focus. "I'm sure I've made the ballad a ripper," he wrote to Watts, early in March, referring to *The King's Tragedy*, "and want therefore to print *Rose Mary, White Ship* and *Kate Barlass* at once and see how far they go towards a volume." And before the close of the month he had begun to put his project into effect.

Unfortunately his new poems did not "go far" enough towards making such a volume as he desired, and he found himself, as he had done at the time of his first volume eleven years before, without sufficient material. His muse, save under the urge of immediate passion, was ever lethargic, and how real his need of additional verse was if he were to produce a new volume, how little his poetic power was now able to meet the need, he showed by his sparing rearrangement of old material which had already appeared in *Poems*, 1870, in order to fill out with what later verse he had, two "new" volumes, his *Ballads and Sonnets* on the one hand, and on the other a new version of *Poems*, which now appeared with very considerable alterations, particularly of omission. In this way, Rossetti obtained two "new" volumes out of a body of new and old verse which might easily have been contained in one.

In 1870 Rossetti had not been blind to the virtues in such a case of thick paper, large print and wide spacing, and these he again employed. Nevertheless, he was forced to remove from the new *Poems*, all the sonnets which in 1870 had constituted *The House of Life*, and to transfer all but one[1] of them, together with six sonnets also from the 1870 volume, but outside *The House of Life*, to *Ballads and Sonnets*, where, with the addition of forty-seven hitherto unpublished sonnets, they constituted a new *House of Life*, which was thus almost doubled. The gap, however, that this must make in the new *Poems* must be filled, and for this reason, in his dearth of material, he

---

[1] *Nuptial Sleep*, omitted from all editions after 1879, because of Buchanan's criticisms, until 1904 and onwards.

inserted Part 1, all that was ever finished, of *The Bride's Prelude*, begun in 1848 as *The Bride's Chamber* or *Bride Chamber Talk*, and occasionally continued in later years. Rossetti was under no delusion that *The Bride's Prelude* provided readers of *Poems* with adequate compensation for the loss of *The House of Life*. At first he had thought of including it in *Ballads and Sonnets* in order "to make it as big as I can"; but considering the theme of the poem "unelevated and repulsive" and wishing to put his best material into the new *Ballads and Sonnets*, he relegated *The Bride's Prelude* to the new edition of *Poems*, declaring: "Its picturesqueness is sufficient to make it pass muster, though it has no other quality to recommend it. Besides," he added conclusively, "I don't see how it can be spared as the space must be filled."

Similarly, he had recently inserted in his poem *Rose Mary*, the Beryl Songs, "more chaunts than songs," he said, and despite the objections of William and others, had refused to remove them. The name *Rose Mary* he chose, he said, because it was "a specially *virginal*[1] name appropriate to the seeress of the Beryl." For *Rose Mary* was a return to the obsessive theme of chastity.

The King's Tragedy, a long ballad on Catherine Douglas and her brave but vain attempt to prevent the murder of James I of Scotland, Rossetti thought "really a success." His first knowledge of the historical incident was doubtless gained from Bell Scott's wall paintings at Penkill, suggested by James's famous poem *The King's Quair*. James interested Rossetti as a poet-king. His championship of the common people against oppression appealed to Gabriel's liberal sympathies. With what intensity of feeling Gabriel wrote the poem he revealed in his comment to Caine: "It was as though my own life ebbed out with it." Yet this confession, in relation to so emotionally sterile a poem, was an unconscious revelation of Rossetti's poetic decline. No longer was he inspired by personal passion, and his present attempts to reanimate historical events by means of pseudo-balladry, although they won for him great respect amongst contemporaries, were in fact, at one time merely academic and cold, at another, rant and doggerel. In

---

[1] Italics are Rossetti's.

fostering this tendency, Watts, who himself loved the sentimental and sensational, must have exercised over Rossetti an unfortunate influence.

It was now, in mid-May, that Rossetti after much doubt and hesitation prefaced *The House of Life* with the misleading statement previously quoted,[1] to the effect that many of the sonnets now added were evidently also of early date, so again attempting to associate the love-sonnets with his own youth and, by implication, with the woman who became his wife.

Finally, Gabriel gave to the faithful William the minor honour of a dedication in the revised *Poems*, and decided in the interests of publicity and sales, and with Christina's approval, to postpone publication of the volumes until the more important autumn publishing season began in October. Until his departure for the Lakes in late September, indeed, he had continued to send occasional new verses for inclusion in *Ballads and Sonnets*, for despite his morbid state, or perhaps because of it, he was now showing some renewal of poetic energy in contrast to the dearth of recent years. "Of poetry I have written a fair amount for a year past," he told Davies in the early days of 1881, and his works justify his assertion. On January 1st his latest sonnet, on Michelangelo's *Holy Family*, had appeared in the *Athenaeum*. A fortnight later he sent his mother "a new one," *Michaelangelo's Kiss*, and in March or April he had written a sonnet on the assassination of the Czar of Russia. Between the opening of the year and his departure for the Vale of St. John he had also in other sonnets mused over the fates of Sir Walter Raleigh, of Cicero, of Antony and Cleopatra, and returned to the theme of the sentimentalized prostitute with a sonnet to the unfinished picture he had now resumed, *Found*. In August he wrote a sequence of three sonnets, *True Woman,—Herself, Her Love, Her Heaven*.

In Rossetti's art, from first to last, woman was to be his primary inspiration:

> The flower of life . . .
> What Man can know
> But as a sacred secret!

[1] *v. sup.* p. 380.

as he now wrote. Woman's love, in Rossetti's narcissistic conception, was the reflection of man's ardour:—

> Passion in her is
> A glass facing his fire, where the bright bliss
> Is mirrored, and the heat returned.

So he relived, in retrospect, amidst these gloomy days of his decline, the passionate, love-intoxicated past which had gradually led him to the desert in which he now dwelt alone amongst memories. Yet even amidst his life's frustrations and futility, he still clung at times to the tremulous hope that earthly love and passion held in them an immortal promise, would find their ultimate justification beyond the dark gateway of death:—

> The sunrise blooms and withers on the hill
> Like any hill-flower; and the noblest troth
> Dies here to dust. Yet shall Heaven's promise clothe
> Even yet those lovers who have cherished still
> This test for love:—in every kiss sealed fast
> To feel the first kiss and forebode the last.

So greatly did these three sonnets on woman appeal to Rossetti that almost his last act before leaving for Cumberland had been specially to direct his mother's attention to them, and she had duly replied, particularly admiring the first, as did Christina also, "who," wrote Mrs. Rossetti, "is loud in admiration of them all."

Gabriel was particularly tender to his mother just now, accused and excused himself for neglect of her. "The sight of you yesterday," he had written, shortly before his departure, "was very dear to me, and I will not hide from you how painfully conscious I am of the many neglected opportunities of seeing you. But I have lately been much more than usually out of sorts, and will hope, if I return from the country somewhat improved, to see you more frequently, and also to get you and Christina to stay here again. I will write to you as soon as I am settled." To which Mrs. Rossetti had replied with characteristic urbanity: "How truly I hope that you will return with renewed strength from your excursion, but though I deeply enjoy the sight of you, knowing your state, I am satisfied with occasional glimpses, as I am sure I am not shut out of your remembrance."

Strangely enough, there were persons, weak, wicked and wilful, no doubt, who disliked the strong-minded, admirably balanced and practical old lady, Mrs. Rossetti. Philip Bourke Marston, the blind poet, Gabriel's friend, was one. "I suppose you know Mrs. Rossetti is dead," he wrote to a friend, five years later, when the old lady died, aged eighty-six years almost to the day. "I don't mean," he added, "Mrs. William Rossetti. I am sorry because I know it will be a great trouble to Miss Rossetti, and William Michael Angelo and Gabriel Rossetti too, were much attached to her. She never seemed to me a very lovable old lady, but I suppose she was, since she won the hearts of her children. . . ." In this last remark, Marston was at least beyond question. "The pattern to me of everything that is simple, sweet, kind and noble," wrote Christina in her diary, three days after her mother's death, and with that verdict the other children would have wholeheartedly agreed. Perhaps Marston's antipathy was due to something unimaginative, unsympathetic, in Mrs. Rossetti; the detachment perhaps which had brought the self-contained old lady safely through so many domestic woes to a sturdy and serene old age, and led her when seventy-three to declare: "I always had a passion for intellect, and my wish was that my husband should be distinguished for intellect, and my children too. I have had my wish and I now wish that there were a little less intellect in the family, so as to allow for a little more common sense." "I have always set store by that utterance of my mother," wrote William, after her death, "as equally sound and characteristic." But perhaps weaker vessels, meeting her, found good Mrs. Rossetti's invulnerability a trifle trying. . . .

Amidst his writing of poems and various other preparations for the appearance of *Ballads and Sonnets*, Rossetti did not neglect during the months preceding his departure from London to repeat, so far as he was able, the meticulous precautions against attack he had taken when publishing his first volume eleven years before. No longer could he bring such an army of friendly critics into the field as then, nor did his highly established reputation as a poetic leader now require so elaborate

precautions in defence. Yet none the less, so far as lay in his
power, he employed his former tactics, getting Watts to review
his volume in the *Athenaeum*, and Caine elsewhere, and when,
"by some blunder," copies were again sent to the reviewers
too early, angry, he anxiously ordered Watts to publish his
review at once, but not to let it suffer in length or quality. "A
fine critique," he described it when Watts's review appeared,
and he wrote gratefully to his friend, thanking him for "the
finest review that ever came from critical or friendly man."
But whatever the provocation, his persecutory complex, his
fears and suspicions of a conspiracy against himself were still
active. "I begin to suspect," he added, "that in other quarters
the book will be ignored by conspiracy—but I always said
yours was the only one I cared for. Gosse wrote me that they
had refused him the book 'in an influential journal'—I suppose the *Saturday*."

Watts, early in the field, had certainly attempted in the
Athenaeum of October 8th to set the right note of adulation of
Rossetti's genius. *Ballads and Sonnets*, he declared, was "certainly
as rich in poetic beauties" as Tennyson's recent "marvellous"
volume, *Ballads and Other Poems*; his additions to *The House of
Life* were "finer than the finest" of their predecessors, and his
power as a sonneteer, akin to Shakespeare's "in the gift of
rendering by means of highly figurative language a passion
still vital and palpitating." Nevertheless, Gabriel's fears proved
not unjustified. Despite his established reputation, or perhaps
because of it, the general reception accorded to *Ballads and
Sonnets* by the professional critics was barely cordial, and
although on the one hand he encountered no repetition of
such an attack as Buchanan's, its consequences and the
malice of jealous rivals did, as he had anticipated, prevent
any approach to such an organized paean of praise as he had
enjoyed upon the publication of his first volume of original
verse eleven years before.

Some of the mud Buchanan had thrown certainly still
stuck, as Rossetti so morbidly complained. Even the admiring
Alice Meynell, while enthusiastically declaring in *The Art
Journal* for March 1882 that both Rossetti's "poems and pictures are a poet's," sorrowfully concluded: "The best of the

sonnets will not be generally considered those in which a foreboding and pathetically passionate love is celebrated with
what we can only call an immoderation which offends against
virile self-control," although she admitted, "others in the
volume—sonnets old and new—are magnificent."

For the most part, however, such strictures were lost upon
Rossetti, who, mindful of his earlier experience with Buchanan,
now refused to see or hear adverse criticism of his work. Thus
he probably never learned of the scarcely veiled hostility of an
anonymous critic who in *The Edinburgh Review* for April 1882,
a few days before Gabriel's death, delivered his verdict upon
the now old volume of 1870, as well as upon the recent *Ballads
and Sonnets*. This began with a condemnation of the "modern
movement" in poetry and painting, due, the critic asserted, to
the influence of Rossetti and his "Preraphaelite" following,
who, he declared, kept a band of critics specially to praise
them, a clique posing as public opinion. Had Rossetti's two
volumes, he graciously conceded, represented no more than
the "artificial sensuousness" of the movement they would not
have deserved notice; but there were in them higher elements,
although "clogged with the morbid sensuousness against
which we have protested."

Rossetti was, he continued, so "conspicuous among poets of
this school for picturesque choice of language, that it is worth
while to consider what matter of real value as poetic literature is
to be extracted from the somewhat chequered contents of these
two volumes; and the unquestionable fact that the repute of
the first volume was largely forced by the advocacy of the
poet's too friendly critics seems to place us under a kind of
moral obligation to deliver Mr. Rossetti, if possible, from his
friends." This jibe was immediately followed by another, suggesting that Rossetti's fame as an artist was merely on the
ground of unseen paintings hidden amongst his admirers,
which, if made public, would fail to substantiate their claims,
and consequently Rossetti's reputation.

Rossetti's verse he also dismissed as the "result of self-
conscious elaboration, rather than of genuine poetic fervour,"
and although he highly praised *Jenny*, particularly for its freedom from "affected elaboration," even defending it from

charges of "indelicacy," he complained that *The House of Life* left him with "a sense of absolute bewilderment," and contrasted the noble treatment of degraded womanhood in *Jenny* —as he saw it—with the conception *The House of Life* gave him, of one who "should treat the subject of conjugal love so as to lower it more than we remember to have seen it lowered in any serious poetry before; should substitute for true affection the languors of sickly and unwholesome passion, in language which, however overlaid with far-fetched and fantastic metaphor, comes at times little short of absolute pruriency." And on this note the critic concluded. Certainly Rossetti in his nervous state, was wise to avoid the strictures of such unfriendly critics. . . .

For whatever momentary satisfaction and distraction the publication of *Ballads and Sonnets* brought Rossetti was quickly submerged in a renewed desolation of spirit beyond all consolation or cure. Even self-expression now failed the sick man amidst these unfamiliar, mountain solitudes, for it was surely now that he scribbled in his note-book of this time those last broken, bitter couplets, reflecting in their very confused intensity his own unhappy state.

> . . . Inexplicable blight,
> And mad revulsion of the tarnished light,

he scrawled painfully, with trembling hand, and twice he wrote of

> Plaintive days that haunt the haggard hills
> With bleak-unspoken woe, . . .

but got no further.

Emotionally, intellectually, physically exhausted, imprisoned within the narrow cage of his own passionate experience, for him there was no escape, and as before he merely continued to repeat the old, ever-revolving cycle of thoughts and moods—past happiness, present misery and decay, a tremulous, intermittent hope of love's final, perfect consummation beyond death. These themes, so long laboured, endlessly repeated as the kindred themes of his paintings were repeated, were his inspiration to the end. They had formed the content of his very last poems in *Ballads and Sonnets*, of *Alas, So Long!* plaintively lamenting the passing of

> . . . the days we never again shall know,

voicing his disgust with the present and with increasing age, the time when

> . . . days and years have never a song,

and finally his passionate, unquenchable desire for love's perfect fulfilment beyond the frustrations of time.

Was it a sudden pang awakened by some momentary vivid memory of Lizzie in her early idealized youth and beauty that inspired the poem's close?

> Ah! dear one, you've been dead so long,—
> How long until we meet again,
> Where hours may never lose their song
> Nor flowers forget the rain,
> In glad noonlight that never shall wane?
> Alas, so long!
> Ah! shall it be then Spring weather,
> And ah! shall we be young together?

Through all his sufferings of body and spirit Rossetti's love-dream still held him, his "one dream alone." That it remained with him to the end he revealed in another of these last poems, *Insomnia*, a picture of the long agony of sleepless nights which had haunted his later years—

> Thin are the night-skirts left behind
> By daybreak hours that onward creep,
> And thin, alas! the shred of sleep
> That wavers with the spirit's wind:
> But in half-dreams that shift and roll
> And still remember and forget,
> My soul this hour has drawn your soul
> A little nearer yet.[1]

Ever more clearly in these last days of his decline, the marks of his frustration show themselves in his verse—an unassuageable, neurotic intensity of passion, the bitterness of "Willow-wood," of the lost years, the poignancy of love snatched from the hand of adverse destiny, the compensatory, unquenchable

---

[1] *cf.* the *Proserpine* sonnet quoted *sup.* p. 543.

longing for the complete realization of his love hereafter, where
no bitterness shall thwart its full perfection of moral and
intellectual beauty—these still dominate Rossetti's verse:—

> Is there a home where heavy earth
>   Melts to bright air that leaves no pain,
>   Where water leaves no thirst again
> And springing fire is Love's new birth?
> If faith long bound to one true goal
>   May there at length its hope beget,
> My soul that hour shall draw your soul
>   For ever nearer yet.

So throughout his verse, and with an ever-growing intensity
until the end, Rossetti expressed his bitter regret that the circumstances of his life had so largely blighted those moral and
spiritual fruits of his passion which were for him the very
essence and perfection of love.

In the last two of his poems in *Ballads and Sonnets, Possession*
and *Spheral Change,* he pursued this theme with even greater
emotional intensity, voicing for the last time his passionate,
unassuaged desire, his realization that there was

> in possession still
> A further reach of longing,

a passionate desire which in *Spheral Change,* his last published
poem, rises to the poignant cry:—

> O dearest! while we lived and died
>   A living death in every day,
> Some hours we still were side by side,
>   When where I was you too might stay
>   And rest and need not go away.
>
> O nearest, furthest! Can there be
>   At length some hard-earned heart-won home,
> Where,—exile changed for sanctuary,—
>   Our lot may fill indeed its sum,
>   And you may wait and I may come?

To the end it was Janey (evidently absent when he wrote
these verses) who held him, although, as scraps of unfinished
poems suggest, sometimes the faded memory of that earlier,
unhappy love emerged, or blended with that of the later, both

his love for Lizzie and for Janey being to him, as he had sung in *The Love-moon*, two distinct revelations of the one absolute power, Love itself, indivisible. . . .

Haunted, in this mood, by thoughts and memories, Gabriel soon found the peace he had sought in these sequestered mountain solitudes unbearable. Illness, misery, intolerable craving quickly followed his attempts to reduce the quantities of chloral he was taking, and with Caine absent for a day and a half each week lecturing in Liverpool, with Watts, whom Rossetti had anxiously expected, at last regretfully explaining that he would not be able to come, Gabriel came increasingly to desire a speedy return to London. Caine, rightly, thought the isolation a harmful influence, telling on Rossetti's nerves.

Yet even now there were occasional relaxations of tension, though only temporary. One such was when Caine, with the indefatigable Fanny, climbed another "mountain," "twice as high," Rossetti proudly told Watts, "as the one we went up before." Rossetti himself had not been well enough to attempt the feat, but he boasted of Fanny's achievement. "She climbs," he told Watts, "as if she had done it all her life, and is looking wonderfully better. I wish," he added, "I could give as good an account of myself. I have, however, considerably decreased the drug with Fanny's assistance." This voluntary testimony of Gabriel's completely discredits Caine's later melodramatic accounts of this visit to the Lakes, in which Fanny appears as a fiend of darkness, a necessary foil to intensify the effect of Caine himself as an angel of light, battling with Fanny as well as with Gabriel, trying to prevent her secretly giving Rossetti chloral and whisky and trying to force him to make a will in her favour. "Excessively attentive and friendly, and . . . really quite an abnegator of self," was Gabriel's description of her, and he was in no mood to give undeserved praise. That at least Caine well knew!

Rossetti rapidly grew worse. Each day his walks became shorter, more reluctant. He refused to visit the many places of literary interest in the neighbourhood, nor could Caine rouse him to fulfil his recent intention to write ballads about local legends and scenery. "That's good, very good," was his invariable, mechanical reply to Caine's accounts of the welcome

PLATE XVIII

DANTE GABRIEL ROSSETTI READING POETRY TO T. WATTS-DUNTON
IN THE PARLOUR OF ROSSETTI'S HOUSE AT 16 CHEYNE WALK, CHELSEA
BY H. T. DUNN
1882

KELMSCOTT MANOR

PLATE XIX

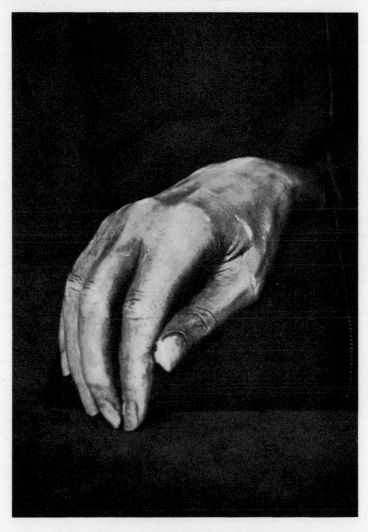

THE HAND OF DANTE GABRIEL ROSSETTI
From a plaster cast taken after death

now being given to his books and pictures, for even to these things now he was indifferent, sitting indoors, brooding, sunk in depression. "You'll be welcome back, Sir," the driver of the station fly would significantly murmur each time Caine returned from Liverpool.

Such were the days; but as night fell Gabriel's melancholy deepened as they sat together through the interminable hours, anxiously awaiting the critical, belated moment when, with some chance of snatching three or four hours' sleep and not awakening before dawn, Rossetti could take his first dose of chloral. During these nightly vigils, Caine, preparing his lectures, would sometimes read to him from the works of the great eighteenth-century novelists, Richardson, Fielding or Sterne; but more often, at Caine's request, Gabriel would repeat, in the once so beautiful but now failing voice, selections from his own verses: *Cloud Confines*, or *The King's Tragedy*, or from Poe's *Ulalume* or *Raven*. It was then he told Caine that he had written *The Blessed Damozel* as a sequel to Poe's *Raven* because: "I saw that Poe had done the utmost it was possible to do with the grief of the lover on earth, and so determined to reverse the conditions, and give utterance to the yearning of the loved one in heaven."

Early in October Caine, on his return from one of his lectures in Liverpool, found that Fanny had gone. Gabriel, disappointed by Watts's absence and unable to endure the solitude longer, now decided—to the weary Caine's "unspeakable relief"—to return at once to Cheyne Walk. On October 17th, a month after their arrival, they set out on their return journey. For this there had been no little preparation. A special saloon, half filled with the easels and canvases Rossetti had brought but not used, was sent from the neighbouring junction to their wayside station, to prevent the inconvenience of changing trains later, and to avoid being seen they travelled by night. . . .

It was during that dreary journey—if we accept Caine's unconvincing account, first given many years later, when the chief incidents involved were already current gossip—that Rossetti, usually so reticent, revealed to this very new acquaintance whose relationship to him was almost that of a menial, what he had apparently hitherto never spoken of to any of his intimate, life-long friends, the secret of his life's frustration, his passion for Janey.[1] In the depth of his depression, said Caine, Rossetti poured out to him during that night journey the tale of how, at Oxford, in 1857, during the "Jovial Campaign," he and Jane Burden had fallen in love, but Gabriel felt himself too deeply committed to his engagement to Lizzie to allow of a withdrawal and a new engagement to Jane. From this had come the bitterness of the years of separation, the barren years in "willow-wood." . . .

In a cold, dreary dawn Rossetti and Caine reached London. At Cheyne Walk the blinds were still down when they entered. As Gabriel, assisted by Caine, crossed the gloomy threshold, with a sigh of relief he murmured: "Thank God! Home at last, and never shall I leave it again."

[1] Janey, though not mentioned by name is clearly indicated, *v.* Caine's *Recollections of Rossetti*, 1928 edn. pp. 141–2, 200–1.

VI

"A DEATH ON EASTER DAY"
1881–1882

And lo! thy spirit understands
Life shaken and shower'd and flown, and Death drawn near.

Fiammetta D. G. ROSSETTI

ROSSETTI'S RETURN TO CHEYNE WALK was not entirely un-cheered. Presentation copies of *Ballads and Sonnets* brought messages of thanks, appreciation and congratulation from the few remaining friends to whom he had sent them. "A goodly volume of noble stuff," wrote Bell Scott from Penkill: "*The King's Tragedy* is to me the crowning work, not the *Beryl Stone* although it has from a different point of view the mastery. . . . Of *The House of Life* as now complete I can hardly trust myself to speak in writing, I feel an interest in every one sonnet, in fact, more as yours and as characteristic of you than as inde-pendent works." Was that last comment a guarded reference to the circumstances inspiring most of the sonnets of *The House of Life*?

"A blessed and divine book," wrote Jones, fulsomely, to Gabriel. "I have been bad again—physically, not otherwise particularly, and couldn't get out—else I should have been to thank you for it. It only reached me a few days ago, but I had got it already of course, as soon as it was published. Tell me when I may see you, I can go out now on days that are not positively devilish, and I do want to see you—it is eight months since I did." But in answer to Jones's effusion came only a short, pitiful note written in a poor, trembling hand: "Thanks, but I am very ill, and not well enough to see you. I can hardly write."

In similar vein, and probably of this time, are the last of the undated notes Gabriel sent Fanny . . . upon whose companion-ship he was apparently as dependent as ever. "My dear Fan," he wrote in what seems to be the latest of these, a note obviously written under the influence of chloral, in a straggling, almost illegible hand: "You know I have not written very many letters written [sic]—but the idea that I may not be seeing your kind face to-night makes me so sincerely miserable that I cannot but sit down to write this. Do come to dinner. Do pray come at once. What I said and did has not satisfied. I am very ill and write this from bed.—Your loving R."

But now, in Gabriel's sickness and financial need, the Rossetti family were evidently trying to take Fanny from him, as a short note dated November 27, 1881, his last dated note to her (that has come down to us at least), shows. "Dear F.," he wrote. "Such difficulties are now arising with my family that it will be impossible for me to see you here till I write again.—D. G. R."

The play, in fact, which had begun so lightheartedly amidst romantic ideals and aspirations some thirty years before, was now nearing its *dénouement* in the mocking degradation of harsh reality, amidst physical, mental and moral decay. Rossetti's spirits sank lower than ever before; his need of friends, his fear of solitude increased, and Caine at last perceived that Rossetti was by nature an eminently social being, that fear of the world, not desire for solitude, had gradually imposed upon him the isolation of his later life.

New fears indeed as well as old now beset him: fears of envious, conspiratorial rivals, hereditary fears, the fears that had haunted his father's life as well as his own, renewed fears, also like his father's, that his again failing sight would end in blindness, fears of poverty since he could no longer paint, and above all fear of death which he now rightly believed not far distant. His fear of poverty might well have been justified had he lived, for his ample revenue in recent years had somehow been squandered, despite the comparative simplicity of his way of life. Fanny may have been a fairly expensive item, though there is no real evidence of that; Miss Wilding received from Gabriel a retaining fee, as he did not wish her to sit to other painters, and both his china and private zoo upon which he had spent so much had apparently been sold at the time of his breakdown in 1872, as William Rossetti stated in an article written shortly after his brother's death. Yet in his *Memoir* of Rossetti, William said the china was sold in 1877 for £650, while Gabriel's friend and dealer, Murray Marks, said the china was sold after Rossetti's death for £700, that it was then catalogued for sale purposes and that the catalogue "still exists." William Rossetti, to relieve Gabriel's anxiety and distress, now assured him that at the worst Gabriel would always be welcome to the shelter of his home.

More insistent now than all other phobias was Rossetti's fear of death. Five years before, in his depression, death had seemed welcome, and in his poem *Adieu* he had cried:

> Sinking suffering heart
> That know'st how weary thou art,—
> Soul so fain for a flight,—
> Aye, spread your wings to depart,
> Sad soul and sorrowing heart,—
> Adieu, Farewell, Good-night.

But now he felt a wild fear of dying rather than any intense desire to live. Both life and death he dreaded, but above all, the nothingness which death meant for him. No longer, in his new realism, did he see Love's final consummation beckoning him beyond the shadow. Never, Caine thought, and rightly, did conventional religion support Rossetti in these last days. Rather indeed the very mention of it irritated him as a futility, so that he disliked even the sound of church bells pealing for Sunday services. Yet he always professed (and sincerely) "faith in God," although beyond that, even towards the vaguest definition of his meaning, he could not go.

In this empty present, overshadowed by ill-omens of the future, he brooded over the past, again yielded—as so often before—to that sense of guilt, a conspicuous element in his malady which had so often brought him the sadistic satisfaction of pleasure in pain, and in this mood he now recalled the unhappiness of his broken friendships. Now, too, following unconsciously a psychological tendency of his type, he lamented (after thirty years of apparent forgetfulness and indifference), his adolescent revolt against his father, and the reproaches his father had made to him.*

Acting upon an emotional rather than intellectual impulse, he suddenly demanded the solace of confession and absolution

* *v.* Notes to p. 142.

at the hands of some Catholic priest, answering Scott's obtuse remonstrances with: "I can make nothing of Christianity, but I only want a confessor to give me absolution for my sins." Scott, psychologically undiscerning, misinterpreted Gabriel's petition as a part of his pseudo-mediaeval "pose"; but Christina understood and approved her brother's wish, urged him to see one of her own favourite Anglican clergy, and touching in a passage of rare self-revelation the heart of Gabriel's own misery, assured him: "however harassed by memory or by anxiety you may be, I have (more or less) gone through the same ordeal. I have borne myself till I became unbearable by myself, and then I have found help in confession and absolution and spiritual counsel, and relief inexpressible." For the time, however, Gabriel abandoned his intention, and consulted neither Catholic nor Protestant priest.

His chief defence against fear and frustration was indeed less spiritual than chemical—chloral! Against his increasing recourse to it, Caine fought in vain. In the daytime, when cheered by the company of one or another of his few remaining friends, Rossetti appeared normal; but with night and solitude his spirits sank into depths of depression from which the drug alone offered escape. Increasingly it was destroying his health, and now, especially at night after a dose was taken, he was seized with violent fits of coughing which shook his whole frame. As the year 1881 closed, his strength rapidly waned. Bell Scott, on his return from Penkill, was "shocked" to find Gabriel prostrate on a sofa, in deep dejection, and believed him dying. And once again Rossetti's paranoiac suspicions revived. For a time he even suspected Watts was robbing him.

In this manner, while autumn gradually changed to winter, Rossetti's life slowly, almost imperceptibly, ebbed away, until on Sunday, December 11th, as he lay on a sofa before the fire, with friends about him, he suddenly exclaimed that his left side was paralysed and he could not rise. Westland Marston, the dramatist, and Caine, who were present, at once carried him back to bed, and Dr. Marshall, summoned, installed one of his medical students in the house for a time to help the nurse, Mrs. Abrey, to watch and control Rossetti. By substituting injections of morphia and secretly increasing the dilution of the choral with water, "that fatal chloral," as Christina called it, was again reduced, and eight days after this seizure the chloral was totally abolished and never resumed, while at the same time the whisky was reduced to a wine-glassful a day. "God help us, for human help is but a very helpless thing," wrote Christina, refusing on the grounds of Gabriel's illness, Lucy and William's invitation to herself and her mother to join them on Christmas Day. And indeed when Christmas Day 1881 arrived, Rossetti was too ill even to receive his mother and sister, but, save for a short visit from William, remained alone with the now chafing, exasperated and disconsolate Caine.

At first the new year brought some improvement in Rossetti's state. For a short time he was even able to do a little painting, finishing for Valpy a duplicate *Joan of Arc*. He again received friends in his studio, and in mid-January even visited his mother and sister. But this apparent recovery soon passed. His left hand and arm remained paralysed, and to Caine his increasing irritability and depression became "almost insupportable." Once again a change of scene was prescribed, and as Gabriel's old acquaintance John Seddon, who had formed one of the early Preraphaelite circle, offered him the use of his roomy bungalow, Westcliff, at Birchington-on-Sea, near Margate, Gabriel went there in February 1882, with Mrs. Abrey the nurse, Caine and Caine's twelve-year-old sister Lily as sole companions.

At the undistinguished seaside bungalow, which delighted Caine and disgusted Gabriel, the last act of Rossetti's life-drama was to be played. Its opening scene was unpropitious, for Rossetti arrived in no amiable mood. The doctor had forbidden his mother, now almost eighty-two years old, to risk a seaside winter at Birchington, and as Christina must remain with her, Rossetti now found himself dependent for company upon the nurse and the Caines. Little Lily Caine, despite her age, closely observed Rossetti whom she now saw for the first time, and in later years wrote an interesting account of her experience, an account endorsed by some who best knew Rossetti and were best qualified to judge. Lily noticed that Gabriel wore a black glove on his paralysed left hand, and that the nurse was kind and good. It was Lily who heard of the ghost at Cheyne Walk, the figure of a woman, seen by the servants but never, she believed, by Rossetti, who however never laughed at it.

To herself as a child, Lily found Gabriel extraordinarily sweet and tender, even playful. When they reached the London, Chatham and Dover Railway Station, on their way to Birchington, Rossetti joked about it to her, saying the initials stood for Lily Caine and Dante Rossetti; but a minute later he turned nervous, was frightened by the noise and bustle of the station, wanted to return home to the quiet of Cheyne Walk. Immediately afterwards the train drew up, and it needed all Caine's persuasion to get him to enter and take a seat. During the journey to Birchington, Rossetti changed his mind continually on every point he discussed, and, as they walked through the entrance gate of Westcliff, their new home, he stooped down and whispered in Lily's ear, so that her brother should not hear him, "Lily, I don't think this looks like a house. Do you? It's more like another L. C. & D. R. station!"

Birchington and the ugly though "cosy" bungalow he detested, and at once demanded to return to town, He changed his mind again and again that first evening, continually demanding to know why he had been brought to such a place, without beauty or comfort, then becoming reconciled to it for a short time, but only to revert to his attitude of restless discontent and disgust. At dinner that first evening he sat silent, but later, by the fire, wondered why he had ever left home. "We must really go back to-morrow, Caine," he said, till at last Caine appeared to satisfy him by promising to return to Cheyne Walk if Rossetti still disliked Birchington after a week's trial. Whereupon Rossetti, pacified, sat for an hour or two in silence, his legs crossed, his head buried in his chest, looking straight into the fire, motionless save for a sudden straightening of himself from time to time, when he would hastily take off the black glove and warm his paralysed hand at the fire.

His nervous instability showed itself in everything he did, and made life almost impossible for those about him. At one moment he would complain of being too hot, and then the fire must be put out; immediately afterwards he would complain with equal bitterness that the room was cold. Then the fire had to be relit and piles of blankets put on his bed; but even then he was not satisfied until Mrs. Abrey, to please him, placed the hearthrug over all as a top quilt. Angry at Caine's refusal to return at once to Cheyne Walk, Rossetti brought whatever charges he could think of against him—accusing him, for example, of not talking to him, Rossetti, yet being ever ready to talk to Watts, William, or "that damned old beast Scott!" until even the submissive Caine soon reached the point of rebellion.

Life at Birchington quickly took on some form of routine. Gabriel breakfasted in bed, and usually came into the drawing-room about noon. He dined in the evening, early, the meal being finished about seven o'clock, and breakfast and dinner were all the meals he took each day. When strong enough, he relapsed into his old habit of walking about the house in slippers, pacing up and down the drawing-room which was now his studio, with head bent forwards and shoulders slightly stooping, dressed in the shabby clothes he loved, particularly his old sack coat, his "painting-coat," bedaubed with paint and now almost threadbare.

Characteristically, he allowed some time to pass before he even thought of going out to explore Birchington, although he listened with interest to the accounts of sea, shore, cliff and countryside that Lily brought back from her excursions. But one evening, attracted by some description of the neighbouring cliffs given him by Hall Caine, he declared he must see them the next day, and although the next day proved stormy, and he was advised to postpone his outing, he refused and, putting on his favourite slouch hat and black Inverness cape, set off with Caine, only to be forced back by the wind before he had gone fifty yards. The weather was generally stormy, but in intervals of brilliant sunshine, with his two companions, he took short and feeble walks along the cliffs or down the neigh-bouring road which drearily wound its way through the grey, flat, treeless countryside to Birchington churchyard, the road along which he was soon to be carried to his grave.

On his first morning at Birchington, Gabriel's easel had been set up, with some little difficulty, in a position with a north light, so that he might continue to paint his *Joan of Arc*, and although in his earliest days in the bungalow he tried to apply himself to his painting, Lily Caine never saw him work at it for more than a quarter of an hour at a time. His mood would suddenly change, passing from dejection and silence to high spirits, and even to the end there were occasional diversions. Mid-February brought a more animated week-end when Watts and the young poetic aspirant Sharp came to see him. The weather was warm, the sea placid and beautiful, and larks were singing in the sky, when Rossetti, Caine and Sharp lay basking on the cliff-top in the early spring sunshine. "Oh, dear me," wrote Sharp, for once "supremely content," "all a-quiver with the delight of it all," to his *fiancée*, "I shall hate to go back to-morrow. Caine is writing a sonnet in your book, Watts is writing a review for the *Athenaeum*, Rossetti is about to go on with painting his *Joan of Arc*, and I am writing the last lines of this note to you." Even to the last it was Rossetti's destiny to kindle adolescent ecstasies.

The seriousness of Gabriel's state was not at first detected by his friends, accustomed as they were to his hypochondria, and his complaints of nervous pains were consequently dismissed as the result of imagination. Was Gabriel really ill or only "acting" in order to keep his friends in suspense? Morris asked Scott. Even William, much less sympathetic to his brother since his own marriage, far from suspecting that Gabriel's letter of February 17th declaring: "my state is decidedly worse" was the last he would receive from his hand, provoked Christina to remonstrate with an unusual touch of asperity: "Pray do not ascribe all his doings and non-doings to foundationless fidgeti-ness, poor dear fellow. Don't you think neither you nor I can quite appreciate all he is undergoing at present, what between wrecked health at least in some measure, nerves which appear to falsify facts, and most anxious money-matters? It is trying to have to do with him at times, but what must it be TO BE himself? And he in so many ways the head of our family—it doubles the pity." Rossetti, however, undeceived by transitory appearances of recovery, intuitively recognized the seriousness of his condition. "There has strictly been no relapse," he told Watts, "as there was never any improvement. It has been a steady decline throughout." He tried "galvanism" for a short time, without benefit, and at the close of February he told his mother: "My state is faint and feeble to a degree; full of pains and unable to walk to any purpose."

As his strength declined and walks became more difficult, he remained increasingly within doors, and, without friends or the power to paint, he turned to reading. Miss Braddon's novels he found much better than he had anticipated, and he even granted her "some genius as apart from mere talent." During Watts's visits Gabriel's spirits rose visibly; but alone, and bored, he groaned in plaintive misery: "Letters out here must soon come to an end for nothing happens." In his boredom he sometimes found relief in a cynical humour which seemed to carry an oblique reference to his own situation. In this mood he told Lily Caine a story of a dying man whose neighbour had sent a clergyman to visit him. "Do you know why Christ died?" asked the clergyman. "Oh! Sir!" replied the dying man in a weak, exhausted voice: "Is this the time to ask me conundrums?" And Gabriel imitated the speech of both persons, laughing over the tale. In this same mood, surely, he turned now to finish the grimly facetious ballad begun long before, about the well-known wager of the Dutchman, Jan Van Hunks, who lost his soul in a smoking match with the Devil. Rossetti intended it to appear in a long-projected but never achieved volume of poems and tales to be produced by Watts and himself, a scheme now much in his mind. Something of his old spirit of fun and laughter returned as he worked on the poem, and at the end of March it was done.

Other ways too he found to lighten the dreariness of life at Birchington, during the long evenings that followed the early dinner. To Lily he recited Poe's *Raven*, in his still rich voice, with much dramatic energy, pouring a sinister emotion into the raven's "Nevermore." On another occasion, finding Lily reading *The Arabian Nights*, Gabriel made her put the book down and told her some of the tales himself, in simple language. Similarly, he told her tales of the great names in literature. Lily would watch him as he sat in a big chair before the fire, his legs crossed, shaking his foot for an hour or more at a time, faster than she had ever believed possible. He had too a habit of cracking his thumb-nail with the nail of the first finger. Lily's attempts to emulate these accomplishments were a dismal failure.

Although Rossetti's reputation meant little to him now, it was in fact not only reviving but increasing. Within a month of publication, twelve thousand copies of *Ballads and Sonnets* had been sold, and the painting *Dante's Dream* was receiving warm and universal praise. The American *Atlantic Monthly* published a laudatory article on Gabriel and Christina, the *Guardian* enthusiastically applauded his works, and his old acquaintance Joseph Knight pleased him with an appreciative article in the Paris journal *Le Livre*, while Ernest Chesneau the French critic was now requesting information about the old Preraphaelite circle and a photograph of *Dante's Dream* for inclusion in a forthcoming study of English painting. Yet Gabriel's hypersensitiveness to criticism remained. "I suspect," he said, on hearing that the Scotch critic Thomas Bain was writing an article on his work for *Fraser's Magazine*, "this may prove nasty, in which case the light of a certain Twilight Hour might be its illuminating medium." Since the Buchanan affair, Rossetti had been particularly suspicious of Scotch critics!

As for the miserable Buchanan, overwhelmed by Rossetti's fame, the anger of Gabriel's friends and his own reverses, he had long since turned from outraged moralist to his more natural role of lickspittle and sycophant. Still trying to "cash in" on Rossetti's reputation—whether as detractor or adulator mattered nothing to Buchanan, so long as he got free advertisement—he had but a few months before, in dedicating his romance *God and Man* to Rossetti as "An Old Enemy," publicly craved his pardon in the unctuous and cringing verses already quoted.[1]

As Rossetti's strength declined and the misery of his ennui increased, his invitations to Watts, his entreaties to his mother and sister grew ever more insistent, until, with the advent of March, Mrs. Rossetti, facing the risks of the inclement season, arrived with Christina at Birchington. With pain they noted how wasted, suffering and depressed he was. His left side, arm and hand still paralysed, his strength steadily ebbing away, he

[1] *v. sup.* pp. 502–3.

was unable to do more than occasionally move from his bedroom to the drawing-room for short intervals. Christina admired his *Proserpine* and *Joan of Arc* as they stood on their
easels in the large drawing-room that was now his studio,
awaiting completion. Soon, as his sight declined, he abandoned
reading and Christina read aloud to him instead. Shortly after
his mother and sister's arrival he began to suffer from pains
in one foot, and remained in bed.

Lily Caine noticed a change gradually coming over the
bungalow at Birchington. The house became very quiet and
people spoke in whispers. Nothing that was done could stop
Rossetti's gradual loss of strength, his continual wasting away;
but his mind was now stronger and clearer than it had ever
been since his breakdown in 1872. "His intellect," said Caine,
"was as powerful as in his best days, and freer than ever of
hallucinations." Christina found him so clear and composed in
mind that "I could not even (judging by appearances)," she
wrote, "suspect its ever having been otherwise." "Pray," she
adjured the still sceptical William, "do not doubt the *reality* of
Gabriel's illness: do not let any theory or any opinion" (this
last doubtless a discreet reference to Lucy), "influence you to
entertain such a doubt." Meanwhile, Gabriel, "chatty and
reasonably cheerful" as he lay in bed, said Christina, revived
old memories in talk with his sister, as he loved to do, while
she, closely watching him, perceived that "not a shadow of
delusion comes to light." But the nurse, watching his wasting
away, suspected deep mischief below the symptoms.

Early in March, Lily Caine returned home. Nurse Abrey
took her into Rossetti's room to say goodbye. He was reading
in bed when she entered, propped up by pillows. For about a
week she had not seen him, and she at once noticed how much
he had altered in that short interval. He was much thinner;
his beard was thickly sprinkled with grey, and was barely more
than half its former length. Though very weak, Rossetti bade
her goodbye with all the warmth his strength would allow,
adding many a good wish for her safe journey. And in those
later years Lily recalled the "fixed glassy stare" of his eyes upon
her as she left the room. She recalled also, with pleasure,
Christina's kindness, her gift of a little desk and the writing of

her own and Lily's name on the inside lid. Even more vivid was her memory of Rossetti's mother, "very little, with a soft, beautiful, spirituelle face—a dear old soul! going about on her daughter's arm in a long sealskin jacket, the gift of her son Gabriel. I recall," wrote Lily Caine, "her deep religious feeling, and that, though fully eighty years old, she would sometimes be coming in from early Sunday morning sacrament when I was getting down to breakfast. . . ."

In mid-March, Sharp came again to spend another week-end with Rossetti. It was probably their last meeting. Two incidents which occurred during this visit Sharp never forgot. On the evening of his arrival, Christina, who had been reading to her brother until he was wearied, was sitting with Sharp in the semi-twilight of the low-ceilinged room, while Gabriel, depressed and silent, sat in his great armchair before the fire. Suddenly and silently, Christina beckoned Sharp to come over to the window to see a very beautiful but quiet-hued sunset. Hearing her exclamation, Rossetti too, feebly moved to the window, but only to stare blankly at the "dove-tones and pale amethyst of the sky," and then, after glancing curiously at his sister and again long and earnestly at the sunset, he turned pettishly away, exclaiming in disgusted tones that all was "grey and gloom," with nothing to admire. "Poor Gabriel," whispered Christina, "I wish he could have at least one hopeful hour again. . . ."

The one "hopeful hour" came indeed, the next day, as if in answer to Christina's prayer; was indeed the second incident of this visit to remain permanently in Sharp's memory. That afternoon the weather was perfect; and Sharp, taking Gabriel's arm, drew him out for a short stroll on the cliff-top in the sun-light. Everywhere spring odours mingled with the salt tang of the sea stretching away below their feet to the horizon, while above, in a blue, cloudless sky, larks sang loudly. As Gabriel stood gazing, momentarily cheered by the warmth, beauty and renewal of life about him, his gloomy indifference suddenly melted, and yielding to a mood of the moment as he drank in the loveliness of the scene, he murmured in his now habitually tired voice, but with a new, sudden note of intensity: "It is beautiful—the world and life itself. I am glad I have lived."

For the rest of that day and night the shadow of his depression lifted, and Christina, taking Sharp's hand a moment, before retiring for the night, whispered: "I am so glad about Gabriel, and grateful!"

For that evening, it seemed to Sharp, the shadow of Death had receded; but henceforth it was to advance inexorably to the not distant end. A few days later, so ill was Gabriel, restless, depressed, constantly sick, in "a truly pitiable state" said Christina, that on her advice the local doctor, Mr. Harris, was called in to supplement the care of Dr. Marshall in London. Dr. Harris, suspecting softening of the brain, ordered, said Christina, "absolute cessation of chloral and Co." which apparently meant the whisky and morphia recently adopted as a substitute for the abandoned chloral. Apparently fearing surreptitious resort to the drug, Harris ordered a careful watch to be kept on his patient, and suggested distraction, some occupation, exertion or amusement, as beneficial. He sensibly remarked that Rossetti would be as well in Chelsea (and better still in a private nursing-home, amongst others), as in the dull seclusion of this Birchington bungalow.

Like his father, Gabriel to the last surprised everyone by the unexpected strength of his recuperative powers, and when a few days later Watts spent a day with him, Rossetti amazed the family by an apparently marvellous rally inspired by the infectious geniality of his visitor. With Watts (momentarily abandoning his guard over Swinburne), Gabriel not only laughed once more—especially when reading to him *Jan Van Hunks*—but even burst at times into snatches of comic song.

April came and with it William, at last alarmed by Christina's reports. He found his brother "barely capable of tottering a few steps, half blind and suffering a great deal of pain." Gabriel, talking quite rationally but without animation, vainly tried to resume his unfinished adolescent tale, *St. Agnes of Intercession*. For some weeks now, finding painting impossible, he had turned again to poetry. All day on April 4th, he remained in his room, in pain, while Caine read to him Wilkie Collins' *Moonstone*, until 1 a.m. The next day, still confined to his room, he dictated to Caine two feeble sonnets on his drawing, *The Sphinx* (also named *The Question*), which he wished to give, together with the drawing, and *Jan Van Hunks*, to Watts for their projected joint volume.

That drawing, *The Sphinx*, was a sore subject for Bell Scott, who believed it, as he had before believed the title of *The Stream's Secret*, and the theme of *Jenny*, to be a plagiarism from his own work. "When he and I were alone," wrote Scott in his *Autobiographical Notes*, describing Rossetti near the close of 1881, "he wept and complained, and made unkind speeches, or showed me things he thought would wound me, as when he made his servant lay before me a large chalk sketch he called *Questioning the Sphinx*. This wounded me, because it happened that I had made an illustration in my first issue of *The Year of the World*, that juvenile 'poem with a purpose,' of the hero traveller leaning on an augural staff with his ear to the mouth of a Sphinx, which I called by that name, and which the beloved D. G. R. of that early time used to make game of, as if I had mistaken the ancient fable in which the Sphinx was the questioner, not the questioned. I had besides written a poem called *To the Sphinx considered as the symbol of religious mystery*. Lying on the sofa dying, as he was, I saw that singular expression of ferocity that used to take possession of his face if he surmised a quarrel was coming. I laid the sketch aside, but he kept staring at me; I refused to take up the gauntlet, and I could not venture to speak of the sketch itself, the style of drawing being so bad as to show his illness was destroying his work."

Such, apparently, was the source of those two despairing, poetically weak, and (save for the privately printed version issued by Mr. Wise) still unpublished sonnets entitled *The Question*, written on April 5, 1882, the last verses from Rossetti's pen. The question they ask and cannot answer is that so long haunting Rossetti's own mind, an indication of his obsessive desire for the non-existent key to the riddle of human life. Like the design to which they refer, these sonnets emphasize the intellectual frustration, the apparent futility as Rossetti saw it, of each period in the life of man—youth, middle and old age.

The day after he had dictated these sonnets to Caine, Rossetti became much worse. In the morning Caine found him

drowsy and sinking, his speech so thick as to be barely intel-
ligible. Yet his mind still ran on poetry, and to Caine he spoke
of his love for the old English ballads, adding that when he
first read them he told himself: "There lies your line." That
night, as Dr. Harris had now diagnosed kidney disease, Marshall, William Rossetti and Watts were summoned by telegram,
and the next morning Shields, Scott and Brown were informed
by letter of Gabriel's state. Until midnight old Mrs. Rossetti
sat with Gabriel, and Christina continued the vigil throughout
that and the following nights. Most of the time Rossetti sat up
in bed, crooning over odd lines of verse, for a sort of stupefaction
had now banished pain. "My own verses torment me," he
said, significantly surely, and turned to half singing, half
reciting snatches from one of Iago's songs in *Othello*. "Strange
things to come into one's head at such a moment," he said, and
when Caine told him Watts was coming on the morrow, he
exclaimed: "Then you really think that I am dying? At *last*
you think so; but *I* was right from the first." That night Caine
telegraphed to Watts: "Come down to-morrow if you can, or
to-night if possible; he is much worse."

The next day, Good Friday, William and Watts arrived.
Throughout the day Gabriel remained in a drowsy state, but
in the evening, helped by Watts, he made his will. Later that
night the rector of Birchington, who had called some weeks
before but by Gabriel's orders had been refused admittance,
called again, having heard that Rossetti would no longer
refuse to see him, and prayed with Gabriel, his mother and
Watts.

To Shields, the next day, William sent news of his brother's
alarming state. "A few sad words in haste," he wrote. "On
Monday I told you Gabriel was dying, but did not know how
very close I spoke to the very fact. He is now dying—I don't
particularly expect him to survive to-day. He is calm, patient,
conscious, rational but somewhat lethargic through weakness—
suffering we may infer, no acute pain, and not any very excessive inconvenience. The doctor says that most probably he
will pass off unconscious. My mother and sister, Watts and
Caine, and myself are here. Leyland looked in yesterday and is
expected to-day. Not many minutes ago—say at noon—Gabriel,

hearing I was going to write you, asked with his half extinct voice that I would tell you that he knows he has neglected you of late, but it was not through any feeling of indifference. Don't let anything I say beguile you into coming down here: it would be of no use."

By that time, however, the anxious Shields was already hastening to the bedside of his dying friend, and shortly afterwards arrived at the bungalow. So too did Marshall, hampered by many unavoidable delays. Gabriel, with whom the rector had again prayed, was still inert and drowsy, was suffering, Marshall declared, from uraemia, but there was no such mental malady as Dr. Harris had feared. Hot sheets and poultices ordered by Marshall brought little improvement, and throughout the night Christina and Mrs. Abrey watched the motionless, barely conscious figure on the bed.

The next evening, Sunday, April 9th, Easter Day, 1882, Rossetti died. Marshall, who had really no hope, dashed away early to London to other duties, saying Gabriel was at least holding his own, and when able must return at once to town as Birchington was too cold. Leyland, a constant caller in recent days, called again, and the rector paid another visit.

Slowly and sadly for the little group in the bungalow, Easter Sunday passed. Christina, wearied out by her nightly vigils, too tired even for church, remained with the rest at home. Early in the day there seemed a change for the better, and hope revived. Gabriel seldom spoke and then but indistinctly, was languid rather than melancholy, and did not rouse himself to any serious effort of attention. But twice during the day, in a calm, unemotional voice, he said: "I believe I shall die to-night. Yesterday I wished to die, but to-day I must confess that I do not." The well-meaning attempts of the atheist William to read parts of Ecclesiastes to him Gabriel rejected, but he yielded, though reluctantly and protestingly, to the rubbings and poulticings ordered by the doctor.

Resting in the drawing-room shortly after nine o'clock that night, in preparation for renewed watching over the sick man, William was suddenly startled by Shields dashing into the room and calling to him to come at once to his brother. Gabriel, seized by some convulsive fit, had screamed several times and collapsed, and now lay apparently unconscious, breathing hard with twitching mouth and half-closed eyes. Shields ran for Dr. Harris, who, on arriving half an hour later, at first pronounced Rossetti to be alive, but on applying the stethoscope declared life extinct, and that the uraemic poison had touched the brain. He died at 9.31 p.m. said William, with Watts, Mrs. Rossetti, Christina and the nurse present. Watts, indeed, at Gabriel's right side, was partly supporting him, while Caine and Shields were passing in and out of the room, helping in various ways.

That night, the agonizing Shields melodramatically confided to his diary the events of the day:—"April 9th—Change for the better. Hope. At a quarter to ten—the loud clang of Fate —and in five minutes the great soul was gone!"

VII

VICTORIAN AFTERMATH

As in a gravegarth, count to see
The monuments of memory.

Soothsay D. G. ROSSETTI

IMMEDIATELY UPON ROSSETTI'S DEATH, much of the pomp and circumstance of Victorianism, which in life he had so consistently evaded, began to gather about his memory. The devoted little band at Birchington at once turned their attention to what they considered the adequate recognition of his genius and preservation of his fame. The day after his death, despite Rossetti's specific prohibition of six years before, a cast of his face was taken, and also one of his small, sensitive, almost feminine hand, with its slender, tapering fingers. On the same day, Shields, at William's request, made a drawing of Gabriel, —"a melancholy, tearful task" Shields described it in his diary—and also, what Shields called "two copies in misery" for Christina and Watts. Shields, indeed, already tortured with the growing conviction that he had not done his utmost to convert Gabriel to Calvinism and so save his soul, found but minor consolation in the knowledge that the local clergyman had visited Rossetti at the last. Having completed his task at Birchington, Shields at once set off for Fulham, in order to give Jones a first-hand report of Rossetti's death, and, as he said, "to weep with him."

William Rossetti, plunged almost automatically into practical affairs by his brother's death, had little opportunity for the indulgence of sentiment. The financial embarrassments which had increasingly beset Gabriel's last years still largely remained to hamper William's arrangements, even for the last rites and the execution of his brother's will. For these reasons, as well as because of Rossetti's isolation during years of solitude, the funeral was almost private. Even the date was carefully suppressed, not only because of Gabriel's creditors but also to prevent the attendance of Fanny, who called several times at Cheyne Walk to enquire but was refused an answer. Watts, indeed, feared that if Gabriel's bank heard of his death, it might refuse to cash a cheque of £300 he had given William for immediate expenses until probate of will was granted; and as, in the event, Ellis the publisher temporarily advanced the sum required, the bank apparently *did* refuse.

It was no doubt these circumstances, as well as Gabriel's prohibition of burial at Highgate where Lizzie was buried, the prohibition he had made during his illness six years before, that determined the choice of Birchington churchyard as his last resting-place. About two o'clock on Friday afternoon, April 14th, a little band of mourners, consisting of old Mrs. Rossetti, wonderfully bearing her eighty-two years, Christina, William, Lucy, Aunt Charlotte (loyal to the last), Watts, Caine, Shields, Hueffer, Sharp, blind Philip Marston, John Seddon, Vernon Lushington (Gabriel's former colleague of The Working Men's College, and now a High Court Judge), three former patrons, Graham, Leyland, and Aldam Heaton, two of the early "Preraphaelite" circle, Stephens and Boyce, the art-dealer Murray Marks, Dr. Harris, and the rector of Birchington, Mr. Alcock, wended its way with Rossetti's remains, down the winding road he had so often and so painfully trodden in recent months, to the little churchyard, bright with spring flowers, that surrounded the old, grey stone church looking out over the flat landscape and the sea. In the churchyard, awaiting them, was an uninvited but welcome mourner, Herbert Gilchrist. Jones, who would have been present, had been taken ill on the way.

To Scott, who had not seen Rossetti since his departure from Cheyne Walk, and who, on a plea of illness, had absented himself from the funeral, Lushington that night described the simple ceremony of Rossetti's burial. "The church at Birchington," he wrote, "stands back about three-quarters of a mile from the sea, on slightly rising ground, which looks over the open land and the sea. It is of grey country flint, built in the twelfth or thirteenth century, and restored a few years ago, I thought simply; it is nicely kept, and to-day was full of Easter flowers. It had an old grey tower, and grey shingle spire, which went up, as I noticed during the ceremony, into a pure bright sky. The churchyard is nicely kept too; it was bright with irises and wallflowers in bloom, and close to Gabriel's grave there was a laurestinus and a lilac. The grave is on the south side close to the porch; it was cut so clearly it seemed carved out of the chalk. Altogether it was a sweet open spot, I thought. At the graveside, wonderful to say, was the old mother, supported by William on one side and Christina on the other—a most pathetic sight. She was very calm, extraordinarily calm, but whether from self-command or the passivity of age, I do not know.—Probably from both. But she followed all the proceedings with close interest. Then around was a company of about fifteen or twenty, many of them friends of yours, and several whom I did not know. The service was well read by the vicar. Then we all looked into the resting-place of our friend, and thought and felt our last farewells—many flowers, azaleas and primroses, were thrown in. I saw William throw in his lily of the valley. This is all I have to tell you. Sad it was, very sad, but simple and full of feeling, and the fresh beauty of the day made itself felt with all the rest. I shook hands with William and went home with Mr. Graham. Dear Gabriel, I shall not forget him. . . ."

That same evening, Aunt Charlotte, Christina, William, Lucy and Shields returned to the churchyard to place a specially beautiful wreath, brought, they believed, (but perhaps mistakenly) by Graham from Lady Mount-Temple, on Gabriel's grave. The next day, Christina returned to town. Her sonnet, *Birchington Churchyard*, written then or immediately afterwards, preserves for us the mood and the environment of the scene:—

> A lowly hill which overlooks a flat,
> Half sea, half country-side;
> A flat-shored sea of low-voiced creeping tide
> Over a chalky weedy mat.
>
> A hill of hillocks, flowery and kept green
> Round crosses raised for hope,
> With many-tinted sunsets where the slope
> Faces the lingering western sheen.
>
> A lowly hope, a height that is but low,
> While Time sets solemnly,
> While the tide rises of Eternity,
> Silent and neither swift nor slow.

Although not of her best verse, Christina's sonnet far sur-
passes the other effusions inspired by Rossetti's death. Sharp's
sentimental verses, quickly produced, and placed—apparently
in unhappy imitation of Gabriel's own impulsive gesture on the
death of his wife—in Rossetti's coffin, were bad. So too was
Watts's quintet of sonnets entitled *A Grave by the Sea,* of which
the sole interest is non-poetic, and lies in the sestet of the concluding sonnet. For that suggests that Rossetti, moved by the
popular interest in spiritualistic enquiry, had made some
arrangement with Watts for indicating, if possible, his survival
after death, so resolving that question of personal immortality
which haunted Rossetti and his age. That, surely is the only
possible meaning of Watts's description of himself in the
solitude of his loss, vainly awaiting throughout the night, the
"promised sign" to be given by Gabriel's voice:—

> . . . night, whom we two loved, seemed strange and dumb;
>   And, waiting till the dawn, the promised sign,
>   I watched—I listened for that voice of thine,
> Though Reason said: "Nor voice nor face can come."

Young Edmund Gosse, too, wrote platitudinous valedictory
verses on Rossetti immediately the news of his death reached
him, verses which he published twelve years later, in his
volume *In Russet and Silver.* The concluding stanzas reveal the
general attitude towards Rossetti as an influence upon the art
and thought and feeling of his day and the day after:—

> Farewell! though time hath vanquished our desire,
>   We shall not be as though he had not been.
> Some love of mystic thought in strange attire,
>   Of things unseen reflected in the seen,
> Of heights towards which the sons of flesh aspire,
>   Shall haunt us with a yearning close and keen.
>
> Farewell! upon the marble of his tomb
>   Let some great sculptor carve a knight in prayer,
> Who dreams he sees the holy vision come.
>   Now let the night-wind pass across his hair;
> Him can no more vain backward hope consume,
>   Nor the world vex him with her wasting care.

Already the Rossetti legend was gathering impetus, entering a
new phase, that of canonization!

With all the bitterness of thwarted affection, Swinburne

learnt the news of Gabriel's death. Scott, also alienated from Gabriel in recent months, sent Swinburne, two days after Rossetti's death, a letter written in a strangely derogatory vein, and falsely stating that "not one of the old circle of friends, admirers and equals, who used to surround him went to see the last of him." Scott's use of the word "equals" is a clear, and more significant because unconscious, revelation of his jealousy, that jealousy amongst Rossetti's acquaintance which had wrought so much havoc with his friendships and mental health. Scott's bait immediately brought a response from Swinburne, with the tale of his own injuries. "Under the circumstances," wrote Swinburne, "I felt that my attendance at his funeral could have been but a painful mockery." Yet at the same time he sent Scott a commemorative sonnet on Rossetti, written on the day of the funeral, and entitled *A Death on Easter Day*, in which Swinburne's new-found belief in immortality appeared in somewhat too sentimental and rhetorical a form, particularly in relation to Gabriel, who, despite a basic sentimentality in his attitude to life, was at the same time too much of a Latin realist for the openly grandiloquent and sentimental to be other than out of place when applied to himself.

That, indeed, was largely the measure of Rossetti, too individual, too independent of contemporary fashions and conventions to fit into any orthodox or conventional setting of commemorative verse. This, Christina had doubtless felt when confining herself to the vague and consequently somewhat weak generalities of *Birchington Churchyard*. In contrast to the subdued, reflective mood of Christina's poem, Swinburne sang over his dead friend a song of victory:—

> A light more bright than ever bathed the skies
> Departs for all time out of all men's eyes.
>   The crowns that girt last night a living head
>   Shine only now, though deathless, on the dead:
> Art that mocks death, and Song that never dies.
> Albeit the bright sweet mothlike wings be furled,
>   Hope sees, past all division and defection,
>   And higher than swims the mist of human breath,
> The soul most radiant once in all the world
>   Requickened to regenerate resurrection
>   Out of the likeness of the shadow of death.

Immediately after Rossetti's funeral, the so long silent house in Cheyne Walk began to hum with mundane human activities. William, to whose share ever fell the commonplace, practical details of his brother's life, even after Gabriel's death, was at once immersed in a flood of accounts and busy settling his brother's debts, including an unexpected claim for fifty-two pounds from a firm of chemists in New Bond Street, for chloral secretly bought by Gabriel in addition to his open purchases from another firm. Dunn, now temporarily back in Cheyne Walk, made water-colour sketches of the familiar rooms before all was changed, and then helped Brown to touch up and complete for sale Rossetti's unfinished works. Old Mrs. Rossetti and Christina, together with aunts Charlotte and Eliza, came to take a last look at the place and choose mementos. Each chose a book from the library, as arranged, and Mrs. Rossetti and Christina a drawing each as well. Caine, at Birchington, was busy despatching Rossetti's belongings to London. A few pieces he bought privately for himself, and with them established himself in Clifford's Inn as a journalist.

One other piece of "clearing up" William had done at the first possible moment when it might be done safely. He had sent to Fanny, on the morning of the funeral, when there could be no chance of her arriving as an undesired and undesirable mourner, the following little note:—"Dear Madam, —Your letter of the 12th only reached me this morning about 9. The coffin had been closed last evening, and the funeral takes place early this afternoon—there is nothing further to be done.—Faithfully yours, W. M. Rossetti." And apart from some vain attempts to extract from Fanny pictures which in some cases at least she had no difficulty in proving from Gabriel's notes had been freely given to her by him, the Rossetti family had no more dealings with the woman whose life had been so strangely linked to Rossetti's. With similar trenchancy, William now replied to the overtures of Howell, refusing all relations save those of business. "I will," said William, in reply to a suggestion from Howell of a personal visit, "however awkward for myself and perhaps not kindly taken by you—say that I had rather not renew any visiting or family intimacy between your house and mine. Our intimacy was severed some years ago by circumstances in which I was not personally concerned, and I think we had better leave it on that footing—mutual helpfulness in any business relations which may be advantageous to both of us, without renewal of familiar visiting, etc." . . .

On July 5th, and the two following days, the sale of Rossetti's household effects took place at Cheyne Walk. To William's pleased surprise it produced, together with some of the pictures sold privately, about three thousand pounds. Shields, inconsolable since his friend's death, attended the second day of the sale, and the next day he drew for Leyland a head of Rossetti. Three days later, when the sale was over, Shields bade the empty house in Cheyne Walk a sad farewell. "To Cheyne Walk," he wrote that night in his diary. "The things all removed. All bare. The last look." The earlier part of the evening he had spent at Mrs. Rossetti's, where Christina had shown him a medallion of Gabriel at eighteen and other souvenirs, including a lock of his hair as a child, when it was still golden, not as later dark. . . . It chanced to be Gabriel's birthday, May 12, 1883, when the remaining paintings were sold at Christie's for about the same sum as the household sale had realized; the total thus raised, almost six thousand pounds, proved sufficient to pay Rossetti's debts and even to leave a small balance in hand.

Nor was public recognition of Rossetti's achievement lacking. Exhibitions of his works were sponsored by the Royal Academy and Burlington Fine Arts Club respectively, and, although Shields and Brown grumbled that the Academy's selection was inadequate, Jones and old Mrs. Rossetti were well pleased. Lady Mount-Temple, comparing Gabriel's paintings with those of the early Italian masters "rejoiced . . . in the thought of the triune angels—the mighty Michael, the beautiful Raphael, and our Messenger of promise," a "thought" which would have much amused so unangelic an individual as Gabriel. Amidst the deluge of compliments Lady Eastlake— widow of the former President of the Royal Academy who, in 1850, had sworn to exterminate the rebels—maintained an adamantine contempt for Rossetti and his works. "Horrors,"

without a single merit, she thought them. Layard, the archaeologist, she declared, "calls them 'women with cadaverous
bodies and sensual mouths.' I say," she added, "that part look
as if they were going to be hanged, wringing their hands and
poking out their chins—and others look as if they had been
hanged and were partially decomposed." Six months later
William Rossetti observed with satisfaction that some of
these despised paintings were now in the South Kensington
Museum.

The Rossettis must have been less appreciative of another
memorial exhibition of Rossetti's works, that held at the
"Rossetti Gallery," 1a Old Bond Street, by Fanny's husband
Schott, probably at the suggestion of Howell. Schott exhibited
whatever works and photographs of works by Gabriel Fanny
had acquired, including two chalk portraits of Fanny and two
of Janey, as well as the famous portrait of Gabriel by G. F.
Watts, a portrait which William had vainly tried to extract
from Fanny, who loudly protested that it was Gabriel's gift to
her—as indeed Rossetti's own notes clearly prove. Gabriel's
reason for these gifts had been his fear that Fanny might be
left without any means of support if anything happened to
himself.

Such public honours, however, did not exhaust the *pietas* of
the Rossetti family. Old Mrs. Rossetti got Brown to design a
Celtic cross for Gabriel's headstone, and Shields to design a
memorial window for the church at Birchington. Attracted as
by some spell of the dead, the old lady spent the summer
months of 1883 and 1884 at Birchington, making daily visits to
her son's grave. "This beautiful air and quiet change," wrote
Christina, the first year, "in combination with the heart's ease
of being near Gabriel's grave, seem to have revived her."
"Very fine," Mrs. Rossetti thought Brown's cross with its runic
bas-relief symbolizing Gabriel's life and work, when she first
saw it in 1884, and so too thought Christina.

Caine's Liverpool friend, the sonnet enthusiast, J. H. Noble,
pointed out in a detailed description of the cross, published in
The Bookman, that each of the four angles is covered with a
design showing the Lilith of Eden Bower, while below is a
marriage ceremony performed by a blindfolded priest. "It may

be assumed," wrote Noble, who doubtless learned much about Rossetti from Caine, "that the designer's conception has a symbolical and personal reference to the real life of Rossetti. . . . This assumption is supported by two significant details. The bridegroom carries in his hand a book which recalls the volume that Rossetti buried in the coffin of his dead wife; and the priest who officiates with bandaged eyes seems to play the part of a blind presiding destiny." Below this was carved a "winged Assyrian bull," recalling Rossetti's *Burden of Nineveh,* and below that was depicted an old monk painter falling dead at his easel. Nor was Brown yet satisfied with his orgy of symbolism, for below all came what in Noble's words "appears to be the ground plan of a maze or labyrinth —fit image of the mystery of life—the involved curves shaping themselves at one spot into a monogram formed of the initials D. G. R."

Planting roses about the grave and making new flower-crosses, in that summer of 1884, Mrs. Rossetti and Christina wondered who had laid there that nameless cross of artificial flowers, and who was the nameless, mysterious lady the sexton spoke of who, in her distress, had actually fainted by the graveside. . . .

On a day of late October, that same year, Shields' memorial window was placed in Birchington church, but Shields looked on it with exasperation. With his usual ill-luck, he had once again unwittingly challenged a Victorian taboo. "I do not think this picture is likely to inspire devotional thoughts and feelings, and fear that in some cases it might rather do the reverse," the vicar had written to him, vetoing Shields' first design for the window, an adaptation of Rossetti's exquisite *Magdalene at the door of Simon.* To this the exasperated artist had replied:—"My friend Rossetti himself would have shrunk with shuddering at any supposition that the design could have an impure effect. Mrs. and Miss Rossetti could not have anticipated, even in dreams, such an objection arising, for they had been accustomed to regard the design as directly opponent to evil, and so it is. I perceive that the freedom of the design from the dead unhelpful conventionality common to religious art has astonished you." The Calvinistic artist's protest however

failed to assuage the worthy vicar's fear of untoward consequence to his flock, and the angry Shields was forced to substitute a design based on Gabriel's *Passover in the Holy Family.*
The second light of the window, an entirely original design by
Shields, showing Christ healing the blind, was accepted by
the vicar as innocuous. "Beautiful beyond my expectation,"
said Mrs. Rossetti, on seeing the window. A day or two later
she left for London, with Christina, and never saw Birchington
again.

Nearly three years later, in July 1887, another plan for the
perpetuation of Rossetti's fame came to fruition, when Holman
Hunt, in a little ceremony on the Chelsea Embankment
opposite 16 Cheyne Walk, unveiled a bronze medallion of
Gabriel, designed by Ford Madox Brown, which surmounted a
drinking fountain designed by John Seddon. "Accepting the
duty," wrote Hunt afterwards, "I determined therefore to
give the fullest measure of admiration possible." But those who
heard Hunt's niggling or ambiguous praise of the dead painter
once his friend, saw that the old jealousy had not died with
Rossetti's death.

Hunt might with some reason protest against the public
exaltation of Gabriel as "leader" of the Preraphaelites, but
despite Rossetti's own denials of ever being a Preraphaelite at
all, so closely was the movement associated in general opinion,
and rightly, with the genius, personality and romantic legend
of Rossetti that upon his death public interest in Preraphaelitism rapidly waned. Preraphaelite influence certainly long
persisted, but French Impressionism and English "aestheticism"
increasingly dominated the thought and artistic outlook of the
nineties as one after another the original Preraphaelite circle
passed away. Their fates, like Rossetti's, were largely determined by their temperaments. Scott, still vain, disappointed
and jealous, died at Penkill in 1890. Brown, stubbornly contemptuous of the Academy to the last, died three years later,
shortly after completing his Manchester frescoes, and still
bravely struggling to master his debts. Millais, although at one
of his own exhibitions he shed tears on seeing how far he had
failed to fulfil the artistic promise of his youth, was supremely
"successful" in his profession, became President of the Academy

he had once pretended to despise, and died a wealthy, influential and widely esteemed man. To the end, despite his momentary tears, he argued with Hunt that "a man should adapt himself to the temper of his time," that "a painter must work for the taste of his own day . . . I want proof," he said, "that the people of my day enjoy my work, and how can I get this better than by finding people willing to give me money for my productions, and that I win honours from contemporaries? What good would recognition of my labours hundreds of years hence do me? I should be dead, buried and crumbled into dust. Don't let us bother ourselves about the destinies of our work in the world, but as it brings us fortune and recognition." So, painting firemen and infants blowing bubbles, amidst universal applause, Millais lived and died a wealthy man in 1896, and was buried in St. Paul's. Two years later, Jones (who had become Sir Edward Burne-Jones), died. But Holman Hunt, first and last of the Preraphaelite Brotherhood, lived on, blind, helpless, but with his wonderful memory unimpaired, until 1910, still resentful of Rossetti's reputed "leadership," still an obstinate opponent of the Academy, but with the Order of Merit as a solace to his pride.

It was Shields, a year before Hunt's death, who in a letter to Charles Rowley, the Preraphaelites' friend and patron in Manchester, penned the Preraphaelites' swan-song. Thanking his friend for a series of designs, Shields particularly appreciated "a precious reprint of the Preraphaelite designs to Tennyson, which sent my memory back to young days when these were a stimulus and a delight of the fullest kind. An awakening to higher aims and effort, and the effect yet remains. Those wonderful Rossetti drawings—ah me! There has been none in my age like to him, and life has been impoverished since he passed away—the great mind, the generous soul. And one after another has gone. . . ."

Whatever the praise and dispraise showered upon Rossetti during the years following his death, his grave in Birchington churchyard long remained a place of pilgrimage. Justin McCarthy, the historian, often visited it during these and later years. "Beautifully placed," he described it in a letter of

October 1888, to Mrs. Campbell Praed, the then famous novelist, "in a quiet old churchyard not wholly unlike that at Battersea." "Yesterday," he wrote again to the same friend, in November 1891, "we walked to Birchington and went into the dear little churchyard and saw Dante Rossetti's grave. You will easily imagine that my mind went back to that other day when you and I were there—shortly before I went to Algeria." And yet again, in July 1893 he told her: "I am going next Saturday to stay until Monday at Quex Park, Birchington. Do you remember Birchington and Dante Rossetti's grave?" Certainly Mrs. Campbell Praed no more forgot Birchington than did her friend. "There seems," she wrote two months after McCarthy's visit there in 1888, "always to have been an association with Justin McCarthy in my winter visits to the Isle of Thanet. I find some notes of an excursion with him to Birchington to see Dante Rossetti's grave, when I felt the first touch of a certain eerie fascination, that deepened with later familiarity, which in my mind hangs over that bit of Kentish coast—the long stretches of grassy land, greyish brown, tinging to yellow in the winter season, almost treeless and apparently level with the horizon, only a solitary farmhouse or windmill or hayrick standing here and there silhouetted in dull grey against fainter-hued grey sky. Grey is the predominant note of that wintry landscape—grey earth, grey heaven, and grey sea blending in the dull grey mist.

"As we entered the church gates, an old sexton who was rolling the gravel walk came up and asked us if we were looking for the tomb of that gentleman as died at Birchington whose grave so many people came to see. He took us to the spot. The headstones in the churchyard were grey, too, and pallidly grey was the granite cross designed by Ford Madox Brown to mark the last resting place of his friend. We stood there for a long time while McCarthy talked of the dead poet-painter, and then we went into the church to see the memorial window. 'There's not another bit of glass in the church to compare with that un,' said the sexton proudly, 'and the left-hand side is after one of the gentleman's own pictures. They're Grills, Matheson and Grind of Birmingham as put it up—and I helped un myself,' added the sexton. Mr. McCarthy smiled and quoted from Byron:

> ... they come to pay
> Homage to him, to myself—whatever
> Your honour pleases.

'Rossetti was a frank atheist,' he went on, 'yet see—he has come to the consecrated ground and the cross and the memorial window!' "

NOTES

p. 28. In justice to Gabriele Rossetti it should be stated that some present-day scholars in Italy believe his theories were not without some justification as regards Dante. See *Gabriele Rossetti in England*, by E. R. Vincent, Oxford, 1936.

p. 127. Of Lizzie's visit to Hastings in 1854 there is abundant evidence; but my sole evidence for this visit two years earlier is D. G. Rossetti's remark in a letter to Christina, dated 4, August, 1852—"I shall very possibly be going to Hastings in a few days," and William Rossetti's comment: "My brother's proposed trip to Hastings was for the purpose of rejoining Miss Siddal, who stayed there at times for Health's sake." *Family Letters of Christina Rossetti*, ed. W. M. Rossetti, London, 1908, pp. 21–2. Part of this letter, including this passage but without editorial comment, had appeared in W. M. Rossetti's *Memoir* of D. G. Rossetti, vol. II, pp. 95–6.

p. 142. Rossetti's antagonism to his father during his lifetime followed by a reversal of attitude after his death, as shown in the sonnet *Dantis Tenebrae* (1861), would doubtless be explained by the modern psychologist as a case of the Oedipus Complex in the light of the following interesting lines from the sonnet *Inclusiveness* (1869).

> Say, hast thou bent o'er thy son's sleep to brood
> How his face shall watch thine when cold it lies?
> *Or pondered when thy mother kissed thine eyes*
> *Of what her kiss was when thy father wooed?*

(The italics are mine.)

The strong personal note of this MS. version was softened on publication (as with so many of these sonnets), by changing the question from the second to the third person: "What man," etc. Rossetti's affection for his mother above all others throughout his life was remarked by his family and friends. See also *sup.* p. 653.

p. 156. Giacomo ("Jocopo" in Rossetti's translation) da Lentino's authorship of this poem is now disputed. See *The Poetry of Giacomo da Lentino*, ed. E. Langley, London, 1915.

p. 241. These mural paintings in the Oxford Union have been admirably restored. See *Manchester Guardian*, March 9 and 11, 1936.

p. 245. "The price paid for the triptych may probably have been £400." *D. G. Rossetti as Designer and Writer*, by W. M. Rossetti. London, 1889, p. 34.

Some years later, said W. M. Rossetti, Gabriel "went to Llandaff and there retouched the picture, and 'much improved' (as he considered) 'the centre-piece by lightening the Virgin and Child.'" *Ibid.*, p. 67.

p. 251. Other facts that may support this suggestion as to Fanny's profession besides her domicile in so notorious a street as Dean Street, Soho, Rossetti's (?) speedy removal of her to Tennyson Street, and Boyce's discovery of her, (evidently without escort, so important in the mid-Victorian period) in the Argyle [*sic*] Rooms[1], (*v. inf.* p. 253) are the frequent allusions in Rossetti's works to the prostitute theme, up to the date of his renewal of close acquaintance with Mrs. Morris on

---

[1] *The Argyll Rooms*. Since writing the above, I find my suspicion of Fanny's profession supported, if not almost proved, upon investigating the associations of The Argyll Rooms in the mid-Victorian period. "The Argyll Rooms (now the Trocadero) in Windmill Street obtained a very unsavoury reputation, and have no history worthy of relation," *London, Past and Present*, by H. B. Wheatley, 3 vols., London, 1891, Vol. I, p. 60. "In the nineteenth century, when night life was confined to men, in the company of ladies of the town, London was a profligate and drunken city. Supper houses and dancing places, like the Piccadilly, Jessops, or the Argyll, would be open all night, and young men about town were carried to bed with the dawn." *Society Racket*, by P. Balfour, London, 1932, p. 162. *v.* also Sala's association of *Jenny* with Fanny (evidently) in Note to p. 257 *inf.*

the Morrises return to London and her sitting to him for her portrait in 1868, the time when Rossetti began to write the many sonnets of that and the next few years in *The House of Life*. The various works in which the prostitute or similar theme appears are as follows:—

Poems

1. Dante at Verona (1849–50 and 1869–70).
2. Jenny (1848, "mostly 1858–69," W. M. R.). Sharp (*D. G. Rossetti*, p. 332) dates *Jenny* as 1858.
3. A Last Confession (1849, also 1869–70).
4. The Burden of Nineveh (1850 and later).
5. After the French Liberation of Italy (1859).
6. Body's Beauty (Lilith) (1866).
7. Mary Magdalene at the Door of Simon the Pharisee (1869).
8. The Orchard Pit (1869).
9. After the German Subjugation of France (1871).
10. Found (1881).
11. Translation of *Lo Marinaio oblia che passa per tal via* (1853?).

Paintings, etc.

1. Hesterna Rosa (1850).
2. Lo Marinaio oblia che passa per tal via (1853).
3. Found (1853 and onwards).
4. Mary Magdalene at the Door of Simon the Pharisee (1858). Pen and ink. Repeated in oil, 1865, and again in water-colour, 1865.
5. Bocca Baciata (1859).
6. Lady Lilith (1864). Also two water-colours and two crayons (1867–8).
7. Head of a Magdalen (1867).

Prose

1. The Orchard Pit (1869).

To these should be added the prose outline entitled *The Doom of the Sirens* (1869) and the corresponding painting, *Ligeia Siren* (1873), which are merely variations upon the same theme.

p. 257. Annie Miller seems to have been the model for *The Magdalene at the Door of Simon the Pharisee*, but evidence is confused. W. M. Rossetti implicitly denies that Fanny was the model, for after enumerating a series of pictures in which Fanny appears, he continues: "I proceed to other sitters not as yet mentioned. For *The Magdalene at the Door of Simon the Pharisee*, and for *Helen of Troy*, an Englishwoman sat, remarkable for beauty, but not for depths of expression. Her head appears also in the water-colour . . . of *Dante's Dream*." *Family Letters with a Memoir*, by W. M. Rossetti, 2 vols., London, 1895, Vol. I, p. 242.

Similarly in *The Art Journal* for June, 1884 (p. 167), W. M. Rossetti distinguishes the model for the Magdalene as different from both Miss Wilding and Fanny. If, as W. M. R. asserts, the model for the Magdalene was the same as that for Helen of Troy, then according to Boyce, she must have been Annie Miller, since Boyce's Diary for March 13, 1863, records: "D. G. R. is going on with Annie Miller's head, which he has converted into *Helen of Troy*—ships burning in the background." *Extracts from Boyce's Diaries*, Old Water-Colour Society's Club, 1941. George Augustus Sala, however, the well-known journalist, who at that time saw much of Rossetti, suggests that the Magdalene is a blending of two models, apparently Miss Herbert and Fanny. Rossetti, he wrote, was one of his "most frequent visitors, . . . who gave us a photo of his wonderful pen-and-ink drawing of Mary Magdalene at the House of Simon the Pharisee. . . . Those who are familiarly cognizant with Rossetti's works are aware that for the face and figure of the Magdalen he used two models: the head and arms of the figure were studied from a delightful actress who is still living, and whom I had the honour to know for many years: the remainder was studied from the typically Preraphaelite model, immortalized by the artist in his poem called *Jenny*." *The Life and Adventures of George Augustus Sala*,

NOTES

2 vols., London, 1895, I, 407. Although *Jenny* was begun long before Rossetti met Fanny, he was revising the poem at this time, and Sala's apparent association of *Jenny* with Fanny is another of the vague suggestions that Jenny's and Fanny's professions were the same, as also perhaps is the close resemblance between the two names. *v.* also *On Rossetti's "Jenny,"* Notes and Queries, July 10, 1937, vol. 173, pp. 20–1, and also *sup.* pp. 249–50.

p. 274. The following is the passage in Swinburne's *A Year's Letters*: "When I am looking at Mademoiselle Philomène, and letting myself go to the sound of her voice like a song to the tune, unhappily there gets up between us such an invincible, exquisite memory of a face ten times more beautiful and lovable to have in sight of one: pale when I saw it last, as if drawn down by its hair, heavily weighted about the eyes with a presage of tears, sealed with sorrow, and piteous with an infinite, unaccomplished desire. The old deep-gold hair and luminous grey-green eyes shot through with colours of sea-water in sunlight, and threaded with faint keen lines of fire and light about the pupil, beat for me the blue-black of Mademoiselle de Rochelaurier's. Then that mouth of hers and the shadow made almost on the chin by the underlip—such sad, perfect lips, full of tender power and faith, and her wonderful way of lifting and dropping her face imperceptibly, flower-fashion, when she begins or leaves off speaking: I shall never hear such a voice in the world, either. I cannot, and need not now, pretend to dissemble or soften down what I feel about her. I do love her with all my heart and might. And now that, after happy years, she is fallen miserable and ill, dangerously ill, for aught I know, and incurably miserable—who can say?—it is not possible for me, sitting here in her house . . . to think very much of anything else, or to think at all of any other woman in the way of liking. This is mere bare truth, not sentiment or excited fancy by any means, and you will not take it for such a sort of thing. If I can never marry the one woman perfectly pleasant to me and faultlessly fit for me in the whole beautiful nature of her, I will never insult her and my own heart by marrying at all."

p. 281. The resemblance between the close of the sonnet *Memorial Thresholds* (1873) and D. G. R.'s letter to Mrs. Gilchrist (1862).

> City, of thine a single simple door,
>   By some new Power reduplicate, must be
>   Even yet my life-porch in eternity,
> Even with one presence filled, as once of yore:
> Or mocking winds whirl round a chaff-strown floor
>   Thee and thy years and these my words and me.

In a letter of condolence, dated January 15, 1862, to Mrs. Gilchrist, whose husband had just died, Rossetti wrote: " . . . But in these feelings as in all other respects, what can be done except to trust to what is surely a natural instinct in all . . . that is, that such terrible partings from love and work must be, unless all things are a mere empty husk of nothing,—a guide to belief in a new field of effort and a second communion with those loved and lost?" *Anne Gilchrist*, by H. H. Gilchrist, London, 1887, p. 111. See also *sup.* p. 554.

p. 286. "*The Beloved* was finished in 1866, but was painted upon again in 1873, this time happily without injurious effects. Amongst other changes which took place while the picture was in progress, Rossetti at one point substituted the little negro boy for his first conception of the foremost figure, a brown mulatto girl." *D. G. Rossetti*, by H. C. Marillier, 3rd ed., p. 97.

p. 317. "*Venus Verticordia*—I think this title has been discussed with you before. Lemprière makes a very startling statement: 'Venus was also surnamed . . . Verticordia because she could turn the hearts of women to cultivate chastity.' If this is at all correct, it is clear that the Verticordian Venus is, technically, just the contrary sort of Venus from the one you contemplate—she must be a phase of Venus

683

Urania." W. M. R. to D. G. R., August 24, 1869, *Rossetti Papers*, ed. W. M. Rossetti, London, 1903, p. 456. "We may notice an especially interesting form of the worship of Venus, where she appears under the title of Verticordia. In the year 114 B.C. three Vestal Virgins were condemned to death for transgressing with Roman knights the rigid law against sexual intercourse. To atone for their misdeeds, a shrine was dedicated to Venus Verticordia in the hope that she would turn the hearts of women and girls against licentiousness and towards chastity. Hence her name Verticordia, which means turner of hearts. Under this title she was especially worshipped by married women. . . ." *Sexual Life in Ancient Rome*, by Otto Kiefer. Translated by Gilbert and Helen Highet, London, 1934, pp. 113–14.

p. 326. Since writing the above, I have read *The Order of Release*, ed. by Sir William James, London, 1947, but consider that it would be premature to change my description of Ruskin until *his* case has been presented with equal clarity. In any case, I give Ruskin as he appeared to himself.

p. 327. The editors of Ruskin's *Works* were misled by W. M. Rossetti's belief that the photograph by Downey to which Ruskin objected was not the well-known one of Ruskin, Rossetti and W. B. Scott, but "a different one, representing Ruskin (alone) seated and leaning on a walking-stick," *Rossetti Papers*, ed. W. M. Rossetti, London, 1903, p. 136. Both William Rossetti and Ruskin's editors, however, overlooked Ruskin's remark to his father in a letter of September 18, 1863: "I have written to Rossetti to scold him for letting that photo get abroad. The broad-hatted individual I always forget to tell you is Scott, the painter of Lady Trevelyan's hall. . . ." Ruskin's *Works*, ed. Cook and Wedderburn, 39 vols., London, 1903–12, Vol. 36, pp. 454 and 491.

p. 339. "Widowhood" it should be noted, is as applicable to a widower as to a widow, since it connotes *a state of bereavement* without reference to the sex of the bereaved. Indeed so comprehensive a dictionary as *Annandale's* published in 1907, significantly omits "widowerhood," defining "widowhood" as "the state of a man or woman whose husband or wife is dead, and who has not married again." Rossetti doubtless uses the term poetically and metaphorically for Janey and poetically, metaphorically and literally for himself. Where my references are specifically to Rossetti, I use the term "widowerhood" (reluctantly), to prevent possible misunderstanding.

p. 343. John Henry Middleton (1846–96) was an architect and archaeologist. In 1886 he was appointed Slade Professor of Fine Art at the University of Cambridge, and in 1892 Art Director of the South Kensington Museum. The following passage from Wilfrid Scawen Blunt's *My Diaries*, 2 vols., London, 1919, is my authority: "on to Kelmscott, where I stayed a couple of nights. I found there my friend John Henry Middleton, the Cambridge Professor, an old ally of Morris's, and intimate in former days with Rossetti. . . . Middleton had known Kelmscott Manor in the early days when Rossetti and Morris first took the house together at a rent of £60 a year. The tapestry room, which is now the sitting-room, used to be Rossetti's own room, and it was there that he wrote his poetry. Rossetti, he tells me, was addicted to loves of the most material kind both before and after his marriage, with women, generally models, without other soul than their beauty. It was remorse at the contrast between his ideal and his real loves that preyed on him and destroyed his mind. It is touching to see still on the table at meals napkins marked with the initials D. G. R. His ghost seems to be present in all the rooms" (August, 1892), pp. 86, 88.

"He (Morris) had little patience with fools, and the prettiest woman in the world could not seduce him into listening to nonsense if there was nothing of fact behind it. His time was too precious to waste on them; and the fine ladies who affected artistic tastes in his company without real knowledge put him straightway to flight. To such he was rude and repellent. . . . In his domestic life Morris was too busy to be unhappy, and of too sanguine a temperament to worry himself much over past disappointments; yet disappointments cannot but have been his.

He had a strong and affectionate heart, and had vented his home affections on his two children. . . . Kelmscott Manor was a romantic house, and the life there extremely primitive. There were few of the conveniences of modern life. The rooms below and also on the upper floor were all passage rooms opening one into another, and in order to reach the tapestried chamber in which we sat in the evenings, it was necessary to pass to and fro through Morris's own bedroom, in which he lay at night in a great square Elizabethan four-post bed. . . ." (1889), *Ibid.*, pp. 28–9. "One thing only, I think, he did not know, much as he had written about it, the love of women, and that he never cared to discuss." *Ibid.*, pp. 30–1.

p. 370. For a list of Rossetti's designs for stained glass and comments thereon, see Marillier's *Dante Gabriel Rossetti*, 2nd ed., London, 1901, pp. 83–6. This and later editions correct the errors in the list as given in the 1st ed., 1899, pp. 111–15.

p. 377. As quoted by Marillier in the various editions of his *Dante Gabriel Rossetti*. W. M. Rossetti in the 1911 edition of his brother's *Works*, gives "formâ" for "vultu."

p. 378. W. M. Rossetti considered that D. G. Rosssetti used the expression *House of Life* in an astrological sense, "Youth (Love?) Change and Fate" being in the House of Life, "as the sun is said to be 'in the house of Leo.' *v. The Works of D. G. Rossetti*, 1911, p. 651. It may well be that Rossetti was indebted to the painter G. F. Watts's grandiose conception of a picture to be called *The House of Life. v. G. F. Watts*, by W. S. Watts, London, 2 vols. 1912, I, 101–2. "A queer sort of picture about God and Creation," was Rossetti's comment on it. *v, Memorials of Sir Edward Burne-Jones* by Lady Burne-Jones, 2 vols., London, 1912, I, 159.

p. 381. Similarly, the original *Love's Compass* became *Heart's Compass*, *Love and Worship*, became *Passion and Worship*, *Love's Pageant* became *Beauty's Pageant*, *Love-light* became *Soul Light*, *Love-measure* became *Equal Troth*, *Sleepless Love* became *Sleepless Dreams*, and as stated in the text, *The Love-lamp* became *The Lamp's Shrine*, *Love's Antiphony* became *Youth's Antiphony*. Thus *Youth's Spring Tribute* was probably originally *Love's Spring Tribute*.

William Rossetti's dating of the sonnets sometimes differs considerably from the dates he gives on other occasions, as a comparison of his edition of the *Collected Works* (1887), with his *Dante Gabriel Rossetti as Designer and Writer* (1889), the *Memoir* (1895), and the *Works* (1911), shows. Even in the last of these, the only one in which he claims accurate knowledge, there are occasional demonstrable inaccuracies, thus—Sonnets 49–52, *Willow-wood*, dated 1869, in 1911, should be 1868, as an entry in W. M. Rossetti's Diary for December 18, 1868, shows. *v. Rossetti Papers*, p. 339. The relevant extract is also quoted in this present work, p. 687. Sonnet 64, *Ardour and Memory*, is dated 1873 in 1911, but was in fact sent to Rosssetti's friend Davies in a letter dated "Xmas 1879" and there described as "written just now." Sharp prints a facsimile of the manuscript version of the sonnet, written in Rossetti's hand and dated "Xmas 1879," in his *D. G. Rossetti*, p. 426. Sonnet 77, *Soul's Beauty*, dated 1867 in 1911, was written in 1866, as a reference to it in an unpublished letter of Rossetti's dated May of that year, shows. Sonnet 97, *A Superscription*, dated 1868 in 1911, was written early in 1869, as an entry in W. M. Rossetti's Diary for January 24, shows. *v. Rossetti Papers*, p. 380. The relevant extract is also quoted in the present work, p. 687.

Sonnet 29, *The Moonstar*, and 55, *Stillborn Love*, dated respectively in 1911, as 1871 and 1870, appear in fact in the First Trial Book of 1869. Sonnet 8, *Love's Lovers*, described in 1911 as first published in 1881, appeared in *Poems* (1870). Sonnets 74–76, *Old and New Art*, are all dated in 1911, as 1849; yet in a note on p. 656 of that same edition, the second and third of these sonnets are dated 1848. All three are also described in 1911 as first published in 1870, yet only No. 1 was published at that date, Nos. 2 and 3 being first published in *Ballads and Sonnets* in 1881. Sonnet 86, *Lost Days*, is described in 1911 as first published in 1863; yet nowhere is any indication given of the medium of such publication, nor does it appear as published under this date in William Michael Rossetti's bibliographies of his brother's works.

Nevertheless, as we shall see, all the biographical evidence suggests that the dating of the sonnets in the *Works*, 1911, is substantially correct.

p. 385. The following extracts from *Rossetti Papers*, ed. W. M. Rossetti, London, 1903, clearly reveal the dating of some of these sonnets, as well as the work he was then doing on his picture *Pandora*.

W. M. Rossetti's Diary—1868

Friday, 27 November.—Gabriel, being still, from the state of his eyes, unable to resume painting, has been looking up his poems of old days, with some floating idea of offering some of them to the *Fortnightly Review*, and at any rate with a degree of zest which looks promising for *some* result with them. . . .

Monday, 7 December.—Gabriel has now resumed work; having begun some crayon heads of Mrs. Morris as *Pandora*, etc. . .

Friday, 18 December.—Gabriel has just written a series of four sonnets—*Willow-wood*—about the finest thing he has done. I see the poetical impulse is upon him again: he says he ought never to have been a painter, but a poet instead.

Saturday, 19 December.—Gabriel wrote a sonnet on Death at Euston Square. (This must be the first of the two sonnets entitled *Newborn Death*, both of which W. M. Rossetti dates "December 1868," in a note in the 1911 edition of Rossetti's *Works*.) *Rossetti Papers*, pp. 336-9.

W. M. Rossetti's diary for 1869 is again of interest as regards these sonnets :—

Sunday, 24 January.—Gabriel has written another sonnet, *A Superscription*: has selected sixteen sonnets, and sent them to the *Fortnightly* for the March number. He thinks he must have by him altogether at least fifty sonnets which he would be willing to publish.

Sunday, 21 February.—Gabriel called in Euston Square: he is engaged on a *Pandora* from Mrs. Morris.

Saturday, 6 March.—According to Sandys, Payne (J. B. Payne, managing partner of Moxon and Co., publishers of Swinburne's *Poems and Ballads*) has disseminated all sorts of scandal about Gabriel among others.

Thursday, 18 March.—Gabriel has done two new sonnets—*Pandora* (for his picture now in progress) and *Vain Virtues*.

Thursday, 6 May.—Gabriel has written several new sonnets.

Saturday, 5 June.—Gabriel showed me a song he has written, *Dark Lily* (published as *Love-Lily*) and two Italian sonnets. (*v.* Note to p. 391.)

Sunday, 18 July.—Gabriel has begun his three-quarter picture of *Pandora*; but wants to carry out the same subject whole-length.

Wednesday, 21 July.—Met Brown who tells me Morris and his wife who are going to Ems for the health of the latter, along with her sister and Lucy Brown (both of whom will return after reaching Cologne or Coblenz), started the other day, and had arrived at Calais. . . . [The Morrises in fact left England on July 14th.—O. D.]

Wednesday, 4 August.—Gabriel is having his various poems—such as he values sufficiently—printed for future use in any way he may like.

Tuesday, 18 September.—Gabriel's pictures of *Lilith* and *Venus* (*Verticordia*) are now sent off to their owners . . . *Sibylla Palmifera* has been a good deal worked on of late, and there are some fresh crayon-drawings of Mrs. Morris. . . .

Tuesday, 21 September.—Gabriel returned to Chelsea yesterday, and I saw him this evening. He looks to me well enough; but he says he has been very weak, perspiring excessively, losing sleep, and that his health is breaking up. He has done a good deal of poetry—ballads of *Helen* and *Lilith* [*Troy Town* and *Eden Bower* were their published titles.—O. D.], both very fine (the latter not yet finished), sonnets, etc. He seems more anxious just now to achieve something permanent in poetry than in painting—in which he considers that at any rate two living Englishmen, Millais and Jones, show a higher innate *executive* power than himself.

Monday, 27 September.—Gabriel called in Euston Square; read us his poem of *Lilith*, just completed, and some others.

Tuesday, 28 September.—Gabriel writes and works at his poems a good deal, and has not yet resumed painting. He seems not by any means indisposed to publish the poems soon with Ellis, whose printer is doing the printing work.

Thursday, 7 October.—Gabriel read several of his poems, and expresses a distinct intention of soon publishing.

Wednesday, 13 October.—Scott informs me that the uncoffining of Gabriel's MS. poems has now been effected.

Tuesday, 26 October.—Gabriel called. He has now finished copying what he wants out of the unearthed MS. book of poems; and read me the old compositions —*Jenny, Last Confession, Dante in Verona, Portrait* and *Bride Chamber Talk* (*The Bride's Prelude*).

Monday, 8 November.—Gabriel, who called in Euston Square, complains very much of a constant shaking of the hand, etc., with corresponding internal sensations. He supposes it to be a nervous disease, and even has some apprehensions of impending paralysis: the symptoms have now been going on several days, but don't seem particularly to affect his steadiness of hand in drawing or writing. He has consulted Marshall, who orders iron and other tonics.

Monday, 15 November.—Dined at Brown's, with Miss Spartali, Stillman, and Gabriel. The chief *raison d'être* of the gathering was for Gabriel to read some of his poems to Miss Spartali, which he did: *Last Confession, Lilith, Dante,* some minor poems.

Monday, 22 November.—Dined at Chelsea with Tebbs and Knight (Joseph Knight, dramatic Critic and Editor of *Notes and Queries*), who came more particularly to hear some of Gabriel's poems. Gabriel has made some additions to the *Dante* poem, etc.: has not yet resumed painting to any extent.

Friday, 10 December.—He (Gabriel) is himself bent on getting out his volume of poems in the Spring. . . . *Rossetti Papers*, pp. 380–417.

The sonnets written at this time, according to the dates given in the 1911 edition of Rossetti's works, are as follows:—

Year 1866.—Soul's Beauty (dated 1867 in 1911 edition *Works*, but letter of May 1866 proves date).

Year 1867.—Body's Beauty.

Year 1868.—The Portrait, Willow-wood* (4 Willow-wood sonnets), all written in December, 1868. See Diary above). *Inclusiveness,* Newborn Death* (2 Newborn Death sonnets, No. 1 written December 19, 1868. See Diary above). (Also in this year, though not included in *The House of Life*, Venus Verticordia. Soul's Beauty, Body's Beauty and Venus Verticordia were all published in *Academy Notes*, 1868, by W. M. R. and Swinburne.

Year 1869.—Bridal Birth, Love's Testament, Lovesight, The Kiss, Nuptial Sleep (*Placata Venere*), Love's Lovers, Winged Hours,* The Love Moon, The Morrow's Message, Sleepless Dreams,* Secret Parting, Parted Love (written September, 1869. v. Family Letters, II, 216), Death in Love, Farewell to the Glen (written September, 1869, v. Sharp's Rossetti, pp. 27, 429), Vain Virtues (v. March 18th, *R.P. sub.*), The Sun's Shame (No. 1), The Vase of Life* (entitled *Run and Won* in *Fortnightly Review*), A Superscription* (written January 24, 1869, see Diary above, and not in 1868 as given in 1911 edition *Works*) To these *House of Life* Sonnets of 1869 should be added *Stillborn Love* and *The Moonstar*, undated, by W. H. R. v. Note to p. 381 *sup.* (Also in this year, but not included in *The House of Life*, Pandora, Sea Spell, Cassandra, Mary Magdalene, Michael Scott's Wooing, Troy Town, First Love Remembered, An Old Song Ended).

p. 389. "About Gabriel—the short ending to his ills, in the worst case, was of course often spoken of by him. . . . I could not strongly dissuade him. . . ." W. B. Scott to W. M. Rossetti, *Rossetti Papers*, p. 373.

---

* Indicates one of the sixteen sonnets published in the *Fortnightly Review* for March, 1869. The remaining five sonnets of the sixteen were of early dates:— *Broken Music* (1852), *Known in Vain* (1853), *The Landmark* (1854), *Lost on Both Sides* (1854), Lost Days (1862).

p. 391. The two Italian sonnets are as follows:—

I

O bocca che nell' ora del compenso
Tante volte baciai, e tante volte
Sentii da te, con mille voti accolte,
Quelle parole d'immortal consenso:—
O possa dei tuoi baci il sacro incenso
Ravvoger sempre in nuvole più folte
Le antiche tante omai larve sepolte,
Empiendo il ciel del nostro amore immenso!
Vieni, beata bocca, O vieni ancora!
Pensando a te, l'amor da te disia
Dolce rugiada in ben rosata via.
Non sei tu quella in cui ora ed ogni ora
Io vivo sol,—cui sol nell' alma mia
La vita, e la morte, e l'amore, adora?

II

O bocca che nell' ora del disìo
Tante volte guardai e tenri pace,—
Che i tanti spirti dell' occhio tenace
Baciar tutt' ora, e mai l labbrio mio,—
Ahi da te bocca, che piacer vogl' io
O che speranza che non sia fallace,—
Qual tuo sorriso, dimmi se ti piace,
E qual parole, per l' amor di Dio?
Deh povera speranza! e come vuoi
Raggiungere il piacer con ale avorte
Alle gemelle sorridenti porte?
Ogni parola che verebbe poi
Più amorosa ahi più sarìa per noi
Radice del silenzio della morte.

(From *Dante Gabriel Rossetti*: an analytical list of Manuscripts in the Duke University Library, with hitherto Unpublished Verse and Prose, ed. P. F. Baum, Duke University Press, Durham, North Carolina, 1931, pp. 53–4.)

p. 398. *At Last, First Fire* and *Threefold Homage* are privately printed in *The Ashley Library*. A Catalogue of printed books, manuscripts and autograph letters collected by Thomas James Wise, 11 vols, 1922–36. *Threefold Homage* is also in *D. G. R., an analytical list of MSS., etc.*, mentioned in preceding note.

p. 401. How closely the salient physical characteristics of the beloved in many of Rossetti's sonnets resemble those in descriptions of Janey left by various persons who knew her, the following references and quotations show. That the contrast of her crisp, dark hair, bunched over her pale forehead particularly struck observers, is very evident. Henry James's description of it, in 1869 (*v. sup.* pp. 371–2) is almost identical with that in William Morris's poem to Janey, written two years before (*v. sup.* pp. 238–9). Others who particularly noticed these characteristics (in addition to James's later comment, *v. sup.* p. 627, on meeting Janey again, after an interval of twelve years), were Allingham (*v. sup.* p. 318). Conway (*v. sup.* p. 334), Lady Burne-Jones (*v. sup.* p. 373), Rothenstein (*v. sup.* p. 373), Le Gallienne (*v. sup.* p. 373) and Robertson (*v. sup.* p. 375). "In his (Burne-Jones's) earlier pictures there is a reflection of my grandmother in large-eyed women of normal, or almost low stature, as against the excessively long-limbed women of his later style. But the hair of these early women is not hers, it is the hair of Rossetti's women, the masses of thick wavy hair which we knew in "Aunt Janey," the beautiful Mrs. William Morris. When I remember her, Aunt Janey's hair was nearly white, but there were still the same masses of it, waving from head to tip. To any one who knew her, Rossetti's pictures—with the exception of his later exaggerated types—were absolutely true. The large deep-set eyes, the full lips, the curved throat, the overshadowing hair, were all there. Even in her old age she looked like a queen as she moved avout the house in long white draperies, her hands in a white muff, crowned by her glorious hair," *Three Houses*, by Angela Thirkell, London, 1947.

The authoress is the granddaughter of Burne-Jones. Note the resemblance of this description to those in Rossetti's sonnets, even to such verbal resemblances as "overshadowing" and "queen," clear indications of the strong impression these characteristics made upon observers. *cf.* also the "thick wavy hair" with Rossetti's "rippling," in the original version of *Youth's Spring Tribute*, p. 434, footnote 2. Compare with these descriptions the following extracts from Rossetti's sonnets :—

Hair—
    "The shadowed eyes remember and foresee . . ."   *The Portrait*, 1868.
      (Admittedly a description of Janey; *v. sup.* p. 377.)
    "Then the dark ripples spread to waving hair . . ."   *Willow-wood I.* (1869).
      cf. sup. p. 434, footnote 2.
    "Thine eyes grey lit in shadowing hair above. . ."   *Love's Lovers* (1869).
      cf. Angela Thirkell's description above.
    "Warmed by her hand and shadowed by her hair . . ." *The Love Letter* (1870)
    ". . . this sovereign face whose love-spell breathes
      Even from its shadowed contour on the wall."   *Genius in Beauty* (1870).
      (Demonstrably of Janey; *v. sup.* p. 401.)
    "In the warm darkness underneath thine hair . . ."   *At Last.*
      (*v. sup.* p. 398.)
    "Amid the clustering hair that shrines her brow . . ."   *First Fire.*
      (*v. sup.* p. 400.)
    See also the quotation from *Her Gifts*, below, under *Eyes*.

Other physical characteristics noted by observers and also described in Rossetti's sonnets are :—

Face—"a thin pale face" (James, *v.* p. 371); "colourless perfection" (Lady Burne-Jones, *v.* p. 373). *cf. Her Gifts* :—

    "Such thrilling pallor of cheek as doth enthral
      The heart; . . ."

Eyes—"strange, sad, deep, Swinburnian eyes" (James, *v.* pp. 371); "eyes of mystery" (Robertson, *v.* p. 375). *cf. Her Gifts* :—

    "A glance like water brimming with the sky
      Or hyacinth-light where forest-shadows fall . . ."
    See also the quotation from *The Portrait*, and Angela Thirkell's description, above.

    Mouth—"like the Oriana in our illustrated Tennyson" (James, *v.* p.371.)
cf.   "The mouth's mould testifies of voice and kiss . . ."   *The Portrait.*
    "And her deep freighted lips expect me now . . ."   *First Fire.*
    "Seals with thy mouth his immortality . . ."   *Love's Lovers.*
    "The delicate love-lines of her mouth . . ."   *A Day of Love.*
    "Her mouth's culled sweetness . . ."   *Love-Sweetness.*
    "And as she kissed her mouth became her soul."   *Secret Parting.*
    ". . . a mouth whose passionate forms imply
    All music and all silence held thereby . . ."   *Her Gifts.*
See also Note to p. 391 for the two Italian sonnets to her mouth.

Silence—The silence mentioned in the preceding quotation from *Her Gifts*, is another noticeable quality of the beloved of the sonnets; see the following :—

Love's Testament, Youth's Antiphony, Youth's Spring Tribute, Silent Noon, Gracious Moonlight, Heart's Compass, The Morrow's Message, Severed Selves, Willow-wood I, He and I. The early sonnet, *The Birthbond*, written in 1854, also mentions silence. With these *cf.* Shaw's description of Mrs. Morris—"the silentest woman I have ever met . . ." (*v. sup.* p. 371).

Neck—"A long neck without any collar . . ." (James, *v.* p. 371); "a 'neck like a tower' . . ." (Robertson, quoting Rossetti's poem on Fanny, *The Song of the Bower*). *v.* p. 375). (*cf.* Angela Thirkell's description, above.)

cf. ". . . the enthroning throat . . ."   *The Portrait.*
    "A round reared neck, meet column of Love's shrine
        To cling to when the heart takes sanctuary . . ."   *Her Gifts.*
    ". . . her neck ten kisses long . . ."   *First Fire.*
    "Up your warm throat to your warm lips . . ."   *Youth's Spring Tribute.*

Her Gifts, the best single complete portrait in words of the beloved, strikingly resembles the descriptions of Janey, save for the gold hair, substituted before publication for the original "deep locks". As regards this, it is noteworthy that he repainted the dead Beatrice in *Dante's Dream*, for which Mrs. Morris was the model, with light instead of dark hair (*v.* Marillier, 2nd ed. p. 131), as also in *Proserpine*, and in the sonnet *Venus Victrix* which first gave "deep-shadowed," for the later "gold-shadowed." (See footnote to p. 400). The general incompatibility of the two types, evident in the pictures, is also almost inevitably present in the two sonnets, in the combination of "hyacinth-light," "forest-shadows" and "thrilling pallor of cheek" with "golden locks," and in the phrase "gold-*shadowed* in thy hair." The psychological origin of this curious, and to the normal person surely somewhat unpleasant, combination of the chief physical attraction of his first and now dead love with those of his later one, is doubtless to be found in his sonnet *The Love Moon*, in which he describes his different love experiences as but various aspects of Love itself.

For references and quotations illustrating other of Janey's qualities reflected in Rossetti's sonnets, see footnotes to pp. 400–1.

p. 410. "Wednesday, 20 October (1869).—Scott called, just back from Penkill. He says that Gabriel, when at Penkill, used to be composing in an upper room frequently while Scott and Miss Boyd were in a lower room, and his movements, etc., used to be audible. After he was gone, the same sounds continued distinctly audible to Scott and Miss Boyd, and also to the Catholic priest Mr. Reid (on at least one occasion). Miss Boyd was much startled in one instance, and went into the upper room to satisfy herself about the matter. This is curious. . . ." W. M. R.'s Diary, *Rossetti Papers*, p. 412.

Scott repeated this story in his *Autobiographical Notes*, and it afterwards received a wide currency through various writings about Rossetti. What is little known, however, is that William Sharp, criticizing the *Autobiographical Notes* in *The Academy* for December 3, 1892, asserted that Scott later discovered the simple explanation of these noises, and described it in detail to Sharp himself.

Evidently Rossetti's overwrought state and supernaturalism had affected the nerves and imaginations of his friends!

p. 417. *Life in Love* is dated 1870 by W. M. Rossetti in D. G. R.'s *Works*, 1911. It first appeared in the 1870 volume, and as it obviously refers to the exhumation after it had taken place must have been written between October 1869 and the close of April 1870. *v. also footnote to* p. 400 *sup.*

p. 431. Even the Rossetti family were uncertain as to the time when Rossetti first used chloral. Christina, suspecting William of antedating it somewhat, enquired: ". . . had he then come in contact with Mr. Stillman? to whom I understood the introduction of chloral was innocently owing. . . ." *The Family Letters of Christina Georgina Rossetti*, ed. W. M. Rossetti, London, 1908, p. 178. (Letter dated 9 March, 1891.) It was probably because of this that W. M. Rossetti, in his *Memoir* of D. G. R., published four years later, imputed the introduction of chloral to

Stillman, and gave the date (consequently?) as 1870 (pp. 286-8). Hall Caine, in his *Recollections of Dante Gabriel Rossetti*, 1882 (p. 48), wrote: "Towards 1868 he heard of the then newly found drug chloral, which was accredited with all the virtues and none of the vices of other known narcotics. Here then was the thing he wanted; this was the blessed discovery that was to save him from days of weariness and nights of misery and tears. Eagerly he procured it, took it nightly in single small doses of ten grains each, and from it he received pleasant and refreshing sleep. He made no concealment of his habit. . . . It was not, however, for some years after he began the use of it that chloral produced any sensible effects of an injurious kind." W. M. Rossetti in his edition of Rossetti's *Poetical Works*, in 1895, shortly after the publication of his *Memoir*, wrote of "insomnia . . . coped with by far too free a use of chloral, which may have begun towards the end of 1869."

p. 434. The sonnets in *The House of Life* dated 1870 by W. M. R. in the 1911 edition of D. G. R.'s *Works*, are as follows:—*Supreme Surrender, Passion and Worship, The Love-letter, A Day of Love, Love-sweetness, Love's Baubles, Life in Love,- Stillborn Love,*. (*Stillborn Love* was written in 1869. v. *Note* to p. 381 *sup.*) *The Monochord, Hoarded Joy, Barren Spring, Death's Songsters, He and I, The One Hope*. All these appeared in the 1870 volume. Another sonnet dated 1870, *Youth's Spring Tribute* did not appear until the 1881 volume, and was probably written too late for insertion in that of 1870. For original titles, v. *Note* to p. 381.

p. 436. *The Monochord*. William Rossetti, shortly before the publication of his *Dante Gabriel Rossetti as Designer and Writer*, in 1889, sent proofs of the book to Christina for comment. She found his explanation of *The Monochord* too merely literal to show the essential significance of the poem, and replied: "Abandoning verbal particulars—don't you think the point may be the common essence (so to say) of all these outward and inward matters?—as if one thread (the musical 'monochord,' but not in the sense of any weight or measure) ran through all, vibrated through all? Thus we should get the sort of truth which the blind man so neatly conveyed who likened *scarlet* to the sound of the trumpet . . ." [*sic*] *The Family Letters of Christina Rossetti*, ed. W. M. Rossetti, London, 1908, p. 173. Christina evidently saw that Gabriel's conception of Love as an entity in itself, apart from its individual manifestations, that Dantesque conception which permeates his work, was again finding expression in this poem.

The note on the poem which ultimately appeared on publication, suggests that William incorporated something of Christina's suggestion into his original note, while the wording in the first sentences is as often, ambiguous—strangely consistent with both the literal interpretation he at least appears to accept, and also with the referential significance to which Christina evidently alluded. Even William, towards the close of the note, becomes as occasionally he does, surprisingly outspoken when he paraphrases one portion as relating to "reminiscences of" his brother's "past emotional life," etc. My own interpretation of the sonnet as evident autobiography, was made before I made acquaintance with these glosses.

William's comment on the poem, in *Dante Gabriel Rossetti as Designer and Writer*, is as follows:—"Of all the sonnets in the *House of Life*, this is the one which seems to me most obscure. In fact, I do not think that its meaning can be seized by a reader unfurnished with some information which the sonnet itself does not supply. I had forgotten (or possibly I never knew) what the inspiring motive of the verses had been; and I was considerably baffled by them until, consulting Mr. Theodore Watts, I was apprised that the idea of the sonnet had come to my brother on an occasion when he was listening to music. Hence the adoption for the title of the musical term Monochord, which is defined as 'an instrument of one string, used to ascertain and demonstrate the several lengths of the string required to produce the several notes of the musical scale.' " (This seems to have been the original note upon which Christina commented. What follows evidently owes much to her remarks and was no doubt added afterwards.)

"Evidently, however, the word Monochord is not here applied in this literal sense, but may rather indicate 'the power of music in eliciting and meting out the emotions of the human soul.' Even after one knows the primary subject-matter of the sonnet, it remains (to me at least) a very difficult one in its particular images and form of expression. Its theme might perhaps be expressed thus—'The mutual response of music and of the human soul.' In the opening lines the poet seems to intimate that the grand strains of the music conjure before his mental eye a vision of sky and sea. Or, taking a larger view of the whole subject, we might say that the point of the sonnet is the common essence of all these outward and inward matters; as if one thread (monochord) ran through all—vibrated through all. With these rather dubious preliminaries I proceed.

"Is it this sky's vast vault, or is it this ocean's sound, which is Life's self, and which draws my life from me, and which, by instinct (self-inherent) ineffable decree, holds my breath quailing on the bitter bound? Nay, is it Life, or death, thus thunder-crowned (crowned with the thundrous raptures of music), which, amid the tide of all emergency, now notes my separate wave (appeals to my individual consciousness, 'finds me out' as a single personal existence), and notes towards what sea its difficult eddies labour in the ground? Oh what is this that knows the road along which I came (evokes so many reminiscences of my past emotional life), the flame turned cloud, the cloud re-turned to flame (light and obscurity, happiness and unhappiness), the lifted shifted steeps, and all the way? this which draws round me at last this wind-warmed space (lulls me into meditative quietude), and turns my face, in regenerate rapture, upon the devious coverts of dismay (lifts me out of despondency, and makes me contemplate even past sorrow with a thrill of bliss)?"

William's note to the poem in the 1911 edition of D. G. Rossetti's works, is strangely different from the above. All suggestion of personal references in the poem has disappeared. The note runs thus:—"Of all the sonnets in *The House of Life*, this is the one which seems to me the most obscure. It was published in the *Poems* of 1870; not as forming part of *The House of Life*, but as a separate sonnet, the last in the volume, with the additional heading 'Written during Music' [*cf.* with his entirely inconsistent statement in the preceding note that but for Watts-Dunton's informing him that it was written during music, he might never have known it, or guessed the subject!] The first line stood at that time thus— 'Is it the moved air or the moving sound.' In that form the sonnet would naturally be understood as indicating, in very figurative language, the power of music over the human soul. The question arises—When Rossetti substituted the present opening, 'Is it this sky's vast vault or ocean's sound,' did he intend to retain the idea of music under a metaphor, or did he discard that idea, and truly deal with the vast influences of nature, sky and sea? I fancy the latter. If so, I understand the general purport of the sonnet to be this: There is an unspeakably mysterious bond between the universe and the soul of man (macrocosm and microcosm): the phenomena of nature search the inmost recesses of the soul, inspiring awe, administering solace.

"The musical term 'Monochord' is defined as 'an instrument of one string, used to ascertain and demonstrate the several lengths of the string required to produce the several notes of the musical scale.' Evidently, however, the word 'Monochord' is not (even in the original form of the sonnet) applied in this literal sense; it may now rather indicate the mysterious bond above-named, unifying nature and the soul."

Hall Caine, in his *Recollections of Rossetti*, ed. 1882, pp. 132–3, speaks of a copy of the Tauchnitz edition of Rossetti's poems, in which the poet inserted whatever alterations he wished to make in his poems. In this copy Caine found a comment on *The Monochord* by Rossetti himself, one which closely agrees, of course, with the interpretation of the poem as expressive of a mood of personal retrospect. Caine's note runs thus: "In the same private copy of the *Poems* the following explanatory passage was written over the much-discussed sonnet, entitled *The Monochord*— 'That sublimated mood of the soul in which a separate essence of itself seems as it were to oversoar and survey it.' "

p. 475. The sonnets in *The House of Life* dated 1871 by W. M. Rossetti in the

1911 edition of D. G. R.'s *Works* are as follows:—*Love Enthroned, Heart's Hope, Lovers' Walk,* Youth's Antiphony, Beauty's Pageant, Genius in Beauty, Silent Noon, Gracious Moonlight, Heart's Haven,* Pride of Youth, Mid-rapture, Heart's Compass, Soul Light, The Moonstar,*[1] *Last Fire, Her Gifts, Equal Troth, Venus Victrix, The Dark Glass,* The Lamp's Shrine, Severed Selves, Through Death to Love,* Hope Overtaken, Love and Hope, Cloud and Wind, Without Her, Loves' Fatality, Love's Last Gift.* (The sonnets marked * can be accurately dated, as Rossetti sent them, together with *Cloud Confines* and *Sunset Wings*, in a letter to W. B. Scott of August 13, 1871, describing them as recent compositions.) Another poem of this year was *Soothsay*. For original titles, *v. Note* to p. 381.

p. 489. "Whether, if Rossetti had lived later, he would have availed himself more of the freedom accorded to painters we cannot, of course, say. With his intense and passionate love of feminine beauty, and a sensual southern strain in his blood besides, it seems rather remarkable how chary he was of painting the nude form. I only know of one entire nude figure (besides, of course, studies) amongst all his works, and that is the crayon called *Spirit of the Rainbow* . . . also a half-length nude done from the same model, a companion drawing in fact." Marillier's *D. G. Rossetti*, 1st ed., p. 135. The "companion drawing" was named *Forced Music. Ibid.*, pp. 191–2.

p. 555. Cathy was Brown's daughter by his second wife Emma, née Hill. Lucy was Brown's daughter by his first wife and cousin, Elizabeth Bromley, who died in 1846.

[1] *The Moonstar* was written in 1869. *v. Note* to p. 381 *sup.*

SELECT BIBLIOGRAPHY

I. MANUSCRIPT SOURCES
(mostly unpublished holographs)

I. *The Brotherton Collection*

(a) Three volumes consisting chiefly of 123 letters from D. G. Rossetti to W. M. Rossetti.

(b) Seven volumes consisting chiefly of 316 letters from D. G. Rossetti to W. T. Watts. (Later Watts-Dunton.)

(c) One volume consisting chiefly of 27 letters from D. G. Rossetti to William Davies.

(d) One volume consisting chiefly of 22 letters from D. G. Rossetti to Dr. F. Hueffer.

II. *The Wise Collection*

(a) A volume of twenty-one letters from Dante Gabriel Rossetti to W. M. Rossetti.

(b) A volume of thirty-three letters from D. G. Rossetti to W. T. Watts.

(c) A volume of ten letters from D. G. Rossetti to A. C. Swinburne.

(d) A volume consisting chiefly of eighteen letters relating to D. G. Rossetti and Fanny Schott.

(e) A volume consisting of Notes and Letters by D. G. Rossetti, on Charles Wells.

(f) A volume consisting of eight letters from D. G. Rossetti to W. T. Watts, and notes on Chatterton.

(g) A volume consisting of three letters by D. G. Rossetti concerning his marriage.

(h) A volume consisting chiefly of four letters from D. G. Rossetti to W. T. Watts.

(i) A volume consisting of three letters from D. G. Rossetti to Swinburne, regarding the attacks made upon the latter by Mortimer Collins and upon both by Robert Buchanan. (Privately printed for T. J. Wise, 1921.)

(j) A volume consisting of five letters from D. G. Rossetti, Ruskin, Morris and (Burne-)Jones to Swinburne. (Privately printed for T. J. Wise, 1919.)

(k) A volume consisting of five letters from D. G. Rossetti to H. B. Forman, containing criticisms and comments on Keats. (Privately printed for T. J. Wise, 1919.)

(l) A volume of two letters, one from D. G. Rossetti to Swinburne, one from Swinburne to Rossetti, relating to the exhumation of Rossetti's poems. (Privately printed by T. J. Wise, 1919, and entitled *A Romance of Literature*.)

(m) A volume containing extracts from five letters from Swinburne to Howell, with ten letters from and to various correspondents, and details o Howell's death from his death certificate.

(n) A letter from Meredith to W. M. Rossetti.

(o) A volume of sixteen letters from Hall Caine to W. M. Rossetti and one from Mary E. Madox Rossetti to T. J. Wise.

(p) Two letters from Swinburne to W. M. Rossetti containing recollections of Mrs. D. G. Rossetti.

(q) A volume consisting of thirty letters from W. M. Rossetti to W. T. Watts.

(r) Three letters from Hall Caine to W. T. Watts.

(s) Twenty-two letters from W. M. Rossetti to Swinburne.

(t) Seven letters from Scott to W. T. Watts. One letter from Alice Boyd to Swinburne.

(u) A volume consisting of four letters of Browning to various correspondents (Privately printed for T. J. Wise, 1919.)

(*v*) A volume containing a fragment of a MS. by Swinburne, briefly describing his friendship with D. G. Rossetti and his wife. (Privately printed for T. J. Wise, and entitled *A Record of Friendship*, 1910.)

(*w*) A volume of forty-one miscellaneous letters relating to D. G. Rossetti.

III. British Museum Collection

(*a*) An album containing ninety-two letters from D. G. Rossetti to his publisher, F. S. Ellis. (These letters, edited by Oswald Doughty, were published as *The Letters of D. G. Rossetti to his Publisher, F. S. Ellis*, London, 1928.)

(*b*) A holograph sonnet by D. G. Rossetti, *Love's Compass*, published in *The House of Life* as *Heart's Compass*.

IV. Documents in the Guildhall Library, London, being The Coroner's Record of the Inquest on the Death of Mrs. Rossetti, held on February 12, 1862.

V. Letters and Documents in the Pierpont Morgan Library, New York

Seventy Letters from D. G. Rossetti to various correspondents, etc., and Unpublished Portions of Ford Madox Brown's Diary.

VI. Letters in Harvard College Library

Three letters of D. G. Rossetti to various correspondents.

VII. Letters in the Boston Public Library

Three letters of D. G. Rossetti to various correspondents.

VIII. Letters in the Janet Camp Troxell Collection

Sixteen letters of D. G. Rossetti to various correspondents, and two letters of Miss Siddal to D. G. Rossetti.

IX. Worcester College Collection, Oxford

Forty letters of D. G. Rossetti to W. T. Watts, etc.

X. Letters from Various Sources

Fifteen Letters of D. G. Rossetti to Miss Boyd (edited and published later by *The Fortnightly Review* for May 1928, by John Purves), etc.

XI. The Fitzwilliam Museum Collection, Cambridge

Including amongst other items, the two "Trial Books" of 1869, of Rossetti's poems, the "third proof" of the *Poems* (1870) and in a separate volume *The House of Life* with variations in text and titles from the published versions.

XII. Copies of the two unpublished sonnets on *The Sphinx* subject.

II. PUBLISHED SOURCES

(*N.B.—Where not stated the place of publication is London*)

(A) BIBLIOGRAPHIES

1. BATESON, F. W.: *The Cambridge Bibliography of English Literature*, 4 vols., Cambridge, 1940.
2. EHRSAM, T. G., DEILY, R. H., and SMITH, R. M.: *Bibliographies of Twelve Victorian Authors*, New York, 1936.
3. ROSSETTI, W. M.: *Bibliography of the Works of Dante Gabriel Rossetti*, 1905.
4. ROSSETTI, W. M.: *Dante Gabriel Rossetti: Classified Lists of his Writings*, 1906.
5. VAUGHAN, C. E.: *Bibliographies of Swinburne, Morris, Rossetti*, etc., 1914. (*Pamphlets of the English Association, No.* 29.)
6. WISE, T. J.: *The Ashley Library*. A catalogue of printed books, manuscripts and autograph letters collected by Thomas James Wise, 11 vols., 1922–36.

(B) WORKS ON THE PRERAPHAELITE MOVEMENT

7. GAUNT, W.: *The Preraphaelite Tragedy*, 1942.
8. HUEFFER, FORD MADOX ("Ford Madox Ford"): *The Preraphaelite Brotherhood*, n.d.
9. HUEFFER, FORD MADOX ("Ford Madox Ford"): *Ancient Lights and Certain New Reflections*, 1911. (Also contains extracts from Ford Madox Brown's diary, not published elsewhere.)
10. HUNT, W. HOLMAN: *Preraphaelitism and the Preraphaelite Brotherhood*, 2 vols., 1905.
11. HUNT, W. HOLMAN: *The Story of the Painting of the Pictures on the Walls and the Decoration on the Ceiling of the Old Debating Hall (now the Library) of the Union Society, Oxford, in the years 1857-8-9*, Oxford and London, 1906.
12. WELBY, T. E.: *The Victorian Romantics, 1850–1870*. 1929.

(C) WORKS OF D. G. ROSSETTI

(a) Collected Works
13. *Collected Works*, ed. W. M. Rossetti, 2 vols., 1887-8.
14. *The Works of Dante Gabriel Rossetti*, ed. W. M. Rossetti, 1911.

(b) Poems and Translations
15. *The Oxford and Cambridge Magazine*, 1856. (Contains Rossetti's work, sometimes in early versions not repeated later.)
16. *The Early Italian Poets*, 1861.
17. *Dante and his Circle*, 1874.
18. *Poems*, 1870.
19. *Poems: A new Edition*, 1881.
20. *Ballads and Sonnets*, 1882.
21. *The House of Life*. With an Introduction and Notes by P. F. Baum, Cambridge, U.S.A., 1928.
22. *The Ballad of Jan Van Hunks*. With an Introduction by Mackenzie Bell, 1929.
23. *Dante Gabriel Rossetti. An Analytical List of Manuscripts in the Duke University Library with hitherto Unpublished Verse and Prose*, ed. P. F. Baum, Duke University Press, Durham, North Carolina, U.S.A., 1931.
24. *The Germ*. A Facsimile Reprint, with an Introduction by W. M. Rossetti, 1901.

(D) CORRESPONDENCE OF D. G. ROSSETTI

25. *D. G. Rossetti's Family Letters with a Memoir*, by W. M. Rossetti, 2 vols., 1895.
26. *Letters of Dante Gabriel Rossetti to William Allingham, 1854-70*, ed. G. B. Hill, 1897.
27. *Ruskin: Rossetti: Preraphaelitism*, ed. W. M. Rossetti, 1899.
28. *Preraphaelite Diaries and Letters*, ed. W. M. Rossetti, 1900.
29. *Rossetti Papers, 1862-70*, ed. W. M. Rossetti, 1903.
30. *Letters of Dante Gabriel Rossetti to his Publisher, F. S. Ellis*, ed. with Introduction and Notes by Oswald Doughty, 1928.
31. *Dante Gabriel Rossetti: Letters to Miss Alice Boyd*. Chosen and arranged by John Purves, *Fortnightly Review*, May, 1928.
32. *Unpublished Letters from Theodore Watts-Dunton to Swinburne*, ed. H. G. Wright, *Review of English Studies*, April, 1934. (Includes letters by D. G. R.)
33. *Three Rossettis: Unpublished Letters to and from Dante Gabriel, Christina, William*, ed. Janet Camp Troxell, Cambridge, U.S.A., 1937.
34. *Portraits and Personalities*, by A. Compton-Rickett, 1937. (Includes letters of D. G. R. to Swinburne, first published in the *Times Literary Supplement*, October 16th and 23rd, 1919, by T. J. Wise.)
35. *Dante Gabriel Rossetti's Letters to Fanny Cornforth*, ed. P. F. Baum, Baltimore, 1940.

(E) BIOGRAPHICAL AND CRITICAL STUDIES OF D. G. ROSSETTI AND HIS WORKS

36. BENSON, A. C.: *Rossetti*, 1906 (English Men of Letters Series).
37. CAINE, T. HALL: *Recollections of Dante Gabriel Rossetti*, 1882.
38. CAINE, T. HALL: *Recollections of Dante Gabriel Rossetti*, 1928. (A reprint of the preceding number, with additions, omissions, and discrepancies.)
39. CAINE, T. HALL: *My Story*, 1908. (Includes much of the "Recollections.")
40. CARR, J. COMYNS: *Some Eminent Victorians: Personal Recollections*, etc., 1908.
41. CECIL, LORD DAVID: *D. G. Rossetti*. In *The Great Victorians*, ed. Massingham, H. J., and Massingham, H., 1932.
42. COLVIN, SIDNEY: *Memories and Notes of Persons and Places*, 1922.
43. DUNN, H. T.: *Recollections of Dante Gabriel Rossetti and his Circle*, 1904.
44. FORBES-ROBERTSON, SIR JOHNSTON: *A Player Under Three Reigns*, 1925.
45. HUEFFER, FORD MADOX (Ford Madox "Ford"): *Rossetti: A Critical Essay on his Art*, 1902.
46. KNIGHT, J.: *Life of Dante Gabriel Rossetti*, 1887.
47. LUCAS, F. L.: *Ten Victorian Poets*, Cambridge, 1930.
48. LYND, ROBERT: *Rossetti and Ritual*. In *Old and New Masters*, 1919.
49. MACCARTHY, DESMOND: *Rossetti and Hall Caine*. In *Portraits*, 1931.
50. MARILLIER, H. C.: *Dante Gabriel Rossetti*, 1st edition, 1899.
51. MARILLIER, H. C.: *Dante Gabriel Rossetti*, 2nd edition (abridged and revised), 1901.
52. MEGROZ, R. L.: *Dante Gabriel Rossetti*, 1928.
53. MYERS, F. W. H.: *Rossetti and the Religion of Beauty*. In *Essays, Modern*, 1883. (Originally appeared in The Cornhill Magazine, February 1883.)
54. PATER, W. H.: *Dante Gabriel Rossetti*. In *The English Poets*, ed. T. H. Ward, 1883 (vol. 4). Reprinted in *Appreciations*, 1889.
55. PATMORE, C. K. D.: *Rossetti as a Poet*. In *Principles in Art*, etc., 1907.
56. QUILTER, H.: *Sententiae Artis*, 1886.
57. QUILTER, H.: *Preferences in Art, Life and Literature*, 1892.
58. ROSSETTI, W. M.: *Dante Gabriel Rossetti as Designer and Writer*, 1889.
59. ROSSETTI, W. M.: *Some Reminiscences*, 2 vols., 1906.
60. RUTTER, F.: *Dante Gabriel Rossetti*, n.d.
61. SHARP, W.: *Dante Gabriel Rossetti*, 1882.
62. SHARP, W.: *Papers Critical and Reminiscent*, 1912.
63. SITWELL, SACHEVERELL: *Dance of the Quick and the Dead*, 1936.
64. SKELTON, J.: *The Table Talk of Shirley* (1st series), 1895.
65. STEPHENS, F. G.: *Dante Gabriel Rossetti*, 1908. (A reprint of the original study published in *Portfolio Monographs*, 1894.)
66. SUDDARD, M.: *The House of Life*. In *Studies and Essays*, Cambridge, 1912.
67. SYMONS, A.: *Studies in Strange Souls*, 1929.
68. WALLER, R. D.: *The Rossetti Family*, 1824-1854, Manchester, 1932.
69. WATTS-DUNTON, W. T.: *D. G. Rossetti*. In *Encyclopaedia Britannica*, 11th edition, Cambridge, 1911, vol. 23.
70. WATTS-DUNTON, W. T.: *Old Familiar Faces*, 1916.

(F) MEMOIRS, LETTERS, BIOGRAPHIES, ETC., RELATING TO ROSSETTI AND HIS FRIENDS

71. *William Allingham: A Diary*, ed. H. Allingham and D. Radford, 1907.
72. *Extracts from G. P. Boyce's Diaries*, 1851-1875. In The Old Water-colour Society's Club. Nineteenth Annual Volume, 1941.
73. *Ford Madox Brown*, by Ford Madox Hueffer ("Ford"), 1896.
74. *The Fleshly School of Poetry*, by Thomas Maitland (alias of R. Buchanan), *Contemporary Review*, October 1871.

75. *The Fleshly School of Poetry*, by Robert Buchanan, 1872. (An expanded version, in pamphlet form, of the preceding.)
76. *Memorials of Sir Edward Burne-Jones*, by Lady G. Burne-Jones, 2 vols., 1912.
77. *Memoirs of Eighty Years*, by Thomas Gordon Hake, 1892.
78. *Murray Marks and his Friends*, by G. C. Williamson, 1919.
79. *The Life and Letters of Sir John Everett Millais*, by J. G. Millais, 2 vols., 1899.
80. *Collected Works of William Morris*, 26 vols., 1915–1936.
81. *The Life of William Morris*, by J. W. Mackail, 2 vols., 1899.
82. *Family Letters of Christina Rossetti*, ed. W. M. Rossetti, 1908.
83. *A Versified Autobiography*, by Gabriele Rossetti. Translated and Supplemented by W. M. Rossetti, 1061.
84. *Gabriele Rossetti in England*, by E. R. Vincent, Oxford, 1936.
85. *Ruskin's Works*, ed. Sir E. T. Cook and A. Wedderburn, 39 vols., 1903–12.
86. *Life of John Ruskin*, by Sir E. T. Cook, 2 vols., 1912.
87. *Autobiographical Notes of the Life of W. B. Scott*, ed. W. Minto, 2 vols., 1892.
88. *The Life and Letters of Frederick Shields*, by Ernestine Mills, 1912.
89. *The Letters of A. C. Swinburne*, ed. Sir Edmund Gosse and T. J. Wise, 2 vols., 1918.
90. *The Letters of A. C. Swinburne*, ed. T. Hake and A. Compton-Rickett, 1918.
91. *The Life of Algernon Charles Swinburne*, by Sir Edmund Gosse, 1917.
92. *La Vie et l'oeuvre de Swinburne*, by G. Lafourcade, 2 vols., 1928.
93. *Swinburne: A Literary Biography*, by G. Lafourcade, 1932.
94. *Theodore Watts-Dunton, Poet, Novelist, Critic*, by James Douglas, 1904.
95. *The Life and Letters of Theodore Watts-Dunton*, by T. Hake and A. Compton-Rickett, 2 vols., 1916.
96. *The Whistler Journal*, ed. E. R. Pennell and J. Pennell, Philadelphia, 1921.
97. *The Life of J. M. Whistler*, by E. R. Pennell and J. Pennell, 2 vols., 1909.
98. *Oscar Wilde: A Critical Study*, by A. Ransome, 1912.
99. *Aspects of Wilde*, by V. O'Sullivan, 1936.
100. *Thomas Woolner: His Life and Letters*, by Amy Woolner, 1917.

(G) PERIODICAL LITERATURE

Burlington Magazine

101. 1903. May. "Dante Rossetti and Elizabeth Siddal," by W. M. Rossetti.
102. 1916. June "Rossetti's Water-Colours of 1857," by Roger Fry.

Contemporary Review

103. 1886. Apr.–June. "The Preraphaelite Brotherhood," by W. Holman Hunt.

English Review

104. 1909. Jan. "A Note on Cheyne Walk," by George Meredith. (The story of Meredith's leaving Cheyne Walk.)
105. 1909. Jan. "Rossettiana. A Glimpse of Rossetti and Morris at Kelmscott," by T. Watts-Dunton.

Fortnightly Review

106. 1869. Mar. "Of Life, Love and Death: Sixteen Sonnets," by D. G. Rossetti.
107. 1928. May. "Dante Gabriel Rossetti: Letters to Miss Alice Boyd," Chosen and arranged by John Purves.

Good Words

108. 1897. Aug. "A Memorable Art Class," by Thomas Sulman. (Interesting reminiscences of Rossetti's class at The Working Men's College.)

Lippincott's Monthly Magazine (Philadelphia)

109. 1901. Nov. "Recollections of Rossetti," by Herbert H. Gilchrist.

London Mercury

110. 1928. May "Dante Gabriel Rossetti," by E. Shanks. (An excellent article.)

Magazine of Art

111. 1904. Feb. "A Chapter from a Painter's Reminiscences: The Oxford Circle," by Val Prinsep.

Manchester Guardian

112. 1936. Mar. 9, 11. "The Restoration of the Paintings at the Oxford Union.

Modern Language Notes (Baltimore, Maryland, U.S.A.)

113. 1929. May "The Bancroft Manuscripts of Rossetti's Sonnets," by R. Wallenstein.

Modern Philology (Chicago)

114. 1917. Sept. "Rossetti's House of Life," by F. M. Tisdel. (An attempt to discover the correct chronology of the sonnet sequence.)

Musical World

115. 1890. July 5. "Memories of Rossetti," by W. H. Hunt.

New Review

116. 1894. Sept. "A Child's Recollections of Rossetti," by Lily Hall Caine.

Nineteenth Century Review

117. 1883. Mar. "The Truth about D. G. Rossetti," by T. Watts-Dunton.

Scribner's Magazine (New York and London)

118. 1920. Jan. "Some Personal Recollections," by Sir Sidney Colvin.

Spectator

119. 1904. Aug. 13. An unintentionally amusing review of Benson's "Rossetti." ("Love, his controlling theme, is not an English obsession. We love in the intervals of other business.")

120. 1928. May 12. A review of Waugh's "Rossetti," by Rachel Armand Taylor. (An admirable study of Rossetti by the reviewer.)

Times

121. 1928. May 11. "D. G. Rossetti, 1828–1928: The Tribute of a Friend," by Sir Johnston Forbes-Robertson.

Times Literary Supplement

122. 1919. Oct. 16, and 23. "Letters of D. G. Rossetti to Swinburne."

INDEX

Aberdare, Lord (*see* Bruce)
Abrey, Mrs., 654, 655
Academicians, Royal, 67
Academy, Royal, 487, 674
    Exhibitions, 63, 78–9, 99–101, 109, 113–4
    Schools, 53, 60, 78, 146
Academy, The, 443, 503
Acland, Dr. Henry, 173–9, 192, 235
Adelphi Theatre, 59
Aesthetic Movement, 234, 446, 616
Agnosticism, 575
Alboni, M., 59
Aldwick Lodge, 574
Allingham, William, 102, 110, 144, 155, 182, 299, 309, 357, 426, 453, 513
    Day and Night Songs, 164
    The Maids of Elfinmere, 205
Alveston (Warwickshire), 139
Antwerp, 84–5
Arabian Nights, 49, 659
Argosy, The, 497
Ariosto, L., 39, 50
Arnold, Matthew, 351, 392, 571
Art and Poetry, 94
Art Journal, 93, 97, 644
Artists' Rifle Corps, 260
Ashburton, Lady, 513
Astley's Amphitheatre, 344
Athenaeum, The, 77, 93, 98–9, 100–1, 216, 235, 331, 443, 488, 496, 506, 561, 643
Atlantic Monthly, 660
Austin, Afred, 448
Australia, 108
Azeglio, Marquis d', 313

Bader, Mr., 363
Bain, Thomas, 660
Ballyshannon, 102
Balzac, H. de, 563
Bateman, Edward, 114, 127
Bath, Marchioness of, 81, 157
Bath, 198
Bible, 39, 43, 46, 207
Birchington-on-Sea, 655, 669
Birchington, the Rector of, 665, 669
Birrell, Mrs. Sarah, 294, 295, 320
Black Friday, 338
Blackwood's Magazine, 99, 508
Blake, William, 55, 613
Blunt, William S., 456, 460
Boccaccio, G., 33, 254
Bodichon, Mme., 426

Bognor, 573
Boswell, J., 474
Botticelli, S., *Spring*, 613
Boulogne, 52
Bowman, Sir William, 360
Boyce, George P., 129, 247, 253, 259, 269, 308, 669
Boyd, Alice, 363–4, 472
Boyle, Hon. Mrs., 129
Brighton, 269
British Museum, 54
"Broadlands," 287
Brooke, Stopford, *Riquet of the Tuft*, 622
Brown, Ford M., 61–4, 69, 72–3, 88, 92, 94, 97, 113, 159–61, 181, 190, 195–6, 213, 217–8, 219, 241, 243, 260, 293, 332, 333–5, 342, 370, 453, 478, 526, 561, 591, 599, 629, 675, 677
    Writings:—
    The Love of Beauty (Sonnet), 92
    The Mechanism of an Historical Picture, 94
    Paintings:—
    Christ Washing Peter's Feet, 113, 487
    The Last of England, 363
    Lear, 72
    The Seraphs' Watch, 62
    The Spirit of Abstract Justice, 80
    Work, 213, 363
Brown, Cathy, *see* Hueffer, Mrs. Francis
Brown, Lucy, 333, 453, 476, 562, 563, 565, 582 589, 669
Browning, Robert, 55, 83, 168, 182, 183, 185, 294, 312, 395, 408, 449, 500–1, 515–6, 609
    Balaustion's Adventure, 516–7
    Bells and Pomegranates, 55
    The Blot on the Scutcheon, 55
    Fifine at the Fair, 516
    Men and Women, 186
    Paracelsus, 55, 82
    Pauline, 182
    Pippa Passes, 55
    Prince Hohenstiel Schwangau, 491
    Sordello, 55
Browning, Mrs. Robert, 184, 185, 260
Bruce, H. A. (later Lord Aberdare), 416
Bruges, 85–6
Brussels, 84